HAMMOND

DISCOVERY

WORLD ATLAS

HAMMOND INCORPORATED
MAPLEWOOD, NEW JERSEY 07040

Hammond Publications Advisory Board

Library of Congress Cataloging-in-Publication Data
Hammond Incorporated.
    Hammond discovery world atlas.
    "Terrain maps of land forms and ocean floors": p.
    Includes indexes.
    1. Atlases. 2. Zip code – United States. I Title.
II. Title: Discovery world atlas.
G1021.H2683 1988   912   88-675304
ISBN 0-8437-1224-4
ISBN 0-8437-1223-6 (pbk.)

CONTENTS

Introduction to the World Atlas

The current edition of the Hammond World Atlas features an outstanding new section devoted to THE PHYSICAL WORLD — a series of terrain maps of land forms and ocean floors. These physical maps were originally produced as sculptured terrain models, thus simulating the earth's surface in a highly realistic manner. The three-dimensional effect is both instructive and pleasing to the eye.

As in previous editions, the atlas is organized to make the retrieval of information as simple and quick as possible. The guiding principle in organizing the atlas material has been to present separate subjects on *separate* maps. In this way, each individual map topic is shown with the greatest degree of clarity, unencumbered with extraneous information that is best revealed on separate maps. Of equal importance from the standpoint of good atlas design is the treatment of all current information on a given country as a single atlas unit. Thus, the basic reference map of an area is accompanied on adjacent pages by all supplementary information pertaining to that area. For example, except for individual United States maps, the detailed index for a given map always appears on the same page as, or on the pages immediately following, the reference map. This same map index provides population data for the many cities, towns and villages shown on the map. Highlight information on the area, i.e., the total population and area, the capital, the highest point, is listed in the summary fact listings accompanying each unit. An adjacent locator map relates the subject area to the larger world beyond. A three-dimensional picture of the area is exhibited by means of the accompanying full-color topographic map. A separate economic map defines the vital agricultural, industrial and mineral resources of the area. In the case of the foreign maps, the flag of each independent nation appears on the appropriate page. Finally, certain country units contain special subject maps dealing with the history, climate, demography and vegetation of the area.

The back of the book contains a second type of index. This is a multi-paged "A-to-Z" index of places that appear on the maps. The use of this map index is essential when the name of a place is known but its country, state, or province is unknown.

Of course, the maps have been thoroughly updated. These revisions echo the new nations, shifting boundaries and the fluid internal divisions of many countries. New communities generated by the opening up of resources in the developing nations are also noted. Up-to-date geographical information, both foreign and domestic, is received daily by the atlas editors. A worldwide correspondence and thorough research brings to the atlas user the latest geographical and demographic information obtainable.

In closing it may be said that the atlas has truly been designed for contemporary use. Just as the information presented on the following pages is as current and up to date as the editors and cartographers could issue it, so the design and organization has been as well planned as possible to create a work useful to present generations.

President
HAMMOND INCORPORATED

Introduction to the Maps and Indexes

The following notes have been added to aid the reader in making the best use of this atlas. Though he may be familiar with maps and map indexes, the publisher believes that a quick review of the material below will add to his enjoyment of this reference work.

Arrangement — The Plan of the Atlas. The atlas has been designed with maximum convenience for the user as its objective. The first part of the atlas is devoted to the physical world — terrain maps of land forms and the sea floor. The rest of the atlas contains the general political reference maps, area by area. All geographically related information pertaining to a country or region appears on adjacent pages, eliminating the task of searching throughout the entire volume for data on a given area. Thus, the reader will find, conveniently assembled, political, topographic, economic and special maps of a political area or region, accompanied by detailed map indexes, statistical data, and illustrations of the national flags of the area.

The sequence of country units in this American-designed atlas in international in arrangement. Units on the world as a whole are followed by a section on the polar regions which, in turn, is followed by pages devoted to Europe and its countries. Following the maps of the European continent and its countries, the geographic sequence plan proceeds as follows: Africa, Asia, the Pacific and Australia, South America, North America, and ends with detailed coverage on the United States.

Political Maps — The Primary Reference Tool. The most detailed maps in each country unit are the *political maps.* It is our feeling that the reader is likely to refer to these maps more often than to any other in the book when confronted by such questions as — Where? How big? What is it near? Answering these common queries is the function of the political maps. Each political map stresses *political* phenomena — countries, internal political divisions, boundaries, cities and towns. The major political unit or units, shown on the map, are banded in distinctive colors for easy identification and delineation. First-order political subdivisions (states, provinces, counties on the state maps) are shown, scale permitting.

The reader is advised to make use of the *legend* appearing under the title on each political map. Map *symbols,* the special "language" of maps, are explained in the legend. Each variety of dot, circle, star or interrupted line has a special meaning which should be clearly understood by the user so that he may interpret the map data correctly.

Each country has been portrayed at a *scale* commensurate with its political, areal, economic or tourist importance. In certain cases, a whole map unit may be devoted to a single nation if that nation is considered to be of prime interest to most atlas users. In other cases, several nations will be shown on a single map if, as separate entities, they are of lesser relative importance. Areas of dense settlement and important significance within a country have been enlarged and portrayed in inset maps inserted on the margins of the main map. The reader is advised to refer to the linear or "bar" scale appearing on each map or map inset in order to determine the distance between points.

The *projection* system used for each map is noted near the title of the map. Map projections are the special graphic systems used by cartographers to render the curved three-dimensional surface of the globe on a flat surface. Optimum map projections determined by the attributes of the area have been used by the the publishers for each map in the atlas.

A word here as to the choice of place names on the maps. Throughout the atlas names appear, with a few exceptions, in their local official spellings. However, conventional Anglicized spellings are used for major geographical divisions and for towns and topographic features for which English forms exist;

i.e., "Spain" instead of "España" or "Munich" instead of "München." Names of this type are normally followed by the local official spelling in parentheses. As an aid to the user the indexes are cross-referenced for all current and most former spellings of such names.

Names of cities and towns in the United States follow the forms listed in the *Post Office Directory* of the United States Postal Service. Domestic physical names follow the decisions of the Board on Geographic Names, U.S. Department of the Interior, and of various state geographic name boards.

It is the belief of the publishers that the boundaries shown in a general reference atlas should reflect current geographic and political realities. This policy has been followed consistently in the atlas. The presentation of *de facto* boundaries in cases of territorial dispute between various nations does not imply the political endorsement of such boundaries by the publisher, but simply the honest representation of boundaries as they exist at the time of the printing of the atlas maps.

Indexes — Pinpointing a Location. Each political map (except for individual United States maps) is accompanied by a comprehensive index of the place names appearing on the map. If you are unfamiliar with the location of a particular geographical place and wish to find its position within the confines of the subject area of the map, consult the map index as your first step. The name of the feature sought will be found in its proper alphabetical sequence with a key reference letter-number combination corresponding to its location on the map. After noting the key reference letter-number combination for the place name, turn to the map. The place name will be found within the square formed by the two lines of latitude and the two lines of longitude which enclose the co-ordinates — i.e., the marginal letters and numbers, the diagram below illustrates the system of indexing.

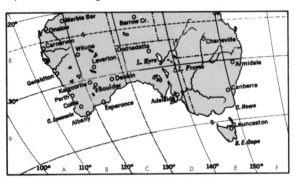

Where space on the map has not permitted giving the complete form of the place name, the complete form is shown in the index. Where a place is known by more than one name or by various spellings of the same name, the different forms have been included in the index. Physical features are listed under their proper names and not according to their generic terms; that is to say, Rio Negro will be found under Negro and not under Rio Negro. On the other hand, Rio Grande will be found under Rio Grande. Accompanying most index entries for cities and towns, and for other political units, are *population figures* for the particular entries. The large number of population figures in the atlas makes this work one of the most comprehensive statistical sources available to the public today. The population figures have been taken from the latest official censuses and estimates of the various nations.

Population and area figures for countries and major political units are listed in bold type *fact lists* on the margins of the indexes. In addition, the capital, largest city, highest point, monetary unit, principal languages and the prevailing religions of the country concerned are also listed. The Gazetteer-Index of the World on the following pages provides a quick reference

index for countries and other important areas. Though population and area figures for each major unit are also found in the map section, the Gazetteer-Index provides a conveniently arranged statistical comparison contained in two pages.

Relief Maps. Accompanying each political map is a relief map of the area. These are in addition to the terrain maps of land forms in the front of the atlas. The purpose of the relief map is to illustrate the surface configuration (TOPOGRAPHY) of the region. A shading technique in color simulates the relative ruggedness of the terrain — plains, plateaus, valleys, hills and mountains. Graded colors, ranging from greens for lowlands, yellows for intermediate elevations to browns in the highlands, indicate the height above sea level of each part of the land. A vertical scale at the margin of the map shows the approximate height in meters and feet represented by each color.

Economic Maps — Agriculture, Industry and Resources. One of the most interesting features that will be found in each country unit is the economic map. From this map one can determine the basic activities of a nation as expressed through its economy. A perusal of the map yields a full understanding of the area's economic geography and natural resources.

The agricultural economy is manifested in two ways: color bands and commodity names. The color bands express broad categories of *dominant land use*, such as cereal belts, forest lands, livestock range lands, nonagricultural wastes. The red commodity names, on the other hand, pinpoint the areas of production of *specific* crops; i.e., wheat, cotton, sugar beets, etc.

Major mineral occurrences are denoted by standard letter symbols appearing in blue. The relative size of the letter symbols signifies the relative importance of the deposit.

The manufacturing sector of the economy is presented by means of diagonal line patterns expressing the various *industrial* areas of consequence within a country.

The fishing industry is represented by names of commercial fish species appearing offshore in blue letters. Major waterpower sites are designated by blue symbols.

The publishers have tried to make this work the most comprehensive and useful atlas available, and it is hoped that it will prove a valuable reference work. Any constructive suggestions from the reader will be welcomed.

Sources and Acknowledgments

A multitude of sources goes into the making of a large-scale reference work such as this. To list them all would take many pages and would consume space better devoted to the maps and reference materials themselves. However, certain general sources were very useful in preparing this work and are listed below.

STATISTICAL OFFICE OF THE UNITED NATIONS.
Demographic Yearbook. New York. Issued annually.

STATISTICAL OFFICE OF THE UNITED NATIONS.
Statisical Yearbook. Nw York. Issued annually.

THE GEOGRAPHER, U.S. DEPARTMENT OF STATE
International Boundary Study papers. Washington. Various dates.

THE GEOGRAPHER, U.S. DEPARTMENT OF STATE.
Geographic Notes. Washington. Various dates.

UNITED STATES BOARD ON GEOGRAPHIC NAMES.
Decisions on Geographic Names in the United States. Washington. Various dates.

UNITED STATES BOARD ON GEOGRAPHIC NAMES.
Official Standard Names Gazetteers. Washington. Various dates.

CANADIAN PERMANENT COMMITTEE ON GEOGRAPHICAL NAMES.
Gazetteer of Canada series. Ottawa. Various dates.

UNITED STATES POSTAL SERVICE.
National Five Digit ZIP Code and Post Office Directory. Washington. Issued annually.

UNITED STATES POSTAL SERVICE.
Postal Bulletin. Washington. Issued weekly.

UNITED STATES DEPARTMENT OF THE INTERIOR.
BUREAU OF MINES.
Minerals Yearbook. 4 vols. Washington. Various dates.

UNITED STATES GEOLOGICAL SURVEY.
Elevations and distances in the United States. Reston, Va. 1980.

CARTACTUAL.
Cartactual — Topical Map Service. Budapest. Issued bi-monthly.

AMERICAN GEOGRAPHICAL SOCIETY.
Focus. New York. Issued ten times a year.

THE AMERICAN UNIVERSITY.
Foreign Area Studies. Washington. Various dates.

CENTRAL INTELLIGENCE AGENCY.
General reference maps. Washington. Various dates.

A sample list of sources used for specific countries follows:

Afghanistan
CENTRAL STATISTICS OFFICE.
Preliminary Results of the First Afghan Population Census 1979. Kabul.

Albania
DREJTORIA E STATISTIKES.
1979 Census. Tiranë.

Argentina
INSTITUTO NACIONAL DE ESTADISTICA Y CENSOS.
Censo Nacional de Población y Vivienda 1980. Buenos Aires.

Australia
AUSTRALIAN BUREAU OF STATISTICS.
Census of Population and Housing 1981. Canberra.

Brazil
FUNDACAO INSTITUTO BRASILEIRO DE GEOGRAFIA E ESTATISTICA.
IX Recenseamento Geral do Brasil 1980. Rio de Janeiro.

Canada
STATISTICS CANADA.
1981 Census of Canada. Ottawa.

Cuba
COMITE ESTATAL DE ESTADISTICAS.
Censo de Población y Viviendas 1981. Havana.

Hungary
HUNGARIAN CENTRAL STATISTICAL OFFICE.
1980 Census. Budapest.

Indonesia
BIRO PUSAT STATISTIK.
Sensus Penduduk 1980. Jakarta.

Kuwait
CENTRAL OFFICE OF STATISTICS.
1980 Census. Al Kuwait.

New Zealand
DEPARTMENT OF STATISTICS.
New Zealand Census of Population and Dwellings 1981. Wellington.

Panama
DIRECCIÓN DE ESTADISTICA Y CENSO.
Censos Nacionales de 1980. Panamá.

Papua New Guinea
BUREAU OF STATISTICS.
National Population Census 1980. Port Moresby.

Philippines
NATIONAL CENSUS AND STATISTICS OFFICE.
1980 Census of Population. Manila.

Saint Lucia
CENSUS OFFICE.
1980 Population Census. Castries.

Singapore
DEPARTMENT OF STATISTICS.
Census of Population 1980. Singapore.

U.S.S.R.
CENTRAL STATISTICAL ADMINISTRATION.
1979 Census. Moscow.

United States
BUREAU OF THE CENSUS.
1980 Census of Population. Washington.

Vanuatu
CENSUS OFFICE.
1979 Population Census. Port Vila.

Zambia
CENTRAL STATISTICAL OFFICE.
1980 Census of Population and Housing. Lusaka.

Gazetteer—Index of the World

This alphabetical list of grand divisions, countries, states, colonial possessions, etc., gives page numbers and index references on which they are shown on the largest scale as well as area and population of each unit. The index reference shows the square on the respective map in which the name of the entry may be located.

Country	Page No.	Index Ref.	Area Square Miles	Area Square Kilometers	Population
*Afghanistan	70	A 2	250,775	649,507	15,540,000
Africa	54, 57	.....	11,707,000	30,321,130	469,000,000
Alabama, U.S.A.	129	.....	51,705	133,916	3,893,888
Alaska, U.S.A.	130	.....	591,004	1,530,700	401,851
*Albania	43	E 5	11,100	28,749	2,590,600
Alberta, Canada	114	.....	255,285	661,185	2,237,724
*Algeria	54	F 6	919,591	2,381,740	17,422,000
American Samoa	89	J 7	77	199	32,297
Andorra	31	G 1	188	487	31,000
*Angola	57	K14	481,351	1,246,700	7,078,000
Anguilla	124	F 3	35	91	6,519
Antarctica	5	.....	5,500,000	14,245,000	.....
*Antigua and Barbuda	124	G 3	171	443	72,000
*Argentina	93	H10	1,072,070	2,776,661	28,438,000
Arizona, U.S.A.	131	.....	114,000	295,260	2,718,425
Arkansas, U.S.A.	132	.....	53,187	137,754	2,286,435
Aruba	124	E 3	75	193	55,148
Ascension Island, St. Helena	1	.....	34	88	719
Asia	58	.....	17,128,500	44,362,815	2,633,000,000
*Australia	86	.....	2,966,136	7,682,300	14,576,330
*Austria	38	B 3	32,375	83,851	7,507,000
*Bahamas	124	C 1	5,382	13,939	209,505
*Bahrain	60	F 4	240	622	358,857
*Bangladesh	70	F 3	55,126	142,776	87,052,024
*Barbados	125	G 4	166	430	248,983
*Belgium	25	E 7	11,781	30,513	9,855,110
*Belize	122	C 2	8,867	22,966	144,857
*Benin	54	G10	43,483	112,620	3,338,240
Bermuda	125	H 3	21	54	67,761
Bhutan	70	G 3	18,147	47,000	1,298,000
Bolivia	90	G 7	424,163	1,098,582	5,600,000
*Botswana	57	L16	224,764	582,139	819,000
*Brazil	90	K 6	3,284,426	8,506,663	119,098,992
British Columbia, Canada	117	.....	366,253	948,596	2,744,467
British Indian Ocean Terr.	58	L10	29	75	2,000
Brunei	83	E 4	2,226	5,765	192,832
*Bulgaria	43	F 4	42,823	110,912	8,862,000
*Burkina Faso	54	F 9	105,869	274,200	6,908,000
*Burma	81	B 2	261,789	678,034	32,913,000
*Burundi	57	M12	10,747	27,835	4,021,910
California, U.S.A.	133	.....	158,706	411,049	23,667,565
*Cambodia (Kampuchea)	81	E 4	69,898	181,036	5,200,000
*Cameroon	54	J10	183,568	475,441	8,503,000
*Canada	96-97	.....	3,851,787	9,976,139	24,343,181
*Cape Verde	1	.....	1,557	4,033	324,000
Cayman Islands	124	B 3	100	259	16,677
*Central African Republic	54	K10	242,000	626,780	2,284,000
Central America	122-123	.....	197,480	511,475	21,000,000
Ceylon, see Sri Lanka					
*Chad	54	K 8	495,752	1,283,998	4,309,000
Channel Islands	11	E 8	75	194	133,000
*Chile	93	F10	292,257	756,946	11,275,440
*China, People's Rep. of	77	.....	3,691,000	9,559,690	958,090,000
China, Republic of (Taiwan)	77	K 7	13,971	36,185	16,609,961
*Colombia	90	F 3	439,513	1,138,339	27,520,000
Colorado, U.S.A.	134	.....	104,091	269,596	2,889,735
*Comoros	57	P14	719	1,862	290,000
*Congo, Rep. of	57	J12	132,046	342,000	1,537,000
Connecticut, U.S.A.	135	.....	5,018	12,997	3,107,576
Cook Islands	89	K 7	91	236	17,695
*Costa Rica	122	E 5	19,575	50,700	2,245,000
*Cuba	124	B 2	44,206	114,494	9,706,369
*Cyprus	64	E 5	3,473	8,995	629,000
*Czechoslovakia	39	C 2	49,373	127,876	15,276,799
Delaware, U.S.A.	146	R 3	2,044	5,294	594,317
*Denmark	19	.....	16,629	43,069	5,124,000
District of Columbia, U.S.A.	146	F 5	69	179	638,432
*Djibouti	55	P 9	8,880	23,000	386,000
*Dominica	125	G 4	290	751	74,089
*Dominican Republic	124	D 3	18,704	48,443	5,647,977
*Ecuador	90	E 4	109,483	283,561	8,354,000
*Egypt	54	M 6	386,659	1,001,447	41,572,000
*El Salvador	122	C 4	8,260	21,393	4,813,000
England, U.K.	11	.....	50,516	130,836	46,220,955
*Equatorial Guinea	57	H11	10,831	28,052	244,000
*Ethiopia	54-55	O 9	471,776	1,221,900	31,065,000
Europe	6	.....	4,057,000	10,507,630	676,000,000
Faerøe Islands, Denmark	19	B 2	540	1,399	41,969
Falkland Islands & Dependencies	93	H14	6,198	16,053	1,812
*Fiji	89	H 8	7,055	18,272	588,068
*Finland	16	O 6	130,128	337,032	4,788,000
Florida, U.S.A.	136	.....	58,664	151,940	9,746,342
*France	26	.....	210,038	543,998	53,788,000
French Guiana	90	K 3	35,135	91,000	73,022
French Polynesia	89	L 8	1,544	4,000	137,382
*Gabon	57	J12	103,346	267,666	551,000
*Gambia	54	C 9	4,127	10,689	601,000
Georgia, U.S.A.	137	.....	58,910	152,577	5,463,105
*Germany, East (German Democratic Republic)	20	.....	41,768	108,179	16,737,000
*Germany, West (Federal Republic)	20	.....	95,985	248,601	61,658,000
*Ghana	54	F10	92,099	238,536	11,450,000
Gibraltar	31	D 4	2.28	5.91	29,760
*Great Britain & Northern Ireland (United Kingdom)	8	.....	94,399	244,493	55,672,000
*Greece	43	F 6	50,944	131,945	9,599,000
Greenland	4	B12	840,000	2,175,600	49,773
*Grenada	125	G 4	133	344	103,103
Guadeloupe & Dependencies	124	F 3	687	1,779	328,400
Guam	89	E 4	209	541	105,979
*Guatemala	122	B 3	42,042	108,889	7,262,419
*Guinea	54	D 9	94,925	245,856	5,143,284
*Guinea-Bissau	54	C 9	13,948	36,125	777,214
*Guyana	90	J 2	83,000	214,970	820,000
*Haiti	124	D 3	10,694	27,697	5,009,000
Hawaii, U.S.A.	130	.....	6,471	16,760	964,691
Holland, see Netherlands					
*Honduras	122	D 3	43,277	112,087	3,691,000
Hong Kong	77	H 7	403	1,044	5,022,000
*Hungary	39	E 3	35,919	93,030	10,709,536
*Iceland	19	B 1	39,768	103,000	228,785
Idaho, U.S.A.	138	.....	83,564	216,431	944,038
Illinois, U.S.A.	139	.....	56,345	145,934	11,426,596
*India	70	D 4	1,269,339	3,287,588	683,810,051
*Indiana, U.S.A.	140	.....	36,185	93,719	5,490,260
*Indonesia	83	D 7	788,430	2,042,034	147,490,298
Iowa, U.S.A.	141	.....	56,275	145,752	2,913,808
*Iran	68	F 4	636,293	1,648,000	37,447,000
*Iraq	68	C 4	172,476	446,713	12,767,000
*Ireland	15	.....	27,136	70,282	3,440,427
Ireland, Northern, U.K.	15	F 2	5,452	14,121	1,543,000
Isle of Man	11	C 3	227	588	64,000
*Israel	67	B 4	7,847	20,324	3,878,000
*Italy	32	.....	116,303	301,225	57,140,000
*Ivory Coast	54	E10	124,504	322,465	7,920,000
*Jamaica	124	C 3	4,411	11,424	2,161,000
*Japan	75	.....	145,730	377,441	117,057,485
*Jordan	67	D 3	35,000	90,650	2,152,273
*Kampuchea (Cambodia)	81	E 4	69,898	181,036	5,200,000
Kansas, U.S.A.	142	.....	82,277	213,097	2,364,236
Kentucky, U.S.A.	143	.....	40,409	104,659	3,660,257
*Kenya	57	O11	224,960	582,646	15,327,061
Kiribati	89	J 6	291	754	57,500
Korea, North	74	D 3	46,540	120,539	17,914,000
Korea, South	74	D 5	38,175	98,873	37,448,836
*Kuwait	60	E 4	6,532	16,918	1,355,827
*Laos	81	D 3	91,428	236,800	3,721,000
*Lebanon	64	F 6	4,015	10,399	3,161,000
*Lesotho	57	M17	11,720	30,355	1,339,000
*Liberia	54	E10	43,000	111,370	1,873,000
*Libya	54	J 6	679,358	1,759,537	2,856,000
Liechtenstein	37	J 2	61	158	25,220
Louisiana, U.S.A.	144	.....	47,752	123,678	4,206,312
*Luxembourg	25	J 9	999	2,587	364,000
Macau	77	H 7	6	16	271,000
*Madagascar	57	R16	226,657	587,041	8,742,000
Maine, U.S.A.	145	.....	33,265	86,156	1,125,027
*Malawi	57	N14	45,747	118,485	5,968,000
Malaya, Malaysia	81	D 6	50,806	131,588	11,138,227

*Member of the United Nations

Gazetteer—Index of the World

HAMMOND

THE PHYSICAL WORLD
Terrain Maps of Land Forms and Ocean Floors

CONTENTS

RELIEF MODELS BY ERNST G. HOFMANN, ASSISTED BY RAFAEL MARTINEZ

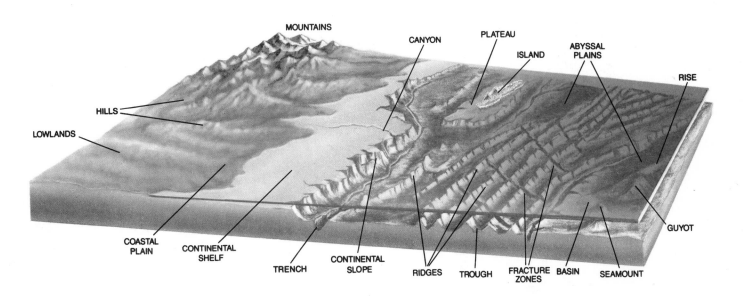

The oblique view diagram above is designed to provide a detailed view of the ocean floor as if seen through the depth of the sea. Graduating blue tones are used to contrast ocean floor depths: from light blue to represent shallow continental shelves to dark blues in the greater depths. Land relief is shown in conventional hypsometric tints.

In this dramatic collection of topographic maps of continents, oceans and major regions of the world, Hammond introduces a revolutionary new technique in cartography.

While most maps depicting terrain are created from painted artwork that is then photographed, Hammond now premiers the use of a remarkable sculptured model mapping technique created by one of our master cartographers.

The process begins with the sculpting of large scale three-dimensional models. Once physical details have been etched on the models and refinements completed, relief work is checked for accurate elevation based on a vertical scale exaggerated for visual effect.

Finished models are airbrushed and painted, then photographed using a single northwesterly light source to achieve a striking three-dimensional effect. The result is the dynamic presentation of mountain ranges and peaks on land, and canyons, trenches and seamounts on the ocean floor. Never before have maps conveyed such rich beauty while providing a realistic representation of the world as we know it.

G H I J K L M

ARCTIC   OCEAN

FRANZ JOSEF LAND   SEVERNAYA
                          ZEMLYA   NEW SIBERIAN IS.   1

SVALBARD   Wrangel
                    NOVAYA   Laptev   I.
Nordkapp   ZEMLYA   Kara   Sea
        Barents   Sea
            Sea   Bering Sea   2
                                                                        Kamchatka   ALEUTIAN
L. Ladoga   S i b e r i a   Pen.   BASIN
Baltic Sea   ALEUTIAN ISLANDS
                    Ob   Yenisey   Sea
EUROPE   Ural Mountains   Lena   Aldan   of   KURIL-KAMCHATKA TRENCH ALEUTIAN TRENCH
        Volga   Angara   L. Baikal   Amur   Okhotsk   3
Dnieper   Aral   Irtysh Ob   Sakhalin
Danube Black Sea Caspian Sea   Honshu   NORTHWEST
        L. Balkhash   Gobi   Japan   PACIFIC
Mediterranean Sea   JAPAN BASIN
                    Kunlun   Hwang   East   TRENCH
                Himalaya Mt. Everest Chang China
AFRICA   Nile Euphrates Indus Ganges   Sea   Tropic of Cancer
        Nile   Arabian   Bay of   South   MARIANA
            Sea   Sea   ARABIAN   Bengal   China   PHILIPPINE MARIANA TRENCH MARSHALL IS. CENTRAL 4
                    BASIN   C. Comorin Sea   IS. Luzon Challenger   PACIFIC
                                  Ceylon   Borneo   BASIN Mindanao Deep   BASIN
        SOMALI   CENTRAL CEYLON   CAROLINE IS.
Victoria BASIN   PLAIN Sumatra   Java Celebes   New Guinea MELANESIAN Equator
Kilimanjaro   INDIAN   JAVA TRENCH   BASIN   5
        Tanga   RIDGE   Coral
                Madagascar   Sea   Fiji Is.
OLA   North Cape
VALVIS RIDGE   AUSTRALIA   Tasman
CAPE   SOUTHEAST INDIAN RIDGE BROKEN   C. Leeuwin   Sea North I.
C. of Good Hope   PLATEAU   South I.
BASIN   INDIAN   OCEAN   S. AUSTRALIA BASIN   Tasmania
AGULHAS RIDGE   6
                KERGUELEN   SOUTHEAST INDIAN RIDGE
                PLATEAU
        ENDERBY ABYSSAL PLAIN   AUSTRALIAN-ANTARCTIC BASIN
                                                      Antarctic Circle   7
                Amery
                Ice Shelf   C. Adare
        ANTARCTICA   Ross Sea

0 500 1000 1500 2000 2500 3000 MILES at Equator
0 500 1000 1500 2000 2500 3000 KILOMETERS at Equator

© Copyright 1987 by HAMMOND INCORPORATED, Maplewood, N.J.   Ross Ice Shelf

G H I J K L M

LEGEND FOR TERRAIN MAPS

International Boundaries ___.___   Mountain Peaks ▲
State and Provincial Boundaries _.._   National Capitals ⊛
Other Boundaries ____   Other Capitals ⊛
Boundaries Along Rivers   Canals

ICELAND BASIN

REYKJANES RIDGE

IRMINGER BASIN

ICELAND

Reykjavik

DENMARK STRAIT

Arctic Circle

GREENLAND
(Denmark)

BAFFIN BAY

DAVIS STRAIT

Nuuk

Baffin Island

Cumberland Pen.

Cumberland Sd.

Frobisher Bay

Foxe Pen.

LABRADOR BASIN

LABRADOR SEA

NEWFOUNDLAND

C. Race

GRAND BANKS OF NEWFOUNDLAND

St. John's

Newfoundland

Hamilton

Ungava Bay

Goose Bay

Churchill

C. Chidley

Smallwood Res.

C. Breton I.

Cape Breton I.

NOVA SCOTIA

CONTINENTAL SHELF

ATLANTIC OCEAN

ARCTIC OCEAN

C. Columbia

QUEEN ELIZABETH ISLANDS

Ellef Ringnes I.

N. Mag. Pole

Axel Heiberg Island

Ellesmere Island

Peel Sd.

Devon I.

Bylot I.

Brodeur Pen.

Somerset I.

Boothia Pen.

Gulf of Boothia

M'Clintock Chan.

Pt. Charles

Foxe Basin

Foxe Chan.

Mansel I.

Southampton I.

Coats I.

Melville Pen.

Rankin Inlet

Hudson Strait

Ungava Peninsula

Belcher Is.

James Bay

Akimiski I.

HUDSON BAY

Churchill

QUÉBEC

ONTARIO

La Grande

Caniapiscau

Canapiscau

Peribonca

Rupert

Mistassini

St-Jean

Québec

Montréal

Ottawa

Ottawa

Toronto

Hamilton

Niagara Falls

L. Ontario

L. Erie

Cleveland

Detroit

Windsor

Lake Huron

Georgian Bay

Sudbury

Timmins

Abitibi

Lake Superior

Sault Ste. Marie

Thunder Bay

L. Nipigon

Lake Michigan

Milwaukee

Chicago

Gulf of St. Lawrence

P.E.I.

Charlottetown

NEW BR.

Fredericton

Halifax

Boston

C. Cod

New York

Philadelphia

Pittsburgh

UNITED STATES

Hudson

St. Lawrence

NORTHWIND RIDGE

CANADA BASIN

BEAUFORT SEA

Banks Island

Prince Patrick I.

Melville I.

Bathurst I.

Prince of Wales I.

Victoria Island

Cambridge Bay

Amundsen Gulf

Coppermine

Back

Kazan

Dubawnt

Thelon

L a u r e n t i a n

C a n a d i a n   S h i e l d

Great Bear Lake

Great Slave Lake

Yellowknife

MANITOBA

SASKATCHEWAN

NORTHWEST TERRITORIES

Reindeer L.

So. Indian L.

Nelson

Lake Winnipeg

L. Winnipegosis

Winnipeg

Brandon

Red

L. Manitoba

L. of the Woods

Lake Winnipeg

Minneapolis

St. Paul

Mississippi

Missouri

BEAUFORT SHELF

Pt. Barrow

Brooks Range

ALASKA

UNITED STATES

Yukon

Tanana

Kobuk

Porcupine

Inuvik

Mackenzie

Liard

Ft. Nelson

Peace

Athabasca

Hay

L. Athabasca

ALBERTA

Edmonton

Calgary

Lethbridge

Bow

YUKON TERRITORY

BRITISH COLUMBIA

Whitehorse

Stikine

Liard

Prince George

Fraser

Columbia

Churchill

N. Sask.

Prince Albert

Saskatoon

Regina

Swift Current

S. Sask.

Yellowstone

Missouri

R o c k y   M o u n t a i n s

CHUKCHI SEA

USSR

Bering Strait

Nome

Gulf of Alaska

Alexander Archipelago

Queen Charlotte Is.

Queen Charlotte Sd.

Vancouver I.

Vancouver

Victoria

C. Flattery

Portland

CASCADE RANGE

PACIFIC OCEAN

Prince Rupert

Alaska Range

Anchorage

C O R D I L L E R A

100   200   300   400   500 MILES

100 200 300 400 500 600 700 KILOMETERS

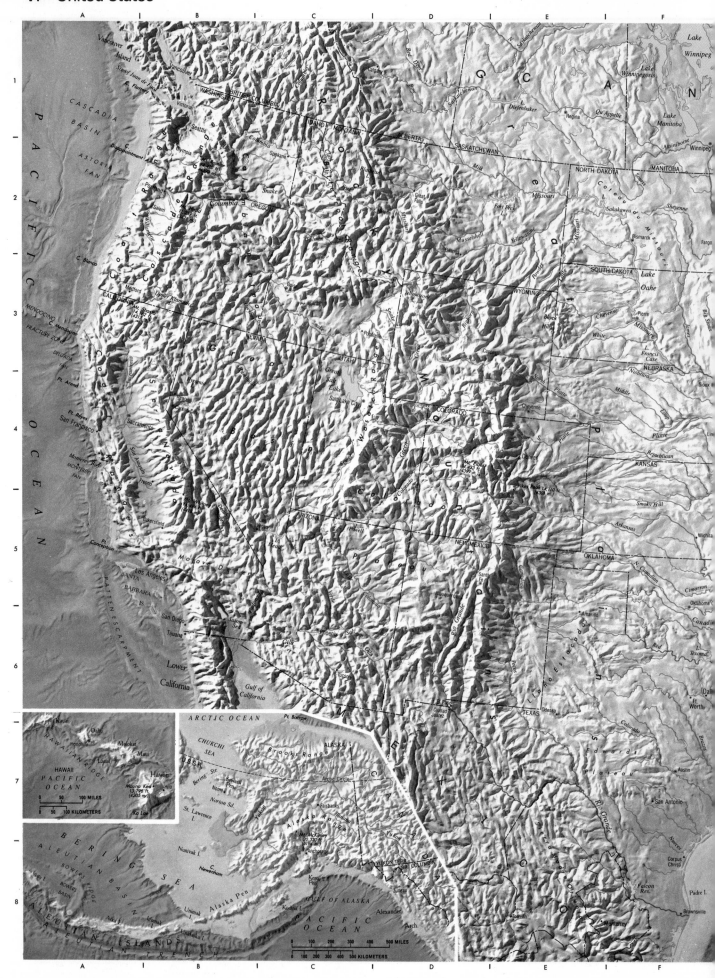

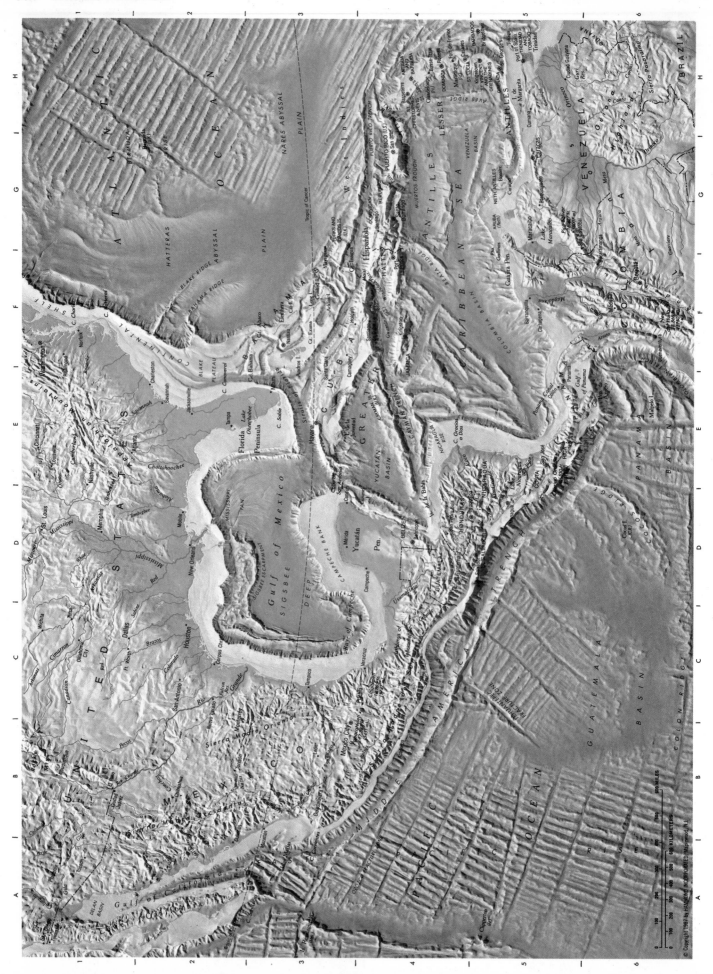

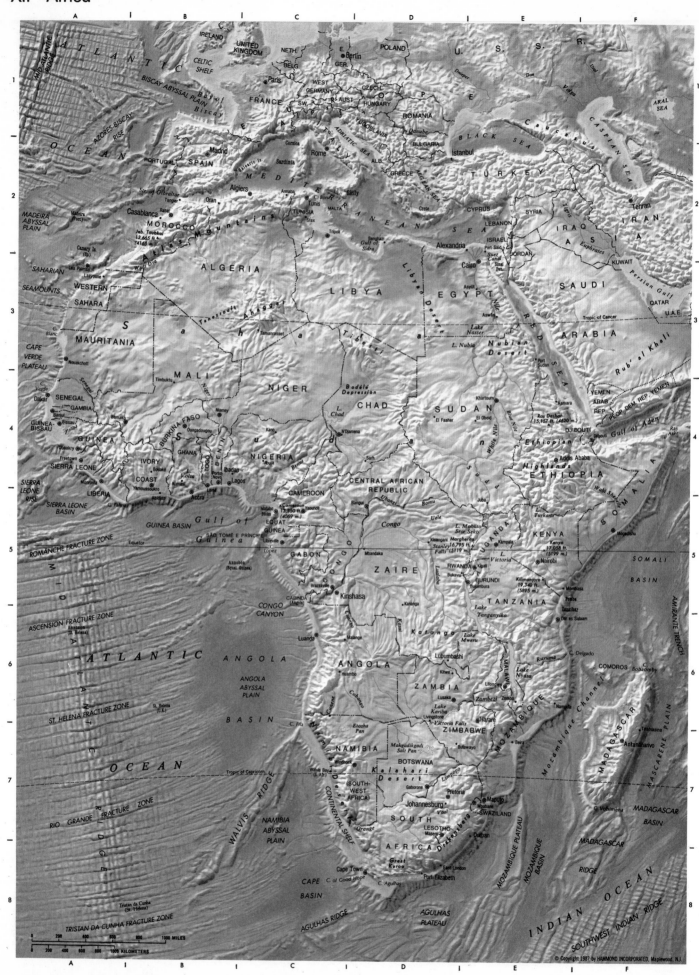

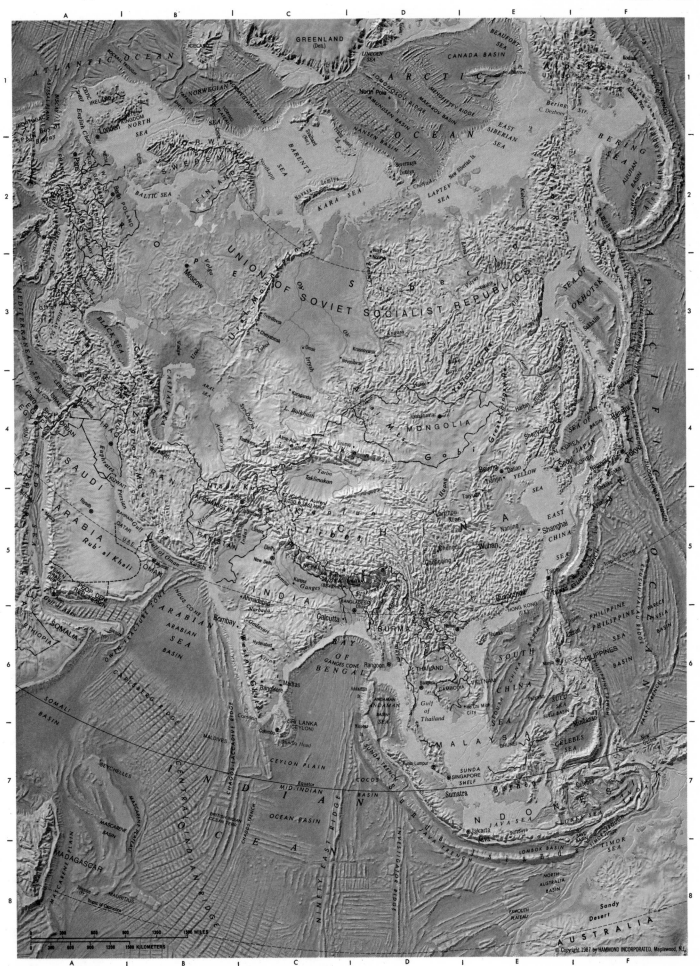

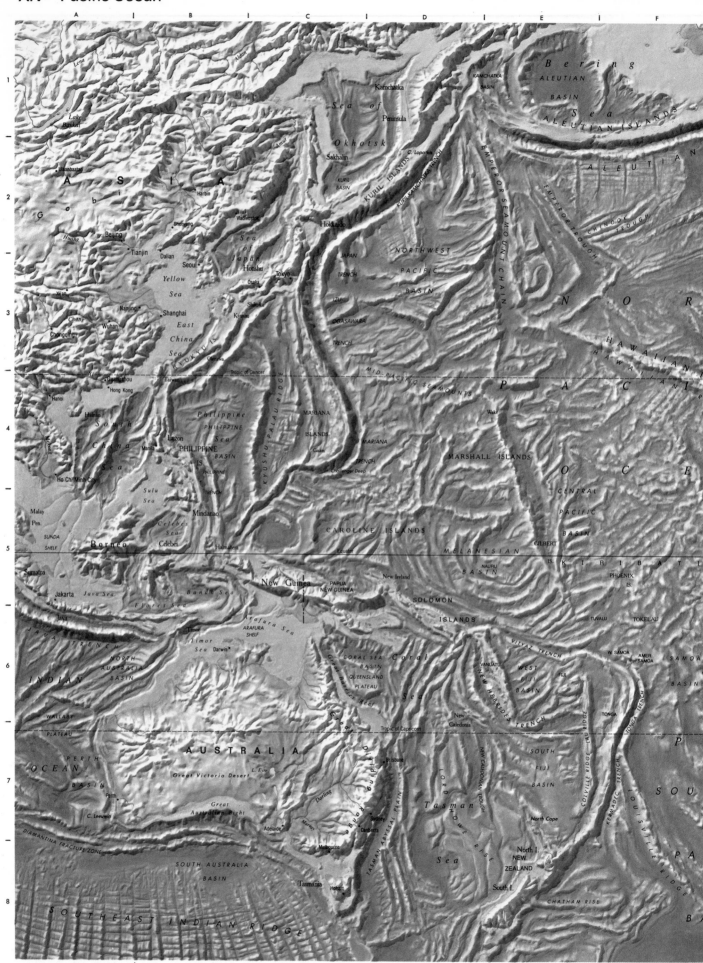

A · I · B · I · C · I · D · I · E · I · F

Lena

Aldan

1

Kamchatka

Sea of

Bering

KAMCHATKA

ALEUTIAN

Lake Baikal

Amur

Okhotsk

Peninsula

BASIN

Sea

C. Lopatka

ALEUTIAN ISLANDS

Sakhalin

KURIL-KAMCHATKA TRENCH

EMPEROR SEAMOUNT CHAIN

A L E U T I A N

Ulaanbaatar

A S I A

Harbin

KURIL BASIN

KURIL ISLANDS

Hokkaido

EMPEROR TROUGH

CHINOOK TROUGH

2

G *o   b   i*

Shenyang

Vladivostok

JAPAN TRENCH

NORTHWEST

Huang

Beijing

Sea

N   *O*   *R*   *R*

Tianjin

Dalian

of

PACIFIC

Xian

Seoul

Japan

Honshu

IZU

BASIN

HAWAIIAN

Yellow

Osaka

Tokyo

HAWAIIAN

3

Nanjing

Shanghai

Sea

Shikoku

OGASAWARA

Chang

Wuhan

East

Kyushu

TRENCH

Chongqing

China

RYUKYU IS.

MID-PACIFIC SEAMOUNTS

P   *A*   *C*   *I*

Sea

Okinawa

Tropic of Cancer

Guangzhou

Taiwan

Hanoi

Hong Kong

Philippine

MARIANA

Wake

Hainan

South

PHILIPPINE

Sea

ISLANDS

MARIANA

4

China

Luzon

PHILIPPINE

Manila

MARSHALL ISLANDS

O   *C*   *E*

Sea

PHILIPPINE

BASIN

Guam

Ho Chi Minh City

IS.

MARIANA

KYUSHU-PALAU RIDGE

TRENCH

Malay

PHILIPPINE

Challenger Deep

CENTRAL

Pen.

Sulu

TRENCH

SUNDA

Sea

PACIFIC

SHELF

Celebes

Mindanao

BASIN

GILBERT

5

Borneo

Sea

Celebes

Halmahera

CAROLINE ISLANDS

MELANESIAN

Sumatra

Equator

NAURU

BASIN

Jakarta

Java Sea

Banda Sea

New Ireland

K *I* *R* *I* *B* *A* *T* *I*

PHOENIX

Java

Flores Sea

New Guinea

PAPUA

SOLOMON

IS.

JAVA

Arafura

NEW GUINEA

TUVALU

TOKELAU

TRENCH

Timor

Sea

ISLANDS

VITYAZ TRENCH

6

NORTH

ARAFURA

Darwin

W. SAMOA

AUSTRALIA

Timor

SHELF

CORAL SEA

VANUATU

WEST

AMER.

SAMOA

BASIN

Sea

BASIN

FIJI

SAMOA

INDIAN

CORAL

NEW HEBRIDES TRENCH

FIJI

BASIN

BASIN

QUEENSLAND

Coral

WALLABY

PLATEAU

Sea

New

TONGA

PLATEAU

Great Barrier Reef

Caledonia

Tropic of Capricorn

P

PERTH

AUSTRALIA

Brisbane

SOUTH

OCEAN

Great Victoria Desert

L. Eyre

Great Dividing Range

FIJI

7

BASIN

Perth

BASIN

COLVILLE RIDGE-LAU RIDGE

SOU

C. Leeuwin

Great

Darling

NEW CALEDONIAN TROUGH

Australian Bight

Tasman

North Cape

Adelaide

Murray

Sydney

Sea

LORD HOWE RISE

TONGA TRENCH

Canberra

LOUISVILLE RIDGE

KERMADEC TRENCH

Melbourne

TASMAN ABYSSAL PLAIN

North I.

P

DIAMANTINA FRACTURE ZONE

SOUTH AUSTRALIA

NEW

Tasmania

BASIN

Hobart

ZEALAND

PA

South I.

8

S O U T H E A S T   I N D I A N   R I D G E

CHATHAM RISE

B

A · I · B · I · C · I · D · I · E · I · F

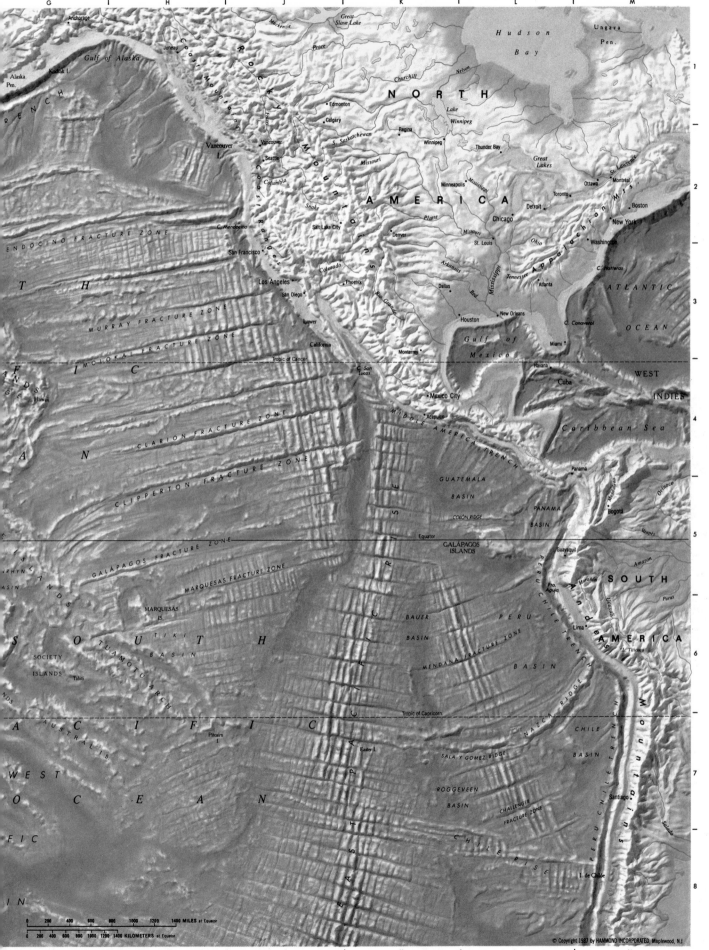

G H I H I J I J K I K L I L M I M

FRENCH

Anchorage
Juneau

Gulf of Alaska

Alaska
Pen.
Kodiak I.

Coast Mountains

ROCKY

Mackenzie

Great
Slave Lake

Peace

Churchill

Hudson
Bay

Ungava
Pen.

1

Edmonton

Calgary

Fraser

Regina

Nelson

NORTH

Lake
Winnipeg

Vancouver
Vancouver

Seattle

Coast Ranges

Columbia

S. Saskatchewan

Winnipeg

Missouri

Thunder Bay

AMERICA

Great
Lakes

St. Lawrence

Ottawa
Montréal

Appalachian Mts.

Boston

2

Snake

Minneapolis

Mississippi

Detroit

Toronto

New York

C. Mendocino

Salt Lake City

Denver

Platte

Chicago

St. Louis

Ohio

Washington

ENDOCINO FRACTURE ZONE

Missouri

ATLANTIC

San Francisco

Colorado

Arkansas

Tennessee

Atlanta

C. Hatteras

T H

Los Angeles

Phoenix

Dallas

Red

Mississippi

OCEAN

3

MURRAY FRACTURE ZONE

San Diego

Lower

Rio Grande

Houston

New Orleans

C. Canaveral

MOLOKAI FRACTURE ZONE

California

Gulf of
Mexico

Miami

Tropic of Cancer

C. San
Lucas

Havana

WEST

I C

Cuba

INDIES

ENDS

Hawaii

Mexico City

Acapulco

Caribbean Sea

4

A

CLARION FRACTURE ZONE

MIDDLE AMERICA TRENCH

N

CLIPPERTON FRACTURE ZONE

GUATEMALA
BASIN

Panamá

Magdalena

Orinoco

PANAMA
BASIN

COLON RIDGE

Bogotá

Vaupés

5

Equator

GALAPAGOS
ISLANDS

Guayaquil

Amazon

GALAPAGOS FRACTURE ZONE

SOUTH

RHYN

MARQUESAS FRACTURE ZONE

Pta.
Aguja

Marañón

ISLANDS

MARQUESAS
IS.

EAST

PACIFIC

BAUER

PERU

Purus

Ucayali

AMERICA

6

SOUTH

TIKIT

RISE

BASIN

BASIN

Lima

L. Titicaca

SOCIETY

TUAMOTU

BASIN

MENDANA FRACTURE ZONE

BASIN

ISLANDS

Tahiti

ARCH

Tropic of Capricorn

NDS

AUSTRALIS

Pitcairn
I.

NAZCA RIDGE

CHILE

7

WEST

Easter I.

SALA Y GOMEZ RIDGE

BASIN

OCEAN

ROGGEVEEN

Santiago

BASIN

CHALLENGER

FRACTURE ZONE

FIC

CHILE RISE

I. de Chiloé

8

Salado

IN

200 400 600 800 1000 1200 1400 MILES at Equator
0 200 400 600 800 1000 1200 1400 KILOMETERS at Equator

© Copyright 1987 by HAMMOND INCORPORATED, Maplewood, N.J.

G I G H I H I J I J K I K L I L M I M

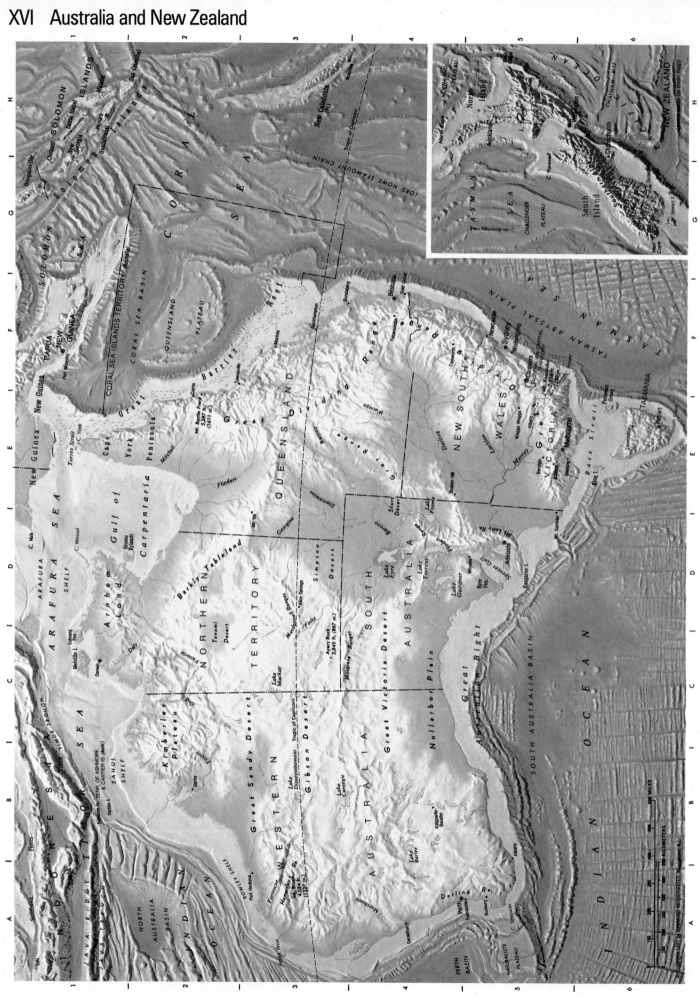

NEW ZEALAND

PACIFIC OCEAN

NORTHLAND PLATEAU

North Cape

North Island

Auckland

L. Taupo

Wellington

TASMAN SEA

CHALLENGER PLATEAU

C. Farewell

Christchurch

South Island

Dunedin

Stewart I.

West Cape

CHATHAM RISE

SOLOMON ISLANDS

Bougainville

Choiseul   Santa Isabel   Malaita

New Georgia   Honiara   San Cristobal

Guadalcanal

SOLOMON SEA

SOLOMON ISLANDS

PAPUA NEW GUINEA

Port Moresby

New Guinea

NEW GUINEA

INDONESIA

Flores

Sumbawa

Timor

JAVA TRENCH

TIMOR TROUGH

TIMOR SEA

ARAFURA SEA

ARAFURA SHELF

Bathurst I.   TERR. OF ASHMORE & CARTIER IS. (Austl.)

Cartier I.

SAHUL SHELF

ROWLEY SHELF

NORTH AUSTRALIA BASIN

INDIAN OCEAN

North West C.

Port Hedland

Forrestie

Mt. Bruce 4,024 ft. (1227 m.)

Hamersley Ra.

WESTERN

Murchison

Geraldton

C. Leeuwin

PERTH BASIN

Perth
Fremantle

Bunbury

Albany

NATURALISTE PLATEAU

Kimberley Plateau

Derby

Ord

Victoria

Fitzroy

Great Sandy Desert

Lake Disappointment

Tropic of Capricorn

Gibson Desert

Lake Carnegie

AUSTRALIA

Great Victoria Desert

Lake Barlee

Kalgoorlie-Boulder

Nullarbor Plain

CORAL SEA

New Caledonia (Fr.)

Tropic of Capricorn

Noumea

LORD HOWE SEAMOUNT CHAIN

C O R A L   S E A

Barrier   Reef

Great

CORAL SEA BASIN

CORAL SEA ISLANDS TERRITORY (Australia)

QUEENSLAND PLATEAU

QUEENSLAND

Cape York Peninsula

C. York

Torres Strait

C. Vels

C. Wessel

Melville I.

Coburg Pen.

Arnhem Land

Darwin

Daly

Gulf of Carpentaria

Groote Eylandt

Mitchell

Flinders

Barkly Tableland

Tanami Desert

NORTHERN TERRITORY

Lake Mackay

Macdonnell Ranges

Alice Springs

Finke

Ayers Rock 2,845 ft. (867 m.)

Musgrave Ranges

SOUTH

Lake Eyre

Cooper

Barcoo

Sturt Desert

Diamantina

Georgina

Mt. Isa

Cloncurry

Cairns

Mt. Bartle Frere 5,287 ft. (1611 m.)

Townsville

Mackay

Rockhampton

Bundaberg

Gladstone

Brisbane
Gold Coast

Toowoomba

Warrego

Condamine

Great

Dividing

Range

Darling

NEW SOUTH WALES

Newcastle

Sydney
Wollongong

AUSTRALIAN CAPITAL TERRITORY

Canberra

Grey

Range

Warrego

Tamworth

Murray

Wagga Wagga

Albury

Mt. Kosciusko 7,316 ft. (2230 m.)

Hume Res.

Leigh Creek

Lake Frome

Flinders Range

Mt. Lofty Ra.

Lake Torrens

Lake Gairdner

Eyre Pen.

Whyalla

Spencer Gulf

Kangaroo I.

Adelaide

C. Gambier

VICTORIA

Bendigo

Ballarat

Geelong

Melbourne

Bass Strait

King I.

Furneaux Group

TASMANIA

Launceston

Hobart

South Cape

Great Australian Bight

AUSTRALIAN BIGHT

SOUTH AUSTRALIA BASIN

INDIAN OCEAN

TASMAN SEA

TASMAN ABYSSAL PLAIN

Murray

Darling R.

0   100   200   300   400   500 MILES

0   100   200   300   400   500   600   700   800 KILOMETERS

Copyright 1967 by HAMMOND INCORPORATED, Maplewood, N.J.

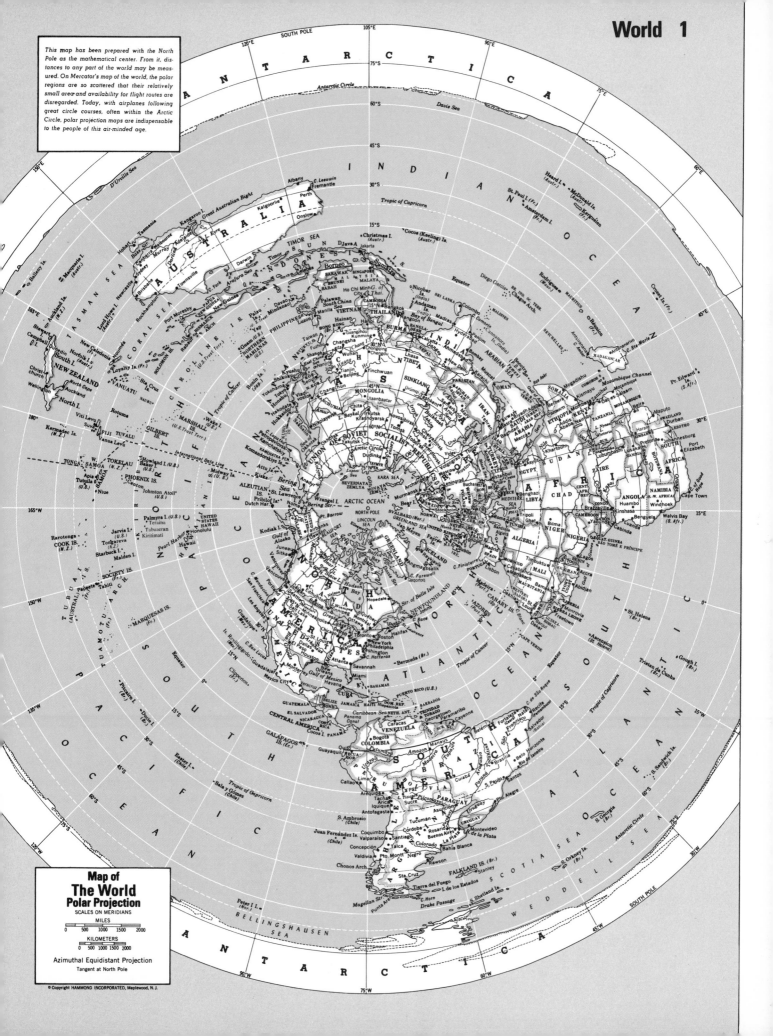

This map has been prepared with the North Pole as the mathematical center. From it, distances to any part of the world may be measured. On Mercator's map of the world, the polar regions are so scattered that their relatively small area and availability for flight routes are disregarded. Today, with airplanes following great circle courses, often within the Arctic Circle, polar projection maps are indispensable to the people of this air-minded age.

Map of The World Polar Projection

SCALES ON MERIDIANS

MILES
0   500   1000   1500   2000

KILOMETERS
0   500 1000 1500 2000

Azimuthal Equidistant Projection
Tangent at North Pole

© Copyright HAMMOND INCORPORATED, Maplewood, N.J.

The World

BRIESEMEISTER ELLIPTICAL
EQUAL-AREA PROJECTION

Capitals of Countries ....⊛
Other Capitals............................⊛
International Boundaries..... − − −

Scale 1:80,000,000

Time Zones

STANDARD	Areas using half hour deviations.
TIME	
ZONES	Areas not using zone system.

NOTE: Standard time zones in the U.S.S.R. are always advanced one hour.

LAND AREA 57,970,000 sq. mi.
(150,142,300 sq. km.)
WATER AREA 139,781,000 sq. mi.
(362,032,790 sq. km.)
TOTAL SURFACE AREA 197,751,000 sq. mi.
(512,175,090 sq. km.)
POPULATION 4,415,000,000

Antarctica
AZIMUTHAL EQUIDISTANT PROJECTION
Scale 1:62,000,000

© Copyright HAMMOND INCORPORATED, Maplewood, N. J.

4 Arctic Ocean

Arctic Ice

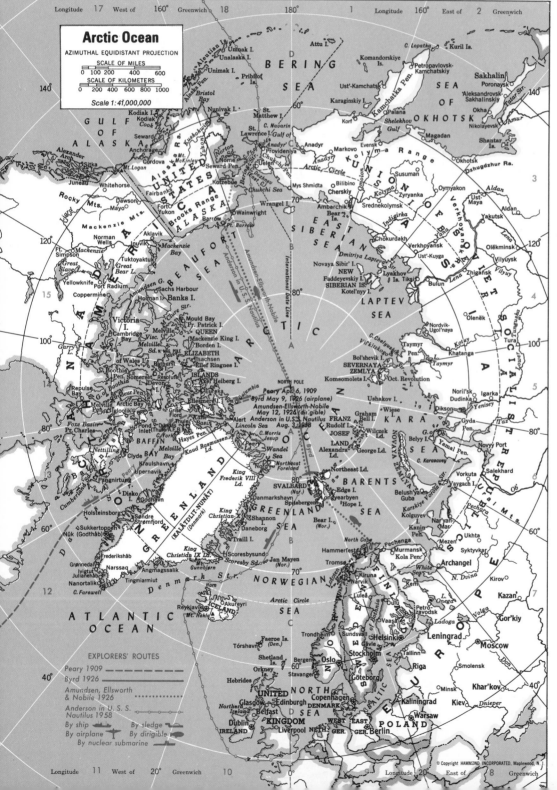

Arctic Ocean — AZIMUTHAL EQUIDISTANT PROJECTION
SCALE OF MILES 0 100 200 400 600
SCALE OF KILOMETERS 0 200 400 600 800 1000
Scale 1:41,000,000

EXPLORERS' ROUTES
Peary 1909
Byrd 1926
Amundsen, Ellsworth & Nobile 1926
Anderson in U.S.S. Nautilus 1958
By ship   By sledge
By airplane   By dirigible
By nuclear submarine

© Copyright HAMMOND INCORPORATED, Maplewood, N.J.

© C.S. Hammond & Co.

Antarctica
AZIMUTHAL EQUIDISTANT PROJECTION

SCALE OF MILES
0 200 400 600 800

KILOMETERS
0 200 400 600 800 1000

© Copyright HAMMOND INCORPORATED, Maplewood, N.J.

Map labels

Amundsen Dec. 14, 1911
Scott Jan. 18, 1912
Byrd Nov. 29, 1929 (airplane)
Fuchs Jan. 19, 1958

AREA OF POLE OF INACCESSIBILITY

SOUTH POLE
South Polar Plateau

EXPLORERS' ROUTES

Palmer 1820
Amundsen 1910-12
Scott 1910-13
Byrd 1928-30
Fuchs 1957-58
By ship   By sledge   By airplane
By snow tractor

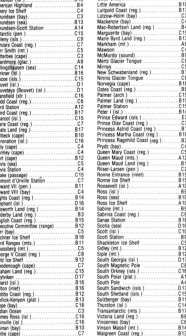

Weddell Sea
Traverse of Cross Section Shown Below
SOUTH POLE
ANTARCTICA
Ross Sea

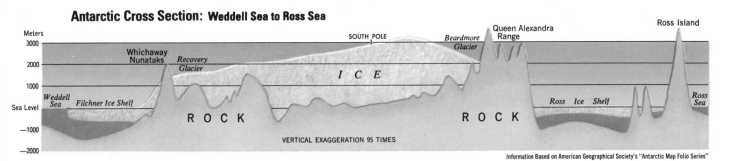

Antarctic Cross Section: Weddell Sea to Ross Sea

Meters
3000 — SOUTH POLE — Queen Alexandra Range — Ross Island
Beardmore Glacier
2000 — Whichaway Nunataks — Recovery Glacier — ICE
1000
Sea Level — Weddell Sea — Filchner Ice Shelf — Ross Ice Shelf — Ross Sea
-1000 — R O C K — R O C K
-2000

VERTICAL EXAGGERATION 95 TIMES

Information Based on American Geographical Society's "Antarctic Map Folio Series"

Europe

POLYCONIC PROJECTION

SCALE OF MILES

0   100   200   300   400

KILOMETERS

0   100 200 300 400

Capitals of Countries	⊛
Other Capitals	●
International Boundaries	
Internal Boundaries	
Canals	

AREA 4,057,000 sq. mi.
(10,507,630 sq. km.)
POPULATION 676,000,000
LARGEST CITY Paris
HIGHEST POINT El'brus 18,510 ft.
(5,642 m.)
LOWEST POINT Caspian Sea -92 ft.
(-28 m.)

Population Distribution

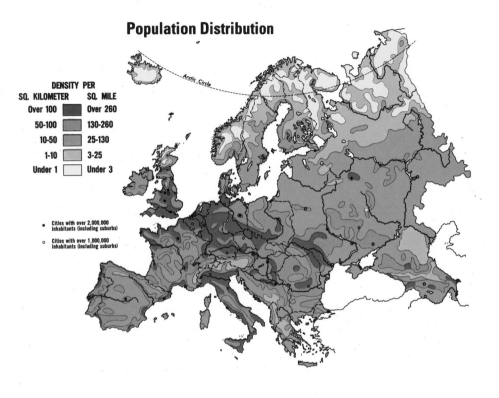

DENSITY PER

SQ. KILOMETER	SQ. MILE
Over 100	Over 260
50-100	130-260
10-50	25-130
1-10	3-25
Under 1	Under 3

• Cities with over 2,000,000
  inhabitants (including suburbs)

○ Cities with over 1,000,000
  inhabitants (including suburbs)

Vegetation

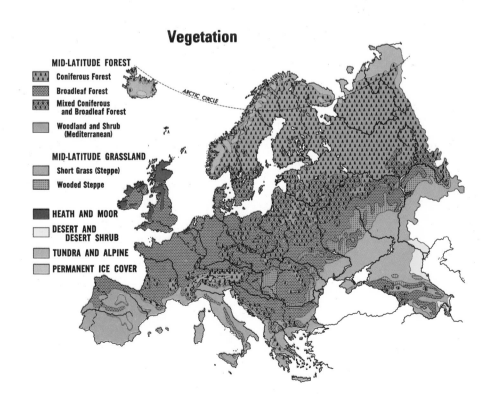

MID-LATITUDE FOREST
  Coniferous Forest
  Broadleaf Forest
  Mixed Coniferous
  and Broadleaf Forest
  Woodland and Shrub
  (Mediterranean)

MID-LATITUDE GRASSLAND
  Short Grass (Steppe)
  Wooded Steppe

HEATH AND MOOR
DESERT AND
DESERT SHRUB
TUNDRA AND ALPINE
PERMANENT ICE COVER

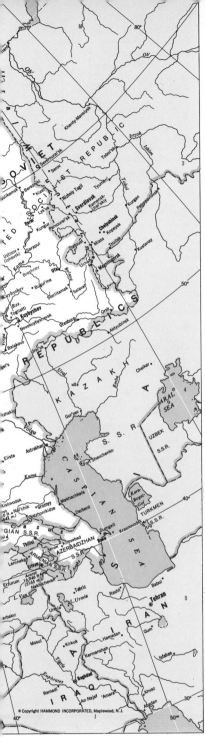

© Copyright HAMMOND INCORPORATED, Maplewood, N.J.

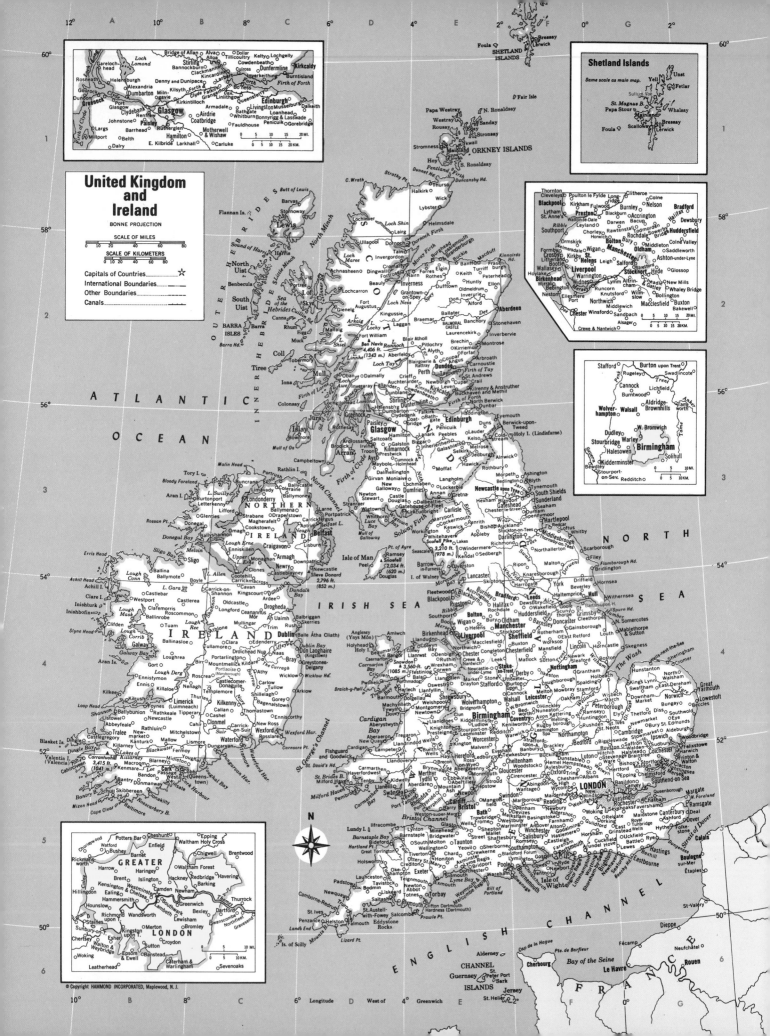

UNITED KINGDOM

AREA 94,399 sq. mi. (244,493 sq. km.)
POPULATION 55,672,000
CAPITAL London
LARGEST CITY London
HIGHEST POINT Ben Nevis 4,406 ft. (1,343 m.)
MONETARY UNIT pound sterling
MAJOR LANGUAGES English, Gaelic, Welsh
MAJOR RELIGIONS Protestantism, Roman Catholicism

IRELAND

AREA 27,136 sq. mi. (70,282 sq. km.)
POPULATION 3,440,427
CAPITAL Dublin
LARGEST CITY Dublin
HIGHEST POINT Carrantuohill 3,415 ft. (1,041 m.)
MONETARY UNIT Irish pound
MAJOR LANGUAGES English, Gaelic (Irish)
MAJOR RELIGION Roman Catholicism

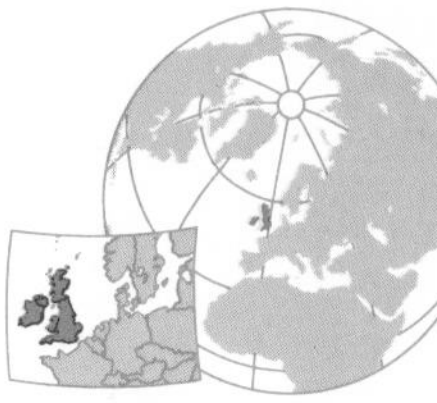

UNITED KINGDOM

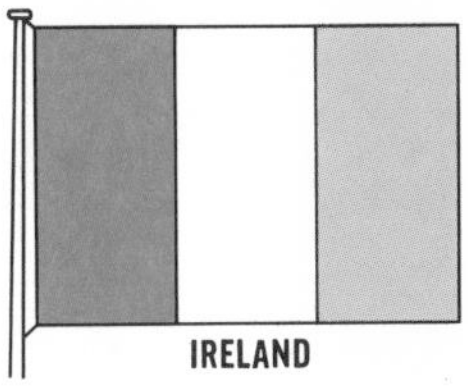

IRELAND

ENGLAND

COUNTIES

Avon, 920,200 ... E 6
Bedfordshire, 491,700 ... G 5
Berkshire, 659,000 ... F 6
Buckinghamshire, 512,000 ... G 6
Cambridgeshire, 563,000 ... G 5
Cheshire, 916,400 ... E 4
Cleveland, 567,900 ... F 3
Cornwall, 405,200 ... C 7
Cumbria, 473,600 ... D 3
Derbyshire, 887,600 ... F 5
Devon, 942,100 ... D 7
Dorset, 575,800 ... E 7
Durham, 610,400 ... F 3
East Sussex, 655,600 ... H 7
Essex, 1,426,200 ... H 6
Gloucestershire, 491,500 ... E 6
Greater London, 7,028,200 ... H 8
Greater Manchester, 2,684,100 ... H 2
Hampshire, 1,456,100 ... F 6
Hereford and Worcester, 594,200 ... E 5
Hertfordshire, 937,300 ... G 6
Humberside, 848,600 ... G 4
Isle of Wight, 111,300 ... F 7
Isles of Scilly, 1,900 ... A 7
Kent, 1,448,100 ... H 6
Lancashire, 1,375,500 ... E 4
Leicestershire, 837,900 ... F 5
Lincolnshire, 524,500 ... G 4
London, Greater, 7,028,200 ... H 8
Manchester, Greater, 2,684,100 ... H 2
Merseyside, 1,578,000 ... G 2
Norfolk, 662,500 ... H 5
Northamptonshire, 505,900 ... G 5
Northumberland, 287,300 ... E 2
North Yorkshire, 653,000 ... F 3
Nottinghamshire, 977,500 ... F 4
Oxfordshire 541,800 ... F6
Shropshire (Salop) 359,000 ... E5
Somerset 404,400 ... E6
South Yorkshire 1,318,300 ... F4
Staffordshire 997,600 ... E5
Suffolk 577,600 ... H5
Surrey 1,002,900 ... G6
Sussex, East 655,600 ... H7
Sussex, West 623,400 ... G7
Tyne and Wear 1,182,900 ... H3
Warwickshire 471,000 ... F5
West Midlands 2,743,300 ... F5
West Sussex 623,400 ... G7
West Yorkshire 2,072,500 ... J1
Wiltshire 512,800 ... E6
Yorkshire, North 653,000 ... F3
Yorkshire, South 1,318,300 ... F4
Yorkshire, West 2,072,500 ... J1

CITIES and TOWNS

Abingdon, 20,130 ... F 6
Accrington, 36,470 ... H 1
Adwick le Street, 17,650 ... K 2
Aldeburgh, 2,750 ... J 5
Aldershot, 33,750 ... G 8
Aldridge Brownhills, 89,370 ... E 5
Alfreton, 21,560 ... F 4
Alnwick, 7,300 ... F 2
Altrincham, 40,800 ... H 2
Amersham, ⊙17,254 ... G 7
Andover, 27,620 ... F 6
Appleby, 2,240 ... E 3
Arnold, 35,090 ... F 4
Arundel, 2,390 ... G 7
Ashford, 36,380 ... H 6
Ashington, 24,720 ... F 2
Ashton-under-Lyne, 48,500 ... H 2
Axminster, ⊙4,515 ... D 7
Aycliffe, ⊙20,203 ... F 3
Aylesbury, 41,420 ... G 7
Bacup, 14,990 ... H 1
Bakewell, 4,100 ... J 2
Banbury, 31,060 ... F 5
Banstead, 44,100 ... H 8
Barking, 153,800 ... H 8
Barnet, 305,200 ... H 7
Barnsley, 74,730 ... J 2
Barnstaple, 17,820 ... D 6
Barrow-in-Furness, 73,400 ... D 3
Barton-upon-Humber, 7,750 ... G 4
Basildon, 135,720 ... J 8
Basingstoke, 60,910 ... F 6
Bath, 83,100 ... E 6
Batley, 41,630 ... J 1
Battle, ⊙4,987 ... H 7
Bebington, 62,500 ... G 2
Bedford, 74,390 ... G 5
Bedlington, 27,200 ... F 2
Bedworth, 41,600 ... F 5
Beeston and Stapleford, 65,360 ... F 5
Benfleet, 49,180 ... J 8
Bentley with Arksey, 22,320 ... F 4
Berkhamsted, 15,920 ... G 7
Beverley, 16,920 ... G 4
Bexhill, 34,680 ... H 7
Bexley, 213,500 ... H 8
Biddulph, 18,720 ... H 2
Birkenhead, 135,750 ... G 2
Birmingham, 1,058,800 ... F 5
Bishop Auckland, 32,940 ... E 3
Bishop's Stortford, 21,720 ... H 6
Blackburn, 101,670 ... H 1
Blackpool, 149,000 ... G 1
Blaydon, 31,940 ... H 3
Blyth, 35,390 ... F 2
Bodmin, 10,430 ... C 7
Bognor Regis, 34,620 ... G 7
Boldon, 24,430 ... J 3
Bolton, 154,480 ... H 2
Bootle 71,160 ... G2
Boston 26,700 ... G5
Bournemouth 144,100 ... F7
Bracknell† 34,067 ... G8
Bradford 458,900 ... J1
Braintree and Bocking 26,300 ... H6
Brent 256,500 ... H8
Brentwood 58,690 ... J8
Bridgwater 26,700 ... E6
Bridlington 26,920 ... G3
Bridport 6,660 ... E7
Brigg 4,870 ... G4
Brighouse 35,320 ... J1
Brightlingsea 7,170 ... J6
Brighton 156,500 ... G7
Bristol 416,300 ... E6
Broadstairs and Saint Peter's 21,670 ... J6
Bromley 299,100 ... H8
Bromsgrove 41,430 ... E5
Buckfastleigh 2,870 ... C7
Buckingham 5,290 ... G6
Bude-Stratton 5,750 ... C7
Bungay 4,120 ... J5
Burgess Hill 20,030 ... G7
Burnham-on-Crouch 4,920 ... H6
Burnley 74,300 ... H1
Burntwood† 23,088 ... F5
Burton upon Trent 49,480 ... F5
Bury 69,550 ... H2
Bury Saint Edmunds 26,800 ... H5
Bushey 24,500 ... H7
Buxton 20,050 ... J2
Caister-on-Sea† 6,287 ... J5
Camborne-Redruth 43,970 ... B7
Cambridge 106,400 ... G5
Camden 185,800 ... H8
Cannock 56,440 ... E5
Canterbury 115,600 ... H6
Canvey Island 29,550 ... J8
Carlisle, 99,600 ... D 3
Carlton, 46,690 ... F 5
Caterham and Warlingham, 35,840 ... H 8
Chatham, 59,550 ... J 8
Cheadle and Gatley, 62,460 ... H 2
Chelmsford, 58,320 ... J 7
Cheltenham, 75,910 ... E 6
Chertsey, 45,070 ... G 8
Chesham, 20,830 ... G 7
Cheshunt, 45,750 ... H 7
Chester, 117,200 ... G 2
Chesterfield, 69,480 ... J 2
Chester-le-Street, 20,720 ... J 3
Chichester, 20,940 ... G 7
Chigwell, 54,220 ... H 8
Chippenham, 18,550 ... E 6
Chorley, 31,800 ... G 2
Christchurch, 31,610 ... F 7
Cirencester, 14,500 ... E 6
Clacton, 39,380 ... J 6
Clay Cross, 9,630 ... J 2
Cleator Moor, ⊙7,686 ... D 3
Cleethorpes, 37,200 ... H 4
Clevedon, 15,140 ... D 6
Clun, ⊙1,261 ... D 6
Coalville, 28,740 ... F 5
Cockermouth, 6,480 ... D 3
Colchester, 79,600 ... H 6
Colne, 19,030 ... H 1
Colne Valley, 21,190 ... J 2
Congleton, 21,500 ... H 2
Consett, 35,080 ... H 3
Corby, 48,850 ... G 5
Coventry, 336,800 ... F 5
Cowes, 19,190 ... F 7
Crawley, 72,600 ... G 6
Crewe and Nantwich, 98,100 ... E 4
Cromer, 5,720 ... J 5
Crook and Willington, 21,120 ... E 3
Crosby, 56,750 ... G 2
Croydon, 330,600 ... H 8
Cuckfield, 26,500 ... G 6
Darlington, 85,120 ... F 3
Dartford, 44,130 ... J 8
Darton, 15,710 ... J 2
Darwen, 29,290 ... H 1
Deal, 26,840 ... J 6
Dearne, 24,780 ... K 2
Denton, 38,110 ... H 2
Derby, 213,700 ... F 5
Dewsbury, 50,560 ... J 1
Didcot, ⊙14,277 ... F 6
Doncaster, 81,530 ... F 4
Dorking, 22,410 ... G 8
Dover, 34,160 ... J 6
Downham Market, 4,120 ... H 5
Droitwich, 13,950 ... E 5
Dronfield, 20,000 ... J 2
Dudley, 187,110 ... E 5
Dunstable, 32,090 ... G 6
Durham, 88,800 ... J 3
Ealing, 293,800 ... H 8
Eastbourne, 73,200 ... H 7
East Grinstead, 19,420 ... G 6
Eastleigh, 46,340 ... F 7
East Retford, 18,260 ... G 4
Egham, 30,320 ... G 8
Egremont, ⊙7,253 ... D 3
Eling, ⊙20,006 ... F 7
Ellesmere, ⊙2,630 ... E 5
Ellesmere Port, 63,870 ... G 2
Enfield, 260,900 ... H 7
Epsom and Ewell, 70,700 ... G 8
Esher, 63,970 ... H 8
Eston, ⊙46,219 ... F 3
Eton, 4,950 ... G 8
Evesham, 14,090 ... F 5
Exeter, 93,300 ... D 7
Exminster, ⊙3,181 ... D 7
Exmouth, 26,840 ... D 7
Falmouth, 17,530 ... B 7
Fareham, 86,300 ... F 7
Farnborough, 43,520 ... G 8
Farnham, 33,140 ... G 8
Farnworth, 26,110 ... H 2
Faversham, 15,010 ... H 6
Felixstowe, 19,460 ... J 6
Felling, 38,990 ... J 3
Filey, 5,660 ... G 3
Fleet, 22,930 ... G 8
Fleetwood, 30,070 ... D 4
Folkestone, 45,610 ... J 6
Formby, 24,850 ... G 2
Framlingham, ⊙2,258 ... J 5
Frimley and Camberley, 47,390 ... G 8
Fulwood, 22,910 ... G 1
Gainsborough, 17,440 ... G 4
Gateshead, 91,230 ... J 3
Gillingham, Dorset, ⊙4,050 ... E 6
Gillingham, Kent, 93,900 ... J 8
Glastonbury, 6,580 ... E 6
Glossop, 24,820 ... J 2
Gloucester, 91,600 ... E 6
Godalming, 18,840 ... G 8
Golborne, 28,720 ... G 2
Goole, 17,920 ... G 4
Gosport, 82,300 ... F 7
Grange, 3,520 ... E 3
Grantham 27,830 ... G5
Gravesend 53,500 ... J8
Great Grimsby 93,800 ... G4
Great Torrington 3,430 ... C7
Great Yarmouth 49,410 ... J5
Greenwich 207,200 ... H8
Guildford 58,470 ... G8
Guisborough 14,860 ... F3
Hackney 192,500 ... H8
Hale 17,080 ... H2
Halesowen 54,120 ... E5
Halifax 88,580 ... J1
Haltemprice 54,850 ... G4
Haltwhistle† 3,511 ... E2
Hammersmith 170,000 ... H8
Haringey 228,200 ... H8
Harlow 79,160 ... H7
Harrogate 64,620 ... F4
Harrow 200,200 ... B5
Hartlepool 97,100 ... F3
Harwich 15,280 ... J6
Haslingden 15,140 ... H1
Hastings 74,600 ... H7
Hatfield† 25,359 ... H7
Havant and Waterloo 112,430 ... G7
Haverhill 14,550 ... H5
Havering 239,200 ... J8
Hayle† 5,378 ... B7
Hazel Grove and Bramhall 40,400 ... H2
Heanor 24,590 ... F4
Hebburn 23,150 ... J3
Hedon 3,010 ... G4
Hemel Hempstead 71,150 ... G7
Hereford 47,800 ... E5
Hertford 20,760 ... H7
Hetton 16,810 ... J3
Hexham 9,820 ... E3
Heywood 31,720 ... H2
High Wycombe 61,190 ... G8
Hillingdon 230,800 ... G8
Hinckley 49,310 ... F5
Hinderwell† 2,551 ... G3
Hitchin 29,190 ... G6
Hoddesdon 27,510 ... H7
Holmfirth 19,790 ... J2
Horley† 18,593 ... H8
Hornsea 7,280 ... G4
Horsham 26,770 ... G6
Horwich 16,670 ... G2
Houghton-le-Spring 33,150 ... J3
Hounslow, 199,100 ... G 8
Hove, 72,000 ... G 7
Hoylake, 32,000 ... G 2
Hoyland Nether, 15,500 ... J 2
Hucknall, 27,110 ... F 4
Huddersfield, 130,060 ... J 2
Hugh Town, ⊙1,958 ... A 8
Hull, 276,600 ... G 4
Hunstanton, 4,140 ... H 5
Huntingdon and Godmanchester, 17,200 ... G 5
Huyton-with-Roby, 65,950 ... G 2
Hyde, 37,040 ... H 2
Ilfracombe, 9,350 ... C 6
Ilkeston, 33,690 ... F 5
Immingham, ⊙10,259 ... G 4
Ipswich, 121,500 ... J 5
Islington, 171,600 ... H 8
Jarrow, 28,510 ... J 3
Kendal, 22,440 ... E 3
Kenilworth, 19,730 ... F 5
Kensington and Chelsea, 161,400 ... G 8
Keswick, 4,790 ... D 3
Kettering, 44,480 ... G 5
Keynsham, 18,970 ... E 6
Kidderminster, 49,960 ... E 5
Kidsgrove, 22,690 ... E 4
King's Lynn, 29,990 ... H 5
Kingston upon Thames, 135,600 ... H 8
Kingswood, 30,450 ... E 6
Kirkburton, 20,320 ... J 2
Kirkby, 59,100 ... G 2
Kirkby Lonsdale, ⊙1,506 ... E 3
Kirkby Stephen, ⊙1,539 ... E 3
Knutsford, 14,840 ... H 2
Lambeth, 290,300 ... H 8
Lancaster, 126,300 ... E 3
Leatherhead, 40,830 ... G 8
Leeds, 744,500 ... J 1
Leek, 19,460 ... H 2
Leicester, 289,400 ... F 5
Leigh, 46,390 ... H 2
Leighton-Linslade, 22,590 ... F 7
Letchworth, 31,520 ... G 6
Lewes, 14,170 ... H 7
Lewisham, 237,300 ... H 8
Leyland, 23,690 ... G 1
Lichfield, 23,690 ... F 5
Lincoln, 73,700 ... G 4
Liskeard, 5,360 ... C 7
Litherland, 23,530 ... G 2
Littlehampton, 20,320 ... G 7

(continued on following page)

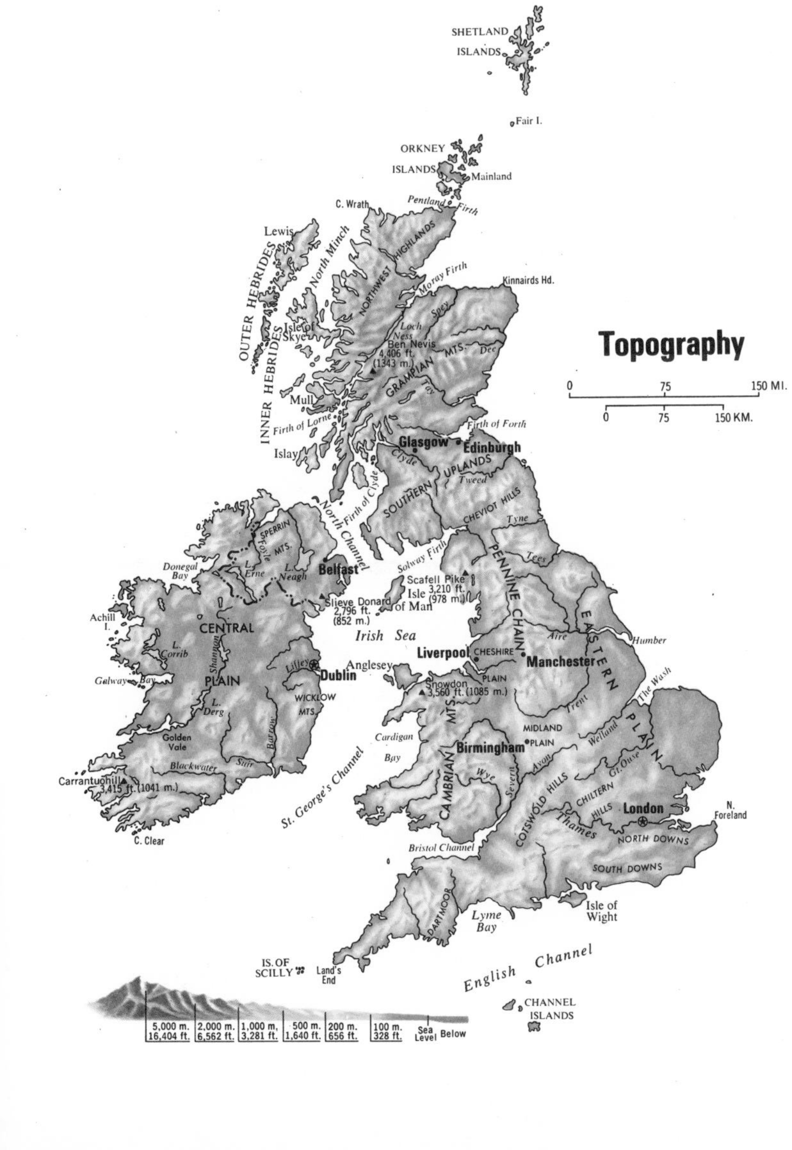

ENGLAND

AREA 50,516 sq. mi. (130,836 sq. km.)
POPULATION 46,220,955
CAPITAL London
LARGEST CITY London
HIGHEST POINT Scafell Pike 3,210 ft. (978 m.)

WALES

AREA 8,017 sq. mi. (20,764 sq. km.)
POPULATION 2,790,462
CAPITAL Cardiff
LARGEST CITY Cardiff
HIGHEST POINT Snowdon 3,560 ft. (1,085 m.)

SCOTLAND

AREA 30,414 sq. mi. (78,772 sq. km.)
POPULATION 5,117,146
CAPITAL Edinburgh
LARGEST CITY Glasgow
HIGHEST POINT Ben Nevis 4,406 ft. (1,343 m.)

NORTHERN IRELAND

AREA 5,452 sq. mi. (14,121 sq. km.)
POPULATION 1,543,000
CAPITAL Belfast
LARGEST CITY Belfast
HIGHEST POINT Slieve Donard 2,796 ft. (852 m.)

10 United Kingdom and Ireland

(continued)

Liverpool, 539,700 G 2
Loftus, 7,850 G 3
London (cap.), 7,028,200 H 8
London, ★12,332,900 H 8
Long Eaton, 33,560 F 5
Longbenton, 50,120 J 3
Looe, 4,060 C 7
Loughborough, 49,010 F 5
Lowestoft, 53,260 J 5
Ludlow, ⊙7,466 E 5
Luton, 164,500 G 6
Lydd, 4,670 H 7
Lyme Regis, 3,460 E 7
Lymington, 36,780 F 7
Lynton, 1,770 D 6
Lytham Saint Anne's, 42,120 G 1
Mablethorpe and Sutton, 6,750 H 4
Macclesfield, 45,420 H 2
Maidenhead, 48,210 G 8
Maidstone, 72,110 J 8
Maldon, 14,350 H 6
Malmesbury, 2,550 E 6
Malton, 4,010 G 3
Malvern, 30,420 E 5
Manchester, 490,000 H 2
Mangotsfield, 23,000 E 6
Mansfield, 58,450 K 2
Mansfield Woodhouse, 25,400 F 4
March, 14,560 H 5
Margate, 50,290 J 6
Market Harborough, 15,230 G 5
Marlborough, 6,370 F 6
Matlock, 20,300 J 2
Melton Mowbray, 20,680 G 5
Merton, 169,400 H 8
Middlesbrough, 153,900 F 3
Middleton, 53,340 H 2
Middlewich, 7,600 H 2
Mildenhall, ⊙9,269 H 5
Millom, ⊙7,101 D 3
Milton Keynes, 89,900 F 5
Minehead, 8,230 D 6
Moretonhampstead, ⊙1,440 C 7
Morpeth, 14,450 F 2
Mundesley, ⊙1,536 J 5
Nelson, 31,220 H 1
Neston, 18,210 G 2
Newark, 24,760 G 4
Newbury, 24,850 F 6
Newcastle upon Tyne, 295,800 H 3
Newcastle-under-Lyme, 75,940 E 4
Newham, 228,900 H 8
Newhaven, 9,970 H 7
Newport, 22,430 F 7
New Romney, 3,830 J 7
Newton Abbot, 19,940 D 7
Newton-le-Willows, 21,780 H 2
New Windsor, 29,660 G 8
Northallerton F 3
Northam, 8,310 C 6
Northampton, 128,290 F 5
Northfleet, 27,150 J 8
North Sunderland, ⊙1,725 F 2
Northwich, 17,710 H 2
Norton, 5,580 G 3
Norton-Radstock, 15,900 E 6
Norwich, 119,200 J 5
Nottingham, 280,300 F 5
Nuneaton, 69,210 F 5
Oadby, 20,700 F 5
Oakham, 7,280 G 5
Okehampton, 4,000 D 7
Oldham, 103,690 H 2
Ormskirk, 28,860 G 2
Oswaldtwistle, 14,270 H 1
Oxford, 117,400 F 6
Padstow, ⊙2,802 B 7
Penryn, 5,660 B 7
Penzance, 19,360 B 7
Peterborough, 118,900 G 5
Peterlee, ⊙21,846 J 3
Plymouth, 259,100 C 7
Polperro, ⊙1,491 C 7
Poole, 110,600 E 7
Porlock, ⊙1,290 D 6
Portishead, 9,680 E 6
Portland, 14,860 E 7
Portslade-by-Sea, 18,040 G 7
Portsmouth, 198,500 F 7
Potters Bar, 24,670 H 7
Poulton-le-Fylde, 16,340 G 1
Preston, 94,760 G 1
Prestwich, 32,850 H 2
Queenborough, 31,550 H 6
Radcliffe, 29,630 H 2
Ramsbottom, 16,710 H 2
Ramsgate, 40,090 J 6
Rawtenstall, 20,950 H 1
Rayleigh, 26,740 J 8
Reading, 131,200 G 8
Redbridge, 231,600 H 8
Redcar, ⊙46,325 F 3
Redditch, 44,750 E 5
Reigate, 55,600 H 8
Richmond upon Thames, 166,800 H 8
Rickmansworth, 29,030 G 8
Ripley, 18,060 F 4
Rochdale, 93,780 H 2
Rochester, 56,030 J 8
Rothbury, ⊙1,818 E 2
Rotherham, 84,770 K 2
Royal Leamington Spa, 44,950 F 5
Royal Tunbridge Wells, 44,800 H 6
Rugby, 60,380 F 5
Rugeley, 24,440 E 5
Runcorn, 42,730 G 2
Rushden, 21,840 G 5
Ryde, 23,170 F 7
Rye, 4,530 H 7
Ryton, 15,170 H 3
Saddleworth, 21,340 J 2
Saint Agnes, ⊙4,747 B 7
Saint Albans, 123,800 H 7
Saint Austell-with-Fowey, 32,710 C 7
Saint Columb Major, ⊙3,953 B 7
Saint Helens, 104,890 G 2
Saint Ives, Cornwall, 9,760 B 7
Saint Neots, 17,940 G 5
Salcombe, 2,370 D 7
Sale, 59,060 H 2
Salford, 261,100 H 2
Salisbury, 35,460 F 6
Saltburn and Marske-by-the-Sea, 21,170 G 3
Sandbach, 14,280 H 2
Sandown-Shanklin, 14,800 F 7
Sandwich, 4,420 J 6
Saxmundham, 1,820 J 5
Scarborough, 43,300 G 3
Scunthorpe, 68,100 G 4
Seaford, 18,020 H 7
Seaham, 22,470 J 3
Seascale, ⊙2,106 D 3
Seaton, 4,500 D 7
Seaton Valley, 35,880 J 3
Sedbergh, ⊙2,741 E 3
Selsey, ⊙6,491 G 7
Sevenoaks, 18,160 J 8
Shaftesbury, 4,180 E 7
Sheffield, 558,000 J 2
Sherborne, 9,230 E 7
Sheringham, 4,940 J 5
Shildon, 15,360 F 3
Shoreham-by-Sea, 19,620 G 7
Shrewsbury, 56,120 E 5
Silloth, ⊙2,662 D 3
Sittingbourne and Milton, 32,830 H 6
Skelmersdale, 35,850 G 2
Skelton and Brotton, 15,930 G 3
Sleaford, 8,050 G 5
Slough, 89,060 G 8
Solihull, 108,230 F 5
Southampton, 213,700 F 7
Southend-on-Sea, 159,300 H 6
Southport, 86,030 G 1
South Shields, 96,900 J 3
Southwark, 224,900 H 8
Southwold, 1,960 J 5
Sowerby Bridge, 15,700 H 1
Spalding, 17,040 G 5
Spenborough, 41,460 J 1
Spennymoor, 19,050 F 3
Stafford, 54,860 E 5
Staines, 56,380 G 8
Stamford, 14,980 G 5
Stanley, 42,280 H 3
Staveley, 17,620 K 2
Stevenage, 72,600 G 6
Stockport, 138,350 H 2
Stockton-on-Tees, 165,400 F 3
Stoke-on-Trent, 256,200 E 4
Stourbridge, 56,530 E 5
Stourport-on-Severn, 19,430 E 5
Stowmarket, 9,020 J 5
Stratford-upon-Avon, 20,080 F 5
Stretford, 52,450 H 2
Stroud, 19,600 E 6
Sudbury, 8,860 H 5
Sunbury-on-Thames, 40,070 G 8
Sunderland, 214,820 J 3
Sutton, 166,700 H 8
Sutton Bridge, ⊙3,113 H 5
Sutton in Ashfield, 40,330 K 2
Swadlincote, 21,060 F 5
Swanage, 8,000 E 7
Swindon, 90,680 F 6
Tamworth, 46,960 F 5
Taunton, 37,570 D 6
Tavistock, ⊙7,620 C 7
Telford, ⊙79,451 E 5
Tenbury, ⊙2,151 E 5
Tewkesbury, 9,210 E 6
Thetford, 15,690 H 5
Thirsk, ⊙2,884 F 3
Thornaby-on-Tees, ⊙42,385 F 3
Thorne, ⊙16,694 F 4
Thornton Cleveleys, 27,090 G 1
Thurrock, 127,700 J 8
Tiverton, 16,190 D 7
Todmorden, 14,540 H 1
Tonbridge, 31,410 H 8
Torbay, 109,900 D 7
Torpoint, 6,840 C 7
Tower Hamlets, 146,100 H 8
Tow Law, 2,460 H 4
Trowbridge, 20,120 E 6
Truro, 15,690 B 7
Turton, 22,800 H 2
Tynemouth, 67,090 J 3
Upton upon Severn, ⊙2,048 E 5
Urmston, 44,130 H 2
Uttoxeter, 9,100 E 5
Ventnor, 6,980 F 7
Wainfleet All Saints, ⊙1,116 H 4
Wakefield, 306,500 J 2
Wallasey, 94,520 G 2
Wallsend, 45,490 J 3
Walsall, 182,430 E 5
Waltham Forest, 223,700 H 8
Waltham Holy Cross, 14,810 H 7
Walton and Weybridge, 51,270 G 8
Walton-le-Dale, 27,660 G 1
Wandsworth, 284,600 H 8
Wantage, 8,490 F 6
Ware, 14,900 H 7
Wareham, 4,630 E 7
Warley, 161,260 E 5
Warminster, 14,440 E 6
Warrington, 65,320 G 2
Warwick, 17,870 F 5
Washington, 27,720 J 3
Watchet, 2,980 D 6
Watford, 77,000 H 7
Wellingborough, 39,570 G 5
Wells, 8,960 E 6
Wells-next-the-Sea, 2,450 H 5
Welwyn, 39,900 H 7
Wem, ⊙3,411 E 5
West Bridgford, 28,340 F 5
West Bromwich, 162,740 F 5
West Mersea, 4,730 H 6
Westminster, 216,100 H 8
Weston-super-Mare, 51,960 D 6
Weymouth and Melcombe Regis, 41,080 E 7
Whickham, 29,710 J 3
Whitchurch, ⊙7,142 E 5
Whitehaven, 26,260 D 3
Whitley Bay, 37,010 J 3
Widnes, 58,330 G 2
Wigan, 80,920 G 2
Wigston, 31,650 F 5
Wilmslow, 31,250 H 2
Wilton, 4,090 F 6
Winchester, 88,900 F 6
Windermere, 7,860 E 3
Winsford, 26,920 G 2
Wirral, 27,510 G 2
Wisbech, 16,990 H 5
Witham, 19,730 H 6
Withernsea, 6,300 H 4
Wivenhoe, 5,630 J 6
Woking, 79,300 G 8
Wokingham, 22,390 G 8
Wolverhampton, 266,400 E 5
Wombwell, 17,850 K 2
Woodhall Spa, 2,420 G 4
Woodley and Sandford, ⊙24,581 G 8
Woodstock, 2,070 F 6
Wooler, ⊙1,833 F 2
Worcester, 73,900 E 5
Workington, 28,260 D 3
Worksop, 36,590 F 4
Worsbrough, 15,180 J 2
Worsley, 49,530 H 2
Worthing, 89,100 G 7
Wymondham, 9,390 J 5
Yateley, ⊙16,505 G 8
Yeovil, 26,180 E 7
York, 101,900 F 4

OTHER FEATURES

Aire (riv.) F 4
Atlantic Ocean A 7
Avon (riv.) F 5
Avon (riv.) F 7
Axe Edge (mt.) H 2
Barnstaple (bay) C 6
Beachy (head) H 7
Bigbury (bay) C 7
Blackwater (riv.) H 6
Bristol (chan.) C 6
Brown Willy (mt.) C 7
Cheviot (hills) E 2
Cheviot, The (mt.) E 2
Chiltern (hills) G 6
Cleveland (hills) F 3
Colne (riv.) G 8
Cornwall (cape) B 7
Cotswold (hills) E 6
Cross Fell (mt.) E 3
Cumbrian (mts.) D 3
Dart (riv.) D 7
Dartmoor National Park C 7
Dee (riv.) D 4
Derwent (riv.) G 3
Derwent (riv.) H 3
Don (riv.) F 4
Dorset Heights (hills) E 7
Dove (riv.) J 2
Dover (str.) J 7
Dungeness (prom.) J 7
Dunkery (hill) D 6
Eddystone (rocks) C 7
Eden (riv.) E 3
English (chan.) D 8
Esk (riv.) D 2
Exe (riv.) D 7
Exmoor National Park D 6
Fens, The (reg.) G 5
Flamborough (head) G 3
Formby (head) G 2
Foulness Island (pen.) J 6
Gibraltar (pt.) H 4
Great Ouse (riv.) H 5
Hartland (pt.) C 6
High Willhays (mt.) C 7
Hodder (riv.) H 1
Holderness (pen.), 43,900 G 4
Holy (isl.), 189 F 2
Humber (riv.) G 4
Irish (sea) B 4
Kennet (riv.) F 6
Lake District National Park D 3
Land's End (prom.) B 7
Lea (riv.) G 6
Lincoln Wolds (hills) G 4
Lindisfarne (Holy) (isl.), 189 F 2
Liverpool (bay) D 4
Lizard, The (pen.), 7,371 B 8
Lundy (isl.), 49 C 6
Lune (riv.) E 3
Lyme (bay) D 7
Manacle (pt.) C 7
Medway (riv.) H 6
Mendip (hills) E 6
Mersea (isl.), 4,423 J 6
Mersey (riv.) G 2
Morecambe (bay) D 3
Mounts (bay) B 7
Naze, The (prom.) J 6
Nene (riv.) H 5
New (for.) F 6
North (sea) J 4
North Downs (hills) G 6
North Foreland (prom.) J 6
Northumberland National Park E 2
North York Moors National Park G 3
Orford Ness (prom.) J 5
Ouse (riv.) G 4
Ouse (riv.) G 6
Parrett (riv.) E 6
Peak District National Park F 4
Peak, The (mt.) J 2
Peel Fell (mt.) E 2
Pennine Chain (range) E 3
Plymouth (sound) C 7
Portland, Bill of (pt.) E 7
Prawle (pt.) D 7
Purbeck, Isle of (pen.), 39,500 F 7
Ribble (riv.) E 4
Saint Alban's (head) F 7
Saint Bees (head) D 3
Saint Martin's (isl.), 106 A 8
Saint Mary's (isl.), 1,958 A 8
Scafell Pike (mt.) D 3
Scilly (isls.), 1,900 A 7
Selsey Bill (prom.) G 7
Severn (riv.) E 6
Sheppey (isl.), 31,550 J 6
Sherwood (for.) F 4
Skiddaw (mt.) D 3
Solent (chan.) F 7
Solway (firth) D 3
South Downs (hills) G 7
Spithead (chan.) F 7
Spurn (head) H 4
Stonehenge (ruins) F 6
Stour (riv.) E 7
Stour (riv.) H 6
Stour (riv.) J 6
Swale (riv.) F 3
Tamar (riv.) C 7
Taw (riv.) D 7
Tees (riv.) F 3
Test (riv.) F 6
Thames (riv.) H 6
Tintagel (head) C 7
Torridge (riv.) C 7
Trent (riv.) G 4
Tresco (isl.), 246 A 8
Tweed (riv.) E 2
Tyne (riv.) F 3
Ure (riv.) F 3
Ver (riv.) H 7
Walney, Isle of (isl.), 11,241 D 3
Wash, The (bay) H 5
Weald, The (reg.) H 6
Wear (riv.) F 3
Weaver (riv.) G 2
Welland (riv.) G 5
Wey (riv.) G 6
Wharfe (riv.) E 3
Wirral (pen.), 432,900 G 2
Witham (riv.) G 4
Wolds, The (hills) G 4
Wye (riv.) D 5
Wyre (riv.) G 1
Yare (riv.) J 5
Yorkshire Dales National Park E 3

CHANNEL ISLANDS

CITIES and TOWNS

Saint Anne E 8
Saint Helier (cap.), Jersey, ⊙28,135 E 8
Saint Peter Port (cap.), Guernsey, ⊙16,303 E 8
Saint Sampson's, ⊙6,534 E 8

OTHER FEATURES

Alderney (isl.), 1,686 E 8
Guernsey (isl.), 51,351 E 8
Herm (isl.), 96 E 8
Jersey (isl.), 72,629 E 8
Sark (isl.), 590 E 8

ISLE of MAN

CITIES and TOWNS

Castletown, 2,820 C 3
Douglas (cap.), 20,389 C 3
Laxey, 1,170 C 3
Michael, 408 C 3
Onchan, 4,807 C 3
Peel, 3,081 C 3
Port Erin, 1,714 C 3
Port Saint Mary, 1,508 C 3
Ramsey, 5,048 C 3

OTHER FEATURES

Ayre (pt.) C 3
Calf of Man (isl.) C 3
Langness (prom.) C 3
Snaefell (mt.) C 3
Spanish (head) C 3

WALES

COUNTIES

Clwyd, 376,000 D 4
Dyfed, 323,100 C 6
Gwent, 439,600 D 6
Gwynedd, 225,100 C 4
Mid Glamorgan, 540,400 D 6
Powys, 101,500 D 5
South Glamorgan, 389,200 A 7
West Glamorgan, 371,900 D 6

CITIES and TOWNS

Aberaeron, 1,340 C 5
Abercarn, 18,370 B 6
Aberdare, 38,030 A 6
Abertillery, 20,550 B 6
Amlwch, 3,630 C 4
Bala, 1,650 D 5
Bangor, 16,030 C 4
Barmouth, 2,070 C 5
Barry, 42,780 B 7
Beaumaris, 2,090 C 4
Bedwellty, 25,460 B 6
Bethesda, 4,180 D 4
Betws-y-Coed, 720 D 4
Brecknock (Brecon), 6,460 D 6
Brecon, 6,460 D 6
Bridgend, 14,690 A 7
Brynmawr, 5,970 B 6
Builth Wells, 1,480 D 5
Burry Port, 5,990 C 6
Caernarfon, 8,840 C 4
Caerphilly, 42,190 B 6
Cardiff, 281,500 B 7
Cardigan, 3,830 C 5
Chepstow, 8,260 E 6
Chirk, ⊙3,564 D 5
Colwyn Bay, 25,370 D 4
Criccieth, 1,590 C 5
Cwmamman, 3,950 D 6
Cwmbran, 32,980 B 6
Denbigh, 8,420 D 4
Dolgellau, 2,430 D 5
Ebbw Vale, 25,670 B 6
Ffestiniog, 5,510 D 5
Fishguard and Goodwick, 5,020 B 5
Flint, 15,070 G 2
Gelligaer, 33,820 A 6
Harlech, ⊙332 C 5
Haverfordwest, 8,930 B 6
Hawarden, ⊙20,389 G 2
Hay, 1,200 D 5
Holywell, 8,570 G 2
Kidwelly, 3,090 C 6
Knighton, 2,190 D 5
Llandeilo, 1,780 C 6
Llandovery, 2,040 D 5
Llandrindod Wells, 3,460 D 5
Llandudno, 17,700 D 4
Llanelli, 25,870 C 6
Llanfairfechan, 3,800 D 4
Llangefni, 4,070 C 4
Llangollen, 3,050 D 5
Llanguicke, ⊙15,029 D 6
Llanidloes, 2,390 D 5
Llantrisant, ⊙27,490 A 7
Llanwrtyd Wells, 460 D 5
Llwchwr, 27,530 D 6
Machynlleth, 1,830 D 5
Maesteg, 21,100 D 6
Menai Bridge, 2,730 C 4
Merthyr Tydfil, 61,500 A 6
Milford Haven, 13,960 B 6
Mold, 8,700 G 2
Montgomery, 1,000 D 5
Mountain Ash, 27,710 A 6
Mynyddislwyn, 15,590 B 6
Narberth, 970 C 6
Neath, 27,280 D 6
Nefyn, ⊙2,086 C 5
Newcastle Emlyn, 690 C 5
Newport, Dyfed, ⊙1,062 C 5
Newport, Gwent, 110,090 B 6
New Quay, 760 C 5
Newtown, 6,400 D 5
Neyland, 2,690 B 6
Ogmore and Garw, 19,680 A 6
Pembroke, 14,570 C 6
Penarth, 24,180 B 7
Penmaenmawr, 4,050 C 4
Pontypool, 36,710 B 6
Pontypridd, 34,180 A 6
Porthcawl, 14,980 D 6
Porthmadog, 3,900 C 5
Port Talbot, 58,200 D 6
Prestatyn, 15,480 D 4
Presteigne, 1,330 D 5
Pwllheli, 4,020 C 5
Rhondda, 85,400 A 6
Rhyl, 22,150 D 4
Risca, 15,780 B 6
Ruthin, 4,780 D 4
Saint David's, ⊙1,638 B 6
Swansea, 190,800 C 6
Tenby, 4,930 C 6
Tredegar, 17,450 B 6
Tywyn, 3,850 C 5
Welshpool, 7,370 D 5
Wrexham, 39,530 E 4

OTHER FEATURES

Anglesey (isl.), 64,500 C 4
Aran Fawddwy (mt.) C 5
Bardsey (isl.), 9 C 5
Berwyn (mts.) D 5
Black (mts.) D 6
Braich-y-Pwll (prom.) C 5
Brecon Beacons (mt.) D 6
Brecon Beacons National Park D 6
Caldy (isl.), 70 C 6
Cambrian (mts.) D 5
Cardigan (bay) C 5
Carmarthen (bay) C 6
Cemmaes (head) C 5
Dee (riv.) D 4
Dovey (riv.) D 5
Ely (riv.) B 7
Gower (pen.), 17,220 C 6
Great Ormes (head) C 4
Holy (isl.), 13,715 C 4
Lleyn (pen.), 25,800 C 5
Menai (str.) C 4
Milford Haven (inlet) B 6
Pembrokeshire Coast National Park C 6
Plynlimon (mt.) D 5
Preseli (mts.) C 6
Radnor (for.) D 5
Rhymney (riv.) B 6
Saint Brides (bay) B 6
Saint David's (head) B 6
Saint George's (chan.) B 5
Saint Gowans (head) C 6
Severn (riv.) E 5
Snowdon (mt.) D 4
Snowdonia National Park D 4
Taff (riv.) B 7
Teifi (riv.) C 5
Towy (riv.) D 6
Tremadoc (bay) C 5
Usk (riv.) B 6
Wye (riv.) D 5
Ynys Môn (Anglesey) (isl.), 64,500 C 4

★Population of met. area.
⊙Population of parish.

SCOTLAND

(map on page 13)

REGIONS

Borders, 99,409 E 5
Central, 269,281 D 4
Dumfries and Galloway, 143,667 E 5
Fife, 336,339 E 4
Grampian, 448,772 F 3
Highland, 182,044 D 3
Lothian, 754,008 E 5
Orkney (islands area), 17,675 E 1
Shetland (islands area), 18,494 F 2
Strathclyde, 2,504,909 C 4
Tayside, 401,987 E 4
Western Isles (islands area) 29,615 A 3

CITIES and TOWNS

Aberchirder, 877 F 3
Aberdeen, 210,362 F 3
Aberdour, 1,576 D 1
Aberfeldy, 1,552 E 4
Aberfoyle, 793 D 4
Aberlady, 737 F 4
Aberlour, 842 E 3
Abernethy, 776 E 4
Aboyne, 1,040 F 3
Acharacle, ⊙764 C 4
Achiltibuie, ⊙1,564 C 3
Achnasheen, ⊙1,078 C 3
Ae, 239 E 5
Airdrie, 38,491 C 2
Alexandria, 9,758 A 1
Alford, 764 F 3
Alloa, 13,558 C 1
Alness, 2,560 D 3
Altnaharra, ⊙1,227 D 2
Alva, 4,593 C 1
Alyth, 1,738 E 4
Ancrum, 266 F 5
Annan, 6,250 E 6
Annat, ⊙550 C 3
Annbank Station, 2,530 D 5
Applecross, ⊙550 C 3
Arbroath, 22,706 F 4
Ardavasar, ⊙449 B 3
Ardersier, 942 E 3
Ardgay, 193 D 3
Ardrishaig, 946 C 4
Ardrossan, 11,072 D 5
Armadale, 7,200 C 2
Arrochar, 543 D 4
Ascog, 230 A 2
Auchenblae, 339 F 4
Auchencairn, 215 E 6
Auchinleck, 4,883 D 5
Auchterarder, 1,738 E 4
Auchtermuchty, 1,426 E 4
Auldearn, 405 E 3
Aviemore, 1,224 E 3
Avoch, 776 D 3
Ayr, 47,990 D 5
Ayton, 410 F 5
Bailivanish, 347 A 3
Baillieston, 7,671 B 2
Balallan, 283 B 2
Balerno, 3,576 D 2
Balfron, 1,149 B 1
Ballantrae, 262 C 5
Ballater, 981 F 3
Ballingry, 4,332 D 1
Ballinluig, 188 E 4
Balloch, Highland, 572 D 3
Balloch, Strathclyde, 1,484 B 1
Baltasound, 246 G 2
Banchory, 2,435 F 3
Banff, 3,832 F 3
Bankfoot, 868 E 4
Bankhead, 1,492 F 3
Bannockburn, 5,889 C 1
Barrhead, 18,736 B 2
Barrhill, 236 D 5
Barvas, 279 B 2
Bathgate, 14,038 C 2
Bayble, 543 B 2
Bearsden, 25,128 B 2
Beattock, 309 E 5
Beauly, 1,141 D 3
Beith, 5,859 D 5
Bellsbank, 3,066 D 5
Bellshill, 18,166 C 2
Berriedale, ⊙1,927 E 2
Bieldside, 1,137 F 3
Biggar, 1,718 E 5
Birnam, 659 E 4
Bishopbriggs, 21,570 B 2
Bishopton, 2,931 B 2
Blackburn, 7,636 C 2
Blackford, 529 E 4
Blair Atholl, 437 E 4
Blairgowrie and Rattray, 5,681 E 4
Blanefield, 835 B 1
Blantyre, 13,992 B 2
Blyth Bridge, ⊙441 E 5
Bo'ness, 12,959 C 1
Boat of Garten, 406 E 3
Boddam, 1,429 G 3
Bonar Bridge, 519 D 3
Bonhill, 4,385 B 1
Bonnybridge, 5,701 C 1
Bonnyrigg and Lasswade, 7,429 D 2
Bowmore, 947 B 5
Braemar, 394 E 3
Breasclete, 234 B 2
Brechin, 6,759 F 4
Bridge of Allan, 4,638 C 1
Bridge of Don, 4,086 F 3
Bridge of Weir, 4,724 A 2
Brightons, 3,106 C 1
Broadford, 310 B 3
Brodick, 630 C 5
Brora, 1,436 E 2
Broxburn, 7,776 D 1
Buchlyvie, 412 B 1
Buckhaven and Methil, 17,930 F 4
Buckie, 8,145 E 3
Bucksburn, 6,567 F 3
Bunessan, ⊙585 B 4
Burghead, 1,321 E 3
Burnmouth, 300 F 5
Burntisland, 5,626 D 1
Cairndow, ⊙874 D 4
Cairnryan, 199 D 6
Callander, 1,805 D 4
Cambuslang, 14,607 B 2
Campbeltown, 6,428 C 5
Cannich, 203 D 3
Canonbie, 234 F 5
Caol, 3,719 C 4
Carbost, ⊙772 B 3
Cardenden, 6,802 D 1
Carloway, 178 B 2
Carluke, 8,864 E 5
Carnoustie, 6,838 F 4
Carnwath, 1,246 E 5
Carradale, 262 C 5
Carrbridge, 416 E 3
Carron, 2,626 C 1
Carsphairn, 186 D 5
Castlebay, 284 A 4
Castle Douglas, 3,384 E 6
Castle Kennedy, 307 D 6
Castletown, 902 E 2
Catrine, 2,681 D 5
Cawdor, 111 E 3
Chirnside, 888 F 5
Chryston, 8,322 C 2
Clackmannan, 3,248 C 1
Clarkston, 8,404 B 2
Closeburn, 225 E 5
Clovulin, ⊙315 C 4
Clydebank, 47,538 B 2
Coalburn, 1,460 E 5
Coatbridge, 50,806 C 2
Cockburnspath, 233 F 5
Cockenzie and Port Seton, 3,539 D 1
Coldingham, 423 F 5
Coldstream, 1,393 F 5
Coll, 305 B 2
Colmonell, 218 D 5
Comrie, 1,119 E 4
Connel, 300 C 4
Cononbridge, 914 D 3
Corpach, 1,296 C 4
Coupar Angus, 2,010 E 4
Cove and Kilcreggan, 1,402 A 1
Cove Bay, 765 F 3
Cowdenbeath, 10,215 D 1
Cowie, 2,751 C 1
Craigellachie, 382 E 3
Craignure, ⊙544 C 4
Crail, 1,033 F 4
Crawford, 384 E 5
Creetown, 769 D 6
Crieff, 5,718 E 4
Crimond, 313 G 3
Crinan, ⊙462 C 4
Cromarty, 492 E 3
Crosshill, 535 D 5
Crossmichael, 317 D 6
Cruden Bay, 528 G 3
Cullen, 1,199 F 3
Culross, 504 C 1
Cults, 3,336 F 3
Cumbernauld, 41,200 C 1
Cumnock and Holmhead, 6,298 D 5
Cupar, 6,607 E 4
Currie, 6,764 D 2
Dailly, 1,258 D 5
Dalbeattie, 3,659 E 6
Daliburgh, 261 A 3
Dalkeith, 9,713 D 2
Dalmally, 283 D 4
Dalmellington, 1,949 D 5
Dalry, 5,833 D 5
Dalrymple, 1,336 D 5
Darvel, 3,177 D 5
Daviot, ⊙513 D 3
Denholm, 581 F 5
Denny and Dunipace, 10,424 C 1
Dervaig, ⊙1,081 B 4
Dingwall, 4,275 D 3
Dollar, 2,573 E 4
Dornoch, 880 D 3
Douglas, 1,843 E 5
Doune, 859 D 4
Drongan, 3,609 D 5
Drumbeg, ⊙833 C 2
Drummore, 336 D 6
Drumnadrochit, 359 D 3
Drymen, 659 B 1
Dufftown, 1,481 E 3
Dumbarton, 25,469 B 1
Dumfries, 29,259 E 5
Dunbar, 4,609 F 4
Dunbeath, 161 E 2
Dunbeg, 939 C 4
Dunblane, 5,222 E 4
Dundee, 194,732 F 4
Dundonald, 2,256 D 5
Dunfermline, 52,098 D 1
Dunkeld, 273 E 4
Dunning, 564 E 4
Dunoon, 8,759 A 2
Dunragit, 323 D 6
Duns, 1,812 F 5
Duntochter, 3,532 B 2
Dunure, 452 D 5
Dunvegan, 301 B 3
Dyce, 2,733 F 3
Eaglesfield, 581 E 5
Eaglesham, 2,788 D 5
Earlston, 1,415 F 5
East Calder, 2,690 D 2
East Kilbride, 71,200 B 2
East Linton, 882 F 5
Eastriggs, 1,455 E 5
Ecclefechan, 844 E 5
Edinburgh (cap.), 470,085 D 1
Edzell, 658 F 4
Elderslie, 5,204 B 2
Elgin, 17,042 E 3
Elie and Earlsferry, 807 F 4
Ellon, 2,855 F 3
Embo, 260 E 3
Errol, 762 E 4
Evanton, 562 D 3
Eyemouth, 2,704 F 5
Fairlie, 1,029 D 5
Falkirk, 36,901 C 1
Falkland, 998 E 4
Fallin, 3,159 C 1
Fauldhouse, 5,247 C 2
Ferness, ⊙287 E 3
Ferryden, 740 F 4
Findhorn, 664 E 3
Findochty, 1,229 E 3
Fintry, 296 B 1
Fochabers, 1,238 E 3
Forfar, 11,179 F 4
Forres, 5,317 E 3
Fort Augustus, 670 D 3
Forth, 2,929 C 2
Fortrose, 1,150 D 3
Fort William, 4,370 C 4
Foyers, 276 D 3
Fraserburgh, 10,930 G 3
Friockheim, 807 F 4
Furnace, 220 C 4
Fyvie, 405 F 3
Gairloch, 125 C 3
Galashiels, 12,808 F 5
Galston, 4,256 D 5
Gardenstown, 892 F 3
Garelochhead, 1,552 A 1
Gargunnock, 457 B 1
Garlieston, 385 D 6
Garmouth, 352 E 3
Garrabost, 307 B 2
Gartmore, 253 B 1
Gatehouse-of-Fleet, 835 D 6
Giffnock, 10,987 B 2
Gifford, 575 F 5
Girvan, 7,597 D 5
Glamis, 190 F 4
Glasgow, 880,617 B 2
Glasgow, ★1,674,789 B 2
Glenbarr, ⊙691 C 5
Glencaple, 275 E 5
Glencoe, 195 C 4
Glenelg, ⊙1,468 C 3
Glenluce, 725 D 6
Glenrothes, 31,400 E 4
Golspie, 1,374 E 3
Gordon, 320 F 5
Gorebridge, 3,426 D 2
Gourock, 11,192 A 1
Grangemouth, 24,430 C 1
Grantown-on-Spey, 1,578 E 3
Greenlaw, 574 F 5
Greenock, 67,275 A 2
Gretna, 1,907 E 5
Gullane, 1,701 F 4
Haddington, 6,767 F 5
Halkirk, 679 E 2
Hamilton, 45,495 C 2
Hamnavoe, 307 G 2
Harthill, 4,712 C 2
Hatton, 315 G 3
Hawick, 16,484 F 5
Heathhall, 1,365 E 5
Helensburgh, 13,327 A 1
Helmsdale, 727 E 2
Hill of Fearn, 233 D 3
Hillside, 692 F 4
Hillswick, ⊙696 G 2
Hopeman, 1,248 E 3
Huntly, 4,078 F 3
Hurlford, 4,294 D 5
Inchnadamph, ⊙833 D 2
Innellan, 922 A 2
Innerleithen, 2,293 E 5
Insch, 881 F 3
Inveraray, 473 C 4
Inverbervie, 853 F 4
Invercassley, ⊙1,067 D 3
Invergordon, 2,385 D 3
Invergowrie, 1,389 E 4
Inverie, ⊙1,468 C 3
Inverkeithing, 6,102 D 1
Inverness, 35,801 D 3
Inverurie, 5,534 F 3
Irvine, 48,500 D 5
Isle of Whithorn, 222 D 6
Jedburgh, 3,953 F 5
John O'Groats, 195 E 2
Johnshaven, 544 F 4
Johnstone, 23,251 B 2
Kames, 230 C 5
Keiss, 344 E 2
Keith, 4,192 F 3
Kelso, 4,934 F 5
Kelty, 6,573 D 1
Kemnay, 1,042 F 3
Kenmore, 211 E 4
Kilbarchan, 2,669 A 2
Kilbirnie, 8,259 A 2
Kilchoan, ⊙764 B 4
Kildonan, ⊙1,105 E 2
Killearn, 1,086 B 1
Killin, 600 D 4
Kilmacolm, 3,348 A 2
Kilmarnock, 50,175 D 5
Kilmaurs, 2,518 D 5
Kilninver, ⊙247 C 4
Kilrenny and Anstruther, 2,951 F 4
Kilsyth, 10,210 B 1
Kilwinning, 8,460 D 5
Kinbrace, ⊙1,105 E 2
Kincardine, 3,278 C 1
Kinghorn, 2,163 D 1
Kingussie, 1,036 D 3
Kinlochewe, ⊙1,794 C 3
Kinlochleven, 1,243 D 4
Kinloch Rannoch, 241 D 4
Kinloss, 2,378 E 3
Kinross, 2,829 E 4
Kintore, 970 F 3
Kippen, 529 B 1
Kirkcaldy, 50,207 D 1
Kirkcolm, 346 C 6
Kirkconnel, 3,318 E 5
Kirkcowan, 354 D 6
Kirkcudbright, 2,690 E 6
Kirkhill, 210 D 3
Kirkintilloch, 26,664 B 2
Kirkmuirhill, 2,575 E 5
Kirkton of Glenisla, ⊙331 E 4
Kirkwall, 4,777 E 2
Kirriemuir, 4,295 E 4
Kyleakin, 268 C 3
Kyle of Lochalsh, 687 C 3
Kylestrome, ⊙745 D 2
Ladybank, 1,216 E 4
Laggan, 393 D 3
Lairg, 572 D 2
Lamlash, 613 C 5
Lanark, 8,842 E 5
Langholm, 2,509 E 5
Larbert, 4,922 C 1
Largs, 9,461 A 2
Larkhall, 15,926 E 5
Lauder, 639 F 5
Laurencekirk, 1,416 F 4

(continued)

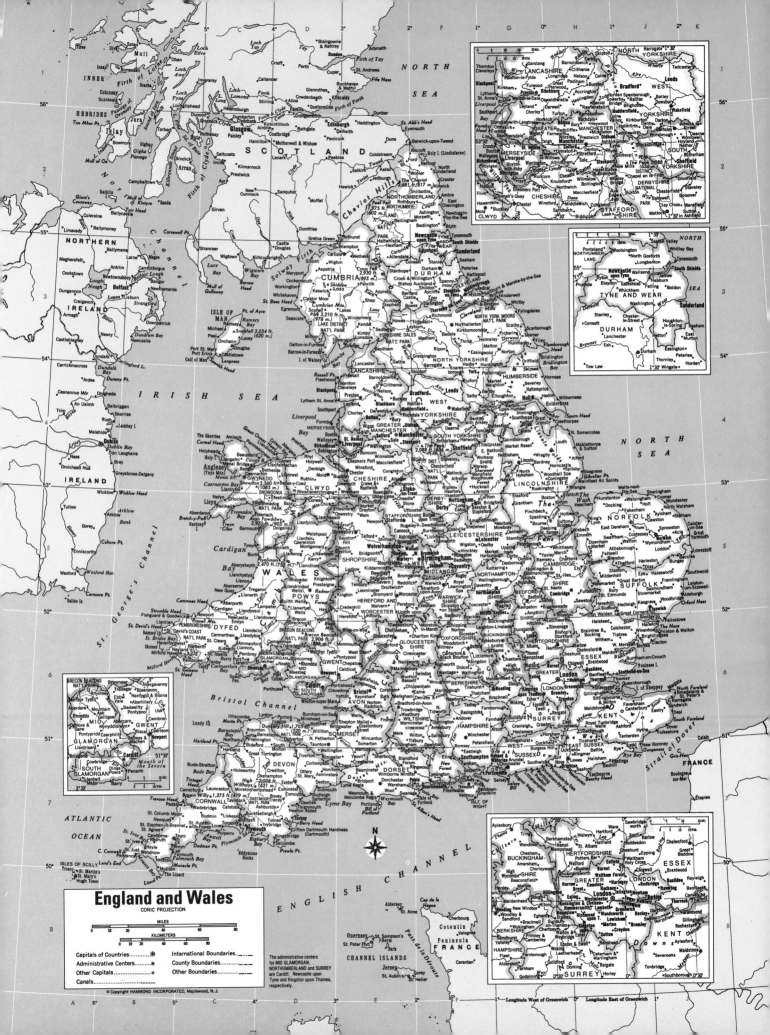

England and Wales

CONIC PROJECTION

MILES
0 10 20 40 60 80

KILOMETERS
0 20 40 60 80

Capitals of Countries.............
Administrative Centers.............
Other Capitals.............
Canals

International Boundaries.......
County Boundaries.......
Other Boundaries.......

The administrative centers for MID GLAMORGAN, NORTHUMBERLAND and SURREY are Cardiff, Newcastle upon Tyne and Kingston upon Thames, respectively.

© Copyright HAMMOND INCORPORATED, Maplewood, N.J.

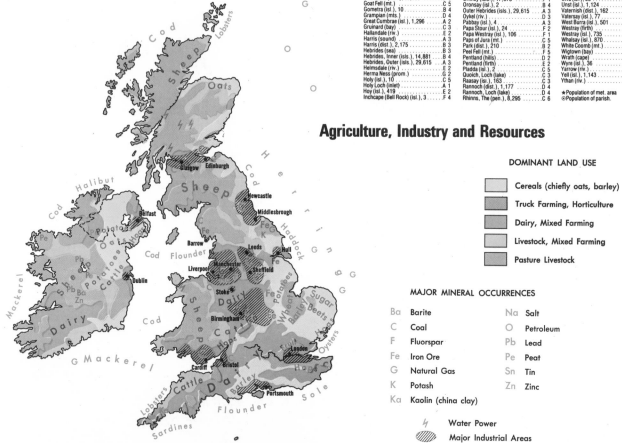

Agriculture, Industry and Resources

DOMINANT LAND USE

Cereals (chiefly oats, barley)

Truck Farming, Horticulture

Dairy, Mixed Farming

Livestock, Mixed Farming

Pasture Livestock

MAJOR MINERAL OCCURRENCES

Ba Barite
C Coal
F Fluorspar
Fe Iron Ore
G Natural Gas
K Potash
Ka Kaolin (china clay)

Na Salt
O Petroleum
Pb Lead
Pe Peat
Sn Tin
Zn Zinc

⚡ Water Power

░ Major Industrial Areas

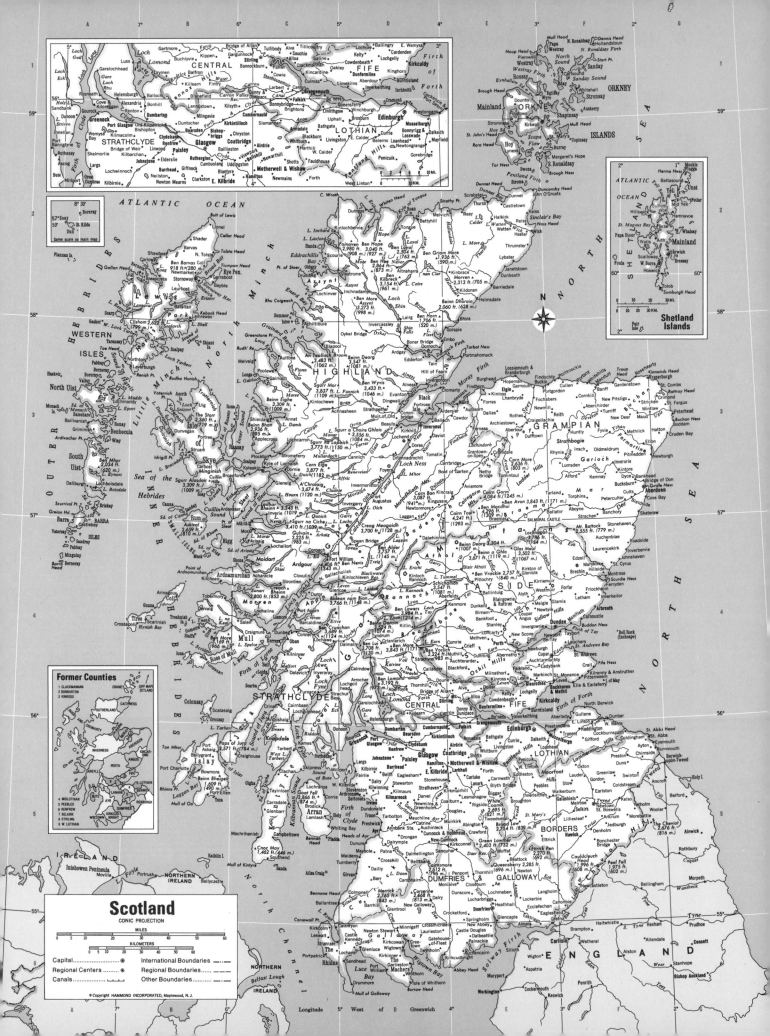

Scotland

CONIC PROJECTION

MILES

KILOMETERS

Capital .... ⊛
Regional Centers .... ⊙
Canals

International Boundaries
Regional Boundaries
Other Boundaries

© Copyright HAMMOND INCORPORATED, Maplewood, N.J.

Former Counties

1 CLACKMANNAN
2 DUMBARTON
3 KINROSS
4 MIDLOTHIAN
5 PEEBLES
6 RENFREW
7 SELKIRK
8 STIRLING
9 W. LOTHIAN

Shetland Islands

14 United Kingdom and Ireland
(continued)

IRELAND

Carlow 34,237 H6
Cavan 52,618 G4
Clare 75,008 D6
Cork 352,883 D7
Donegal 108,344 K2
Dublin 852,219 J5
Galway 149,223 D5
Kerry 112,772 B7
Kildare 71,977 H5
Kilkenny 61,473 G6
Laois 45,259 G6
Leitrim 28,360 E3
Leix (Laois) 45,259 G6
Limerick 140,459 D7
Longford 28,250 F4
Louth 74,951 J4
Mayo 109,525 C4
Meath 71,729 H4
Monaghan 46,242 H3
Offaly 51,829 F5
Roscommon 53,519 E4
Sligo 50,275 D3
Tipperary 123,565 F6
Waterford 77,315 F7
Westmeath 53,570 G5
Wexford 86,351 H7
Wicklow 66,295 J5

CITIES and TOWNS

Abbeydorney, 188 B 7
Abbeyfeale, 1,337 C 7
Abbeylara, ‡290 F 4
Abbeyleix, 1,033 G 6
Achill Sound, ‡1,163 B 4
Aclare, ‡336 D 3
Adare, 545 D 6
Aghada-Farsid-Rostellan, 461 E 8
Aghadoe, ‡497 B 7
Aghagower, ‡693 C 4
Ahascragh, 221 E 5
Annagry, 201 E 1
Annascaul, 236 B 7
An Uaimh, 4,605 H 4
An Uaimh, *6,665 H 4
Ardagh, Limerick, 213 C 7
Ardagh, Longford, ‡974 F 4
Ardara, 683 E 2
Ardee, *3,183 H 4
Ardee, 3,096 H 4
Ardfert, 286 B 7
Ardfinnan, 510 F 7
Ardmore, 233 F 8
Ardrahan, ‡239 D 5
Arklow, 6,948 J 6
Arthurstown, 1,188 H 7
Arva, 370 F 4
Ashford, 341 J 5
Askeaton, 844 D 6
Athboy, 705 H 4
Athea, 328 C 7
Athenry, 1,240 D 5
Athleague, ‡955 E 4
Athlone, 9,825 F 5
Athlone, *11,611 F 5
Athy, 4,270 H 6
Athy, *4,654 H 6
Aughrim, 451 J 6
Avoca, ‡620 J 6
Bagenalstown (Muinebeag), 2,321 H 6
Baile Átha Cliath (Dublin) (cap.), 567,866 K 5
Bailieborough, 1,293 G 4
Balbriggan, 3,741 J 4
Balla, 293 C 4
Ballaghaderreen, 1,121 E 4
Ballina, Mayo, 6,063 C 3
Ballina, *6,369 C 3
Ballina, Tipperary, 336 E 6
Ballinagh, 459 G 4
Ballinakill, 300 G 6
Ballineen D 8
Ballinamore, 808 F 3
Ballinasloe, 5,969 E 5
Ballincollig-Carrigrohane, 2,110 D 8
Ballindine, 232 C 4
Ballingarry, Limerick, 422 D 7
Ballingarry, Tipperary, ‡574 F 6
Ballinlough, 242 D 4
Ballinrobe, 1,272 C 4
Ballintober, ‡867 E 4
Ballintra, 197 E 2
Ballisodare, 486 E 3
Ballivor, 287 H 4
Ballybay, 754 G 3
Ballybay, *1,159 G 3
Ballybofey-Stranorlar, 2,214 F 2
Ballybunion, 1,287 B 7
Ballycanew, ‡460 J 6
Ballycarney, ‡294 J 6
Ballycastle, ‡724 C 3
Ballyconnell, 421 F 3
Ballycotton, 389 F 8
Ballydehob, 253 C 8
Ballyduff, 406 B 7
Ballygar, 359 E 4
Ballygeary, 725 J 7
Ballyhaise, 274 G 3
Ballyhaunis, 1,093 D 4
Ballyheigue, 450 B 7
Ballyjamesduff, 673 G 4
Ballylanders, 266 E 7
Ballylongford, 504 B 6
Ballymahon, 707 F 4
Ballymakeery, 272 C 8
Ballymore, ‡447 F 5
Ballymore Eustace, 433 J 5
Ballymote, 952 D 3
Ballyporeen, ‡810 E 7
Ballyragget, 519 G 6
Ballyroan, ‡478 G 6
Ballyshannon, 2,325 E 3
Ballytore, ‡580 H 5
Baltimore, 200 C 9
Baltinglass, 909 H 6
Baltray, 236 J 4
Banagher, 1,052 F 5
Bandon, 2,257 D 8
Bandon, *4,071 D 8
Bannow, ‡798 H 7
Bansha, 184 E 7
Bantry, 2,579 C 8
Barna, ‡1,734 C 5
Belmullet, 744 B 3
Belturbet, 1,092 G 3
Bennettsbridge, 367 G 6
Birr, 3,319 F 5
Birr, *3,881 F 5
Blanchardstown, 3,279 H 5
Blarney, 1,128 D 8
Blessington, 637 J 5
Boherbue, 372 C 7
Borris, 430 H 6
Borris-in-Ossory, 276 F 6
Borrisokane, 769 E 6
Borrisoleigh, 471 E 6
Boyle, 1,727 E 4
Boyle, *1,939 E 4
Bray, 14,467 K 5
Bray, *15,841 K 5
Brí Chualann (Bray), 14,467 K 5
Broadford, 226 C 7
Brosna, 250 C 7
Bruff, 547 D 7
Bruree, 243 D 7
Bunbeg-Derrybeg, 878 E 1
Bunclody-Carrickduff, 929 H 6
Buncrana, 2,955 G 1
Buncrana, *3,334 G 1
Bundoran, 1,337 E 3
Burtonport, ‡1,288 E 2
Buttevant, 1,045 D 7
Cahir, 1,747 F 7
Cahirciveen, 1,547 A 8
Callan, 1,283 G 7
Camolin, 306 J 6
Campile, 231 H 7
Cappamore, 567 E 6
Cappawhite, 305 E 6
Cappoquin, 872 F 7
Carbury, ‡894 H 5
Carlingford, 559 J 3
Carlow, 9,588 H 6
Carlow, *10,399 H 6
Carndonagh, 1,146 G 1
Carnew, 570 H 6
Carrickmacross, 2,100 H 4
Carrickmacross, *2,475 H 4
Carrick-on-Shannon, 1,854 F 4
Carrick-on-Suir, 5,006 F 7
Carrigaholt, ‡493 B 6
Carrigaline, 951 E 8
Carrigallen, 230 F 4
Carrigart, ‡753 F 1
Carrigtwohill, 622 E 8
Carrowkeel, ‡326 G 1
Cashel, 2,692 F 7
Castlebar, 5,979 C 4
Castlebar, *6,476 C 4
Castlebellingham, 407 J 4
Castleblayney, 2,118 H 3
Castleblayney, *2,395 H 3
Castlecomer-Donaguile, 1,244 G 6
Castledermot, 583 H 6
Castlefin, 610 F 2
Castlegregory, 216 A 7
Castleisland, 1,929 B 7
Castlemartyr, 491 E 8
Castlepollard, 693 G 4
Castlerea, 1,752 D 4
Castletown, ‡504 F 6
Castletownbere, 812 B 8
Castletownroche, 399 D 7
Castletownshend, 170 C 9
Causeway, 215 B 7
Cavan, 3,273 G 3
Cavan, *4,312 G 3
Ceanannus Mór, 2,391 G 4
Ceanannus Mór, *2,653 G 4
Celbridge, 1,568 H 5
Charlestown-Bellahy, 677 D 4
Charleville (Rathluirc), 2,232 D 7
Clara, 2,156 F 5
Claregalway, ‡594 D 5
Claremorris, 1,718 C 4
Clashmore, ‡379 F 8
Clifden, 790 B 5
Cloghan, 404 F 5
Clogh-Chatsworth, 324 G 6
Clogheen, 530 F 7
Clogherhead, 649 J 4
Clonakilty, 2,430 D 8
Clonaslee, 285 F 5
Clondalkin, 7,009 J 5
Clonegal, 202 H 6
Clones, 2,164 G 3
Clonfert, ‡430 E 5
Clonmany, ‡936 G 1
Clonmel, 11,622 F 7
Clonmel, *12,291 F 7
Clonmellon, 328 H 4
Clonroche, 222 H 7
Clontuskert, 351 E 4
Cloone, ‡460 F 4
Cloughjordan, 480 E 6
Cloyne, 654 E 8
Coachford, 290 D 8
Cóbh, 6,076 E 8
Cóbh, *7,141 E 8
Coill Dubh, 920 H 5
Collon, 262 J 4
Collooney, 546 E 3
Cong, 233 C 4
Convoy, 654 F 2
Coolaney, ‡352 D 3
Coolgreany, ‡603 J 6
Cootehill, 1,415 G 3
Cootehill, *1,542 G 3
Cork, 128,645 E 8
Cork, *134,430 E 8
Corofin, 342 C 6
Courtmacsherry, 210 D 8
Courtown Harbour, 291 J 6
Creeslough, 269 F 1
Crookhaven, ‡400 B 9
Croom, 756 D 6
Crosshaven, 1,222 E 8
Crossmolina, 1,077 C 3
Crusheen, ‡405 D 6
Culdaff, ‡621 G 1
Daingean, 492 G 5
Delvin, 223 G 4
Dingle, 1,401 A 7
Doaghbeg, ‡701 F 1
Donabate, 426 J 5
Donegal, 1,725 F 2
Doneraile, 799 D 7
Dooagh-Keel, 649 A 4
Doon, 387 E 6
Douglas, ‡4,448 D 8
Drimoleague, 415 C 8
Drishane, ‡1,548 C 7
Drogheda, 19,762 J 4
Drogheda, *20,095 J 4
Droichead Nua, 5,053 H 5
Droichead Nua, *6,444 H 5
Dromahair, 177 E 3
Drumcar, ‡1,215 J 4
Drumconrath, ‡1,044 H 4
Drumkeerin, ‡467 E 3
Drumlish, 205 F 4
Drumshanbo, 576 E 3
Dublin (cap.), 567,866 K 5
Dublin, *679,748 K 5
Duleek, 658 J 4
Duncannon, 228 H 7
Dundalk, 21,672 H 3
Dundalk, *23,816 H 3
Dunfanaghy, 303 F 1
Dungarvan, 5,583 F 7
Dungloe, 940 E 2
Dunkineely, 288 E 2
Dún Laoghaire, 53,171 K 5
Dún Laoghaire, *98,379 K 5
Dunlavin, 423 H 5
Dunleer 855 J4
Dunmanway 1,392 C8
Dunmore 522 D4
Dunmore East 656 G7
Dunshaughlin⊙ 283 H5
Durrow, Laois 596 G6
Durrow, Offaly⊙ 441 F5
Easky 184 D3
Edenderry 2,953 G5
Edenderry* 3,116 G5
Elphin 489 E4
Emyvale 281 G3
Ennis 5,972 D6
Ennis* 10,840 D6
Enniscorthy 5,704 J7
Enniscorthy* 6,642 J7
Enniskerry 772 J5
Ennistymon 1,013 C6
Eyrecourt 314 E5
Fahan⊙ 1,023 G1
Falcarragh 506 E1
Feakle⊙ 398 D6
Fenit 360 B7
Ferbane 1,064 F5
Fermoy 3,237 E7
Fermoy* 4,033 E7
Ferns 712 J6
Fethard, Tipperary 1,064 F7
Fethard, Wexford⊙ 637 H7
Foxford 868 C4
Foynes 624 C6
Frankford (Kilcormac) 1,089 F5
Frenchpark⊙ 693 E4
Freshford 585 G6
Galbally 258 E7
Galway 27,726 C5
Galway* 29,375 C5
Geashill⊙ 751 G5
Glandore⊙ 695 C8
Glanmire-Riverstown 1,113 E8
Glanworth 335 E7
Glenamaddy 315 D4
Glenbeigh 266 B7
Glencolumbkille⊙ 787 D2
Glengarriff 244 C8
Glenties 734 E2
Glenville⊙ 264 D7
Glin 623 C6
Golden⊙ 640 F7
Gorey 2,946 J6
Gorey* 3,024 J6
Gormanston⊙ 1,384 J4
Gort 975 D5
Gowran 402 G6
Graiguenamanagh-Tinnahinch 1,303 H6
Granard 1,054 F4
Greencastle 322 H1
Greenore 882 J4
Greystones-Delgany 4,517 K5
Gurteen 165 D3
Hacketstown 574 H6
Headford 673 C5
Holycross⊙ 902 F6
Hospital 525 E7
Inchigeelagh⊙ 516 C8
Inishannon 190 D8
Inistioge 179 G7
Inniscrone 582 C3
Johnstown 303 G6
Kanturk 2,063 D7
Keel-Dooagh 649 A4
Kells⊙ 423 G6
Kells (Ceanannus Mór) 2,391 G4
Kenmare 903 B8
Kilbaha⊙ 471 B6
Kilbeggan 635 G5
Kilcar 273 D2
Kilcock 827 H5
Kilconnell⊙ 629 E5
Kilcoole 679 K5
Kilcormac 1,089 F5
Kilcullen 880 H5
Kildare 3,137 H5
Kildysart 239 C6
Kilfenora⊙ 441 C6
Kilfinane 561 D7
Kilgarvan 228 B8
Kilkee 1,287 B6
Kilkelly 225 D4
Kilkenny 9,838 G6
Kilkenny* 13,306 G6
Killala 368 C3
Killaloe 871 D6
Killarney 7,184 C7
Killarney* 7,541 C7
Killavullen 221 D7
Killenaule 592 F6
Killeshandra 432 F3
Killimor 221 E5
Killinaboy⊙ 297 C6
Killorglin 1,150 B7
Killucan-Rathwire 290 G4
Killybegs 1,094 E2
Kilmacrennan 274 F1
Kilmacthomas 396 G7
Kilmallock 1,170 D7
Kilmeadan⊙ 262 G7
Kilmihill 284 C6
Kilmoganny 181 G7
Kilmore Quay 273 H7
Kilmurry⊙ 387 C6
Kilnaleck 273 G4
Kilronan 243 B5
Kilrush 2,671 C6
Kilsheelan⊙ 665 F7
Kiltimagh 978 C4
Kilworth 360 E7
Kingscourt 1,016 H4
Kingstown (Dún Laoghaire) 53,171 K5
Kinlough 160 E3
Kinnegad 362 G5
Kinnitty⊙ 420 F5
Kinsale 1,622 D8
Kinsale* 1,989 D8
Kinvara 293 D5
Knightstown 236 A8
Knock⊙ 1,202 D4
Knocklong 248 D7
Knocknagashel 168 C7
Labasheeda⊙ 468 C6
Laghy⊙ 625 E2
Lahinch 455 C6
Lanesborough-Ballyleague 906 E4
Laracor⊙ 404 H4
Laytown-Bettystown-Mornington 1,882 J4
Leenane⊙ 271 B4
Leighlindridge 379 H6
Leitrim⊙ 544 F3
Leixlip 2,402 H5
Letterkenny 4,930 F2
Letterkenny* 5,207 F2
Lifford 1,121 F2
Limerick 57,161 D6
Limerick* 63,002 D6
Liscarroll 231 D7
Lisdoonvarna 459 C5
Lismore 884 F7
Lismore⊙ 1,041 F7
Listowel 3,021 C7
Littleton 322 F6
Longford 3,876 F4
Longford* 4,791 F4
Lorrha⊙ 685 E5
Loughrea 3,075 E5
Louisburgh 310 B4
Louth 208 J4
Lucan-Doddsborough 4,245 J5
Luimneach (Limerick) 57,161 D6
Lusk 553 J4
Macroom 2,256 C8
Malahide 3,834 J5
Malin⊙ 552 G1
Mallow 5,901 D7
Mallow* 6,506 D7
Manorhamilton 858 E3
Manulla⊙ 660 C4
Maryborough (Portlaoise) 3,902 G5
Maynooth 1,296 H5
Meathas Truim 546 G4
Midleton 3,075 E8
Midleton* 4,666 E8
Milford 763 F1
Millstreet 1,319 D7
Milltown 260 A7
Miltown-Malbay 677 C6
Minard⊙ 397 A7
Mitchelstown 2,783 E7
Moate 1,378 F5
Mohill 868 F4
Monaghan 5,256 G3
Monasterevan 1,619 H5
Moneygall 282 F6
Monivea⊙ 405 D5
Mooncoin 413 G7
Mount Bellew 275 D5
Mountcharles 445 E2
Mountmellick 2,595 G5
Mountmellick* 2,864 G5
Mountrath 1,098 F5
Moville 1,089 G1
Moycullen⊙ 498 C5
Moynalty⊙ 583 H4
Muff 240 G1
Muinebeag 2,321 H6
Mullagh 293 H4
Mullaghmore⊙ 629 D3
Mullinahone 262 F7
Mullinavat 343 G7
Mullingar 6,790 G4
Mullingar* 9,245 G4
Naas 5,078 H5
Navan (An Uaimh) 4,605 H4
Nenagh 5,085 E6
Nenagh* 5,174 E6
Newbliss⊙ 547 G3
Newbridge (Droichead Nua) 5,053 H5
Newcastle 2,549 D7
Newcastle* 2,680 D7
Newmarket 886 C7
Newmarket-on-Fergus 1,052 D6
New Pallas⊙ 1,271 E6
Newport, Mayo 420 C4
Newport, Tipperary 582 E6
New Ross 4,775 H7
New Ross* 5,153 H7
Newtown Forbes⊙ 495 F4
Newtownmountkennedy 882 J5
Newtownsandes 268 C6
O'Briensbridge-Montpelier 237 D6
Oldcastle 759 G4
Old Leighlin⊙ 309 G6
Oola 348 E6
Oranmore 440 D5
Oughterard 628 C5
Passage East 408 G7
Passage West 2,709 E8
Patrickswell 415 D6
Pettigo 332 F2
Piltown 456 G7
Portarlington 3,117 G5
Portlaoise 3,902 G5
Portlaoise* 6,470 G5
Portlaw 1,166 G7
Portmarnock 1,726 J5
Portumna 913 E5
Queenstown (Cóbh) 6,076 E8
Rahan⊙ 531 F5
Ramelton 807 F1
Raphoe 945 F2
Rathangan 868 G5
Rathcoole 1,740 J5
Rathcormac 191 E7
Rathdowney 892 F6
Rathdrum 1,141 J6
Rathgormuck⊙ 231 F7
Rathkeale 1,543 D7
Rathluirc 2,232 D7
Rathmore 437 J5
Rathmullen 486 F1
Rathnew-Merrymeeting 954 J6
Rathowen⊙ 294 F4
Rathvilly 230 H6
Ratoath 300 J5
Riverstown 236 E3
Rockcorry 233 H3
Rosapenna⊙ 822 F1
Roscommon 1,556 E4
Roscommon* 2,821 E4
Roscrea 3,855 F6
Rosscarbery 309 C8
Rosses Point 464 D3
Rosslare 588 J7
Rosslare Harbour (Ballygeary) 725 J7
Roundstone 204 A5
Roundwood 260 J5
Rush 2,633 J4
Saint Johnston 463 F2
Scarriff 619 E6
Schull 457 B8
Scotstown 264 H3
Shanagolden 231 C6
Shannon Airport 3,657 D6
Shannon Bridge 188 F5
Shercock 313 G4
Shillelagh 246 J6
Shinrone 365 F5
Shrule 288 C4
Sixmilebridge 567 D6
Skerries 3,044 J4
Skibbereen 2,104 C8
Slane 483 H4
Sligo 14,080 E3
Sligo* 14,456 E3
Sneem 285 B8
Spiddal⊙ 819 C5
Stepaside 748 J5
Stradbally, Laois 891 G5
Stradbally, Waterford 158 F7
Strokestown 563 E4
Swanlinbar 257 F3
Swinford 1,105 C4
Swords 4,133 J5
Taghmon 369 H7
Tallaght 6,174 J5
Tallow, 883 F 7
Tarbert, 485 C 6
Teltown, ‡739 H 4
Templemore, 2,174 F 6
Templetuohy, 197 F 6
Termonfeckin, 328 J 4
Thomastown, 1,270 G 7
Thurles, 6,840 F 6
Thurles, *7,087 F 6
Timoleague, 257 D 8
Tinahely, 450 H 6
Tipperary, 4,631 E 7
Tipperary, *4,717 E 7
Toomevara, 272 E 6
Tralee, 12,287 B 7
Tralee, *13,263 B 7
Tramore, 3,792 G 7
Trim, 1,700 H 4
Trim, *2,255 H 4
Tuam, 3,808 D 4
Tuam, *4,952 D 4
Tubbercurry, 959 D 3
Tulla, 415 D 6
Tullamore, 6,809 G 5
Tullamore, *7,474 G 5
Tullaroan, ‡301 G 6
Tullow, 1,838 H 6
Tullow, *1,945 H 6
Tynagh, ‡452 E 5
Tyrrellspass, 289 G 5
Urlingford, 652 F 6
Virginia, 583 G 4
Waterford, 31,968 G 7
Waterford, *33,676 G 7
Waterville, 547 A 8
Westport, 3,023 C 4
Wexford, 11,849 H 7
Wexford, *13,293 H 7
Whitegate, 370 E 8
Wicklow, 3,786 K 6
Wicklow, *3,915 K 6
Woodenbridge, ‡620 J 6
Woodford, 198 E 5
Youghal, 5,445 F 8
Youghal, *5,626 F 8

OTHER FEATURES

Achill (isl.), 3,129 A 4
Allen (lake) E 3
Allen, Bog of (marsh) H 5
Aran (isl.), 773 D 2
Aran (isls.), 1,499 B 5
Arklow (bank) K 6
Arrow (lake) E 3
Awbeg (riv.) D 7
Ballinskelligs (bay) A 8
Ballycotton (bay) F 8
Ballyheige (bay) B 7
Ballyhoura (hills) E 7
Ballyteige (bay) H 7
Bandon (riv.) D 8
Bann (riv.) J 6
Bantry (bay) B 8
Barrow (riv.) H 7
Baurtregaum (mt.) A 7
Bear (isl.), 288 B 8
Blacksod (bay) A 3
Blackstairs (mt.) H 6
Blackwater (riv.) D 7
Blackwater (riv.) H 4
Blasket (isls.) A 7
Bloody Foreland (prom.) E 1
Blue Stack (mts.) E 2
Boderg (lake) E 4
Boggeragh (mts.) D 7
Boyne (riv.) J 4
Brandon (head) A 7
Bride (riv.) E 7
Broad Haven (harb.) B 3
Brosna (riv.) F 5
Bull, The (isl.), 5 A 8
Caha (mts.) B 8
Carlingford (inlet) J 3
Carnsore (pt.) J 7
Carrantuohill (mt.) B 7
Clare (riv.) D 5
Clare (isls.), 168 A 4
Clear (cape) B 9
Clear (isl.), 192 C 9
Clew (bay) B 4
Comeragh (mts.) F 7
Conn (lake) C 3
Connacht (prov.), 390,902 C 4
Connemara (dist.), 7,599 B 5
Cork (harb.) E 8
Corrib (lake) C 5
Courtmacsherry (bay) D 8
Curragh, The H 5
Dee (riv.) H 4
Deel (riv.) D 7
Deele (riv.) F 2
Derg (lake) E 6
Derravaragh (lake) G 4
Derryveagh (mts.) E 2
Dingle (bay) A 7
Donegal (bay) D 3
Drum (hills) F 7
Dublin (bay) J 5
Dundalk (bay) J 4
Dunmanus (bay) B 8
Dursey (isl.), 38 A 8
Ennell (lake) G 5
Erne (riv.) E 3
Errigal (mt.) E 1
Erris (head) A 3
Fanad (head) F 1
Fastnet Rock (isl.), 3 B 9
Feale (riv.) C 7
Fergus (riv.) D 6
Finn (riv.) F 2
Finn (riv.) G 3
Flesk (riv.) C 7
Foyle (inlet) G 1
Foyle (riv.) G 2
Galley (head) D 9
Galtee (mts.) E 7
Galtymore (mt.) E 7
Galway (bay) C 5
Gara (lake) D 4
Garadice (lake) F 3
Gill (lake) E 3
Glyde (riv.) H 4
Golden Vale (plain) E 7
Gorumna (isl.), 1,108 B 5
Gowna (lake) G 4
Grand (canal) G 5
Greenore (pt.) J 7
Gweebarra (bay) D 2
Hags (head) B 6
Helvick (head) G 7
Hook (head) H 7
Horn (head) E 1
Iar Connacht (dist.), 10,774 C 5
Inishbofin (isl.), 236 A 4
Inishbofin (isl.), 103 E 1
Inisheer (isl.), 313 B 5
Inishmaan (isl.), 319 C 5
Inishmore (isl.), 864 B 5
Inishowen (head) H 1
Inishowen (pen.), 24,109 G 1
Inishtrahull (isl.), 3 G 1
Inishturk (isls.), 83 A 4
Inny (riv.) A 8
Inny (riv.) F 4
Inver (bay) E 2
Ireland's Eye (isl.) K 5
Irish (sea) K 4
Joyce's Country (dist.), 2,021 B 4
Kenmare (riv.) A 8
Kerry (head) A 7
Key (lake) E 3
Kilkieran (bay) B 5
Killala (bay) C 3
Killary (harb.) A 4
Kinsale (harb.) E 8
Kippure (mt.) J 5
Knockboy (mt.) B 8
Knockmealdown (mts.) F 7
Lady's Island Lake (inlet) J 7
Lambay (isl.), 24 K 4
Laune (riv.) B 7
Leane (lake) B 7
Leane (lake) G 4
Lee (riv.) D 8
Leinster (mt.) H 6
Leinster (prov.), 1,498,140 G 5
Lettermullan (isl.), 221 B 5
Liffey (riv.) H 5
Liscannor (bay) B 6
Long Island (bay) B 9
Loop (head) A 6
Lugnaquillia (mt.) J 5
Macgillicuddy's Reeks (mts.) B 7
Macnean (lake) F 3
Maigue (riv.) D 6
Maine (riv.) C 7
Malin (head) F 1
Mask (lake) C 4
Maumturk (mts.) B 5
Melvin (lake) E 3
Mizen (head) B 9
Moher (cliffs) B 6
Monavullagh (mts.) F 7
Moy (riv.) C 3
Mulkear (riv.) E 6
Mullaghareirk (mts.) C 7
Mulroy (bay) F 1
Munster (prov.), 882,002 D 7
Mweelrea (mt.) B 4
Mweenish (isl.), 198 B 5
Nagles (mts.) E 7
Nenagh (riv.) E 6
Nephin (mt.) C 3
Nore (riv.) G 7
North (sound) B 5
Omey (isl.), 34 A 5
Oughter (lake) G 3
Ovoca (riv.) J 6
Owenmore (riv.) D 3
Owey (isl.), 51 D 1
Paps, The (mt.) C 7
Partry (mts.) C 4
Pollaphuca (res.) J 5
Punchestown H 5
Rathlin O'Birne (isl.), 3 C 2
Ree (lake) F 5
Roaringwater (bay) B 9
Rosses (bay) D 1
Rosskeeragh (pt.) D 3
Royal (canal) G 4
Saint Finan's (bay) A 8
Saint George's (chan.) K 7
Saint John's (pt.) D 2
Saltee (isls.) H 7
Seven (heads) D 8
Seven Hogs, The (isls.) A 7
Shannon (riv.) E 6
Sheeffry (hills) B 4
Sheelin (lake) G 4
Sheep Haven (harb.) F 1
Sheeps (head) B 8
Sherkin (isl.), 82 C 9
Silvermine (mts.) E 6
Slaney (riv.) H 7
Slieve Aughty (mts.) D 5
Slieve Bloom (mts.) F 5
Slieve Gamph (mts.) D 3
Slievenaman (mt.) F 7
Sligo (bay) D 3
Slyne (head) A 5
South (sound) C 5
Stacks (mts.) B 7
Suck (riv.) E 5
Suir (riv.) G 7
Swilly (inlet) F 1
Tara (hill) H 4
Tory (isl.), 273 E 1
Tory (sound) E 1
Tralee (bay) B 7
Trawbreaga (bay) F 1
Ulster (part) (prov.), 207,204 G 2
Valencia (Valentia) (isl.), 770 A 8
Valentia (isl.), 770 A 8
Waterford (harb.) G 7
Wexford (bay) J 7
Wicklow (head) K 6
Wicklow (mts.) J 6
Youghal (bay) F 8

NORTHERN IRELAND

DISTRICTS

Antrim, 37,600 J 2
Ards, 52,100 K 2
Armagh, 47,500 H 3
Ballymena, 52,200 J 2
Ballymoney, 22,700 J 1
Bainbridge, 28,800 J 3
Belfast, 368,200 J 2
Carrickfergus, 27,500 K 2
Castlereagh, 63,600 K 2
Coleraine, 44,900 H 1
Cookstown, 27,500 H 2
Craigavon, 71,200 J 3
Down, 48,800 K 3
Dungannon, 43,000 H 3
Fermanagh, 50,900 F 3
Larne, 29,000 K 2
Limavady, 25,000 H 1
Lisburn, 80,800 J 2
Londonderry, 86,600 G 2
Magherafelt, 32,200 H 2
Mourne (Newry and Mourne), 75,300 J 3
Moyle, 13,400 J 1
Newtownabbey, 71,500 J 2
North Down, 59,600 K 2
Omagh, 41,800 G 2
Strabane, 35,500 G 2

CITIES and TOWNS

Ahoghill, ‡1,929 J 2
Annalong, 1,001 K 3
Antrim, 8,351 J 2
Ardglass, 1,052 K 3
Armagh, 13,606 H 3
Armoy, ‡1,051 J 1
Augher, ‡1,986 G 3
Aughnacloy, ‡1,885 H 3
Ballycastle, 2,899 J 1
Ballyclare, 5,155 J 2
Ballygawley, ‡2,165 G 3
Ballykelly, 1,116 G 1
Ballymena, 23,386 J 2
Ballymoney, 5,697 J 1
Ballynahinch, 3,485 J 3
Banbridge, 7,968 J 3
Bangor, 35,260 K 2
Belfast (cap.), 353,700 J 2
Belfast, *551,940 J 2
Bellaghy, ‡2,265 H 2
Belleek, ‡2,487 E 3
Beragh, ‡2,137 G 2
Bessbrook, 2,619 J 3
Brookeborough, ‡2,534 G 3
Broughshane, 1,288 J 2
Bushmills, 1,288 J 1
Caledon, ‡1,828 H 3
Carnlough, 1,416 J 2
Carrickfergus, 16,603 K 2
Carrowdore, 2,548 K 2
Castledawson, 1,162 H 2
Castlederg, 1,766 F 2
Castlewellan, 1,488 K 3
Claudy, ‡2,507 G 2
Clogher, ‡1,888 G 3
Coalisland, 3,614 H 2
Coleraine, 16,354 H 1
Comber, 5,575 K 2
Cookstown, 6,965 H 2
Craigavon, 12,740 J 3
Crossgar, 1,098 K 3
Crossmaglen, 1,085 H 3
Crumlin, 1,450 J 2
Cullybackey, 1,649 J 2
Derrygonnelly, ‡2,539 F 3
Dervock, ‡1,191 J 1
Donaghadee, 4,008 K 2
Downpatrick, 7,918 K 3
Draperstown, ‡2,247 H 2
Dromore, Bainbridge, 2,848 J 3
Dromore, Omagh, ‡2,224 G 3
Drumquin, ‡1,982 F 2
Dundrum, ‡2,245 K 3
Dungannon, 8,190 H 3
Dungiven, 1,536 H 2
Dunnamanagh, ‡2,242 G 2
Ederny and Kesh, ‡2,497 F 2
Enniskillen, 9,679 F 3
Feeny, ‡1,459 H 2
Fintona, 1,190 G 3
Fivemiletown, ‡1,649 G 3
Garvagh, ‡2,363 H 2
Gilford, 1,592 J 3
Glenarm, ‡1,728 J 2
Glenavy, ‡2,360 J 2
Glynn, ‡1,872 K 2
Gortin, ‡2,033 G 2
Greyabbey, ‡2,646 K 2
Hillsborough, 1,021 J 3
Holywood, 9,892 K 2
Irvinestown, 1,457 F 3
Keady, 2,145 H 3
Kells, ‡2,560 J 2
Kesh, ‡2,497 F 3
Kilkeel, 4,090 K 3
Killough, ‡3,295 K 3
Killyleagh, 2,359 K 3
Kilrea, 1,196 H 2
Kircubbin, 1,075 K 3
Larne, 18,482 K 2
Limavady, 6,004 H 1
Lisburn, 31,836 J 2
Lisnaskea, 1,443 G 3
Londonderry, 51,200 G 2
Loughbrickland, ‡2,056 J 3
Maghera, 2,085 H 2
Magherafelt, 4,704 H 2
Markethill, ‡2,352 H 3
Millisle, 1,172 K 2
Moneymore, 1,178 H 2
Moy, ‡2,349 H 3
Moygashel, 1,086 H 3
Newcastle, 4,647 J 3
Newry, 20,279 J 3
Newtownabbey, 58,114 K 2
Newtownards, 15,484 K 2
Newtownbutler, ‡2,663 G 3
Newtownhamilton, ‡1,936 H 3
Newtownstewart, 1,433 G 2
Omagh, 14,594 G 2
Pomeroy, ‡1,786 H 2
Portaferry, 1,730 K 3
Portavogie, 1,310 K 3
Portglenone, ‡2,061 H 2
Portrush, 5,376 H 1
Portstewart, 5,085 H 1
Randalstown, 2,799 J 2
Rathfriland, 1,886 J 3
Rostrevor, 1,617 J 3
Saintfield, ‡2,198 K 3
Sion Mills, 1,588 G 2
Sixmilecross, ‡1,980 G 2
Stewartstown, ‡1,759 H 2
Strabane, 9,413 G 2
Strangford, ‡1,987 K 3
Tandragee, 1,725 J 3
Tempo, ‡2,282 G 3
Trillick, ‡2,167 G 3
Warrenpoint, 4,291 J 3
Whitehead, 2,642 K 2

OTHER FEATURES

Bann (riv.) H 2
Belfast (inlet) K 2
Blackwater (riv.) H 3
Bush (riv.) H 1
Derg (riv.) F 2
Divis (mt.) J 2
Dundrum (bay) K 3
Erne (lake) F 3
Foyle (inlet) G 1
Foyle (riv.) G 2
Giant's Causeway H 1
Lagan (riv.) K 2
Larne (inlet) K 2
Magee, Island (pen.), 1,581 K 2
Magilligan (pt.) H 1
Main (riv.) J 2
Mourne (mts.) J 3
Mourne (riv.) G 2
Neagh (lake) J 2
North (chan.) K 1
Rathlin (isl.), 109 J 1
Red (bay) K 1
Roe (riv.) H 1
Saint John's (pt.) K 3
Slieve Donard (mt.) K 3
Sperrin (mts.) G 2
Strangford (inlet) K 3
Torr (head) K 1
Ulster (part) (prov.), 1,537,200 G 2
Upper Lough Erne (lake) F 3

*City and suburbs.
‡Population of district.

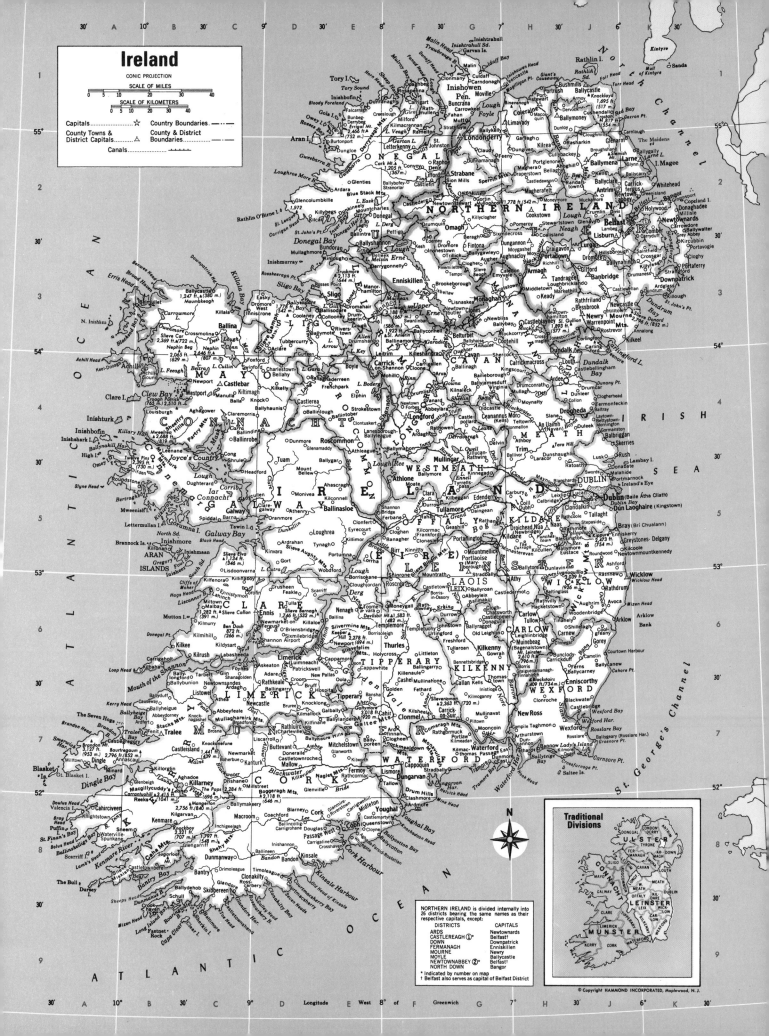

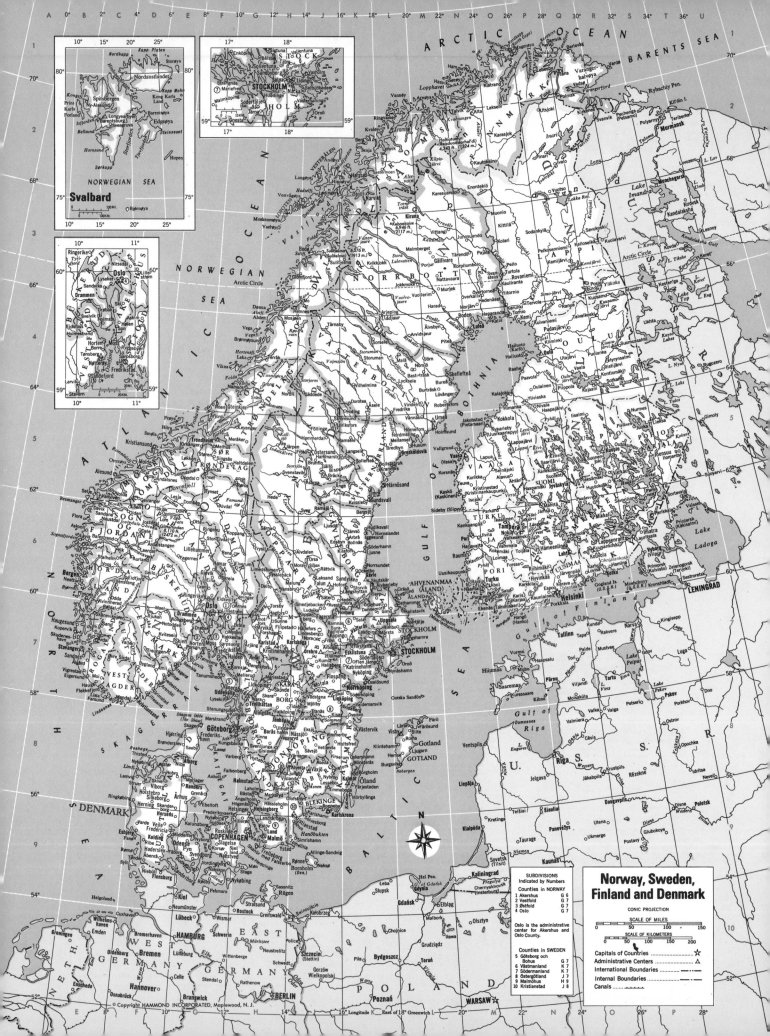

Norway, Sweden, Finland and Denmark

CONIC PROJECTION

SCALE OF MILES

SCALE OF KILOMETERS

Capitals of Countries .... ☆
Administrative Centers .... △
International Boundaries .... —·—·—
Internal Boundaries .... —·—·—
Canals .... ———

SUBDIVISIONS
Indicated by Numbers

Counties in NORWAY

1 Akershus   G 6
2 Vestfold   G 7
3 Østfold   G 7
4 Oslo   G 7

Oslo is the administrative
center for Akershus and
Oslo County.

Counties in SWEDEN

5 Göteborg och
   Bohus   G 7
6 Västmanland   K 7
7 Södermanland   K 7
8 Östergötland   J 7
9 Malmöhus   J 8
10 Kristianstad   J 8

© Copyright HAMMOND INCORPORATED, Maplewood, N.J.

Svalbard

NORWEGIAN SEA

AREA 125,053 sq. mi. (323,887 sq. km.)
POPULATION 4,092,000
CAPITAL Oslo
LARGEST CITY Oslo
HIGHEST POINT Glittertinden 8,110 ft. (2,472 m.)
MONETARY UNIT krone
MAJOR LANGUAGE Norwegian
MAJOR RELIGION Protestantism

AREA 173,665 sq. mi. (449,792 sq. km.)
POPULATION 8,320,000
CAPITAL Stockholm
LARGEST CITY Stockholm
HIGHEST POINT Kebnekaise 6,946 ft. (2,117 m.)
MONETARY UNIT krona
MAJOR LANGUAGE Swedish
MAJOR RELIGION Protestantism

AREA 130,128 sq. mi. (337,032 sq. km.)
POPULATION 4,788,000
CAPITAL Helsinki
LARGEST CITY Helsinki
HIGHEST POINT Haltiatunturi 4,343 ft. (1,324 m.)
MONETARY UNIT markka
MAJOR LANGUAGES Finnish, Swedish
MAJOR RELIGION Protestantism

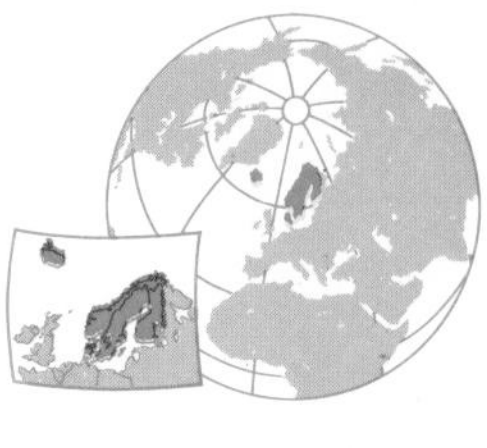

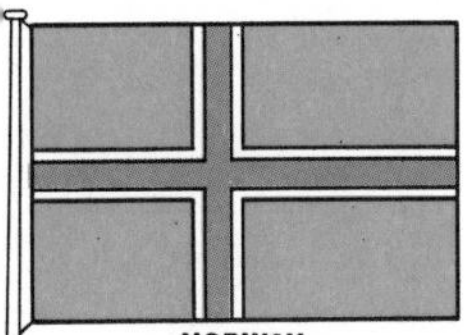

NORWAY

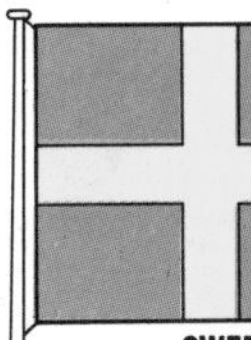

SWEDEN

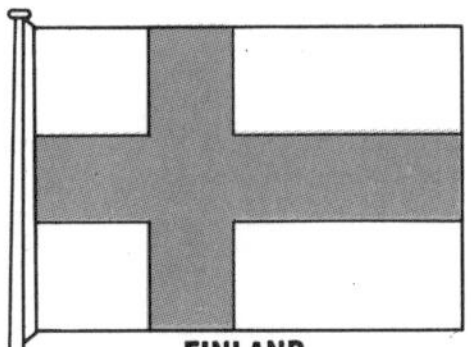

FINLAND

FINLAND

PROVINCES

Ahvenanmaa 22,380 ..... L6
Åland (Ahvenanmaa) 22,380 ..... L6
Häme 662,500 ..... O6
Keski-Suomi 241,770 ..... O5
Kuopio 252,023 ..... P5
Kymi 346,478 ..... Q6
Lappi 196,792 ..... P3
Mikkeli 211,453 ..... P6
Oulu 406,309 ..... P4
Pohjois-Karjala 179,065 ..... Q5
Turku ja Pori 697,988 ..... N6
Uusimaa 1,085,625 ..... O6
Vaasa 425,283 ..... N5

CITIES and TOWNS

Äänekoski 10,725 ..... O5
Åbo (Turku) 164,857 ..... N6
Alavus 10,285 ..... N5
Borgaå 18,740 ..... O6
Ekenäs 7,391 ..... N6
Espoo 117,090 ..... O6
Forssa 18,442 ..... N6
Haapajärvi 7,791 ..... O5
Hämeenlinna 40,761 ..... O6
Hamina 11,055 ..... P6
Hangö 10,374 ..... N7
Hanko (Hangö) 10,374 ..... N7
Harjavalta 8,445 ..... M6
Heinola 15,350 ..... P6
Helsinki (cap.) 502,961 ..... O6
Helsinki* 794,746 ..... O6
Huutokoski† 6,458 ..... P5
Hyvinkää 35,865 ..... O6
Iisalmi 21,159 ..... P5
Ikaalinen 8,364 ..... N6
Imatra 35,590 ..... Q6
Ivalo 2,661 ..... P2
Jakobstad 20,397 ..... N5
Jämsä 12,526 ..... O6
Järvenpää 16,259 ..... O6
Joensuu 41,429 ..... R5
Jyväskylä 61,209 ..... O5
Jyväskylä* 84,185 ..... O5
Kajaani 20,583 ..... P4
Kalajoki 3,624 ..... N4
Kankaanpää 12,564 ..... M6
Karhula 21,834 ..... P6
Karis 8,152 ..... N6
Karjaa (Karis) 8,152 ..... N6
Karkkila 8,678 ..... N6
Kauniainien 6,219 ..... O6
Kauttua 3,297 ..... M6
Kelloselkä† 8,200 ..... Q3
Kemi 27,893 ..... O4
Kemijärvi 12,951 ..... P3
Kerava 19,966 ..... O6
Kokemäki 10,188 ..... N6
Kokkola 22,096 ..... N5
Kotka 34,026 ..... P6
Kotka* 60,235 ..... P6
Kouvola 29,383 ..... P6
Kouvola* 59,507 ..... P6
Kristiinankaupunki (Kristinestad) 9,331 ..... N5
Kristinestad 9,331 ..... N5
Kuhmo 4,150 ..... Q4
Kuopio 71,684 ..... Q5
Kurikka 11,177 ..... M5
Kuusamo 4,449 ..... Q4
Kuusankoski 22,342 ..... P6
Lahti 94,864 ..... O6
Lahti* 112,129 ..... O6
Lappeenranta 52,682 ..... P6
Lapua 15,189 ..... N5
Lieksa 20,274 ..... R5
Loimaa 6,575 ..... N6
Lovisa 8,674 ..... P6
Maarianhamina (Mariehamn) 9,574 ..... M7
Mänttä 7,910 ..... O6
Mariehamn 9,574 ..... M7
Mikkeli 27,112 ..... P6
Naantali 7,814 ..... M6
Nokia 22,308 ..... N6
Nurmes 11,721 ..... Q5
Nykarleby 7,408 ..... N5
Oulainen 7,322 ..... O4
Oulu 93,707 ..... O4
Oulu* 103,044 ..... O4
Outokumpu 10,736 ..... Q5
Parainen 10,170 ..... M6
Parkano 8,518 ..... N6
Pieksämäki 12,923 ..... P5
Pietarsaari (Jakobstad) 20,397 ..... N5
Pori 80,343 ..... M6
Pori* 86,635 ..... M6
Posio† 6,205 ..... Q3
Pudasjärvi† 12,594 ..... P4
Raahe 15,379 ..... O4
Raisio 14,271 ..... M6
Rauma 29,081 ..... M6
Riihimäki 24,106 ..... O6
Rovaniemi 28,411 ..... O3
Saarijärvi 2,714 ..... O5
Salo 19,176 ..... N6
Savonlinna 28,336 ..... Q6
Seinäjoki 22,123 ..... N5
Sodankylä 3,304 ..... P3
Sotkamo 2,316 ..... Q4
Suolahti 5,936 ..... O5
Suonenjoki 9,286 ..... P5
Tammisaari (Ekenäs) 7,391 ..... N6
Tampere 168,118 ..... N6
Tampere* 220,920 ..... N6
Toijala 8,080 ..... N6
Tornio 19,971 ..... O4
Turku 164,857 ..... N6
Turku* 217,423 ..... N6
Turtola† 5,852 ..... O3
Ulvila† 8,040 ..... N6
Uusikaarlepyy (Nykarleby) 7,408 ..... N5
Uusikaupunki 11,915 ..... M6
Vaasa 54,402 ..... M5
Vaasa* 58,224 ..... M5
Valkeakoski 22,588 ..... N6
Vammala 16,363 ..... N6
Varkaus 24,450 ..... Q5
Vasa (Vaasa) 54,402 ..... M5
Vuotso† 10,186 ..... P2
Ylivieska 10,827 ..... O4

OTHER FEATURES

Åland (isls.) L6
Baltic (sea) K9
Bothnia (gulf) M5
Finland (gulf) P7
Hailuoto (isl.) O4
Haltiatunturi (mt.) M2
Hangöudd (prom.) N7
Haukivesi (lake) Q5
Iijoki (riv.) O4
Inari (lake) P2
Ivalojoki (riv.) P2
Juojärvi (lake) Q5
Kalajoki (riv.) O4
Kallavesi (lake) P5
Karlö (Hailuoto) (isl.) O4
Keitele (lake) O5
Kemijärvi (lake) Q3
Kemijoki (riv.) O3
Kiantajärvi (lake) Q4
Kilpisjärvi (lake) M2
Kitinen (riv.) P3
Kivijärvi (lake) O5
Koitere (lake) R5
Kuusamojärvi (lake) Q4
Längelmävesi (lake) O6
Lapland (reg.) O2
Lappajärvi (lake) O5
Lapuanjoki (riv.) N5
Lestijärvi (lake) O5
Lokka (res.) Q3
Muojärvi (lake) R4
Muonio (riv.) M2
Näsijärvi (lake) O6
Onkivesi (lake) P5
Orihvesi (lake) Q5
Oulujärvi (lake) P4
Oulujoki (riv.) O4
Ounasjoki (riv.) O3
Päijänne (lake) O6
Pielinen (lake) Q5
Puruvesi (lake) Q6
Puulavesi (lake) P5
Pyhäjärvi (lake) O5
Pyhäjärvi (lake) M6
Saimaa (lake) Q6
Siikajoki (riv.) O4
Simojärvi (lake) P3
Simojoki (riv.) O4
Tana (riv.) P2
Tornio (riv.) O3
Vallgrund (isl.) M5
Ylikitka (lake) Q3

NORWAY

COUNTIES

Akershus 355,196 ..... G6
Aust-Agder 86,216 ..... E7
Buskerud 209,684 ..... F6
Finnmark 79,373 ..... O2
Hedmark 183,465 ..... G6
Hordaland 386,492 ..... E6
Møre og Romsdal 231,944 ..... E5
Nordland 243,233 ..... J3
Nord-Trøndelag 122,886 ..... H4
Oppland 178,259 ..... F6
Oslo (city) 462,732 ..... D3
Østfold 228,546 ..... G7
Rogaland 287,653 ..... E7
Sogn og Fjordane 103,135 ..... E6
Sør-Trøndelag 241,361 ..... G5
Telemark 158,853 ..... F7
Troms 144,111 ..... L2
Vest-Agder 131,659 ..... E7
Vestfold 182,433 ..... G7

CITIES and TOWNS

Ålesund 40,868 ..... D5
Ålgård 2,322 ..... D7
Alta 5,582 ..... N2
Åndalsnes 2,574 ..... F5
Årdalstangen 2,360 ..... F6
Arendal 11,701 ..... F7
Arendal* 21,228 ..... F7
Årnes 2,267 ..... G6
Askim 8,413 ..... E4
Bamble† 7,031 ..... F7
Barentsburg C2
Bergen 213,434 ..... D6
Bodø 31,077 ..... J3
Borge† 3,294 ..... H2
Brønnøysund 3,130 ..... G4
Dombås 1,114 ..... F5
Drammen 50,777 ..... C4
Drammen* 56,521 ..... C4
Drøbak 4,538 ..... D4
Eidsvoll 2,906 ..... G6
Eigersund 11,379 ..... D7
Elverum 7,391 ..... G6
Farsund 8,908 ..... E7
Flekkefjord 8,750 ..... E7
Flora 8,822 ..... D6
Fredrikstad 29,024 ..... D4
Fredrikstad* 51,141 ..... D4
Gjøvik 25,963 ..... G6
Grimstad 13,091 ..... F7
Halden 27,087 ..... G7
Hamar 16,418 ..... G6
Hamar* 25,138 ..... G6
Hammerfest 7,610 ..... N1
Hammerfest* 8,005 ..... N1
Harstad 21,125 ..... K2
Haugesund 27,386 ..... D7
Haugesund* 29,277 ..... D7
Hermansverk 706 ..... E6
Holmestrand 8,246 ..... C4
Holmsbu 273 ..... D4
Honningsvag 3,780 ..... O1
Horten 13,746 ..... D4
Horten* 17,246 ..... D4
Kirkenes 4,466 ..... Q2
Kongsberg 19,854 ..... F7
Kongsvinger 16,146 ..... H6
Kopervik 4,221 ..... D7
Kornsjø† 6,079 ..... G7
Kragerø 5,249 ..... F7
Kristiansand 59,488 ..... F8
Kristiansund 18,847 ..... E5
Kvinnherad† 2,898 ..... E6
Larvik 9,097 ..... C4
Larvik* 19,202 ..... C4
Lenvik† 11,098 ..... L2
Levanger 5,066 ..... G5
Lillehammer 21,248 ..... F6
Lillesand 3,028 ..... F7
Lillestrøm† 11,550 ..... E3
Longyearbyen D2
Lysaker† 81,612 ..... D3
Mandal 11,579 ..... E7
Meråker† 2,907 ..... G5
Mo 21,033 ..... J3
Molde 20,334 ..... E5
Mosjøen 9,341 ..... H4
Moss 25,786 ..... D4
Moss* 27,430 ..... D4
Mysen 3,760 ..... G7
Namsos 11,452 ..... G4
Narvik 19,582 ..... K2
Nesttun† 11,519 ..... D6
Nittedal† 8,889 ..... D3
Notodden 12,970 ..... F7
Nøtterøy 11,944 ..... D4
Ny-Ålesund C2
Odda 7,401 ..... E6
Oppdal 2,173 ..... F5
Orkanger 3,685 ..... F5
Oslo (cap.) 462,732 ..... D3
Oslo* 645,413 ..... D3
Porsgrunn 31,709 ..... G7
Rakkestad 2,392 ..... G7
Ringerike 30,156 ..... C3
Risør 6,560 ..... F7
Rjukan 5,334 ..... F7
Røros 3,041 ..... G5
Sandefjord 33,350 ..... C4
Sandnes 33,934 ..... D7
Sandvika† 34,337 ..... C3
Sarpsborg 12,889 ..... D4
Sarpsborg* 36,449 ..... D4
Selje† 3,386 ..... D5
Ski 9,081 ..... D4
Skien 47,105 ..... F7
Stavanger 86,639 ..... D7
Stavern 2,604 ..... D4
Steinkjer 20,553 ..... G4
Stor-Elvdal† 2,993 ..... G6
Sunndalsøra 5,114 ..... F5
Sveagruva D2
Svolvaer 3,942 ..... J2
Tønsberg 9,964 ..... D4
Tønsberg* 36,374 ..... D4
Tromsø 43,830 ..... L2
Trondheim 134,910 ..... F5
Ullensvang† 2,326 ..... E6
Vadsø 6,019 ..... Q1
Vardø 3,875 ..... R1
Vik 1,019 ..... E6
Volda 3,511 ..... E5
Voss 5,944 ..... E6

OTHER FEATURES

Alsten (isl.) H4
Andøya (isl.) J2
Barduelv (riv.) L2
Bellsund C2
Bjørnafjorden (fjord) D6
Bjornøya (isl.) D3
Boknafjord (fjord) D7
Bremanger (isl.) D6
Dønna (isl.) H3
Dovrefjell (hills) F5
Edgeøya (isl.) E2
Femundsjø (lake) G5
Folda (fjord) G4
Folda (fjord) J3
Frohavet (bay) F5
Frøya (isl.) F5
Glittertinden (mt.) F6
Hardangervidda (plat.) E6
Hardangerfjord (fjord) D7
Hinlopenstreten (str.) C1
Hinnøya (isl.) K2
Hitra (isl.) F5
Hopen (isl.) E2
Isfjorden (fjord) C2
Jostedalsbreen (glac.) E6
Kjölen (mts.) K3
Kongsfjorden (fjord) B2
Kvaløya (isl.) O1
Lågen (riv.) G6
Laksefjorden (fjord) P1
Langøy (isl.) J2
Lapland (reg.) K2
Leka (isl.) G4
Lindesnes (cape) E8
Lista (pen.) E7
Lofoten (isls.) H2
Lopphavet (bay) M1
Magerøya (isl.) P1
Moskenesøya (isl.) H3
Namsen (riv.) H4
Nordaustlandet (isl.) D1
Nordfjord (fjord) E6
Nordkapp (pt.) C1
Nordkinn (headland) Q1
Nordkinn (pen.) P1
North Cape (Nordkapp) (pt.) P1
Norwegian (sea) F3
Ofotfjorden (fjord) K2
Oslofjord (fjord) D4
Otra (riv.) E7
Otterøya (isl.) E5
Pasvikelv (riv.) Q2
Platen, Kapp (pt.) D1
Porsangen (fjord) O1
Rana (fjord) H3
Rauma (riv.) F5
Ringvassøy (isl.) L2
Romsdalsfjorden (fjord) E5
Saltfjorden (fjord) J3
Seiland (isl.) N1
Senja (isl.) K2
Skagerrak (str.) F8
Smøla (isl.) E5
Sognafjorden (fjord) D6
Sørkapp (pt.) C2
Sorøya (isl.) N1
Spitsbergen (isl.) C2
Storfjorden (fjord) D2
Sulitjelma (mt.) J3
Svalbard (isls.) C3
Tana (riv.) P1
Tanafjord (fjord) Q1
Tokke (riv.) F7
Trondheimsfjorden (fjord) G5
Tyrifjord (lake) C3
Vaerøy (isl.) H3
Vagåvatn (lake) F6
Vannøy (isl.) L1
Varangerhalvøya (pen.) Q1
Varangerfjord (fjord) Q2
Vega (isl.) G4
Vesterålen (isls.) J2
Vestfjord (fjord) H3
Vestvågøya (isl.) H3
Vikna (isls.) G4

SWEDEN

COUNTIES

Älvsborg 418,150 ..... H7
Blekinge 155,391 ..... J8
Gävleborg 294,595 ..... K6
Göteborg och Bohus 714,660 ..... G7
Gotland 54,447 ..... L8
Halland 219,767 ..... H8
Jämtland 133,559 ..... J5
Jönköping 301,905 ..... H8
Kalmar 240,768 ..... K8
Kopparberg 281,082 ..... J6
Kristianstad 272,090 ..... J8

(continued on following page)

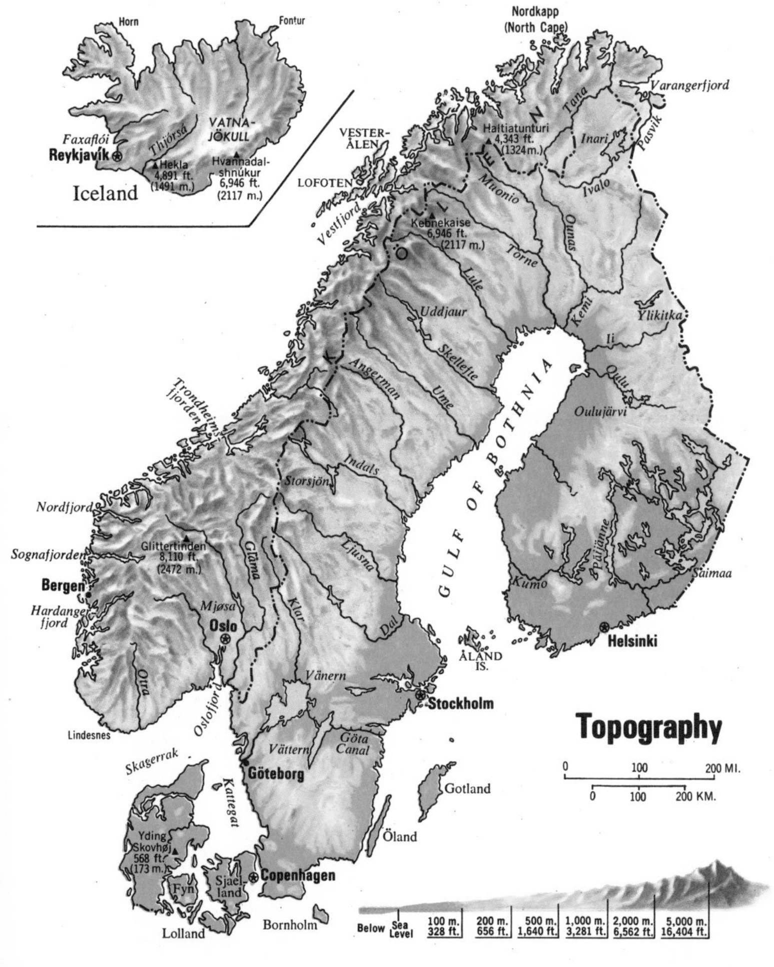
Horn
Fontur
Faxaflói
Reykjavík
Thjórsá
VATNA-JÖKULL
Hekla 4,891 ft. (1491 m.)
Hvannadal-shnúkur 6,946 ft. (2117 m.)
Iceland
Nordkapp (North Cape)
Varangerfjord
VESTER-ÅLEN
LOFOTEN
Vestfjord
Haltiatunturi 4,343 ft. (1324 m.)
Tana
Inari
Pasvik
Ivalo
Muonio
Ounas
Kebnekaise 6,946 ft. (2117 m.)
Torne
Lule
Kemi
Ylikitka
Uddjaur
Skellefte
Ume
Ångerman
Oulu
Oulujärvi
Trondheimsfjorden
GULF OF BOTHNIA
Indals
Storsjön
Nordfjord
Ljusna
Päijänne
Saimaa
Glittertinden 8,110 ft. (2472 m.)
Sognafjorden
Glåma
Bergen
Hardanger fjord
Mjøsa
Oslo
Klar
Dal
Kumo
Helsinki
ÅLAND IS.
Otra
Vänern
Stockholm
Oslofjord
Lindesnes
Topography
Skagerrak
Vättern
Göta Canal
Göteborg
Gotland
Kattegat
0 100 200 MI.
0 100 200 KM.
Öland
Yding Skovhøj 568 ft. (173 m.)
Fyn
Sjaelland
Copenhagen
Lolland
Bornholm
Below Sea Level
100 m. 328 ft.
200 m. 656 ft.
500 m. 1,640 ft.
1,000 m. 3,281 ft.
2,000 m. 6,562 ft.
5,000 m. 16,404 ft.

Kronoberg 169,454 ....J8	Gimo 3,154 ....K6	Lycksele 8,586 ....L4	Strängnäs 10,255 ....F1	Kalmarsund (sound) K8	Århus 245,941 ....D5
Malmöhus 740,137 ....H9	Gislaved 8,564 ....H8	Lysekil 7,815 ....G7	Strömstad 4,735 ....G7	Kattegat (str.) G8	
Norrbotten 264,215 ....L3	Gnesta 3,835 ....G2	Malmberget 10,239 ....M3	Strömsund 4,119 ....K5	Kebnekaise (mt.) L3	

Agriculture, Industry and Resources

DOMINANT LAND USE

- Cash Cereals, Dairy
- Dairy, Cattle, Hogs
- Dairy, General Farming
- General Farming (chiefly cereals)
- Nomadic Sheep Herding
- Forests, Limited Mixed Farming
- Nonagricultural Land

MAJOR MINERAL OCCURRENCES

Ag	Silver	Ni	Nickel
Au	Gold	O	Petroleum
Co	Cobalt	Pb	Lead
Cr	Chromium	Ti	Titanium
Cu	Copper	U	Uranium
Fe	Iron Ore	V	Vanadium
Mg	Magnesium	Zn	Zinc
Mo	Molybdenum		

⚡ Water Power

Major Industrial Areas

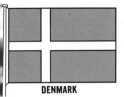

DENMARK

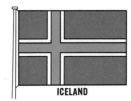

ICELAND

DENMARK
AREA 16,629 sq. mi. (43,069 sq. km.)
POPULATION 5,124,000
CAPITAL Copenhagen
LARGEST CITY Copenhagen
HIGHEST POINT Yding Skovhøj
568 ft. (173 m.)
MONETARY UNIT krone
MAJOR LANGUAGE Danish
MAJOR RELIGION Protestantism

ICELAND
AREA 39,768 sq. mi. (103,000 sq. km.)
POPULATION 228,785
CAPITAL Reykjavík
LARGEST CITY Reykjavík
HIGHEST POINT Hvannadalshnúkur
6,952 ft. (2,119 m.)
MONETARY UNIT króna
MAJOR LANGUAGE Icelandic
MAJOR RELIGION Protestantism

Møgeltønder 711 ....B8	Vraå 2.652 ....C3
Næstved 35.011 ....E7	
Nakskov 16.393 ....E8	**OTHER FEATURES**
Neksø 3.527 ....F9	
Nibe 2.796 ....C4	Ærø (isl.) D8
Nordborg 4.132 ....C7	Als (isl.) C8
Nordby, Ribe 2.084 ....B7	Amager (isl.) F6
Nørre Åby 2.165 ....C7	Anholt (isl.) E4
Nørre Alslev 1.338 ....E8	Årø (isl.) C7
Nørre Broby 904 ....D7	Baåge (isl.) C7
Nørre Nebel 901 ....B6	Baltic (sea) E9
Nørre Snede 1.461 ....C6	Bornholm (isl.) F9
Nørre Vorupør 644 ....D7	Endelave (isl.) D7
Nyborg 14.181 ....D7	Falster (isl.) E8
Nykøbing, Storstrøm 20.059 ....F8	Fanø (isl.) B7
Nykøbing,	Fehmarn (str.) E8
Vestsjælland 4.996 ....E6	Fejø (isl.) E8
Nykøbing, Viborg 9.066 ....B4	Femø (isl.) E8
Nysted 1.229 ....E8	Frisian, North (isls.) B7
Odder 6.617 ....D6	Fyn (isl.) D7
Odense 168.178 ....D7	Gelsaå (riv.) C7
Øløod 2.258 ....B7	Gudenaå (riv.) C5
Ølsted 1.093 ....D5	Isefjord (fjord) E6
Øster Vrå 906 ....D3	Jutland (pen.) C5
Otterup 2.673 ....D7	Jylland (Jutland)
Ovtrup 602 ....B7	(pen.) C5
Pandrup 1.525 ....C3	Kattegat (str.) E4
Præstø 2.789 ....E7	Læsø (isl.) D3
Ramme 506 ....B4	Langeland (isl.) D8
Randers 58.409 ....C5	Lille Bælt (chan.) C7
Ranum 1.472 ....C4	Limfjorden (fjord) A4
Rødby 5.296 ....E8	Løgstør Bredning (fjord) C4
Rødding 2.102 ....B7	Lolland (isl.) E8
Rødekro 2.246 ....C7	Møn (isl.) F8
Rødkaersbro 1.098 ....C5	Mors (isl.) B4
Rødvig 1.115 ....F7	North (sea) B9
Rømø 816 ....B7	North Frisian (isls.) B7
Rønde 1.523 ....D5	Omø (isl.) E8
Rønne 14.736 ....F9	Øresund (sound) F6
Roskilde 44.248 ....E6	Rømø (isl.) B7
Roslev 1.058 ....B4	Samsø (isl.) D6
Rudkøbing 4.080 ....D7	Sejerø (isl.) E6
Ruds Vedby 1.071 ....E7	Sjælland (isl.) E6
Ry 2.699 ....C5	Skagens Odde (cape) D2
Ryomgård 1.000 ....D5	Skagerrak (str.) C2
Saeby 5.430 ....D3	Skaw, The (Skagens Odde) (cape) D2
Sakskøbing 4.102 ....E8	Storaa (riv.) B5
Silkeborg 29.015 ....C5	Store Bælt (chan.) D6
Sindal 2.406 ....D3	Susaå (riv.) E7
Skaelskør 4.585 ....E7	The Skaw (Skagens Odde)
Skaerbaek 2.483 ....B7	(cape) D2
Skagen 11.620 ....C4	Tranebjerg (mt.) D6
Skals 960 ....C4	Yding Skovhøj (mt.) C6
Skanderborg 11.344 ....D5	
Skårup 1.216 ....D7	**FAEROE ISLANDS**
Skibby 1.549 ....E6	
Skive 17.015 ....B4	**CITIES and TOWNS**
Skjern 6.056 ....B6	
Skodborg 935 ....C7	Klaksvík 4.536 ....B2
Skørping 1.675 ....C4	Tórshavn (cap.), Faeroe
Slagelse 26.851 ....E7	Is. 11.618 ....A3
Slangerup 3.036 ....E6	
Snedsted 1.105 ....B4	**OTHER FEATURES**
Søllested 960 ....E8	
Sønderborg 24.526 ....C8	Faeroe (isls.) B2
Sønder Omme 1.393 ....B6	Sandoy (isl.) B3
Sønderstee 885 ....D7	Streymoy (isl.) B3
Sorø 8.683 ....E7	Sudhuroy (isl.) B3
Stege 3.869 ....F8	
Stenille 1.014 ....E6	**ICELAND**
Stenstrup 1.245 ....D7	
Stoholm 1.224 ....C5	**CITIES and TOWNS**
Store Heddinge 2.630 ....F7	
Støvring 2.366 ....C4	Akranes 4.253 ....B1
Strandby 1.017 ....D3	Akureyri 10.755 ....C1
Struer 10.848 ....B5	Hafnarfjördhur 9.696 ....B2
Stubbekøbing 2.031 ....E8	Húsavík 1.993 ....C1
Svanke 1.193 ....F8	Ísafjördhur 2.680 ....B1
Svendborg 24.203 ....D7	Keflavík 5.663 ....B1
Svinninge 1.797 ....E6	Kópavogur 11.165 ....B1
Tarm 3.150 ....B6	Nes (Neskaupstadhur) 1.552 ....D1
Tårbæk 45.661 ....F6	Neskaupstadhur 1.552 ....D1
Tåstrup 30.608 ....F6	Ólafsfjördhur 1.086 ....C1
Them 511 ....C5	Reykjavík (cap.) 81.693 ....B1
Thisted 11.252 ....B4	Reykjavík* 98.521 70
Thyborøn 2.425 ....A4	Sauthárkrókur 1.600 ....B1
Thyregod 1.001 ....C6	Seydhisfjördhur 884 ....D1
Tim 553 ....B5	Siglufjördhur 2.161 ....C1
Tinglev 1.531 ....C8	Vestmannaeyjar 5.186 ....B2
Tistrup 762 ....B6	
Toftlund 2.147 ....C7	**OTHER FEATURES**
Tølløse 1.982 ....E6	
Tommerup 1.439 ....D7	Bjargtangar (pt.) A1
Tønder 7.469 ....B8	Breidhafjördhur (fjord) B1
Tørring 1.537 ....C6	Faxaflói (bay) B1
Tranebjerg 657 ....D6	Fontur (pt.) D1
Troense 771 ....D7	Gerpir (cape) D1
Trustrup 794 ....D5	Grímsey (isl.) C1
Uldum 885 ....C6	Hekla (vol.) B1
Ulfborg 1.357 ....B5	Horn (cape) B1
Vamdrup 3.111 ....C7	Húnaflói (bay) B1
Varde 11.615 ....B6	Hvannadalshnúkur (mt.) B1
Vejen 6.213 ....C7	North (Horn) (cape) B1
Vejle 43.976 ....C6	Reykjanesta (cape) A2
Vemb 989 ....B5	Surtsey (isl.) B2
Vester Skerninge 603 ....D7	Thjorsá (riv.) C1
Vestervig 747 ....B4	Vatnajökull (glac.) C1
Viborg 27.441 ....C5	
Viby 1.549 ....F6	*City and suburbs.
Vig 1.037 ....E6	
Vildbjerg 1.500 ....B5	
Vinderup 2.284 ....B5	
Vojens 5.595 ....C7	
Vorbasse 791 ....B6	
Vordingborg 11.639 ....E7	

Germany

CONIC PROJECTION

SCALE OF MILES

SCALE OF KILOMETERS

Capitals of Countries .... ☆
State and District Capitals .... ◉
International Boundaries ....
State and District Boundaries ....
Canals ....

East Germany is divided into districts bearing the same name as their respective capitals.

© Copyright HAMMOND INCORPORATED, Maplewood, N.J.

AREA 95,985 sq. mi. (248,601 sq. km.)
POPULATION 61,658,000
CAPITAL Bonn
LARGEST CITY Berlin (West)
HIGHEST POINT Zugspitze 9,718 ft. (2,962 m.)
MONETARY UNIT Deutsche mark
MAJOR LANGUAGE German
MAJOR RELIGIONS Protestantism, Roman Catholicism

AREA 41,768 sq. mi. (108,179 sq. km.)
POPULATION 16,737,000
CAPITAL Berlin (East)
LARGEST CITY Berlin (East)
HIGHEST POINT Fichtelberg 3,983 ft. (1,214 m.)
MONETARY UNIT East German mark
MAJOR LANGUAGE German
MAJOR RELIGIONS Protestantism, Roman Catholicism

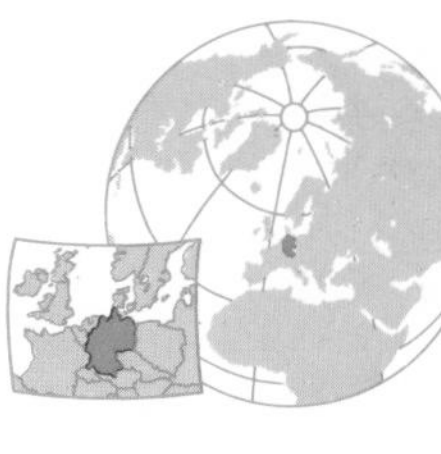

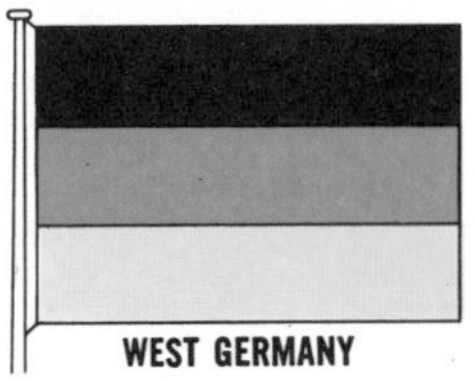

Topography

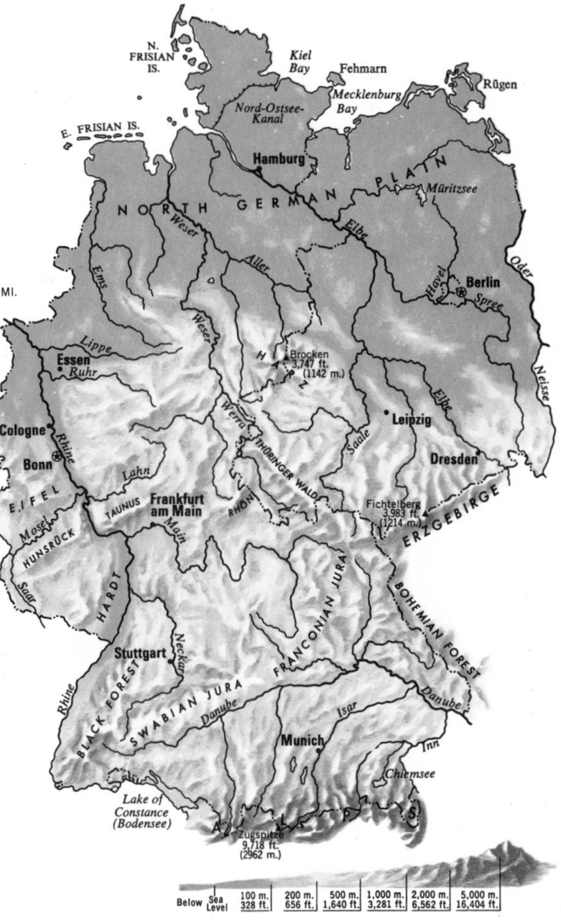

EAST GERMANY

DISTRICTS

Berlin 1,094,147	F4
Cottbus 872,242	F3
Dresden 1,845,459	E3
Erfurt 1,247,213	D3
Frankfurt 688,637	F2
Gera 738,847	D3
Halle 1,890,187	D3
Karl-Marx-Stadt 1,994,115	E3
Leipzig 1,457,817	E3
Magdeburg 1,297,881	D2
Neubrandenburg 628,686	E2
Potsdam 1,124,892	E2
Rostock 867,806	E1
Schwerin 592,334	D2
Suhl 550,497	D3

CITIES and TOWNS

Aken 11,742	D3
Altenburg 51,193	E3
Angermünde 11,786	E2
Anklam 19,099	E2
Annaberg-Buchholz 26,561	E3
Apolda 28,649	D3
Arnstadt 29,462	D3
Aschersleben 36,674	D3
Aue 32,622	E3
Auerbach 18,168	E3
Bad Doberan 12,541	D1
Bad Dürrenberg 15,192	D3
Bad Langensalza 166,282	D3
Bad Salzungen 17,277	C3
Barth 12,069	E1
Bautzen 45,851	F3
Bergen 13,244	E1
Berlin, East (cap.) 1,094,147	F4
Bernau bei Berlin 15,749	E2
Bernburg 44,428	D3
Bischofswerda 11,540	F3
Bitterfeld 27,062	E3
Blankenburg am Harz 18,784	D3
Boizenburg an der Elbe 12,428	D2
Borna 21,807	E3
Brandenburg 94,071	E2
Burg bei Magdeburg 29,027	D2
Calbe 15,976	D3
Chemnitz (Karl-Marx-Stadt) 303,811	E3
Coswig, Dresden 22,149	E3
Coswig, Halle 12,473	E3
Cottbus 94,293	F3
Crimmitschau 28,845	E3
Delitzsch 24,076	E3
Demmin 17,270	E2
Dessau 100,820	E3
Döbeln 27,624	E3
Dresden 507,692	E3
Ebersbach 12,694	F3
Eberswalde-Finow 47,141	E2
Eilenburg 22,245	E3
Eisenach 49,954	D3
Eisenberg 13,450	D3
Eisenhüttenstadt 46,455	F2
Eisleben 29,297	D3
Erfurt 202,979	D3
Falkensee 25,295	E3
Falkenstein 14,367	E3
Finsterwalde 22,466	E3
Forst 28,084	F3
Frankfurt an der Oder 70,817	F2
Freiberg 50,815	E3
Freital 46,061	E3
Friedland	E2
Fürstenwalde 31,065	F2
Gardelegen 12,987	D2
Genthin 15,916	E2
Gera 113,108	E3
Glauchau 30,927	E3
Görlitz 84,658	F3
Gotha 59,243	D3
Greifswald 53,940	E1
Greiz 37,612	E3
Grevesmühlen 12,005	D2
Grimma 17,100	E3
Grimmen 14,571	E1
Grossenhain 18,712	E3
Grossräschen 12,889	E3
Guben (Wilhelm-Pieck-Stadt) 32,731	F3
Güstrow 36,824	E2
Halberstadt 46,669	D3
Haldensleben 19,194	D2
Halle 241,425	D3
Halle-Neustadt 67,956	D3
Havelberg	D2
Heidenau 21,315	E3
Heiligenstadt 13,931	D3
Hennigsdorf bei Berlin 24,853	E3
Hettstedt 20,291	D3
Hildburghausen 11,372	D3
Hoyerswerda 64,904	F3
Ilmenau 22,021	D3
Jena 99,431	D3
Johanngeorgenstadt 10,328	E3
Jüterbog 13,477	E3
Kamenz 18,221	F3
Karl-Marx-Stadt 303,811	E3
Kleinmachnow 14,059	E4
Klingenthal 13,614	E3
Königs Wusterhausen 11,825	E2
Köpenick 130,987	F4
Köthen 35,451	E3
Kühlungsborn	D1
Lauchhammer 26,939	E3
Leipzig 570,972	E3
Lichtenberg 192,063	F4
Limbach-Oberfrohna 25,706	E3
Löbau 18,077	F3
Lübben 14,224	E3
Lübbenau 22,350	F3
Luckenwalde 28,544	E2
Ludwigslust 13,280	D2
Magdeburg 276,089	D2
Markkleeberg 22,380	E3
Meerane 25,037	E3
Meiningen 26,134	D3
Meissen 43,561	E3
Merseburg 54,269	D3
Meuselwitz 13,585	E3
Mittweida 19,259	E3
Mühlhausen (Thomas-Müntzer-Stadt) 44,106	D3
Nauen 11,940	E2
Naumburg 36,358	D3
Neubrandenburg 59,971	E2
Neuenhagen bei Berlin 12,603	F4
Neuruppin 24,888	E2
Neustrelitz 27,074	E2
Nordhausen 44,442	D3
Oelsnitz 15,084	E3
Oelsnitz im Erzgebirge 16,063	E3
Olbernhau 13,479	E3
Oranienburg 24,452	E2
Oschatz 18,974	E3
Oschersleben 17,377	D2
Pankow 136,527	F3
Parchim 22,927	D2
Pasewalk 15,099	F2
Peenemünde	E1
Perleberg 15,029	D2
Pirna 49,771	E3
Plauen 80,353	E3
Pössneck 18,648	D3
Potsdam 117,236	E2
Prenzlau 22,738	E2
Pritzwalk 11,887	E2
Quedlinburg 29,796	D3
Radeberg 18,528	E3
Radebeul 38,383	E3
Rathenow 32,011	E2
Reichenbach 27,440	E3
Ribnitz-Damgarten 17,254	E1
Riesa 49,989	E3
Rosslau 16,520	E3
Rostock 210,167	E1
Rudolstadt 31,698	D3
Saalfeld 33,648	D3
Salzwedel 21,741	D2
Sangerhausen 32,721	D3
Sassnitz 13,857	E1
Schkeuditz 15,585	E3
Schmalkalden 15,017	D3
Schmölln 13,406	E3
Schneeberg 20,376	E3
Schönebeck 45,197	D2
Schwedt 45,729	F2
Schwerin 104,984	D2
Sebnitz 13,470	F3
Senftenberg 29,953	F3
Sömmerda 20,712	D3
Sondershausen 23,383	D3
Sonneberg 29,193	D3
Spremberg 22,862	F3
Stassfurt 26,225	D3
Stendal 39,647	D2
Stralsund 72,167	E1
Strausberg 21,334	F2
Suhl 36,642	D3
Tangermünde 12,898	D2
Teltow 16,171	E4
Templin 11,718	E2
Thale 17,248	D3
Thomas-Müntzer-Stadt 44,106	D3
Torgau 21,613	E3
Torgelow 14,320	F2
Treptow 127,448	F4
Ueckermünde 11,423	F2
Waldheim 11,925	E3
Waltershausen 13,893	D3
Waren 22,921	E2
Weida 11,816	D3
Weimar 63,144	D3
Weissenfels 43,191	D3
Weissensee 78,451	F3
Weisswasser 25,910	F3
Werdau 22,249	E3
Wernigerode 34,658	D3
Wilhelm-Pieck-Stadt 32,731	F3
Wismar 56,765	D2
Wittenberg 51,364	E3
Wittenberge 32,907	D2
Wolfen 27,570	E3
Wolgast 16,384	E1
Wurzen 20,501	E3
Zehdenick 12,651	E2
Zeitz 44,582	E3
Zella-Mehlis 16,301	D3
Zerbst 19,356	E3
Zeulenroda 13,452	D3
Zittau 42,298	F3
Zwickau 123,069	E3

OTHER FEATURES

Altmark (reg.)	D2
Arkona (cape)	E1
Baltic (sea)	E1
Black Elster (riv.)	E3
Brandenburg (reg.)	E2
Elbe (riv.)	D2
Elde (riv.)	D2
Elster, Black (riv.)	E3
Elster, White (riv.)	E3
Erzgebirge (mts.)	E3
Fichtelberg (mt.)	E3
Harz (mts.)	D3
Havel (riv.)	E2
Lusatia (reg.)	F3
Mecklenburg (bay)	D1
Mecklenburg (reg.)	E2
Mulde (riv.)	E3
Neisse (riv.)	F3
Oder (riv.)	F2
Peene (riv.)	E2
Pomerania (reg.)	E2
Pomeranian (bay)	F1
Rhön (mts.)	D3
Rügen (isl.)	E1
Saale (riv.)	D3
Saxony (reg.)	E3
Spree (riv.)	F3
Spreewald (for.)	F3
Thüringer Wald (for.)	D3
Thuringia (reg.)	D3
Ücker (riv.)	E2
Unstrut (riv.)	D3
Usedom (isl.)	F1
Warnow (riv.)	D2
Werra (riv.)	D3
White Elster (riv.)	E3

WEST GERMANY

STATES

Baden-Württemberg 9,152,700	C4
Bavaria 10,810,400	D4
Berlin (West) (free city) 1,984,800	E4
Bremen 716,800	C2
Hamburg 1,717,400	D2
Hesse 5,549,800	C3
Lower Saxony 7,238,500	C2
North Rhine-Westphalia 17,129,600	B3
Rhineland-Palatinate 3,665,800	B4
Saarland 1,096,300	B4
Schleswig-Holstein 2,582,400	C1

CITIES and TOWNS

Aachen 242,453	B3
Aalen 64,735	D4
Ahaus 27,126	B2
Ahlen 54,214	B3
Ahrensburg 24,964	D2
Alfeld 24,273	C2
Alsdorf 47,473	B3
Alsfeld 18,091	C3
Altena 26,753	B3
Altona	C2
Alzey 15,190	C4
Amberg 46,934	D4
Andernach 27,132	B3
Ansbach 39,117	D4
Arnsberg 80,287	C3
Arolsen 15,619	C3
Aschaffenburg 55,398	C4
Augsburg 249,943	D4
Aurich 34,194	B2
Backnang 29,614	C4
Bad Berleburg 20,415	C3
Bad Driburg 17,478	C3
Bad Dürkheim 16,133	C4
Bad Ems 10,487	B3
Baden-Baden 49,718	C4
Bad Gandersheim 11,614	D3
Bad Harzburg 25,786	D3
Bad Hersfeld 29,248	C3
Bad Homburg vor der Höhe 51,196	C3
Bad Honnef 20,903	B3
Bad Kissingen 22,279	D3
Bad Kreuznach 42,588	B4
Bad Lauterberg im Harz 14,715	D3
Bad Mergentheim 19,895	C4
Bad Münstereifel 14,340	B3
Bad Nauheim 25,916	C3
Bad Neuenahr-Ahrweiler 26,371	B3
Bad Oldesloe 19,640	D2
Bad Pyrmont 21,896	C3
Bad Reichenhall 13,048	E5
Bad Salzuflen 50,924	C2
Bad Schwartau 18,696	D2
Bad Segeberg 13,320	D2
Bad Tölz 12,458	D5
Bad Vilbel 25,012	C3
Bad Waldsee 14,296	C5
Bad Wildungen 15,418	C3
Bad Wimpfen 5,536	C4
Baiersbronn 14,845	C4
Balingen 29,310	C4
Bamberg 74,236	D4
Barsinghausen 32,873	C2
Bassum 14,113	C2
Bayreuth 67,035	D4
Bayrischzell 1,639	E5
Bebra 15,740	C3
Bendorf 15,943	B3
Bensheim 32,653	C4
Bentheim 13,681	B2
Berchtesgaden 8,558	E5
Bergisch Gladbach 99,517	B3
Berleburg (Bad Berleburg) 20,415	C3
Berlin (West) 1,984,837	E4
Biberach an der Riss 28,891	C4
Bielefeld 316,058	C2
Bietigheim-Bissingen 34,042	C4
Bingen 24,541	B4
Birkenfeld 5,883	B4
Blaubeuren 11,652	C4
Böblingen 40,547	C4
Bocholt 65,460	B3
Bochum 414,842	B3
Bonn (cap.) 283,711	B3
Boppard 16,888	B3
Borghorst 17,238	B2
Borken 30,212	B3
Bornheim 32,847	B3
Bottrop 101,495	B3
Brake 18,089	C2
Bramsche 24,119	B2
Braunschweig (Brunswick) 268,519	D2
Breisach am Rhein 9,230	B4
Bremen 572,969	C2
Bremerhaven 143,836	C2
Bremervörde 17,565	C2
Bretten 22,140	C4
Brilon 24,595	C3
Bruchsal 38,929	C4
Brühl 44,305	B3
Brunsbüttel 11,451	C2
Brunswick 268,519	D2
Buchholz in der Nordheide 25,713	C2
Bückeburg 21,393	C2
Büdingen 16,845	C3
Bühl 21,596	C4
Bünde 40,021	C2
Büren 17,352	C3
Burg auf Fehmarn 5,874	D1
Burghausen 16,892	E4
Burgsteinfurt 31,367	B2
Butzbach 20,592	C3
Buxtehude 30,249	C2
Castrop-Rauxel 82,373	B3
Celle 74,347	D2
Cham 12,423	E4
Charlottenburg 201,732	E4
Clausthal-Zellerfeld 16,690	D3
Cloppenburg 19,757	B2
Coburg 46,244	D3
Coesfeld 30,617	B3
Cologne 1,013,771	B3
Crailsheim 24,506	D4
Cuxhaven 60,353	C2
Dachau 33,207	D4
Dahlem	E4
Darmstadt 137,018	C4
Deggendorf 25,188	E4
Delmenhorst 71,488	C2
Detmold 65,629	C3
Diepholz 14,201	C2
Dillenburg 14,068	C3
Dillingen 21,369	B4
Dillingen an der Donau 11,601	D4
Dingolfing 13,325	E4
Dinkelsbühl 10,034	D4
Donaueschingen 17,578	C5
Donauwörth 17,077	D4
Dorsten 65,718	B3
Dortmund 630,609	B3
Duderstadt 23,255	D3
Dudweiler 27,877	B4
Duisburg 591,635	B3
Dülmen 37,013	B3
Düren 87,774	B3
Düsseldorf 664,336	B3
Eberbach 15,834	C4
Ebingen 22,594	C4
Eckernförde 22,938	D1
Ehingen 21,600	C4
Eichstätt 13,080	D4
Einbeck 29,821	C3
Eiserfeld 22,346	C3
Ellwangen 21,994	D4
Elmshorn 41,355	C2
Emden 53,509	B2
Emmendingen 24,722	B4
Emmerich 29,113	B3
Emsdetten 30,195	B2
Erlangen 100,671	D4
Eschwege 24,882	C3
Eschweiler 53,603	B3
Espelkamp 22,670	C2
Essen 677,568	B3
Esslingen am Neckar 95,298	C4
Ettlingen 35,159	C4
Euskirchen 43,558	B3
Eutin 17,701	D1
Fellbach 42,501	C4
Flensburg 93,213	C1
Forchheim 23,430	D4
Frankenberg-Eder 15,337	C3
Frankenthal 43,684	C4
Frankfurt am Main 636,157	C3
Frechen 41,453	B3
Freiburg im Breisgau 175,371	B5
Freising 31,524	D4
Freudenstadt 19,454	C4
Friedberg 24,762	C3
Friedrichshafen 51,544	C5
Fritzlar 15,079	C3
Fulda 58,976	C3
Fürstenfeldbruck 27,194	D4
Fürth 101,639	D4
Füssen 10,506	D5
Gaggenau 28,846	C4
Garbsen 56,337	C2
Garmisch-Partenkirchen 26,831	D5
Gatow	E4
Geesthacht 24,745	D2
Geislingen an der Steige 28,693	C4
Geldern 24,082	B3
Gelnhausen 17,889	C3
Gelsenkirchen 322,584	B3
Georgsmarienhütte 30,259	B2
Geretsried 17,330	D5
Germersheim 12,041	C4
Gerolstein 6,857	B3
Gifhorn 31,635	D2
Glückstadt 12,159	C2
Goch 28,213	B3
Göggingen 15,980	D4
Göppingen 54,365	C4
Goslar 53,957	D3
Göttingen 123,797	D3
Greven 27,479	B2
Grevenbroich 56,392	B3
Griesheim 18,548	C4
Gronau 40,527	B2
Gummersbach 49,316	B3
Günzburg 13,528	D4
Gunzenhausen 13,565	D4
Gütersloh 77,128	C3
Haar 18,824	D4
Hagen 229,224	B3
Haltern 29,750	B3
Hamburg 1,717,383	D2
Hameln 61,066	C2
Hamm 172,210	B3
Hammelburg 12,350	C3
Hanau 86,676	C3
Hannover 552,955	C2
Harburg-Wilhelmsburg	C2
Hassloch 17,752	C4
Haunstetten 21,810	D4
Hechingen 15,926	C4
Heide 21,918	C1
Heidelberg 129,368	C4
Heidenheim an der Brenz 49,943	D4
Heilbronn 113,177	C4
Helmstedt 28,095	D2
Hennef 27,815	B3
Herford 64,385	C2
Herne 190,561	B3
Hildesheim 105,290	D2
Hockenheim 16,890	C4
Hof 54,357	D3
Hofgeismar 13,380	C3
Holzminden 23,650	C3
Homburg 41,861	B4
Horn-Bad Meinberg 16,927	C3
Höxter 32,759	C3
Hückelhoven 34,865	B3
Hünfeld 13,873	C3
Hürth 51,692	B3
Husum 24,984	C1
Hüttental 39,561	C3
Ibbenbüren 42,202	B2
Idar-Oberstein 37,179	B4
Immenstadt im Allgäu 13,720	C5
Ingolstadt 88,500	D4
Iserlohn 96,174	B3
Isny im Allgäu 12,367	D5
Itzehoe 35,077	C2
Jever 12,096	B2
Jülich 31,564	B3
Kaiserslautern 100,886	B4
Karlsruhe 280,448	C4
Kassel 205,534	C3
Kaufbeuren 42,224	D5
Kehl 29,861	B4
Kelheim 11,996	D4
Kempten 56,944	D5
Kevelaer 20,971	B3
Kiel 262,164	D1
Kirchheim unter Teck 31,666	C4
Kitzingen 19,116	C4
Kleve 44,043	B3
Koblenz 118,394	B3
Köln (Cologne) 1,013,771	B3
Königswinter 34,586	B3
Konstanz 70,152	C5
Korbach 22,998	C3
Kornwestheim 27,771	C4
Krefeld 228,463	B3
Kreutztal 30,473	C3
Kronach 11,538	D3
Kulmbach 25,711	D3
Lage 31,724	C3
Lahnstein 19,725	B3
Lahr 35,570	B4
Lampertheim 31,993	C4
Landau in der Pfalz 37,661	C4
Landsberg am Lech 15,862	D4
Landshut 55,858	E4
Langen 30,227	C4
Langenhagen 47,092	C2
Lauenburg an der Elbe 11,077	D2
Lauf an der Pegnitz 19,443	D4
Lauingen 8,778	D4
Lauterbach 15,007	C3
Leer 32,785	B2
Lehrte 38,272	D2
Lemgo 39,664	C2
Lengerich 20,836	B2
Leverkusen 165,947	B3
Lichtenfels 13,719	D3
Limburg an der Lahn 28,606	C3
Lindau 23,930	C5

(continued on following page)

Germany Before World War I 1871-1914

DENMARK · SWEDEN · NETH. · Berlin ☆ · RUSSIA · BELG. · LUX. · FRANCE · AUSTRIA-HUNGARY · SWITZ. · ITALY

Germany Between Wars 1919-1937

DENMARK · SWEDEN · LITH. · DANZIG · NETH. · Berlin ☆ · POLAND · BELG. · LUX. · Saar (To Germany 1935) · CZECHOSLOVAKIA · FRANCE · AUSTRIA · SWITZ. · ITALY · YUGO. · HUNG.

Occupied Germany 1945-1949

DENMARK · SWEDEN · U.S.S.R. · NETH. · BRITISH ZONE · BERLIN · RUSSIAN ZONE · POLAND · BELG. · LUX. · FRENCH ZONE · SAAR · AMERICAN ZONE · CZECHOSLOVAKIA · FRANCE · AUSTRIA · SWITZ. · ITALY · YUGO. · HUNG.

Agriculture, Industry and Resources

DOMINANT LAND USE

- Wheat, Sugar Beets
- Cereals (chiefly rye, oats, barley)
- Potatoes, Rye
- Dairy, Livestock
- Mixed Cereals, Dairy
- Truck Farming
- Grapes, Fruit
- Forests

MAJOR MINERAL OCCURRENCES

Ag	Silver	K	Potash
Ba	Barite	Lg	Lignite
C	Coal	Na	Salt
Cu	Copper	O	Petroleum
Fe	Iron Ore	Pb	Lead
G	Natural Gas	U	Uranium
Gr	Graphite	Zn	Zinc

⚡ Water Power
▨ Major Industrial Areas

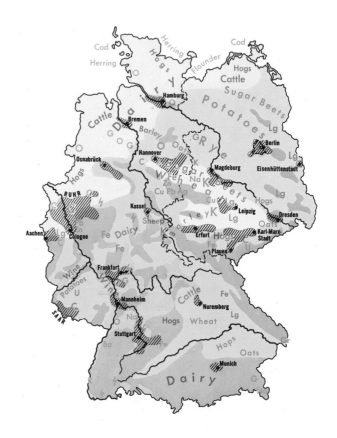

AREA 15,892 sq. mi. (41,160 sq. km.)
POPULATION 14,227,000
CAPITALS The Hague, Amsterdam
LARGEST CITY Amsterdam
HIGHEST POINT Vaalserberg 1,056 ft. (322 m.)
MONETARY UNIT guilder (florin)
MAJOR LANGUAGE Dutch
MAJOR RELIGIONS Protestantism, Roman Catholicism

AREA 11,781 sq. mi. (30,513 sq. km.)
POPULATION 9,855,110
CAPITAL Brussels
LARGEST CITY Brussels (greater)
HIGHEST POINT Botrange 2,277 ft. (694 m.)
MONETARY UNIT Belgian franc
MAJOR LANGUAGES French (Walloon), Flemish
MAJOR RELIGION Roman Catholicism

AREA 999 sq. mi. (2,587 sq. km.)
POPULATION 364,000
CAPITAL Luxembourg
LARGEST CITY Luxembourg
HIGHEST POINT Ardennes Plateau 1,825 ft. (556 m.)
MONETARY UNIT Luxembourg franc
MAJOR LANGUAGES Luxembourgeois (Letzeburgisch), French, German
MAJOR RELIGION Roman Catholicism

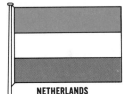

NETHERLANDS

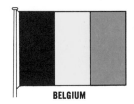

BELGIUM

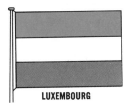

LUXEMBOURG

BELGIUM

PROVINCES

Antwerp 1,533,249	F6
Brabant 2,176,373	F7
East Flanders 1,310,117	D7
Hainaut 1,317,453	D7
Liège 1,008,905	H7
Limburg 652,547	G7
Luxembourg 217,310	G9
Namur 380,561	F8
West Flanders 1,054,429	B7

CITIES and TOWNS†

Aalst 46,659	D7
Aalter 9,173	C6
Aarlen (Arlon) 13,745	H9
Aarschot 12,474	F7
Aat (Ath) 11,842	D7
Alken 8,677	G7
Alost (Aalst) 46,659	D7
Amay 7,617	G7
Andenne 8,091	G8
Anderlecht 103,796	B9
Anderlues 12,176	E8
Ans	H7
Antoing 3,426	C7
Antwerp 224,543	E6
Antwerp* 928,000	E6
Antwerpen (Antwerp) 224,543	E6
Ardooie 7,081	C7
Arendonk 9,919	G6
Arlon 13,745	H9
As 5,496	H6
Asse 6,583	E7
Ath 11,842	D7
Attert	H9
Aubange 3,761	H9
Audenarde (Oudenaarde) 26,615	D7
Auderghem 34,546	C9
Auvelais 8,287	F8
Aywaille 3,850	H8
Baarle-Hertog	F6
Balen 15,110	G6
Basse-Sambre	F8
Bastenaken (Bastogne) 6,816	H9
Bastogne 6,816	H9
Beernem	C6
Beloeil	D7
Berchem 50,241	F6
Berchem-Sainte-Agathe 19,087	B9
Bergen (Mons) 59,362	E8
Beringen	G6
Bertogne	H8
Bertrix 4,562	G9
Beveren 15,913	E6
Bilzen 7,178	G7
Binche 10,098	E8
Blankenberge 13,969	C6
Bocholt 6,497	H6
Boom 16,584	E6
Borgerhout 49,002	E6
Borgloon 3,412	G7
Borgworm (Waremme) 10,956	G7
Bourg-Léopold (Leopoldsburg) 9,593	G6
Boussu 11,474	D8
Braine-l'Alleud 18,531	E7
Braine-le-Comte 11,957	D7
Brecht	F6
Bredene 9,244	B6
Bree 10,389	H6
Bruges 117,220	C6
Brugge (Bruges) 117,220	C6
Brussels (cap.)* 1,054,970	C9
Bruxelles (Brussels) (cap.)* 1,054,970	C9
Cerfontaine	E8
Charleroi 23,689	E8
Charleroi* 458,000	E8
Chastre	F7
Châtelet 14,752	F8
Chièvres 3,283	D7
Chimay 3,288	E8
Chiny	G9
Ciney 7,536	G8
Comblain-au-Pont 3,582	G8
Comines 8,192	B7
Courcelles 17,015	E8
Courtrai (Kortrijk) 44,961	C7
Couvin 4,234	F8
Damme	C6
De Haan	C6
Deinze 16,711	D7
Denderleeuw 9,925	E7
Dendermonde 22,119	E6
De Panne 6,985	B6
Dessel 7,505	G6
Destelbergen	D6
Deurne 80,766	F6
Diest 10,799	F7
Diksmuide 6,669	B6
Dilbeek 15,108	B9
Dilsen	H6
Dinant 9,747	G8
Dison 8,466	H7
Dixmude (Diksmuide) 6,669	B6
Doische	F8
Doornik (Tournai) 32,794	C7
Dour 10,059	D8
Drogenbos 4,840	B10
Duffel 13,802	F6
Durbuy	G8
Ecaussinnes 6,630	E7
Edingen (Enghien) 4,115	D7
Eeklo 19,144	D6
Eghezée	F7
Eigenbrakel (Braine-l'Alleud) 18,531	E7
Ekeren 27,648	E6
Ellezelles 3,556	D7
Enghien 4,115	D7
Erezée	G8
Erquelinnes 4,471	E8
Esneux 6,183	H7
Essen 10,795	F6
Estampuis	D7
Etterbeek 51,030	B9
Eupen 14,879	J7
Evere 26,957	C9
Evergem 12,886	D6
Farciennes	E8
Fernelmont	F7
Ferrières	H8
Flémalle 8,135	G7
Fleurus 8,523	F8
Florennes 4,107	F8
Forest 55,135	B9
Fosses-La-Ville 3,972	F8
Franieries 11,224	D8
Froidchapelle	E8
Furnes (Veurne) 9,496	B6
Ganshoren 21,147	B9
Geel 29,346	F6
Geldenaken (Jodoigne) 4,132	F7
Gembloux-sur-Orneau 11,249	F7
Genk 57,913	H7
Gent (Ghent) 148,860	D6
Geraardsbergen 17,533	D7
Gerpinnes	F8
Ghent 148,860	D6
Ghent* 477,000	D6
Gistel	B6
Gooik	B9
Gouvy	H8
Grammont (Geraardsbergen) 17,533	D7
Grez-Doiceau	F7
Grimbergen	E7
Haacht 4,436	F7
Habay	H9
Hal (Halle) 20,017	E7
Halen 5,322	G7
Halle 20,017	E7
Hamme 17,559	E6
Hamois	G8
Hamont-Achel 6,893	H6
Hannut (Hannut) 7,232	G7
Hannut 7,232	G7
Harelbeke 18,498	C7
Hasselt 39,663	G7
Hastière	F8
Heist-Knokke 27,582	C6
Heist-op-den-Berg 13,472	F6
Hensies	D8
Herentals 18,639	F6
Herne	D7
Herselt 7,412	F6
Herstal 29,600	H7
Herve 4,118	H7
Heuvelland	B7
Hoboken 33,693	E6
Hoei (Huy) 12,736	G8
Hoeselt 6,884	G7
Honnelles	D8
Hoogstraten 4,381	F6
Horebeke	D7
Huy 12,736	G8
Ichtegem	B6
Ieper 20,825	B7
Ingelmunster 10,245	C7
Itter	E7
Ixelles 86,450	C9
Izegem 22,928	C7
Jabbeke	C6
Jemappes 18,632	D8
Jette 40,013	B9
Jodoigne 4,132	F7
Kalmthout 12,724	F6
Kapellen 13,352	E6
Kasterlee	F6
Kinrooi	H6
Knokke-Heist 27,582	C6
Koekelare 7,807	B6
Koekelberg 17,570	B9
Koksijde	B6
Kontich 14,432	F6
Kortemark 5,904	C6
Kortrijk 44,961	C7
Kraainem 11,390	C9
La Louvière 23,310	E8
La Louvière* 113,259	E8
Lanaken 8,659	H7
Landen 5,740	G7
Langemark-Poelkapelle 5,457	B7
Lasne	F7
Lede 10,316	D7
Léglise	H9
Leopoldsburg 9,593	G6
Le Roeulx	E8
Lessen (Lessines) 8,906	D7
Lessines 8,906	D7
Leuze-en-Hainaut 7,185	C7
Libin	G9
Libramont-Chevigny 2,975	G9
Lichtervelde 7,807	C6
Liedekerke 10,482	E7
Liège 145,573	H7
Liège* 622,000	H7
Lier (Lier) 28,416	F6
Lierre (Lier) 28,416	F6
Limbourg 3,762	J7
Limburg (Limbourg) 3,762	J7
Linkebeek 4,265	C10
Linter	G7
Lochristi	D6
Lokeren 26,740	D6
Lommel 21,984	G6
Lontzen	H9
Looz (Borgloon) 3,412	G7
Lo-Reninge	B7
Louvain (Leuven) 30,623	F7
Luik (Liège) 145,573	H7
Lummen	G7
Maaseik 8,622	H6
Maasmechelen	H7
Machelen 7,057	C9
Maldegem 14,474	C6
Malines (Mechelen) 65,466	F6
Malmédy 6,464	J8
Manage	E7
Manhay	H8
Marche-en-Famenne 4,567	G8
Marchin 4,206	G8
Mechelen 65,466	F6
Meerhout 8,567	G6
Meise	E7
Menen 22,037	C7
Menin (Menen) 22,037	C7
Merchtem 8,998	E7
Merelbeke 13,837	D7
Merksem 39,768	E6
Merksplas 5,065	F6
Messancy 3,150	H9
Mettet 3,372	F8
Meulebeke 10,458	C7
Middelkerke	B6
Moeskroen (Mouscron) 37,311	C7
Mol 28,823	G6
Molenbeek-Saint-Jean 68,411	B9
Momignies	E8
Mons 59,362	E8
Montigny-le-Tilleul	E8
Moorslede	B7
Mortsel 28,012	E6
Mouscron 37,311	C7
Namen (Namur) 32,269	F8
Namur 32,269	F8
Nassogne	G8
Nazareth	D7
Neerpelt 8,771	G6
Neufchâteau 2,670	G9
Nevele	D7
Nieuport (Nieuwpoort) 8,273	B6
Nieuwpoort 8,273	B6
Nijvel (Nivelles) 16,126	E7
Ninove 12,428	D7
Nivelles 16,126	E7
Ohey	G8
Onhaye	F8
Oostende (Ostend) 71,227	B6
Oostkamp 8,999	C6
Opwijk 9,699	E7
Ostend 71,227	B6
Oudenaarde 26,615	D7
Oudenburg	C6
Oud-Turnhout 9,245	H7
Oupeye	H7
Overijse 16,181	F7
Overpelt 10,470	G6
Paliseul	G9
Peer 7,201	G6
Péruwelz 7,878	D8
Philippeville 2,076	E8
Plombières	J7
Pont-à-Celles	E8
Poperinge 12,671	B7
Profondeville	F8
Putte 6,953	F6
Quaregnon 17,688	D8
Quévy	D8
Quiévrain 5,510	D8
Raeren 3,655	J7
Ravels	G6
Rebecq 3,744	E7
Renaix (Ronse) 25,056	D7
Rendeux	G8
Retie 6,619	G6
Rochefort 4,357	G8
Roeselare 40,428	C7
Ronse 25,056	D7
Roulers (Roeselare) 40,428	C7
Rouvroy	G9
Ruislede	D6
Sainte-Ode	H8
Saint-Georges-sur-Meuse 6,003	G7
Saint-Gilles 55,055	B9
Saint-Hubert 3,091	G8
Saint-Josse-ten-Noode 23,633	C9
Saint-Nicolas	
Saint-Trond (Sint-Truiden) 21,473	G7
Saint-Vith (Sankt Vith) 3,001	J8
Sankt Vith 3,001	J8
Schaerbeek 118,950	C9
Schoten 29,914	F6
Seraing 40,545	G7
's-Gravenbrakel (Braine-le-Comte) 11,957	D7
Sint-Laureins	D6
Sint-Niklaas 49,214	E6

(continued on following page)

Agriculture, Industry and Resources

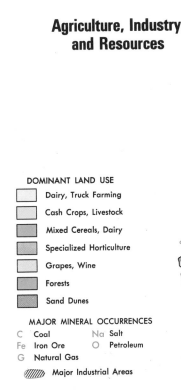

DOMINANT LAND USE

- Dairy, Truck Farming
- Cash Crops, Livestock
- Mixed Cereals, Dairy
- Specialized Horticulture
- Grapes, Wine
- Forests
- Sand Dunes

MAJOR MINERAL OCCURRENCES

C	Coal	Na	Salt
Fe	Iron Ore	O	Petroleum
G	Natural Gas		

Major Industrial Areas

*City and suburbs.
†Population of cities in Belgium & Netherlands are communes.

Land from the Sea

NORTH SEA — WEST FRISIAN ISLANDS — WADDENZEE

Enclosing Dam 1932

Leeuwarden

1600 · 1400 · 1280 · 1242 · 1200 · 1427

1847 · 1824 · 1599 · 1610 · 1456 · 1844 · 1927 · 1564 · 1631 · 1608 · 1635 · 1683 · 1612 · 1626 · 1622 · 1628 · 1872

Wieringermeer Polder 1930

IJSSELMEER (ZUIDER ZEE)

NORTH EAST POLDER 1942

Markerwaard (planned)

East Flevoland 1957

Amsterdam

South Flevoland 1969

Haarlemmer Lake 1852

Reclaimed Land and Dates of Completion

Future Polders

□ = 10 Square Miles

For centuries the Dutch have been renowned for the drainage of marshes and the construction of polders, i.e., arable land reclaimed from the sea. Future projects will convert much of the present IJsselmeer to agricultural land.

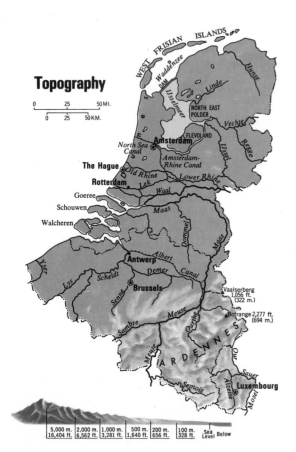

Topography

Netherlands, Belgium and Luxembourg

CONIC PROJECTION

SCALE OF MILES

SCALE OF KILOMETRES

Capitals of Countries
Provincial Capitals
International Boundaries
Provincial Boundaries
Canals

© Copyright HAMMOND INCORPORATED, Maplewood, N.J.

DEPARTMENTS

Ain 376,477 F4
Aisne 533,862 E3
Allier 378,406 E4
Alpes-de-Haute-Provence 112,178 G5
Alpes-Maritimes 816,681 G6
Ardèche 257,065 F5
Ardennes 309,306 F3
Ariège 137,857 D6
Aube 284,823 E3
Aude 272,366 E6
Aveyron 278,306 E5
Bas-Rhin 882,121 G3
Belfort (terr.) 128,125 G4
Bouches-du-Rhône 1,632,974 F6
Calvados 560,967 C3
Cantal 166,549 E5
Charente 337,064 D5
Charente-Maritime 497,859 C5
Cher 316,350 E4
Corrèze 240,363 D5
Corse du Sud 128,634 B6
Côte-d'Or 456,070 F4
Côtes-du-Nord 525,556 B3
Creuse 146,214 D4
Deux-Sèvres 335,829 C4
Dordogne 373,179 D5
Doubs 471,082 G4
Drôme 361,847 F5
Essonne 923,063 E3
Eure 422,952 D3
Eure-et-Loir 335,151 D3
Finistère 804,088 A3
Gard 494,575 F6
Gers 175,366 D6
Gironde 1,061,480 C5
Haute-Corse 161,208 B6
Haute-Garonne 777,431 D6
Haute-Loire 205,491 E5
Haute-Marne 212,304 F3
Hautes-Alpes 97,358 G5
Haute-Saône 222,254 G4
Haute-Savoie 447,795 G5
Hautes-Pyrénées 227,222 D6
Haute-Vienne 352,149 D5
Haut-Rhin 635,209 G4
Hauts-de-Seine 1,438,930 A2
Hérault 648,202 E6
Ille-et-Vilaine 702,199 C3
Indre 248,523 D4
Indre-et-Loire 478,601 D4
Isère 860,339 F5
Jura 238,856 F4
Landes 288,323 C5
Loire 742,396 F5
Loire-Atlantique 934,499 C4
Loiret 490,189 E4
Loir-et-Cher 283,686 D4
Lot 150,778 D5
Lot-et-Garonne 292,616 D5
Lozère 74,825 E5
Maine-et-Loire 629,849 C4
Manche 451,662 C3
Marne 530,399 F3
Mayenne 261,789 C3
Meurthe-et-Moselle 722,588 G3
Meuse 203,904 F3
Morbihan 563,588 B4
Moselle 1,006,373 G3
Nièvre 245,212 E4
Nord 2,510,738 E2
Oise 606,320 E3
Orne 293,523 C3
Paris (city) 2,299,830 B2
Pas-de-Calais 1,403,035 E2
Puy-de-Dôme 580,033 E5
Pyrénées-Atlantiques 534,748 C6
Pyrénées-Orientales 299,506 E6
Rhône 1,429,647 F5
Saône-et-Loire 569,810 F4
Sarthe 490,385 D3
Savoie 305,118 G5
Seine-et-Marne 755,762 E3
Seine-Saint-Denis 1,322,127 C1
Somme 538,462 E3
Tarn 338,024 E6
Tarn-et-Garonne 183,314 D5
Val-de-Marne 1,215,713 C1
Val-d'Oise 840,885 E3
Var 626,093 G6
Vaucluse 390,446 F6
Vendée 450,641 C4
Vienne 357,366 D4
Vosges 397,957 G3
Yonne 299,851 E4
Yvelines 1,082,255 D3

CITIES and TOWNS

Abbeville 25,252 D2
Agde 9,856 E6
Agen 33,763 D5
Aix-en-Provence 91,665 F6
Aix-les-Bains 21,884 G5
Ajaccio 47,065 B7
Albert 11,746 E2
Albertville 16,630 G5
Albi 43,942 E6
Alençon 32,917 D3
Alès 33,315 E5
Ambérieu-en-Bugey 9,294 F5
Amboise 10,498 D4
Amiens 129,453 D3
Ancenis 6,689 C4
Angers 136,603 C4
Angoulême 46,293 D5
Annecy 53,058 G5
Annonay 19,234 F5
Antibes 44,226 G6
Antony 57,450 B2
Apt 9,735 F6
Arcachon 13,856 C5
Argentan 16,063 D3
Argenteuil 101,542 A1
Arles 37,337 F6
Armentières 23,850 E2
Arras 45,804 E2
Asnières-sur-Seine 75,328 A1
Aubagne 26,145 F6
Aubenas 11,967 F5
Aubervilliers 72,859 B1
Auch 18,767 D6
Audincourt 18,570 G4
Aulnay-sous-Bois 77,982 B1
Auray 10,006 B4
Aurignac 744 D6
Aurillac 29,458 E5
Autun 19,441 F4
Auxerre 36,039 E4
Auxonne 6,414 F4
Avallon 8,518 E4
Avignon 73,482 F6
Avion 22,860 E2
Avranches 10,128 C3
Ax-les-Thermes 1,456 D6
Bagnères-de-Bigorre 9,080 D6
Bagnolet 35,858 B2
Bagnols-sur-Cèze 13,111 F5
Barbizon 1,189 E3
Barcelonnette 2,523 G5
Barfleur 701 C3
Bar-le-Duc 19,188 F3
Bar-sur-Aube 7,227 F3
Bastia 45,387 B6
Bayeux 13,381 C3
Bayonne 41,281 C6
Beaucaire 10,189 F6
Beaune 16,386 F4
Beauvais 53,493 E3
Belfort 54,469 G4
Belley 6,612 F5
Berck 14,104 D2
Bergerac 25,488 D5
Bernay 9,928 D3
Besançon 119,803 G4
Béthune 26,208 E2
Béziers 79,213 E6
Biarritz 27,453 C6
Blois 49,134 D4
Bobigny 43,041 B1
Bogny-sur-Meuse 6,845 F3
Bolbec 12,347 D3
Bondy 48,285 B1
Bonneville 6,717 G4
Bordeaux 220,830 C5
Boulogne-Billancourt 103,527 A2
Boulogne-sur-Mer 48,309 D2
Bourg-en-Bresse 40,052 F4
Bourges 75,200 E4
Bourgoin-Jallieu 18,504 F5
Bressuire 9,778 C4
Brest 163,940 A3
Briançon 8,523 G5
Brignoles 8,784 G6
Brioude 7,756 E5
Brive-la-Gaillarde 49,276 D5
Bruay-en-Artois 25,544 E2
Caen 116,987 C3
Cahors 19,288 D5
Calais 73,009 D2
Caluire-et-Cuire 43,024 F5
Cambrai 38,706 E2
Cannes 70,226 G6
Carcassonne 38,887 D6
Carmaux 11,970 E5
Carpentras 20,169 F5
Castelnaudary 8,947 E6
Castelsarrasin 6,562 D6
Castres 41,037 E6
Cavaillon 17,383 F6
Châlons-sur-Marne 50,870 F3
Chalon-sur-Saône 55,495 F4
Chambéry 52,286 F5
Chambord 166 D4
Chamonix-Mont-Blanc 6,246 G5
Champigny-sur-Marne 80,189 C2
Chantilly 10,517 E3
Charenton-le-Pont 20,383 B2
Charleville-Mézières 59,513 F3
Chartres 38,574 D3
Châteaubriant 12,417 C4
Château-du-Loir 5,598 D4
Châteaudun 14,634 D3
Château-Gontier 8,301 C4
Châteauroux 53,166 D4
Château-Thierry 13,379 E3
Châtellerault 33,811 D4
Châtillon 26,562 B2
Châtillon-sur-Seine 7,367 F4
Chatou 26,415 A1
Chaumont 26,568 F3
Chauny 14,324 E3
Chelles 24,192 C1
Cherbourg 31,333 C3
Chinon 5,378 D4
Choisy-le-Roi 38,629 B2
Cholet 49,887 C4
Clamart 52,881 A2
Clermont 7,834 E3
Clermont-Ferrand 153,379 E5
Clichy 47,731 B1
Cluny 4,335 F4
Cluses 12,713 G4
Cognac 21,567 C5
Colmar 58,585 G3
Colombes 83,241 A1
Commentry 8,074 E4
Commercy 6,918 F3
Compiègne 37,009 E3
Concarneau 15,096 A4
Cosne-Cours-sur-Loire 9,768 E4
Coudekerque-Branche 24,702 E2
Coulommiers 11,363 E3
Courbevoie 54,391 A1
Coutances 8,286 C3
Creil 31,893 E3
Crépy-en-Valois 10,661 E3
Créteil 58,665 B2
Cusset 13,672 E4
Dax 18,019 C6
Deauville 5,655 C3
Decazeville 9,318 E5
Decize 6,853 E4
Denain 26,096 E2
Dieppe 25,607 D3

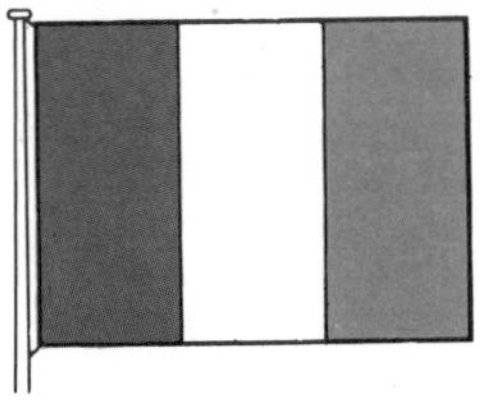

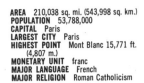

AREA 210,038 sq. mi. (543,998 sq. km.)
POPULATION 53,788,000
CAPITAL Paris
LARGEST CITY Paris
HIGHEST POINT Mont Blanc 15,771 ft. (4,807 m.)
MONETARY UNIT franc
MAJOR LANGUAGE French
MAJOR RELIGION Roman Catholicism

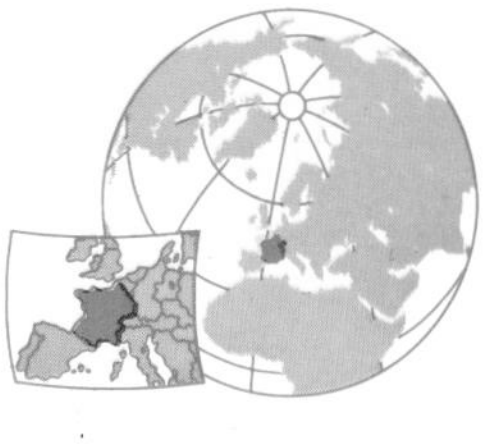

Topography

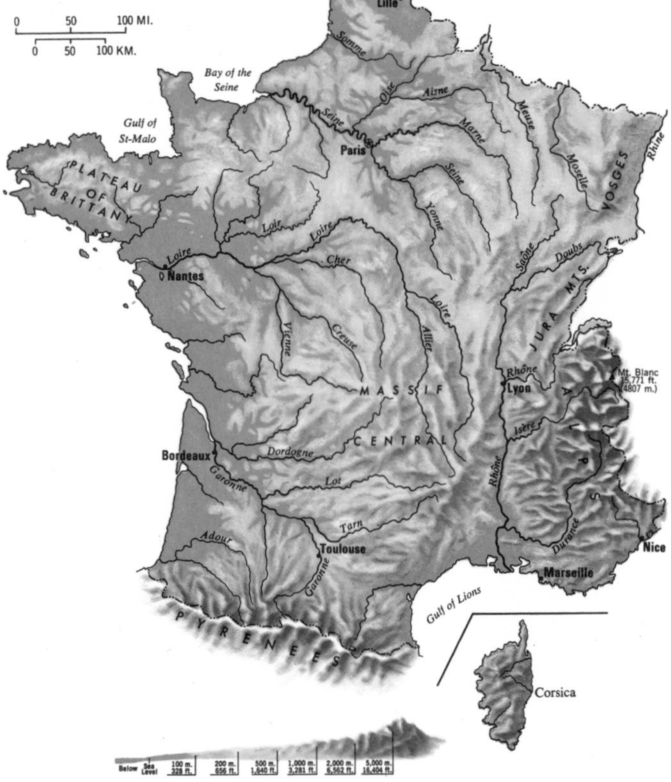

Historic Provinces

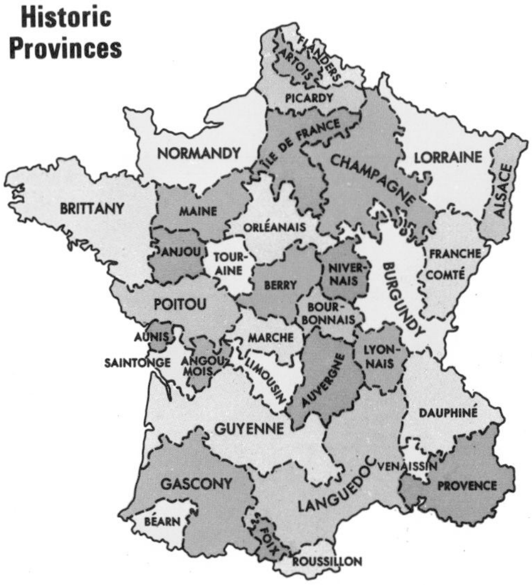

A resident of the city of Caen thinks of himself as a Norman rather than as a citizen of the modern department of Calvados. In spite of the passing of nearly two centuries, the historic provinces which existed before 1790 command the local patriotism of most Frenchmen.

Digne 13,140 G5
Digoin 10,449 F4
Dijon 149,899 F4
Dinan 13,303 B3
Dinard 9,211 B3
Dôle 28,109 F4
Domrémy-la-Pucelle 190 F3
Douai 43,954 E2
Douarnenez 17,851 A3
Doullens 6,806 E2
Draguignan 19,653 G6
Drancy 64,258 B1
Dreux 31,503 D3
Dunkirk (Dunkerque) 78,171 E2
Elbeuf 18,642 D3
Épernay 29,286 E3
Épinal 39,000 G3
Épinay-sur-Seine 46,458 B1
Erstein 6,494 G3
Étampes 18,810 E3
Étaples 10,423 D2
Eu 8,349 D3
Évreux 46,181 D3
Évry 15,300 E3
Falaise 8,133 C3
Fécamp 20,835 D3
Figeac 8,675 D5
Firminy 23,776 F5
Flers 18,590 C3
Foix 9,569 D6
Fontainebleau 16,436 E3
Fontenay-le-Comte 12,301 C4
Fontenay-sous-Bois 46,200 C2
Forbach 24,812 G3
Fougères 26,260 C3
Fourmies 15,318 F2
Fréjus 27,805 G6
Gagny 36,714 C1
Gaillac 7,653 D6
Gap 24,962 G5
Gardanne 8,175 F6
Gennevilliers 50,154 B1
Gentilly 16,843 B2
Gex 3,959 G4
Gien 13,817 E4
Gif 10,866 E3
Gisors 7,591 D3
Givet 7,787 F2
Givors 19,356 F5
Granville 12,869 C3
Grasse 24,260 G6
Graulhet 11,099 E6
Gray 8,718 F4
Grenoble 165,431 F5
Guebwiller 10,477 G4
Guéret 14,418 D4
Guingamp 9,269 B3
Guise 6,642 E3
Haguenau 23,023 G3
Harfleur 9,857 D3
Hautmont 19,130 F2
Hayange 8,479 F3
Hazebrouck 18,867 E2
Hendaye 9,404 C6
Hénin-Beaumont 26,296 E2
Hennebont 8,978 B4
Héricourt 8,481 G4
Hirson 11,909 F3
Honfleur 8,995 D3
Hyères 29,366 G6
Issoire 13,560 E5
Issoudun 15,065 D4
Issy-les-Moulineaux 47,355 A2
Istres 10,127 F6
Ivry-sur-Seine 62,804 B2
Joigny 10,825 E3
La Baule-Escoublac 13,854 B4
La Ciotat 29,290 F6
La Courneuve 37,917 B1
La Flèche 12,743 C4
La Grand-Combe 9,406 E5
L'Aigle 9,198 D3
Landerneau 13,983 B3
Langres 10,745 F4
Lannion 13,692 B3
Laon 27,420 E3
La Pallice C4
La Rochelle 72,936 C4
La Roche-sur-Yon 40,789 C4
La Seyne-sur-Mer 50,059 F6
Laval 50,734 C3
Lavelanet 9,278 E6
Le Blanc 7,431 D4
Le Blanc-Mesnil 49,062 B1
Le Bourget 10,520 B1
Le Cateau 8,680 E2
Le Chesnay 24,590 A2
Le Creusot 31,643 F4
Le Havre 216,917 C3
Le Mans 150,289 C3
Lens 39,973 E2
Le Puy 24,793 F5
Les Andelys 7,524 D3
Les Sables-d'Olonne 17,157 B4
Le Teil 7,993 F5
Le Tréport 6,463 D2
Levallois-Perret 52,460 A1
Lézignan-Corbières 6,929 E6
Libourne 21,265 C5
Liévin 33,040 E2
Lille 171,010 E2
Limoges 136,059 D5
Limoux 9,595 E6
Lisieux 24,972 D3
Livry-Gargan 32,879 C1
Lodève 7,131 E6
Longwy 20,107 F3
Lons-le-Saunier 20,897 F4
Lorient 68,655 B4
Loudéac 7,173 B3
Loudun 7,060 D4
Lourdes 17,685 C6
Louviers 17,919 D3
Luçon 8,834 C4
Lunel 12,392 E6
Lunéville 22,438 G3
Lure 8,538 G4
Luxeuil-les-Bains 10,061 G4
Lyon 454,265 F5
Mâcon 39,130 F4
Maisons-Alfort 53,963 B2
Maisons-Laffitte 23,465 A1
Malakoff 34,100 A2
Manosque 17,256 G6
Mantes-la-Jolie 42,403 D3
Marmande 13,223 C5
Marseille 901,421 F6
Martigues 26,850 F6
Maubeuge 34,152 F2
Mayenne 11,278 C3
Mazamet 13,148 E6
Meaux 41,831 E3
Mehun-sur-Yèvre 6,533 E4
Melun 36,913 E3
Mende 10,040 E5
Menton 24,736 G6
Metz 110,939 G3
Meudon 31,294 A2
Millau 20,401 E5
Mimizan 6,826 C5
Mirecourt 7,160 G3
Moissac 7,403 D5
Montargis 18,021 E3
Montauban 35,344 D5
Montbard 7,477 F4
Montbéliard 29,968 G4
Montbrison 9,945 E5
Montceau-les-Mines 28,093 F4
Mont-de-Marsan 24,812 C6
Mont-Dore 2,074 E5
Montélimar 25,422 F5
Montfort 2,701 C3
Montigny-les-Metz 24,208 G3
Montluçon 56,337 E4
Montmédy 1,859 F3
Montpellier 178,136 E6
Montreuil, Seine-Saint-Denis 96,441 B2
Montrouge 40,189 B2
Mont-Saint-Michel 88 C3
Morlaix 15,919 B3
Morteau 6,515 G4
Moulins 25,856 E4
Moyeuvre-Grande 12,448 G3
Mulhouse 116,494 G4
Muret 13,041 D6
Nancy 106,906 G3
Nanterre 94,441 A1
Nantes 252,537 C4
Narbonne 36,525 E6
Nemours 11,159 E3
Neufchâteau 8,582 F3
Neuilly-sur-Seine 65,941 A1
Nevers 45,122 E4
Nice 331,002 G6
Nîmes 123,914 F6
Niort 59,297 C4
Nogent-le-Rotrou 12,284 D3
Noisy-le-Sec 37,674 B1
Noyon 13,784 E3
Oloron-Sainte-Marie 11,616 C6
Orange 19,847 F5
Orléans 88,503 D3
Orly 26,090 B2
Orthez 9,639 C6
Oullins 27,731 F5
Oyonnax 22,548 F4
Pamiers 12,906 D6
Pantin 42,651 B1
Paray-le-Monial 11,523 F4
Paris (cap.) 2,291,554 B2
Parthenay 12,549 C4
Pau 81,560 C6
Périgueux 34,779 D5
Péronne 8,358 E3
Perpignan 101,198 E6
Pessac 50,333 C5
Pézenas 6,768 E6
Pithiviers 9,976 E3
Poitiers 78,739 D4
Pont-à-Mousson 14,461 G3
Pontarlier 17,778 G4
Pontivy 9,478 B3
Pont-l'Abbe 6,618 A4
Pontoise 26,702 E3
Port-de-Bouc 20,448 F6
Port-Saint-Louis-du-Rhône 9,649 F6
Port-Vendres 5,448 E6
Privas 9,385 F5
Provins 12,281 E3
Puteau 35,366 A2
Quimper 50,856 A4
Quimperlé 9,783 B4
Rambouillet 18,446 D3
Redon 9,528 C4
Reims 177,320 E3
Remiremont 10,250 G3
Rennes 194,094 C3

(continued on following page)

MONACO

CITIES and TOWNS

* City and suburbs

MONACO

AREA 368 acres
(149 hectares)
POPULATION 25,029

Wine Regions

Climate, soil and variety of grape planted determine the quality of wine. Long, hot and fairly dry summers with cool, humid nights constitute an ideal climate. The nature of the soil is such a determining influence that identical grapes planted in Bordeaux, Burgundy and Champagne, will yield wines of widely different types.

Agriculture, Industry and Resources

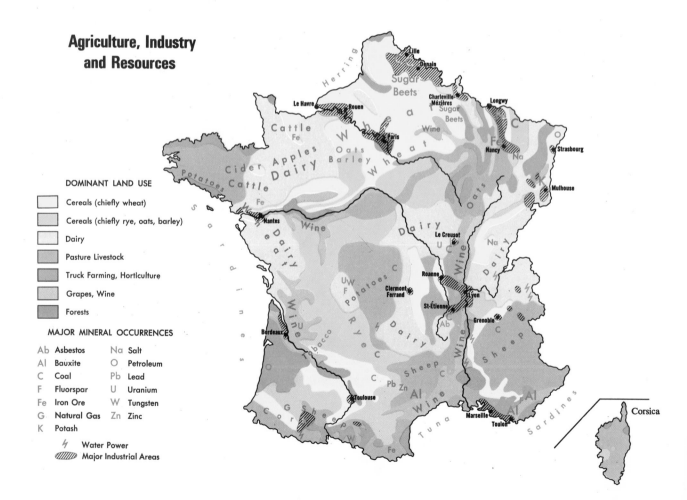

DOMINANT LAND USE

- Cereals (chiefly wheat)
- Cereals (chiefly rye, oats, barley)
- Dairy
- Pasture Livestock
- Truck Farming, Horticulture
- Grapes, Wine
- Forests

MAJOR MINERAL OCCURRENCES

Ab	Asbestos	Na	Salt
Al	Bauxite	O	Petroleum
C	Coal	Pb	Lead
F	Fluorspar	U	Uranium
Fe	Iron Ore	W	Tungsten
G	Natural Gas	Zn	Zinc
K	Potash		

⚡ Water Power
▨ Major Industrial Areas

ANDORRA

SPAIN

PORTUGAL

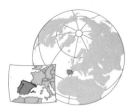

Agriculture, Industry and Resources

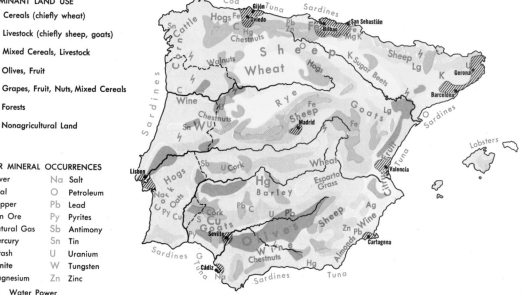

SPAIN

AREA 194,881 sq. mi. (504,742 sq. km.)
POPULATION 37,430,000
CAPITAL Madrid
LARGEST CITY Madrid
HIGHEST POINT Pico de Teide 12,172 ft. (3,710 m.)
(Canary Is.); Mulhacén 11,411 ft. (3,478 m.)
(mainland)
MONETARY UNIT peseta
MAJOR LANGUAGES Spanish, Catalan, Basque,
  Galician, Valencian
MAJOR RELIGION Roman Catholicism

ANDORRA

AREA 188 sq. mi. (487 sq. km.)
POPULATION 31,000
CAPITAL Andorra la Vella
MONETARY UNITS French franc, Spanish peseta
MAJOR LANGUAGE Catalan
MAJOR RELIGION Roman Catholicism

PORTUGAL

AREA 35,549 sq. mi. (92,072 sq. km.)
POPULATION 9,933,000
CAPITAL Lisbon
LARGEST CITY Lisbon
HIGHEST POINT Malhão da Estrela
  6,532 ft. (1,991 m.)
MONETARY UNIT escudo
MAJOR LANGUAGE Portuguese
MAJOR RELIGION Roman Catholicism

GIBRALTAR

AREA 2.28 sq. mi. (5.91 sq. km.)
POPULATION 29,760
CAPITAL Gibraltar
MONETARY UNIT pound sterling
MAJOR LANGUAGES English, Spanish
MAJOR RELIGION Roman Catholicism

(continued on following page)

(continued)

San Lorenzo de El Escorial 8,098	E2	Tobarra 5,887	F3	Barros 12,610	C3
Sanlúcar de Barrameda 29,483	C4	Toledo 43,905	F3	Villagarcla 6,601	B1
Sanlúcar la Mayor 6,121	C4	Tolosa 15,164	F1	Villajoyosa 12,573	G3
San Roque 8,224	D4	Tomelloso 26,041	E3	Villanueva de Córdoba 11,270	D3
San Sebastián 159,557	F1	Tordesillas 5,815	D2	Villanueva del Arzobispo 8,076	E3
Santa Cruz de la Palma 10,393	B4	Toro 8,455	D2	Villanueva de la Serena 16,687	D3
Santa Cruz de Mudela 6,354	E3	Torredonjimeno 12,507	D4	Villanueva de los Infantes 8,154	E3
Santa Cruz de Tenerife 74,910	B4	Torrejón de Ardoz 21,081	G4	Villanueva y Geltrú 35,714	G2
Santa Eugenia 5,946	B1	Torrelavega 19,933	D1	Villarreal de los Infantes 29,482	G3
Santa Fe 8,990	E4	Torremolinos 20,484	D4	Villarrobledo 19,696	E3
Santander 130,019	D1	Torrente 38,397	G3	Villarrubia de los Ojos 9,144	E3
Santiago 51,620	B1	Torrevieja 9,431	F4	Villaverde	F4
Santo Domingo de la Calzada 5,638	E1	Torrijos 6,362	D2	Villena 23,483	F3
Santoña 9,546	E1	Tortosa 5,583	G2	Vinaroz 13,727	G3
San Vicente de Alcántara 7,006	C3	Totana 12,714	E4	Vitoria 124,791	E1
Saragossa 449,319	F2	Triguéros 5,280	C4	Yecla 19,352	F3
Saragossat 500,000	F2	Trujillo 9,024	D3	Zafra 11,583	C3
Segorbe 6,962	G3	Tudela 20,942	F1	Zalamea de la Serena 6,017	D3
Segovia 41,880	D2	Úbeda 28,306	E3	Zamora 48,791	D2
Seo de Urgel 6,604	G1	Ubrique 13,166	D4	Zaragoza (Saragossa) 449,319	F2
Seville 511,447	D4	Utiel 9,168	F3		
Seville† 560,000	D4	Utrera 28,287	D4	**OTHER FEATURES**	
Sitges 5,906	G2	Valdemoro 6,263	F4		
Socuéllamos 12,610	E3	Valdepeñas 24,018	E3	Alborán (isl.)	E5
Sóller 6,470	H3	Valencia 626,675	G3	Alcaraz, Sierra de (range)	E3
Solsona 5,346	G2	Valencia† 700,000	G3	Alcudia (bay)	H3
Sonseca 6,594	D3	Valencia de Alcántara 5,963	C3	Almanzor (mt.)	D2
Soria 24,744	E2	Valladolid 227,511	D2	Almanzora (riv.)	F4
Sotrondio 5,914	D1	Vall de Uxó 23,976	F3	Almenara (riv.)	E1
Sueca 20,019	G3	Vallecas	G2	Andalusia (reg.)	G1
Tabernes de Valldigna 13,962	G3	Valls 14,189	G2	Aneto (peak)	F2
Tafalla 8,858	F1	Valverde del Camino 10,566	C4	Aragón (riv.)	F1
Talavera de la Reina 39,889	D2	Vejer de la Frontera 6,184	C4	Arosa, Ría de (est.)	B1
Tarancón 8,238	E3	Vélez-Málaga 20,794	E4	Asturias (reg.)	A5
Tarazona 11,067	E2	Vendrell 7,951	G2	Balaítous (mt.)	F1
Tarazona de la Mancha 5,952	F3	Vera 4,903	F4	Balearic (Baleares) (isls.)	H3
Tarifa 9,201	D4	Vergara 11,541	E1	Barbate (riv.)	D4
Tarragona 53,548	G2	Vicálvaro	H2	Biscay (bay)	E1
Tarrasa 134,481	G2	Vich 25,449	H2	Cabrera (isl.)	H3
Tárrega 9,036	G2	Vigo 114,526	B1	Cala Burras (pt.)	D4
Tauste 6,832	F2	Vilafranca del Penadés 16,875	G2	Canary (isls.)	B4
Teide 13,257	B5	Villacañas 9,883	E3	Cantabrian (range)	C1
Teruel 20,614	F2	Villacarrillo 9,452	E3	Catalonia (reg.)	G2
		Villafranca de los			

Cinca (riv.)	G2	Mancha, La (reg.)	E3	Rosas (gulf)	H1
Columbretes (isls.)	G3	Manzanares (riv.)	F4	San Jorge (gulf)	G2
Costa Brava (coast)	H2	Marismas, Las (marsh)	C4	Segre (riv.)	F3
Costa de Sola (Costa del Sol) (reg.)	D4	Mar Menor (lag.)	F4	Segura (riv.)	E3
Creus (cape)	H1	Mayor (cape)	C1	Sil (riv.)	C1
Cuenca, Sierra de (range)	E1	Menorca (Minorca) (isl.)	B1	Tagus (riv.)	D3
Demanda, Sierra de la (range)	E1	Miño (riv.)	B1	Tajo (Tagus) (riv.)	D3
Douro (riv.)	C2	Minorca (isl.)	J2	Teide, Pico de (peak)	B5
Duero (Douro) (riv.)	C2	Moncayo, Sierra de (range)	F2	Tenerife (isl.)	B5
Ebro (riv.)	G2	Montserrat (mt.)	H1	Ter (riv.)	H1
Eresma (riv.)	D2	Morena, Sierra (range)	E3	Tinto (riv.)	C4
Esla (riv.)	D1	Nao (cape)	G3	Toledo (mts.)	D3
Estats (peak)	G1	Navia (riv.)	C1	Tortosa (cape)	G2
Estremadura (reg.)	B2	Nevada, Sierra (mts.)	E4	Trafalgar (cape)	C4
Finisterre (cape)	B1	Oca (riv.)	E1	Turia (riv.)	F3
Formentera (isl.)	G3	Órbigo (riv.)	D1	Ulla (riv.)	B1
Formentor (cape)	H2	Oiel (riv.)	C4	Urgel, Llanos de (plain)	G2
Fuerteventura (isl.)	C4	Old Castile (reg.)	D2	Valencia (gulf)	G3
Galicia (reg.)	B1	Palos (cape)	F4	Valencia (reg.)	F3
Gata (cape)	F4	Peñalara (mt.)	D2	Valencia, Albufera de (lag.)	G3
Genil (riv.)	D4	Peña Vieja (mt.)	D1	Vascongadas (reg.)	E1
Gibraltar (str.)	D5	Peñíbetica, Sistema (range)	E4		
Gomera (isl.)	B5	Perdido (mt.)	G1	**PORTUGAL**	
Gran Canaria (isl.)	B5	Pyrenees (range)	F1		
Gredos, Sierra de (range)	D2			**DISTRICTS**	
Guadalimar (riv.)	H3				
Guadalquivir (riv.)	E3			Aveiro 545,230	B2
Guadarrama, Sierra de (range)	E2				
Guadarrama (riv.)	F3				
Guadiana (riv.)	D3				
Gúdar, Sierra de (range)	F2				
Henares (riv.)	G4				
Hierro (isl.)	A5				
Ibiza (isl.)	G3				
Ibiza (isl.)	F1				
Jalón (riv.)	E2				
Jarama (riv.)	E2				
Júcar (riv.)	F3				
Lanzarote (isl.)	C4				
La Palma (isl.)	A4				
León (riv.)	C1				
Llobregat (riv.)	H2				
Majorca (isl.)	H3				
Mallorca (Majorca) (isl.)	H3				

Beja 204,440	C3
Braga 609,415	C2
Braganca 180,395	D2
Castelo Branco 254,355	C2
Coimbra 399,380	B2
Évora 178,475	C3
Faro 268,040	C4
Guarda 210,720	C2
Leiria 375,540	B3
Lisbon 1,568,020	A1
Oporto (Porto)	B2
1,309,560	
Portalegre 145,545	C3
Porto 1,309,560	B2
Santarém 427,995	B3
Setúbal 469,555	B3
Viana do Castelo	
250,510	C2
Vila Real 265,605	C2
Viseu 410,795	C2

CITIES and TOWNS

Abrantes 11,775	B3
Agueda 9,343	B2
Albufeira 7,479	B3
Alcácer do Sal 13,187	B3
Alcântara 23,699	A1

Topography

Scale: 0 — 50 — 100 MI. / 0 — 50 — 100 KM.

Below Sea Level	100 m. 328 ft.	200 m. 656 ft.	500 m. 1,640 ft.	1,000 m. 3,281 ft.	2,000 m. 6,562 ft.	5,000 m. 16,404 ft.

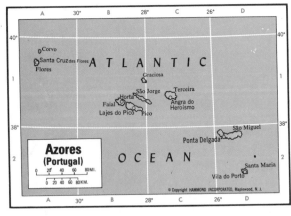

Azores (Portugal)

Scale: 0 20 40 60 80 MI. / 0 20 40 60 80 KM.

© Copyright HAMMOND INCORPORATED, Maplewood, N.J.

AZORES

INTERNAL DIVISIONS

Angra do Heroísmo (dist.) 83,500	C1
Horta (dist.) 38,700	A1
Ponta Delgada (dist.) 153,700	D2

CITIES and TOWNS

Angra do Heroísmo 13,795	C1
Horta 6,145	B1
Lajes do Pico 2,147	B1
Ponta Delgada 20,195	D2
Santa Cruz das Flores 1,880	A1
Vila do Porto 4,149	D2

OTHER FEATURES

Azores (isls.)	A2
Corvo (isl.)	A1
Faial (isl.)	B1
Flores (isl.)	A1
Graciosa (isl.)	C1
Pico (isl.)	C1
Santa Maria (isl.)	D2
São Jorge (isl.)	B1
São Miguel (isl.)	D2
Terceira (isl.)	C1

PORTUGAL is divided into 18 mainland districts bearing the same names as their respective capitals. The Azores and Madeira are offshore autonomous regions.

Alcobaça 4,799	B3	Campo Maior 7,405	C3	Grândola 9,698	B3	Moura 9,351	C3	Salvaterra de Magos 6,265	B3	Vila Nova de Gaia	B2	Sado (riv.)	B3
Aldeia Nova de São		Cantanhede 6,734	B2	Guarda 9,735	C2	Nazaré 8,553	B3	Santa Cruz 6,348	A2	Vila Real Real 10,050	C2	São Vincent (cape)	B4

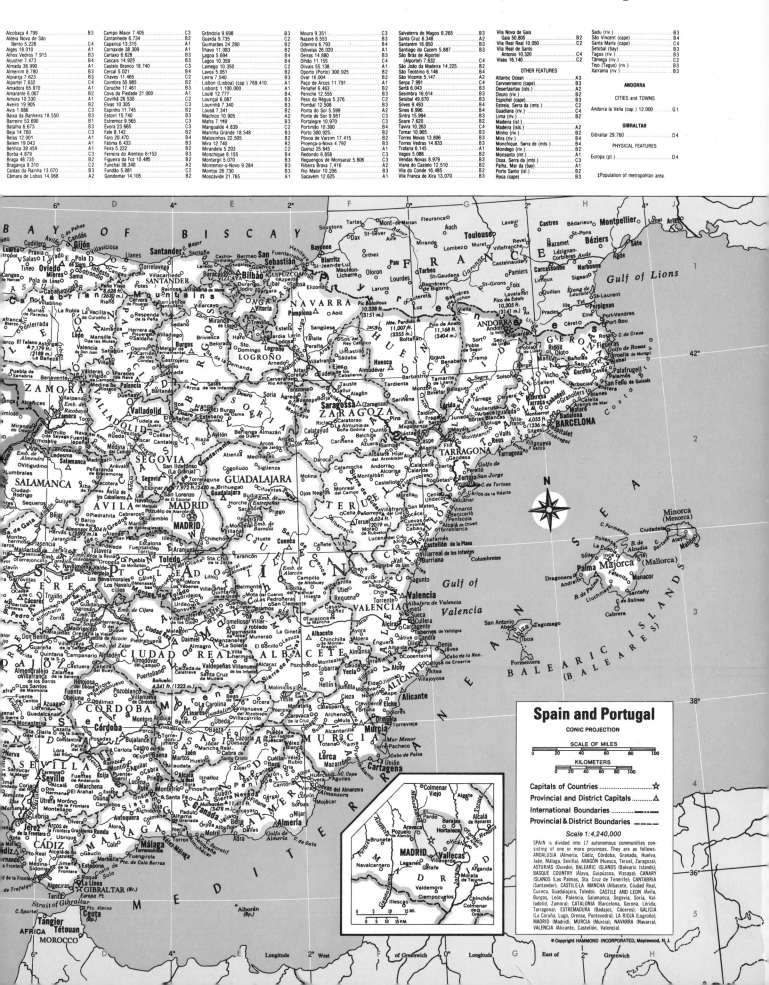

Italy

CONIC PROJECTION

SCALE OF MILES

SCALE OF KILOMETERS

Capitals of Countries	☆
Regional Capitals	⊞
Provincial Capitals	△
International Boundaries	— · · —
Regional Boundaries	— · —

The regions are subdivided into provinces bearing the same names as their respective capitals, except:

PROVINCE	CAPITAL
MASSA-CARRARA	Massa
PESARO-URBINO	Pesaro

Vatican City

SCALE

Rome and Environs

© Copyright HAMMOND INCORPORATED, Maplewood, N.J.

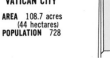

VATICAN CITY

AREA 108.7 acres (44 hectares)
POPULATION 728

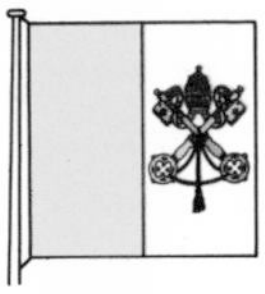

SAN MARINO

AREA 23.4 sq. mi. (60.6 sq. km.)
POPULATION 19,149

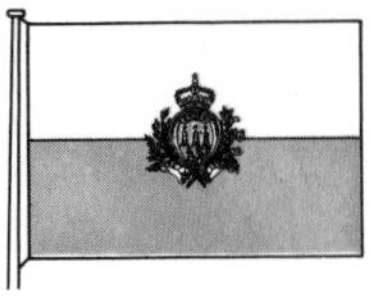

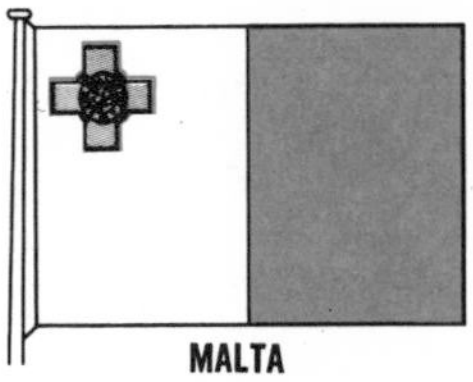

MALTA

AREA 122 sq. mi. (316 sq. km.)
POPULATION 343,970
CAPITAL Valletta
LARGEST CITY Sliema
HIGHEST POINT 787 ft. (240 m.)
MONETARY UNIT Maltese pound
MAJOR LANGUAGES Maltese, English
MAJOR RELIGION Roman Catholicism

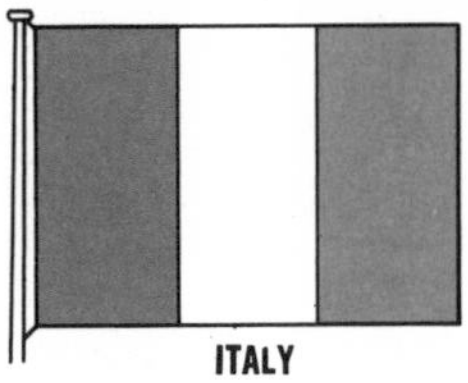

ITALY

AREA 116,303 sq. mi. (301,225 sq. km.)
POPULATION 57,140,000
CAPITAL Rome
LARGEST CITY Rome
HIGHEST POINT Dufourspitze (Mte. Rosa) 15,203 ft. (4,634 m.)
MONETARY UNIT lira
MAJOR LANGUAGE Italian
MAJOR RELIGION Roman Catholicism

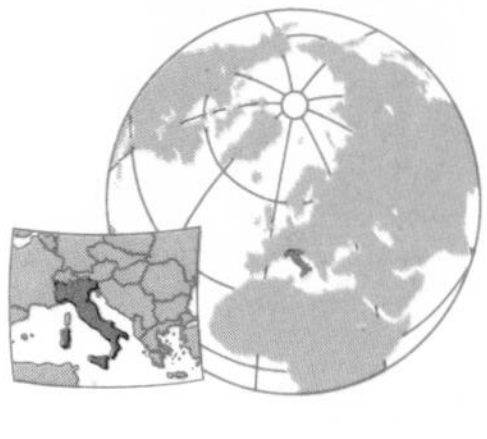

ITALY

REGIONS

Abruzzi 1,166,664 D3
Aosta 109,150 A2
Apulia (Puglia) 3,582,787 F4
Basilicata 603,064 F4
Calabria 1,988,051 F5
Campania 5,059,348 E4
Emilia-Romagna 3,846,755 C2
Friuli-Venezia Giulia 1,213,532 D1
Latium (Lazio) 4,689,482 D3
Liguria 1,853,578 B2
Lombardy 8,543,657 B2
Marche 1,359,907 D3
Molise 319,807 E4
Piedmont 4,432,313 A2
Sardinia 1,473,800 B4
Sicily 4,680,715 D6
Trentino-Alto Adige 841,886 C1
Tuscany 3,473,097 C3
Umbria 775,783 D3
Veneto 2,109,502 D3

PROVINCES

Agrigento 454,045 D6
Alessandria 483,183 B2
Ancona 416,611 D3
Aosta 109,150 A2
Arezzo 306,340 C3
Ascoli Piceno 340,758 D3
Asti 218,547 B2
Avellino 427,509 E4
Bari 1,351,288 F4
Belluno 221,155 D1
Benevento 286,499 E4
Bergamo 829,019 B2
Bologna 918,844 C2
Bolzano-Bozen 414,041 C1
Brescia 957,686 C2
Brindisi 366,027 G4
Cagliari 802,888 B5
Caltanissetta 282,069 D6
Campobasso 227,641 E4
Caserta 677,959 E4
Catania 938,273 E6
Catanzaro 718,069 F5
Chieti 351,567 E3
Como 720,463 B2
Cosenza 691,659 F5
Cremona 334,281 B2
Cuneo 540,504 A2
Enna 202,131 E6
Ferrara 383,639 C2
Florence 1,146,367 C3
Foggia 657,292 E4
Forlì 565,470 D2
Frosinone 422,630 D4
Genoa 1,087,973 B2
Gorizia 142,412 D2
Grosseto 216,315 C3
Imperia 225,127 B3
Isernia 92,166 E4
L'Aquila 293,066 D3
La Spezia 244,435 B2
Latina 376,238 D4
Lecce 696,503 G4
Leghorn 335,265 C3
Lucca 380,356 C3
Macerata 286,155 D3
Mantua 376,892 C2
Massa-Carrara 200,955 C2
Matera 194,629 F4
Messina 654,703 E5
Milan 3,903,685 B2
Modena 553,852 C2
Naples 2,709,929 E4
Novara 496,811 B2
Nuoro 273,021 B4
Padua 762,998 C2
Palermo 1,124,015 D5
Parma 395,497 C2
Pavia 526,389 B2
Perugia 552,936 D3
Pesaro e Urbino 316,383 D3
Pescara 264,981 E3
Piacenza 284,881 B2
Pisa 375,933 C3
Pistoia 254,335 C2
Pordenone 253,906 D2
Potenza 408,435 E4
Ragusa 255,047 E6
Ravenna 351,876 D2
Reggio di Calabria 578,323 E5
Reggio nell'Emilia 392,696 C2
Rieti 143,162 D3
Rome 3,490,377 F6
Rovigo 251,908 C2
Salerno 957,452 E4
Sassari 397,891 B4
Savona 296,043 B2
Siena 257,221 C3
Sondrio 169,149 B1
Syracuse 365,039 E6
Taranto 511,677 F4
Teramo 257,080 D3
Terni 222,847 D3
Trapani 405,393 D5
Trento 427,845 C1
Treviso 668,620 D2
Trieste 300,304 E2
Turin 2,287,016 A2
Udine 516,910 D1
Varese 725,823 B2
Venice 807,251 D2
Vercelli 406,252 B2
Verona 733,595 C2
Vicenza 677,884 C2
Viterbo 257,075 C3

CITIES and TOWNS

Acireale 34,081 E6
Acqui Terme 20,099 B2
Acri 8,150 F5
Adrano 31,988 E6
Adria 11,951 D2
Agira 11,262 E6
Agnone 3,965 E4
Agrigento 40,513 D6
Agropoli 9,413 E4
Alassio 13,512 A2
Alatri 5,710 D4
Alba 23,522 B2
Albano Laziale 15,561 F7
Albenga 13,397 B3
Albino 8,837 B2
Alcamo 41,448 D6
Alessandria 78,644 B2
Alghero 28,454 B4
Altamura 44,879 F4
Amalfi 4,205 E4
Amantea 6,132 E5
Amelia 4,331 D3
Ancona 88,427 D3
Andria 76,405 F4
Anguillara Sabazia 3,241 F6
Anzio 14,966 D4
Aosta 35,053 A2
Aprilia 18,412 D4
Aragona 11,213 D6
Arezzo 56,693 C3
Argenta 6,682 D2
Ariano Irpino 9,796 E4
Ariccia 7,287 F7
Artena 5,034 F7
Ascoli Piceno 43,041 D3
Assisi 4,630 D3
Asti 62,277 B2
Atessa 3,079 E3
Atri 4,686 D3
Augusta 32,501 E6
Avellino 44,750 E4
Aversa 46,536 E4
Avezzano 26,456 D3
Avigliano 5,400 E4
Avola 29,089 E6
Bagheria 32,465 D5
Barcellona Pozzo di Gotto 25,280 E5
Bari 339,110 F4
Barletta 75,116 F4
Bassano del Grappa 33,002 C2
Bellagio 3,258 B2
Belluno 22,180 D1
Benevento 48,523 E4
Bergamo 127,553 B2
Biancavilla 18,743 E6
Biella 46,453 B2
Bisceglie 45,014 F4
Bitonto 39,714 F4
Bitti 4,606 B4
Bologna 493,282 C2
Bolzano (Bolzen) 102,806 C1
Bondeno 7,451 C2
Bonorva 5,232 B4
Bordighera 8,994 A3
Borgo 4,013 C1
Borgomanero 16,655 B2
Bôrgo San Lorenzo 7,699 C2
Bosa 8,045 B4
Boves 3,896 A2
Bra 18,399 A2
Bracciano 7,681 C3
Brescia 189,092 C2
Bressanone 12,261 C1
Brindisi 76,612 G4
Bronte 17,823 E6
Brunico 5,175 D1
Budrio 5,635 C2
Busto Arsizio 72,400 B2
Cagli 4,356 D3
Cagliari 211,015 B5
Caltagirone 34,444 E6
Caltanissetta 52,838 D6
Camaiore 8,578 C3
Camerino 4,644 D3
Campobasso 35,551 E4
Campo Tures 1,325 C1
Canicatti 28,761 E6
Canosa di Puglia 30,263 E4
Cantù 28,617 B2
Capua 13,938 E4
Caravaggio 11,298 B2
Carbonia 23,031 B5
Carini 14,255 D5
Carloforte 6,671 B5
Carmagnola 16,469 A2
Carpi 41,789 C2
Carrara 56,236 C2
Casale Monferrato 35,156 B2
Casalmaggiore 6,374 C2
Cascina-Navacchio 28,263 C3
Caserta 51,621 E4
Cassano allo Ionio 9,661 F5
Cassino 14,747 D4
Castelfranco Veneto 16,042 D2
Castel Gandolfo 2,965 F7
Castellammare del Golfo 13,144 D5
Castellammare di Stabia 64,341 E4
Castel San Pietro Terme 6,985 C2
Castelvetrano 29,167 D6
Castiglion Fiorentino 3,797 C3
Castrovillari 15,207 F5
Catania 403,390 E6
Catanzaro 52,054 F5
Caulonia 3,402 F5
Cava de'Tirreni 33,868 E4
Cavarzere 7,917 D2
Cecina 19,415 C3
Cefalù 11,043 E5
Ceglie Messapico 17,512 F4
Celano 9,531 D3
Cerignola 44,648 E4
Cernobbio 8,026 B2
Cerveteri 5,239 E6
Cesano 2,883 F6
Cesena 49,915 D2
Cesenatico 12,805 D2
Chiari 12,017 C2
Chiavari 29,950 B2
Chieri 27,548 A2
Chieti 31,895 E3
Chioggia 24,044 D2
Chivasso 21,369 A2
Ciampino 36,728 F7
Cittadella 9,321 C2
Città di Castello 18,880 C3
Cittanova 11,045 F5
Cividale del Friuli 8,345 D1
Civitavecchia 41,305 C3
Clusone-Fiorine 6,428 C2
Codroipo 6,117 D2
Colle di Val d'Elsa 8,657 C3
Comacchio 10,437 D2
Comiso 24,508 E6
Como 73,257 B2
Conegliano 28,635 D2
Conversano 16,805 F4
Corato 38,163 F4
Cori 6,829 F7
Corigliano Calabro 14,518 F5
Corleone 11,057 D6
Correggio 11,415 C2
Cortina d'Ampezzo 7,285 D1
Cortona 3,482 C3
Cosenza 94,565 F5
Courmayeur 1,401 A2
Crema 26,061 B2
Cremona 75,988 B2
Crotone 44,081 F5
Cuneo 41,633 A2
Cuorgnè 6,752 A2
Desenzano del Garda 14,624 C2
Diano Marina 6,001 B3
Domodossola 18,562 A1
Dorgali 6,714 B4
Eboli 19,787 E4
Edolo 3,707 C1
Empoli 30,526 C3
Enna 27,351 E6
Este 12,992 C2
Fabriano 18,355 D3
Faenza 36,241 D2
Fano 31,238 D3
Fasano 21,247 F4
Favara 27,940 D6
Feltre 11,806 C1
Fermo 17,521 D3
Ferrandina 8,372 F4
Ferrara 97,507 C2
Fidenza 18,064 B2
Fiesole 3,772 C3
Finale Emilia 7,474 C2
Finale Ligure 11,461 B2
Firenze (Florence) 441,654 C3
Fiumicino 13,180 F7
Florence 441,654 C3
Floridia 16,562 E6
Foggia 136,436 E4
Foligno 26,887 D3
Fondi 16,472 D4
Forlì 83,303 D2
Formia 18,978 D4
Fossano 15,857 A2
Fossombrone 5,882 D3
Francavilla Fontana 30,347 F4
Frascati 14,217 F7
Frosinone 34,066 D4
Gaeta 21,973 D4
Galatina 22,137 G4
Galatone 13,880 F4
Gallarate 43,773 B2
Gallipoli 16,878 F4
Garessio 3,359 A2
Gela 66,845 E6
Gemona 6,863 D1
Genoa 787,011 B2
Genova (Genoa) 787,011 B2
Genzano di Roma 14,147 F7
Giarre 18,233 E6
Gioia del Colle 23,299 F4
Gioiosa Ionica 3,811 F5
Giovinazzo 17,768 F4
Giulianova 17,926 E3
Gorizia 35,912 D2
Gravina in Puglia 32,006 F4
Grosseto 48,309 C3
Grottaferrata 10,639 F7
Grottaglie 23,556 F4
Guardiagrele 4,122 E3
Guastalla 7,639 C2
Gubbio 12,371 D3
Guidonia 8,413 F6
Iglesias 24,472 B5
Imola 42,111 C2
Imperia 37,585 B3
Isernia 12,290 E4
Ivrea 26,530 B2
Jesi 33,011 D3
Ladispoli 6,625 E6
Lagonegro 5,613 E4
La Maddalena 10,405 B4
Lanciano 19,652 E3
Lanusei 5,508 B5
Lanuvio 2,970 F7
L'Aquila 36,233 D3
Larino 5,166 E4
La Spezia 121,254 B2
Latina 53,003 D4
Lauria 4,927 E4
Lavello 11,486 E4
Lecce 80,114 G4
Lecco 53,165 B2
Leghorn 170,369 C3
Legnago 15,534 C2
Lendinara 7,079 C2
Lentini 31,429 E6
Leonforte 16,317 E6
Lerici 5,407 B2
Licata 40,997 D6
Lido di Ostia 61,492 F7
Lido di Venezia 18,794 D2
Lipari 3,886 E5
Livigno 2,135 C1
Livorno (Leghorn) 170,369 C3
Lodi 42,489 B2
Lonigo 6,368 C2
Lucca 54,280 C3
Lucera 29,355 E4
Lugo 19,497 D2
Macerata 33,470 D3
Macomer 9,433 B4
Maglie 13,326 G4
Manduria 25,194 F4
Manfredonia 44,463 F4
Mantua 59,529 C2
Marino 12,135 F7
Marsala 34,150 D6
Marsciano 5,372 D3
Martina Franca 31,811 F4
Massa 56,591 C2
Massafra 22,610 F4
Massa Marittima 6,438 C3
Matera 43,026 F4
Mazara del Vallo 37,441 D6
Mazzarino 14,981 E6
Melfi 13,355 E4
Menfi 12,386 D6
Merano 30,951 C1
Mesagne 26,955 G4
Messina 203,937 E5
Mestre 184,818 D2
Milan 1,724,557 B2
Milazzo 18,576 E5
Minturno 2,428 D4
Mirandola 11,551 C2
Mira Taglio 10,194 D2
Mistretta 6,631 E6
Modena 149,029 C2
Modica 31,074 E6
Mola di Bari 23,778 F4
Molfetta 63,250 F4
Moncalieri 49,953 A2
Mondovì Breo 12,524 A2
Monfalcone 29,589 D2
Monopoli 29,776 F4
Monreale 19,348 D5
Monselice 9,047 C2
Montalto Uffugo 3,173 E5
Montebelluna 9,573 D2
Montefiascone 6,885 D3
Montepulciano 4,069 C3
Monterotondo 15,869 F6
Monte Sant'Angelo 17,756 F4
Montevarchi 16,849 C3
Monza 110,735 B2
Mortara 13,929 B2
Naples 1,214,775 E4
Nardò 24,142 F4
Narni 6,213 D3
Naro 13,171 D6
Nettuno 20,927 D4
Nicastro 27,206 F5
Nicosia 13,982 E6
Niscemi 23,925 E6
Nizza Monferrato 7,532 B2
Nocera Inferiore 44,415 E4
Noto 21,606 E6
Novara 92,634 B2
Novi Ligure 29,944 B2
Nuoro 30,551 B4
Olbia 20,998 B4
Oliena 7,030 B4
Orbetello 6,884 C3
Oristano 20,966 B5
Ortona 11,966 E3
Orvieto 8,813 D3
Osimo 12,034 D3
Ostia Antica 2,583 F7
Ostuni 27,241 F4
Otranto 3,707 G4
Ozieri 9,149 B4
Pachino 20,427 E6
Padua 210,950 C2
Palazzolo Acreide 8,981 E6
Palermo 556,374 D5
Palestrina 9,239 F7
Palma di Montechiaro 22,381 D6
Palmi 14,405 E5
Palombara Sabina 5,292 F6
Pantelleria 3,116 C6
Paola 11,330 E5
Parma 151,967 C2
Partanna 10,303 D6
Partinico 25,447 D6
Paterno 41,504 E6
Patti 7,500 E5
Pavia 80,639 B2
Pavullo nel Frignano 5,026 C2
Penne 5,889 D3
Pergine Valsugana 6,248 C1
Pergola 3,866 D3
Perugia 65,975 D3
Pesaro 72,104 D3
Pescara 125,391 E3
Pescia 9,918 C3
Piacenza 100,001 B2
Piazza Armerina 21,754 E6
Pietrasanta 6,620 B3
Pinerolo 33,935 A2
Piombino 35,641 C3
Piove di Sacco 7,035 C2
Pisa 91,156 C3
Pisticci 11,239 F4
Pistoia 55,403 C2
Poggibonsi 21,271 C3
Pomezia 11,915 F7
Pont Canavese 4,075 A2
Pontecorvo 5,986 D4
Pontinia 3,166 D4
Pontremoli 5,222 B2
Popoli 5,372 E3
Pordenone 43,230 D2
Portocivitanova 25,773 D3
Porto Empedocle 15,986 D6
Portoferraio 7,579 C3
Portofino 720 B2
Portogruaro 12,258 D2
Portomaggiore 6,343 C2
Porto Recanati 5,389 D3
Porto Torres 15,422 B4
Potenza 46,869 E4
Pozzallo 12,199 E6
Pozzuoli 53,546 D4
Prato 108,385 C3
Prima Porta 11,393 F6
Priverno 9,950 D4
Putignano 19,290 F4
Quartu Sant'Elena 29,715 B5
Ragusa 55,751 E6
Rapallo 22,272 B2
Ravenna 75,153 D2
Recanati 10,176 D3
Reggio di Calabria 110,291 E5
Reggio nell'Emilia 102,337 C2
Rho 39,206 B2
Riesi 15,855 E6
Rieti 26,775 D3
Rimini 101,579 D2
Rionero in Vulture 11,230 E4
Riva del Garda 8,513 C2
Roccastrada 2,629 C3
Rome (cap.) 2,535,018 F6
Ronciglione 5,900 C3
Rossano 12,119 F5
Rovereto 26,827 C2
Rovigo 31,124 C2
Ruvo di Puglia 23,133 F4

(continued on following page)

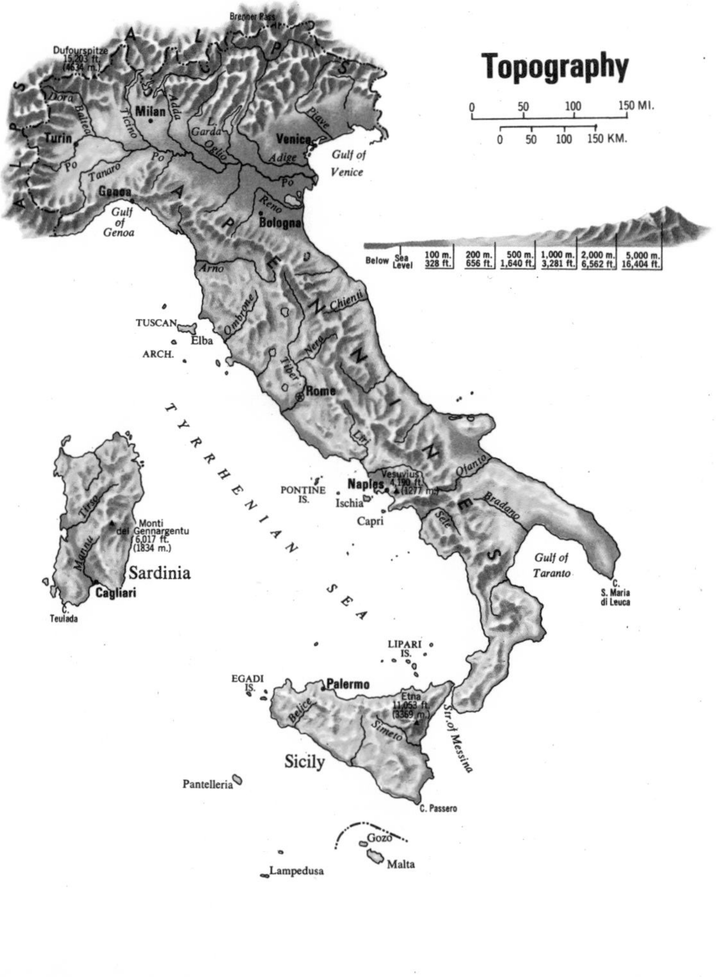

Agriculture, Industry and Resources

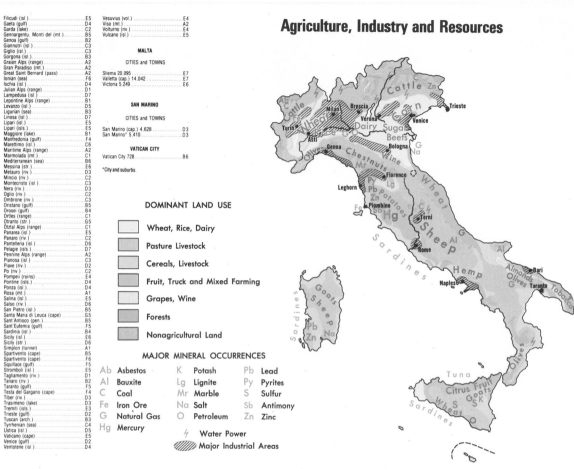

DOMINANT LAND USE

- Wheat, Rice, Dairy
- Pasture Livestock
- Cereals, Livestock
- Fruit, Truck and Mixed Farming
- Grapes, Wine
- Forests
- Nonagricultural Land

MAJOR MINERAL OCCURRENCES

Ab	Asbestos	K	Potash	Pb	Lead
Al	Bauxite	Lg	Lignite	Py	Pyrites
C	Coal	Mr	Marble	S	Sulfur
Fe	Iron Ore	Na	Salt	Sb	Antimony
G	Natural Gas	O	Petroleum	Zn	Zinc
Hg	Mercury				

Water Power

Major Industrial Areas

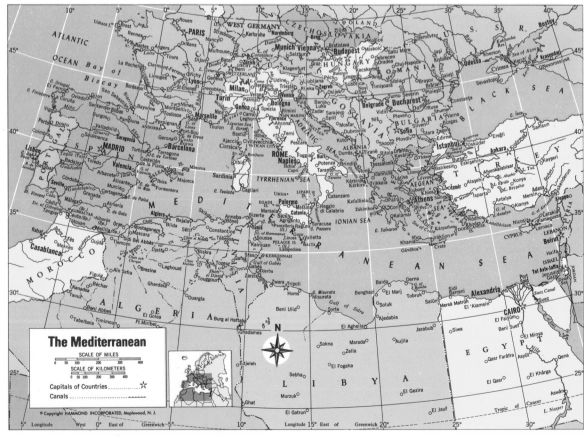

The Mediterranean

SCALE OF MILES
0 50 100 200 300 400

SCALE OF KILOMETERS
0 50 100 200 300 400

Capitals of Countries ....☆
Canals ....

© Copyright HAMMOND INCORPORATED, Maplewood, N.J.

SWITZERLAND

AREA 15,943 sq. mi. (41,292 sq. km.)
POPULATION 6,365,960
CAPITAL Bern
LARGEST CITY Zürich
HIGHEST POINT Dufourspitze
(Mte. Rosa) 15,203 ft. (4,634 m.)
MONETARY UNIT Swiss franc
MAJOR LANGUAGES German, French,
Italian, Romansch
MAJOR RELIGIONS Protestantism,
Roman Catholicism

LIECHTENSTEIN

AREA 61 sq. mi. (158 sq. km.)
POPULATION 25,220
CAPITAL Vaduz
LARGEST CITY Vaduz
HIGHEST POINT Grauspitze 8,527 ft.
(2,599 m.)
MONETARY UNIT Swiss franc
MAJOR LANGUAGE German
MAJOR RELIGION Roman Catholicism

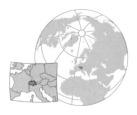

SWITZERLAND

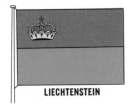

LIECHTENSTEIN

Languages

- German
- French
- Italian
- Romansch

Switzerland is a multilingual nation with four
official languages. 70% of the people speak
German, 19% French, 10% Italian and 1% Romansch.

SWITZERLAND

CANTONS

Aargau 442,400 .... F2
Appenzell, Ausser
Rhoden 46,700. .... H2
Appenzell, Inner Rhoden 13,500 .... H2
Baselland 219,500 .... E2
Baselstadt 209,700 .... E1
Bern 920,900. .... D2
Fribourg 181,600 .... D3
Geneva (Genève) 338,600 .... B4
Glarus 35,700 .... H3
Graubünden (Grisons) 164,300 ...... H3
Grisons (Graubünden) 164,300 ...... H3
Jura 67,200 .... D2
Lucerne (Luzern) 292,900 .... F2
Luzern 292,900 .... F2
Neuchâtel 162,200 .... F3
Nidwalden 26,900 .... G3
Obwalden 25,400 .... F3
Sankt Gallen 385,000 .... H2
Schaffhausen 69,300 .... G1
Schwyz 93,100 .... G2
Soleure (Solothurn) 221,800 .... E2
Solothurn 221,800 .... E2
Thurgau 183,500 .... H1
Ticino 264,400 .... G4
Uri 34,000 .... G3
Valais 214,000 .... D4
Vaud 523,500 .... B3
Zug 73,600 .... G2
Zürich 1,117,300 .... G2

CITIES and TOWNS

Aadorf 3,022 .... G2
Aarau 16,881 .... F2
Aarau* 51,800 .... F2
Aarberg 3,122 .... D2
Aarburg 5,943 .... E2
Adelboden 3,326 .... E3
Adliswil 15,920 .... F2
Aeschi bei Spiez 1,402 .... E3
Affoltern am Albis 7,363 .... F2
Affoltern im Emmental 1,223 ..... E2
Aigle 6,532 .... C4
Airolo 2,140 .... G3
Alle 1,615 .... D2
Allschwil 17,638 .... D1
Alpnach 3,277 .... F3
Altdorf 8,647 .... G3
Altstätten 9,084 .... J2
Amriswil 7,601 .... H1
Andelfingen 1,453 .... G1
Andermatt 1,589 .... G3
Appenzell 5,217 .... H2
Arbedo-Castione 2,456 .... G4
Arbon 12,227 .... H1
Arbon* 15,400 .... H1
Ardon 1,498 .... D4
Arosa 2,717 .... J3
Arth 7,580 .... F2
Ascona 4,086 .... G5
Attalens 1,116 .... C3
Au 4,944 .... J2
Aubonne 1,983 .... B4
Avenches 2,235 .... D3
Baar 14,074 .... F2
Baden 14,115 .... F2
Baden* 66,800 .... F2
Bad Ragaz 3,713 .... H2
Balerna 3,885 .... G5
Balsthal 5,607 .... E2
Bäretswil 2,733 .... G2
Basel 199,600 .... E1
Basel* 379,700 .... E1
Bassecourt 2,985 .... D2
Bätterkinden 1,757 .... E2
Bauma 3,159 .... G2
Beatenberg 1,263 .... E3
Beinwil am See 2,520 .... F2
Belfaux 1,075 .... D3
Bellinzona 16,979 .... H4
Bellinzona* 31,000 .... H4
Belp 6,981 .... D3
Berg 1,039 .... H1
Bern (cap.) 154,700 .... D3
Bern* 285,300 .... D3
Beromünster 1,552 .... F2
Bettlach 4,046 .... D2
Bex 5,069 .... D4
Biasca 4,696 .... H4
Biberist 7,769 .... D2
Biel 63,400 .... D2
Biel*89,900 .... D2
Bière 1,252 .... B3
Binningen 15,344 .... D1
Bischofszell 4,233 .... H1
Blumenstein 1,049 .... E3
Bodio 1,425 .... G4
Bolligen 26,121 .... E3
Boltigen 1,519 .... D3
Bonaduz 1,289 .... H3
Boncourt 1,528 .... D2
Bönigen 1,738 .... E3
Boswil 1,904 .... F2
Boudry 4,372 .... C3
Bourg Saint-Pierre 236 ... D5
Breil-Brigels 1,215 ...... H3
Breitenbach 2,455 .... E2
Bremgarten 4,873 .... F2
Brienz 2,796 .... F3
Brig 5,191 .... F4
Brissago 2,120 .... G4
Brittnau 2,888 .... E2
Broc 1,842 .... D3
Brugg 8,635 .... F2
Brusio 1,344 .... K4
Bubendorf 2,070 .... E2
Bubikon 3,244 .... G2
Buchs 8,454 .... H2
Bülach 11,043 .... G1
Bulle 7,556 .... D3
Buochs 3,232 .... F3
Büren an der Aare 3,085 .. D2
Burgdorf 15,888 .... E2
Burgdorf* 18,400 ...... E2
Bürglen, Thurgau 1,920 .. H1
Bürglen, Uri 3,401 .... G3
Bussigny-près-Lausanne 4,509 .. B3
Bütschwil 3,270 ...... H2
Carouge 14,055 .... B4
Castagnola 4,430 ..... G4
Cazis 1,687 .... H3
Cernier 1,717 .... C2
Chalais 1,651 .... E4
Cham 8,209 .... F2
Chamoson 2,049 ..... D4
Charmey 1,155 ...... D3
Château-d'Oex 3,203 .. D4
Châtel-Saint-Denis 2,842 .. C3
Chêne-Bougeries 8,670 .. B4
Chavornay 1,521 .... C3
Chexbres 1,607 ..... C3
Chiasso 8,868 ...... G5
Chippis 1,561 ...... E4
Chur 32,400 .... J3
Churwalden 1,052 .. J3
Claro 1,143 .... G4
Collombey-Muraz 2,279 .. C4
Collonge-Bellerive 3,541 .. B4
Conthey 4,259 ..... D4
Coppet 1,097 ...... B4
Corcelles-près-Payerne 1,256 .. C3
Corgémont 1,645 ... D2
Cossonay 1,529 .... B3
Courgenay 1,954 ... D2
Courrendlin 2,656 .. D2
Courroux 1,788 .... D2
Courtelary 1,462 .. D2
Courtételle 1,864 .. D2
Couvet 3,481 ..... C3
Cully 1,535 ...... C4
Davos 10,238 .... J3
Degersheim 3,400 .. H2
Delémont 11,797 .. D2
Derendingen 4,917 .. E2
Dielsdorf 2,691 .. F1
Diemtigen 1,913 .. D3
Diepoldsau 3,311 .. J2
Diessenhofen 2,532 .. G1
Dietikon 22,705 .. F2
Disentis-Mustér 2,319 .. G3
Domat-Ems 5,701 .. H3
Dombresson 1,109 .. C2
Dornach 5,258 .... E2
Döttingen 3,380 .. F1
Dübendorf 19,639 .. G2
Düdingen 4,932 ... D3
Dürnten 4,820 .... G2
Dürrenroth 1,084 .. E2
Ebnat-Kappel 5,131 .. H2
Echallens 1,643 .. C3
Ecublens 6,379 ... B3
Egg 5,250 ...... G2
Eggiwil 2,391 ... E3
Eglisau 2,160 ... G1
Egnach 3,466 .... H1

(continued on following page)

Agriculture, Industry and Resources

DOMINANT LAND USE

- Cereals, Dairy
- Pasture Livestock
- General Farming, Livestock
- Fruit, Truck, Mixed Farming
- Forests
- Nonagricultural Land

⚡ Water Power

Major Industrial Areas

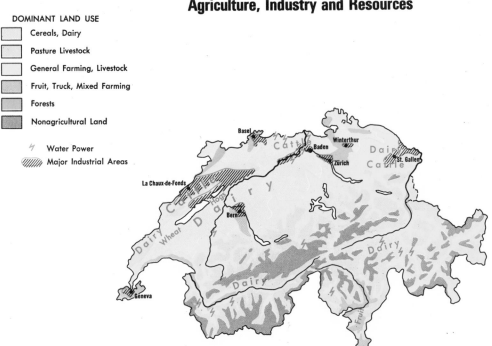

Topography

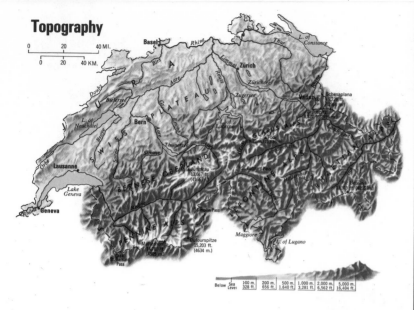

0   20   40 MI.
0   20   40 KM.

| Below Sea Level | 100 m. 328 ft. | 200 m. 656 ft. | 500 m. 1,640 ft. | 1,000 m. 3,281 ft. | 2,000 m. 6,562 ft. | 5,000 m. 16,404 ft. |

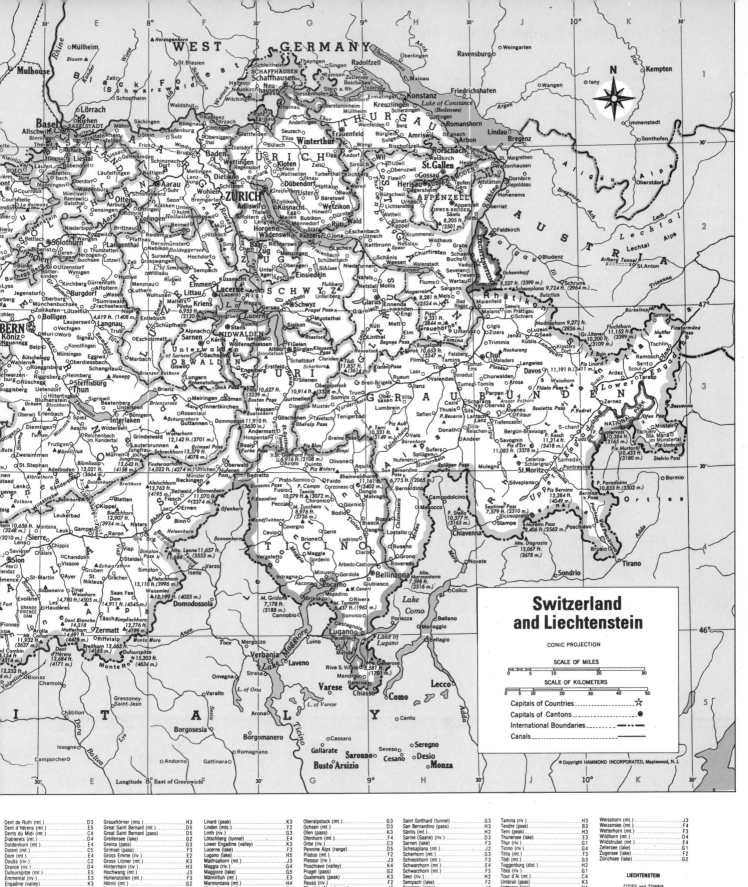

Switzerland and Liechtenstein

CONIC PROJECTION

SCALE OF MILES

0   5   10   20   30

SCALE OF KILOMETERS

0 5 10   20   30   40   50

Capitals of Countries .... ☆
Capitals of Cantons .... ◉
International Boundaries ....
Canals ....

© Copyright HAMMOND INCORPORATED, Maplewood, N.J.

Dent de Ruth (mt.) D3	Grauehörner (mts.) H3	Linard (peak) K3	Oberalpstock (mt.) G3	Saint Gotthard (tunnel) G3	Tamina (riv.) H3	Weisshorn (mt.) J3
Dent d'Hérens (mt.) E5	Great Saint Bernard (mts.) D5	Linden (mts.) F2	Ochsen (mt.) K3	San Bernardino (pass) H4	Tendre (peak) B3	Weissmies (mt.) F4
Dents du Midi (mt.) C4	Great Saint Bernard (pass) D5	Linth (riv.) G2	Ofen (pass) K3	Säntis (mt.) H2	Terri (mt.) H3	Wetterhorn (mt.) F3
Diablerets (mt.) D4	Greifensee (lake) G2	Lötschberg (tunnel) E4	Ofenhorn (mt.) F4	Sarine (Saane) (riv.) D3	Thunersee (lake) E3	Wildhorn (mt.) D4
Doldenhorn (mt.) E4	Greina (pass) G3	Lower Engadine (valley) K3	Orbe (riv.) C3	Sarnen (mt.) G1	Thur (riv.) G1	Wildstrubel (mt.) E4
Dolent (mt.) C5	Grimsel (pass) F3	Lucerne (lake) F3	Pennine Alps (range) D5	Schesaplana (mt.) J2	Ticino (riv.) G4	Zellersee (lake) G1
Dom (mt.) E4	Gross Emme (riv.) E2	Lugano (lake) H5	Pilatus (mt.) F3	Scherhorn (mt.) G3	Titlis (mt.) F3	Zugersee (lake) F2
Doubs (riv.) C2	Gross Litzner (mt.) K3	Madrisahorn (mt.) J3	Plessur (riv.) J3	Schreckhorn (mt.) F3	Tödi (mt.) G3	Zürichsee (lake) G2
Drance (riv.) C4	Hinterrhein (riv.) H3	Maggia (riv.) G4	Poschiavo (valley) K4	Schwarzhorn (mt.) E3	Toggenburg (dist.) H2	
Dufourspitze (mt.) E5	Hochwang (mt.) J3	Maggiore (lake) G5	Pragel (pass) G2	Schwarzhorn (mt.) F3	Toss (riv.) G1	**LIECHTENSTEIN**
Emmental (riv.) E3	Hohenstollen (mt.) F3	Männlifluh (mt.) E3	Quatervals (peak) K3	Seez (riv.) H2	Tour d'Aï (mt.) D4	
Engadine (valley) K3	Hörnli (mt.) G2	Marmontana (mt.) H4	Reuss (riv.) F2	Sempach (lake) E2	Umbrail (pass) K3	CITIES and TOWNS
Err (mt.) J3	Inn (riv.) K3	Matterhorn (mt.) E5	Rhaetian Alps (range) J3	Septimer (pass) J4	Untersee (lake) H1	
Finsteraarhorn (mt.) F3	Jorat (mt.) C3	Mauvoisin (dam) D4	Rhätikon (mts.) J2	Sesvenna (peak) K3	Unterwalden (reg.) F3	Schaan 4,552 .... H2
Finstermünz (pass) K3	Jungfrau (mt.) E3	Moësa (riv.) G4	Rheinwaldhorn (mt.) G4	Sihlsee (lake) G2	Upper Engadine (valley) J4	Triesen 2,971 .... H2
Fletschhorn (mt.) F4	Jura (mts.) B3	Morat (lake) C3	Rhine (riv.) G1	Silvretta (mts.) K3	Urirotstock (mt.) F3	Vaduz (cap.) 4,614 .... H2
Fluchthorn (mt.) K3	Kaisereg (mt.) D3	Mürg (riv.) G1	Rhône (riv.) D4	Simme (riv.) D3	Vadret (peak) J3	
Fluela (pass) J3	Kesch (peak) J3	Murtaröl (mt.) K3	Rigi (mt.) F2	Simplon (pass) F4	Valserrhein (riv.) H3	OTHER FEATURES
Furka (pass) F3	La Dôle (mt.) B4	Muttler (mt.) K3	Rimpfischhorn (mt.) E4	Simplon (tunnel) F4	Vanil Noir (mt.) D3	
Generoso (mt.) H5	Landquart (riv.) J3	Naafkopf (mt.) J2	Ringelspitz (mt.) H3	Sonnenhorn (mt.) F4	Vélan (mt.) D4	Grauspitz (mt.) J2
Geneva (lake) C4	Le Chasseral (mt.) C2	Napf (mt.) E2	Risoux (mt.) B3	Splügen (pass) H4	Visp (riv.) E4	Ochsenkopf (mt.) J2
Glärnisch (mt.) G2	Le Gros Crêt (mt.) B3	National Park K3	Rosa (mt.) E5	Stockhorn (mt.) E3	Vorab (mt.) H3	Rhätikon (mts.) J2
Glarus Alps (range) G3	Léman (Geneva) (lake) C4	Neuchâtel (lake) C3	Rosstock (mt.) G3	Sufzfluh (mt.) J3	Vorderrhein (riv.) G3	Rhine (riv.) J2
Grand Combin (mt.) D5	Leone (riv.) F4	Noirmont (mt.) B3	Rothorn (mt.) E4	Susten (pass) F3	Wandfluhhorn (mt.) G4	
Grande Dixence (dam) D4	Lepontine Alps (range) F2	Oberalp (pass) G3	Saane (Sarine) (riv.) D3	Sustenhorn (mt.) F3	Weissenstein (mt.) D2	*City and suburbs.
Grand Muveran (mt.) D4			Saint Gotthard (pass) G3	Tamaro (mt.) G4	Weissmies (mt.) E4	

AUSTRIA

PROVINCES

Burgenland 272,119 ....D3
Carinthia 525,728 ....B3
Lower Austria 1,414,161 ....C2
Salzburg 401,766 ....B3
Styria 1,192,442 ....C3
Tirol 540,771 ....A3
Upper Austria 1,223,444 ....B2
Vienna (city) 1,614,841 ....D2
Vorarlberg 271,473 ....A3

CITIES and TOWNS†

Admont 3,126 ....C3
Allentsteig 2,783 ....C2
Altheim 4,766 ....B2
Althofen 3,886 ....C3
Amstetten 13,330 ....C2
Andau 3,058 ....D3
Arnoldstein 6,740 ....B3
Aspang Markt 2,316 ....D3
Attnang-Puchheim 7,837 ....B2
Bad Aussee 5,039 ....C3
Baden 22,631 ....D2
Badgastein 5,228 ....B3
Bad Goisern 6,360 ....B3
Bad Hofgastein 5,525 ....B3
Bad Ischl 12,740 ....B3
Bad Leonfelden 2,712 ....C2
Bad Sankt-Leonhard im
   Lavanttal 4,882 ....C3
Berndorf 8,371 ....D2
Bischofshofen 9,417 ....B3
Bludenz 12,050 ....A3
Bramberg am Wildspiegel 3,129 ....B3
Braunau am Inn 16,432 ....B2
Bregenz 22,839 ....A3
Bruck an der Leitha 7,506 ....D2
Bruck an der Mur 16,359 ....C3
Deutsch Feistritz 3,820 ....C3
Deutschkreutz 3,673 ....D3
Deutsch Landsberg 6,614 ....C3
Deutsch Wagram 4,481 ....D2
Dornbirn 33,810 ....A3
Eberharth 2,272 ....D3
Ebensee 9,413 ....B3
Eferding 3,014 ....B2
Eggenburg 3,730 ....C2
Ehrwald 2,198 ....A3

Horn 6,264 ....C2
Hüttenberg 3,251 ....C3
Imst 5,855 ....A3
Innsbruck 115,800 ....A3
Innsbruck* 167,200 ....A3
Jenbach 5,868 ....A3
Jennersdorf 4,210 ....C3
Judenburg 11,346 ....C3
Kapfenberg 26,001 ....C3
Kappl 2,156 ....A3
Kaprun 2,604 ....B3
Kindberg 6,128 ....C3
Kirchdorf an der Krems 3,471 ....C3
Kitzbühel 7,995 ....B3
Klagenfurt 74,326 ....C3
Klagenfurt* 112,600 ....C3
Klosterneuburg 21,912 ....D2
Knittelfeld 14,517 ....C3
Koflach 12,612 ....C3
Königswiesen 2,921 ....C2
Kornenburg 8,892 ....C2
Kössen 2,764 ....B3
Kötschach-Mauthen 3,740 ....B3
Krems an der Donau 21,733 ....C2
Kufstein 12,766 ....A3
Kundl 3,020 ....A3
Laa an der Thaya 5,455 ....D2
Laakirchen 7,664 ....B3
Lambach 3,401 ....B2
Landeck 7,388 ....A3
Langenfeld 2,838 ....A3
Langenlois 4,957 ....C2
Langenwang 4,071 ....C3
Lavamünd 4,120 ....C3
Leibnitz 6,646 ....C3
Lenzing 5,385 ....B3
Leoben 35,153 ....C3
Lienz 11,696 ....B3
Liezen 6,244 ....C3
Lilienfeld 3,126 ....C3
Linz 205,700 ....C2
Linz* 356,500 ....C2
Lustenau 15,239 ....A3
Mannersdorf am
   Leithagebirge 4,012 ....D3
Marcheg 2,678 ....D2
Mariazell 2,298 ....C3
Matrei in Osttirol 4,003 ....B3
Mattersburg 5,417 ....D3
Mattighofen 4,344 ....B2
Mauerkirchen 2,237 ....B2
Mautern in Steiermark 2,536 ....C3

Sankt Valentin 8,715 ....C2
Sankt Veit an der Glan 11,047 ....C3
Sankt Wolfgang im
   Salzkammergut 2,746 ....B3
Schärding 5,874 ....B2
Scheibbs 4,419 ....C2
Schladming 3,460 ....B3
Schrams 3,393 ....A3
Schruns 3,607 ....A3
Schwarzach im Pongau 3,616 ....B3
Schwaz 10,253 ....A3
Schwechat 14,997 ....D2
Schwertberg 3,881 ....C2
Sierning 8,162 ....C2
Sillian 1,988 ....B3
Solbad Hall in Tirol 12,335 ....A3
Spittal an der Drau 13,690 ....B3
Spital am Pyhrn 2,315 ....C3
Steinach 2,698 ....A3
Steyr 40,578 ....C2
Stockerau 12,634 ....C2
Strassburg 2,850 ....C3
Tamsweg 5,060 ....B3
Telfs 6,589 ....A3
Ternitz 10,287 ....D3
Traiskirchen 8,878 ....D2
Traun 20,843 ....C2
Trieben 4,639 ....C3
Trofaiach 8,731 ....C3
Tulln 7,705 ....C2
Velden am Wörthersee 7,306 ....C3
Vienna (cap.) 1,700,000 ....D2
Vienna* 1,858,700 ....D2
Villach 50,979 ....B3
Vöcklabruck 10,627 ....B2
Voitsberg 11,094 ....C3
Völkermark 10,772 ....C3
Vordernberg 2,508 ....C3
Waidhofen an der Thaya 4,200 ....C2
Waidhofen an der Ybbs 5,218 ....C2
Weitensfeld-Flattnitz 5,206 ....B3
Weitra 3,250 ....C2
Weiz 8,241 ....C3
Weit 47,279 ....C2
Weyer Markt 2,518 ....C2
Wien (Vienna) (cap.) 1,700,000 ....D2
Wiener Neustadt 34,774 ....D3
Wildon 2,002 ....C3
Wilhelmsburg 6,307 ....C2
Wolfberg 31,176 ....C3
Wörgl 7,811 ....A3
Ybbs an der Donau 6,422 ....C2

Zams 3,120 ....A3
Zell am See 7,456 ....B3
Zell am Ziller 1,882 ....A3
Zeltweg 8,431 ....C3
Zirl 4,157 ....A3
Zistersdorf 3,412 ....D2
Zwettl-Niederösterreich 11,624 ....C2

OTHER FEATURES

AllgÄu Alps (mts.) A3
Bavarian Alps (mts.) A3
Bodensee (Constance) (lake) A3
Brenner (pass) A3
Carnic Alps (mts.) B3
Constance (lake) A3
Danube (riv.) C2
Donau (Danube) (riv.) C2
Drau (riv.) B3
Drava (riv.) C3
Enns (riv.) C3
Grossglockner (mt.) B3
Hohe Tauern (range) B3
Inn (riv.) A3
Karawanken (range) C3
March (riv.) D2
Mühlviertel (reg.) C2
Mur (riv.) C3
Neusiedler See (lake) D3
Niedere Tauern (range) B3
Ötztal Alps (mts.) A3
Raab (riv.) C3
Rhine (riv.) A3
Salzach (riv.) B2
Salzkammergut (reg.) B3
Semmering (pass) C3
Thaya (riv.) C2
Traun (riv.) C2
Wildspitze (mt.) A3
Zugspitze (mt.) A3

CZECHOSLOVAKIA

REPUBLICS

Czech Socialist Rep. 9,964,338 ....B1
Slovak Socialist Rep. 4,670,409 ....E2

REGIONS

Bratislava 333,000 ....D2
Jihočeský 662,002 ....C2
Jihomoravský 1,966,850 ....D2
Praha (city) 1,161,200 ....C1

Severočeský 1,122,035 ....C1
Severomoravský 1,849,286 ....D2
Středočeský 1,193,041 ....C2
Středoslovenský 1,436,351 ....E2
Východočeský 1,214,581 ....C1
Východoslovenský 1,298,481 ....F2
Západočeský 865,094 ....C2
Západoslovenské 1,610,542 ....D2

CITIES and TOWNS

Aš 120,000 ....B1
Austerlitz (Slavkov) E2
Bánovce nad Bebravou 11,400 ....E2
Banská Bystrica 53,000 ....E2
Banská Štiavnica 7,486 ....E2
Bardejov 14,800 ....F2
Benešov 11,100 ....C2
Beroun 17,600 ....B2
Bílina 17,800 ....C1
Blansko 13,800 ....D2
Boskovice 8,531 ....D2
Brandýs nad Labem-Stará
   Boleslav 333,000 ....C1
Bratislava 333,000 ....D2
Břeclav 21,100 ....D2
Brezno 14,800 ....E2
Brno 335,700 ....D2
Broumov 7,782 ....D1
Bruntál 12,300 ....D2
Bystřice nad
   Pernštejnem 6,471 ....D2
Bystřice pod
   Hostýnem 6,681 ....D2
Bytča 6,922 ....C1

Čadca 16,800 ....E2
Čálovo 6,591 ....D3
Čáslav 10,200 ....C2
Česká Lípa 18,600 ....C1
Česká Třebová 14,700 ....D2
České Budějovice 80,800 ....C2
Český Brod 6,640 ....C2
Český Krumlov 12,000 ....C2
Český Těšín 17,200 ....E2
Cheb 27,000 ....B1
Chocen̆ 8,198 ....D1
Chodov 14,400 ....B1
Chomutov 44,200 ....B1
Chotěboř 6,692 ....C2
Chrudim 18,800 ....C2
Čierny Balog 6,435 ....E2
Děčín 46,500 ....C1
Detva 13,100 ....E2
Dobříš 6,378 ....C2
Dobruška 5,779 ....D1
Dolný Kubín 9,900 ....E2
Domažlice 9,100 ....B2
Dubnica nad Váhom 11,300 ....E2
Duchcov 9,712 ....B1
Dunajská Streda 13,000 ....D3
Dvory nad Žitavou 5,847 ....E3
Dvě Králové nad
   Labem 16,300 ....D1
Falknov (Sokolov) 23,900 ....B1
Fil'akovo 7,800 ....E2
Frenštát pod
   Radhoštěm 8,516 ....E2
Frýdek-Místek 43,800 ....E2
Frýdlant v. C1

Frýdlant nad
   Ostravicí 6,250 ....E2
Galanta 12,300 ....D3
Goldwaldov 84,300 ....D2
Handlová 16,200 ....E2
Havířov 85,800 ....E2
Havličkův Brod 19,200 ....C2
Hlinsko 8,890 ....C2
Hlohovec 15,200 ....D2
Hluĉín 15,300 ....E2
Hnúšt'a-Likier E2
Hodonín 22,600 ....D2
Holešov 9,091 ....D2
Holič 7,602 ....D2
Holice 6,151 ....C2
Horažd'ovice C2
Horice v
   Podkrkonoší 7,715 ....C1
Horná Štubňa E2
Horní Benešov D1
Horní Líbina D1
Hořovice 5,665 ....C2
Horšovský Týn B2
Hostinné C1
Hradec Králové 85,600 ....C1
Hranice 13,300 ....D2
Hrínova 7,800 ....E2
Hronov 9,767 ....D1
Hrušovany C2
Humenné 22,200 ....F2
Humpolec 7,810 ....C2
Hurbanovo E3
Ilava D2
Ivančice 7,314 ....D2

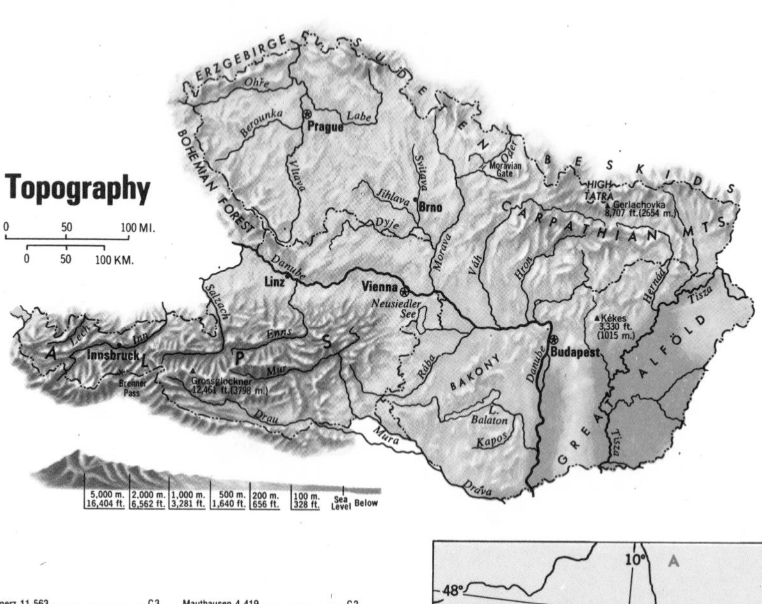

Eisenerz 11,563 ....C3
Eisenkappel-Vellach 3,761 ....C3
Eisenstadt 10,059 ....D3
Enns 9,622 ....C2
Feldbach 3,887 ....C3
Feldkirch 21,214 ....A3
Feldkirchen in
   Kärnten 11,188 ....B3
Ferlach 7,621 ....C3
Feldbach 3,651 ....C3
Fohsdorf 11,169 ....C3
Frankenmarkt 2,960 ....B2
Frauenkirchen 2,749 ....D3
Freistadt 5,956 ....C2
Freidberg 2,504 ....C3
Friesach 7,257 ....C3
Frohnleiten 5,081 ....C3
Fulpmes 2,553 ....A3
Fürstenfeld 6,054 ....C3
Gaming 4,181 ....C2
Gänserndorf 4,211 ....D2
Gleisdorf 4,921 ....C3
Gloggnitz 7,078 ....C3
Gmünd, Carinthia 2,267 ....B3
Gmünd, Lower Austria 6,323 ....C2
Gmunden 12,270 ....B3
Golling an der Salzach 3,089 ....B3
Götzis 7,931 ....A3
Gratwein 2,747 ....C3
Graz 251,900 ....C3
Graz* 314,200 ....C3
Grein 2,767 ....C2
f21Grieskirchen 4,519 ....B2
Grossgleigharts 3,288 ....C2
Grünburg 3,775 ....C2
Güssing 3,803 ....D3
Haag 5,060 ....C2
Hainburg an der Donau 6,009 ....D2
Hainfeld 3,897 ....C2
Hallein 14,371 ....B3
Hallstatt 1,303 ....B3
Hartberg 5,702 ....C3
Haslach an der Mühl 2,636 ....C2
Heidenreichstein 4,340 ....C2
Heiligenblut 1,308 ....B3
Hermagor-Presseggersee 7,531 ....B3
Herzogenburg 7,299 ....C2
Hohenau an der March 3,591 ....D2
Honenberg 2,016 ....C3
Hohenems 11,487 ....A3
Hollabrunn 6,563 ....C2
Hopfgarten in Nordtirol 4,784 ....B3

Mauthausen 4,419 ....C2
Mauthen-Kötschach 3,750 ....B3
Mayrhofen 3,174 ....A3
Melk 5,108 ....C2
Mistelbach an der Zaya 6,306 ....D2
Mittersill 4,361 ....B3
Mödling 18,712 ....D2
Mondsee 2,141 ....B3
Murau 2,710 ....C3
Mürzzuschlag 11,564 ....C3
Neuberg an der Mürz 2,183 ....C3
Neumarkt am Wallersee 3,267 ....B3
Neunkirchen 10,922 ....C3
Neusiedl am See 3,999 ....D3
Neustift im Stubaital 2,789 ....A3
Ober Grafendorf 4,109 ....C2
Oberndorf bei Salzburg 3,293 ....B3
Obervellach 2,420 ....B3
Oberwart 5,661 ....D3
Paternion 5,805 ....B3
Perg 4,872 ....C2
Peuerbach 2,161 ....B2
Pfunds 2,043 ....A3
Pinkafeld 4,610 ....C3
Pöchlarn 3,199 ....C2
Pörtschach am
   Wörthersee 2,511 ....C3
Poysdorf 5,772 ....D2
Pregarten 3,249 ....C2
Raabs an der Thaya 4,194 ....C2
Radenthein 6,847 ....B3
Radkersburg 2,000 ....C3
Radstadt 3,585 ....B3
Rankweil 8,440 ....A3
Rechnitz 3,412 ....D3
Reichenau an der Rax 4,053 ....C3
Retz 4,780 ....C2
Ried im Innkreis 10,534 ....B2
Rottenmann 4,781 ....C3
Saalfelden am Steinernen
   Meer 10,172 ....B3
Salzburg 122,100 ....B3
Salzburg* 213,430 ....B3
Sankt Aegyt am Neuwalde 3,165 ....C3
Sankt Anton am Arlberg 2,086 ....A3
Sankt Johann in Tirol 5,942 ....A3
Sankt Michael im Lungau 2,839 ....C3
Sankt Michael im
   Oberstdermark 3,717 ....C3
Sankt Michael im Lungau 2,839 ....C3
Sankt Paul im Lavanttal 6,721 ....C3
Sankt Pölten 43,300 ....C2

Topography

0   50   100 MI.

0   50   100 KM.

5,000 m. · 2,000 m. · 1,000 m. · 500 m. · 200 m. · 100 m. · Sea
16,404 ft. · 6,562 ft. · 3,281 ft. · 1,640 ft. · 656 ft. · 328 ft. · Level · Below

AREA 32,375 sq. mi. (83,851 sq. km.)
POPULATION 7,507,000
CAPITAL Vienna
LARGEST CITY Vienna
HIGHEST POINT Grossglockner 12,457 ft. (3,797 m.)
MONETARY UNIT schilling
MAJOR LANGUAGE German
MAJOR RELIGION Roman Catholicism

AREA 49,373 sq. mi. (127,876 sq. km.)
POPULATION 15,276,799
CAPITAL Prague
LARGEST CITY Prague
HIGHEST POINT Gerlachovka 8,707 ft. (2,654 m.)
MONETARY UNIT koruna
MAJOR LANGUAGES Czech, Slovak
MAJOR RELIGIONS Roman Catholicism, Protestantism

AREA 35,919 sq. mi. (93,030 sq. km.)
POPULATION 10,709,536
CAPITAL Budapest
LARGEST CITY Budapest
HIGHEST POINT Kékes 3,330 ft. (1,015 m.)
MONETARY UNIT forint
MAJOR LANGUAGE Hungarian
MAJOR RELIGIONS Roman Catholicism, Protestantism

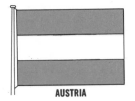

AUSTRIA

CZECHOSLOVAKIA

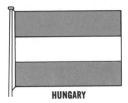

HUNGARY

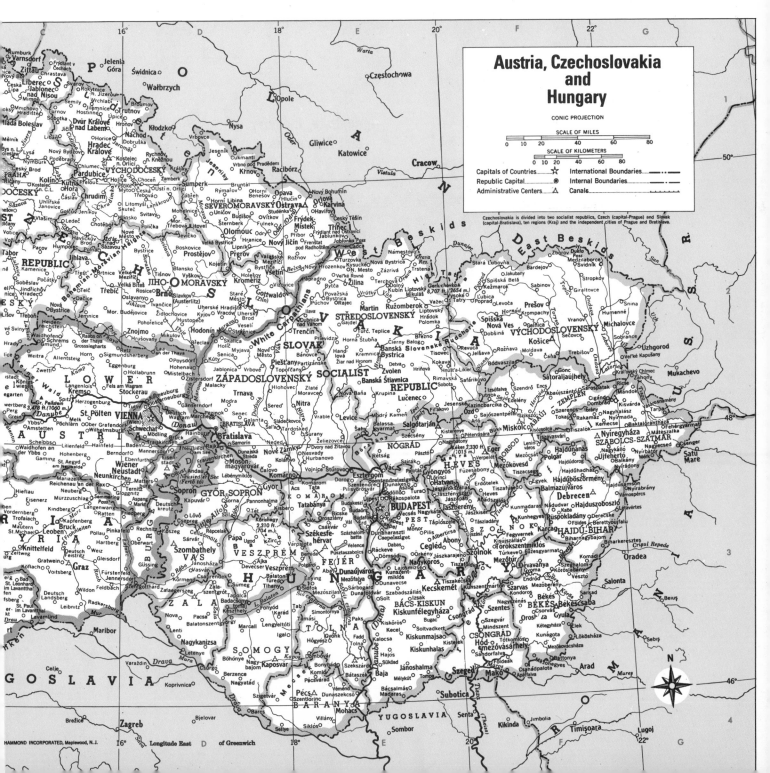

Austria, Czechoslovakia and Hungary

CONIC PROJECTION

SCALE OF MILES
0 10 20   40   60   80

SCALE OF KILOMETERS
0 10 20   40   60   80

Capitals of Countries................☆   International Boundaries........
Republic Capital.........................◉   Internal Boundaries...............
Administrative Centers..............△   Canals......................................

Czechoslovakia is divided into two socialist republics, Czech (capital-Prague) and Slovak (capital-Bratislava), ten regions (Kraj) and the independent cities of Prague and Bratislava.

40 Austria, Czechoslovakia and Hungary

(continued)

Jablonec nad Nisou 36,300 ... C1
Jablonica ... D2
Jablunkov 9,405 ... E2
Jáchymov ... B1
Jakubany ... F2
Jaroměř 11,600 ... C1
Jelšava ... F2
Jemnice ... C2
Jeseník 10,900 ... D1
Jesenské ... F2
Jevíčko ... D2
Jičín 13,200 ... C1
Jihlava 44,500 ... C2
Jilemnice ... C1
Jindřichův Hradec 15,700 ... C2
Jiřkov 11,400 ... B1
Kadaň 18,100 ... B1
Kamenice ... C2
Kaplice ... C2
Karlovy Vary 43,300 ... B1
Karviná 79,100 ... E2
Kdyně ... B2
Kežmarok 11,000 ... F2
Kladno 61,200 ... B1
Klatovy 18,500 ... B2
Kojetín 5,852 ... D2
Kokava nad Rimavicou 5,391 ... E2
Kolárovo 10,500 ... D3
Kolín 29,100 ... C1
Komárno 28,200 ... D3
Košice 169,100 ... F2
Kostelec nad Orlicí 5,575 ... D1
Kráľovský Chlmec 5,329 ... G2
Kralupy nad Vltavou 16,900 ... C1
Kraslice 6,733 ... B1
Kremnica 5,941 ... E2
Krnov 25,000 ... D1
Kroměříž 23,200 ... D2
Krompachy 6,332 ... F2
Krupina 6,627 ... E2
Krupka 8,301 ... B1
Kutná Hora 19,200 ... C2
Kyjov 10,700 ... D2
Kynšperk 5,524 ... B1
Kysucké Nové Mesto 11,700 ... E2
Lanškroun 8,683 ... D2
Levice 19,000 ... E2
Levoča 10,100 ... F2
Libáň ... C1
Liberec 75,600 ... C1
Lidice ... C1
Lipník nad Bečvou 7,358 ... D2
Liptovský Mikuláš 19,400 ... E2
Litoměřice 19,700 ... C1
Litomyšl 8,112 ... D2
Litovel 5,805 ... D2
Litvínov 23,300 ... B1
Lomnice ... C2
Louny 15,200 ... B1
Lovosice 9,323 ... C1
Ľubica ... F2
Lučenec 23,300 ... E2
Lysá nad Labem 9,920 ... C1
Malacky 13,200 ... D2
Mariánské Lázně 14,600 ... B2
Martin 47,800 ... E2
Medzilaborce ... F2
Mělník 17,800 ... C1
Michalovce 23,600 ... G2
Mikulov 6,267 ... D2
Milevsko 7,091 ... C2
Mimoň 6,773 ... C1
Mladá Boleslav 36,900 ... C1
Mladá Vožice ... C2
Mnichovo Hradiště 5,239 ... C1
Modra 7,219 ... D2
Modrý Kameň 6,200 ... E2
Mohelnice 6,050 ... D2
Moldava nad Bodvou 5,397 ... F2
Moravská Třebová 9,052 ... D2
Moravské Budějovice 5,576 ... D2
Most 59,400 ... B1
Myjava 6,657 ... D2
Náchod 19,300 ... D1
Námestovo ... E2
Neded ... D2
Nejdek 8,187 ... B1
Nepomuk ... B2
Nesvady 5,453 ... E3
Netolice ... C2
Nitra 50,000 ... E2
Nová Baňa 6,218 ... E2
Nová Bystrica ... E2
Nová Bystřice ... C2
Nové Hrady ... C2
Nové Město na Moravě 6,581 ... D2
Nové Město nad Váhom 15,900 ... D2
Nové Strašecí ... B1
Nové Zámky 27,300 ... D3
Nový Bohumín 16,700 ... E2
Nový Bor 7,621 ... C1
Nový Bydžov 6,824 ... C1
Nový Hrozenkov ... E2
Nový Jičín 21,400 ... E2
Nymburk 13,600 ... C1
Nýřany 6,204 ... B2
Nýrsko ... B2
Odry ... D2
Olomouc 82,800 ... D2
Opava 53,800 ... E2
Orlová 25,500 ... E2
Ostrava 293,500 ... E2
Ostrov 18,200 ... B1
Pardubice 78,500 ... C1
Partizánske 15,100 ... E2
Pelhřimov 11,900 ... C2
Pezinok 13,100 ... D2
Piešťany 25,400 ... D2
Písek 25,100 ... C2
Plzeň 155,000 ... B2
Počátky ... C2
Podbořany ... B1
Poděbrady 13,400 ... C1
Pohořelice ... D2
Polička 6,529 ... D2
Polná ... C2
Polomka ... E2
Poprad 25,800 ... F2
Považská Bystrica 19,300 ... E2
Prachatice 7,900 ... B2
Prague (Praha) (cap.) 1,161,200 ... C1
Přelouč 6,251 ... C1
Přerov 43,500 ... D2
Prešov 61,000 ... F2
Přeštice ... B2
Příbor 7,726 ... E2
Příbram 31,300 ... B2
Prievidza 30,900 ... E2
Prostějov 44,200 ... D2
Protivín ... C2
Púchov 9,306 ... E2
Radnice ... B2
Rajec ... E2
Rakovník 14,200 ... B1
Revúca 5,901 ... F2
Říčany u Prahy 8,407 ... C2
Rimavská Sobota 5,800 ... E2
Rokycany 12,800 ... B2
Rokytnice nad Jizerou ... C1
Rosice ... D2
Roudnice nad Labem 11,800 ... C1
Rožňava 12,400 ... F2
Rožnov pod Radhoštěm 11,600 ... E2
Rumburk ... C1
Ružomberok 22,600 ... E2
Rychnov nad Kněžnou 7,500 ... D1
Rýmařov 7,522 ... D2
Sabinov 5,473 ... F2
Šafárikovo ... F2
Šahy 5,049 ... E2
Šaľa 15,200 ... D2
Šamorín 8,287 ... D2
Sečovce 5,744 ... F2
Sedlčany ... C2
Semily 8,200 ... C1
Senec 8,544 ... D2
Senica 12,300 ... D2
Sereď 12,500 ... D2
Skalica 11,100 ... D2
Skuteč ... D2
Sládečkovce 5,598 ... D2
Slaný 13,200 ... C1
Slavkov ... D2
Snina 10,900 ... G2
Soběslav 6,140 ... C2
Sobotka ... C1
Sobrance ... G2
Sokolov 23,900 ... B1
Spišská Belá ... F2
Spišská Nová Ves 26,100 ... F2
Stará Ľubovňa 5,800 ... F2
Staré Město 6,293 ... D2
Šternberk 13,700 ... D2
Stod ... B2
Strakonice 19,000 ... B2
Strážnice 5,482 ... D2
Stříbro ... B2
Stropkov 5,645 ... F2
Studénka 9,744 ... D2
Štúrovo 8,287 ... E3
Šumperk 25,900 ... D1
Šurany 6,693 ... E2
Sušice 10,300 ... B2
Svárov ... C1
Svidník 4,600 ... F2
Svitavy 15,000 ... D2
Tábor 28,100 ... C2
Tachov 11,400 ... B2
Telč 5,285 ... C2
Teplice 52,300 ... B1
Tišnov 8,263 ... D2
Topoľčany 17,500 ... D2
Třebíč 23,900 ... C2
Trebišov 13,700 ... F2
Třeboň 6,068 ... C2
Trenčín 38,800 ... E2
Třešť 5,053 ... C2
Třinec 32,000 ... E2
Trnava 48,600 ... D2
Trutnov 24,500 ... D1
Turnov 13,600 ... C1
Turzovka 6,107 ... E2
Uherské Hradiště 32,100 ... D2
Uherský Brod 12,800 ... D2
Uničov 10,800 ... D2
Úpice 6,323 ... C1
Ústí nad Labem 74,900 ... C1
Ústí nad Orlicí 13,700 ... D2
Valašské Meziříčí 19,400 ... D2
Varnsdorf 14,700 ... C1
Važec ... E2
Vejprty ... B1
Velká Bíteš ... D2
Velká Bystřice ... D2
Veľké Kapušany ... G2
Velké Meziříčí 7,590 ... D2
Veľké Rovné ... E2
Veselí nad Lužnicí ... C2
Veselí nad Moravou 11,500 ... D2
Vimperk 5,749 ... B2
Vítkov 5,138 ... D2
Vizovice ... D2
Vlašim 8,873 ... C2
Vodňany 5,620 ... C2
Vojnice ... E3
Volary ... B2
Volyně ... B2
Votice ... C2
Vráble ... E2
Vracov ... D2
Vranov nad Teplou 14,700 ... F2
Vrbno pod Pradědem 5,594 ... D1
Vrbovce ... D1
Vrbové ... D2
Vrchlabí 11,700 ... C1
Vrútky 5,756 ... E2
Vsetín 24,100 ... D2
Vyškov 15,100 ... D2
Vysoké Mýto 8,830 ... D2
Vysoké Tatry ... F2
Vyšší Brod ... C2
Zábřeh 11,300 ... D2
Žamberk 5,040 ... D1
Žatec 17,400 ... B1
Zázrivá ... E2
Zbiroh ... B2
Zborov ... F2
Žďár nad Sázavou 17,800 ... C2
Želiezovce 5,478 ... E2
Žiar nad Hronom 14,800 ... E2
Židlochovice ... D2
Žilina 56,000 ... E2
Zlaté Moravce 10,300 ... E2
Zlín (Gottwaldov) 84,300 ... D2
Žlutice ... B1
Znojmo 28,500 ... D2
Zvolen 29,000 ... E2

OTHER FEATURES

Berounka (riv.) ... C2
Beskids, East (mts.) ... F1
Beskids, West (mts.) ... E2
Bohemian (for.) ... B2
Bohemian-Moravian Heights (hills) ... C2
Danube (riv.) ... C2
Dunajec (riv.) ... F2
Dyje (riv.) ... D2
Erzgebirge (mts.) ... B1
Gerlachovka (mt.) ... E2
Hornád (riv.) ... F2
Hron (riv.) ... E2
Ipeľ (riv.) ... E2
Jablunka (pass) ... E2
Jeseníky (mts.) ... D1
Jihlava (riv.) ... D2
Krušné Hory (Erzgebirge) (mts.) ... B1
Labe (riv.) ... C1
Lipno (res.) ... C2
Lužnice (riv.) ... C2
Moldau (Vltava) (riv.) ... C2
Morava (riv.) ... D2
Nitra (riv.) ... E2
Oder (Odra) (riv.) ... D2
Ohře (riv.) ... B1
Ondava (riv.) ... F2
Orava (riv.) ... E2
Orlická (res.) ... C2
Sázava (riv.) ... C2
Slovenské Rudohorie (mts.) ... E2
Sudeten (mts.) ... C1
Svitava (riv.) ... D2
Svratka (riv.) ... D2
Tatra, High (mts.) ... E2
Torysa (riv.) ... F2
Úhlava (riv.) ... B2
Váh (riv.) ... D2
Vltava (riv.) ... C2
White Carpathians (mts.) ... E2

HUNGARY

COUNTIES

Bács-Kiskun 568,532 ... E3
Baranya 434,030 ... E4
Békés 436,987 ... F3
Borsod-Abaúj-Zemplén 808,924 ... F2
Budapest (city) 2,060,170 ... E3
Csongrád 456,862 ... F3
Fejér 421,568 ... E3
Győr-Sopron 428,476 ... D3
Hajdú-Bihar 552,417 ... F3
Heves 350,874 ... F3
Komárom 321,579 ... E3
Nógrád 239,907 ... E3
Pest 973,486 ... E3
Somogy 360,308 ... D3
Szabolcs-Szatmár 593,746 ... G3
Szolnok 446,379 ... F3
Tolna 266,414 ... E3
Vas 285,527 ... D3
Veszprém 386,740 ... D3
Zala 316,610 ... D3

CITIES and TOWNS

Aba 4,271 ... E3
Abádszalók 6,386 ... F3
Abaújszántó 4,209 ... F2
Abony 15,624 ... E3
Ács 8,423 ... E3
Ajka 29,601 ... D3
Albertirsa 11,252 ... E3
Alsózsolca 5,045 ... F2
Arló 4,203 ... F2
Aszód 6,218 ... E3
Bácsalmás 9,025 ... E3
Badacsonytomaj 2,933 ... D3
Baja 38,456 ... E3
Baktalórántháza 3,736 ... G2
Balassagyarmat 18,534 ... E2
Balatonfüred 12,599 ... D3
Balkány 7,667 ... G3
Balmazújváros 17,371 ... F3
Barcs 11,448 ... D4
Bátaszék 7,274 ... E3
Battonya 9,324 ... F3
Békés 22,287 ... F3
Békéscsaba 67,266 ... F3
Berettyóújfalu 16,406 ... F3
Berzence 3,406 ... D3
Bicske 10,720 ... E3
Biharkeresztes 4,788 ... F3
Biharnagybajom 4,093 ... F3
Böhönye 3,215 ... D3
Bonyhád 14,841 ... E3
Budafok 40,623 ... E3
Budaörs 13,958 ... E3
Budakeszi 10,429 ... E3
Budapest (cap.) 2,060,170 ... E3
Bugak 4,989 ... E3
Cegléd 40,567 ... E3
Celldömölk 12,533 ... D3
Cigánd 4,767 ... F2
Csabrendek 3,045 ... D3
Csákvár 5,238 ... E3
Csanádpalota 4,642 ... F3
Csenger 4,792 ... G3
Csepel 71,693 ... E3
Csepreg 4,079 ... D3
Csongrád 22,202 ... E3
Csorna 12,131 ... D3
Csorvás 6,826 ... F3
Csurgó 5,463 ... D3
Dabas 13,075 ... E3
Debrecen 192,484 ... F3
Derecske 9,579 ... F3
Dévaványa 11,208 ... F3
Devecser 5,482 ... D3
Dombóvár 19,917 ... E3
Dombrád 6,328 ... F2
Dömsöd 6,545 ... E3
Dorog 10,754 ... E3
Dunaföldvár 10,318 ... E3
Dunaharaszti 15,788 ... E3
Dunakeszi 25,187 ... E3
Dunaszekcső 2,999 ... E3
Dunaújváros 60,694 ... E3
Dunavecse 4,521 ... E3
Edelény 9,559 ... F2
Eger 61,283 ... F3
Egyek 7,956 ... F3
Elek 6,032 ... F3
Enes 2,565 ... F2
Endrőd 8,136 ... F3
Enying 7,518 ... E3
Érd 41,210 ... E3
Erdőtelek 4,250 ... F3
Esztergom 30,476 ... E3
Fadd 4,805 ... E3
Fegyvernek 8,421 ... F3
Fehérgyarmat 6,729 ... G3
Földeák 3,855 ... F3
Földes 5,293 ... F2
Fonyód 3,957 ... D3
Füzesabony 6,965 ... F3
Füzesgyarmat 7,097 ... F3
Gödöllő 28,057 ... E3
Gönc 2,875 ... F2
Gyoma 10,392 ... F3
Gyöngyös 36,927 ... E3
Gyönk 2,507 ... E3
Győr 123,618 ... D3
Gyula 34,514 ... F3
Hajdúböszörmény 32,145 ... F3
Hajdúdorog 10,118 ... F3
Hajdúhadház 13,626 ... F3
Hajdúnánás 18,146 ... F3
Hajdúsámson 7,492 ... F3
Hajdúszoboszló 23,374 ... F3
Hajós 5,113 ... E3
Hatvan 24,790 ... E3
Heves 10,943 ... F3
Hódmezővásárhely 54,481 ... F3
Hőgyész 3,534 ... E3
Ibrány 7,037 ... F2
Izsák 7,686 ... E3
Izsófalva 6,816 ... F2
Jánoshalma 12,534 ... E3
Jánosháza 3,274 ... D3
Jászapáti 10,424 ... E3
Jászárokszállás 10,139 ... E3
Jászberény 31,347 ... E3
Jászfényszaru 6,869 ... E3
Jászkarajenő 4,101 ... E3
Jászkisér 6,816 ... F3
Jászladány 7,823 ... F3
Kaba 6,654 ... F2
Kalocsa 18,613 ... E3
Kaposvár 72,330 ... D3
Kapuvár 11,243 ... D3
Karád 2,754 ... D3
Karcag 25,264 ... F3
Kazincbarcika 37,481 ... F2
Kecel 10,493 ... E3
Kecskemét 91,929 ... E3
Kemecse 4,583 ... F2
Keszthely 21,671 ... D3
Kétegyháza 4,728 ... F3
Kisbér 4,562 ... D3
Kiskőrös 15,499 ... E3
Kiskunfélegyháza 35,339 ... E3
Kiskunhalas 30,552 ... E3
Kiskunmajsa 14,439 ... E3
Kispest 65,106 ... E3
Kistelek 8,544 ... E3
Kisterenye 6,844 ... E2
Kisújszállás 13,699 ... F3
Kisvárda 17,828 ... G2
Komádi 8,765 ... F3
Komárom 19,955 ... E3
Komló 30,301 ... E3
Kondoros 7,319 ... F3
Körmend 11,787 ... D3
Körösladány 6,565 ... F3
Kőszeg 12,705 ... D3
Kunágota 4,622 ... F3
Kunhegyes 10,116 ... F3
Kunmadaras 7,343 ... F3
Kunszentmárton 11,103 ... F3
Kunszentmiklós 7,952 ... E3
Lajosmizse 12,872 ... E3
Lébénymiklós 6,190 ... D3
Lengyeltóti 3,389 ... D3
Leninváros 18,667 ... F3
Lenti 8,106 ... D3
Létavértes 9,106 ... G3
Letenye 4,395 ... D3
Lökösháza 2,514 ... F3
Lőrinci 10,679 ... E3
Madaras 4,519 ... E3
Makó 29,943 ... F3
Mándok 5,093 ... G2
Marcali 12,485 ... D3
Mátészalka 17,709 ... G3
Mélykút 7,640 ... E3
Mérk 3,211 ... G3
Mezőberény 12,702 ... F3
Mezőcsát 6,729 ... F3
Mezőfalva 5,008 ... E3
Mezőhegyes 8,631 ... F3
Mezőkovácsháza 7,473 ... F3
Mezőkövesd 18,435 ... F3
Mezőszilas 2,792 ... E3
Mezőtúr 22,018 ... F3
Mindszent 8,730 ... F3
Miskolc 206,727 ... F2
Mohács 21,385 ... E4
Monor 16,838 ... E3
Mór 12,066 ... E3
Mosonmagyaróvár 29,732 ... D3
Nádudvar 9,447 ... F3
Nagyatád 12,946 ... D3
Nagybajom 4,402 ... D3
Nagyecsed 8,225 ... G3
Nagyhalász 6,437 ... F2
Nagykálló 11,282 ... F3
Nagykanizsa 48,494 ... D3
Nagykáta 11,922 ... E3
Nagykőrös 27,900 ... E3
Nagyszénás 7,124 ... F3
Nyírábrány 4,509 ... G3
Nyíradony 7,146 ... G3
Nyírbátor 13,388 ... G3
Nyíregyháza 108,156 ... F3
Nyírmada 4,744 ... F2
Örkény 5,013 ... E3
Orosháza 36,243 ... F3
Oroszlány 20,604 ... E3
Ózd 48,521 ... F2
Pacsa 1,984 ... D3
Paks 19,514 ... E3
Pannonhalma 3,731 ... D3
Pápa 32,202 ... D3
Pásztó 7,962 ... E3
Pécs 168,788 ... E3
Pécsvárad 3,672 ... E3
Pétervására 2,753 ... F3
Pilis 9,055 ... E3
Pilisvörösvár 10,217 ... E3
Polgár 9,429 ... F3
Polgárdi 5,767 ... E3
Püspökladány 15,730 ... F3
Pusztaszabolcs 5,794 ... E3
Putnok 7,103 ... F2
Ráckeve 7,534 ... E3
Rajka 2,448 ... D3
Rakamaz 5,407 ... F2
Rákospalota 60,983 ... E3
Répcelak 1,997 ... D3
Ricse 2,992 ... G2
Sajószentpéter 13,992 ... F2
Salgótarján 49,320 ... E2
Sándorfalva 5,949 ... F3
Sárbogárd 11,178 ... E3
Sarkad 11,937 ... F3
Sárospatak 15,316 ... F2
Sárvár 15,126 ... D3
Sátoraljaújhely 19,252 ... F2
Sellye 2,804 ... D4
Siklós 10,567 ... E4
Simontornya 4,892 ... E3
Siófok 20,084 ... E3
Solt 6,911 ... E3
Soltvadkert 7,934 ... E3
Sopron 53,930 ... D3
Sükösd 4,430 ... E3
Sümeg 6,229 ... D3
Szabadszállás 8,223 ... E3
Szarvas 20,598 ... F3
Szécsény 5,690 ... E2
Százhalombatta 13,963 ... E3
Szeged 171,342 ... E3
Szeghalom 9,736 ... F3
Szegvár 6,395 ... F3
Székesfehérvár 103,197 ... E3
Szekszárd 34,592 ... E3
Szendrő 4,098 ... F2
Szentendre 16,844 ... E3
Szentes 35,326 ... F3
Szentgotthárd 5,837 ... D3
Szentlőrinc 3,926 ... E3
Szerencs 8,612 ... F2
Szigetvár 12,114 ... D3
Szikszó 6,419 ... F2
Szil 2,073 ... D3
Szolnok 75,203 ... F3
Szombathely 82,830 ... D3
Tab 3,922 ... E3
Tamási 7,602 ... E3
Tápiószele 5,575 ... E3
Tapolca 17,161 ... D3
Tarpa 3,436 ... G2
Tata 24,114 ... E3
Tatabánya 75,942 ... E3
Tét 4,441 ... D3
Tiszacsege 6,263 ... F3
Tiszaföldvár 12,560 ... F3
Tiszafüred 12,259 ... F3
Tiszakécske 12,378 ... E3
Tiszalök 6,230 ... F2
Tiszavasvári 13,292 ... F3
Tokaj 4,845 ... F2
Tolna 8,997 ... E3
Tompa 5,365 ... E3
Törökszentmiklós 25,551 ... F3
Tótkomlós 8,803 ... F3
Tura 8,235 ... E3
Túrkeve 11,393 ... F3
Újfehértó 14,412 ... F3
Újpest 80,384 ... E3
Újszász 7,098 ... F2
Vác 34,837 ... E3
Vál 2,488 ... E3
Vámospércs 5,213 ... F3
Várpalota 28,293 ... E3
Vásárosnamény 8,637 ... G2
Vasvár 4,275 ... D3
Vecsés 19,193 ... E3
Velence 3,463 ... E3
Véménd 2,293 ... E3
Verpelét 4,622 ... F2
Veszprém 54,898 ... D3
Vésztő 9,815 ... F3
Villány 2,764 ... E4
Záhony 3,049 ... G2
Zalaegerszeg 39,671 ... D3
Zalaszentgrót 5,346 ... D3
Zirc 5,980 ... D3

OTHER FEATURES

Bakony (mts.) ... D3
Balaton (lake) ... D3
Berettyó (riv.) ... F3
Bükk (mts.) ... F2
Csepelsziget (isl.) ... E3
Danube (riv.) ... E3
Dráva (riv.) ... D3
Duna (Danube) (riv.) ... E3
Fertő tó (Neusiedler See) (lake) ... D3
Great Alföld (plain) ... F3
Hernád (riv.) ... F2
Kapos (riv.) ... D3
Kékes (mt.) ... E3
Körös (riv.) ... F3
Maros (riv.) ... F3
Mátra (mts.) ... E3
Mecsek (mts.) ... D3
Mura (riv.) ... D3
Rába (riv.) ... D3
Sajó (riv.) ... F2
Sárviz csatorna (canal) ... E3
Sió csatorna (canal) ... E3
Szentendreisziget (isl.) ... E3
Tisza (riv.) ... F3
Zala (riv.) ... D3

*City and suburbs.
†Population of Austrian cities are communes.

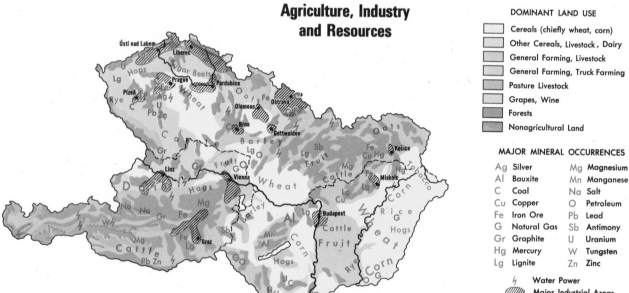

Agriculture, Industry and Resources

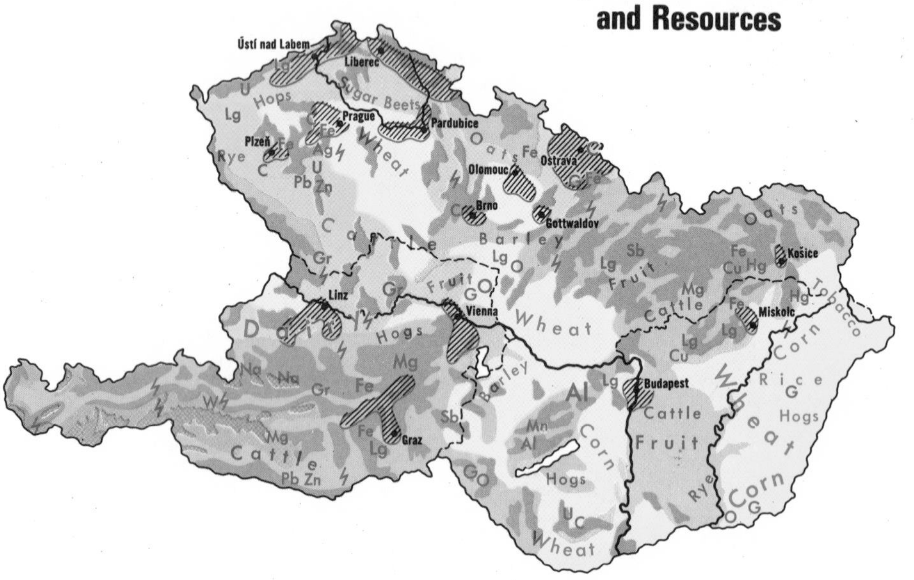

DOMINANT LAND USE

Cereals (chiefly wheat, corn)
Other Cereals, Livestock, Dairy
General Farming, Livestock
General Farming, Truck Farming
Pasture Livestock
Grapes, Wine
Forests
Nonagricultural Land

MAJOR MINERAL OCCURRENCES

Ag Silver
Al Bauxite
C Coal
Cu Copper
Fe Iron Ore
G Natural Gas
Gr Graphite
Hg Mercury
Lg Lignite
Mg Magnesium
Mn Manganese
Na Salt
O Petroleum
Pb Lead
Sb Antimony
U Uranium
W Tungsten
Zn Zinc

Water Power
Major Industrial Areas

YUGOSLAVIA

AREA 98,766 sq. mi. (255,804 sq. km.)
POPULATION 22,471,000
CAPITAL Belgrade
LARGEST CITY Belgrade
HIGHEST POINT Triglav 9,393 ft. (2,863 m.)
MONETARY UNIT Yugoslav dinar
MAJOR LANGUAGES Serbo-Croatian, Slovenian, Macedonian, Montenegrin, Albanian
MAJOR RELIGIONS Eastern Orthodoxy, Roman Catholicism, Islam

ALBANIA

AREA 11,100 sq. mi. (28,749 sq. km.)
POPULATION 2,590,600
CAPITAL Tiranë
LARGEST CITY Tiranë
HIGHEST POINT Korab 9,026 ft. (2,751 m.)
MONETARY UNIT lek
MAJOR LANGUAGE Albanian
MAJOR RELIGIONS Islam, Eastern Orthodoxy, Roman Catholicism

ROMANIA

AREA 91,699 sq. mi. (237,500 sq. km.)
POPULATION 22,048,305
CAPITAL Bucharest
LARGEST CITY Bucharest
HIGHEST POINT Moldoveanul 8,343 ft. (2,543 m.)
MONETARY UNIT leu
MAJOR LANGUAGES Romanian, Hungarian
MAJOR RELIGION Eastern Orthodoxy

BULGARIA

AREA 42,823 sq. mi. (110,912 sq. km.)
POPULATION 8,862,000
CAPITAL Sofia
LARGEST CITY Sofia
HIGHEST POINT Musala 9,597 ft. (2,925 m.)
MONETARY UNIT lev
MAJOR LANGUAGE Bulgarian
MAJOR RELIGION Eastern Orthodoxy

GREECE

AREA 50,944 sq. mi. (131,945 sq. km.)
POPULATION 9,599,000
CAPITAL Athens
LARGEST CITY Athens
HIGHEST POINT Olympus 9,570 ft. (2,917 m.)
MONETARY UNIT drachma
MAJOR LANGUAGE Greek
MAJOR RELIGION Eastern (Greek) Orthodoxy

BULGARIA

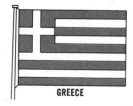

GREECE

YUGOSLAVIA

ALBANIA

ROMANIA

Agriculture, Industry and Resources

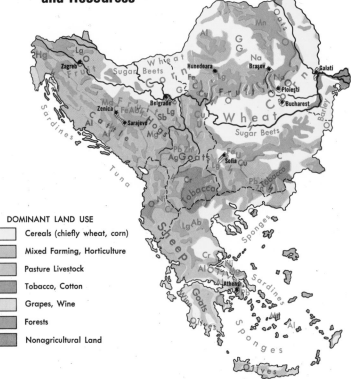

DOMINANT LAND USE

- Cereals (chiefly wheat, corn)
- Mixed Farming, Horticulture
- Pasture Livestock
- Tobacco, Cotton
- Grapes, Wine
- Forests
- Nonagricultural Land

MAJOR MINERAL OCCURRENCES

Ab	Asbestos	Mg	Magnesium
Ag	Silver	Mn	Manganese
Al	Bauxite	Mr	Marble
C	Coal	Na	Salt
Cr	Chromium	Ni	Nickel
Cu	Copper	O	Petroleum
Fe	Iron Ore	Pb	Lead
G	Natural Gas	Sb	Antimony
Hg	Mercury	U	Uranium
Lg	Lignite	Zn	Zinc

⚡ Water Power
▨ Major Industrial Areas

ALBANIA

CITIES and TOWNS

Berat 25,700	D5
Corovode	D5
Burrel	D5
Delvinë 6,000	D6
Durrës (Durazzo) 53,800	D5
Elbasan 41,700	E5
Ersekë	E5
Fier 23,000	D5
Gjirokastër 17,100	D5
Kavajë 18,700	D5
Korçë 47,300	E5
Krujë 7,900	D5
Kuçovë (Stalin) 14,000	D5
Kukës 6,100	E4
Leskovik	E5
Lezhë	D5
Lushnje 18,900	D5
Memaliaj	D5
Peqin	D5
Përmet	E5
Peshkopi 6,600	E5
Pogradec 10,100	E5
Pukë	E4
Sarandë 8,700	E6
Shëngjin	D5
Shijak 6,200	D5
Shkodër 55,300	D5
Stalin 14,000	D5
Tepelenë	D5
Tiranë (Tirana) (cap.) 171,300	E5
Vlorë 50,000	D5

OTHER FEATURES

Adriatic (sea)	B4
Drin (riv.)	E4
Korab (mt.)	E5
Ohrid (lake)	E5
Otranto (str.)	D5
Prespa (lake)	E5
Sazan (isl.)	D5
Scutari (lake)	D4
Vijosë (riv.)	D5

BULGARIA

CITIES and TOWNS

Akhtopol 938	H4
Alfatar 3,249	H4
Ardino 5,080	G5
Asenovgrad 43,049	G5
Aytos 20,967	H4
Balchik 11,070	J4
Bansko 10,011	F5
Belogradchik 6,892	F4
Berkovitsa 16,253	F4
Blagoevgrad 50,043	F5
Botevgrad 17,789	F4
Bregovo 5,567	F3
Breznik 4,699	F4
Burgas 144,449	H4
Byala 10,564	H4
Byala Slatina 15,788	F4
Chirpan 20,595	G4
Devin 7,120	G5
Dimitrovgrad 45,596	G4
Dobrich (Tolbukhin) 86,184	H4
Dryanovo 9,804	G4
Elena 7,008	H4
Elin Pelin 5,499	F4
Elkhovo 12,397	H4
Gabrovo 75,034	G4
General-Toshevo 8,928	H4
Godech 5,225	F4
Gorna Oryakhovitsa 34,157	G4
Gotse Delchev 17,015	F5
Grudovo 9,871	H4
Ikhtiman 11,482	F4
Isperikh 10,500	H4
Ivaylovgrad 3,900	H5
Karapelit	H4
Karlovo 25,472	G4
Karnobat 21,480	H4
Kavarna 10,872	J4
Kazanlŭk 53,607	G4
Kharmanli 19,240	H5
Khaskovo 75,031	G5
Kotel 8,229	H4
Krumovgrad 5,211	G5
Kubrat 9,826	H4
Kula 5,667	F4
Kŭrdzhali 47,757	G5
Kyustendil 48,239	F4
Lom 30,538	F4
Lovech 43,858	G4
Lukovit 10,400	G4
Malko Tŭrnovo 4,233	H4
Maritsa 8,664	H4
Michurin 4,434	H4
Mikhaylovgrad 40,064	F4
Momchilgrad 8,185	G5
Nesebŭr 6,768	H4
Nikopol 5,563	G4
Nova Zagora 21,872	H4
Novi Pazar 15,751	H4
Omurtag 9,067	H4
Oryakhovo 14,012	F4
Panagyurishte 20,649	F4
Pazardzhik 65,577	F4
Pernik 87,432	F4
Peshtera 16,882	G4
Petrich 24,381	F5
Pirdop 8,248	G4
Pleven 107,567	G4
Plovdiv 300,242	G4
Pomorie 11,960	H4
Popina	H3
Popovo 19,428	H4
Provadiya 15,143	H4
Radomir 10,436	F4
Razgrad 42,486	H4
Razlog 13,690	F5
Roistsa	H4
Ruse 160,351	H4
Samokov 25,763	F4
Sandanski 19,003	F5
Sevlievo 24,421	G4
Shabla 4,471	J4
Shumen 83,525	H4
Silistra 58,270	H3
Simeonovgrad (Maritsa) 8,664	G4
Sliven 90,137	H4
Smolyan 29,032	G5
Smyadovo 5,020	H4
Sofia (cap.) 965,728	F4
Sozopol 3,877	H4
Stanke Dimitrov 42,034	F4
Stara Zagora 122,200	G4
Svilengrad 15,143	G5
Svishtov 29,412	G4
Teteven 12,555	G4
Tolbukhin 86,184	H4
Topolovgrad 7,230	H4
Troyan 23,692	G4
Trŭn 3,435	F4
Tŭrgovishte 38,796	H4
Tutrakan 11,447	H4
Varna 251,654	J4
Veliko Tŭrnovo 56,497	G4
Vidin 53,030	F4
Vratsa 61,265	F4
Yambol 75,861	H4
Zimnitsa	H4
Zlatograd 7,732	G5

OTHER FEATURES

Balkan (mts.)	G4
Black (sea)	J4
Danube (riv.)	H4
Dunav (Danube) (riv.)	J4
Emine (cape)	H4
Iskŭr (riv.)	F4
Kaliakra (cape)	J4
Maritsa (riv.)	G5
Mesta (riv.)	F5
Midzhur (mt.)	F4
Musala (mt.)	F4
Osŭm (riv.)	G4
Rhodope (mts.)	G5
Rujen (mt.)	F4
Struma (riv.)	F5
Timok (riv.)	F3
Tundzha (riv.)	G4
Vit (riv.)	G4

GREECE

REGIONS

Aegean Islands 417,813	G6
Athens, Greater 2,566,775	F7
Áyion Óros (aut. dist.) 1,732	G5
Central Greece and Euboea 966,543	F6
Crete 456,642	G8
Epirus 310,334	E6
Ionian Islands 184,443	E6
Macedonia 1,888,952	F5
Peloponnisos 986,912	F7
Thessaly 659,913	F6
Thrace 329,582	G5

CITIES and TOWNS

Agrínion 30,973	E6
Aíyina 5,704	F7
Aíyion 18,829	F6
Alexandroúpolis 22,995	H5
Alivérion 4,414	G6
Almirós 5,680	F6
Amaliás 14,177	E7
Amfíklokhla 4,668	E6
Amfissa 6,605	F6
Andíssa 1,762	H6
Andravídha 3,046	E6
Ándros 1,827	G7
Áno Viánnos 1,431	G8
Anóyia 2,750	G8
Ardhéa 3,555	F5
Areópolis 674	F7
Argalastí 1,621	F6
Árgos 18,890	F7
Argostólion 7,060	E6
Arkhángelos 3,016	J7
Árnala 2,424	F5
Árta 19,498	E6
Astipálaia 787	H7
Athénai 4,581	F6
Athens (cap.) 867,023	F7
Athens* 2,566,775	F7
Ayíá 3,241	F6
Áyios Kírikos 1,083	H7
Áyios Matthaíos 1,596	D6
Áyios Nikólaos 5,002	G8
Candia (Iráklion) 77,506	G8
Canea (Khaniá) 40,564	G8
Corinth 20,773	F7
Delfí 1,185	F6
Delvinákion 1,067	E6
Dhidhimótikhon 8,388	H5
Dhíkaia 1,222	H5
Dhimitsána 996	F7
Dhomokós 1,971	F6
Dráma 29,692	F5
Édhessa 13,967	F5
Elassón 7,200	F6
Elevtheroúpolis 4,888	G5
Ermoúpolis 13,502	G7
Fársala 6,967	F6
Filiátes 2,579	E6
Filiatrá 5,919	E7
Fílippís 3,248	G5
Flórina 11,164	E5
Gargaliánoi 5,888	E7
Grevená 8,106	F5
Ídhra 2,381	F7
Ierápetra 7,055	G8
Igoumenítsa 4,109	E6
Ioánnina 40,130	E6
Íos 1,270	G7
Iráklion 77,506	G8
Istiaía 4,059	F6
Itháki 2,293	E6
Kalámai 39,133	E7
Kalampáka 5,453	E6
Kalávrita 1,948	F6
Kálimnos 6,492	H7
Kándanos 403	F8
Kardhítsa 25,685	F6
Kariá 1,350	E6
Karlaí 301	G5
Kárlstos 3,550	G6
Kárpathos 1,363	H8
Karpenísion 4,414	E6
Kastéllion (Kíssamos) 2,996	F8
Kastéllion 1,152	G6
Kastoría 15,407	E5
Katákolon 690	E7
Kateríni 28,808	F5
Kavála 46,234	G5
Kéa 693	G7
Kérkira 28,630	D6
Khalkís 36,300	F6
Khaniá 40,564	G8
Khíos 24,084	G6
Khóra Sfakíon 246	G8
Kiáton 7,392	F7
Kilkís 10,538	F5
Kími 2,772	G6
Kiparissía 3,882	E7
Kíssamos 2,996	F8
Kíthira 349	F7
Komotiní 28,896	G5
Kónitsa 3,150	E5
Koropí 9,367	G7
Kos 7,828	H7
Kozáni 23,240	F5
Kranídhion 3,657	F7
Lagkadía 1,350	F7
Lamía 37,872	F6
Langadhás 6,707	F5
Langádhia	F7
Lárisa 72,336	F6
Lávrion 8,283	G7
Leonídhion 3,181	F7
Levádhia 15,445	F6
Levkás 6,818	E6
Liménária 1,507	G5

(continued on following page)

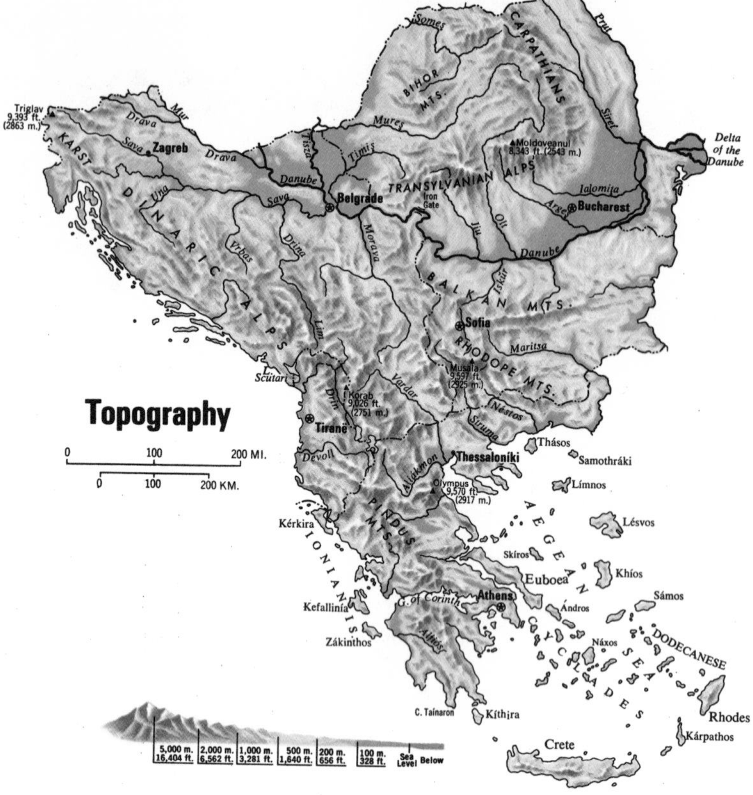
Topography
Triglav 9,393 ft. (2863 m.)
Mur
Drava
Sava
Zagreb
KARST
DINARIC ALPS
Una
Vrbas
Drina
Danube
Belgrade
Tisza
Mureș
Someș
BIHOR MTS.
CARPATHIANS
Prut
Siret
Delta of the Danube
Timiș
TRANSYLVANIAN ALPS
Iron Gate
Moldoveanul 8,343 ft. (2543 m.)
Ialomița
Argeș
Bucharest
Olt
Jiu
Morava
Iskur
BALKAN MTS.
Sofia
Maritsa
RHODOPE MTS.
Musala 9,597 ft. (2925 m.)
Lim
Scutari
Korab 9,026 ft. (2751 m.)
Drin
Tirane
Vardar
Néstos
Struma
Thásos
Samothráki
Thessaloníki
Aliákmon
Devoli
Olympus 9,570 ft. (2917 m.)
Límnos
Kérkira
PINDUS MTS.
IONIAN SEA
AEGEAN SEA
Lésvos
Skíros
Euboea
Khíos
Sámos
Kefallinía
G. of Corinth
Athens
Ándros
Zákinthos
Náxos
DODECANESE SEA
CYCLADES
C. Taínaron
Kíthira
Rhodes
Kárpathos
Crete
0 100 200 MI.
0 100 200 KM.
5,000 m. 16,404 ft.
2,000 m. 6,562 ft.
1,000 m. 3,281 ft.
500 m. 1,640 ft.
200 m. 656 ft.
100 m. 328 ft.
Sea Level
Below

Límni 2,394 F6
Líndos 700 J7
Litókhoron 5,561 F5
Lixoúrion 3,364 E6
Loutrá Aidhipsoú 2,195 F6
Marathón 1,976 G6
Megalópolis 3,357 E7
Mégara 17,294 F6
Meligalá 1,724 F7
Mesolóngion 11,614 E6
Messíni 6,625 E7
Métsovon 2,823 E6
Mikínai 390 F7
Mílos 850 G7
Mírina 3,982 G6
Míthimna 1,414 G6
Mitilíni 23,426 H6
Moírai 2,948 G8
Moláoi 2,484 F7
Monólithos 247 H7
Moúdhros 1,024 G6
Náousa 17,375 F5
Návpaktos 8,170 F6
Návplion 9,281 F7
Náxos 2,892 G7
Neápolis 3,070 F7
Neméa 4,356 F7
Néon Karlóvasi 4,401 H7
Nestórion 1,143 E5
Nigríta 7,301 F5
Oinói 188 F6
Orestías 10,727 H5
Paramithía 2,747 E6
Pátrai 111,607 E6
Pérdika 1,198 E6
Péta 2,116 E6
Pílos 2,258 E7
Piraiévs (Piraeus) 187,362 F7
Pírgos 20,599 E7
Piryí 1,455 G6
Píthion 1,047 H5
Plomárion 4,353 H6
Políkastron 5,279 F5
Políkhnitos 4,152 G6
Políyiros 3,707 F5
Póros 4,051 F7
Préveza 11,439 E6
Psakhná 4,650 F6
Psári 622 E7
Ptolemaís 16,588 E5
Réthimnon 14,969 G8
Rhodes (Ródhos) 32,092 J7
Salamís 18,256 F6
Salonika (Thessaloníki) 345,799 F5
Sámi 957 E6
Sámos 5,146 H7
Samothráki 508 G5
Sápai 2,456 G5
Sérrai 39,897 F5
Sérvia 3,834 F5
Siátista 4,852 E5
Sidhirókastron 6,363 F5
Sími 2,344 H7
Sitía 6,167 H8
Skíathos 3,707 F6
Skíros 1,925 G6
Skópelos 2,545 F6
Souflíon 5,637 H5
Sparta 10,549 F7
Spétsai 3,427 F7
Spíli 789 G8
Stavrós 1,700 F5
Stilís 4,427 F6
Thásos 2,052 G5
Thessaloníki 345,799 F5
Thessaloníki* 482,361 F5
Thíra 1,322 G7
Thívai 15,971 F6
Timbákion 3,229 G8
Tínos 3,423 G7
Tírnavos 10,451 F6
Tríkkala 34,794 E6
Trípolis 20,209 F7
Vámos 652 F8
Vartholomión 3,015 E7
Vathí 2,491 H7
Velvendós 4,063 F5
Vérroia 29,528 F5
Vólos 51,290 F6
Vónitsa 3,324 E6
Vrondádhes 4,253 G6
Xánthi 24,867 G5
Yerolimín 73 F7
Yiannitsá 18,151 F5
Yíthion 4,915 F7
Zákinthos 9,339 E7
Zante (Zákinthos) 9,339 E7

OTHER FEATURES

Aegean (sea) G6
Akrítas (cape) E7
Aktí (pen.) G5
Amorgós (isl.) G7
Anáfi (isl.) G7
Andikíthira (isl.) F8
Ándros (isl.) G7
Árda (riv.) G5
Argolís (gulf) F7
Astipálaia (isl.) H7
Áthos (mt.) G5
Áyios Evstrátios (isl.) G6
Áyios Yeóryios (cape) G5
Cephalonia (Kefallinía) (isl.) E6
Corfu (Kérkira) (isl.) D6
Corinth (gulf) F6
Crete (isl.) G8
Crete (sea) G7
Cyclades (isls.) G7
Día (isl.) G8
Dodecanese (isls.) H8
Euboea (Évvoia) (isl.) G6
Évros (riv.) H5
Évvoia (isl.) G6
Gávdhos (isl.) F8
Ídhi (mt.) G8
Ikaría (isl.) G7
Ionian (sea) D7
Íos (isl.) G7
Itháki (Ithaca) (isl.) E6
Kafirévs (cape) G6
Kálimnos (isl.) H7
Kárpathos (isl.) H8
Kásos (isl.) H8
Kassándra (pen.) F6
Kéa (isl.) G7
Kefallinía (isl.) E6
Kérkira (isl.) D6
Khálki (isl.) H7
Khaniá (gulf) G8
Khíos (isl.) G6
Kímolos (isl.) G7
Kiparissía (gulf) E7
Kíthira (isl.) F7
Kíthnos (isl.) G7
Kos (isl.) H7
Kriós (cape) F8
Kríti (Crete) (isl.) G8
Lakonía (gulf) F7
Léros (isl.) H7
Lésvos (isl.) G6
Levítha (isl.) H7
Levkás (isl.) E6
Límnos (isl.) G6
Maléa (cape) F7
Matapan (Taínaron) (cape) F7
Merabéllou (gulf) H8
Mesará (gulf) G8
Messíni (gulf) E7
Míkonos (isl.) G7
Mílos (isl.) G7
Mirtóön (sea) F7
Náxos (isl.) G7
Néstos (riv.) G5
Nísiros (isl.) H7
Northern Sporades (isls.) F6
Olympia (isls.) E7
Olympus (mt.) F5
Parnassus (mt.) F6
Páros (isl.) G7
Pátmos (isl.) H7
Paxoí (isl.) D6
Pindus (mts.) E6
Piniós (riv.) E6
Prespa (lake) E5
Psará (isl.) G6
Psevdhókavos (cape) G6
Rhodes (isl.) H7
Rhodope (mts.) G5
Salonika (Thermaic) (gulf) F6
Sámos (isl.) H7
Samothráki (isl.) G5
Saría (isl.) H8
Saronic (gulf) F7
Sérifos (isl.) G7
Sídheros (cape) H8
Sífnos (isl.) G7
Sími (isl.) H7
Síros (isl.) G7
Sithoniá (pen.) F5
Skíros (isl.) G6
Spátha (cape) F8
Strimón (gulf) G5
Strofádhes (isls.) E7
Taínaron (cape) F7
Thásos (isl.) G5
Thermaic (gulf) F6
Thíra (isl.) G7
Tílos (isl.) H7
Tínos (isl.) G7
Toronaic (gulf) F5
Vardar (riv.) E5
Voïvís (lake) F6
Vólvi (lake) F5
Voúxa (cape) F8
Zákinthos (Zante) (isl.) E7

ROMANIA

CITIES and TOWNS

Aiud 25,173 F2
Alba Iulia 44,552 F2
Alexandria 38,296 G3
Anina 11,594 E3
Arad 161,568 E2
Babadag 8,423 J3
Bacău 131,413 H2
Baia de Aramă 5,065 F3
Baia Mare 112,893 F2
Băile Herculane 4,606 F3
Băilești 21,246 F3
Balș 16,091 G3
Beiuș 9,992 F2
Berești Tîrg H2
Bicaz 9,490 G2
Bîrlad 59,059 H2
Bistrița 47,562 G2
Bivolari H2
Blaj 21,678 F2
Borșa 25,287 G2
Botoșani 69,881 H2
Brad 18,391 F2
Brăila 203,983 H3
Brașov 259,108 G3
Bucharest (București) (cap.) 1,832,015 G3
Bucharest* 1,960,097 G3
Buhuși 20,204 H2
Buzău 106,738 H3
Buziaș 8,310 E3
Calafat 16,421 F3
Călărași 58,960 H3
Caracal 31,159 G3
Caransebeș 27,429 F3
Carei 24,496 F2
Cernavodă 14,686 J3
Chișineu Criș 9,344 E2
Cîmpeni 7,722 F2
Cîmpia Turzii 23,745 F2
Cîmpina 33,259 H3
Cîmpulung 33,448 G3
Cîmpulung Moldovenesc 19,270 G2
Cisnădie 21,114 G3
Cluj-Napoca 274,095 F2
Cogealac J3
Comanești 18,177 H2
Constanța 279,308 J3
Corabia 20,454 G4
Costești 10,446 G3
Craiova 220,893 F3
Cujmir F3
Curtea de Argeș 23,555 G3
Dăbuleni F4
Dăeni J3
Darabani 12,207 H1
Dej 35,396 F2
Deta 6,956 E3
Deva 68,290 F3
Dorohoi 23,121 H2
Drăgănești Olt 11,606 G3
Drăgășani 16,290 F3
Drobeta-Turnu Severin 80,114 F3
Făgăraș 34,762 G3
Fălciu J2
Fălticeni 22,463 H2
Făurei 3,620 H3
Fetești 28,730 H3
Focșani 62,275 H3
Foltești H3
Găești 13,384 G3
Galați 252,884 H3
Gheorghe Gheorghiu-Dej 41,297 H2
Gheorghieni 20,592 G2
Gherla 19,303 G2
Giurgiu 53,241 G3
Hațeg 9,706 F3
Hîrlău 8,135 H2
Hîrșova 8,434 J3
Huedin 8,557 F2
Hunedoara 83,159 F3
Huși 24,329 J2
Iași 262,493 H2
Ineu 10,414 E2
Isaccea 5,283 J3
Jibou F2
Jimbolia 15,325 E3
Lipova 12,427 E2
Luduș 15,771 G2
Lugoj 48,558 F3
Lupeni 28,251 F3
Mangalia 27,263 J4
Medgidia 43,691 J3
Mediaș 68,442 G2
Miercurea Ciuc 38,097 G2
Mizil 14,294 H3
Mociu G2
Moinești 21,015 H2
Moldova Nouă 18,498 E3
Moreni 17,743 G3
Nădlac 8,407 E2
Năsăud 8,646 G2
Negrești 7,435 H2
Ocna Mureș 16,381 G2
Odobești 8,440 H3
Odorheiu Secuiesc 33,392 G2
Oltenița 25,536 H3
Oradea 175,400 E2
Orăștie 18,769 F3
Oravița 13,628 E3
Orșova 14,873 F3
Panciu 7,772 H3
Pașcani 26,937 H2
Pătulele F3
Pechea H3
Pecica E2
Periam E2
Petrila 25,087 F3
Petroșeni 42,316 F3
Piatra Neamț 84,192 G2
Pincota 7,494 E2
Pitești 125,029 G3
Plenița F3
Ploiești 207,009 H3
Poenari Burchi G3
Poiana Mare F4
Pucioasa 14,056 G3
Rădăuți 24,222 G2
Reghin 31,948 G2
Reșița 90,698 E3
Rîmnicu Sărat 29,815 H3
Rîmnicu Vîlcea 75,070 G3
Roman 56,466 H2
Roșiori de Vede 28,832 G3
Săcele 29,391 G3
Salonta 19,698 E2
Satu Mare 108,152 F2
Săveni 7,913 H1
Sebeș 27,448 F3
Sebiș 6,401 F2
Segarcea 8,783 F3
Sfîntu Gheorghe 51,210 G3
Sfîntu Gheorghe J3
Sibiu 156,854 G3
Sighetu Marmației 38,879 F2
Sighișoara 32,296 G2
Șimleul Silvaniei 14,780 F2
Sinaia 14,215 G3
Sînnicolaul Mare 13,565 E2
Siret 6,677 G1
Slănic 8,017 G3
Slatina 54,954 G3
Slobozia 35,207 H3
Solca 4,835 G2
Sovata 10,745 G2
Ștefănești H2
Strehaia 11,431 F3
Suceava 66,857 G2
Sulina 5,240 J3
Tășnad 10,441 F2
Techirghiol 11,228 J3
Tecuci 37,928 H3
Timișoara 281,320 E3
Tinca F2
Tîrgoviște 71,533 G3
Tîrgu Cărbunești 7,536 F3
Tîrgu Frumos 6,428 H2
Tîrgu Jiu 70,629 F3
Tîrgu Mureș 129,284 G2
Tîrgu Neamț 15,756 G2
Tîrgu Ocna 12,960 H2
Tîrgu Secuiesc 18,265 H2
Tîrnăveni 27,799 F2
Toplița 14,347 G2
Tulcea 67,091 J3
Turda 57,972 F2
Turnu Măgurele 30,003 G4
Urlața 10,900 H3
Urziceni 13,500 H3
Vasile Roaită J3
Vaslui 44,134 H2
Vatra Dornei 16,748 G2
Videle 11,323 G3
Vișeul de Sus 20,697 F2
Viziru H3
Zalău 36,158 F2
Zărnești 23,378 G3
Zimnicea 15,111 G4

OTHER FEATURES

Argeș (riv.) G3
Bîrlad (riv.) H2
Black (sea) J4
Brăila (marshes) H3
Buzău (riv.) H3
Carpathian (mts.) G2
Crișul Alb (riv.) F2
Crișul Repede (riv.) F2
Danube (delta) J3
Danube (riv.) H4
Ialomița (marshes) J3
Ialomița (riv.) H3
Jijia (riv.) H2
Jiu (riv.) F3
Moldoveanul (mt.) G3
Mureș (riv.) E2
Olt (riv.) G3
Peleaga (mt.) F3
Pietrosul (mt.) G2
Prut (riv.) J2
Siret (riv.) H2
Someș (riv.) F2
Timiș (riv.) E3
Tîrnava Mare (riv.) G2
Transylvanian Alps (mts.) G3

YUGOSLAVIA

INTERNAL DIVISIONS

Bosnia and Hercegovina (rep.) 3,710,965 C3
Croatia (rep.) 4,396,397 C3
Kosovo (aut. reg.) 1,240,919 E4
Macedonia (rep.) 1,623,598 E5
Montenegro (rep.) 527,207 D4
Serbia (rep.) 8,401,673 E3
Slovenia (rep.) 1,697,068 B2
Vojvodina (aut. prov.) 1,953,980 D3

CITIES and TOWNS

Aleksinac 11,943 E4
Apatin 17,501 D3
Arendjelovac 15,659 E3
Bačka Topola 16,028 D3
Bakar B3
Banja Luka 85,786 C3
Bar 3,594 D4
Bečej 26,616 E3
Bela Crkva 11,137 E3
Belgrade (cap.) 727,945 E3
Beli Manastir 7,325 D3
Beograd (Belgrade) (cap.) 727,945 E3
Berovo 5,053 F5
Bihać 24,155 B3
Bijeljina 24,888 D3
Bijelo Polje 9,298 D4
Bileća 4,083 D4
Biograd 3,595 B4
Bitola 64,467 E5
Bjelovar 21,019 C3
Blato 5,591 C4
Bled 4,710 A2
Bor 27,520 E3
Bosanska Dubica 9,191 C3
Bosanska Gradiška 9,742 C3
Bosanska Kostajnica 2,535 B3
Bosanska Krupa 8,947 C3
Bosanski Brod 10,113 D3
Bosanski Novi 9,861 C3
Bosanski Petrovac 4,113 C3
Bosanski Šamac 4,949 D3
Brčko 25,575 D3
Brežice 3,271 B3
Budva 2,483 D4
Bugojno 9,079 C3
Čačak 38,890 E4
Čakovec 11,766 C2
Čapljina 4,677 C4
Caribrod (Dimitrovgrad) 5,449 F4
Cazin 1,213 B3
Celje 30,827 B2
Cetinje 12,089 D4
Ćuprija 17,691 E4
Daruvar 8,478 C3
Debar 8,597 E5
Derventa 11,887 C3
Dimitrovgrad 5,449 F4
Djakovica 29,499 E4
Djakovo 15,833 D3
Doboj 18,073 C3
Donji Vakuf 4,928 C3
Drvar 6,237 C3
Dubrovnik 31,213 C4
Fiume (Rijeka) 128,883 B3
Foča 9,370 D4
Gacko 1,641 D4
Gevgelija 9,319 F5
Glamoč 2,627 C3
Gnjilane 21,359 E4
Gornji Milanovac 11,114 D3
Gornji Vakuf 2,429 C4
Gospić 8,238 B3
Gostivar 18,805 E5
Gračac 3,228 B3
Gračanica 9,302 D3
Gradačac 7,571 D3
Grubišno Polje 2,771 C3
Gusinje 2,616 D4
Herceg Novi 6,645 D4
Ivangrad 11,373 E4
Ivanjica 5,719 E4
Jajce 9,221 C3
Jesenice 16,163 A2
Kanjiža 11,348 D2
Karlovac 47,046 B3
Kavadarci 17,974 E5
Kičevo 14,189 E5
Kikinda 37,392 E3
Kladanj 3,255 D3
Ključ 3,466 C3
Knin 7,279 C3
Knjaževac 11,734 F4
Kočani 16,611 F5
Kočevje 7,277 B3
Kolašin 2,111 D4
Konjic 9,161 D4
Koper 16,683 A3
Koprivnica 16,398 C2
Kosovska Mitrovica 42,526 E4
Kostajnica 9,161 C3
Kotor 5,728 D4
Kragujevac 72,080 E3
Kraljevo 28,065 E4
Kranj 26,341 B2
Križevci 8,501 C2
Krk 1,500 B3
Krško 4,451 B3
Kruševac 29,902 E4
Kulen Vakuf 1,078 B3
Kumanovo 44,791 E4
Kutina 10,892 C3
Leskovac 46,050 E4
Livno 7,223 C4
Ljubinje 785 D4
Ljubljana 169,064 B3
Ljubuški 2,891 C4
Loznica 13,513 D3
Maglaj 5,869 D3
Makarska 6,589 C4
Maribor 94,976 B2
Modriča 7,406 D3
Mostar 47,821 D4
Murska Sobota 9,665 C2
Našice 5,836 C3
Negotin 11,325 F3
Nevesinje 3,077 D4
Nikšić 28,940 D4
Nin 1,782 B3
Niš 128,231 F4
Nova Gorizia A2
Nova Gradiška 11,765 C3
Novi 2,682 B3
Novi Pazar 28,696 E4
Novi Sad 143,591 D3
Novo Mesto 9,553 B3
Novska 5,168 C3
Ogulin 9,975 B3
Ohrid 26,352 E5
Omiš 3,515 C4
Opatija 9,238 A3
Osijek 94,989 D3
Pag 2,318 B3
Pančevo 53,979 E3
Paraćin 21,555 E4
Peć 41,783 E4
Petrinja 12,296 B3
Piran 5,485 A3
Pirot 29,658 F4
Plav 3,072 D4
Pljevlja 14,459 D4
Ploče 4,257 C4
Pola (Pula) 47,117 A3
Poreč 4,512 A3
Postojna 6,085 B3
Požarevac 33,336 E3
Preševo 7,634 E4
Priboj 12,556 D4
Prijedor 22,379 C3
Prijepolje 7,960 D4
Prilep 48,045 E5
Priština 71,264 E4
Prizren 41,875 E4
Prokuplje 20,617 E4
Prozor 1,420 C4
Ptuj 9,245 C2
Pula 47,117 A3
Rab 1,675 B3
Radoviš 9,373 F5
Ragusa (Dubrovnik) 31,213 C4
Raška 3,935 E4
Ravne na Koroškem 6,529 B2
Rijeka 128,883 B3
Rogatica 4,801 D4
Rovinj 8,998 A3
Rožaj E4
Ruma 24,180 D3
Šabac 43,539 D3
Samobor 7,821 B3
Sanski Most 8,718 C3
Sarajevo 245,058 D4
Senj 4,927 B3
Senta 24,694 D3
Šibenik 29,619 C4
Šid 11,867 D3
Sinj 4,705 C4
Sisak 37,215 C3
Sjenica 9,118 E4
Škofja Loka 4,971 A2
Skopje 308,117 E5
Skradin 893 B4
Slavonska Požega 18,160 C3
Slavonski Brod 38,829 D3
Smederevo 39,200 E3
Smederevska Palanka 18,837 E3
Sombor 44,210 D3
Split 150,739 C4
Srebrenica 3,101 D3
Sremska Mitrovica 32,569 D3
Štip 27,218 F5
Stolac 3,862 D4
Ston 407 C4
Struga 11,369 E5
Strumica 22,770 F5
Subotica 89,476 D2
Surdulica 7,048 F4
Svetozarevo 27,812 E4
Svilajnac 7,848 E3
Teslić 4,940 C3
Tetovo 35,293 E5
Titograd 54,639 D4
Titovo Užice 35,465 D4
Titov Veles 35,583 E5
Travnik 12,745 C3
Trbovlje 16,393 B2
Trebinje 3,553 D4
Trogir 6,162 C4
Trstenik 7,167 E4
Tržič 4,435 B2
Tuzla 53,836 D3
Ub 3,785 E3
Ulcinj 7,472 D5
Umag 3,228 A3
Uroševac E4
Valjevo 26,655 D3
Varaždin 34,662 B2
Vareš 7,632 D3
Velenje 11,225 B2
Velika Plana E3
Veliki Bečkerek (Zrenjanin) 60,201 E3
Vinkovci 29,257 D3
Virovitica 16,389 C3
Višegrad 4,753 D4
Visoko 9,365 D4
Vlasenica 4,033 D3
Vranje 25,909 F4
Vrbas 22,502 D3
Vršac 33,573 E3
Vučitrn 11,701 E4
Vukovar 29,500 D3
Žabljak 1,023 D4
Zadar 43,588 B3
Zagreb 561,773 C3
Zaječar 27,724 E4
Zara (Zadar) 43,588 B3
Zenica 49,522 C3
Žepče 3,177 D3
Zrenjanin 60,201 E3
Zvornik 8,498 D3

OTHER FEATURES

Adriatic (sea) B4
Bobotov Kuk (mt.) D4
Bosna (riv.) D3
Brač (isl.) C4
Cazma (riv.) C3
Cres (isl.) B3
Čvrsnica (mt.) C4
Dalmatia (reg.) C4
Danube (riv.) E3
Dinaric Alps (mts.) B3
Drava (riv.) C3
Drina (riv.) D3
Dugi Otok (isl.) B3
Hvar (isl.) C4
Ibar (riv.) E4
Istria (pen.) A3
Kamenjak (cape) A3
Kladovo F3
Korab (mt.) E5
Korčula (isl.) C4
Kornat (isl.) B4
Krk (isl.) B3
Kupa (riv.) B3
Kvarner (gulf) B3
Lastovo (Lagosta) (isl.) C4
Lim (riv.) D4
Lošinj (isl.) B3
Midzhur (mt.) F4
Mljet (isl.) C4
Morava (riv.) E3
Mur (riv.) B2
Neretva (riv.) D4
Ohrid (lake) E5
Pag (isl.) B3
Palagruža (Pelagosa) (isl.) C4
Prespa (lake) E5
Rab (isl.) B3
Rujen (mt.) F4
Sava (riv.) D3
Scutari (lake) D4
Slavonia (reg.) C3
Šolta (isl.) C4
Tara (riv.) D4
Timok (riv.) F3
Tisa (riv.) E3
Triglav (mt.) A2
Una (riv.) C3
Vardar (riv.) E5
Vis (isl.) C4
Vrbas (riv.) C3
Žirje (isl.) B4

*City and suburbs.

The Balkan States

CONIC PROJECTION

SCALE OF MILES

0 25 50 75 100 125 150 175

SCALE OF KILOMETERS

0 25 50 75 100 125 150 175

Capitals of Countries _____ ☆
Administrative Centers _____ △
International Boundaries _ _ _ _ _ _
Major Internal Boundaries _ _ _ _ _
Minor Internal Boundaries _ _ _ _ _
Canals _ _ _ _ _ _ _ _ _

BULGARIA and GREECE are divided into counties and
departments, respectively. Because of the scale no
attempt has been made to delimit and name these subdivisions; their administrative centers have, however,
been designated.

The larger divisions named in Greece are well-known
geographical regions, without administrative function.

ROMANIA consists of thirty-nine counties and
three cities of regional status, Bucharest, Constanța
and Petroșeni. Scale does not permit delimiting
these counties.

ALBANIA is divided into twenty-seven districts. Scale
does not permit the delimitation of these divisions.

YUGOSLAVIA is a federation of six republics. The
Serbian republic includes an autonomous province
(Vojvodina), and an autonomous region (Kosovo).

® Copyright HAMMOND INCORPORATED, Maplewood, N. J.

Topography

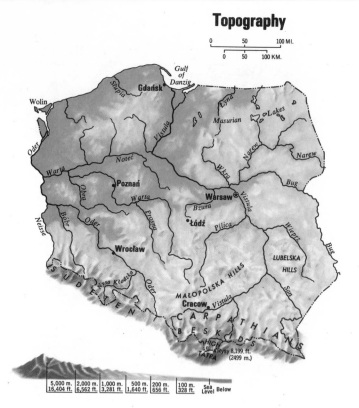

PROVINCES			
Biała Podlaska 283,200	F3	Nowy Sącz 600,300	E4
Białystok 613,800	F2	Olsztyn 654,400	E2
Bielsko 765,500	D4	Opole 961,600	C3
Bydgoszcz 982,100	C2	Ostrołęka 360,700	E2
Chełm 221,000	F3	Piła 414,000	C2
Ciechanów 398,500	E2	Piotrków 581,900	D3
Cracow (Kraków) 1,097,600	E4	Płock 479,700	D2
Cracow (city) 651,300	E4	Poznań 1,156,500	C2
Częstochowa 723,200	D3	Przemyśl 373,100	F4
Elbląg 419,800	D1	Radom 674,400	E3
Gdańsk 1,312,300	D1	Rzeszów 602,200	F4
Gorzów 428,700	B2	Siedlce 602,100	F2
Jelenia Góra 483,400	B3	Sieradz 388,000	D3
Kalisz 640,300	D3	Skierniewice 388,300	E2
Katowice 3,439,700	D3	Słupsk 352,900	C1
Kielce 1,030,400	E3	Suwałki 412,700	F1
Konin 423,700	D2	Szczecin 841,400	B2
Koszalin 428,500	C1	Tarnobrzeg 532,200	E3
Krosno 418,000	E4	Tarnów 573,900	E4
Legnica 405,600	C4	Toruń 580,500	D2
Leszno 340,600	C3	Wałbrzych 709,600	C3
Łódź 1,063,700	D3	Warsaw 2,117,700	E2
Łódź (city) 777,800	D3	Warsaw (city) 1,377,100	E2
Łomża 320,600	F2	Włocławek 402,000	D2
Lublin 875,300	F3	Wrocław 1,014,600	C3
		Zamość 472,300	F3
		Zielona Góra 575,000	B3

CITIES and TOWNS	
Aleksandrów Kujawski 9,600	D2
Aleksandrów	
(Oświęcim) 39,600	D3
Allenstein (Olsztyn) 94,119	E2
Andrespol 12,400	D3
Andrychów 14,300	D4
Augustów 19,784	F2
Auschwitz	
(Oświęcim) 39,600	D3
Bartoszyce 15,500	E1
Będzin 42,787	B3
Beuthen (Bytom) 186,993	A3
Biała Podlaska 26,100	F3
Białogard 20,500	C1
Białystok 166,619	F2
Bielawa 30,900	C3
Bielsk Podlaski 14,000	F2
Bielsko-Biała 105,601	D4
Biłgoraj 12,888	F3
Błonie 12,500	E2
Bochnia 14,500	E4
Bogatynia 11,800	B3
Boguszów-Gorce 11,900	B3
Bolesławiec 30,500	B3

Agriculture, Industry and Resources

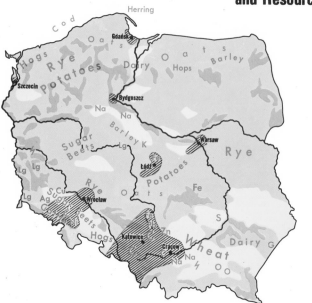

MAJOR MINERAL OCCURRENCES

Ag	Silver	Na	Salt
C	Coal	Ni	Nickel
Cu	Copper	O	Petroleum
Fe	Iron Ore	Pb	Lead
G	Natural Gas	S	Sulfur
K	Potash	Zn	Zinc
Lg	Lignite		

⚡ Water Power
▨ Major Industrial Areas

DOMINANT LAND USE

☐ Cereals (chiefly wheat)

☐ Rye, Oats, Barley, Potatoes

☐ General Farming, Livestock

☐ Forests

Poland 1938

0   50   100
MILES

Poland 1945

0   50   100
MILES

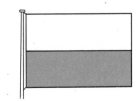

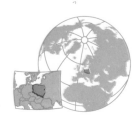

AREA 120,725 sq. mi. (312,678 sq. km.)
POPULATION 35,815,000
CAPITAL Warsaw
LARGEST CITY Warsaw
HIGHEST POINT Rysy 8,199 ft. (2,499 m.)
MONETARY UNIT zloty
MAJOR LANGUAGE Polish
MAJOR RELIGION Roman Catholicism

Braniewo 12,100	D1
Breslau (Wrocław) 461,900	C3
Brieg (Brzeg) 30,780	C3
Brodnica 17,300	D2
Brzeg 30,780	C3
Brzeg Dolny 10,800	C3
Brzesko 9,701	E4
Busko Zdrój 11,100	E3
Bydgoszcz 280,460	C2
Bytom 186,993	A3
Bytów 10,642	C1
Chełm 38,789	F3
Chełmno 17,906	D2
Chełmża 14,200	D2
Chodzież 14,100	C2
Chojnice 23,500	C2
Chojnów 11,000	B3
Chorzów 151,338	B4
Choszczno 9,800	B2
Chrzanów 29,300	B4
Ciechanów 28,500	E2
Cieplice Śląskie-Zdrój 15,400	B3
Cieszyn 25,304	C4
Cracow 651,300	E4
Czechowice-Dziedzice 25,400	D4
Czeladź 31,843	B4
Częstochowa 187,613	D3
Dąbrowa Górnicza 61,660	B3
Danzig (Gdańsk) 364,285	D1
Darłowo 11,200	C1
Dębica 22,900	E3
Deblin 14,600	B2
Debno 10,700	B2
Dzałdowo 10,100	D2
Dzierzoniów 32,800	C3
Elbing (Elbląg) 89,835	D1
Ełk 27,188	F2
Gdańsk 364,285	D1
Gdynia 190,125	D1
Giżycko 18,200	E1
Gleiwitz (Gliwice) 170,912	A4
Głogów (Glogau) 20,226	C3
Głowno 12,800	D3
Głubczyce 13,200	C3
Głuchołazy 13,200	C3
Gniezno 50,643	C2
Goleniów 14,600	B2
Gorlice 15,200	E4
Gorzów Wielkopolski 74,267	B2
Gostyń 13,000	C3
Gostynin 12,000	D2
Grajewo 11,200	F2
Grodzisk Mazowiecki 20,400	E2
Grójec 10,300	E3
Grudziądz 75,511	D2
Grünberg (Zielona Góra) 59,700	B3
Gryfice 13,200	B2
Guben (Gubin) 14,600	B3
Hajnówka m4,345	F2
Hindenburg (Zabrze) 199,400	A4
Hirschberg (Jelenia Góra) 55,720	B3
Hrubieszów 14,999	F3
Iława 16,400	D2
Inowrocław 54,817	D2
Jarocin 18,100	C3
Jarosław 29,000	F4
Jasło 17,025	E4
Jastrzębie Zdrój 34,400	C3
Jaworzno 63,271	B4
Jędrzejów 13,264	E3
Jelenia Góra 55,720	B3
Kalisz 81,227	C3
Kamienna Góra 21,000	B3
Kartuzy 10,558	C1
Katowice 303,264	B4
Kędzierzyn-Koźle 45,600	C3
Kępno 10,151	C3
Kętrzyn 19,300	E1
Kielce 125,962	E3
Kłobuck 12,600	D3
Kłodzko 26,000	C3
Kluczbork 18,000	D3
Knurów 28,400	A4
Kolberg (Kołobrzeg) 25,419	B1
Koło 13,100	D2
Kołobrzeg 25,419	B1
Konin 40,600	D2
Konstantynów Łódzki 12,800	D3
Kościan 18,700	C3
Kościerzyna 18,914	C1
Koszalin (Köslin) 64,414	C1
Kostrzyn 11,200	B2
Koszalin 64,414	C1
Kraków (Cracow) 651,300	E4
Krapkowice 13,800	D3
Kraśnik Fabryczny 14,600	F3
Krasnystaw 12,495	F3
Krosno 26,500	E4
Krotoszyn 21,900	C3
Krynica 10,200	E4
Kustrin 11,200	B2
Kutno 30,000	D2
Kwidzin 23,104	D2
Łańcut 12,049	F3
Landsberg (Gorzów Wielkopolski) 74,267	B2
Łaziska Górne 10,800	A4
Lębork 25,000	C1
Łęczyca 13,900	D2
Legionowo 20,800	E2
Legnica 75,843	C3
Leszno 33,890	C3
Leżajsk 12,200	F3
Libiaż 10,600	B4
Lidzbark Warmiński 14,200	E1
Liegnitz (Legnica) 75,843	C3
Lipno 10,900	D2
Łódź 777,800	D3
Łomża 25,500	F2
Łowicz 20,400	D2
Lubań 17,200	B3
Lubartów 10,000	F3
Lubin 28,400	C3
Lublin 235,937	F3
Lubliniec 19,800	D3
Luboń 16,400	C2
Lubsko 12,600	B3
Łuków 15,500	F3
Malbork (Marienburg) 30,900	D1
Międzyrzec Podlaski 13,500	F3
Międzyrzecz 14,900	B2
Mielec 26,800	E3
Mików 21,300	B4
Mińsk Mazowiecki 24,200	E2
Mława 20,007	E2
Mońki 9,560	F2
Morąg 9,681	D1
Mragowo 13,400	E2
Mysłowice 12,100	E4
Myślenice 44,737	E4
Myszków 18,000	D3
Nakło nad Notecią 16,800	C2
Namysłów 11,076	C3
Nidzica 9,642	D2
Nisko 10,000	F3
Nowa Ruda 18,100	C3
Nowa Sól 33,300	B3
Nowy Dwór Mazowiecki 16,900	E2
Nowy Sącz 41,103	E4
Nowy Targ 21,900	E4
Nysa 31,837	C3
Oborniki 10,200	C2
Oława 17,700	C3
Oleśnica 27,500	C3
Olkusz 15,800	D3
Olsztyn 94,119	D2
Opoczno 12,168	E3
Opole 86,510	C3
Orzesze 9,600	A4
Ostróda 21,300	D2
Ostrołęka 21,981	E2
Ostrów Mazowiecka 15,000	E2
Ostrów Wielkopolski 49,530	C3
Ostrowiec Świętokrzyski 49,958	E3
Oświęcim 39,600	D3
Otwock 39,863	E2
Ozorków 18,200	D3
Pabianice 62,275	D3
Piekary Śląskie 36,300	B4
Pionki 13,600	E3
Piotrków Trybunalski 59,683	D3
Pisz 11,100	E2
Pleszew 13,348	C3
Płock 71,727	D2
Płońsk 11,619	E2
Police 12,700	B2
Poznań 469,085	C2
Prudnik 20,300	C3
Pruszcz Gdański 13,000	D1
Pruszków 42,961	E2
Przasnysz 11,100	E2
Przemyśl 53,228	F4
Puck 9,500	D1
Puławy 34,800	F3
Pułtusk 12,600	E2
Rabka 10,700	D4
Raciborz 40,418	C3
Radom 158,640	E3
Radomsko 31,179	D3
Ratibor (Racibórz) 40,418	C3
Rawa Mazowiecka 9,800	E3
Rawicz 14,100	C3
Ruda Śląska 142,407	B4
Rumia 23,300	D1
Rybnik 43,415	D3
Rypin 10,029	D2
Rzeszów 82,192	F4
Sandomierz 16,800	E3
Sanok 21,600	F4
Schneidemühl (Piła) 36,600	C2
Schweidnitz (Świdnica) 47,542	C3
Siedlce 38,983	F2
Siemianowice Śląskie 67,278	B4
Sieradz 18,500	D3
Sierpc 12,700	D2
Skarzysko-Kamienna 39,194	E3
Skawina 15,800	D4
Skierniewice 25,590	E2
Sławno 10,700	C1
Słubice 12,000	B2
Słupsk 68,311	C1
Sochaczew 20,500	E2
Sokółka 10,023	F2
Sokołów Podlaski 9,569	F2
Sopot 47,573	D1
Sremь 15,600	C2
Środa Śląska 10,259	C3
Środa Wielkopolska 14,800	C2
Stalowa Wola 29,768	F3
Starachowice 42,807	E3
Stargard Szczeciński 44,400	B2
Starogard Gdański 33,400	D1
Stary Sącz 57,400	E4
Stettin (Szczecin) 337,294	B2
Stolp (Słupsk) 68,311	C1
Strzegom 14,000	C3
Strzelce Opolskie 14,700	D3
Strzelin 9,800	C3
Sulechów 10,200	B3
Suwałki 35,360	F1
Swarzędz 12,100	C2
Świdnica 47,542	C3
Świdnik 21,900	F3
Świdwin 12,500	B2
Świebodzice 18,500	C3
Świebodzin 14,900	B2
Świecie 21,300	C2
Świętochłowice 57,633	A4
Świnoujście (Swinemünde) 27,900	B1
Szamotuły 14,600	C2
Szczecin 337,294	B2
Szczecinek 28,600	C2
Szczytno 17,371	E2
Szprotawa 11,200	B3
Tarnobrzeg 18,800	E3
Tarnów 85,514	E4
Tarnowskie Góry 34,200	A3
Tczew 40,794	D1
Tomaszów Lubelski 12,329	F3
Tomaszów Mazowiecki 54,911	E3
Toruń 129,152	D2
Turek 18,500	D2
Tychy 71,384	B4
Ustka 9,900	C1
Wąbrzeźno 11,800	D2
Wadowice 11,700	D4
Wałbrzych 125,048	C3
Wałcz 18,900	C2
Waldenburg (Wałbrzych) 125,048	C3
Warsaw (Warszawa) (cap.) 1,377,100	E2
Wejherowo 33,600	D1
Wieliczka 13,600	E4
Wieluń 14,300	D3
Wisła 9,800	D4
Włocławek 77,169	D2
Wodzisław Śląski 25,600	D4
Wolin 35,458	B2
Wołomin 24,000	E2
Wrocław 523,318	C3
Września 17,800	C2
Wyszków 10,000	E2
Wyszków	E2
Ząbki 16,100	E2
Zabkowice Śląskie 13,800	C3
Zabrze 197,214	A4
Zagan 21,400	B3
Zakopane 27,039	E4
Zambrów 14,082	E2
Zamość 34,734	F3
Żary 28,300	B3
Zawiercie 39,410	D3
Zduńska Wola 29,066	D3
Zgierz 42,838	D3
Zgorzelec 28,400	B3
Zielona Góra 73,156	B3
Złocieniec 10,100	C2
Złotoryja 12,200	C3
Złotów 11,600	C2
Znin 9,600	C2
Żyrardów 33,196	E2
Żywiec 22,400	D4

OTHER FEATURES	
Baltic (sea)	B1
Beskids (range)	D3
Brda (riv.)	B4
Brynica (riv.)	B4
Bug (riv.)	F2
Danzig (Gdańsk) (gulf)	D1
Dukla (pass)	E4
Dunajec (riv.)	E4
Gwda (riv.)	C2
Hel (pen.)	D1
High Tatra (range)	E4
Kłodnica (riv.)	A4
Łyna (riv.)	E1
Mamry, Jezioro (lake)	E1
Narew (riv.)	E2
Neisse (riv.)	B3
Notec (riv.)	C2
Nysa (riv.)	C3
Nysa Kłodzka (riv.)	C3
Nysa Łużycka (Neisse) (riv.)	B3
Oder (riv.)	B2
Oder (res.)	D3
Pilica (riv.)	D3
Pomeranian (bay)	B1
Prosna (riv.)	C3
Przemsza (riv.)	B4
Rysy (mt.)	E4
San (riv.)	F3
Słupia (riv.)	C1
Śniardwy, Jezioro (lake)	E2
Sudeten (range)	B3
Uznam (Usedom) (isl.)	B1
Vistula (riv.)	D1
Warmia (reg.)	E1
Warta (riv.)	C2
Wieprz (riv.)	F3
Wisła (Vistula) (riv.)	E2
Wkra (riv.)	E2
Wolin (Wollin) (isl.)	B2

UNION REPUBLICS

Armenian S.S.R. 3,031,000 ... E6
Azerbaidzhan S.S.R. 6,028,000 ... E5
Estonian S.S.R. 1,466,000 ... C4
Georgian S.S.R. 5,015,000 ... D5
Kazakh S.S.R. 14,684,000 ... G5
Kirgiz S.S.R. 3,529,000 ... H5
Latvian S.S.R. 2,521,000 ... C4
Lithuanian S.S.R. 3,398,000 ... C4
Moldavian S.S.R. 3,947,000 ... C5
Russian S.F.S.R. 137,551,000 ... E4
Tadzhik S.S.R. 3,801,000 ... G6
Turkmen S.S.R. 2,759,000 ... F6
Ukrainian S.S.R. 49,755,000 ... C5
Uzbek S.S.R. 15,391,000 ... G5
White Russian S.S.R. 9,560,000 ... C4

INTERNAL DIVISIONS

Abkhaz A.S.S.R. 505,000 ... E5
Adygey Aut. Obl. 405,000 ... D5
Adzhar A.S.S.R. 354,000 ... E5
Aginsk Buryat Aut. Okr. 69,000 ... M4
Bashkir A.S.S.R. 3,849,000 ... F4
Buryat A.S.S.R. 900,000 ... L4
Chechen-Ingush
A.S.S.R. 1,154,000 ... E5
Chukchi Aut. Okr. 133,000 ... R3
Chuvash A.S.S.R. 1,292,000 ... E4
Dagestan A.S.S.R. 1,628,000 ... E5
Evenki Aut. Okr. 16,000 ... K3
Gorno-Altay Aut. Obl. 172,000 ... J4
Gorno-Badakhshan Aut.
Obl. 127,000 ... H6
Jewish Aut. Obl. 190,000 ... O5
Kabardin-Balkar

A.S.S.R. 674,000 ... E5
Kalmuck A.S.S.R. 294,000 ... E5
Karachay-Cherkess Aut.
Obl. 368,000 ... E5
Karakalpak A.S.S.R. 904,000 ... G5
Karelian A.S.S.R. 736,000 ... D3
Khakass Aut. Obl. 500,000 ... J4
Khanty-Mansi Aut. Okr. 569,000 ... H3
Komi A.S.S.R. 1,119,000 ... F3
Komi-Permyak Aut. Okr. 173,000 ... F4
Koryak Aut. Okr. 34,000 ... R3
Mari A.S.S.R. 703,000 ... E4
Mordvinian A.S.S.R. 991,000 ... E4
Nagorno-Karabakh Aut.
Obl. 161,000 ... E6
Nakhichevan' A.S.S.R. 239,000 ... E6
Nenets Aut. Okr. 47,000 ... F3
North Ossetian
A.S.S.R. 597,000 ... E5
South Ossetian Aut.
Obl. 98,000 ... E5
Tatar A.S.S.R. 3,436,000 ... F4
Taymyr Aut. Okr. 44,000 ... K2
Tuvinian A.S.S.R. 267,000 ... K4
Udmurt A.S.S.R. 1,494,000 ... F4
Ust'-Ordynsky Buryat Aut.
Okr. 133,000 ... L4
Yakut A.S.S.R. 839,000 ... N3
Yamal-Nenets Aut. Okr. 158,000 ... H3

CITIES and TOWNS

Abakan 128,000 ... K4
Abay 34,245 ... H5
Abaza 15,202 ... J4
Achinsk 117,000 ... K4
Agata ... K3
Aginskoye 7,922 ... M4
Akmolinsk
(Tselinograd) 234,000 ... H4
Aksay 10,010 ... F4
Aktas ... H4
Aktash ... J5
Aktyubinsk 191,000 ... F4
Aldan 17,689 ... N4
Aleksandrovsk-Sakhalinskiy
20,342 ... P5
Alekseyevka 18,041 ... H4
Aleysk 32,487 ... J4
Alga 12,000 ... F4
Aliskerovo ... R3
Allakh-Yun' ... O3
Alma-Ata 910,000 ... H5
Almazny ... M3
Ambarchik ... F3
Amderma ... F3
Amursk 24,010 ... O4
Anadyr' 7,703 ... S3
Andizhan 230,000 ... H5
Andropov 239,000 ... D4
Angarsk 239,000 ... L4
Angren ... H5
Anzhero-Sudzhensk
105,000 ... J4
Aral'sk 37,722 ... G5
Archangel (Arkhangel'sk)
385,000 ... E3
Arkalyk 15,108 ... G4
Armavir 162,000 ... E5
Arsen'yev 60,000 ... O5
Artem 69,000 ... O5
Artemovsky ... L4
Arys' 26,414 ... G5
Arzamas 93,000 ... E4
Asbest 79,000 ... G4
Ashkhabad 312,000 ... F6
Asino 29,395 ... J4
Astrakhan' 461,000 ... E5
Atbasar 37,228 ... H4
Atka ... O3
Ayagus 35,827 ... J5
Ayan ... N4
Aykhal ... M3
Bagdarin ... M4
Baku 1,022,000 ... E5
Baku* 1,550,000 ... F5
Balakovo 152,000 ... F4
Balashov 93,000 ... E4
Baley 27,215 ... M4
Balkhash 78,000 ... H5
Balykshi 22,397 ... F5
Barabinsk 37,274 ... H4
Baranovichi 131,000 ... C4
Barnaul 533,000 ... J4
Batagay 10,000 ... O3
Batumi 123,000 ... E5
Baykit ... K3
Baykonyr ... G5
Bayram-Ali 31,987 ... G6
Belgorod 240,000 ... D4
Belogorsk 63,000 ... N4
Belomorsk 16,595 ... D3
Beloretsk 71,000 ... F4
Belovo 112,000 ... J4
Berdichev 80,000 ... C5
Berdsk 67,000 ... J4
Berezniki 185,000 ... F4
Berezovo 6,000 ... G3
Beringovsky ... T3
Bikin 17,473 ... O5
Bira ... O5
Birobidzhan 69,000 ... O5
Biruni ... G5
Biysk 212,000 ... J4
Blagoveshchensk 172,000 ... N4
Bobruysk 192,000 ... C4
Bodaybo 19,000 ... M4
Borisoglebsk 68,000 ... E4
Borzya 27,815 ... M4
Bratsk 214,000 ... L4
Brest 177,000 ... C4
Brindakit ... N4
Bryansk 394,000 ... D4
Bugul'ma 80,000 ... F4
Bukachacha 10,000 ... M4
Bukhara 185,000 ... G5
Bulun ... N2
Buzuluk 76,000 ... F4
Chadan ... K4
Chapayevsk 85,000 ... F4
Chara ... M4
Chardzhou 140,000 ... G6
Charsk 10,100 ... J5
Cheboksary 308,000 ... E4
Chegdomyn 16,499 ... O4
Chelkar 19,377 ... F5
Chelyabinsk 1,030,000 ... G4
Cheremkhovo 77,000 ... L4
Cherepovets 266,000 ... D4
Cherkessk 91,000 ... E5
Chernigov 238,000 ... D4
Chernogorsk 71,000 ... K4
Chernovtsy 219,000 ... C5
Chernyshevsk 10,000 ... M4
Cherskiy ... Q3
Chimbay 18,899 ... F5
Chimkent 322,000 ... H5
Chirchik 132,000 ... H5
Chita 303,000 ... M4
Chokurdakh ... P2
Chumikan ... O4
Dal'negorsk 33,506 ... O5
Dal'nerechensk 28,224 ... O5
Daugavpils 116,000 ... C4
Denau ... G6
Dikson ... J2
Dimitrovgrad 106,000 ... F4
Dnepropetrovsk 1,066,000 ... D5
Donetsk 1,021,000 ... D5
Drogobych 66,000 ... C5
Druzhba ... J5
Druzhina ... P3
Dudinka 19,701 ... J3
Dushanbe 494,000 ... G6
Dzerzhinsk 257,000 ... E4
Dzhalal-Abad 55,000 ... H5
Dzhalinda ... M4
Dzhambul 264,000 ... H5
Dzhelinda ... M2
Dzhetygara 32,169 ... G4
Dzhezkazgan 89,000 ... G5
Dzhusaly 20,658 ... G5
Egvekinot ... S3
Ekibastuz 66,000 ... H4
Ekimchan ... O4
El'dikan ... O3
Elista 70,000 ... E5
Emba 17,820 ... F5
Engel's 161,000 ... F4
Erivan 1,019,000 ... E6
Evensk ... Q3
Fergana 176,000 ... H5
Fort-Shevchenko 12,000 ... F5
Frolovo 33,398 ... E5
Frunze 533,000 ... H5
Gasan-Kuli ... F6
Gol'chikha ... J2
Gomel' 383,000 ... D4
Gor'kiy 1,344,000 ... E4
Gorno-Altaysk 34,413 ... J4
Gornyak 16,643 ... J4
Grodno 195,000 ... C4
Groznyy 375,000 ... E5
Gubakha 33,243 ... F4
Gulistan 30,879 ... G5
Gur'yev 131,000 ... F5
Gusinoozersk 10,000 ... L4
Gyda ... M2
Igarka 15,624 ... J3
Igrim ... G3
Ilansky 22,852 ... K4
Indiga ... E3
Inta 51,000 ... G3
Iolotan' 10,000 ... G6
Irkutsk 550,000 ... L4
Ishim 63,000 ... H4
Isil'kul' 25,958 ... H4
Iul'tin ... T3
Ivano-Frankovsk
149,000 ... C5
Ivanovo 465,000 ... E4
Ivdel 15,308 ... G3
Izhevsk (Ustinov)
549,000 ... F4
Izmail 83,000 ... C5
Kachug ... L4
Kagan 34,117 ... G6
Kalachinsk 20,809 ... H4
Kalakan ... M4
Kalinin 412,000 ... D4
Kaliningrad 355,000 ... B4
Kalmykovo ... F5
Kaluga 265,000 ... D4
Kamen'-na-Obi 35,604 ... H4

AREA 8,649,490 sq. mi. (22,402,179 sq. km.)
POPULATION 262,436,227
CAPITAL Moscow
LARGEST CITY Moscow
HIGHEST POINT Communism Peak 24,599 ft. (7,498 m.)
MONETARY UNIT ruble
MAJOR LANGUAGES Russian, Ukrainian, White Russian, Uzbek,
Azerbaidzhani, Tatar, Georgian, Lithuanian, Armenian, Yiddish,
Latvian, Mordvinian, Kirgiz, Tadzhik, Estonian, Kazakh, Moldavian
(Romanian), German, Chuvash, Turkmenian, Bashkir
MAJOR RELIGIONS Eastern (Russian) Orthodoxy, Islam, Judaism,
Protestantism (Baltic States)

Kamenskoye	R3
Kamensk-Ural'skiy 187,000	G4
Kamyshin 112,000	E4
Kandalaksha 42,656	C3
Kansk 101,000	K4
Kapchagay	H5
Kara	G3
Karaganda 572,000	H5
Karasuk 22,637	H4
Karatau 26,962	H5
Karazhal 17,702	H5
Kargasok	J4
Karpinsk	F4
Karshi 108,000	G6
Kartaly 42,801	G4
Katangli	P4
Kattakurgan 53,000	G5
Kaunas 370,000	C4

Kavalerovo 16,415	O5
Kazan' 993,000	F4
Kem' 21,025	D3
Kemerovo 471,000	J4
Kentau 52,000	G5
Kerki 10,000	G6
Khabarovsk 528,000	O5
Khandyga	O3
Khanty-Mansiysk 24,754	H3
Khar'kov 1,444,000	D4
Khatanga	L2
Kherson 319,000	D5
Khilok 17,000	M4
Khiva 24,139	F5
Khodzheyli 36,435	F5
Kholmsk 37,412	P5
Khorog 12,295	H6
Kiev 2,144,000	D4

UNION REPUBLICS

	AREA (sq. mi.)	AREA (sq. km.)	POPULATION	CAPITAL and LARGEST CITY
RUSSIAN S.F.S.R.	6,592,812	17,075,400	137,551,000	Moscow 7,831,000
KAZAKH S.S.R.	1,048,300	2,715,100	14,684,000	Alma-Ata 910,000
UKRAINIAN S.S.R.	233,089	603,700	49,755,000	Kiev 2,144,000
TURKMEN S.S.R.	188,455	488,100	2,759,000	Ashkhabad 312,000
UZBEK S.S.R.	173,591	449,600	15,391,000	Tashkent 1,780,000
WHITE RUSSIAN S.S.R.	80,154	207,600	9,560,000	Minsk 1,262,000
KIRGIZ S.S.R.	76,641	198,500	3,529,000	Frunze 533,000
TADZHIK S.S.R.	55,251	143,100	3,801,000	Dushanbe 494,000
AZERBAIDZHAN S.S.R.	33,436	86,600	6,028,000	Baku 1,022,000
GEORGIAN S.S.R.	26,911	69,700	5,015,000	Tbilisi 1,066,000
LITHUANIAN S.S.R.	25,174	65,200	3,398,000	Vilna 481,000
LATVIAN S.S.R.	24,595	63,700	2,521,000	Riga 835,000
ESTONIAN S.S.R.	17,413	45,100	1,466,000	Tallinn 430,000
MOLDAVIAN S.S.R.	13,012	33,700	3,947,000	Kishinev 503,000
ARMENIAN S.S.R.	11,506	29,800	3,031,000	Erivan 1,019,000

Kirensk 10,000	L4
Kirov 390,000	E4
Kirovabad 232,000	E5
Kirovograd 237,000	D5
Kirovskiy	H5
Kiselevsk 122,000	J4
Kishinev 503,000	C5
Kizel 46,264	F4
Kizyl-Arvat 21,671	F6
Klaipeda 176,000	B4
Kokand 153,000	H5
Kokchetav 103,000	H4
Kolomna 147,000	D4
Kolpashevo 24,911	J4
Komsomol'sk 15,385	O4
Komsomol'sk-na-Amure 264,000	O4
Kondopoga 27,908	D3
Kopeysk 146,000	G4
Korf	R3
Korsakov 38,210	P5
Koslan	E3
Kostroma 255,000	E4
Kotlas 61,000	E3
Korf 33,351	F6
Kovrov 143,000	E4
Kovel' 33,351	C4
Kozhevnikovo	L2
Krasino	F2
Krasnodar 560,000	E5
Krasnokamensk 51,000	M4

Krasnokamsk 56,000	F4
Krasnotur'insk 61,000	G3
Krasnoural'sk 39,743	G4
Krasnovodsk 53,000	F5
Krasnoyarsk 796,000	K4
Kremenchug 210,000	D5
Krivoy Rog 650,000	D5
Kudymkar 26,350	F4
Kul'sary 16,427	F5
Kulunda 15,264	H4
Kulyab 55,000	H6
Kum-Dag 10,000	F6
Kungur 80,000	F4
Kupino 20,799	H4
Kurgan 310,000	G4
Kurgan-Tyube 34,620	G6
Kursk 375,000	D4
Kushka	G6
Kustanay 165,000	G4
Kutaisi 194,000	E5
Kuybyshev 1,216,000	F4
Kuybyshev 40,166	H4
Kyakhta 15,316	L4
Kyusyur	N2
Kyzyl 66,000	K4
Kzyl-Orda 156,000	G5
Labytnangi	G3
Lebedinyy	N4
Leninabad 130,000	G5

Leninakan 207,000	E5
Leningrad 4,073,000	D4
Leningrad* 4,588,000	D4
Leninogorsk 54,000	J5
Leninsk	G5
Leninsk-Kuznetskiy 132,000	K4
Leninskoye	M3
Lenkoran 35,505	E6
Lensk 16,758	M3
Lesosibirsk	K4
Lesozavodsk 34,957	O5
Liepāja 108,000	B4
Lipetsk 396,000	E4
Luga 31,905	D4
Lutsk 137,000	C4
L'vov 667,000	C4
Lys'va 75,000	F4
Magadan 121,000	P4
Magdagachi 15,059	N4
Magnitogorsk 406,000	G4
Makhachkala 251,000	E5
Makinsk 22,850	H4
Mama	M3
Markovo	S3
Mary (Merv) 74,000	G6
Maykop 128,000	D5
Mednogorsk 38,024	F4
Medvezh'yegorsk 17,465	D3
Mezen'	E3

Miass 150,000	G4
Michurinsk 101,000	E4
Millerovo 34,627	E5
Minsk 1,262,000	C4
Minsk* 1,276,000	C4
Minusinsk 56,000	K4
Mirnyy 23,826	M3
Mogilev 290,000	D4
Mogocha 17,884	N4
Molodechno 73,000	C4
Monchegorsk 51,000	C3
Moscow (cap.) 7,831,000	D4
Moscow* 8,011,000	D4
Motygino 10,300	K4
Mozyr' 73,000	C4
Murgab	H6
Murmansk 381,000	D3
Moynak 12,000	F5
Mys Shmidta	T3
Nadym	H3
Nagornyy	N4
Nakhichevan' 33,279	E6
Nakhodka 133,000	O5
Nal'chik 207,000	E5
Namangan 227,000	H5
Naminga	M4
Nar'yan-Mar 16,864	F3
Naryn 21,098	H5
Navoi 84,000	G6

Nazarovo 54,000	K4
Nazyvayevsk 15,792	H4
Nebit-Dag 71,000	F6
Nefteyugansk 52,000	H3
Nel'kan	O4
Nepa	L4
Neryungri	N4
Nevel'sk 20,726	P5
Nevel 440,000	D5
Nikolayev 440,000	D5
Nikolayevsk-na-Amure 30,082	P4
Nikol'skoye	R4
Nizhneudinsk 39,743	K4
Nizhnevartovsk 109,000	H3
Nizhneyansk	O3
Nizhniy Tagil 398,000	G4
Nordvik-Ugol'naya	M2
Noril'sk 180,000	J3
Novaya Kazanka	F5
Novgorod 186,000	D4
Novokazalinsk 34,815	G5
Novokuznetsk 541,000	J4
Novomoskovsk 147,000	E4
Novorossiysk 159,000	D5
Novosibirsk 1,312,000	J4
Novozybkov 34,433	D4
Novyy Port	H3
Novyy Uzen' 18,073	F5
Novyy Urengoy	H3
Nukus 109,000	G5

Topography

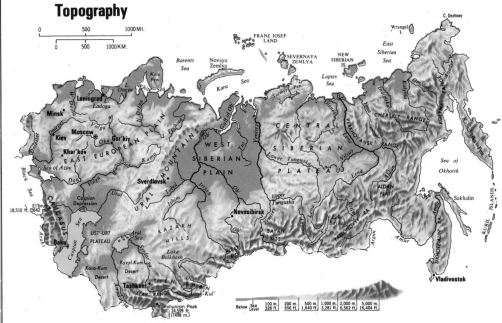

(continued)

Nyandoma 23,366 .... E3
Nyurba M3
Obluch'ye 17,000 .... N5
Odessa 1,046,000 .... D5
Okha 30,890 .... P4
Okhotsk P4
Olëkminsk N3
Olënek M3
Omsk 1,014,000 .... H4
Omsukchan Q3
Omutninsk 28,777 .... F4
Onega 25,047 .... D3
Ordzhonikidze 279,000 .... E5
Orel 305,000 .... D4
Orenburg 459,000 .... F4
Orotukan Q3
Orsk 247,000 .... F4
Osh 169,000 .... H5
Ostrogozhsk 29,921 .... D4
Oymyakon O3
Ozernovskiy Q4
Palana 2,735 .... R4
Panfilov 19,173 .... H5
Pärnu 51,000 .... C4
Partizansk 48,345 .... O5
Pavlodar 273,000 .... H4
Pechenga D2
Pechora 56,000 .... F3
Peleduy M4
Penza 483,000 .... E4
Perkatkin T2
Perm' 999,000 .... F4
Pervoural'sk 129,000 .... F4
Petropavlovsk 207,000 .... G4
Petropavlovsk-Kamchatskiy 215,000 .... R4
Petrovsk-Zabaykal'skiy 28,313 .... L4
Petrozavodsk 234,000 .... D3
Pevek S3
Pikol'skiy 32,862 .... G5
Pinsk 90,000 .... C4
Plastun O5
Podol'sk 202,000 .... D4
Pokrovsk N3
Poligus K3
Poltava 279,000 .... D5
Polyarnyy 15,321 .... D3
Ponoy E3
Poronaysk 23,610 .... P5
Prikumsk 35,768 .... E5
Progress 10,000 .... O5
Prokop'yevsk 266,000 .... J4
Provideniya T3
Przheval'sk 51,000 .... H5
Pskov 176,000 .... C4
Pushkin 90,000 .... C4
Raychikhinsk 25,157 .... N5
Riga 835,000 .... C4
Rostov-na-Donau 934,000 .... E5
Rovno 179,000 .... C4
Rubtsovsk 157,000 .... J4
Ruch'i E3
Rudnyy 110,000 .... G4
Ryazan' 453,000 .... E4
Rybach'ye H5
Rybinsk (Andropov) 239,000 .... D4
Rzhev 69,000 .... D4
Saksaul'sky F5
Salekhard 21,929 .... G3
Sal'sk 57,000 .... E5
Samagaltay K4
Samarkand 477,000 .... G6
Sangar N3
Saran' 55,000 .... H5
Saransk 263,000 .... E4
Sarapul 107,000 .... F4
Saratov 856,000 .... E4
Sarkand 18,296 .... J5
Segezha 28,810 .... D3
Semipalatinsk 283,000 .... H4
Serakhs G6
Serov 101,000 .... G4
Serpukhov 140,000 .... D4
Sevastopol' 301,000 .... D5
Severobaykal'sk M4
Severodvinsk 197,000 .... E3
Severo-Kuril'sk 8,000 .... Q4
Severoural'sk 29,880 .... G3
Severo-Yeniseysk K3
Shadrinsk 82,000 .... G4
Shakhtinsk 50,000 .... H5
Shakhty 209,000 .... E5
Shar'ya 25,788 .... E4
Shchuchinsk 40,432 .... H4
Shenkursk E3
Shevchenko 111,000 .... F5
Shilka 16,065 .... M4
Shimanovsk 16,880 .... N4
Shushenskoye 10,000 .... K4
Šiauliai 118,000 .... C4
Siktyakh N3
Simferopol' 302,000 .... D5
Skovorodino 10,000 .... N4
Slavgorod 32,908 .... H4
Slobodskoy 34,374 .... E4
Slyudyanka 20,639 .... L4
Smolensk 276,000 .... D4
Snezhnogorsk J3
Sochi 287,000 .... D5
Sokol 48,253 .... E4
Solikamsk 101,000 .... F3
Sortavala 22,188 .... C3
Sosnogorsk 24,688 .... F3
Sosnovo-Ozerskoye M4
Sovetskaya Gavan' 28,455 .... P5
Spassk-Dal'niy 53,000 .... O5
Srednekolymsk Q3
Sretensk 16,000 .... M4
Stalingrad (Volgograd) 929,000 .... E5
Stavropol' 258,000 .... E5
Stepanakert 30,293 .... E6
Sterlitamak 220,000 .... F4
Strezhevoy H3
Sukhana M3
Sukhumi 114,000 .... D5
Sumy 228,000 .... D4
Suntar M3
Surgut 107,000 .... H3
Susuman 12,000 .... P3
Sverdlovsk 1,211,000 .... F4
Svobodnyy 75,000 .... N4
Syktyvkar 171,000 .... F3
Syzran' 178,000 .... E4
Taganrog 276,000 .... D5
Takhiatash F5
Takhta-Bazar G6
Taksimo M4
Taldy-Kurgan 88,000 .... H5
Talgar 31,273 .... H5
Tallinn 430,000 .... C4
Tambey G2
Tambov 270,000 .... E4
Tara 22,358 .... H4
Tarko-Sale H3
Tartu 105,000 .... C4
Tashauz 84,000 .... F5
Tashkent 1,780,000 .... G5
Tatarsk 29,589 .... H4
Tavda G4
Tayshet 34,232 .... K4
Tazovskiy J3
Tbilisi 1,066,000 .... E5
Tedzhen 25,708 .... F6
Tekeli 29,846 .... H5
Temirtau 213,000 .... H4
Termez 57,000 .... G6
Ternopol' 144,000 .... C5
Tiksi N2
Tobol'sk 62,000 .... G4
Togliatti (Tol'yatti) 502,000 .... F4
Tokmak 59,000 .... H5

Tommot 8,000 .... N4
Tomsk 421,000 .... J4
Tot'ma E4
Troitsk 88,000 .... G4
Tselinograd 234,000 .... H4
Tskhinvali 30,311 .... E5
Tula 514,000 .... D4
Tulun 52,000 .... L4
Tura 3,528 .... L3
Turan K4
Turgay G5
Turkestan 67,000 .... G5
Tynda N4
Tyumen' 359,000 .... G4
Uelen T3
Ufa 969,000 .... F4
Uglegorsk 17,921 .... P5
Ukhta 87,000 .... F3
Ulan-Ude 300,000 .... L4
Ul'yanovsk 464,000 .... E4
Ural'sk 167,000 .... F4
Uray 17,385 .... G3
Urgench 100,000 .... G5
Ushtobe 24,484 .... H5
Usol'ye-Sibirskoye 103,000 .... L4
Ussuriysk 147,000 .... O5
Ust'-Ilimsk 69,000 .... L4
Ustinov 549,000 .... F4
Ust'-Kamchatsk 10,000 .... R4
Ust'-Kamenogorsk 274,000 .... J5
Ust'-Kut 50,000 .... L4
Ust'-Kuyga O3
Ust'-Maya O3
Ust'-Nera P3
Ust'-Omchug P3
Ust'-Olenëk M2
Ust'-Ordynskiy 10,693 .... L4
Ust'-Port J2
Vanavara L3
Vanino 15,401 .... P5
Velikiye Luki 102,000 .... D4
Velikiy Ustyug 36,737 .... E3
Vel'sk 21,899 .... E3
Ventspils 40,467 .... B4
Verkhnevilyuysk N3
Verkniy At-Uryakh Q3
Verkhoyansk 2,000 .... N3
Vilna (Vilnius) 481,000 .... C4
Vilyuysk N3
Vinnitsa 314,000 .... C5
Vitebsk 297,000 .... D4
Vitimskiy M4
Vladimir 296,000 .... D4
Vladivostok 550,000 .... O5
Volgograd 929,000 .... E5
Volochanka K2
Vologda 237,000 .... E4
Vorkuta 100,000 .... G3
Voronezh 783,000 .... E4
Voroshilovgrad 463,000 .... E5
Vostochnyy O5
Votkinsk 90,000 .... F4
Voy-Vozh 10,000 .... F3
Vyazemskiy 18,365 .... O5
Vyborg 76,000 .... C3
Vyshniy Volochek 72,000 .... D4
Yakutsk 152,000 .... N3
Yalutorsk 25,426 .... G4
Yamsk Q4
Yaroslavl' 597,000 .... D4
Yartsevo J4
Yelets 112,000 .... D4
Yelizovo 10,000 .... Q4
Yeniseysk 19,880 .... K4
Yermak 28,133 .... H4
Yermentau 15,276 .... H4
Yesil' 15,000 .... G4
Yessey L3
Yoshkar-Ola 201,000 .... E4
Yurga 78,000 .... J4
Yuzhno-Sakhalinsk 140,000 .... P5
Zabaykal'sk M5
Zakamensk 10,000 .... L4
Zaozernyy 27,216 .... K4
Zaporozh'ye 781,000 .... D5
Zarafshan G5
Zavitinsk 19,009 .... O4
Zaysan 10,000 .... J5
Zeya 16,684 .... N4
Zhatay O3
Zhdanov 503,000 .... D5
Zheleznogorsk-Ilimskiy 22,179 .... L4
Zhigalovo L4
Zhigansk N3
Zhitomir 244,000 .... C4
Zima 41,567 .... L4
Zlatoust 198,000 .... F4
Zyryanka Q3

OTHER FEATURES

Alakol' (lake) J5
Alazeya (riv.) Q3
Aldan (plat.) N4
Aldan (riv.) O3
Alexandra Land (isl.) E1
Altay (mts.) J5
Amga (riv.) O3
Amgun' (riv.) O4
Amudar'ya (riv.) G5
Amur (riv.) O4
Anabar (riv.) M2
Anadyr' (gulf) T3
Anadyr' (range) S3
Anadyr' (riv.) S3
Angara (riv.) K4
Aral (sea) F5
Arctic Ocean K1
Argun (riv.) M4
Arkticheskiy Institut (isls.) H2
Atrek (riv.) F6
Ayon (isl.) R2
Azov (sea) D5
Balkhash (lake) H5
Baltic (sea) B4
Barents (sea) D2
Baykal (lake) L4
Baykal (mts.) L4
Beloye (lake) D3
Belyy (isl.) G2
Bering (isl.) R4
Bering (sea) S4
Bering (strait) U3
Bet-Pak-Dala (des.) H5
Black (sea) D5
Bol'shevik (isl.) K2
Bol'shoy Lyakhovskiy (isl.) P2
Bolvanskiy Nos (cape) G2
Bratsk (res.) L4
Caspian (sea) F6
Caucasus (mts.) E5
Chelyuskin (cape) M2
Cherskiy (range) P3
Chu (riv.) H5
Chukchi (pen.) T3
Chukchi (sea) T2
Chulym (riv.) J4
Chuna (riv.) K4
Chunya (riv.) K3
Communism (peak) H6
Crimea (pen.) D5
Dezhnev (cape) T3
Dmitriya Lapteva (strait) O2
Dnieper (riv.) D5
Dniester (riv.) C5
Don (riv.) E5
Donets (riv.) D5
Dulgalakh (riv.) O3
Dvina, Northern (riv.) E3

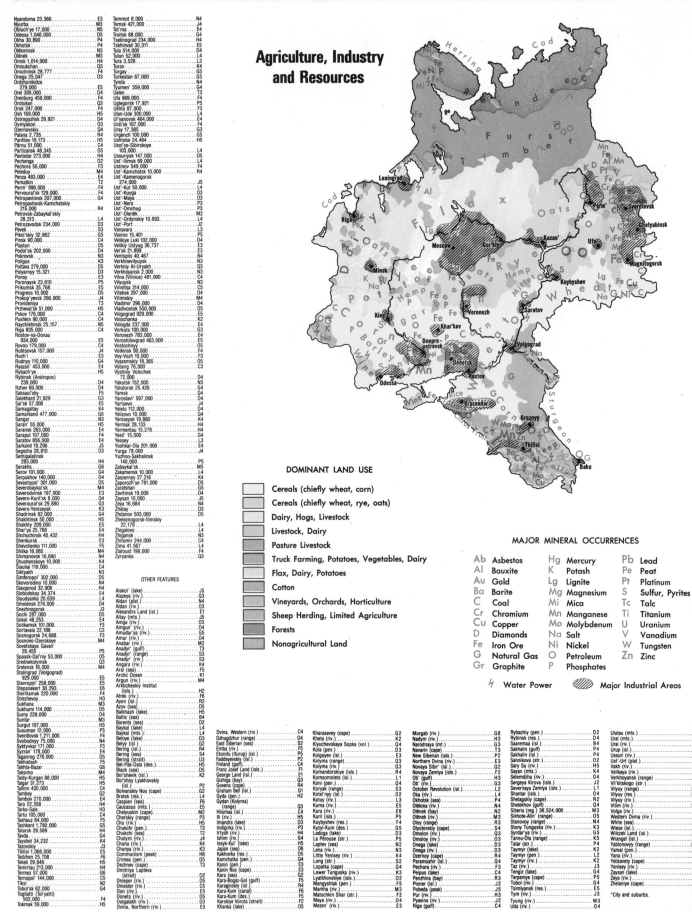

Agriculture, Industry and Resources

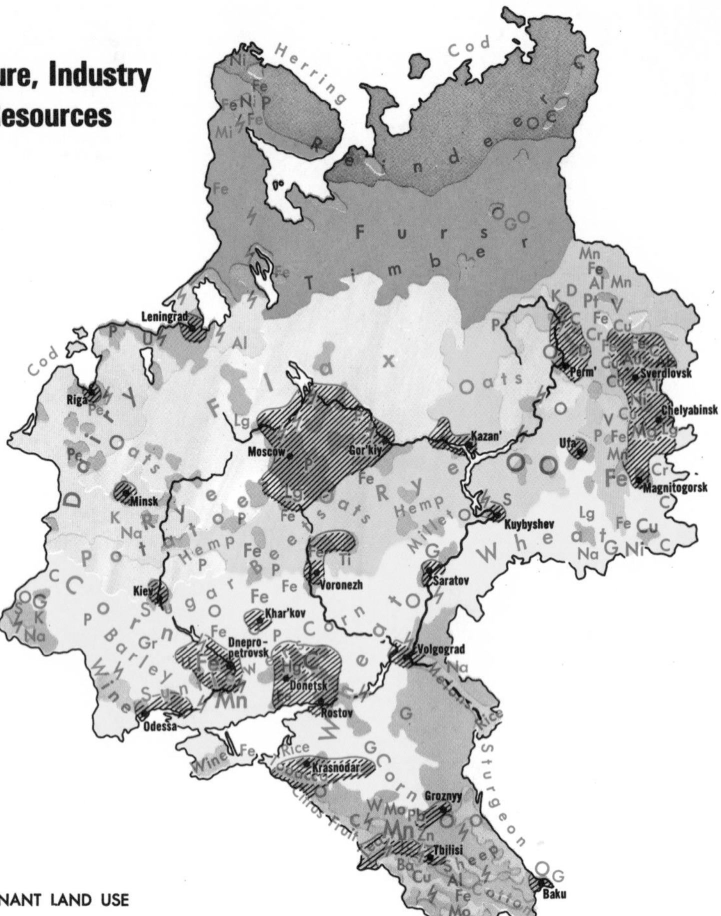

DOMINANT LAND USE

- Cereals (chiefly wheat, corn)
- Cereals (chiefly wheat, rye, oats)
- Dairy, Hogs, Livestock
- Livestock, Dairy
- Pasture Livestock
- Truck Farming, Potatoes, Vegetables, Dairy
- Flax, Dairy, Potatoes
- Cotton
- Vineyards, Orchards, Horticulture
- Sheep Herding, Limited Agriculture
- Forests
- Nonagricultural Land

MAJOR MINERAL OCCURRENCES

Ab	Asbestos	Hg	Mercury	Pb	Lead
Al	Bauxite	K	Potash	Pe	Peat
Au	Gold	Lg	Lignite	Pt	Platinum
Ba	Barite	Mg	Magnesium	S	Sulfur, Pyrites
C	Coal	Mi	Mica	Tc	Talc
Cr	Chromium	Mn	Manganese	Ti	Titanium
Cu	Copper	Mo	Molybdenum	U	Uranium
D	Diamonds	Na	Salt	V	Vanadium
Fe	Iron Ore	Ni	Nickel	W	Tungsten
G	Natural Gas	O	Petroleum	Zn	Zinc
Gr	Graphite	P	Phosphates		

Water Power
Major Industrial Areas

Dvina, Western (riv.) C4
Dzhugdzhur (range) O4
East Siberian (sea) S2
Emba (riv.) F5
Etorofu (Iturup) (isl.) P5
Faddeyevskiy (isl.) P2
Finland (gulf) C4
Franz Josef Land (isls.) F1
George Land (isl.) E1
Gizhiga (bay) Q3
Govena (cape) R4
Graham Bell (isl.) G1
Gyda (pen.) H2
Gydan (Kolyma) (range) Q3
Hiiumaa (isl.) C4
Ili (riv.) H5
Imandra (lake) D3
Indigirka (riv.) P3
Irtysh (riv.) H4
Ishim (riv.) G4
Issyk-Kul' (lake) H5
Japan (sea) O6
Kakhovka (res.) D5
Kamchatka (pen.) Q4
Kanin (pen.) E3
Kanin Nos (cape) E3
Kara (sea) G2
Kara-Bogaz-Gol (gulf) F5
Karaginskiy (isl.) R4
Kara-Kum (canal) F6
Kara-Kum (des.) F5
Karskiye Vorota (strait) F2
Khanka (lake) O5

Kharasavey (cape) G2
Kheta (riv.) K2
Klyuchevskaya Sopka (vol.) Q4
Kola (pen.) D3
Kolguyev (isl.) E3
Kolyma (range) Q3
Kolyma (riv.) Q3
Komandorskiye (isls.) R4
Komsomolets (isl.) L1
Koni (pen.) Q4
Koryak (range) S3
Kotel'nyy (isl.) O2
Kotuy (riv.) L3
Kuma (riv.) E5
Kura (riv.) E6
Kuril (isls.) P5
Kuybyshev (res.) F4
Kyzyl-Kum (des.) G5
Ladoga (lake) D3
La Pérouse (str.) P5
Laptev (sea) N2
Lena (riv.) N3
Little Yenisey (riv.) K4
Long (str.) S2
Lopatka (cape) Q4
Lower Tunguska (riv.) K3
Lyatkhovskiye (isls.) O2
Mangyshlak (pen.) F5
Markha (riv.) M3
Matochkin Shar (str.) F2
Maya (riv.) O4
Mezen' (riv.) E3

Murgab (riv.) G6
Nadym (riv.) H3
Narodnaya (mt.) G3
Navarin (cape) T3
New Siberian (isls.) P2
Northern Dvina (riv.) E3
Novaya Sibir' (isl.) Q2
Novaya Zemlya (isls.) F2
Ob' (gulf) H3
Ob' (riv.) G3
October Revolution (isl.) L2
Oka (riv.) L4
Okhotsk (sea) P4
Olëkma (riv.) N4
Olënek (bay) N2
Olënek (riv.) M3
Oloy (range) R3
Olyutorskiy (cape) S4
Omolon (riv.) Q3
Omoloy (riv.) O3
Onega (lake) D3
Onega (riv.) D3
Ozernoy (cape) R4
Paramushir (isl.) Q4
Pechora (riv.) F3
Peipus (lake) C4
Penzhina (bay) R3
Pioner (isl.) J2
Pobeda (peak) J5
Pur (riv.) H3
Pyasina (riv.) J2
Riga (gulf) C4

Rybachiy (pen.) D2
Rybinsk (res.) D4
Saaremaa (isl.) B4
Sakhalin (gulf) P4
Sakhalin (isl.) P4
Sannikova (str.) O2
Sary Su (riv.) H5
Sayan (mts.) K4
Selemdzha (riv.) O4
Sergeya Kirova (isls.) J2
Severnaya Zemlya (isls.) L1
Shantar (isls.) O4
Shelagskiy (cape) R2
Shelekhov (gulf) Q4
Siberia (reg.) 38,524,000 .... M3
Sikhote-Alin' (range) O5
Stanovoy (range) N4
Stony Tunguska (riv.) K3
Syrdar'ya (riv.) G5
Tannu-Ola (range) K5
Tatar (str.) P4
Taymyr (lake) K2
Taymyr (pen.) L2
Taymyr (riv.) K2
Taz (riv.) J3
Tengiz (lake) G4
Terpeniye (cape) P5
Tobol (riv.) G4
Tsimlyansk (res.) E5
Tym (riv.) J3
Tyung (riv.) M3
Uda (riv.) O4

Ulutau (mts.) ....
Ural (mts.) ....
Ural (riv.) ....
Urup (isl.) ....
Ussuri (riv.) ....
Ust'-Urt (plat.) ....
Vakh (riv.) ....
Velikaya (riv.) ....
Verkhoyansk (range) ....
Vil'kitskogo (str.) ....
Vilyuy (range) ....
Vilyuy (res.) ....
Vilyuy (riv.) ....
Vitim (riv.) ....
Volga (riv.) ....
Western Dvina (riv.) ....
White (sea) ....
Wiese (isl.) ....
Wilczek Land (isl.) ....
Wrangel (isl.) ....
Yablonovyy (range) ....
Yamal (pen.) ....
Yana (riv.) ....
Yelizavety (cape) ....
Yenisey (riv.) ....
Zaysan (lake) ....
Zeya (riv.) ....
Zhelaniye (cape) ....

*City and suburbs.

Agriculture, Industry and Resources

DOMINANT LAND USE

- Cereals (chiefly wheat, corn)
- Livestock, Dairy
- Truck Farming, Potatoes, Vegetables, Dairy
- Cotton
- Sheep Herding, Limited Agriculture
- Forests
- Nonagricultural Land

MAJOR MINERAL OCCURRENCES

Ab	Asbestos	Cu	Copper	Mi	Mica	Pt	Platinum
Au	Silver	D	Diamonds	Mn	Manganese	S	Sulfur, Pyrites
Al	Bauxite	F	Fluorspar	Mo	Molybdenum	Sb	Antimony
Au	Gold	Fe	Iron Ore	Na	Salt	Sn	Tin
Be	Beryl	G	Natural Gas	Ni	Nickel	U	Uranium
C	Coal	Hg	Mercury	O	Petroleum	W	Tungsten
Co	Cobalt	Ka	Kaolin	P	Phosphates	Zn	Zinc
Cr	Chromium	Lg	Lignite	Pb	Lead		

⚡ Water Power   ▨ Major Industrial Areas

U.S.S.R.–Railroads and Navigation

Principal Railroads
Navigable Rivers
Canals
Main Sea Routes
Major Russian Ports ⚓

SCALE OF MILES
0   500   1000

SCALE OF KILOMETERS
0   500   1000

© Copyright HAMMOND INCORPORATED, Maplewood, N.J.

(continued on following page)

Union of Soviet Socialist Republics
European Part

CONIC PROJECTION
SCALE OF MILES
0   50 100   200   300
SCALE OF KILOMETERS
0 50 100   200   300

☆ National Capitals
⬡ Capitals of Union Republics
△ Administrative Centers
International boundaries
Union Republic boundaries
A.S.S.R., Oblast, Kray boundaries
Autonomous Oblast boundaries
Autonomous Okrug boundaries

The government of the United States has not recognized the incorporation of Estonia, Latvia and Lithuania into the Soviet Union.

Administrative Divisions bear same names as their respective Capitals or Centers, except:

Abkhaz A.S.S.R.	Sukhumi	F6
Adygey Aut. Oblast	Maykop	F6
Adzhar A.S.S.R.	Batumi	F6
Bashkir A.S.S.R.	Ufa	J4
Chechen-Ingush A.S.S.R.	Groznyy	G6
Chuvash A.S.S.R.	Cheboksary	G3
Crimean Oblast	Simferopol'	D6
Dagestan A.S.S.R.	Makhachkala	G6
Kabardin-Balkar A.S.S.R.	Nal'chik	F6
Kalmuck A.S.S.R.	Elista	F5
Karachay-Cherkess Aut. Obl.	Cherkessk	F6
Karelian A.S.S.R.	Petrozavodsk	D2
Komi A.S.S.R.	Syktyvkar	H2
Komi-Permyak Aut. Okrug	Kudymkar	H3
Mari A.S.S.R.	Yoshkar-Ola	G3
Mordvinian A.S.S.R.	Saransk	G4
Nagorno-Karabakh Aut. Obl.	Stepanakert	G7
Nenets Aut. Okrug	Nar'yan-Mar	H1
North Ossetian A.S.S.R.	Ordzhonikidze	F6
South Ossetian Aut. Obl.	Tskhinvali	F6
Tatar A.S.S.R.	Kazan'	G3
Trans-Carpathian Oblast	Uzhgorod	B5
Udmurt A.S.S.R.	Ustinov	H3
Volyn Oblast	Lutsk	C4

© Copyright HAMMOND INCORPORATED, Maplewood, N.J.

(continued)

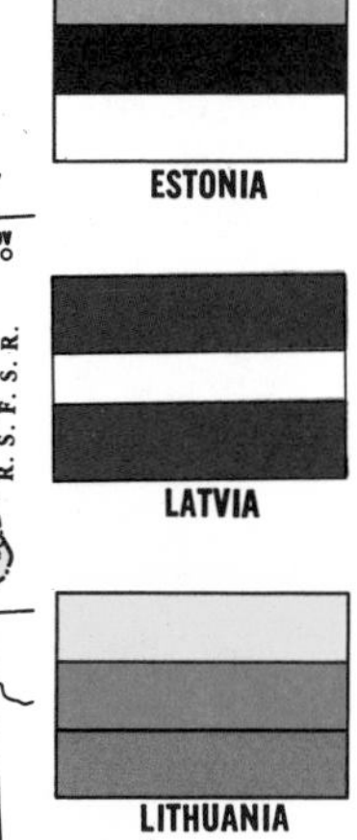

The government of the United States has not recognized the incorporation of Estonia, Latvia and Lithuania into the Soviet Union, nor does it recognize other post-war territorial changes shown on this map. The flags shown here were the official flags of the independent Baltic States prior to 1939.

The Baltic States

SCALE OF MILES 0 25 50 75 100
SCALE OF KILOMETERS 0 30 60 90 120 150 180

Capitals ☆
International Boundaries
Union Republic Boundaries
Prewar boundaries of the Baltic States where divergent from present boundaries

© Copyright HAMMOND INCORPORATED, Maplewood, N. J.

BALTIC STATES

Alytus 55,000 ... C3
Biržai 11,400 ... C2
Cēsis 17,696 ... C2
Daugava (Western Dvina) (riv.) ... D2
Daugavpils 116,000 ... D3
Dobele 10,100 ... B2
Druskininkai 11,200 ... C3
Dvina Western (riv.) ... C2
Finland (gulf) ... D1
Gauja (riv.) ... C2
Haapsalu 11,483 ... B1
Hiiumaa (isl.) ... B1
Jēkabpils 22,400 ... C2
Jelgava 68,000 ... B2
Jonava 14,400 ... C3
Jurmala 61,000 ... B2
Kapsukas 28,763 ... B3
Kaunas 370,000 ... C3
Kedainiai 19,677 ... C3
Kihnu (isl.) ... B1
Kingisepp (Kuressaare) 12,140 ... B1
Kiviõli 11,153 ... D1
Klaipeda 176,000 ... A3
Kohtla-Järve 73,000 ... D1
Kretinga 13,000 ... A3
Kuldīga 12,300 ... A2
Kuressaare 12,140 ... B1
Kuršenai 11,500 ... B2
Liepāja 108,000 ... A2
Lubāna (lake) ... D2
Mažeikiai 13,400 ... A2
Memel (Klaipeda) 176,000 ... A3
Muhu (isl.) ... B1
Narva 73,000 ... E1
Naujoji-Akmene 10,200 ... B2
Niemen (riv.) ... A3
Ogre 15,708 ... C2
Panevežys 102,000 ... C3
Pärnu 51,000 ... C1
Peipus (lake) ... D1
Plunge 13,600 ... B3
Radviliškis 16,841 ... B3
Rakvere 17,891 ... D1
Rēzekne 30,803 ... D2
Riga (cap.), Latvia 835,000 ... C2
Riga (gulf) ... B2
Saaremaa (isl.) ... B1
Saldus 10,000 ... B2
Šiauliai 118,000 ... B3
Sillamäe 13,505 ... D1
Šilute 12,400 ... A3
Tallinn (cap.), Estonia 430,000 ... C1
Tapa 10,037 ... C1
Tartu 105,000 ... D1
Taurage 19,461 ... B3
Telšiai 20,220 ... B2
Tukums 14,800 ... B2
Ukmerge 21,663 ... C3
Utena 13,300 ... C3
Valga 16,795 ... D2
Valmiera 20,331 ... C2
Venta (riv.) ... B2
Ventspils 40,467 ... A2
Viliya (riv.) ... C3
Viljandi 20,814 ... C1
Vilna (Vilnius) (cap.), Lithuania 481,000 ... C3
Vormosi (isl.) ... B1
Võrtsjärv (lake) ... D1
Võru 15,398 ... D2
Western Dvina (riv.) ... C2

U.S.S.R. — EUROPEAN

UNION REPUBLICS

Armenian S.S.R. 3,031,000 ... F6
Azerbaidzhan S.S.R. 6,028,000 ... G6
Estonian S.S.R 1,466,000 ... C3
Georgian S.S.R. 5,015,000 ... F6
Latvian S.S.R 2,521,000 ... B3
Lithuanian S.S.R. 3,398,000 ... B3
Moldavian S.S.R. 3,947,000 ... C5
Russian S.F.S.R. 137,551,000 ... F3
Ukrainian S.S.R. 49,755,000 ... D5
White Russian S.S.R. 9,560,000 ... C4

INTERNAL DIVISIONS

Abkhaz A.S.S.R. 505,000 ... F6
Adygey Aut. Obl. 405,000 ... F6
Adzhar A.S.S.R. 354,000 ... F6
Bashkir A.S.S.R. 3,849,000 ... J4
Chechen-Ingush A.S.S.R. 1,154,000 ... G6
Chuvash A.S.S.R. 1,292,000 ... G3
Crimean Oblast 2,183,000 ... D6
Dagestan A.S.S.R. 1,628,000 ... G6
Kabardin-Balkar A.S.S.R. 674,000 ... F6
Kalmuck A.S.S.R. 294,000 ... F5
Karachay-Cherkess Aut. Obl. 368,000 ... F6
Karelian A.S.S.R. 736,000 ... D2
Komi A.S.S.R. 1,119,000 ... H2
Komi-Permyak Aut. Okr. 173,000 ... H3
Mari A.S.S.R. 703,000 ... G3
Mordvinian A.S.S.R. 991,000 ... G4
Nagorno-Karabakh Aut. Obl. 161,000 ... G7
Nakhichevan' A.S.S.R. 239,000 ... F7
Nenets Aut. Okr. 47,000 ... H1
North Ossetian A.S.S.R. 597,000 ... F6
South Ossetian Aut. Obl. 98,000 ... F6
Tatar A.S.S.R. 3,436,000 ... G3
Trans-Carpathian Oblast 1,155,000 ... B5
Udmurt A.S.S.R. 1,494,000 ... H3
Volyn Oblast 1,015,000 ... C4

CITIES and TOWNS

Abdulino 26,010 ... H4
Agdam 21,277 ... G6
Agryz 19,267 ... H3
Akhaltsikhe 18,972 ... F6
Akhtubinsk 43,466 ... G5
Akhty ... G6
Akhtyrka 41,354 ... E4
Akkerman (Belgorod-Dnestrovskiy) 32,928 ... D5
Alagir 18,161 ... F6
Alatyr' 43,499 ... G4
Alaverdi 21,311 ... F6
Aleksandriya 82,000 ... D5
Aleksandrovsk 18,286 ... J3
Alekseyevka 25,562 ... E4
Aleksin 67,000 ... E4
Ali-Bayramly 33,828 ... G7
Al'met'yevsk 110,000 ... H3
Alushta 22,016 ... D6
Amderma ... K1
Anapa 29,900 ... E6
Andropov 239,000 ... E3
Apatity 62,000 ... D1
Apsheronsk 32,867 ... F6
Archangel (Arkhangel'sk) 385,000 ... F2
Armavir 162,000 ... F5
Arzamas 93,000 ... F3
Astara ... G7
Astrakhan' 461,000 ... G5
Atkarsk 28,881 ... G4
Azov 75,000 ... E5
Bakhchisaray 15,912 ... D6
Baku 1,022,000 ... H6
Balakhna 36,542 ... F3
Balaklava ... D6
Balakovo 152,000 ... G4
Balashov 93,000 ... F4
Baltiysk 20,300 ... A4
Baranovichi 131,000 ... C4
Barysh 20,792 ... G4
Bataysk 90,000 ... E5
Batumi 123,000 ... F6
Belaya Tserkov' 151,000 ... C5
Belebey 32,460 ... H4
Belev 17,733 ... E4
Belgorod 240,000 ... E4
Belgorod-Dnestrovskiy 32,928 ... D5
Belomorsk 16,595 ... D2
Belorechensk 35,970 ... E6
Beloretsk 71,000 ... J4
Belozersk ... E3
Bel'tsy 125,000 ... C5
Belush'ya Guba ... H1
Bendery 101,000 ... C5
Berdichev 80,000 ... C5
Berdyansk 122,000 ... E5
Beregovo 27,308 ... B5
Berezniki 185,000 ... J3
Beslan 26,893 ... F6
Bezhetsk 30,030 ... E3
Birsk 29,607 ... J3
Bobrov 17,977 ... F4
Bobruysk 192,000 ... C4
Bologoye 33,949 ... D3
Bor 63,000 ... F3
Borislav 33,800 ... B5
Borisoglebsk 68,000 ... F4
Borisov 112,000 ... C4
Borovichi 60,000 ... D3
Brest 177,000 ... B4
Brezhnev 301,000 ... H3
Bryansk 394,000 ... D4
Bugul'ma 80,000 ... H4
Buguruslan 54,000 ... H4
Buturlinovka 21,643 ... F4
Buy 29,946 ... F3
Buynaksk 37,946 ... G6
Buzuluk 76,000 ... H4
Bykhov 17,371 ... C4
Cēsis 17,696 ... C3
Chadyr-Lunga 20,474 ... C5
Chapayevsk 85,000 ... G4
Chaykovskiy 48,034 ... H3
Cheboksary 308,000 ... G3
Cherepovets 266,000 ... E3
Cherkassy 228,000 ... D5
Cherkessk 91,000 ... F6
Chernigov 238,000 ... D4
Chernovtsy 219,000 ... C5
Chernushka 21,106 ... J3
Chervonograd 55,000 ... B4
Chiatura 25,474 ... F6
Chistopol' 64,000 ... H3
Chortkov 19,183 ... B5
Chudovo ... D3
Chusovoy 56,000 ... J3
Danilov 17,500 ... E3
Dankov 20,030 ... E4
Daugavpils 116,000 ... C3
Davlekanovo 20,123 ... H4
Derbent 70,000 ... G6
Dimitrovgrad 106,000 ... G4
Dneprodzerzhinsk 250,000 ... D5
Dnepropetrovsk 1,066,000 ... D5
Dobrush 16,809 ... D4
Dobryanka 18,349 ... J3
Donetsk 1,021,000 ... E5
Drogobych 66,000 ... B5
Dubna 55,000 ... E3
Dubna ... E4
Dubno 25,442 ... C4
Dvinsk (Daugavpils) 116,000 ... C3
Dyat'kovo 26,825 ... D4
Dzerzhinsk 257,000 ... F3
Dzhankoy 43,459 ... D5
Dzhul'fa ... G7
Echmiadzin 31,819 ... F6
Elektrostal' 139,000 ... E3
Elista 70,000 ... F5
El'ton ... G5
Engel's 161,000 ... G4
Erivan 1,019,000 ... F6
Fastov 51,000 ... C4
Feodosiya 76,000 ... D5
Frolovo 33,398 ... F5
Furmanov 40,155 ... F3
Gagra 23,025 ... E6
Galich 19,374 ... F3
Gandzha (Kirovabad) 232,000 ... G6
Gatchina 75,000 ... C3
Gay 28,250 ... J4
Gaysin 23,741 ... C5
Gdov ... C3
Gelendzhik 29,086 ... E6
Genichesk 20,031 ... E5
Georgiu-Dezh 52,000 ... E4
Glazov 81,000 ... H3
Glubokoye ... C3
Glukhov 27,096 ... D4
Gomel' 383,000 ... D4
Gori 56,000 ... F6
Gorki 22,117 ... D4
Gor'kiy 1,344,000 ... F3
Gorlovka 336,000 ... E5
Gorodets 34,229 ... F3
Gremikha ... E1
Gremyachinsk 29,975 ... J3
Grodno 195,000 ... B4
Groznyy 375,000 ... G6
Gryazi 41,292 ... F4
Gubakha 33,243 ... J3
Gubkin 65,000 ... E4
Gudauta ... F6
Gudermes 32,445 ... G6
Gukovo 68,000 ... F5
Gus'-Khrustal'nyy 72,000 ... F3
Imishli 17,839 ... G7
Inta 51,000 ... K1
Inza 19,060 ... G4
Ishimbay 57,000 ... J4
Ivano-Frankovsk 150,000 ... B5
Ivanovo 465,000 ... E3
Izberbash 17,299 ... G6
Izhevsk (Ustinov) 549,000 ... H3
Izmail 83,000 ... C5
Izyum 61,000 ... E5
Jēkabpils 22,440 ... C3
Jelgava 68,000 ... B3
Jurmala 61,000 ... B3
Kadiyevka (Stakhanov) 108,000 ... E5
Kafan 29,916 ... G7
Kagul 26,249 ... C5
Kakhovka 28,472 ... D5
Kalach 18,475 ... F4
Kalach-na-Donu 20,795 ... F5
Kalinin 412,000 ... E3
Kaliningrad, Kaliningrad 355,000 ... B4
Kaliningrad, Moscow Oblast 133,000 ... E3
Kalinkovichi 23,918 ... C4
Kaluga 265,000 ... E4
Kalush 60,000 ... B5
Kamenets-Podol'skiy 81,000 ... C5
Kamenka 30,067 ... F4
Kamensk-Shakhtinskiy 72,000 ... F5
Kamyshin 112,000 ... F4
Kanash 40,682 ... G3
Kandalaksha 42,656 ... D1
Kapsukas 28,763 ... B4
Karachayevsk ... F6
Karachev 15,972 ... E4
Kashin 17,678 ... E3
Kasimov 33,066 ... F4
Kaspiysk 38,990 ... G6
Kaunas 370,000 ... B4
Kazan' 993,000 ... G3
Kazatin 26,649 ... C5
Kem' 21,025 ... D2
Kerch' 157,000 ... E5
Keret' ... D1
Khachmas 22,313 ... G6
Khadyzhensk 17,856 ... E6
Khar'kov 1,444,000 ... E5
Khasavyurt 65,000 ... G6
Khashuri 24,469 ... F6
Kherson 319,000 ... D5
Khmel'nitskiy 172,000 ... C5
Khotin 10,319 ... C5
Khust 23,810 ... B5
Khvalynsk 16,249 ... G4
Kiev 2,144,000 ... D4
Kiliya 24,276 ... C5
Kimovsk 44,490 ... E4
Kimry 58,000 ... E3
Kinel' 39,373 ... H4
Kineshma 101,000 ... F3
Kirishi 27,252 ... D3
Kirov, Kaluga 29,355 ... D4
Kirov, Kirov 390,000 ... G3
Kirovabad 232,000 ... G6
Kirovakan 146,000 ... G6
Kirovo-Chepetsk 71,000 ... H3
Kirovograd 237,000 ... D5
Kirovsk 38,484 ... D1
Kirsanov 21,795 ... F4
Kishinev 503,000 ... C5
Kislovodsk 101,000 ... F6
Kizel 46,264 ... J3
Kizlyar 29,745 ... G6
Klaipeda 176,000 ... B3
Klintsy 67,000 ... D4
Kobrin 24,935 ... B4
Kobuleti 18,051 ... F6
Kohtla-Järve 73,000 ... C3
Kolomiya 52,000 ... B5
Kolomna 147,000 ... E4
Kolpino 114,000 ... D3
Kommunarsk 120,000 ... E5
Komrat 21,369 ... C5
Komsomol'skiy 17,078 ... K1
Kondopoga 27,908 ... D2
Königsberg (Kaliningrad) 355,000 ... B4
Konotop 82,000 ... D4
Konstantinovka 112,000 ... E5
Korenovsk 26,323 ... E5
Korosten' 65,000 ... C4
Korostyshev 21,153 ... C4
Koryazhma 33,230 ... G2
Kostopol' 17,548 ... C4
Kostroma 255,000 ... F3
Kotel'nich 29,196 ... G3
Kotel'nikovo 19,063 ... F5
Kotlas 61,000 ... G2
Kotovo 20,553 ... G4
Kotovsk, Odessa 36,463 ... C5
Kotovsk, Tambov 33,347 ... F4
Kovel' 33,351 ... C4
Kovrov 143,000 ... F3
Kovylkino 17,300 ... F4
Kramatorsk 178,000 ... E5
Krasnoarmeysk 60,000 ... G4
Krasnodar 560,000 ... E6
Krasnograd 18,386 ... E5
Krasnokamsk 56,000 ... H3
Krasnoslobodsk 17,749 ... G5
Krasnovishersk ... J2
Krasnyy Kut 17,087 ... G4
Krasnyy Luch 106,000 ... E5
Krasnyy Sulin 41,684 ... F5
Kremenchug 210,000 ... D5
Krichev 25,682 ... D4
Krivoy Rog 650,000 ... D5
Krolevets 18,307 ... D4
Kronshtadt 39,477 ... C3
Kropotkin 70,000 ... F5
Krymsk 41,430 ... E5
Kuba 18,871 ... G6
Kudymkar 26,350 ... H3
Kulebaki 46,252 ... F3
Kumertau 52,000 ... J4
Kunda ... C3
Kungur 80,000 ... J3
Kupyansk 30,055 ... E5
Kuressaare 12,140 ... B3
Kursk 375,000 ... E4
Kutaisi 194,000 ... F6
Kuvandyk 22,914 ... J4
Kuybyshev 1,216,000 ... H4
Kuznetsk 94,000 ... G4
Kuzomen' ... E1
Labinsk 54,000 ... F6
Lakhdenpokh'ya ... C2
Lebedin 29,240 ... D4
Leninakan 207,000 ... F6
Leningrad 4,073,000 ... C3
Leningrad* 4,588,000 ... C3
Leninogorsk 54,000 ... H4
Lenkoran' 35,505 ... G7
L'gov 25,110 ... E4
Lida 66,000 ... C4
Liepāja 108,000 ... B3
Likhoslavl' ... E3
Lipetsk 396,000 ... E4
Lisichansk 119,000 ... E5
Livny 37,290 ... E4
Lodeynoye Pole 19,632 ... D2
Lozovaya 53,000 ... E5
Lubny 54,000 ... D4
Luga 31,905 ... C3
Lutsk 137,000 ... B4
L'vov (Lwów) 667,000 ... B5
Lys'va 75,000 ... J3
Lyubertsy 160,000 ... E3
Lyubotin 33,324 ... E4
Lyudinovo 33,871 ... D4
Makeyevka 436,000 ... E5
Makhachkala 251,000 ... G6
Makharadze 21,679 ... F6
Malaya Vishera 15,381 ... D3
Malgobek 20,548 ... F6
Manturovo 21,510 ... F3
Marganets 50,000 ... E5
Mariupol' (Zhdanov) 503,000 ... E5
Marks 17,132 ... G4
Maykop 128,000 ... F6
Mednogorsk 38,024 ... J4
Medvezh'yegorsk 17,465 ... D2
Melenki 18,545 ... F3
Meleuz 24,851 ... J4
Melitopol' 161,000 ... D5
Memel (Klaipeda) 176,000 ... B3
Merefa 29,985 ... E5
Mezen' ... F1
Michurinsk 101,000 ... F4
Mikhaylovka 58,000 ... F4
Millerovo 34,627 ... F5
Mineral'nye Vody 67,000 ... F6
Mingechaur 60,000 ... G6
Minsk 1,262,000 ... C4
Minsk* 1,276,000 ... C4
Mirgorod 28,407 ... D5
Mogilev 290,000 ... C4
Mogilev-Podol'skiy 26,051 ... C5
Molodechno 73,000 ... C4
Molotov (Perm') 999,000 ... J3
Monchegorsk 51,000 ... D1
Morshansk 44,245 ... F4
Moscow (Moskva) (cap.) 7,831,000 ... E3
Moscow* 8,011,000 ... E3
Mozhaysk 20,321 ... E3
Mozhga 38,930 ... H3
Mozyr' 73,000 ... C4
Mtsensk 27,833 ... E4
Mukachevo 72,000 ... B5
Murmansk 381,000 ... D1
Murom 114,000 ... F3
Mytishchi 141,000 ... E3
Nakhichevan' 33,279 ... F7
Nal'chik 207,000 ... F6
Narva 73,000 ... C3
Nar'yan-Mar 16,864 ... H1
Neftekamsk 70,000 ... J3
Nelidovo 29,813 ... D3
Nerekhta 25,722 ... F3
Nevel' 17,804 ... D3
Nevinnomyssk 104,000 ... F6
Nezhin 70,000 ... D4
Nikel' 21,299 ... C1
Nikolayev 440,000 ... D5
Nikol'sk 20,740 ... G4
Nikopol' 146,000 ... D5
Nizhnekamsk 134,000 ... H3
Nizhniy Lomov 17,460 ... F4
Nizhniy Novgorod (Gor'kiy) 1,344,000 ... F3
Nosovka 19,430 ... D4
Novaya Kakhovka 52,000 ... D5
Novgorod 186,000 ... D3
Novgorod-Severskiy ... D4
Novoanninskiy 20,461 ... F4
Novocherkassk 183,000 ... F5
Novograd-Volynskiy 41,194 ... C4
Novogrudok 19,374 ... C4
Novokuybyshevsk 109,000 ... G4
Novomoskovsk 147,000 ... E4
Novopolotsk 67,000 ... C3
Novorossiysk 159,000 ... E6
Novoshakhtinsk 104,000 ... E5
Novotroitsk 95,000 ... J4
Novoukrainka 19,554 ... D5
Novouzensk ... G4
Novovolynsk 41,187 ... B4
Novovyatsk 26,408 ... G3
Novozybkov 34,433 ... D4
Nurlat 17,533 ... H4
Nyandoma 23,366 ... F2
Nytva 17,491 ... H3
Nyuvchim ... H2
Obninsk 73,000 ... E3
Ochamchira 18,718 ... F6
Odessa 1,046,000 ... D5
Oktyabr'sk 33,981 ... G4
Oktyabr'skiy 88,000 ... H4
Okulovka 19,194 ... D3
Olenegorsk 21,485 ... D1
Olonets ... D2
Omutninsk 28,777 ... H3
Onega 25,047 ... E2
Ordzhonikidze 279,000 ... F6
Orel 305,000 ... E4
Orenburg 459,000 ... J4
Orgeyev 25,798 ... C5
Orsha 112,000 ... C4
Orsk 247,000 ... J4
Osa 15,038 ... J3
Osipenko (Berdyansk) 122,000 ... E5
Osipovichi 19,705 ... C4
Ostashkov 23,419 ... D3
Ostrogozhsk 29,921 ... E4
Ostrov 22,369 ... C3
Otradnyy 44,426 ... H4
Panevežys 102,000 ... B3
Pärnu 51,000 ... C3
Pavlograd 107,000 ... E5
Pavlovo 68,000 ... F3
Pechenga ... D1
Pechora 56,000 ... J1
Penza 483,000 ... G4
Perm' 999,000 ... J3
Pervomaysk 72,000 ... D5
Petrokrepost' ... D3
Petrovsk 30,953 ... G4
Petrozavodsk 234,000 ... D2
Petsamo (Pechenga) ... D1
Pinsk 90,000 ... C4
Podol'sk 202,000 ... E3
Podporozh'ye 21,545 ... D2
Pokhvistnevo 26,125 ... H4
Polonnoye 22,484 ... C4
Polotsk 71,000 ... C3
Poltava 279,000 ... D5
Polyarnyy 15,321 ... D1
Ponoy ... F1
Poti 45,979 ... F6
Povenets ... E2
Povorino 20,591 ... F4
Prikumsk 35,768 ... F6
Priluki 65,000 ... D4
Primorsk ... C2
Primorsko-Akhtarsk 25,981 ... E5
Priozersk 16,652 ... D2
Privolzhskiy 23,041 ... G4
Priyutovo 21,051 ... H4
Prokhladnyy 40,074 ... F6
Pskov 176,000 ... C3
Pugachev 33,963 ... G4
Pushkin 90,000 ... C3
Pyatigorsk 110,000 ... F6
Rabocheostrovsk ... D1
Rakhov ... B5
Rakvere 17,891 ... C3
Rasskazovo 40,038 ... F4
Razdan 26,833 ... G6
Rechitsa 60,000 ... C4
Reni 19,625 ... C5
Revel (Tallinn) 430,000 ... B3
Rězekne 30,803 ... C3
Riga 835,000 ... B3
Romny 53,000 ... D4
Roslavl' 56,000 ... D4
Rossosh' 36,438 ... E4
Rostov 30,815 ... E3
Rostov-na-Donu 934,000 ... F5
Rovno 179,000 ... C4
Rtishchevo 37,146 ... F4
Rubezhnoye 66,000 ... E5
Rustavi 129,000 ... G6
Ruzayevka 41,084 ... F4
Ryazan' 453,000 ... E4
Ryazhsk 25,425 ... F4
Rybinsk (Andropov) 239,000 ... E3
Rybnitsa 32,266 ... C5
Rzhev 69,000 ... D3
Safonovo 53,000 ... D3
Saki 24,208 ... D5
Salavat 137,000 ... H4
Sal'sk 57,000 ... F5
Sal'yany 24,228 ... G7
Samara (Kuybyshev) 1,216,000 ... H4
Sambor 29,253 ... B5
Saransk 263,000 ... G4
Sarapul 107,000 ... H3
Saratov 856,000 ... G4
Sasovo 27,228 ... F4
Segezha 28,810 ... D2
Semenov 23,633 ... F3
Semiluki 18,221 ... E4
Sengiley ... G4
Serdobol (Sortavala) 22,188 ... D2
Serdobsk 33,783 ... F4
Sergach 22,509 ... F3
Serpukhov 140,000 ... E4
Sevastopol' 301,000 ... D6
Severodonetsk 113,000 ... E5
Severodvinsk 197,000 ... E2
Severomorsk 50,000 ... D1
Shakhty 209,000 ... F5
Shakhun'ya 20,009 ... G3
Shar'ya 25,788 ... G3
Shchekino 70,000 ... E4
Shchigry 17,133 ... E4
Sheki 43,158 ... G6
Shemakha 17,986 ... G6
Shepetovka 38,707 ... C4
Shostka 82,000 ... D4
Shpola 19,806 ... D5
Shumerlya 33,816 ... G3
Shuya 72,000 ... F3
Šiauliai 118,000 ... B3
Sibay 37,656 ... J4
Simferopol' 302,000 ... D6
Skadovsk ... D5
Skopin 24,429 ... F4
Slantsy 41,146 ... C3
Slavuta 25,573 ... C4
Slavyansk 140,000 ... E5
Slavyansk-na-Kubani 54,000 ... E5
Slobodskoy 34,374 ... H3
Slonim 30,279 ... B4
Slutsk 35,609 ... C4
Smela 62,000 ... D5
Smolensk 276,000 ... D4
Sochi 287,000 ... E6
Sokol 48,243 ... F3
Soligorsk 65,000 ... C4
Solikamsk 101,000 ... J3
Sol'-Iletsk 22,227 ... J4
Sorochinsk 23,235 ... H4
Soroki 21,924 ... C5
Sortavala 22,188 ... D2
Sosnogorsk 24,688 ... H2
Sovetsk (Tilsit) 38,456 ... B4
Sovetsk 17,027 ... G3
Stakhanov 108,000 ... E5
Stalingrad (Volgograd) 929,000 ... F5
Staraya Russa 34,577 ... D3
Staryy Oskol 115,000 ... E4
Stavropol' 258,000 ... F5
Stepanakert 30,293 ... G7
Sterlitamak 220,000 ... J4
Stupino 70,000 ... E4
Sudak ... E6
Sukhumi 114,000 ... F6
Sumgait 190,000 ... G6
Sumy 228,000 ... E4
Svetlogorsk 55,000 ... C4
Svetlograd 40,265 ... F5
Syktyvkar 171,000 ... H2
Syzran' 178,000 ... G4
Taganrog 276,000 ... E5
Tallinn 430,000 ... B3
Tambov 270,000 ... F4
Tartu 105,000 ... C3
Taurage 19,461 ... B3
Tbilisi 1,066,000 ... F6
Telavi 21,179 ... G6
Telšiai 20,220 ... B3
Temryuk 23,172 ... E5
Ternopol' 144,000 ... C5
Teykovo 41,607 ... E3
Tiflis (Tbilisi) 1,066,000 ... F6
Tighina (Bendery) 101,000 ... C5
Tikhoretsk 64,000 ... F5
Tikhvin 59,000 ... D3
Tilsit (Sovetsk) 38,456 ... B4
Timashevsk 29,055 ... E5
Tiraspol' 139,000 ... D5
Togliatti (Tol'yatti) 502,000 ... G4
Tokmak 59,000 ... E5
Toropets 16,863 ... D3
Torzhok 45,443 ... D3
Troitsko-Pechorsk ... J2
Tskhinvali 30,311 ... F6
Tuapse 60,000 ... E6
Tula 514,000 ... E4
Tutayev 16,839 ... E3
Tuymazy 37,021 ... H4
Tver (Kalinin) 412,000 ... E3
Tyrnyauz 18,253 ... F6
Uchaly 21,808 ... J4
Ufa 969,000 ... J4
Uglich 35,463 ... E3
Ukmerge 21,663 ... C3
Ul'yanovsk 464,000 ... G4
Uman' 79,000 ... D5
Unecha 21,749 ... D4
Ungeny 17,228 ... C5
Uryupinsk 38,192 ... F4
Usinsk ... J1
Usman' 20,150 ... E4
Ustinov 549,000 ... H3
Uvarovo 24,946 ... F4
Uzhgorod 91,000 ... B5
Uzlovaya 65,000 ... E4
Valga 16,795 ... C3
Valmiera 20,331 ... C3
Valuyki 29,093 ... E4
Vasil'kov 26,741 ... D4
Velikiye Luki 102,000 ... D3
Velikiy Ustyug 36,737 ... F2
Vel'sk 21,899 ... F2
Ventspils 40,467 ... B3
Vereshchagino 23,585 ... H3
Vichuga 52,000 ... F3
Viipuri (Vyborg) 76,000 ... C2
Vileyka ... C4
Vilna (Vilnius) 481,000 ... C4
Vinnitsa 314,000 ... C5
Vinogradov 20,580 ... B5
Vitebsk 297,000 ... C3
Vladimir 296,000 ... F3
Vladimir-Volynskiy 28,412 ... B4
Volgodonsk 91,000 ... F5
Volgograd 929,000 ... F5
Volkhov 47,025 ... D3
Volkovysk 28,266 ... B4
Vologda 237,000 ... F3
Vol'sk 66,000 ... G4
Volzhsk 52,000 ... G3
Volzhskiy 209,000 ... G5
Vorkuta 100,000 ... K1
Voronezh 783,000 ... E4
Voroshilovgrad 463,000 ... E5
Voskresensk 76,000 ... E3
Votkinsk 90,000 ... H3
Voznesensk 36,457 ... D5
Vyatskiye Polyany 32,729 ... H3
Vyaz'ma 52,000 ... D3
Vyborg 76,000 ... C2
Vyksa 54,000 ... F3
Vyshniy Volochek 72,000 ... D3
Yalta 80,000 ... D6
Yanaul 20,115 ... J3
Yaroslavl' 597,000 ... E3
Yartsevo 36,662 ... D3
Yefremov 53,000 ... E4
Yelabuga 31,728 ... H3
Yelets 112,000 ... E4
Yenakiyevo 114,000 ... E5
Yershov 21,731 ... G4
Yessentuki 78,000 ... F6
Yevlakh 29,462 ... G6
Yevpatoria 93,000 ... D5
Yeysk 71,000 ... E5
Yoshkar-Ola 201,000 ... G3
Yur'yevets 20,144 ... F3
Zagorsk 107,000 ... E3
Zapolyarnyy 22,084 ... D1
Zaporozh'ye 781,000 ... E5
Zelenodol'sk 85,000 ... G3
Zelenokumsk 29,691 ... F6
Zernograd 20,324 ... F5
Zhdanov 503,000 ... E5
Zheleznodorozhnyy 76,000 ... H2
Zheleznogorsk 65,000 ... E4
Zhigulevsk 52,130 ... G4
Zhitomir 244,000 ... C4
Zhlobin 25,359 ... D4
Zhmerinka 36,195 ... C5
Zhodino 22,083 ... C4
Zhovtnevoye 31,102 ... D5
Znamenka 27,393 ... D5
Zolotonosha 27,639 ... D5
Zugdidi 39,896 ... F6
Zuyevka 17,001 ... H3

OTHER FEATURES

Apsheron (pen.) ... H6
Araks (riv.) ... G7
Azov (sea) ... E5
Baltic (sea) ... B3
Barents (sea) ... E1
Belaya (riv.) ... H3
Beloye (lake) ... E2
Black (sea) ... D6
Bug (riv.) ... B4
Bug (riv.) ... D5
Caspian (sea) ... G6
Caucasus (mts.) ... F6
Crimea (pen.) ... D5
Desna (riv.) ... D4
Dnieper (riv.) ... D5
Dniester (riv.) ... C5
Don (riv.) ... F5
Donets (riv.) ... E5
Dvina (bay) ... E2
Dvina, Northern (riv.) ... F2
Dvina, Western (riv.) ... C3
Dykh-Tau (mt.) ... F6
El'brus (mt.) ... F6
Finland (gulf) ... C3
Hiiumaa (isl.) ... B3
Il'men' (lake) ... D3
Imandra (lake) ... D1
Kakhovka (res.) ... D5
Kama (riv.) ... H2
Kandalaksha (gulf) ... D1
Kanin (pen.) ... G1
Kara (sea) ... K1
Karskiye Vorota (str.) ... J1
Kazbek (mt.) ... F6
Khoper (riv.) ... F4
Kola (pen.) ... E1
Kolguyev (isl.) ... G1
Kuban' (riv.) ... E5
Kura (riv.) ... G6
Kuybyshev (res.) ... G4
Ladoga (lake) ... D2
Lapland (reg.) ... D1
Mezen' (riv.) ... G1
Moksha (riv.) ... F4
Narodnaya (mt.) ... J1
Niemen (riv.) ... B4
Novaya Zemlya (isls.) ... H1
Oka (riv.) ... F4
Onega (bay) ... E2
Onega (lake) ... E2
Onega (riv.) ... E2
Pechora (riv.) ... H1
Peipus (lake) ... C3
Pripet (marshes) ... C4
Pripyat' (riv.) ... C4
Prut (riv.) ... C5
Riga (gulf) ... B3
Rybachiy (pen.) ... D1
Rybinsk (res.) ... E3
Saaremaa (isl.) ... B3
Samara (riv.) ... H4
Sevan (lake) ... G6
Seym (riv.) ... D4
Sura (riv.) ... G4
Svir' (riv.) ... D2
Timan (ridge) ... G1
Tsil'ma (riv.) ... H1
Tsimlyansk (res.) ... F5
Tuloma (riv.) ... D1
Ural (mts.) ... J2
Ural (riv.) ... J4
Usa (riv.) ... K1
Valday (hills) ... D3
Vaygach (isl.) ... K1
Velikaya (riv.) ... C3
Volga (riv.) ... G5
Volga-Don (canal) ... F5
Volgograd (res.) ... G5
Volkhov (riv.) ... D3
Vorskla (riv.) ... E4
Vyatka (riv.) ... H3
Vychegda (riv.) ... G2
Vyg (lake) ... E2
White (sea) ... E1
Yamantau (mt.) ... J4
Yugorskiy (pen.) ... K1

*City and suburbs.

ALGERIA
AREA 919,591 sq. mi. (2,381,740 sq. km.)
POPULATION 17,422,000
CAPITAL Algiers
LARGEST CITY Algiers
HIGHEST POINT Tahat 9,852 ft. (3,003 m.)
MONETARY UNIT Algerian dinar
MAJOR LANGUAGES Arabic, Berber, French
MAJOR RELIGION Islam

ANGOLA
AREA 481,351 sq. mi. (1,246,700 sq. km.)
POPULATION 7,078,000
CAPITAL Luanda
LARGEST CITY Luanda
HIGHEST POINT Mt. Moco 8,593 ft. (2,620 m.)
MONETARY UNIT kwanza
MAJOR LANGUAGES Mbundu, Kongo, Lunda, Portuguese
MAJOR RELIGIONS Tribal religions, Roman Catholicism

BENIN
AREA 43,483 sq. mi. (112,620 sq. km.)
POPULATION 3,338,240
CAPITAL Porto-Novo
LARGEST CITY Cotonou
HIGHEST POINT Atakora Mts. 2,083 ft. (635 m.)
MONETARY UNIT CFA franc
MAJOR LANGUAGES Fon, Somba, Yoruba, Bariba, French, Mina, Dendi
MAJOR RELIGIONS Tribal religions, Islam, Roman Catholicism

BOTSWANA
AREA 224,764 sq. mi. (582,139 sq. km.)
POPULATION 819,000
CAPITAL Gaborone
LARGEST CITY Francistown
HIGHEST POINT Tsodilo Hill 5,922 ft. (1,805 m.)
MONETARY UNIT pula
MAJOR LANGUAGES Setswana, Shona, Bushman, English, Afrikaans
MAJOR RELIGIONS Tribal religions, Protestantism

BURKINA FASO
AREA 105,869 sq. mi. (274,200 sq. km.)
POPULATION 6,908,000
CAPITAL Ouagadougou
LARGEST CITY Ouagadougou
HIGHEST POINT 2,352 ft. (717 m.)
MONETARY UNIT CFA franc
MAJOR LANGUAGES Mossi, Lobi, French, Samo, Gourounsi
MAJOR RELIGIONS Islam, tribal religions, Roman Catholicism

BURUNDI
AREA 10,747 sq. mi. (27,835 sq. km.)
POPULATION 4,021,910
CAPITAL Bujumbura
LARGEST CITY Bujumbura
HIGHEST POINT 8,858 ft. (2,700 m.)
MONETARY UNIT Burundi franc
MAJOR LANGUAGES Kirundi, French, Swahili
MAJOR RELIGIONS Tribal religions, Roman Catholicism, Islam

CAMEROON
AREA 183,568 sq. mi. (475,441 sq. km.)
POPULATION 8,503,000
CAPITAL Yaoundé
LARGEST CITY Douala
HIGHEST POINT Cameroon 13,350 ft. (4,069 m.)
MONETARY UNIT CFA franc
MAJOR LANGUAGES Fang, Bamileke, Fulani, Duala, French, English
MAJOR RELIGIONS Tribal religions, Christianity, Islam

CAPE VERDE
AREA 1,557 sq. mi. (4,033 sq. km.)
POPULATION 324,000
CAPITAL Praia
LARGEST CITY Praia
HIGHEST POINT 9,281 ft. (2,829 m.)
MONETARY UNIT Cape Verde escudo
MAJOR LANGUAGE Portuguese
MAJOR RELIGION Roman Catholicism

CENTRAL AFRICAN REPUBLIC
AREA 242,000 sq. mi. (626,780 sq. km.)
POPULATION 2,284,000
CAPITAL Bangui
LARGEST CITY Bangui
HIGHEST POINT Gao 4,659 ft. (1,420 m.)
MONETARY UNIT CFA franc
MAJOR LANGUAGES Banda, Gbaya, Sangho, French
MAJOR RELIGIONS Tribal religions, Christianity, Islam

CHAD
AREA 495,752 sq. mi. (1,283,998 sq. km.)
POPULATION 4,309,000
CAPITAL N'Djamena
LARGEST CITY N'Djamena
HIGHEST POINT Emi Koussi 11,204 ft. (3,415 m.)
MONETARY UNIT CFA franc
MAJOR LANGUAGES Arabic, Bagirmi, French, Sara, Massa, Moudang
MAJOR RELIGIONS Islam, tribal religions

COMOROS
AREA 719 sq. mi. (1,862 sq. km.)
POPULATION 290,000
CAPITAL Moroni
LARGEST CITY Moroni
HIGHEST POINT Karthala 7,746 ft. (2,361 m.)
MONETARY UNIT CFA franc
MAJOR LANGUAGES Arabic, French, Swahili
MAJOR RELIGION Islam

CONGO
AREA 132,046 sq. mi. (342,000 sq. km.)
POPULATION 1,537,000
CAPITAL Brazzaville
LARGEST CITY Brazzaville
HIGHEST POINT Leketi Mts. 3,412 ft. (1,040 m.)
MONETARY UNIT CFA franc
MAJOR LANGUAGES Kikongo, Bateke, Lingala, French
MAJOR RELIGIONS Christianity, tribal religions, Islam

DJIBOUTI
AREA 8,880 sq. mi. (23,000 sq. km.)
POPULATION 386,000
CAPITAL Djibouti
LARGEST CITY Djibouti
HIGHEST POINT Moussa Ali 6,768 ft. (2,063 m.)
MONETARY UNIT Djibouti franc
MAJOR LANGUAGES Arabic, Somali, Afar, French
MAJOR RELIGIONS Islam, Roman Catholicism

EGYPT
AREA 386,659 sq. mi. (1,001,447 sq. km.)
POPULATION 41,572,000
CAPITAL Cairo
LARGEST CITY Cairo
HIGHEST POINT Jeb. Katherina 8,651 ft. (2,637 m.)
MONETARY UNIT Egyptian pound
MAJOR LANGUAGE Arabic
MAJOR RELIGIONS Islam, Coptic Christianity

EQUATORIAL GUINEA
AREA 10,831 sq. mi. (28,052 sq. km.)
POPULATION 244,000
CAPITAL Malabo
LARGEST CITY Malabo
HIGHEST POINT 9,868 ft. (3,008 m.)
MONETARY UNIT CFA franc
MAJOR LANGUAGES Fang, Bubi, Spanish
MAJOR RELIGIONS Tribal religions, Christianity

ETHIOPIA
AREA 471,776 sq. mi. (1,221,900 sq. km.)
POPULATION 31,065,000
CAPITAL Addis Ababa
LARGEST CITY Addis Ababa
HIGHEST POINT Ras Dashan 15,157 ft. (4,620 m.)
MONETARY UNIT birr
MAJOR LANGUAGES Amharic, Gallinya, Tigrinya, Somali, Sidamo, Arabic, Ge'ez
MAJOR RELIGIONS Coptic Christianity, Islam

GABON
AREA 103,346 sq. mi. (267,666 sq. km.)
POPULATION 551,000
CAPITAL Libreville
LARGEST CITY Libreville
HIGHEST POINT Ibounzi 5,165 ft. (1,574 m.)
MONETARY UNIT CFA franc
MAJOR LANGUAGES Fang and other Bantu languages, French
MAJOR RELIGIONS Tribal religions, Christianity, Islam

GAMBIA
AREA 4,127 sq. mi. (10,689 sq. km.)
POPULATION 601,000
CAPITAL Banjul
LARGEST CITY Banjul
HIGHEST POINT 100 ft. (30 m.)
MONETARY UNIT dalasi
MAJOR LANGUAGES Mandingo, Fulani, Wolof, English, Malinke
MAJOR RELIGIONS Islam, tribal religions, Christianity

GHANA
AREA 92,099 sq. mi. (238,536 sq. km.)
POPULATION 11,450,000
CAPITAL Accra
LARGEST CITY Accra
HIGHEST POINT Togo Hills 2,900 ft. (884 m.)
MONETARY UNIT cedi
MAJOR LANGUAGES Twi, Fante, Dagbani, Ewe, Ga, English, Hausa, Akan
MAJOR RELIGIONS Tribal religions, Christianity, Islam

GUINEA
AREA 94,925 sq. mi. (245,856 sq. km.)
POPULATION 5,143,284
CAPITAL Conakry
LARGEST CITY Conakry
HIGHEST POINT Nimba Mts. 6,070 ft. (1,850 m.)
MONETARY UNIT syli
MAJOR LANGUAGES Fulani, Mandingo, Susu, French
MAJOR RELIGIONS Islam, tribal religions

GUINEA-BISSAU
AREA 13,948 sq. mi. (36,125 sq. km.)
POPULATION 777,214
CAPITAL Bissau
LARGEST CITY Bissau
HIGHEST POINT 689 ft. (210 m.)
MONETARY UNIT Guinea-Bissau escudo
MAJOR LANGUAGES Balante, Fulani, Crioulo, Mandingo, Portuguese
MAJOR RELIGIONS Islam, tribal religions, Roman Catholicism

IVORY COAST
AREA 124,504 sq. mi. (322,465 sq. km.)
POPULATION 7,920,000
CAPITAL Yamoussoukro
LARGEST CITY Abidjan
HIGHEST POINT 5,745 ft. (1,751 m.)
MONETARY UNIT CFA franc
MAJOR LANGUAGES Bale, Bete, Senufu, French, Dioula
MAJOR RELIGIONS Tribal religions, Islam

KENYA
AREA 224,960 sq. mi. (582,646 sq. km.)
POPULATION 15,327,061
CAPITAL Nairobi
LARGEST CITY Nairobi
HIGHEST POINT Kenya 17,058 ft. (5,199 m.)
MONETARY UNIT Kenya shilling
MAJOR LANGUAGES Kikuyu, Luo, Kavirondo, Kamba, Swahili, English
MAJOR RELIGIONS Tribal religions, Christianity, Hinduism, Islam

LESOTHO
AREA 11,720 sq. mi. (30,355 sq. km.)
POPULATION 1,339,000
CAPITAL Maseru
LARGEST CITY Maseru
HIGHEST POINT 11,425 ft. (3,482 m.)
MONETARY UNIT loti
MAJOR LANGUAGES Sesotho, English
MAJOR RELIGIONS Tribal religions, Christianity

LIBERIA
AREA 43,000 sq. mi. (111,370 sq. km.)
POPULATION 1,873,000
CAPITAL Monrovia
LARGEST CITY Monrovia
HIGHEST POINT Wutivi 5,584 ft. (1,702 m.)
MONETARY UNIT Liberian dollar
MAJOR LANGUAGES Kru, Kpelle, Bassa, Vai, English
MAJOR RELIGIONS Christianity, tribal religions, Islam

LIBYA
AREA 679,358 sq. mi. (1,759,537 sq. km.)
POPULATION 2,856,000
CAPITAL Tripoli
LARGEST CITY Tripoli
HIGHEST POINT Bette Pk. 7,500 ft. (2,286 m.)
MONETARY UNIT Libyan dinar
MAJOR LANGUAGES Arabic, Berber
MAJOR RELIGION Islam

MADAGASCAR
AREA 226,657 sq. mi. (587,041 sq. km.)
POPULATION 8,742,000
CAPITAL Antananarivo
LARGEST CITY Antananarivo
HIGHEST POINT Maromokotro 9,436 ft. (2,876 m.)
MONETARY UNIT Madagascar franc
MAJOR LANGUAGES Malagasy, French
MAJOR RELIGIONS Tribal religions, Roman Catholicism, Protestantism

MALAWI
AREA 45,747 sq. mi. (118,485 sq. km.)
POPULATION 5,968,000
CAPITAL Lilongwe
LARGEST CITY Blantyre
HIGHEST POINT Mulanje 9,843 ft. (3,000 m.)
MONETARY UNIT Malawi kwacha
MAJOR LANGUAGES Chichewa, Yao, English, Nyanja, Tumbuka, Tonga, Ngoni
MAJOR RELIGIONS Tribal religions, Islam, Christianity

MALI
AREA 464,873 sq. mi. (1,204,021 sq. km.)
POPULATION 6,906,000
CAPITAL Bamako
LARGEST CITY Bamako
HIGHEST POINT Hombori Mts. 3,789 ft. (1,155 m.)
MONETARY UNIT Mali franc
MAJOR LANGUAGES Bambara, Senufu, Fulani, Soninke, French
MAJOR RELIGIONS Islam, tribal religions

MAURITANIA
AREA 419,229 sq. mi. (1,085,803 sq. km.)
POPULATION 1,634,000
CAPITAL Nouakchott
LARGEST CITY Nouakchott
HIGHEST POINT 2,972 ft. (906 m.)
MONETARY UNIT ouguiya
MAJOR LANGUAGES Arabic, Wolof, Tukolor, French
MAJOR RELIGION Islam

AFRICA
AREA 11,707,000 sq. mi. (30,321,130 sq. km.)
POPULATION 469,000,000
LARGEST CITY Cairo
HIGHEST POINT Kilimanjaro 19,340 ft. (5,895 m.)
LOWEST POINT Lake Assal, Djibouti -512 ft. (-156 m.)

MAURITIUS
AREA 790 sq. mi. (2,046 sq. km.)
POPULATION 959,000
CAPITAL Port Louis
LARGEST CITY Port Louis
HIGHEST POINT 2,711 ft. (826 m.)
MONETARY UNIT Mauritian rupee
MAJOR LANGUAGES English, French, French Creole, Hindi, Urdu
MAJOR RELIGIONS Hinduism, Christianity, Islam

MAYOTTE
AREA 144 sq. mi. (373 sq. km.)
POPULATION 47,300
CAPITAL Dzaoudzi

RÉUNION
AREA 969 sq. mi. (2,510 sq. km.)
POPULATION 491,000
CAPITAL St-Denis

MOROCCO
AREA 172,414 sq. mi. (446,550 sq. km.)
POPULATION 20,242,000
CAPITAL Rabat
LARGEST CITY Casablanca
HIGHEST POINT Jeb. Toubkal 13,665 ft. (4,165 m.)
MONETARY UNIT dirham
MAJOR LANGUAGES Arabic, Berber, French
MAJOR RELIGIONS Islam, Judaism, Christianity

MOZAMBIQUE
AREA 303,769 sq. mi. (786,762 sq. km.)
POPULATION 12,130,000
CAPITAL Maputo
LARGEST CITY Maputo
HIGHEST POINT Mt. Binga 7,992 ft. (2,436 m.)
MONETARY UNIT metical
MAJOR LANGUAGES Makua, Thonga, Shona, Portuguese
MAJOR RELIGIONS Tribal religions, Roman Catholicism, Islam

NAMIBIA (SOUTH-WEST AFRICA)
AREA 317,827 sq. mi. (823,172 sq. km.)
POPULATION 1,200,000
CAPITAL Windhoek
LARGEST CITY Windhoek
HIGHEST POINT Brandberg 8,550 ft. (2,606 m.)
MONETARY UNIT rand
MAJOR LANGUAGES Ovambo, Hottentot, Herero, Afrikaans, English
MAJOR RELIGIONS Tribal religions, Protestantism

NIGER
AREA 489,189 sq. mi. (1,267,000 sq. km.)
POPULATION 5,098,427
CAPITAL Niamey
LARGEST CITY Niamey
HIGHEST POINT Banguezane 6,234 ft. (1,900 m.)
MONETARY UNIT CFA franc
MAJOR LANGUAGES Hausa, Songhai, Fulani, French, Tamashek, Djerma
MAJOR RELIGIONS Islam, tribal religions

NIGERIA
AREA 357,000 sq. mi. (924,630 sq. km.)
POPULATION 82,643,000
CAPITAL Lagos
LARGEST CITY Lagos
HIGHEST POINT Dimlang 6,700 ft. (2,042 m.)
MONETARY UNIT naira
MAJOR LANGUAGES Hausa, Yoruba, Ibo, Ijaw, Fulani, Tiv, Kanuri, Ibibio, English, Edo
MAJOR RELIGIONS Islam, Christianity, tribal religions

RWANDA
AREA 10,169 sq. mi. (26,337 sq. km.)
POPULATION 4,819,317
CAPITAL Kigali
LARGEST CITY Kigali
HIGHEST POINT Karisimbi 14,780 ft. (4,505 m.)
MONETARY UNIT Rwanda franc
MAJOR LANGUAGES Kinyarwanda, French, Swahili
MAJOR RELIGIONS Tribal religions, Roman Catholicism, Islam

SÃO TOMÉ E PRÍNCIPE
AREA 372 sq. mi. (963 sq. km.)
POPULATION 85,000
CAPITAL São Tomé
LARGEST CITY São Tomé
HIGHEST POINT Pico 6,640 ft. (2,024 m.)
MONETARY UNIT dobra
MAJOR LANGUAGES Bantu languages, Portuguese
MAJOR RELIGIONS Tribal religions, Roman Catholicism

SENEGAL
AREA 75,954 sq. mi. (196,720 sq. km.)
POPULATION 5,508,000
CAPITAL Dakar
LARGEST CITY Dakar
HIGHEST POINT Futa Jallon 1,640 ft. (500 m.)
MONETARY UNIT CFA franc
MAJOR LANGUAGES Wolof, Peul (Fulani), French, Mende, Mandingo, Dida
MAJOR RELIGIONS Islam, tribal religions, Roman Catholicism

SEYCHELLES
AREA 145 sq. mi. (375 sq. km.)
POPULATION 63,000
CAPITAL Victoria
LARGEST CITY Victoria
HIGHEST POINT Morne Seychellois 2,993 ft. (912 m.)
MONETARY UNIT Seychellois rupee
MAJOR LANGUAGES English, French, Creole
MAJOR RELIGION Roman Catholicism

SIERRA LEONE
AREA 27,925 sq. mi. (72,325 sq. km.)
POPULATION 3,470,000
CAPITAL Freetown
LARGEST CITY Freetown
HIGHEST POINT Loma Mts. 6,390 ft. (1,947 m.)
MONETARY UNIT leone
MAJOR LANGUAGES Mende, Temne, Vai, English, Krio (pidgin)
MAJOR RELIGIONS Tribal religions, Islam, Christianity

SOMALIA
AREA 246,200 sq. mi. (637,658 sq. km.)
POPULATION 3,645,000
CAPITAL Mogadishu
LARGEST CITY Mogadishu
HIGHEST POINT Surud Ad 7,900 ft. (2,408 m.)
MONETARY UNIT Somali shilling
MAJOR LANGUAGES Somali, Arabic, Italian, English
MAJOR RELIGION Islam

SOUTH AFRICA
AREA 455,318 sq. mi. (1,179,274 sq. km.)
POPULATION 23,771,970
CAPITALS Cape Town, Pretoria
LARGEST CITY Johannesburg
HIGHEST POINT Injasuti 11,182 ft. (3,408 m.)
MONETARY UNIT rand
MAJOR LANGUAGES Afrikaans, English, Xhosa, Zulu, Sesotho
MAJOR RELIGIONS Protestantism, Roman Catholicism, Islam, Hinduism, tribal religions

SUDAN
AREA 967,494 sq. mi. (2,505,809 sq. km.)
POPULATION 18,691,000
CAPITAL Khartoum
LARGEST CITY Khartoum
HIGHEST POINT Jeb. Marra 10,073 ft. (3,070 m.)
MONETARY UNIT Sudanese pound
MAJOR LANGUAGES Arabic, Dinka, Nubian, Beja, Nuer
MAJOR RELIGIONS Islam, tribal religions

SWAZILAND
AREA 6,705 sq. mi. (17,366 sq. km.)
POPULATION 547,000
CAPITAL Mbabane
LARGEST CITY Manzini
HIGHEST POINT Emlembe 6,109 ft. (1,862 m.)
MONETARY UNIT lilangeni
MAJOR LANGUAGES siSwati, English
MAJOR RELIGIONS Tribal religions, Christianity

TANZANIA
AREA 363,708 sq. mi. (942,003 sq. km.)
POPULATION 17,527,560
CAPITAL Dar es Salaam
LARGEST CITY Dar es Salaam
HIGHEST POINT Kilimanjaro 19,340 ft. (5,895 m.)
MONETARY UNIT Tanzanian shilling
MAJOR LANGUAGES Nyamwezi-Sukuma, Swahili, English
MAJOR RELIGIONS Tribal religions, Christianity, Islam

TOGO
AREA 21,622 sq. mi. (56,000 sq. km.)
POPULATION 2,472,000
CAPITAL Lomé
LARGEST CITY Lomé
HIGHEST POINT Agou 3,445 ft. (1,050 m.)
MONETARY UNIT CFA franc
MAJOR LANGUAGES Ewe, French, Twi, Hausa
MAJOR RELIGIONS Tribal religions, Roman Catholicism, Islam

TUNISIA
AREA 63,378 sq. mi. (164,149 sq. km.)
POPULATION 6,367,000
CAPITAL Tunis
LARGEST CITY Tunis
HIGHEST POINT Jeb. Chambi 5,066 ft. (1,544 m.)
MONETARY UNIT Tunisian dinar
MAJOR LANGUAGES Arabic, French
MAJOR RELIGION Islam

UGANDA
AREA 91,076 sq. mi. (235,887 sq. km.)
POPULATION 12,630,076
CAPITAL Kampala
LARGEST CITY Kampala
HIGHEST POINT Margherita 16,795 ft. (5,119 m.)
MONETARY UNIT Ugandan shilling
MAJOR LANGUAGES Luganda, Acholi, Teso, Nyoro, Soga, Nkole, English, Swahili
MAJOR RELIGIONS Tribal religions, Christianity, Islam

WESTERN SAHARA
AREA 102,703 sq. mi. (266,000 sq. km.)
POPULATION 76,425
HIGHEST POINT 2,700 ft. (823 m.)
MAJOR LANGUAGE Arabic
MAJOR RELIGION Islam

ZAIRE
AREA 905,063 sq. mi. (2,344,113 sq. km.)
POPULATION 28,291,000
CAPITAL Kinshasa
LARGEST CITY Kinshasa
HIGHEST POINT Margherita 16,795 ft. (5,119 m.)
MONETARY UNIT zaire
MAJOR LANGUAGES Tshiluba, Mongo, Kikongo, Kingwana, Zande, Lingala, Swahili, French
MAJOR RELIGIONS Tribal religions, Christianity

ZAMBIA
AREA 290,586 sq. mi. (752,618 sq. km.)
POPULATION 5,679,808
CAPITAL Lusaka
LARGEST CITY Lusaka
HIGHEST POINT Sunzu 6,782 ft. (2,067 m.)
MONETARY UNIT Zambian kwacha
MAJOR LANGUAGES Bemba, Tonga, Lozi, Luvale, Nyanja, English
MAJOR RELIGIONS Tribal religions

ZIMBABWE
AREA 150,803 sq. mi. (390,580 sq. km.)
POPULATION 7,360,000
CAPITAL Harare
LARGEST CITY Harare
HIGHEST POINT Mt. Inyangani 8,517 ft. (2,596 m.)
MONETARY UNIT Zimbabwe dollar
MAJOR LANGUAGES English, Shona, Ndebele
MAJOR RELIGIONS Tribal religions, Protestantism

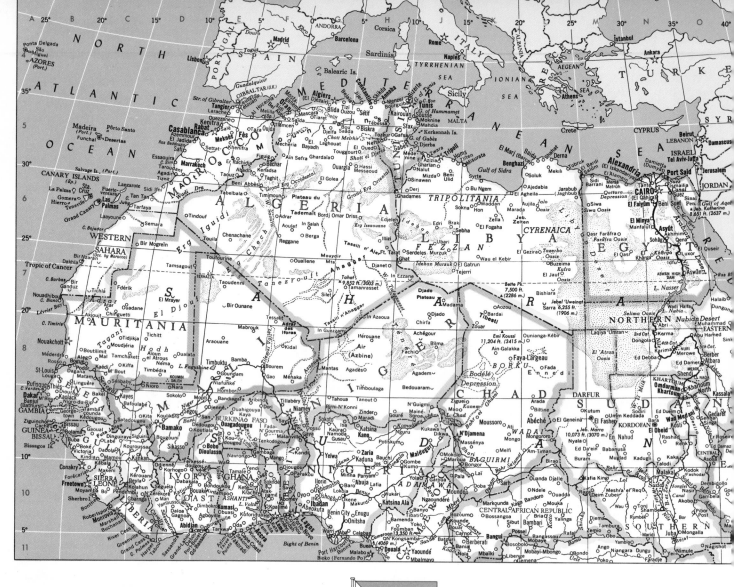

Topography

Below Sea Level | 100 m. 328 ft. | 200 m. 656 ft. | 500 m. 1,640 ft. | 1,000 m. 3,281 ft. | 2,000 m. 6,562 ft. | 5,000 m. 16,404 ft.

0   200   400 MI.
0   200   400 KM.

DJIBOUTI

ZIMBABWE

ALGERIA

CITIES and TOWNS

Ain Sefra 22,400 .... G5
Algiers (cap.) 1,365,400 ..... G4
Annaba 255,900 .... H4
Béchar 72,800 .... F5
Bejaïa 89,500 .... G4
Biskra 90,500 .... H5
Blida 160,900 .... G4
Bou Saâda 50,000 .... G5
Constantine 335,100 .... H4
Djelfa 51,000 .... G5
Ech Cheliff 106,100 .... G4
El Bayadh 38,500 .... G5
El Oued 72,100 .... H5
Ghardaïa 70,500 .... G5
Jijel 49,800 .... H4
Laghouat 59,200 .... G5
Mascara 62,300 .... G4
Mostaganem 101,600 .... F4
Oran 491,900 .... F4
Ouargla 77,400 .... G5
Saïda 62,100 .... G4
Sétif 144,200 .... H4
Sidi Bel Abbès 116,000 .... F4
Skikda 107,700 .... H4
Tamanrasset 23,200 .... H7
Tébessa 67,200 .... H4
Tiaret 62,900 .... G4
Tizi Ouzou 73,100 .... G4
Tlemcen 109,400 .... F5
Touggourt 75,600 .... G5

OTHER FEATURES

Ahaggar (range) H7
Grand Erg Occidental
(des.) G5
Grand Erg Oriental (des.) H5
Sahara (des.) EM7
Tanezrouft (des.) G7

ANGOLA

CITIES and TOWNS

Benguela 40,996 .... J14
Cabinda 21,124 .... J13
Lobito 59,528 .... J14
Luanda (cap.) 475,328 .... J13
Lubango 31,674 .... K13
Malange 31,599 .... K13
Namibe (Moçâmedes) 12,076 .. J15
Saurimo 12,901 .... L13

OTHER FEATURES

Cubango (riv.) K14
Cunene (riv.) J15

BENIN

CITIES and TOWNS

Abomey 38,000 .... G10
Cotonou 178,000 .... G10
Parakou 21,000 .... G10
Porto-Novo (cap.) 104,000 ... G10

BOTSWANA

CITIES and TOWNS

Francistown 22,000 .... M16
Gaborone (cap.) 21,000 ..... M16
Kanye 10,664 .... L6
Mahalapye 12,056 .... M16
Serowe 15,723 .... M16

OTHER FEATURES

Kalahari (des.) L16
Makgadikgadi (salt pan) L16
Ngami (lake) L16
Okovanggo (swamps) L14

BURUNDI

CITIES and TOWNS

Bujumbura (cap.) 141,040 .... N12
Gitega 19,500 .... N12

CAMEROON

CITIES and TOWNS

Buea 24,584 .... H11
Douala 458,426 .... J11
Ebolowa 24,000 .... J11
Foumban 33,944 .... J11
Garoua 63,900 .... J10
Maroua 67,187 .... J9
Ngaoundéré 38,992 .... J11
N'Kongsamba 71,298 .... J11
Yaoundé (cap.) 313,706 ..... J11

OTHER FEATURES

Biafra (bight) H11
Cameroon (mt.) H11
Sanaga (riv.) J11

CENTRAL AFRICAN REPUBLIC

CITIES and TOWNS

Bambari 31,285 .... L1
Bangassou 21,773 .... L1
Bangui (cap.) 279,792 .... K1
Berbérati 27,285 .... K
Bossangoa 25,150 .... K
Bouar 29,528 .... K

OTHER FEATURES

Lobaye (riv.) K1
Shinko (riv.) L

CHAD

CITIES and TOWNS

Abéché 28,100 L
Bongor 14,300 L
Faya-Largeau 6,800 .... K
Moundou 39,600 .... K
N'Djamena (cap.) 179,000 ... K

OTHER FEATURES

Baguirmi (reg.) .... K
Chad (lake) .... K
Emi Koussi (mt.) .... K
Ennedi (plat.) L
Sahara (des.) .... EM
Shari (riv.) .... K
Sudan (reg.) .... EM
Tibesti (mts.) .... K
Wadai (reg.) L

COMOROS

CITIES and TOWNS

Moroni (cap.) 12,000 .... P1

OTHER FEATURES

Mwali (isl.) P1
Njazidja (isl.) P1
Nzwani (isl.) P1

CONGO

CITIES and TOWNS

Brazzaville (cap.) 298,967 ... J1
Impfondo .... K
Ouesso .... J

FLAGS OF AFRICA

Africa
Northern Part
LAMBERT AZIMUTHAL EQUAL-AREA PROJECTION

SCALE OF MILES
0 100 200   400   600

SCALE OF KILOMETERS
0 100 200   400   600

Capitals of Countries .... ☆
Other Capitals .... ◉
International Boundaries .... —·—·—
Internal Boundaries ....
Canals .... ⊣⊢ Wells .... ○

© Copyright by HAMMOND INCORPORATED, Maplewood, N.J.

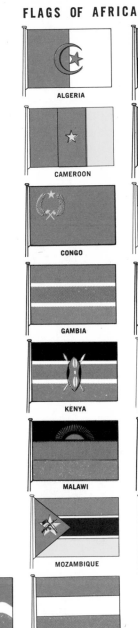

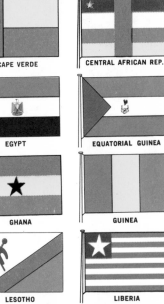

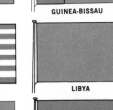
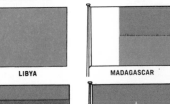

ALGERIA	ANGOLA	BENIN	BOTSWANA	BURUNDI
CAMEROON	CAPE VERDE	CENTRAL AFRICAN REP.	CHAD	COMOROS
CONGO	EGYPT	EQUATORIAL GUINEA	ETHIOPIA	GABON

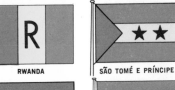

| GAMBIA | GHANA | GUINEA | GUINEA-BISSAU | IVORY COAST |
| KENYA | LESOTHO | LIBERIA | LIBYA | MADAGASCAR |

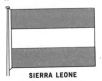

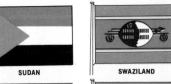

| MALAWI | MALI | MAURITANIA | MAURITIUS | MOROCCO |
| MOZAMBIQUE | NIGER | NIGERIA | RWANDA | SÃO TOMÉ E PRÍNCIPE |

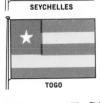
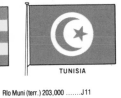

| SENEGAL | SEYCHELLES | SIERRA LEONE | SOMALIA | SOUTH AFRICA | SUDAN | SWAZILAND |
| TANZANIA | TOGO | TUNISIA | UGANDA | BURKINA FASO (UPPER VOLTA) | ZAIRE | ZAMBIA |

(continued on following page)

Agriculture, Industry and Resources

DOMINANT LAND USE

- Cereals, Horticulture, Livestock
- Cash Crops, Mixed Cereals
- Cotton, Cereals
- Diversified Tropical Crops
- Plantation Agriculture
- Oases
- Pasture Livestock
- Nomadic Livestock Herding
- Forests
- Nonagricultural Land

MAJOR MINERAL OCCURRENCES

Ab	Asbestos	Mi	Mica
Ag	Silver	Mn	Manganese
Al	Bauxite	Na	Salt
Au	Gold	O	Petroleum
Be	Beryl	P	Phosphates
C	Coal	Pb	Lead
Co	Cobalt	Pt	Platinum
Cr	Chromium	Sb	Antimony
Cu	Copper	Sn	Tin
D	Diamonds	So	Soda Ash
Fe	Iron Ore	Ti	Titanium
G	Natural Gas	U	Uranium
Gp	Gypsum	V	Vanadium
Gr	Graphite	W	Tungsten
K	Potash	Zn	Zinc

⚡ Water Power

/// Major Industrial Areas

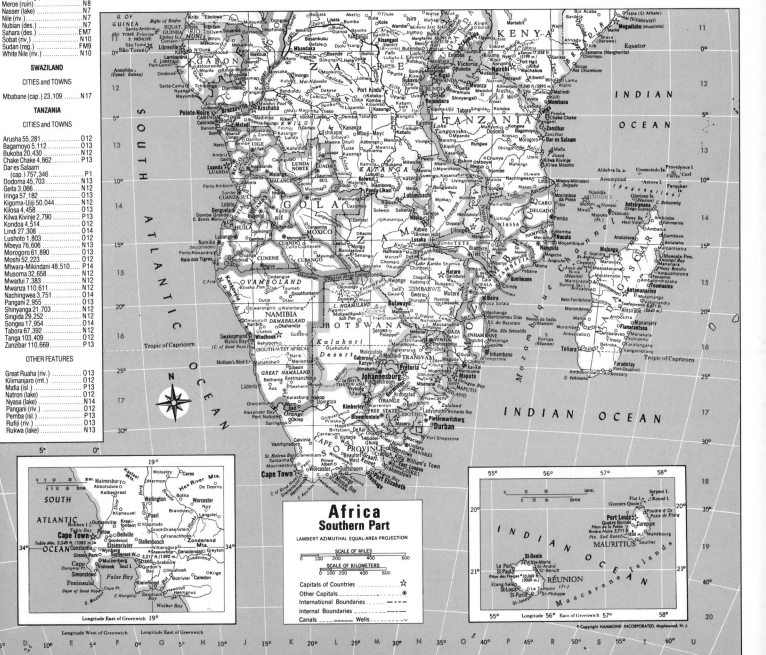

Africa
Southern Part

LAMBERT AZIMUTHAL EQUAL-AREA PROJECTION

SCALE OF MILES
0   100   200   300   400   500   600

SCALE OF KILOMETERS
0   100   200   300   400   500   600

Capitals of Countries ....★
Other Capitals ....◉
International Boundaries ....
Internal Boundaries ....
Canals .... Wells ....

© Copyright HAMMOND INCORPORATED, Maplewood, N.J.

Asia

LAMBERT AZIMUTHAL EQUAL-AREA PROJECTION

SCALE OF MILES

0 100 200   400   600   800   1000   1200

SCALE OF KILOMETERS

0 200 400 600 800 1000 1200

Capitals of Countries .... ⊛

Other Capitals .... ⊙

International Boundaries .... ▬ ▬ ▬

Other Boundaries .... ▬ ▬ ▬

Canals .... ▬ ▬ ▬

Scale 1:46,500,000

© Copyright HAMMOND INCORPORATED, Maplewood, N.J.

Population Distribution

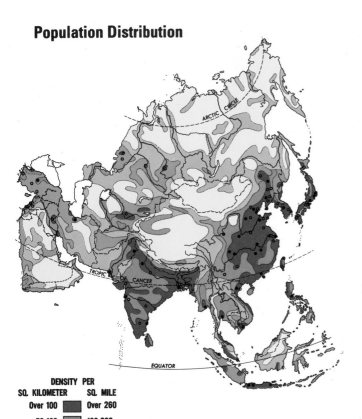

AREA 17,128,500 sq. mi.
(44,362,815 sq. km.)
POPULATION 2,633,000,000
LARGEST CITY Tokyo
HIGHEST POINT Mt. Everest 29,028 ft.
(8,848 m.)
LOWEST POINT Dead Sea -1,296 ft.
(-395 m.)

Vegetation

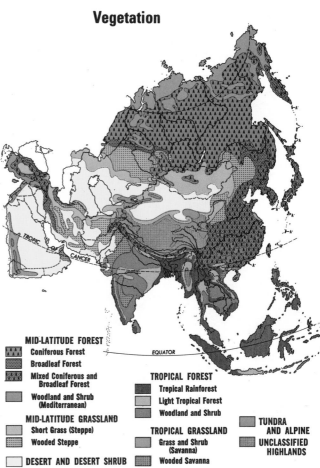

DENSITY PER

SQ. KILOMETER	SQ. MILE
Over 100	Over 260
50-100	130-260
10-50	25-130
1-10	3-25
Under 1	Under 3

- Cities with over 2,000,000 inhabitants (including suburbs)
- Cities with over 1,000,000 inhabitants (including suburbs)

MID-LATITUDE FOREST
Coniferous Forest
Broadleaf Forest
Mixed Coniferous and Broadleaf Forest
Woodland and Shrub (Mediterranean)

MID-LATITUDE GRASSLAND
Short Grass (Steppe)
Wooded Steppe

DESERT AND DESERT SHRUB

TROPICAL FOREST
Tropical Rainforest
Light Tropical Forest
Woodland and Shrub

TROPICAL GRASSLAND
Grass and Shrub (Savanna)
Wooded Savanna

TUNDRA AND ALPINE
UNCLASSIFIED HIGHLANDS

SAUDI ARABIA | KUWAIT | YEMEN ARAB REPUBLIC | BAHRAIN | QATAR | OMAN | PEOPLE'S DEM. REP. OF YEMEN

AFGHANISTAN
CITIES and TOWNS

Anar Darreh	H3	Farsi	J3	Jorm	K2	Lashkar Gah 26.646	H3	Qalat 5.946	J3	Sheberghan 54.870	H2
Andkhvoy	H2	Feyzabad 10.142	K2	Kabul (cap.) 905.108	J3	Mar'uf	J3	Qale'h-ye Now 5.340	H3	Shindand	H3
Aqcheh	J2	Gardez 11.415	J3	Kalat (Qalat) 5.946	J3	Mazar-e Sharif 122.567	J2	Qale'h-ye Panjeh	K2	Spin Buldak	J3
Aybak 33.016	J2	Gereshk	H3	Kandahar (Qandahar) 178.409	J3	Meymaneh 54.954	H2	Qandahar 178.409	J3	Tagab	J3
Baghlan 75.130	J2	Ghazni 30.425	J3	Khanabad	J2	Mirabad	H3	Qonuuz 107.191	J2	Taloqan 46.202	J2
Balkh 7.355	J2	Ghurian	J3	Khugiani	J3	Mogor	J3	Rostag	J2	Teyvareh	H3
Bamian 7.355	J3	Gizab	J3	Kowst	J3	Now Zad	H3	Rudbar	H3	Tulak	H3
Baraki Barak	J3	Hazar Qadam	H3	Kuhestan	K3	Owbeh	H3	Sakhar	J3	Zaranj 6.477	H3
Belcheragh	J2	Herat 163.960	H3	Landay	J3	Panjab	J3	Sar-e Pol	J2	Zibak	K2
Chahar Borjak	H3	Jalalabad 56.384	K3	Lash-e Joveyn	H3	Pol-e Khomri	J2	Shah Juy	J3		
Charikar 25.093	J3										
Dowlat Yar	J3										
Dowlatabad	J2										
Dowshi	J3										
Farah 18.797	H3										

UNITED ARAB EMIRATES

OTHER FEATURES

Farah Rud (riv.) H3
Gowd-e Zerreh (depr.) H4
Namaksar (salt lake) H3
Hariard (riv.) H3
Hindu Kush (mts.) J2
Kabul (riv.) K3
Konar (riv.) K2
Lurah (riv.) J3

Margow, Dasht-e (des.) H3
Murghab (riv.) H2
Namaksar (salt lake) H3
Paropamisus (mts.) H3
Rigestan (reg.) H3

BAHRAIN

CITIES and TOWNS

Manama (cap.) 88,785 ....F4
Muharraq 37,732 ....F4

GAZA STRIP

CITIES and TOWNS

Gaza* 118,272 ....B3

IRAN

CITIES and TOWNS

Abadan 296,081 ....E3
Abadeh 16,000 ....F3
Abarqu 8,000 ....F3
Ahvaz 329,006 ....E3

Amol 68,782 ....F2
Anar 463 ....G3
Anarak 2,038 ....F3
Arak 114,507 ....E2
Ardabil 147,404 ....E2
Ardestan 5,868 ....F3
Asterabad (Gorgan) 88,348 .....F2
Babol 67,790 ....F2
Bafq 5,000 ....G3
Baft 6,000 ....G4

(continued on following page)

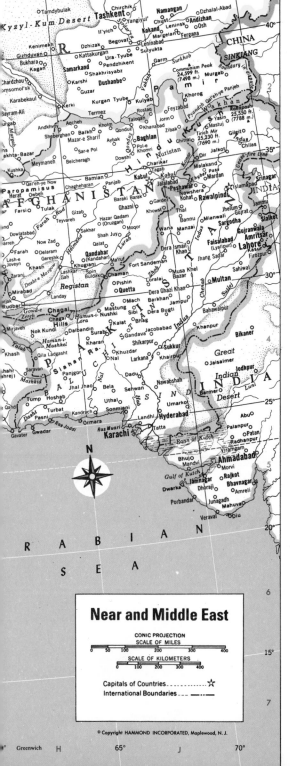

SAUDI ARABIA

AREA 829,995 sq. mi.
(2,149,687 sq. km.)
POPULATION 8,367,000
CAPITAL Riyadh
MONETARY UNIT Saudi riyal
MAJOR LANGUAGE Arabic
MAJOR RELIGION Islam

YEMEN ARAB REPUBLIC

AREA 77,220 sq. mi. (200,000 sq. km.)
POPULATION 6,456,189
CAPITAL San'a
MONETARY UNIT Yemeni rial
MAJOR LANGUAGE Arabic
MAJOR RELIGION Islam

QATAR

AREA 4,247 sq. mi. (11,000 sq. km.)
POPULATION 220,000
CAPITAL Doha
MONETARY UNIT Qatari riyal
MAJOR LANGUAGE Arabic
MAJOR RELIGION Islam

PEOPLE'S DEM. REP. OF YEMEN

AREA 111,101 sq. mi. (287,752 sq. km.)
POPULATION 1,969,000
CAPITAL Aden
MONETARY UNIT Yemeni dinar
MAJOR LANGUAGE Arabic
MAJOR RELIGION Islam

KUWAIT

AREA 6,532 sq. mi. (16,918 sq. km.)
POPULATION 1,355,827
CAPITAL Al Kuwait
MONETARY UNIT Kuwaiti dinar
MAJOR LANGUAGE Arabic
MAJOR RELIGION Islam

BAHRAIN

AREA 240 sq. mi. (622 sq. km.)
POPULATION 358,857
CAPITAL Manama
MONETARY UNIT Bahraini dinar
MAJOR LANGUAGE Arabic
MAJOR RELIGION Islam

OMAN

AREA 120,000 sq. mi. (310,800 sq. km.)
POPULATION 891,000
CAPITAL Muscat
MONETARY UNIT Omani rial
MAJOR LANGUAGE Arabic
MAJOR RELIGION Islam

UNITED ARAB EMIRATES

AREA 32,278 sq. mi. (83,600 sq. km.)
POPULATION 1,040,275
CAPITAL Abu Dhabi
MONETARY UNIT dirham
MAJOR LANGUAGE Arabic
MAJOR RELIGION Islam

Topography

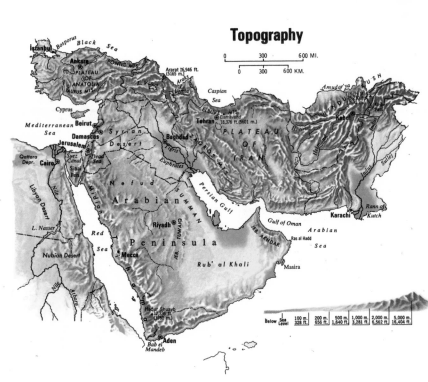

Near and Middle East

CONIC PROJECTION
SCALE OF MILES
0 50 100 200 300 400

SCALE OF KILOMETERS
0 100 200 300 400

Capitals of Countries .... ☆
International Boundaries ___ .___ .___

Bakhtaran 290,861 ....E3	Sabzevar 69,174 ....G2	Al Fathaḥ 15,329 ....D2	Murbat G6	Doga D6	YEMEN ARAB REP.
Bam 22,000 ....G4	Sabzvaran 7,000 ....G4	Al Musaiyib 15,955 ....D3	Muscat (cap.) 7,500 ....G5	Duwadami D5	
Bampur 1,585 ....H4	Sai'dabad 20,000 ....G4	Al Qurna 5,638 ....E3	Nizwa G5	Er Ras D4	CITIES and TOWNS
Bandar 'Abbas 89,103 ....G4	Sanandaj 95,834 ....E2	'Amadiya 2,578 ....D2	Quryat G5	Faid E5	
Bandar-e Anzali (Enzeli) 55,978 ....E2	Saqqez 17,000 ....E2	'Amara 64,847 ....E3	Raysut (Risut) F6	Gail E5	'Amran D6
Bandar-e Khomeyni 6,000 ....F4	Saravan H4	Salala 4,000 ....F6	Haddar D5	Bait al Faqih D7
Bandar-e Lengeh 4,920 ....F4	Sari 70,936 ....F2	An 'Amara 15,729 ....D3	Sarur G5	Hadiya D4	Dhamar 19,467 ....D6
Bandar-e Rig 1,889 ....F4	Saveh 17,565 ....F3	An Najaf 128,096 ....D3	Shinas G5	Hafar al Batin E4	El Beida 5,975 ....D7
Bandar-e Torkeman 13,000 ....F2	Semnan 31,058 ....F2	An Nasiriya 60,405 ....E3	Sohar G5	Hail 40,502 ....D4	Hajja 5,814 ....D6
Bejestan 3,823 ....G3	Shahdad 2,777 ....G3	Arbela (Erbil) 90,320 ....D2	Sur G5	Hamar E5	Harib E7
Birjand 25,854 ....G3	Shahreza 34,220 ....F3	Ar Ramhaliya 1,579 ....D3	Suwaiq G5	Hamda D5	Hodeida 80,314 ....D7
Bojnurd 31,248 ....G2	Shiraz 416,408 ....F4	As Salman 3,584 ....E3		Hanakiya D5	Huth D7
Borazjan 20,000 ....F4	Shirvan 11,000 ....G2	Baghdad (cap.) 502,503 ....D3	OTHER FEATURES	Haql C4	Ibb 19,066 ....D7
Borujerd 100,103 ....E3	Shustar 24,000 ....E3	Baghdad* 1,745,328 ....D3		Harad E5	Luhaiya D6
Bushehr 57,681 ....F4	Sirjan (Sai'dabad) 20,000 ....G4	Ba'quba 34,575 ....D3	Akhdar, Jebel (range) F5	Haraja D6	Marib 292 ....D7
Chah Bahar 1,800 ....H4	Tabas 10,000 ....G3	Basra 313,327 ....E3	Batina (reg.) G5	Harig E5	Mocha D7
Chalus 15,000 ....F2	Tabas-Masina (Tabas) 466 ....H3	Erbil 90,320 ....D2	Dhofar (reg.) F6	Hariq E5	Sa'da 4,252 ....D6
Damghan 13,000 ....F2	Tabriz 598,576 ....E2	Habbaniya 14,405 ....D3	Hadd, Ras al (cape) G5	Hatiba, Ras (cape) C5	Sana' (cap.) 134,588 ....D6
Darab 13,000 ....G4	Tarom 394 ....G4	Haditha 6,870 ....D3	Jibsh, Ras (cape) G5	Hofuf 101,271 ....E4	Sheikh Sa'id D7
Dasht-e Azadegan 21,000 ....E3	Tehran (cap.) 4,496,159 ....F2	Hai 16,988 ....E3	Kuria Muria (isls.) G6	Jabrin E5	Ta'iz 78,642 ....D7
Dashtiari H4	Tonekabon 12,000 ....F2	Hilla 84,717 ....D3	Madraka, Ras (cape) G6	Jauf D4	Yarim D7
Dezful 110,287 ....E3	Torbat-e Heydariyeh 30,106 ....G2	Hit 9,131 ....D3	Masira (gulf) G6	Jidda 561,104 ....C5	Zabid D7
Dezh Shahpur 1,384 ....E2	Torbat-e Jam 13,000 ....H2	Karbal'a 83,301 ....D3	Masira (isl.) G6	Jizan (Qizan) 32,812 ....D6	
Emamshahr 30,767 ....F2	Torud 721 ....G2	Khanaqin 23,522 ....D3	Musandam, Ras (cape) G4	Jubail F4	OTHER FEATURES
Enzeli 55,978 ....E2	Turan G3	Kirkuk 167,413 ....D2	Nus, Ras (cape) G6	Jubba D4	
Estahbanat 18,187 ....F4	Turbat-i-Shaikh Jam 13,000 ....H2	Kirkuk* 176,794 ....D2	Oman (gulf) G4	Junaina D5	Hanish (isls.) D7
Fahrej (Iranshahr)5,000 ....H4	Urmia 163,991 ....D2	Kut 42,116 ....E3	Oman (reg.) G5	Kaf D4	Manar, Jebel (mt.) D7
Fasa 19,000 ....F4	Yazd 135,978 ....F3	Maidan 354 ....E3	Ruus al Jibal (dist.) G4	Khaibar, 'Asir D6	Mandeb, Bab el (str.) D7
Ferdows 11,000 ....G3	Yazdan H3	Mosul 315,157 ....D2	Saugira (bay) F6	Khaibar, Hejaz D5	Red (sea) D7
Gach Saran F4	Zabol 20,000 ....H3	Qala' Sharqat 2,434 ....D2	Saugira, Ras (cape) F6	Khamis Mushait 49,581 ....D6	Sabir, Jebel (mt.) D7
Garmsar 4,723 ....F2	Zahedan 92,628 ....H4	Ramadi 28,723 ....D3	Sham, Jebel (mt.) G5	Khay E5	Tihama (reg.) D7
Golpayegan 20,515 ....F3	Zanjan 99,967 ....E2	Rutba 5,091 ....D3	Sharbatat, Ras (cape) G6	Khurma D5	Zuqar (isl.) D7
Gonabad 8,000 ....G3	Zarand 5,000 ....G3	Samarra 24,746 ....D3		Kuia E5	
Gorgan 88,348 ....F2		Samawa 33,473 ....D3	QATAR	Majmaa' E6	YEMEN, PEOPLE'S DEM. REPUBLIC OF
Hamadan 155,846 ....E3	OTHER FEATURES	Shithatha 2,326 ....D3		Maqna C4	
Iranshahr 5,000 ....H4		Tikrit 9,921 ....D2	CITIES and TOWNS	Marib E6	CITIES and TOWNS
Isfahan 671,825 ....F3	Araks (riv.) E2			Mastaba D6	
Jahrom 38,236 ....F4	Atrek (riv.) G2	OTHER FEATURES	Doha (cap.) 150,000 ....F4	Mastura C5	Aden (cap.) 240,370 ....E7
Kangan 2,682 ....F4	Bazman, Kuh-e (mt.) H4		Dukhan F4	Mecca (cap.) 366,801 ....C5	Ahwar E7
Kangavar 9,414 ....E3	Damavand (mt.) F2	'Aneiza, Jebel (mt.) C3	Umm Sa'id F5	Medain Salih C5	Balhaf E7
Kashan 84,545 ....F3	Dez (riv.) E3	'Ara'r, Wadi (dry riv.) D4		Medina 198,186 ....D5	Bir 'Ali F6
Kashmar 17,000 ....G2	Elburz (mts.) F2	Batin, Wadi al (dry riv.) E4	OTHER FEATURES	Mendak D6	Damqut F6
Kazerun 51,309 ....F4	Gavkhuni (lake) F3	Euphrates (riv.) D3		Mina Sau'd E4	Ghaida F6
Kerman 140,309 ....G4	Gorgan (riv.) F2	Hauran, Wadi (dry riv.) D3	Persian (gulf) F4	Mubarraz 54,325 ....E4	Habban E7
Khash 7,439 ....H4	Halil (riv.) G4	Mesopotamia (reg.) D3	Rakan, Ras (cape) F4	Mudhnib D5	Hadibu F7
Khorramabad 104,928 ....E3	Jaz Murian, Hamun-e (marsh) H4	Syrian (El Hamad) (des.) D3		Muwailih C4	Hajarain E7
Khorramshahr 146,709 ....E3	Karun (riv.) E3	Tigris (riv.) E3	SAUDI ARABIA	Najran (Aba as Sau'd) 47,501 ....D6	Haura E7
Khoy 70,040 ....E2	Kavir, Dasht-e (salt des.) G3			Nisab D4	Hureidha E7
Lar 22,000 ....F4	Kavir-e Namak (salt des.) G3	KUWAIT	CITIES and TOWNS	O'gair E4	I'rqa E7
Mahabad 28,610 ....E2	Lut, Dasht-e (des.) G3			Qadhima C5	Lahej E7
Maragheh 60,820 ....E2	Maidani, Ras (cape) H4	CITIES and TOWNS	Aba as Sau'd 47,501 ....D6	Qafar D4	Lejiun E7
Marand 24,000 ....E2	Mand Rud (riv.) F4		Abaila F5	Qasr al Haiyanya D5	Lodar E7
Meshed 670,180 ....H2	Mashkid (riv.) H4	Al Kuwait (cap.) 181,774 ....E4	Abha 30,150 ....D6	Qatif F4	Madinat ash Shab' E7
Mianeh 28,447 ....E2	Mehran (riv.) F4	Mina al Ahmadi E4	Abqaiq E4	Qizan 32,812 ....D6	Meifa E7
Minab 4,228 ....G4	Namak, Daryacheh-ye (salt lake) F3	Mina Saud E4	Abu 'Arish D6	Qunfidha D6	Mukalla 45,000 ....E7
Mirjaveh 11,000 ....H4	Namaksar (salt lake) H3		Abu Hadriya E4	Qusaiba D5	Nisab E7
Nahavand 24,000 ....E3	Namakzar-e Shahdad (salt lake) G3	OTHER FEATURES	'Ain al Mubarrak C4	Rabigh C5	Nuqub E7
Na'in 5,925 ....F3	Oman (gulf) G5		Al 'Ain F4	Ra's al Khafji E4	Qishn F6
Najafabad (Zaboli) 20,000 ....H3	Persian (gulf) F4	Bubiyan (isl.) E4	Al-'Ala D4	Ras Tanura F4	Riyan E7
Natanz 4,370 ....F3	Qeys (isl.) F4	Persian (gulf) F4	Al 'Auda E4	Riyadh (cap.) 666,840 ....E5	Saihut F6
Nehbandan 2,130 ....G3	Qezel Owzan (riv.) E2		Al Birk D6	Ruman C4	Seiyun 20,000 ....E7
Neyshabur 59,101 ....H2	Qeshm (isl.) G4	OMAN	Al Hilla D5	Sabya D6	Shabwa E7
Nikshahr H4	Safidar, Kuh-e (mt.) F4		Al Lidam D5	Sakaka D4	Shibam E7
Pahlevi (Enzeli) 55,978 ....E2	Shaikh Shua'ib (isl.) F4	CITIES and TOWNS	Al Lith D5	Salwa F5	Shihr E7
Qasr-e Qand 1,879 ....H4	Shir Kuh (mt.) F3		Al Muadhdham C4	Shaqra D5	Shuqra E7
Qayen 6,000 ....G3	Taftan, Kuh-e (mt.) H4	Adam G5	'Anaiza D5	Shuqaiq D6	Tarim E7
Qazvin 138,527 ....F2	Talab (riv.) H4	Buraimi G5	Artawiya D4	Sufeina D5	Yeshhum E7
Qom 246,831 ....F3	Tashk (lake) F4	Dhank G5	Ashaira D5	Sulaiyil D5	Zinjibar E7
Quchan 29,133 ....G2	Urmia (lake) E2	Ibra G5	Ayun C4	Taif 204,857 ....D5	
Qum (Qom) 246,831 ....F3	Zagros (mts.) E3	I'bri G5	Badr C5	Taima C4	OTHER FEATURES
Rafsanjan 21,000 ....G3		Juwara G6	Buraida 69,940 ....D4	Tamra D5	
Rasht 187,203 ....E2	IRAQ	Kamil G5	Dam D4	Tathlith D6	Fartak, Ras (cape) F6
Ravar 5,074 ....G3		Khaluf G5	Dammam 127,844 ....F4	Tebuk (Tabuk) 74,825 ....C4	Hadhramaut (dist.) E7
Rey 102,825 ....F3	CITIES and TOWNS	Khasab G4	Dar al Hamra C4	Truba D4	Hadhramaut, Wadi (dry riv.) E7
Reza'iyeh (Urmia) 163,991 ....D2		Manah G5	Dhaba C4	Umm Lajj C5	Kamaran (isl.) D6
	Al'Aziziya 7,450 ....E3	Masqat (Muscat) (cap.) 7,500 ....G5	Dhahran E5	Wejh C5	Perim (isl.) D7
	Al Falluja 38,072 ....D3	Matrah 15,000 ....G5	Dharma E5	Yamama E5	Socotra (isl.) F7
		Mina al Fahal G5	Dilam E5	Yenbo C5	
				Zahran D6	*City and suburbs.

UNITED ARAB EMIRATES — CITIES and TOWNS
Abu Dhabi (cap.) 347,000 ....C5; 'AJman ....G4; 'Aradah ....F5; Buraimi ....G4; Dubai ....G4; Fujairah ....G4; Jebel Dhanna ....F4; Ras al Khaimah ....G4; Ruwais ....F5; Sharjah ....G4; Umm al Qaiwain G4
OTHER FEATURES — Das -(isl.) ....F4; Oman (gulf) ....G4; Yas (isl.) ....F5; Zirko (isl.) F5

WEST BANK — CITIES and TOWNS — Hebron 38,309 ....C3
OTHER FEATURES — Dead (sea) C3

Zalim ....D5; Zilfi ....E4; Turaba D5

Agriculture, Industry and Resources

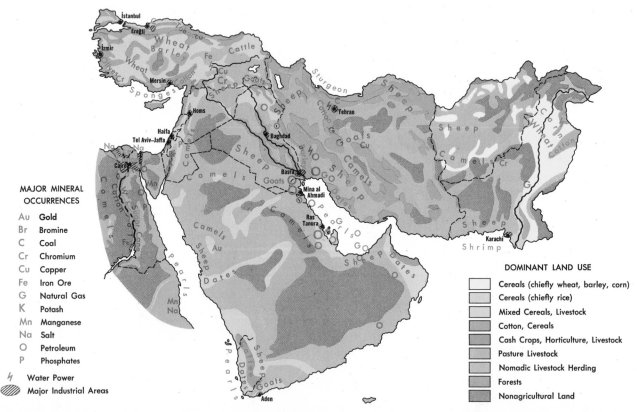

MAJOR MINERAL OCCURRENCES

Au Gold
Br Bromine
C Coal
Cr Chromium
Cu Copper
Fe Iron Ore
G Natural Gas
K Potash
Mn Manganese
Na Salt
O Petroleum
P Phosphates
⚡ Water Power
▨ Major Industrial Areas

DOMINANT LAND USE

Cereals (chiefly wheat, barley, corn)
Cereals (chiefly rice)
Mixed Cereals, Livestock
Cotton, Cereals
Cash Crops, Horticulture, Livestock
Pasture Livestock
Nomadic Livestock Herding
Forests
Nonagricultural Land

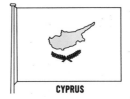

TURKEY

SYRIA

LEBANON

CYPRUS

TURKEY
AREA 300,946 sq. mi. (779,450 sq. km.)
POPULATION 45,217,556
CAPITAL Ankara
LARGEST CITY Istanbul
HIGHEST POINT Ararat 16,946 ft. (5,165 m.)
MONETARY UNIT Turkish lira
MAJOR LANGUAGE Turkish
MAJOR RELIGION Islam

SYRIA
AREA 71,498 sq. mi. (185,180 sq. km.)
POPULATION 8,979,000
CAPITAL Damascus
LARGEST CITY Damascus
HIGHEST POINT Hermon 9,232 ft. (2,814 m.)
MONETARY UNIT Syrian pound
MAJOR LANGUAGES Arabic, French, Kurdish, Armenian
MAJOR RELIGIONS Islam, Christianity

LEBANON
AREA 4,015 sq. mi. (10,399 sq. km.)
POPULATION 3,161,000
CAPITAL Beirut
LARGEST CITY Beirut
HIGHEST POINT Qurnet es Sauda 10,131 ft. (3,088 m.)
MONETARY UNIT Lebanese pound
MAJOR LANGUAGES Arabic, French
MAJOR RELIGIONS Christianity, Islam

CYPRUS
AREA 3,473 sq. mi. (8,995 sq. km.)
POPULATION 629,000
CAPITAL Nicosia
LARGEST CITY Nicosia
HIGHEST POINT Troödos 6,406 ft. (1,953 m.)
MONETARY UNIT Cypriot pound
MAJOR LANGUAGES Greek, Turkish, English
MAJOR RELIGIONS Eastern (Greek) Orthodoxy, Islam

CYPRUS

CITIES and TOWNS

Dhali 2,970 ... E5
Episkopi 2,150 ... E5
Famagusta 38,960 ... E5
Ktima ... E5
Kyrenia 3,892 ... E5
Kythrea 3,400 ... E5
Lapithos 3,600 ... E5
Larnaca 19,608 ... E5
Lefka 3,650 ... E5
Limassol 79,641 ... E5
Morphou 9,040 ... E5
Nicosia (cap.) 115,718 ... E5
Paphos 8,984 ... E5
Polis 2,200 ... E5
Rizokarpasso 3,600 ... F5
Yialousa 2,750 ... F5

OTHER FEATURES

Andreas (cape) ... F5
Arnauti (cape) ... E5
Gata (cape) ... E5
Greco (cape) ... F5
Kormakiti (cape) ... E5
Troödos (mt.) ... E5

LEBANON

CITIES and TOWNS

A'leih 18,630 ... F6
Amyun 7,926 ... F5
Baa'lbek 15,560 ... G5
Batrun 5,976 ... F5
Beirut (cap.) 474,870 ... F6
Beirut* 938,940 ... F6
Hermil 2,652 ... G5
Merj U'yun 9,318 ... G6
Rasheiya 6,731 ... G6
Rayak 1,480 ... G6
Saida 32,200 ... F6
Sidon (Saida) 32,200 ... F6
Sur 16,483 ... F6
Tripoli (Tarabulus) 127,611 ... F5

Tyre (Sur) 16,483 ... F6
Zahle 53,121 ... F6
Zegharta 18,210 ... G5

OTHER FEATURES

Lebanon (mts.) ... F6
Leontes (Litani) (riv.) ... F6
Litani (riv.) ... F6
Sauda, Qurnet es (mt.) ... G5

SYRIA

PROVINCES

Aleppo 1,316,872 ... G4
Damascus 1,457,934 ... H5
Deir ez Zor 292,780 ... H5
Dera' 230,481 ... G6
El Quneitra 16,490 ... F6
Es Suweida 139,650 ... G6
Hama 514,748 ... G5
Haseke 468,506 ... J4
Homs 546,176 ... G5
Idlib 383,695 ... G5
Latakia 389,552 ... F5
Rashid 243,736 ... H5
Tartus 302,065 ... G5

CITIES and TOWNS

Abu Kemal 6,907 ... J5
A'in el A'rab 4,529 ... H4
Aleppo 639,428 ... G4
Azaz 13,923 ... G4
Baniyas 8,537 ... F5
Busra ... G6
Damascus (cap.) 836,668 ... G6
Damascus* 923,253 ... G6
Deir ez Zor 66,164 ... H5
Dera' 27,651 ... G6
Dimashq (Damascus) (cap.) 836,668 ... G6
Duma 30,050 ... G6
El Bab 27,366 ... G4
El Haseke 32,746 ... J4
El Ladhiqiya (Latakia) 125,716 ... F5
El Quryatein ... G5
El Quneitra 17,752 ... F6
El Rashid 37,151 ... H5

Adiyaman 346,892 ... H4
Afyonkarahisar 579,171 ... D3
Agri 330,201 ... K3
Amasya 322,806 ... F2
Ankara 2,585,293 ... E3
Antalya 669,357 ... D4
Artvin 226,026 ... J2
Aydin 609,869 ... B4
Balikesir 789,255 ... B3
Bilecik 137,120 ... D2
Bingöl 210,804 ... J3
Bitlis 218,305 ... J3
Bolu 428,704 ... D2
Burdur 222,896 ... D4
Bursa 961,639 ... C2
Çanakkale 369,385 ... B2
Çankiri 265,468 ... F2
Çorum 547,580 ... F2
Denizli 560,916 ... C4
Diyarbakir 651,233 ... H4
Edirne 340,732 ... B2
Elaziğ 417,924 ... H3
Erzincan 283,683 ... H3
Erzurum 746,666 ... J3
Eskişehir 495,097 ... D3
Gaziantep 715,939 ... G4
Giresun 463,587 ... H2
Gümüşhane 293,673 ... H2
Hakkâri 126,036 ... K4
Hatay 744,113 ... G4
Isparta 322,685 ... D4
Istanbul 3,904,588 ... C2
Izmir 1,673,966 ... B3
Kahramanmaras 641,480 ... G4
Kars 707,398 ... K2
Kastamonu 438,243 ... E2
Kayseri 676,809 ... F3
Kirklareli 268,399 ... B2
Kirşehir 232,853 ... F3
Kocaeli 477,736 ... D2
Konya 1,422,461 ... E4
Kütahya 470,423 ... C3
Malatya 574,558 ... H3
Manisa 872,375 ... B3
Mardin 519,687 ... H4
Muğla 400,796 ... C4
Mus 267,203 ... J3
Nevşehir 249,308 ... F3
Niğde 463,121 ... F4

OTHER FEATURES

A'mrit (ruins) ... F5
Arwad (Ruad) (isl.) ... F5
A'si (Orontes) (riv.) ... G5
Druz, Jebel ed (mts.) ... G6
El Furat (riv.) ... H4
Euphrates (El Furat) (riv.) ... H4
Hermon (mt.) ... F6
Khabur (riv.) ... J5
Orontes (riv.) ... G5
Palmyra (Tadmor) (ruins) ... H5
Ruwaq, Jebel er (mts.) ... G5

TURKEY

PROVINCES

Adana 1,240,475 ... F4

Ordu 664,290 ... G2
Rize 336,278 ... J2
Sakarya 495,649 ... D2
Samsun 906,381 ... F2
Siirt 381,503 ... J4
Sinop 267,605 ... F2
Sivas 741,713 ... G3
Tekirdağ 319,987 ... B2
Tokat 599,166 ... G2
Trabzon 719,008 ... H2
Tunceli 164,591 ... H3
Urfa 597,277 ... H4
Uşak 229,679 ... C3
Van 386,314 ... K3
Yozgat 500,371 ... F3
Zonguldak 836,156 ... D2

CITIES and TOWNS

Acigöl 3,934 ... F3
Acipayam 5,046 ... C4
Adalia (Antalya) 130,774 ... D4
Adana 475,384 ... F4
Adapazari 114,130 ... D2
Adilcevaz 9,022 ... K3
Adiyaman 43,782 ... H4
Afşin 18,231 ... G3
Afyonkarahisar 60,150 ... D3
Ağlasun 4,288 ... D4
Ağri 3,399 ... K3
Ağri (Karaköse) 35,284 ... K3
Ahlat 7,995 ... K3
Akçaabat 10,756 ... H2
Akçadağ 7,366 ... G3
Akçakoca 9,066 ... D2
Akdağmadeni 7,909 ... F3
Akhisar 53,357 ... B3
Aksaray 45,564 ... F3
Akşehir 35,544 ... D3
Akseki 5,141 ... D4
Akviran 3,799 ... E4
Akyazi 12,438 ... D2
Alaca 12,552 ... F2
Alacahan 2,321 ... G3
Aladağ 10,013 ... F2
Alanya 18,520 ... D4
Alaşehir 23,243 ... C3
Alexandretta (Iskenderun) 107,437 ... G4
Aliağa 5,727 ... B3

Alibeyköyü 33,387 ... D6
Almus 4,225 ... G2
Alpu 3,718 ... D3
Altindağ 512,392 ... E2
Altinova 6,980 ... B3
Altintaş 3,386 ... C3
Altinözü 5,158 ... G4
Alucra 7,070 ... H2
Amasra 4,369 ... E2
Amasya 41,496 ... F2
Anamur 21,475 ... E4
Andirin 5,018 ... G4
Ankara (cap.) 1,701,004 ... E3
Antakya 77,518 ... G4
Antalya 130,774 ... D4
Antioch (Antakya) 77,518 ... G4
Araç 3,594 ... E2
Aralik 4,155 ... L3
Arapkir 8,436 ... H3
Ardahan 16,285 ... K2
Ardeşen 7,980 ... J2
Ardanuç 2,942 ... K2
Arguvan 2,664 ... H3
Arhavi 6,311 ... J2
Arpaçay 2,651 ... K2
Arsin 6,557 ... H2
Artova 2,813 ... G2
Arvad 29,218 ... J2
Aşkale 10,817 ... J3
Avanos 8,635 ... F3
Ayancik 7,202 ... F1
Ayaş 4,575 ... E2
Aybasti 13,180 ... G2
Aydin 59,579 ... B4
Aydincik 6,739 ... E4
Ayvacik 2,664 ... B3
Ayvacik 3,120 ... B3
Ayvalik 18,041 ... B3
Badadağ 5,890 ... C4
Babaeski 17,900 ... B2
Bafra 34,288 ... F2
Bahçe 10,212 ... G4
Bakirköy 200,942 ... D6
Balaban 3,327 ... C4
Balâ 4,107 ... E3
Balikesir 99,443 ... B3
Balya 2,362 ... B3
Banaz 6,264 ... C3
Bandirma 45,752 ... B2
Bartin 18,409 ... E2

Başkale 8,558 ... K3
Başmakçi 5,925 ... C4
Batman 64,384 ... J4
Bayat 4,671 ... F2
Bayindir 14,078 ... B3
Baykan 2,890 ... J3
Bayramiç 6,385 ... B3
Bergama 29,749 ... B3
Beşiktaş 174,931 ... D6
Beyağaç 4,165 ... C4
Besni 16,313 ... G4
Beykoz 76,804 ... D5
Beyoğlu 230,532 ... D6
Beyşaari 14,963 ... D2
Beyşehir 15,060 ... D3
Beytüşşebap 2,766 ... K4
Biga 15,188 ... B2
Bigadiç 7,535 ... C3
Bilecik 11,269 ... D2
Bingöl (Çapakçur) 22,047 ... J3
Birecik 20,104 ... H4
Bismil 12,775 ... J4
Bitlis 25,054 ... J3
Bodrum 7,858 ... B4
Boğazliyan 10,329 ... F3
Bolu 32,812 ... D3
Bolvadin 29,218 ... D3
Bor 16,560 ... F4
Borçka 4,636 ... J2
Bornova 45,096 ... B3
Boyabat 13,139 ... F2
Bozdoğan 7,216 ... C4
Bozkir 5,294 ... E4
Bozkurt 2,948 ... F2
Bozova 5,462 ... H4
Bozüyük 15,197 ... C3
Bucak 15,090 ... D4
Bulancak 14,153 ... H2
Bulanik 8,296 ... K3
Bulak 11,115 ... C3
Bünyan 12,277 ... G3
Burdur 36,633 ... D4
Burhaniye 12,800 ... B3
Bursa 346,103 ... C2
Büyükada ... D6
Büyükdere ... D5
Cal 3,274 ... C3
Çala 2,450 ... K2
Çaldiran 3,366 ... K3

(continued on following page)

Agriculture, Industry and Resources

DOMINANT LAND USE

Cereals (chiefly wheat, barley), Livestock
Cash Crops, Horticulture, Livestock
Pasture Livestock
Nomadic Livestock Herding
Forests
Nonagricultural Land

MAJOR MINERAL OCCURRENCES

Ab Asbestos
Al Bauxite
C Coal
Cr Chromium
Cu Copper
Fe Iron Ore
Hg Mercury
Mg Magnesium
Na Salt
O Petroleum
P Phosphates
Pb Lead
Py Pyrites
Sb Antimony
Zn Zinc

Water Power
Major Industrial Areas

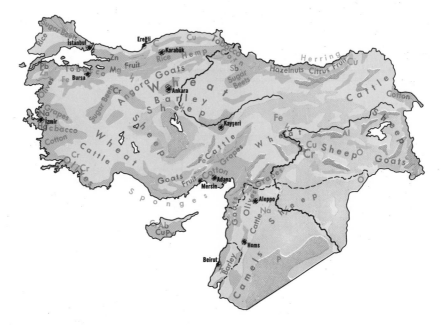

Place	Pop.	Key
Çalköy 3,002		C3
Çamardı 2,419		F4
Çamel 2,502		B3
Çamlidere 4,386		E2
Çan 11,797		B2
Çanakkale 30,788		B6
Çandir 6,986		E2
Çankaya 895,005		E2
Çankiri 28,512		E2
Çapakçur 22,047		J3
Çardak 4,232		G2
Çarşamba 23,973		G2
Çatak 2,366		K4
Çatalca 7,693		C2
Çatalzeytin 2,271		F1
Çay 12,200		D3
Çaycuma 8,118		D2
Çayeli 13,480		J2
Çayiralan 8,071		F3
Çayirli 4,580		J3
Çekerek 7,454		F2
Çelikhan 5,066		H3
Çemişgezek 3,048		H3
Çerkeş 3,780		E2
Çerkezköy 8,428		C2
Çermik 9,749		H3
Çeşme 5,284		B3
Çetinkaya 3,616		G3
Ceyhan 62,909		F4
Ceylanpinar 20,171		H4
Çiçekdaği 3,203		F3
Cide 3,520		E2
Çifteler 8,163		D3
Cihanbeyli 10,079		E3
Çildir 2,260		J2
Çimin 5,341		H3
Çine 11,308		B4
Cizre 15,557		K4
Çivril 7,721		C3
Çorlu 40,134		C2
Çorum 64,852		F2
Çubuk 13,793		E2
Çukur 5,479		J3
Çukurca 3,019		K4
Çumra 19,225		E4
Çüngüş 2,616		H3
Daday 2,528		E2
Darende 8,055		G3
Dazkiri 3,912		C4
Delice 3,462		F3
Demirci 15,016		C3
Demirkent 4,204		E4
Demirköy 4,257		C2
Denizli 106,902		C4
Dereli 6,188		H2
Derik 13,292		J4
Derinkuyu 5,618		F3
Develi 17,323		F3
Devrek 9,164		D2
Devrekani 4,014		E2
Dicle 5,247		H3
Dikili 6,916		B3
Dinar 19,873		C3
Dirmil 3,476		C4
Divriği 12,302		H3
Diyadin 5,094		K3
Diyarbakir 169,535		H4
Doğanbey 3,077		B3
Doğanhisar 3,487		D3
Doğanşehir 10,280		G3
Döger 3,478		D3
Doğubeyazit 17,612		K3
Domaniç 2,729		C3
Dörtyol 19,390		F4
Dumlu 4,206		J2
Duraşan 3,259		F1
Dursunbey 8,615		C3
Düzce 32,129		D2
Eceabat 3,642		B6
Edirne 63,001		B2
Edremit 26,110		B3
Efláni 3,793		E2
Eğridir 9,799		D3
Elâziğ 131,415		H3
Elbistan 26,048		G3
Eleşkirt 8,202		K3
Elmali 10,184		C4
Emet 6,239		C3
Emirdağ 13,184		D3
Emirgazi 5,244		E4
Enez 2,486		B2
Erbaa 20,315		G2
Erciş 22,351		K3
Erdek 8,685		B2
Erdemli 19,936		E4
Ereğli 45,992		D2
Ereğli 50,353		F4
Ergani 21,936		H3
Erkilet 3,924		F3
Ermenak 13,464		D4
Eruh 5,340		K4
Erzin 15,314		G4
Erzincan 60,351		H3
Erzurum 162,973		J3
Eskimalatya 10,182		H3
Eskişehir 259,952		D3
Esme 7,828		C3
Espiye 8,168		H2
Eynesil 6,081		H2
Eyüp 95,486		D6
Ezibider 3,631		H2
Ezine 9,359		B3
Fakili 4,173		F3
Fatih 504,127		D6
Fatsa 19,758		G2
Feke 5,576		F4
Fethiye 12,700		C4
Fevzipaşa 5,495		G4
Findikli 5,008		J2
Finike 4,200		C4
Foça 4,829		B3
Gallipoli 13,466		C5
Gaziantep 300,882		G4
Gazipaşa 6,696		E4
Gebze 33,110		C2
Gediz 10,649		C3
Gelibolu (Gallipoli) 13,466		C5
Gemerek 5,769		G3
Gemlik 20,704		C2
Genezin 4,925		F3
Gerede 8,259		D2
Germencik 10,558		B4
Gerze 7,313		F1
Gevaş 6,333		K3
Geyve 7,806		D2
Giresun 38,236		H2
Gökçe 4,470		C3
Göksun 10,481		G3
Gölbaşi 15,103		D3
Gölcük 33,279		C2
Göle 7,680		K2
Gölköy 10,022		G2
Gölmarmara 11,982		C3
Gölpazari 5,002		D2
Gönen 16,091		B2
Gördes 7,909		C3
Görele 8,075		H2
Göynücek 2,600		F2
Göynük 2,519		D2
Güdül 4,746		E2
Gülnar 6,344		E4
Gülşehir 6,188		F3
Gümüş 3,066		F2
Gümüşhacıköy 12,789		F2
Gümüşhane 11,166		H2
Güney 7,154		C3
Güroymak 9,138		K3
Hacıbektaş 5,032		F3
Hacılar 15,622		F3
Hadim 10,467		E4
Hafik 5,398		G3
Hakkâri (Çölemerik) 11,735		K4
Halfeti 3,689		G4
Hamur 2,267		K3
Hanak 2,581		K2
Hani 7,559		H3
Harput 3,231		H3
Haruniye 12,837		G4
Hassa 10,926		G4
Hatay (Antakya) 77,518		G4
Havran 7,552		B3
Havsa 4,298		B2
Hayrabolu 15,341		C2
Haymana 6,123		E2

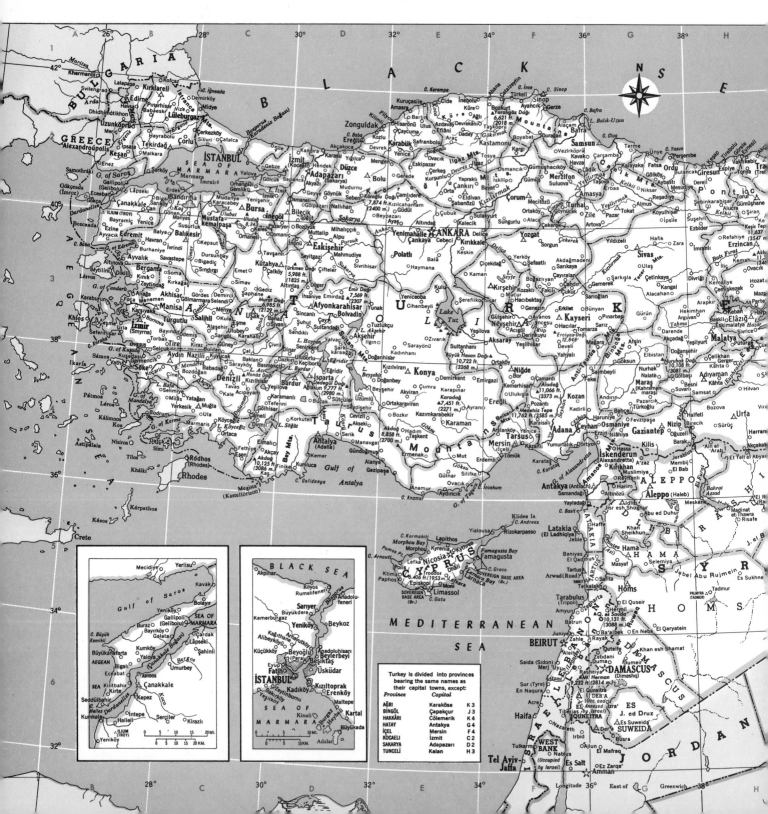

Turkey is divided into provinces bearing the same names as their capital towns, except:

Province	Capital	Key
AĞRI	Karaköse	K3
BİNGÖL	Çapakçur	J3
HAKKÂRİ	Çölemerik	K4
HATAY	Antakya	G4
İÇEL	Mersin	F4
KOCAELİ	İzmit	C2
SAKARYA	Adapazari	D2
TUNCELİ	Kalan	H3

Hayrabolu 12.331 ...B2	İslâhiye 20.683 ...G4
Hazro 4.896 ...J3	Isparta 62.870 ...D4
Hekimhan 11.818 ...G3	İspir 3.929 ...J2
Hendek 15.291 ...H4	İstanbul 2.547.364 ...D6
Hilvan 6.473 ...H4	İvrindi 3.730 ...B3
Hınıs 10.226 ...J3	İzmir 636.834 ...B3
Hisarönü 4.485 ...E2	İzmit 165.483 ...D2
Hizan 2.545 ...K3	İznik 11.614 ...C2
Hopa 9.089 ...K2	Kadınhanı 11.802 ...E3
Horasan 2.724 ...K2	Kadirli 34.779 ...H3
Hozat 5.796 ...H3	Kağıthane 164.448 ...D6
İçel (Mersin) 152.236 ...F4	Kağızman 11.517 ...J4
İdil 4.862 ...J4	Kâhta 15.602 ...H4
Iğdır 29.542 ...K3	Kale 11.637 ...H3
İlgaz 6.624 ...E2	Kale 3.399 ...C4
İliç 11.830 ...D3	Kalecik 4.707 ...E2
İlica 8.947 ...J3	Kaman 16.516 ...E2
İmranlı 5.667 ...H2	Kandıra 10.187 ...D2
İncesu 7.089 ...F3	Kangal 5.937 ...G3
İnebolu 6.824 ...E2	Karabük 69.182 ...E2
İnegöl 37.805 ...C2	Karacabey 21.648 ...C2
İnönü 4.152 ...D3	Karahallı 5.539 ...C3
İpsala 6.829 ...B2	Karaisalı 2.316 ...F4
İpsile 2.328 ...J2	Karaköçan 5.604 ...H3
İskenderun 107.437 ...G4	Karaköse (Ağrı) 35.284 ...K3
İskilip 16.588 ...F2	

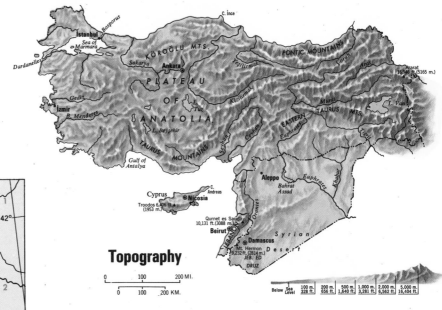

Topography

0   100   200 MI.

0   100   200 KM.

Below Sea Level	100 m. 328 ft.	200 m. 656 ft.	500 m. 1,640 ft.	1,000 m. 3,281 ft.	2,000 m. 6,562 ft.	5,000 m. 16,404 ft.

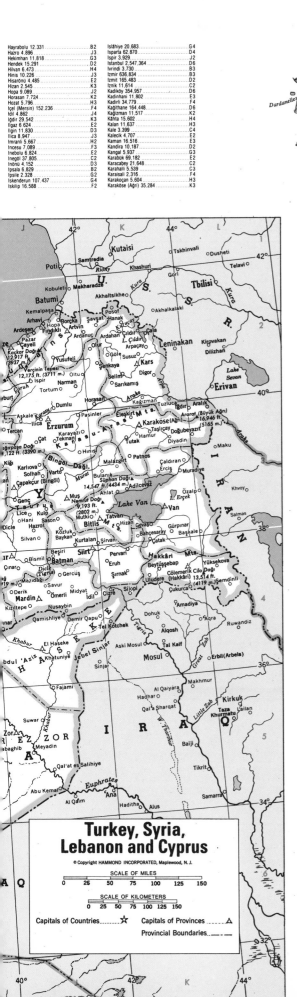

Turkey, Syria, Lebanon and Cyprus

© Copyright HAMMOND INCORPORATED, Maplewood, N.J.

SCALE OF MILES
0   25   50   75   100   150

SCALE OF KILOMETERS
0   25   50   75   100   125   150

Capitals of Countries .... ★

Capitals of Provinces .... △

Provincial Boundaries ....

Karaman 43.759 ...E4	Muğla 24.178 ...C4	Silvan 29.599 ...J3	Yeşilyurt 7.451 ...H3
Karamanlı 5.904 ...C4	Muradiye 6.334 ...K3	Simav 11.601 ...C3	Yıldızeli 7.043 ...G3
Karapınar 19.589 ...E4	Muş 27.761 ...J3	Sincanlı 3.847 ...D3	Yozgat 32.501 ...F3
Karasu 11.600 ...D2	Mustafakemalpaşa 27.706 ...C3	Sındırgı 7.818 ...C3	Yüksekova 7.329 ...L4
Karataş 5.598 ...F4	Mut 11.466 ...E4	Sinop 16.098 ...F2	Yumurtalık 2.442 ...F4
Karayaka 4.242 ...C3	Mutki 2.815 ...J3	Şiran 5.048 ...H2	Yunak 6.187 ...D3
Karayazı 3.595 ...J3	Muttalip 3.917 ...D3	Şırnak 10.587 ...K4	Yusufeli 3.050 ...J2
Kargı 5.021 ...F2	Nallıhan 7.883 ...D2	Sivas 149.201 ...G3	Zara 10.376 ...G3
Karlıova 3.631 ...J3	Narman 4.607 ...J2	Sivaslı 4.394 ...C3	Zeytinburnu 123.548 ...D6
Kars 54.892 ...K2	Nazilli 52.176 ...C4	Siverek 40.990 ...H4	Zeytindağ 3.517 ...B3
Karşıyaka 171.600 ...B3	Nevşehir 30.203 ...F3	Sivrihisar 8.713 ...D3	Zile 32.157 ...G2
Kartal 53.073 ...D6	Niğde 31.844 ...F4	Smyrna (İzmir) 636.834 ...B3	Zivarik 2.703 ...E3
Kaş 2.493 ...C4	Niksar 19.156 ...G2	Söğüt 5.329 ...C2	Zonguldak 90.221 ...D2
Kastamonu 29.993 ...E2	Nizip 36.190 ...G4	Söke 35.407 ...B4	
Kavak, Çanakkale 3.932 ...C5	Nurhak 5.330 ...G4	Solhan 7.014 ...J3	**OTHER FEATURES**
Kavak, Samsun 3.964 ...G2	Nusaybin 23.684 ...J4	Soma 23.713 ...C3	
Kayseri 207.037 ...F3	Ödemiş 37.364 ...C3	Sorgun 14.081 ...F3	Abydos (ruins) ...B6
Kazanlı 4.461 ...F4	Of 10.376 ...J2	Şuhut 8.154 ...D3	Acı (lake) ...C3
Kazımkarabekir 4.086 ...E4	Oğuzeli 7.194 ...G4	Sulakyurt 4.311 ...E2	Adalar (isl.) ...D6
Keban 5.598 ...H3	Oltu 10.093 ...J2	Sultandağı 4.017 ...D3	Aegean (sea) ...A3
Keçiborlu 7.096 ...C3	Ömerli 4.738 ...J4	Sultanhanı 5.112 ...E3	Ağrı, Büyük (Ararat) (mt.) ...L3
Keles 2.423 ...C3	Ordu 47.481 ...G2	Suluova 21.278 ...F2	Akdağ (mt.) ...F3
Kelkit 6.928 ...H2	Orhaneli 3.335 ...C3	Sungurlu 21.641 ...F2	Aladağ (mt.) ...F4
Kemah 3.038 ...H3	Orhangazi 12.181 ...C2	Sürmene 8.096 ...J2	Alexandretta (gulf) ...G4
Kemaliye 3.014 ...H3	Orta 3.596 ...E2	Sürüç 20.395 ...H4	Amanos (mts.) ...G4
Kemalpaşa 7.572 ...J2	Ortaca 8.604 ...C4	Suşehri 10.863 ...H2	Anamur (cape) ...E5
Kemerburgaz 7.234 ...D5	Ortakaraviran 3.856 ...E4	Susurluk 14.000 ...C3	Anatolia (reg.) ...D3
Kemirhisar 6.205 ...F4	Ortaköy, Çorum 2.657 ...F2	Susuz 5.006 ...K2	Ankara (riv.) ...D3
Kepsut 4.704 ...C3	Ortaköy, Niğde 6.371 ...F3	Sütçüler 2.721 ...D4	Antalya (gulf) ...D4
Keşan 27.088 ...B2	Osmancık 11.921 ...F2	Tarsus 102.186 ...F4	Anti-Taurus (mts.) ...G3
Keşap 5.264 ...G2	Osmaneli 4.789 ...D2	Taşkent 7.098 ...E4	Araks (riv.) ...K2
Keskin 10.540 ...E3	Osmaniye 61.581 ...G4	Taşköprü 8.146 ...F2	Ararat (mt.) ...L3
Kığı 5.598 ...J3	Ovacık, Tunceli 2.248 ...H3	Taşlıçay 3.684 ...K3	Arpa (riv.) ...K2
Kilimli 26.649 ...D2	Özalp 4.188 ...L3	Taşova 6.516 ...G2	Baba (cape) ...A3
Kilis 54.055 ...G4	Palu 5.489 ...H3	Tatvan 29.271 ...K3	Batı Fırat (riv.) ...H3
Kınık 11.785 ...B3	Pasinler 14.267 ...J2	Tavas 9.728 ...C4	Beyşehir (lake) ...D4
Kiraz 5.284 ...C2	Patnos 15.918 ...K3	Tavşanlı 19.575 ...C3	Black (sea) ...C1
Kırıkhan 38.118 ...G4	Pazar, Rize 8.956 ...J2	Tefenni 4.280 ...C4	Bosporus (str.) ...C2
Kırıkkale 137.874 ...E3	Pazar, Tokat 4.337 ...G2	Tekirdağ 41.257 ...B2	Bozcaada (isl.) ...A3
Kırkağaç 15.078 ...B3	Pazarcık 15.943 ...G4	Tercan 6.068 ...J3	Burgaz (isl.) ...D6
Kırklareli 33.265 ...C2	Pazaryeri 5.633 ...C3	Terme 15.680 ...G2	Büyük Ağrı (Ararat) (mt.) ...L3
Kırşehir 41.415 ...F3	Pera (Beyoğlu) 230.532 ...D6	Tire 30.694 ...B3	Çanakkale Boğazı (Dardanelles) (str.) ...B6
Kızılcahamam 7.050 ...E2	Perşembe 6.701 ...G2	Tirebolu 7.385 ...H2	Çandarlı (gulf) ...B3
Kızılhisar 11.119 ...C3	Pertek 4.176 ...H3	Tokat 48.588 ...G2	Çanik (gulf) ...G2
Kızıltepe 21.531 ...J4	Pervari 4.126 ...K4	Tomarza 6.548 ...F3	Ceyhan (riv.) ...F4
Kızılviran 3.260 ...E4	Pınarbaşı 9.503 ...G3	Tomük 7.660 ...F4	Cilo Dağı (mt.) ...K4
Kocaeli (İzmit) 165.483 ...D2	Pınarhisar 10.523 ...B2	Tonya 10.564 ...H2	Çoruh (riv.) ...J2
Koçarlı 5.182 ...B3	Polatlı 35.267 ...E3	Torbalı 17.237 ...B3	Dardanelles (str.) ...B6
Konya 246.727 ...E3	Posof 2.209 ...K2	Tortum 4.110 ...J2	Dicle (riv.) ...J4
Korkuteli 10.334 ...D4	Pozantı 5.408 ...F4	Tosya 17.515 ...F2	Eastern Taurus (mts.) ...J3
Köyceğiz 4.612 ...C4	Pütürge 3.442 ...H3	Trabzon 97.210 ...H2	Ephesus (ruins) ...B3
Koyulhisar 3.861 ...G2	Refahiye 6.570 ...H3	Trebizond (Trabzon) 97.210 ...H2	Erciyas Dağı (mt.) ...F3
Kozaklı 6.200 ...F3	Reşadiye 9.022 ...G2	Tunceli (Kalan) 11.637 ...H3	Ergene (riv.) ...B2
Kozan 32.045 ...F4	Reyhanlı 25.749 ...G4	Turgutlu 47.009 ...B3	Euphrates (Fırat) (riv.) ...G4
Kozlu 27.322 ...D2	Rize 36.044 ...J2	Turhal 39.170 ...G2	Gediz (riv.) ...C3
Kozluk 6.197 ...J3	Sabanözü 3.442 ...E2	Türkeli 2.194 ...F2	Gelidonya (cape) ...D4
Küçükköy 56.411 ...C6	Safranbolu 14.793 ...E2	Türkoğlu 9.207 ...G4	Gökçeada (isl.) ...A2
Kula 10.807 ...C3	Saimbeyli 3.622 ...G4	Tutak 4.325 ...K3	Göksu (riv.) ...E4
Kulp 4.474 ...J3	Sakarya (Adapazarı) 114.130 ...D2	Tuzluca 5.209 ...K3	Helles (cape) ...B6
Kulu 11.707 ...E3	Salihli 45.514 ...C3	Tuzluköp 4.613 ...D3	Heybeli (isl.) ...D6
Kumkale 1.752 ...B6	Samandağ 22.540 ...F4	Ula 5.117 ...C4	Ilium (ruins) ...B6
Kumluca 7.704 ...D4	Samsat 2.083 ...H4	Ulaş 2.469 ...G3	İmroz (Gökçeada) (isl.) ...A2
Küre 2.378 ...E2	Samsun 168.478 ...G2	Ulubey 4.161 ...C3	İnce (cape) ...F1
Kurşunlu 6.562 ...E2	Sandıklı 13.181 ...D3	Uluborlu 10.016 ...D3	İstranca (mts.) ...B2
Kurtalan 7.001 ...J3	Sapanca 9.040 ...D2	Uludere 4.050 ...K4	Kaçkar Dağı (mt.) ...J2
Kuşadası 10.269 ...B4	Şaphane 3.919 ...C3	Ulukışla 6.336 ...F4	Karadeniz Boğazı (Bosporus) (str.) ...C2
Kütahya 82.442 ...C3	Sarayköy 10.513 ...C4	Umurbey 2.754 ...C2	Karasu-Aras (mts.) ...J3
Kuyucak 6.039 ...C4	Sarayönü 8.946 ...E3	Ünye 23.366 ...G2	Kelkit (riv.) ...G2
Lâdik 6.785 ...G2	Sarıgöl 6.979 ...C3	Urfa 132.934 ...H4	Kerme (gulf) ...B4
Lâpseki 3.727 ...B2	Sarıkamış 21.262 ...K2	Ürgüp 6.758 ...F3	Keşiş Tepesi (mt.) ...C3
Lice 8.625 ...J3	Sarıkaya 5.160 ...F3	Urla 13.903 ...B3	Kızılırmak (riv.) ...F2
Lüleburgaz 32.401 ...B2	Sarıköy 4.695 ...B2	Uşak 58.578 ...C3	Koca (riv.) ...C2
Maden 15.151 ...H3	Sarıoğlan 3.245 ...F3	Üsküdar 202.957 ...D6	Köroğlu (mts.) ...E2
Mağara 4.314 ...G3	Sarıyer 79.329 ...D5	Üzümlü 4.365 ...H3	Küre (mts.) ...E2
Mahmudiye 5.240 ...D3	Sarız 3.591 ...G3	Uzunköprü 27.005 ...B2	Mandalya (gulf) ...B4
Malatya 154.505 ...H3	Şarkikaraağaç 4.772 ...D3	Vakfıkebir 12.556 ...H2	Marmara (sea) ...C2
Malazgirt 13.094 ...K3	Şarkışla 12.763 ...G3	Van 63.663 ...K3	Menderes, Büyük (riv.) ...C4
Malkara 14.399 ...B2	Şarköy 5.396 ...B2	Varto 5.572 ...J3	Meriç (riv.) ...B2
Maltepe 66.343 ...D6	Sason 3.211 ...J3	Vezirköprü 11.551 ...F2	Murat (riv.) ...H3
Manavgat 10.804 ...D4	Savaştepe 7.179 ...B3	Viranşehir 26.244 ...H4	Pontic (mts.) ...G2
Manisa 78.114 ...B3	Şavşat 3.078 ...K2	Vize 8.203 ...C2	Porsuk (riv.) ...D3
Manyas 4.410 ...B2	Savur 4.983 ...J4	Yahyalı 13.738 ...F3	Prinkipo (Adalar) (isl.) ...D6
Maraş (Kahramanmaraş) 135.782 ...G4	Seben 2.471 ...D2	Yalova, İstanbul 27.289 ...C2	Sakarya (riv.) ...D2
Mardin 36.629 ...J4	Şebinkarahisar 10.214 ...H2	Yalvaç 18.305 ...D3	Saros (gulf) ...B2
Marmaris 5.596 ...C4	Şefaatli 6.769 ...F3	Yapraklı 3.020 ...E2	Seyhan (riv.) ...F4
Mazgirt 3.141 ...H3	Seferihisar 6.484 ...B3	Yatağan 4.903 ...C4	Simav (riv.) ...C3
Mazıdağı 4.842 ...J4	Selçuk 12.251 ...B3	Yayladağı 4.471 ...F5	Sinop (cape) ...F1
Mecitözü 6.066 ...F2	Selendi 4.457 ...C3	Yenice, Çanakkale 4.004 ...B3	Sultan (mts.) ...D3
Menemen 18.464 ...B3	Selim 3.569 ...K2	Yenice, İçel 4.106 ...E4	Süphan Dağı (mt.) ...K3
Mengen 2.459 ...D2	Selimiye 2.989 ...B4	Yenice, Zonguldak 5.791 ...E2	Taurus (mts.) ...E4
Meriç 3.922 ...B2	Senirkent 8.247 ...D3	Yeniceoba 5.740 ...E3	Tigris (Dicle) ...J4
Mersin 152.236 ...F4	Şenkaya 3.190 ...K2	Yeniköy, İstanbul ...D6	Troy (Ilium) (ruins) ...B6
Merzifon 30.801 ...F2	Şereflikoçhisar 20.523 ...E3	Yenimahalle 198.643 ...D6	Tuz (lake) ...E3
Mesudiye 4.294 ...G2	Serik 14.161 ...D4	Yenişehir 15.188 ...C2	Van (lake) ...K3
Midyat 16.905 ...J4	Seydişehir 25.651 ...D3	Yerkesker 2.381 ...F3	Yeşilırmak (riv.) ...G2
Midye 2.003 ...C2	Seyitgazi 2.819 ...D3	Yerköy 19.927 ...F3	
Mihalıççık 4.004 ...D3	Siirt 35.654 ...J3	Yeşilhisar 10.409 ...F3	* City and suburbs
Milâs 17.929 ...B4	Şile 4.062 ...C2	Yeşilova, Burdur 3.685 ...C4	
Mucur 9.398 ...F3	Silifke 19.257 ...E4	Yeşilova, Niğde 5.237 ...E3	
Mudanya 8.399 ...C2	Silivri 9.257 ...C2		
Mudurnu 3.905 ...D2	Silopi 4.460 ...K4		

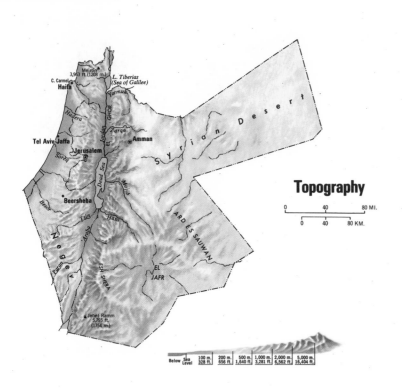

Topography

0   40   80 MI.

0   40   80 KM.

Below Sea Level | 100 m. 328 ft. | 200 m. 656 ft. | 500 m. 1,640 ft. | 1,000 m. 3,281 ft. | 2,000 m. 6,562 ft. | 5,000 m. 16,404 ft.

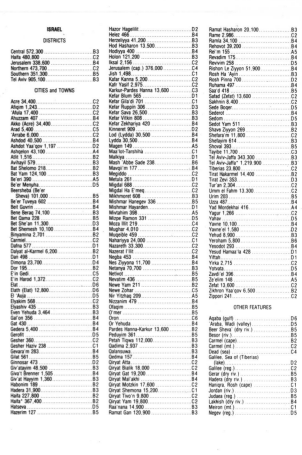

ISRAEL

DISTRICTS

Central 572,300	B3
Haifa 480,800	C2
Jerusalem 338,600	B4
Northern 473,700	C2
Southern 351,300	B5
Tel Aviv 905,100	B3

CITIES and TOWNS

Acre 34,400	C2
Afiqim 1,243	D2
'Afula 17,400	C2
Ahuzzam 407	B4
Akko (Acre) 34,400	C2
Arad 5,400	C5
'Arrabe 6,000	C2
Ashdod 40,500	B4
Ashdot Yaa'qov 1,197	D2
Ashqelon 43,100	A4
Atlit 1,516	B2
Avihayil 579	B3
Bat Shelomo 218	B2
Bat Yam 124,100	B4
Be'eri 390	A5
Be'er Menuha	D5
Beersheba (Be'er Sheva) 101,000	B5
Be'er Tuveya 602	B4
Beit Guvrin	B4
Bene Beraq 74,100	B3
Bet Qama 228	B5
Bet She'an 11,300	D3
Bet Shemesh 10,100	B4
Binyamina 2,701	B2
Carmiel	C2
Dafna 577	D1
Dalyat al-Karmel 6,200	C2
Dan 498	D1
Dimona 23,700	D4
Dor 195	B2
E'in Gedi	C5
E'in Harod 1,372	C2
Elat	D6
Elath (Elat) 12,800	D6
El 'Auja	D5
Elyakim 568	C2
Elyashiv 435	B3
Even Yehuda 3,464	B3
Gal'on 356	B4
Gat 430	B4
Gedera 5,400	B4
Gerofit	D5
Gesher 360	C2
Gesher Haziv 238	C1
Gevara'm 283	A4
Gilat 561	B5
Ginnosar 473	D2
Giv'atayim 48,500	B3
Giva't Brenner 1,505	B4
Giv'at Hayyim 1,360	B3
Habonim 189	B2
Hadera 31,900	B3
Haifa 227,800	B2
Haifa* 367,400	B2
Hatseva	D5
Hazerim 127	B5
Hazor Hagelilit	D2
Helez 466	B4
Herzeliyya 41,200	B3
Hod Hasharon 13,500	B3
Hodiyya 400	B4
Holon 121,200	B3
Iksal 2,156	C2
Jish 1,498	C1
Kafar Kanna 5,200	C2
Kafr Yasif 2,975	C2
Karkur-Pardes Hanna 13,600	C3
Kefar Blum 565	D1
Kefar Gila'di 701	D1
Kefar Ruppin 306	D3
Kefar Sava 26,500	B3
Kefar Vitkin 808	B3
Kefar Zekhariya 420	B4
Kinneret 909	D2
Lod (Lydda) 30,500	B4
Lydda 30,500	B4
Magen 149	A5
Maa'lot-Tarshiha	C1
Malkiya	D1
Mash 'Abbe Sade 238	B6
Mavqii'm 177	A4
Megiddo	C2
Metula 261	D1
Migdal 688	D2
Migdal Ha E'meq	C2
Mikhmoret 608	B3
Mishmar Hanegev 336	B5
Mishmar Hayarden	D1
Mivtahim 398	A5
Mizpe Ramon 331	D5
Moza Illit 219	C4
Mughar 4,010	C2
Mugeible 459	C2
Nahariyya 24,000	C1
Nazareth 33,300	C2
Nazerat I'lit	C2
Negba 453	B4
Nes Ziyyona 11,700	B4
Netanya 70,700	B3
Netivot	B4
Nevatim 436	B5
Newe Yam 211	B2
Newe Zohar	C5
Nir Yitzhaq 209	A5
Nizzanim 479	B4
Ofaqim	B5
O'mer	B5
Oron	C6
Or Yehuda	B4
Pardes Hanna-Karkur 13,600	C3
Peduyim 361	B5
Petah Tiqwa 112,000	B3
Qadima 2,937	B3
Qalansuwa	B3
Qedma 157	B4
Qiryat Atta	C2
Qiryat Bialik 18,000	C2
Qiryat Gat 19,200	B4
Qiryat Mal'akhi	B4
Qiryat Motzkin 17,600	C2
Qiryat Shemona 15,200	C1
Qiryat Tivo'n 9,800	C2
Qiryat Yam 19,800	C2
Raa'nana 14,900	B3
Ramat Gan 120,900	B3
Ramat Hasharon 20,100	B3
Rame 2,986	C2
Ramla 34,100	B4
Rehovot 39,200	B4
Re'm 155	B4
Revadim 175	B4
Revivim 258	B5
Rishon Le Ziyyon 51,900	B4
Rosh Ha 'Ayin	B3
Rosh Pinna 700	D2
Ruhama 497	B4
Saa'd 418	B4
Safad (Zefat) 13,600	C2
Sakhnin 8,400	C2
Sede Boqer	B4
Sederot	B4
Sedom	C5
Sedot Yam 511	B3
Shave Ziyyon 269	C1
Shefara'm 11,800	C2
Shefayim 614	B3
Shoval 393	B4
Tayibe 11,700	C3
Tel Aviv-Jaffa 343,300	B3
Tel Aviv-Jaffa* 1,219,900	B3
Tiberias 23,800	C2
Tirat Hakarmel 14,400	C2
Tirat Zevi 353	D3
Tur'an 2,304	C2
Umm el Fahm 13,300	C2
Urim 203	B5
Uzza 487	B4
Yad Mordekhai 416	A4
Yagur 1,266	C2
Yahav	D5
Yavne 10,100	B4
Yavne'el 1,580	C2
Yehud 8,900	B3
Yeroham 5,800	C5
Yesodot 293	B4
Yesud Hamaa'la 428	D1
Yiftah	D1
Yirka 2,715	C2
Yotvata	D6
Zavdi'el 396	B4
Ze'elim 148	A5
Zefat 13,600	C2
Zikhron Yaa'qov 6,500	B2
Zippori 241	C2

OTHER FEATURES

Aqaba (gulf)	D6
'Araba, Wadi (valley)	D5
Beer Sheva (dry riv.)	B5
Besor (riv.)	B5
Carmel (cape)	B2
Carmel (mt.)	C2
Dead (sea)	C4
Galilee, Sea of (Tiberias) (lake)	D2
Galilee (reg.)	C2
Gerar (dry riv.)	B5
Hadera (dry riv.)	B3
Haniqra, Rosh (cape)	C1
Jordan (riv.)	D3
Judaea (reg.)	C4
Lakhish (dry riv.)	B4
Meiron (mt.)	C1
Negev (reg.)	C5

Archaeological Sites in Palestine

■ Major Excavations

Miles
0   10   20   30

© Copyright HAMMOND INCORPORATED

Agriculture, Industry and Resources

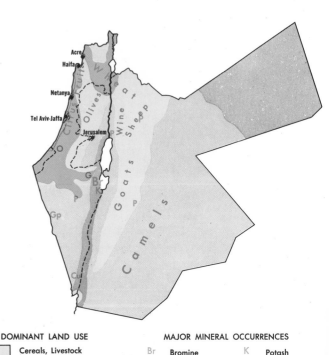

DOMINANT LAND USE

- Cereals, Livestock
- Cash Crops, Horticulture
- Nomadic Livestock Herding
- Nonagricultural Land

MAJOR MINERAL OCCURRENCES

Br	Bromine	K	Potash
Cu	Copper	O'	Petroleum
G	Natural Gas	P	Phosphates
Gp	Gypsum		

▨ Major Industrial Areas

ISRAEL

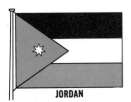

JORDAN

ISRAEL
AREA 7,847 sq. mi. (20,324 sq. km.)
POPULATION 3,878,000
CAPITAL Jerusalem
LARGEST CITY Tel Aviv-Jaffa
HIGHEST POINT Meiron 3,963 ft. (1,208 m.)
MONETARY UNIT shekel
MAJOR LANGUAGES Hebrew, Arabic
MAJOR RELIGIONS Judaism, Islam, Christianity

JORDAN
AREA 35,000 sq. mi. (90,650 sq. km.)
POPULATION 2,152,273
CAPITAL Amman
LARGEST CITY Amman
HIGHEST POINT Jeb. Ramm 5,755 ft. (1,754 m.)
MONETARY UNIT Jordanian dinar
MAJOR LANGUAGE Arabic
MAJOR RELIGION Islam

Israel and Jordan
CYLINDRICAL PROJECTION
© Copyright HAMMOND INCORPORATED, Maplewood, N.J.
SCALE OF MILES
SCALE OF KILOMETERS

Capitals of Countries .... ☆
Internal Capitals .... ◉
International Boundaries ....
Internal Boundaries ....

IRAN

INTERNAL DIVISIONS

Azerbaijan, East
(prov.) 3,194,543 ....E1
Azerbaijan, West
(prov.) 1,404,875 ....D1
Bakhtiari (prov.) 1,016,199 ...E3
Bakhtiari
(governorate) 394,300 ....F4
Boyer Ahmediyeh and Kohkiluyeh
(governorate) 244,750 ....G6
Bushehr (prov.) 345,427 ....G6
Central
(prov.) 6,921,283 ....G3
Esfahan (Isfahan)
(prov.) 1,974,938 ....H4
Fars (prov.) 2,020,947 .....H6
Gilan (prov.) 1,577,800 ....F2
Hamadan (governorate) 1,086,512 ..F3
Hormozgan (prov.) 463,419 .....J7
Ilam (governorate) 244,222 ...E4
Isfahan (prov.) 1,974,938 ...H4
Kerman (prov.) 1,088,045 ....K5
Khorasan (prov.) 3,266,650 ...K3
Khuzestan (prov.) 2,176,612 ...F5
Kordestan (Kurdistan)
(prov.) 781,889 ....E3
Lorestan (Luristan)
(governorate) 924,848 ....F4
Mazandaran (prov.) 2,384,226 ...H2
Semnan (governorate) 485,875 ...J3
Sistan and Baluchestan
(prov.) 659,297 ....M6
Yazd (governorate) 356,218 ...H4
Zanjan (governorate) 579,000 ...F2

CITIES and TOWNS

Abadan 296,081 ....F5
Abadeh 16,000 ....H5
Abarqu 8,000 ....H5
Abhar 24,000 ....F2
Agha Jari 24,195 ....F5
Amol 68,782 ....H2
Anarak 2,038 ....H4
Andimeshk 16,000 ....F4
Aradan 8,978 ....H3
Arak 114,507 ....F3
Ardabil 147,404 ....F1
Ardestan 5,868 ....H4
Asadabad 7,000 ....E3
Asterabad (Gorgan) 88,348 ...J2
Babol 67,790 ....H2
Babol Sar 7,237 ....H2
Baft 6,000 ....K6
Bakhtaran 290,861 ......E3
Bam 22,000 ....L6
Bandar 'Abbas 89,103 ...J7
Bandar-e Anzali
(Enzeli) 55,978 ....F2
Bandar-e Deylam 3,691 ...G5
Bandar-e Khomeyni 6,000 ...F5
Bandar-e Lengeh 4,920 ...J7
Bandar-e Mas hur 17,000 ...F5
Bandar-e Rig 1,889 .....G6
Bandar-e Torkeman 13,000 ...H2
Bandar Shahpur 6,000 ...F5
Bastak 2,473 ....J7
Bastam 3,296 ....J2
Behbehan 39,874 ....G5
Behshahr 26,032 ....H2
Bejestan 3,823 ....K3
Bijar 12,000 ....E3
Birjand 25,854 ....L3
Bojnurd 31,248 ....L2
Borazjan 20,000 ....G6
Borujerd 100,103 ......F4
Bostan 4,619 ....F5
Bowkan 9,000 ....E2
Bushehr (Bushire) 57,681 ...G6
Chalus 15,000 ....G2
Damavand 5,319 ....H3
Damghan 13,000 ....J2
Darab 13,000 ....J6
Daran 4,609 ....G4
Dasht-e Azadegan 21,000 ...F5
Dehkhvaregan 6,000 ....D2
Delijan 6,000 ....G4
Dezful 110,287 ....F4
Dizful (Dezful) 110,287 ...F4
Duzdab (Zahedan) 92,628 ...M6
Emamshahr 30,767 ......J2
Enzeli 55,978 ....F2
Esfahan (Isfahan) 671,820 ...G4
Eslamabad 12,000 ......E4
Estahbanat 18,187 .....J6
Evaz 6,064 ....J7
Ezna 5,000 ....F4
Fahrej (Iranshahr) 5,000 ...M7
Fariman 8,000 ....L3
Farrashband 3,532 .....G6
Fasa 19,000 ....J6
Ferdows 11,000 ....K3
Firuzabad 8,718 ....H6
Firuzkuh 4,881 ....H3
Fowman 9,000 ....F2
Gach Saran G5
Ganaveh 9,000 ....G6
Garmsar 4,723 ....H3
Gavater M8
Ghaemshahr 63,289 .....H2
Golpayegan 20,515 .....G4
Golshan (Tabas) 10,000 ...K4
Gomishan 6,000 ....J2
Gonabad 8,000 ....L3
Gonbad-e Kavus 59,868 ...J2
Gonbadi 531 ....M2
Gorgan (Gurgan) 88,348 ...M2
Haft Gel 10,000 ....F5
Hamadan 155,846 ....F3
Hashtgar 5,000 ....H3
Hormoz 2,569 ....J7
Huzgan 4,722 ....K5
Ilam 15,000 ....E4
Iranshahr 5,000 ....M7
Isfahan 671,825 ....G4
Jahrom 38,236 ....H6
Jajarm 3,641 ....K2
Jask 1,078 ....K8
Kakhk 4,043 ....L3
Kangan 2,682 ....G6
Kangavar 9,414 ....F3
Karaj 138,774 ....G3
Kashan 84,545 ....G3
Kashmar 17,000 ....L3
Kazerun 51,309 ....G6
Kazvin (Qazvin) 138,527 ...F3
Kerman 140,309 ....K5
Khaf 5,000 ....L3
Khalkhal 5,422 ....F2
Khash 7,439 ....M6
Khiyav 9,000 ....E1
Khoman 3,054 ....F2
Khomeinishar 46,836 ....G4
Khorramabad 104,928 ...F4
Khorramshahr 146,709 ...F5
Khvaf 5,000 ....L3
Khvonsar 9,000 ....G4
Khvor 2,912 ....J3
Kord Koy 9,855 ....J2
Lahijan 25,725 ....G2
Lar 22,000 ....J7
Mahabad 28,610 ....D2
Mahallat 12,000 ......G4
Mahan 8,000 ....K5
Malamir (Izeh) 1,983 ...F5
Malayer 28,434 ....F3
Marageh 60,820 ....E2
Marand 24,000 ....D1
Marv Dasht 25,498 ....H6
Mashhad (Meshed) 670,180 ...L2
Masjed Soleyman 77,161 ...F5
Medishahr 9,000 ......H3
Mehran 664 ....E4
Meybod 15,000 ....J4
Miandoab 19,000 .....D2
Mianeh 28,447 ....E2
Minab 4,228 ....K7
Mirjaveh 11,000 .....M6
Naft-e Shah 3,043 ....D4
Nahavand 24,000 .....F3
Na'in 5,925 ....H4
Najafabad 76,236 ....G4
Naraq 2,725 ....G4
Nasratabad (Zabol) 20,000 ...M5
Neyriz 16,114 ....J6
Neyshabur 59,101 ....L2
Nishapur (Neyshabur) 59,101 ...L2
Nosratabad 20,000 ...L6
Now Shahr 8,000 .....G2
Orumiyeh 10,947 .....D1
Orumiyeh (Urmia) 163,991 ...D1
Oshnoviyeh 5,000 ....D2
Pahlevi (Enzeli) 55,978 ...F2
Pazanan 81 ....G5
Qasr-e-Shirin 15,094 ...D4
Qayen 6,000 ....L3
Qazvin 138,527 ......F3
Qom 246,831 ....G3
Qorveh 2,929 ....E2
Quchan 29,133 ....L2
Qum (Qom) 246,831 ...G3
Rafsanjan 21,000 ....K5
Ramhormoz 9,000 .....F5
Rasht 187,203 ....F2
Ravar 5,074 ....K5
Resht (Rasht) 187,203 ...F2
Rey 102,825 ....G3
Reza'iyeh (Urmia) 163,991 ...D2
Rigan 8,255 ....L6
Rud Sar 7,460 ....G2
Sabzevar 69,174 .....K2
Sabzvaran 7,000 .....K6
Saeendey 4,195 ......E2
Sa'idabad 20,000 ....J6
Sanandaj 95,834 .....E2
Saqqez 17,000 ....E2
Sarab 16,000 ....E1
Saraskhs 3,461 ......M2
Saravan 4,012 ....N7
Sar Dasht 6,000 .....D2
Sari 70,936 ....H2
Savanat (Sabzanat) 18,187 ...J6
Semnan 31,058 ....H3
Shadegan 6,000 ......F5
Shahdad 2,777 ....K5
Shahistan (Saravan) 4,012 ...N7
Shahreza 34,220 .....G4
Shahr Kord 24,000 ...G4
Shahrud (Emamshahr) 30,767 ...J2
Sharafkhaneh 1,260 ...D1
Shiraz 416,408 ......H6
Shirvan 11,000 ......L2
Shush 1,433 ....F4
Shushtar 24,000 .....F5
Sinneh (Sanandaj) 95,834 ...E2
Sirjan (Sa'idabad) 20,000 ...J6
Sivand 1,811 ....H5
Songor 10,433 ....E3
Sufian 2,914 ....D1
Sultanabad (Kashmar) 17,000 ...L3
Tabas 10,000 ....K4
Tabriz 598,576 ......D1
Taft 7,000 ....J4
Tajrish 157,486 .....G3
Takestan 13,485 .....F3
Tehran (cap.) 4,496,159 ...G3
Tonekabon 12,000 ....G2
Torbat-e Heydariyeh 30,106 ...L3
Torbat-e Jam 13,000 ...M3
Tun (Ferdows) 11,000 ...K3
Tuysarkan 12,000 ....F3
Urmia 163,991 ....D2
Varamin 11,183 ......G3
Yazd (Yezd) 135,978 ...H4
Yazd-e Khvast 3,544 ...H5
Zabol 20,000 ....M5
Zahedan 92,628 ......M6
Zanjan 99,967 ....F2
Zarand 5,000 ....K5
Zarqam 7,000 ....H6
Zenjan (Zanjan) 99,967 ...F2

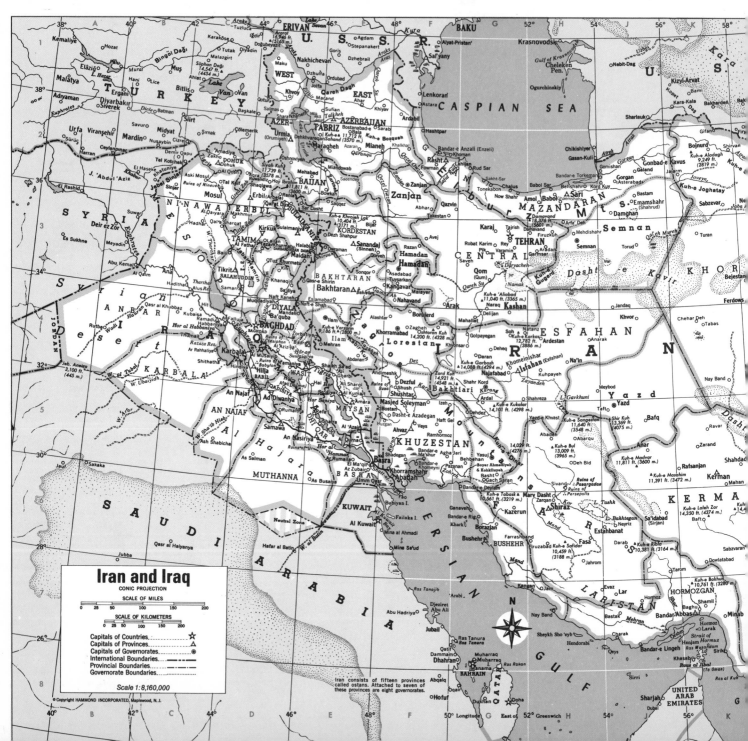

Iran and Iraq
CONIC PROJECTION

SCALE OF MILES
0 25 50   100   150   200

SCALE OF KILOMETERS
0 25 50 100   150   200

Capitals of Countries .... ☆
Capitals of Provinces .... △
Capitals of Governorates .... ◉
International Boundaries ....
Provincial Boundaries ....
Governorate Boundaries ....

Scale 1:8,160,000

Iran consists of fifteen provinces called ostans. Attached to seven of these provinces are eight governorates.

© Copyright HAMMOND INCORPORATED, Maplewood, N.J.

OTHER FEATURES

Aji Chai (riv.) E1
A'rabi (isl.) G7
Araks (Aras) (riv.) E1
Atrak (Atrek) (riv.) J2
Bakhtegan (lake) J6
Baluchistan (reg.) M7
Bampur (riv.) M7
Behistun (ruins) E3
Caspian (sea) G1
Damavand (Demavend) (mt.) H3
Dez (riv.) F4
Elburz (mts.) G2
Farsi (isl.) G7
Gorgan (riv.) J2
Hari Rud (riv.) M3
Kashaf Rud (riv.) M2
Karkheh (riv.) E4
Karun (riv.) F5
Khark (Kharg) (isl.) G6
Kuh (cape) K8
Kurang (riv.) G4
Laristan (reg.) J7
Makran (reg.) M8
Mand Rud (riv.) G6
Mehran (riv.) J7
Namaksar (lake) M3
Nezwar (riv.) E4
Oman (gulf) M8
Pasargadae (ruins) H5
Persepolis (ruins) H6
Persian (gulf) F6
Qareh Su (riv.) G3
Qareh Su (riv.) G3
Qeshm (isl.) J7
Qezel Owzam (riv.) F2
Safid Rud (riv.) F2

Shaikh Shua'ib (isl.) H7
Shelagh (riv.) M5
Shirvan (riv.) E3
Shur (riv.) J7
Siah Kuh (mt.) L3
Silup (riv.) M8
Susa (ruins) F4
Talab (riv.) N6
Tashk (lake) J6
Urmia (lake) D2
Zarineh (riv.) E2
Zilbir (riv.) D1
Zohreh (riv.) F5

IRAQ

GOVERNORATES

Anbar B4
An Najaf C5
Babil D4
Baghdad D4
Basra E5
Dhi Qar E5
Diyala D4
Dohuk C2
Erbil C3
Karbala C4
Maysan E4
Muthanna D5
Ninawa B3
Qadisiya D4
Salahuddin C3
Sulaimaniya D3
Tamin D3
Wasit D4

CITIES and TOWNS

Ad Diwaniya 60,553 .... D5
A'faq 5,390 .... D4
Al A'ziziya 7,450 .... D4
Al Falluja 38,072 .... C4
Al Fathat 15,329 .... C3
A'li Gharbi 15,456 .... D4
A'li Sharqi 8,398 .... E4
Al Kufa 30,862 .... D4
Al Musaiyib 15,955 .... D4
Al Q'aim 3,372 .... B3
Al Qaiyara 3,060 .... C2
Al Qosh 3,863 .... C2
Al Qurna 5,638 .... E5
A'madiya 2,578 .... C2
A'mara 64,847 .... E4
A'na 15,729 .... B3
An Najaf 128,096 .... D5
An Nasiriya 60,405 .... D5
A'qra 8,659 .... D2
Arbela (Erbil) 90,320 .... D2
Aski Mosul 643 .... C2
As Salman 1,789 .... E5
Az Zubair 41,408 .... E5
Badra 3,564 .... D4
Baghdad (cap.) 502,503 .... D4
Baiji 6,785 .... C3
Baq'uba 34,575 .... D4
Basra 313,327 .... E5
Dohuk 16,998 .... C2
Erbil 90,320 .... D2
Fao 15,399 .... F6
Habbaniya 14,405 .... C4
Haditha 6,870 .... C3
Hai 16,988 .... E4
Halabja 11,206 .... D3
Hilla 84,717 .... D4
Hindiya 16,436 .... D4
Hit 9,131 .... C4
Karbal'a 83,301 .... C4
Khanaqin 23,522 .... D3
Kifri 8,500 .... D3
Kirkuk 167,413 .... D3
Kirkuk* 176,794 .... D3
Kubaisa 4,023 .... C4
Kut 42,116 .... D4
Makhmur 2,556 .... C3
Mandali 11,262 .... D4
Mosul 315,157 .... C2
Muqdadiyah 12,181 .... D4
Naft Kaneh D4
Na'maniya 11,943 .... D4
Qal'at Diza 6,250 .... D2
Ramadi 28,723 .... C4
Rania 4,090 .... D2
Refai 7,681 .... E5
Rumaitha 10,222 .... D5
Rutba 5,091 .... B4
Ruwandiz 5,801 .... D2
Sad'iya 5,285 .... D3
Samarra 24,746 .... C3
Samawa 33,473 .... D5
Shaikh Saa'd 2,958 .... E4
Shaqlawa 6,814 .... D2
Shatra 18,822 .... E5
Sinjar 7,942 .... B2
Sulaimaniya 86,822 .... D3
Tal Kaif 7,482 .... C2
Taza Khurmatu 2,681 .... D3
Tikrit 9,921 .... C3
Tuz Khurmatu 13,860 .... D3
Zakho 14,790 .... C2

OTHER FEATURES

Adhaim (riv.) D3
Aneiza, Jebel (mt.) A4
A'rab, Shatt-al- (riv.) F5
A'ra'r, Wadi (dry riv.) B5
Babylon (ruins) D4
Batin, Wadi al (dry riv.) E6
Ctesiphon (ruins) D4
Darbandikhan (dam) D3
Euphrates (riv.) D4
Great Zab (riv.) C2
Hauran, Wadi (dry riv.) B4
Little Zab (riv.) C3
Mesopotamia (reg.) B3
Nineveh (ruins) C2
Sad'iya, Hor (lake) E4
Saniya, Hor (lake) E5
Shai'b Hisb, Wadi (dry riv.) .. C5
Sinjar, Jebel (mts.) B2
Siyah Kuh (mt.) D2
Syrian (des.) B4
Tigris (riv.) E4
Ubaiyidh, Wadi (dry riv.) B5
Ur (ruins) E5

*City and suburbs.
†Population of commune.

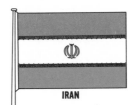

IRAN

IRAQ

AREA 636,293 sq. mi. (1,648,000 sq. km.)
POPULATION 37,447,000
CAPITAL Tehran
LARGEST CITY Tehran
HIGHEST POINT Damavand 18,376 ft. (5,601 m.)
MONETARY UNIT Iranian rial
MAJOR LANGUAGES Persian, Azerbaijani, Kurdish
MAJOR RELIGION Islam

AREA 172,476 sq. mi. (446,713 sq. km.)
POPULATION 12,767,000
CAPITAL Baghdad
LARGEST CITY Baghdad
HIGHEST POINT Haji Ibrahim 11,811 ft. (3,600 m.)
MONETARY UNIT Iraqi dinar
MAJOR LANGUAGES Arabic, Kurdish
MAJOR RELIGION Islam

Topography

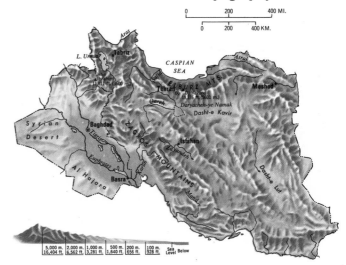

5,000 m. / 16,404 ft.   2,000 m. / 6,562 ft.   1,000 m. / 3,281 ft.   500 m. / 1,640 ft.   200 m. / 656 ft.   100 m. / 328 ft.   Sea Level   Below

Agriculture, Industry and Resources

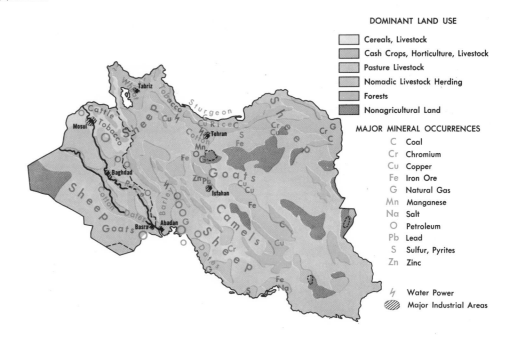

DOMINANT LAND USE

Cereals, Livestock
Cash Crops, Horticulture, Livestock
Pasture Livestock
Nomadic Livestock Herding
Forests
Nonagricultural Land

MAJOR MINERAL OCCURRENCES

C   Coal
Cr   Chromium
Cu   Copper
Fe   Iron Ore
G   Natural Gas
Mn   Manganese
Na   Salt
O   Petroleum
Pb   Lead
S   Sulfur, Pyrites
Zn   Zinc

⚡   Water Power
▨   Major Industrial Areas

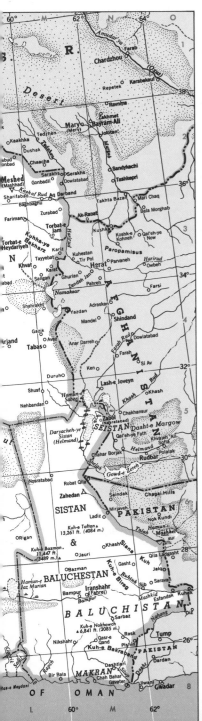

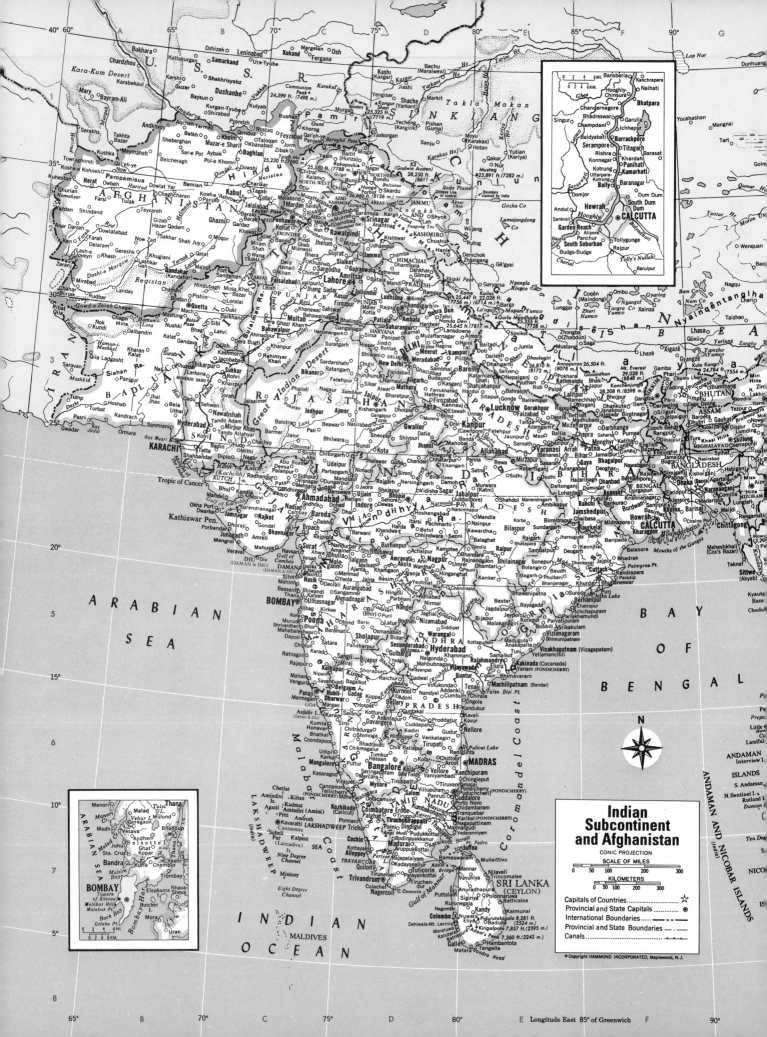

Indian Subcontinent and Afghanistan

CONIC PROJECTION

SCALE OF MILES

0   50   100   200   300

KILOMETERS

0   50   100   200   300

Capitals of Countries.............................☆
Provincial and State Capitals.............⊛
International Boundaries......____ ____ ____
Provincial and State Boundaries......___ _ ___
Canals...

© Copyright HAMMOND INCORPORATED, Maplewood, N.J.

Longitude East 85° of Greenwich

INDIA

AREA 1,269,339 sq. mi. (3,287,588 sq. km.)
POPULATION 683,810,051
CAPITAL New Delhi
LARGEST CITY Calcutta (greater)
HIGHEST POINT Nanda Devi 25,645 ft. (7,817 m.)
MONETARY UNIT Indian rupee
MAJOR LANGUAGES Hindi, English, Bihari, Telugu,
Marathi, Bengali, Tamil, Gujarati, Rajasthani,
Kanarese, Malayalam, Oriya, Punjabi, Assamese,
Kashmiri, Urdu
MAJOR RELIGIONS Hinduism, Islam, Christianity,
Sikhism, Buddhism, Jainism, Zoroastrianism, Animism

PAKISTAN

AREA 310,403 sq. mi. (803,944 sq. km.)
POPULATION 83,782,000
CAPITAL Islamabad
LARGEST CITY Karachi
HIGHEST POINT K2 (Godwin Austen)
28,250 ft. (8,611 m.)
MONETARY UNIT Pakistani rupee
MAJOR LANGUAGES Urdu, English, Punjabi,.
Pushtu, Sindhi, Baluchi, Brahui
MAJOR RELIGIONS Islam, Hinduism, Sikhism,
Christianity, Buddhism

SRI LANKA (CEYLON)

AREA 25,332 sq. mi.
(65,610 sq. km.)
POPULATION 14,850,001
CAPITAL Colombo
LARGEST CITY Colombo
HIGHEST POINT Pidurutalagala
8,281 ft. (2,524 m.)
MONETARY UNIT Sri Lanka rupee
MAJOR LANGUAGES Sinhala, Tamil,
English
MAJOR RELIGIONS Buddhism,
Hinduism, Christianity, Islam

AFGHANISTAN

AREA 250,775 sq. mi.
(649,507 sq. km.)
POPULATION 15,540,000
CAPITAL Kabul
LARGEST CITY Kabul
HIGHEST POINT Nowshak
24,557 ft. (7,485 m.)
MONETARY UNIT afghani
MAJOR LANGUAGES Pushtu, Dari,
Uzbek
MAJOR RELIGION Islam

NEPAL

AREA 54,663 sq. mi.
(141,577 sq. km.)
POPULATION 14,179,301
CAPITAL Kathmandu
LARGEST CITY Kathmandu
HIGHEST POINT Mt. Everest
29,028 ft. (8,848 m.)
MONETARY UNIT Nepalese rupee
MAJOR LANGUAGES Nepali,
Maithili, Tamang, Newari, Tharu
MAJOR RELIGIONS Hinduism,
Buddhism

MALDIVES

AREA 115 sq. mi. (298 sq. km.)
POPULATION 143,046
CAPITAL Male
LARGEST CITY Male
HIGHEST POINT 20 ft. (6 m.)
MONETARY UNIT Maldivian rupee
MAJOR LANGUAGE Divehi
MAJOR RELIGION Islam

BHUTAN

AREA 18,147 sq. mi.
(47,000 sq. km.)
POPULATION 1,298,000
CAPITAL Thimphu
LARGEST CITY Thimphu
HIGHEST POINT Kula Kangri
24,784 ft. (7,554 m.)
MONETARY UNIT ngultrum
MAJOR LANGUAGES Dzongka,
Nepali
MAJOR RELIGIONS Buddhism,
Hinduism

BANGLADESH

AREA 55,126 sq. mi.
(142,776 sq. km.)
POPULATION 87,052,024
CAPITAL Dhaka
LARGEST CITY Dhaka
HIGHEST POINT Keokradong
4,034 ft. (1,230 m.)
MONETARY UNIT taka
MAJOR LANGUAGES Bengali,
English
MAJOR RELIGIONS Islam,
Hinduism, Christianity

INDIA

PAKISTAN

SRI LANKA (CEYLON)

BHUTAN

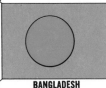
AFGHANISTAN

MALDIVES

BANGLADESH

NEPAL

AFGHANISTAN

CITIES and TOWNS

Bala Murghab 10,000 .... A1
Balkh 15,000 .... B1
Chahardeh B2
Girishk 10,000 .... A2
Kabul (cap.) 318,094 ...... B2
Kabul* 534,350 .... B2
Kuhsan A2
Kushk 10,000 .... A1
Landi Muhammad Amin
Khan 1,000 .... B2
Panjao 3,000 .... B2
Qaleh-i-Kang 17,400 .... A2
Sabzawar 5,000 .... A2
Shindand
(Sabzawar) 5,000 .... A2
Taiwara 5,000 .... A2

OTHER FEATURES

Farah Rud (riv.) A2
Hari Rud (riv.) A1
Helmand (riv.) B2
Hindu Kush (mts.) B1
Jam (mt.) A2
Kabul (riv.) C2
Kunar (riv.) C1
Kunduz (riv.) B1
Lora (riv.) B2
Margo, Dasht-i- (des.) A2
Namaksar (salt lake) A2
Paropamisus (range) A2
Registan (reg.) B2

BANGLADESH

CITIES and TOWNS

Chittagong 416,733 .... G4
Cox's Bazar (Maheshkhali) .. G4
Dhaka (Dacca) (cap.)
1,310,976 .... G4
Dhaka (Dacca) ☐ 2,539,991 . G4
Habiganj G4
Jamalpur F4
Khulna 436,000 .... G4
Kishorganj G4
Madaripur G4
Maheshkhali G4
Narayanganj 176,879 ...... G4
Nawabganj F4
Noakhali 19,874 .... G4
Rangamati 6,416 .... G4

OTHER FEATURES

Bengal, Bay of (sea) F5
Brahmaputra (riv.) G3

BHUTAN

CITIES and TOWNS

Bumthang 10,000 .... G3
Punakha 12,000 .... G3
Taga Dzong 18,000 .... G3
Tongsa Dzong 2,500 .... G3

OTHER FEATURES

Chomo Lhari (mt.) F3
Himalaya (mts.) E2
Kula Kangri (mt.) G3

INDIA

INTERNAL DIVISIONS

Andaman and Nicobar Isls.
(terr.) 115,133 .... G6
Andhra Pradesh
(state) 43,502,708 .... D5
Arunachal Pradesh
(terr.) 467,511 .... G3
Assam (state) 14,625,152 . G3
Bihar (state) 56,353,369 .. F4
Chandigarh
(terr.) 257,251 .... D2
Dadra and Nagar Haveli
(terr.) 74,170 .... C4
Daman and Diu
(terr.) 857,771 .... C4
Delhi (terr.) 4,065,698 ..... D3
Gujarat (state) 26,697,475 . C4
Haryana (state) 10,036,808 . D3
Himachal Pradesh
(state) 3,460,434 .... D2
Jammu and Kashmir
(state) 4,616,632 .... D2
Karnataka
(state) 29,299,014 .... D6
Kerala (state) 21,347,375 .. D6
Lakshadweep
(terr.) 31,810 .... C6
Madhya Pradesh
(state) 41,654,119 .... D4
Maharashtra
(state) 50,412,235 .... C5
Manipur (state) 1,072,753 . G4
Meghalaya
(state) 1,011,699 .... G3
Mizoram (terr.) 332,390 ... G4
Nagaland
(state) 516,449 .... G3

OTHER FEATURES

Ganges (riv.) F3
Sundarbans (reg.) F4

(continued on following page)

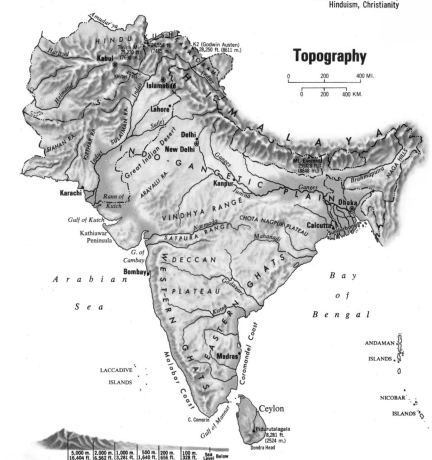

Topography

0   200   400 MI.
0   200   400 KM.

| 5,000 m. | 2,000 m. | 1,000 m. | 500 m. | 200 m. | 100 m. | Sea | Below |
| 16,404 ft. | 6,562 ft. | 3,281 ft. | 1,640 ft. | 656 ft. | 328 ft. | Level | |

Agriculture, Industry and Resources

DOMINANT LAND USE

- Cereals (chiefly wheat, barley, corn)
- Cereals (chiefly millet, sorghum)
- Cereals (chiefly rice)
- Cotton, Cereals
- Pasture Livestock
- Nomadic Livestock Herding
- Forests
- Nonagricultural Land

MAJOR MINERAL OCCURRENCES

Ab	Asbestos	Gr	Graphite
Al	Bauxite	Lg	Lignite
Au	Gold	Mg	Magnesium
Be	Beryl	Mi	Mica
C	Coal	Mn	Manganese
Cr	Chromium	Na	Salt
Cu	Copper	O	Petroleum
D	Diamonds	Pb	Lead
Fe	Iron Ore	Ti	Titanium
G	Natural Gas	U	Uranium
Gp	Gypsum	Zn	Zinc

⚡ Water Power
▨ Major Industrial Areas

AREA 145,730 sq. mi. (377,441 sq. km.)
POPULATION 117,057,485
CAPITAL Tokyo
LARGEST CITY Tokyo
HIGHEST POINT Fuji 12,389 ft. (3,776 m.)
MONETARY UNIT yen
MAJOR LANGUAGE Japanese
MAJOR RELIGIONS Buddhism, Shintoism

AREA 46,540 sq. mi. (120,539 sq. km.)
POPULATION 17,914,000
CAPITAL P'yŏngyang
LARGEST CITY P'yŏngyang
HIGHEST POINT Paektu 9,003 ft. (2,744 m.)
MONETARY UNIT won
MAJOR LANGUAGE Korean
MAJOR RELIGIONS Confucianism, Buddhism, Ch'ondogyo

AREA 38,175 sq. mi. (98,873 sq. km.)
POPULATION 37,448,836
CAPITAL Seoul
LARGEST CITY Seoul
HIGHEST POINT Halla 6,398 ft. (1,950 m.)
MONETARY UNIT won
MAJOR LANGUAGE Korean
MAJOR RELIGIONS Confucianism, Buddhism, Ch'ondogyo, Christianity

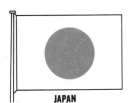

JAPAN

NORTH KOREA

SOUTH KOREA

JAPAN

PREFECTURES

Aichi 5,923,569	H6
Akita 1,232,481	J4
Aomori 1,468,646	K3
Chiba 4,149,147	P2
Ehime 1,465,215	F7
Fukui 773,599	G5
Fukuoka 4,292,963	E7
Fukushima 1,970,616	K5
Gifu 1,867,978	H6
Gumma 1,756,480	E6
Hiroshima 2,646,324	E6
Hokkaido 5,338,206	K2
Hyogo 4,992,140	H7
Ibaraki 2,342,198	K5
Ishikawa 1,069,872	K4
Iwate 1,385,563	K4
Kagawa 961,292	G6
Kagoshima 1,723,902	E8
Kanagawa 6,397,748	O2
Kochi 808,397	F7
Kumamoto 1,715,273	E7
Kyoto 2,424,856	J7
Mie 1,626,002	H6
Miyagi 1,955,267	K4
Miyazaki 1,085,055	E8
Nagano 2,017,564	J5
Nagasaki 1,571,912	D7
Nara 1,077,491	J8
Niigata 2,391,938	J5
Oita 1,190,314	E7
Okayama 1,814,305	F6
Okinawa 1,042,572	N6
Osaka 8,278,925	J8
Saga 837,674	E7

Saitama 4,821,340	O2
Shiga 985,621	J7
Shimane 768,886	F6
Shizuoka 3,308,799	H6
Tochigi 1,698,003	K5
Tokushima 805,166	G7
Tokyo 11,673,554	O2
Tottori 581,311	G6
Toyama 1,070,791	H5
Wakayama 1,072,118	G6
Yamagata 1,220,302	K4
Yamaguchi 1,555,218	E6
Yamanashi 783,050	J6

CITIES and TOWNS

Abashiri 43,825	M1
Ageo 146,358	O2
Aikawa 13,546	H4
Aizuwakamatsu 108,650	J3
Ajigasawa 18,086	J3
Akashi 234,905	H8
Aki 24,480	F7
Akita 261,246	J4
Akkeshi 16,778	M2
Akune 30,295	E7
Amagasaki 545,783	H8
Amagi 42,725	E7
Anan 60,439	G7
Aomori 264,222	K3
Asahi 34,028	K6
Asahikawa 320,526	L2
Ashibetsu 36,520	L2
Ashikaga 162,359	J5
Ashiya 76,211	H8
Atami 51,437	J6
Atsugi 108,955	O2
Awaji 9,623	H8

Ayabe 43,490	G6
Beppu 133,894	E7
Bibai 38,416	L2
Biratori 9,331	L2
Chiba 659,356	P2
Chichibu 61,798	J5
Chigasaki 152,023	O3
Chitose 61,031	K2
Chofu 175,924	O2
Choshi 90,374	K6
Daito 110,829	J8
Ebetsu 77,624	K2
Eniwa 39,884	K2
Esashi, Hokkaido 10,172	L1
Esashi, Hokkaido 14,409	J3
Esashi, Iwate 36,336	K4
Fuchu, Hiroshima 50,217	F6
Fuchu, Tokyo 182,474	O2
Fuji 199,195	J6
Fujieda 90,358	J6
Fujisawa 265,975	O3
Fukagawa 36,000	L2
Fukuchiyama 60,003	D7
Fukue 32,018	J4
Fukuoka 1,002,201	D7
Fukushima 246,531	K5
Fukuyama 329,714	F6
Funabashi 423,101	P2
Furukawa 54,356	K4
Gifu 408,707	H6
Gobo 30,272	G7
Gose 37,554	J8
Gosen 39,376	J5
Goshogawara 49,040	K3
Gotsu 27,992	F6
Habikino 94,160	J8
Haboro 13,624	K1

Hachinohe 224,366	K3
Hachioji 322,580	O2
Hadano 103,663	O3
Hagi 52,724	E6
Hakodate 307,453	K3
Hakui 28,726	H5
Hamada 50,316	E6
Hamamatsu 468,884	H6
Hamakita 65,826	K4
Hanno 55,926	O2
Haramachi 43,483	K5
Hasama 24,026	O3
Higashiosaka 524,750	J8
Himeji 436,086	G6
Himi 61,789	H5
Hino 126,847	O2
Hirara 297,618	J7
Hirara 29,301	L7
Hirata 30,942	F6
Hiratsuka 195,635	O3
Hiroo 11,399	L2
Hirosaki 164,911	J3
Hiroshima 852,611	E6
Hitachi 202,383	K5
Hitachiota 35,322	K5
Hitoyoshi 41,118	E7
Hofu 105,540	E6
Hondo 40,432	D7
Honjo 40,488	J4
Hyuga 53,448	E7
Ibaraki 210,286	J7
Ibusuki 32,339	E8
Ichihara 194,068	P3
Ichikawa 319,291	P2
Ichinohe 21,433	K3
Ichinomiya 238,463	H6
Ichinoseki 59,122	K4

Ide 9,112	J7
Iida 77,112	H6
Iizuka 75,417	E7
Ikeda, Hokkaido 12,306	L2
Ikeda, Osaka 100,268	H7
Ikeda 48,848	J8
Ikuno 6,658	J6
Imabari 119,726	F6
Imari 60,913	D7
Imazu 11,519	G6
Ina 54,468	J6
Isahaya 73,341	D7
Ise 104,957	H6
Ishigaki 34,657	L7
Ishige 19,220	P2
Ishinomaki 115,085	K4
Ishioka 43,679	K5
Itami 171,978	H7
Ito 68,072	J6
Itoigawa 36,646	H5
Itoman 39,363	N6
Iwaizumi 20,219	K4
Iwaki 330,213	K5
Iwakuni 111,069	E6
Iwami 16,063	K5
Iwamizawa 72,305	L2
Iwanai 25,823	K2
Iwasaki 4,437	J3
Iwata 67,665	H6
Iwatsuki 83,825	O2
Iyo 27,805	F7
Izuhara 18,460	D6
Izumi 118,237	J8
Izumiotsu 62,062	J8
Izumisano 86,139	G6
Izumo 71,568	F6
Joetsu 123,418	H5
Joyo 58,923	J7

Kadoma 143,238	J7
Kaga 61,599	H5
Kagoshima 456,827	E8
Kaizuka 79,506	H8
Kakogawa 169,293	G6
Kamaishi 68,981	L4
Kamakura 165,552	O3
Kameoka 58,184	J7
Kamisco 27,229	K4
Kaminoyama 37,858	J4
Kamiyaku 8,668	E8
Kamo 8,953	J7
Kanazawa 395,263	H5
Kanonji 44,131	J6
Kanoya 67,951	E8
Kanuma 81,799	J5
Karatsu 75,224	D7
Kaseda 24,969	D8
Kashihara 95,701	J8
Kashiwa 203,065	P2
Kashiwara 63,586	J8
Kashiwazaki 80,351	J5
Kasugai 213,857	H6
Kasukabe 121,639	O2
Katsuta 79,996	K5
Katsuura 26,755	K6
Kawachinagano 66,936	J8
Kawagoe 225,465	O2
Kawaguchi 345,538	J6
Kawanishi 115,773	H7
Kawasaki 1,014,951	O2
Kikonai 10,034	K3
Kimitsu 76,016	O3
Kiryu 134,239	J5
Kisarazu 96,840	P3
Kishiwada 174,952	J8
Kitaibaraki 44,332	K5

Kitakami 48,759	K4
Kitakata 37,471	J5
Kitakyushu 1,058,058	E6
Kitami 91,519	L2
Kizu 11,890	J7
Kobayashi 38,325	E8
Kobe 1,360,605	H7
Kochi 280,962	F7
Kodaira 156,181	O2
Kofu 193,879	J6
Koga 55,973	J5
Koganei 102,714	O2
Kokubu 31,660	E8
Komagane 30,318	H6
Komatsu 100,273	H5
Koriyama 264,628	K5
Koshigaya 195,917	P2
Koyama 16,394	E8
Kubohama 17,817	K3
Kuji 38,122	K3
Kuki 45,797	O2
Kumagaya 131,485	J5
Kumamoto 488,166	E7
Kumano 27,026	G7
Kumiyama 11,540	J7
Kurashiki 392,755	F6
Kurayoshi 50,785	F6
Kure 242,655	F6
Kuroiso 42,349	K5
Kurume 204,474	E7
Kushiro 30,456	E8
Kushima 30,038	E8
Kushimoto 18,997	G7
Kushiro 206,840	M2
Kyonan 13,067	O3
Kyoto 1,461,059	J7
Machida 255,305	O2
Maebashi 250,241	J5
Maihara 12,845	G6
Maizuru 97,780	G6
Makubetsu 18,444	L2
Makurazaki 29,685	O3
Mashike 9,312	K2
Masuda 50,734	E6
Matane 127,440	H8
Matsubara 132,662	H8
Matsumae 18,307	J3
Matsumoto 185,595	H5
Matsusaka 108,893	H6
Matsuto 36,170	H5
Matsuyama 367,323	F7
Mihara 83,679	F6
Miki 53,731	H7
Mikuni 21,602	G5
Minamata 36,782	E7
Minobu 10,345	J6
Minoo 79,621	J7
Misawa 37,437	K3
Mitaka 164,950	O2
Mito 197,953	K5
Mitsukaido 38,820	P2
Miura 47,888	O3
Miyako 61,912	L4
Miyakonojo 118,289	E8
Miyazaki 234,347	E8
Miyazu 30,194	G6
Miyoshi 37,193	F6
Mizusawa 52,266	K4
Mobara 64,942	K6
Mombetsu 32,825	L1
Mombetsu 15,029	L2
Mooka 47,345	K5
Mori 17,030	K2
Moriguchi 178,383	J7
Morioka 216,223	K4
Motobu 17,823	N6
Muko 45,886	J7
Murakami 32,939	J4
Muroran 158,715	K2
Muroto 26,660	G7
Musashino 139,508	O2
Mutsu 44,646	K3
Nachikatsuura 23,596	H7
Nagahama, Ehime 13,144	F7
Nagahama, Shiga 54,064	H6
Nagano 306,637	J5
Nagaoka, Kyoto 65,557	J7
Nagaoka, Niigata 171,742	J5
Nagaokakyo 65,557	J7
Nagasaki 450,194	D7
Nagato 27,327	E6
Nago 45,210	N6
Nagoya 2,079,740	H6
Naha 295,006	N6
Nakaminato 33,147	K5
Nakamura 34,437	F7
Nakasato 14,248	K3
Nakatsu 59,111	E7
Nanao 49,493	H5
Nankoku 42,832	F7
Nara 257,538	J8
Narashino 117,852	P2
Nayoro 35,145	L1
Naze 46,359	O5
Nemuro 45,817	M2
Neyagawa 254,311	J7
Nichinan 52,171	E8
Niigata 423,188	J5
Niihama 131,712	F6
Niimi 30,014	F6
Niitsu 58,970	J5
Nishinomiya 400,622	H8

(continued on following page)

Agriculture, Industry and Resources

DOMINANT LAND USE

- Cereals, Cash Crops
- Truck Farming, Horticulture
- Mixed Farming, Dairy
- Rice
- Forests, Scrub

MAJOR MINERAL OCCURRENCES

Ag	Silver	Mn	Manganese
Au	Gold	Mo	Molybdenum
C	Coal	O	Petroleum
Cu	Copper	Pb	Lead
Fe	Iron Ore	Py	Pyrites
G	Natural Gas	U	Uranium
Gr	Graphite	W	Tungsten
Mg	Magnesium	Zn	Zinc

⚡ Water Power

▨ Major Industrial Areas

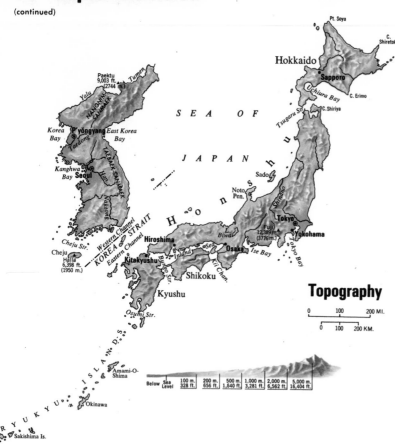

Topography

Below Sea Level | 100 m. 328 ft. | 200 m. 656 ft. | 500 m. 1,640 ft. | 1,000 m. 3,281 ft. | 2,000 m. 6,562 ft. | 5,000 m. 16,404 ft.

Okhotsk (sea) M1
Oki (isls.) F5
Okinawa (isl.) N6
Okinawa (isl.) N6
Okinoerabu (isl.) L7
Okushiri (isl.) J2
Oma (cape) K3
Omono (riv.) J4
Ono (riv.) E7
Ontake (mt.) J5
Osaka (bay) H6
O-Shima (isl.) J6
Osumi (isls.) E8
Osumi (pen.) E8
Osumi (str.) E8
Otakine (mt.) K5
Rikuchu-Kaigan National Park L4
Rishiri (isl.) K1
Ryukyu (isls.) L7
Sado (isl.) J5
Sagami (bay) O3
Sagami (riv.) O2
Sagami (sea) J6
Saikai National Park D7
Sakishima (isls.) K7

San'in Kaigan National Park G6
Sata (cape) E8
Setonaikai National Park H7
Shikoku (isl.) G7
Shikotan (isl.) K2
Shikotsu-Toya National Park K2
Shimane (pen.) G6
Shimokita (pen.) K3
Shinano (riv.) J5
Shiono (cape) H7
Shiragami (cape) J2
Shirane (mt.) J5
Shirane (mt.) H6
Shiretoko (cape) M1
Shiriya (cape) K3
Soya (str.) K1
Suo (sea) G6
Suruga (bay) J6
Suwanose (isl.) O4
Suzu (pt.) H5
Takeshima (isls.) G6
Tama (riv.) O2
Tanega (isl.) E8
Tappi (cape) K3

Nishinoomote 24,266 .... E8
Nobeoka 134,521 .... E7
Noboribetsu 50,885 .... K2
Noda 78,193 .... P2
Nogata 58,551 .... E7
Nose 9,749 .... J7
Noshiro 59,215 .... J3
Noto 15,815 .... H5
Numata 45,255 .... J5
Numazu 199,325 .... J6
Obama 33,890 .... G6
Obihiro 141,774 .... L2
Oda 37,449 .... F6
Odate 71,828 .... K3
Odawara 173,519 .... J6
Ofunato 39,632 .... K4
Oga 39,619 .... J4
Ogaki 140,424 .... H6
Ogi 4,717 .... J5
Ohata 12,632 .... K3
Oita 320,237 .... E7
Ojiya 44,375 .... J5
Okaya 50,395 .... E7
Okaya 61,776 .... H5
Okayama 513,471 .... F6
Okazaki 234,510 .... H6
Omagari 40,581 .... K4
Omiya 327,698 .... O2
Omu 7,407 .... L1
Omura, Bonin Is. 1,507 .... M3
Omura, Nagasaki 60,919 .... E7
Omuta 165,969 .... E7
Onagawa 16,945 .... K4
Ono 41,918 .... H6
Onoda 43,804 .... E6
Onomichi 102,951 .... F6
Osaka 2,778,987 .... J8
Ota 110,723 .... J5
Otaru 184,406 .... K2
Otawara 42,332 .... K5
Otofuke 26,933 .... L2
Otsu 191,481 .... J7
Owase 31,797 .... H6
Oyabe 56,791 .... H5
Oyama 120,264 .... J5
Ozu 37,294 .... F7
Rausu 8,249 .... M1
Rikuzentakata 29,439 .... K4
Rumoi 36,882 .... K2
Ryotsu 22,110 .... J5
Ryugasaki 40,565 .... P2
Sabae 57,252 .... H5
Saga 152,258 .... E7
Sagamihara 377,398 .... O2
Saigo 14,409 .... F5
Sakai 52,863 .... J8
Saito 37,054 .... E7
Sakado 51,232 .... O2
Sakai, Ibaraki 24,347 .... O2
Sakai, Osaka 750,688 .... J8
Sakaide 67,624 .... G6
Sakaiminato 35,821 .... F6
Sakata 97,723 .... J4
Saku 56,143 .... J5
Sakurai 54,814 .... J7
Sanda 35,261 .... H7
Sanjo 81,806 .... J5
Sapporo 1,240,613 .... K2
Sarufutsu 3,552 .... L1
Saroma 250,729 .... L2
Satte 43,083 .... O1
Sawara 48,670 .... K6
Sayama 98,548 .... O2
Sendai, Kagoshima 61,788 .... E8
Sendai, Miyagi 615,473 .... K4
Setouchi 15,290 .... O5
Settsu 76,704 .... J8
Shari 15,996 .... M2
Shibata 74,025 .... J5
Shibetsu 30,028 .... L1
Shimabara 45,179 .... E7
Shimamoto 22,404 .... J7

Shimizu 243,049 .... J6
Shimoda 31,700 .... J6
Shimonoseki 266,593 .... E6
Shingu 39,023 .... H7
Shinjo 42,227 .... J4
Shiogama 59,235 .... K4
Shirakawa 42,685 .... K5
Shiranuka 14,897 .... M2
Shiroishi 40,862 .... K4
Shizunai 24,833 .... L2
Shizuoka 446,952 .... H6
Shobara 23,867 .... F6
Soka 167,177 .... O2
Soma 37,551 .... K5
Sonobe 14,827 .... J7
Suita 300,956 .... J7
Sukagawa 54,922 .... K5
Sukumo 25,340 .... F7
Sumoto 44,137 .... H6
Sunagawa 26,023 .... K2
Susaki 31,019 .... F7
Suttsu 6,511 .... J2
Suwa 49,594 .... J6
Suzu 28,238 .... H5
Suzuka 141,829 .... H6
Tachikawa 138,129 .... O2
Tagawa 61,464 .... E7
Tajimi 68,901 .... H6
Takaishi 66,822 .... J8
Takamatsu 298,999 .... G6
Takaoka 169,621 .... H5
Takarazuka 162,624 .... H7
Takasaki 211,348 .... J5
Takatsuki 330,570 .... J7
Takayama 60,504 .... H5
Takefu 65,012 .... G6
Takikawa 50,098 .... K2
Tanabe, Kyoto 30,022 .... J7
Tanabe, Wakayama 66,999 .... H7
Tateyama 56,139 .... K6
Tendo 48,082 .... K4
Tenri 62,909 .... J7
Teshio 6,509 .... K1
Toba 25,847 .... H6
Tobetsu 17,351 .... K2
Togane 33,406 .... K6
Toi 6,983 .... J6
Tojo 13,796 .... F6
Tokamachi 50,211 .... J5
Tokorozawa 196,870 .... O2
Tokunoshima 35,391 .... O5
Tokushima 239,281 .... G7
Tokuyama 106,967 .... E6
Tokyo (cap.) 8,646,520 .... O2
Tokyo* 11,673,554 .... O2
Tomakomai 132,477 .... K2
Tomiyama 7,389 .... O3
Tondabayashi 91,393 .... J8
Tosa 30,679 .... F7
Tosashimizu 24,856 .... F7
Tosu 50,733 .... E7
Tottori 122,312 .... G6
Towada 54,365 .... K3
Toyama 290,143 .... H5
Toyohashi 284,585 .... H6
Toyonaka 398,384 .... J7
Toyooka 46,210 .... H6
Toyota 248,774 .... H6
Tsu 139,538 .... H6
Tsubame 43,265 .... J5
Tsuchiura 104,028 .... J5
Tsuruga 60,205 .... G6
Tsuruoka 95,932 .... J4
Tsuyama 79,907 .... F6
Ube 161,969 .... E6
Ueda 105,151 .... J5
Ugo 21,956 .... K4
Uji 133,405 .... J7
Uozu 48,419 .... H5
Urakawa 20,213 .... L2
Urawa 331,145 .... O2
Ushibuka 24,250 .... D7

Usuki 39,163 .... F7
Utsunomiya 344,420 .... K5
Uwajima 70,428 .... F7
Wajima 33,234 .... H5
Wakasa 6,989 .... G6
Wakayama 389,717 .... H7
Wakkanai 55,464 .... K1
Warabi 76,311 .... O2
Yaizu 94,102 .... J6
Yamada 19,206 .... J8
Yamagata 219,773 .... K4
Yamaguchi 106,099 .... E6
Yamato 145,881 .... O2
Yamatokoriyama 71,001 .... J8
Yamatotakada 58,637 .... J8
Yao 261,639 .... J8
Yatabe 22,225 .... P2
Yatsushiro 103,691 .... E7
Yawata 50,132 .... J7
Yawatahama 45,259 .... F7
Yoichi 25,816 .... K2
Yokawa 8,015 .... H7
Yokkaichi 247,001 .... H6
Yokohama 2,621,771 .... O3
Yokosuka 389,557 .... O3
Yokote 43,030 .... K4
Yonago 116,332 .... F6
Yonezawa 91,974 .... K5
Yono 71,044 .... O2
Yotsukaido 50,131 .... L2
Yubetsu 6,693 .... L1
Yukuhashi 53,750 .... E7
Yuzawa 38,005 .... K4
Zushi 56,298 .... O3

OTHER FEATURES

Abashiri (riv.) M1
Agano (riv.) J4
Akan National Park M2
Akita (bay) J4
Amami (isls.) L7
Amami-O-Shima (isl.) N5
Ara (riv.) O2
Asahi (mt.) K4
Asama (mt.) J5
Ashizuri (cape) E7
Aso National Park E7
Atsumi (bay) H6
Awa (isl.) J6
Awaji (isl.) H6
Bandai-Asahi National Park K5
Biwa (lake) J6
Bonin (isls.) M3
Boso (pen.) P3
Bungo (strait) E7
Chichi (isl.) M3
Chichibu-Tama National Park J6
Chokai (mt.) J4
Chubu-Sangaku National Park H5
Dai (mt.) F6
Daimanji (mt.) K5
Daio (cape) H6
Daisen-Oki National Park F6
Daisetsu (mt.) L2
Daisetsu-Zan National Park L2
Dogo (isl.) F5
Dozen (isls.) F5
East China (sea) D8
Edo (riv.) P2
Erimo (cape) L3
Esan (pt.) K3
Etorofu (isl.) N1
Fuji (mt.) J6
Fuji-Hakone-Izu National Park J6
Gassan (mt.) J4
Goto (isls.) D7
Habomai (isls.) N2

Hachiro (lag.) J3
Haha (isl.) M3
Hakken (mt.) H6
Haku (mt.) H5
Hakusan National Park H5
Harima (bay) G6
Hida (riv.) H6
Hidaka (mt.) L2
Hokkaido (isl.) L2
Honshu (isl.) J5
Ibuki (mt.) J6
Iheya (isl.) N6
Iki (isl.) D7
Ina (riv.) H7
Inawashiro (lake) K5
Inubo (cape) K6
Iriomote (isl.) K7
Iro (cape) J6
Ise (bay) H6
Ise-Shima National Park H6
Ishigaki (isl.) K2
Ishikari (bay) K2
Ishikari (riv.) L2
Ishizuchi (mt.) F7
Iwaki (mt.) K3
Iwate (mt.) M4
Iwo (isl.) M4
Iyo (sea) F7
Izu (isls.) J6
Izu (pen.) J6
Japan (sea) G4
Joshinetsu-Kogen National Park J5
Kagoshima (bay) E8
Kamui (cape) K2
Kariba (mt.) K2
Kasumiga (lag.) K6
Kazan-retto (Volcano) M4
Kerama (isls.) M6
Kii (isls.) G7
Kii (chan.) H7
Kikai (isl.) O5
Kino (riv.) H7
Kirishima-Yaku National Park E7
Kita Iwo (isl.) M4
Kitakami (riv.) K4
Komaga (mt.) K2
Koshiki (isls.) D8
Kuchino (isl.) O4
Kuju (mt.) E7
Kume (isl.) M6
Kunashiri (isl.) N2
Kutcharo (lake) M2
Kyushu (isl.) E7
Meakan (mt.) L2
Minami Iwo (isl.) M5
Miura (pen.) O3
Miyako (isls.) L7
Miyako (isl.) K7
Mogami (riv.) J4
Motsuta (cape) J2
Muko (isl.) G7
Muko (riv.) H7
Muroto (pt.) G7
Mutsu (bay) K3
Naka (riv.) K5
Nampo-Shoto (isls.) M4
Nansei Shoto (Ryukyu) (isls.) M6
Nantai (mt.) J5
Nasu (mt.) K5
Nemuro (strait) M1
Nii (isl.) J6
Nikko National Park J5
Nojima (pt.) K2
Nosappu (pt.) N2
Noto (pen.) H5
Nyudo (cape) J4
Oani (riv.) K3
Obitsu (riv.) P3
Oga (pen.) J4
Ogasawara-gunto (Bonin) (isls.) M3

JAPAN is divided into prefectures bearing the same names as their capitals except:

Prefecture	Capital	Ref.
AICHI	NAGOYA	H6
EHIME	MATSUYAMA	F7
GUMMA	MAEBASHI	J5
HOKKAIDO	SAPPORO	K2
HYOGO	KOBE	H6
IBARAKI	MITO	K5
ISHIKAWA	KANAZAWA	H5
IWATE	MORIOKA	K4
KAGAWA	TAKAMATSU	G6
KANAGAWA	YOKOHAMA	O3
MIE	TSU	H6
MIYAGI	SENDAI	K4
OKINAWA	NAHA	N6
SAITAMA	URAWA	O2
SHIGA	OTSU	J7
SHIMANE	MATSUE	F6
TOCHIGI	UTSUNOMIYA	K5
YAMANASHI	KOFU	J6

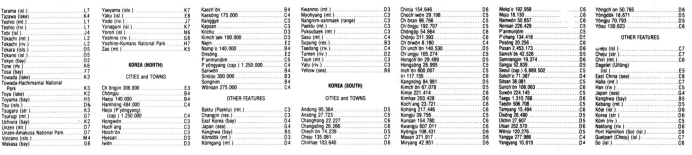

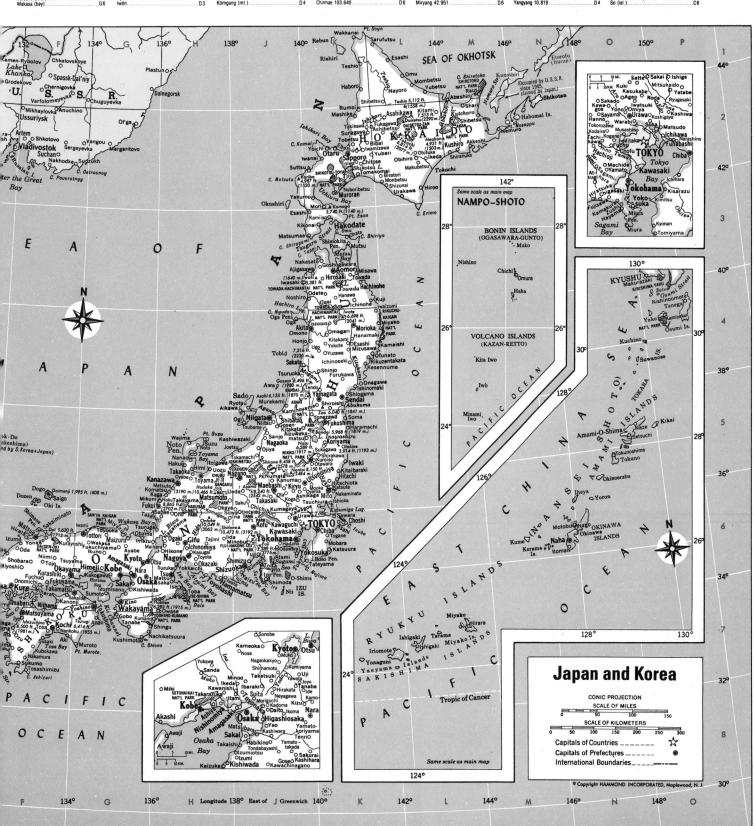

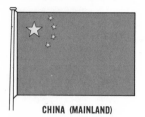

CHINA (MAINLAND)

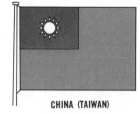

CHINA (TAIWAN)

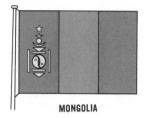

MONGOLIA

CHINA (MAINLAND)
AREA 3,691,000 sq. mi. (9,559,690 sq. km.)
POPULATION 958,090,000
CAPITAL Beijing
LARGEST CITY Shanghai
HIGHEST POINT Mt. Everest 29,028 ft.
(8,848 m.)
MONETARY UNIT yuan
MAJOR LANGUAGES Chinese, Chuang, Uigur,
Yi, Tibetan, Miao, Mongol, Kazakh
MAJOR RELIGIONS Confucianism, Buddhism,
Taoism, Islam

Topography

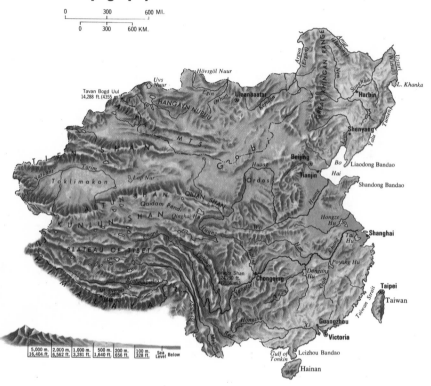

CHINA†

PROVINCES

Anhui (Anhwei) 47,130,000 .... J5
Fujian (Fukien) 24,500,000 ... J6
Gansu (Kansu) 18,730,000 ... E3
Guangdong (Kwangtung)
55,930,000 .... H7
Guangxi Zhuangzu (Kwangsi
Chuang Autonomous Reg.)
34,020,000 .... G7
Guizhou (Kweichow)
26,860,000 .... G6
Heilongjiang
(Heilungkiang) 33,760,000 .. K2
Hebei (Hopei) 50,570,000 .... J4
Henan (Honan) 70,660,000 .. H5
Hubei (Hupei) 45,750,000 ... H5
Hunan 51,660,000 .... H6
Jiangsu (Kiangsu) 58,340,000 . K5
Jiangxi (Kiangsi) 31,830,000 .. J6
Jilin (Kirin) 24,740,000 .... L3
Liaoning 37,430,000 .... K3
Nei Monggol (Inner Mongolian
Aut. Reg.) 18,900,000 ...... H3
Ningxia Huizu (Ningsia Hui Aut.
Reg.) 3,660,000 .... F3
Qinghai (Tsinghai) 3,650,000 .. E4
Shaanxi (Shensi) 27,790,000 .. G5
Shanxi (Shansi) 24,340,000 .. H4
Shandong
(Shantung) 71,600,000 ...... J4
Sichuan
(Szechwan) 97,070,000 ..... F5
Taiwan 16,609,961 .... K7
Xinjiang Uygur (Sinkiang-Uigur
Aut. Reg.) 12,330,000 ...... B3
Xizang (Tibet Aut.
Reg.) 1,790,000 .... B5
Yunnan 30,920,000 .... F7
Zhejiang
(Chekiang) 37,510,000 ...... K6

CITIES AND TOWNS

Aihui (Aigun) (Heihe) L1
Amoy (Xiamen) 400,000 ...... J7
Anqing (Anking) 160,000 ..... J5

Anshan 1,500,000 .... K3
Anyang 225,000 .... H4
Aqsu (Aksu) B3
Baoding (Paoting) 350,000 ... J4
Baoji (Paoki) 275,000 .... G5
Baoshan E7
Baotou (Paotow) 800,000 .... G3
Bei'an (Pehan) 130,000 ...... L2
Beihai (Pakhoi) 175,000 ...... G7
Beijing (Peking) (cap.)
8,500,000 .... J3
Bengbu (Pengpu) 400,000 ... J5
Benxi (Penki) 750,000 .... K3
Canton (Guangzhou)
2,300,000 .... H7
Chamdo (Qamdo) E5
Changchun 1,500,000 .... L3
Changde (Changteh) 225,000 . H6
Changhua 137,236 .... K7
Changsha 850,000 .... H6
Changzhi (Changchih) H4
Changzhou (Changchow)
400,000 .... K5
Chankiang (Zhanjiang)
220,000 .... H7
Chao'an (Chaochow) J7
Charkhlia (Ruoqiang) C4
Chefoo (Yantai) 180,000 ..... K4
Chengchow (Zhengzhou)
1,500,000 .... H5
Chengde (Chengteh) 200,000 . J3
Chengdu (Chengtu)
2,000,000 .... F5
Cherchen (Qiemo) C4
Chiai 238,713 .... K7
Chinchow (Jinzhou) 750,000 . K3
Chinkiang (Zhenjiang)
250,000 .... J5
Chinwangtao (Qinhuangdao)
400,000 .... K4
Chongqing (Chungking)
3,500,000 .... G6
Chüanchow (Quanzhou)
130,000 .... J7
Chuchow (Zhuzhou) 350,000 . H6
Chuguchak (Tacheng) B2
Chungshan (Zhongshan)
135,000 .... H7

Dali E6
Dalian 1,480,240 .... K4
Dandong (Tantung) 450,000 . K3
Datong (Tatung) 300,000 ..... H3
Erenhot H2
Foshan (Fatshan) H7
Fushun 1,700,000 .... K3
Fuxin (Fusin) 350,000 .... K3
Fuzhou (Foochow) 900,000 .. J6
Ganzhou (Kanchow) 135,000 . H6
Garyarsa (Gartok) B5
Gejiu (Kokiu) 250,000 .... F7
Golmud (Golmo) D4
Guangzhou (Canton)
2,300,000 .... H7
Guilin (Kweilin) 225,000 ...... G6
Guiyang (Kweiyang) 1,500,000 . G6
Gulja (Yining) 160,000 .... B3
Gyangzê C6
Haikou (Hoihow) 500,000 .... H8
Hailar J2
Hami (Kumul) D3
Handan (Hantan) 500,000 .... H4
Hangzhou (Hangchow)
1,100,000 .... J5
Hanzhong (Hanchung)
120,000 .... G5
Harbin 2,750,000 .... L2
Hefei (Hofei) 400,000 .... J5
Hegang (Hokang) 3,530,000 . L2
Heihe (Aihui) (Aigun) L1
Hengyang 310,000 .... H6
Hohhot (Huhehot) 700,000 .. H3
Horqin Youyi Qianqi (Ulanhot)
110,000 .... K2
Hotan B4
Huainan 350,000 .... J5
Huangshi 200,000 .... J5
Ichang (Yichang) 150,000 .... H5
Ichun (Yichun) 200,000 .... L2
Ipin (Yibin) 275,000 .... F6
Jiamusi (Kiamusze) 275,000 .. M2
Ji'an (Kian) 100,000 .... J6
Jiangmen (Kongmoon)
150,000 .... H7
Jiaozuo (Tsiaotso) 300,000 .. H4
Jilin (Kirin) 1,200,000 .... L3
Jinan (Tsinan) 1,500,000 ..... J4

Jingdezhen (Kingtehchen)
300,000 .... J6
Jining (Tsining) 160,000 ...... H3
Jinshi (Tsingshih) 100,000 ... H6
Jinzhou (Chinchow) 750,000 . K3
Jiujiang (Kiukiang) 120,000 .. J5
Jixi (Kisi) 350,000 .... M2
Juichin (Ruijin) J6
Kaifeng 330,000 .... H5
Kalgan (Zhangjiakou)
1,000,000 .... J3
Kanchow (Ganzhou) 135,000 . H6
Kaohsiung 1,028,334 .... J7
Karakax (Kara Kash) (Moyu) .. A4
Karghalik (Yecheng) A4
Kashi (Kashgar) 175,000 ..... A4
Kaxgar (Kashi) 175,000 ...... A4
Keelung 342,604 .... K6
Keriya (Yutian) B4
Khotan (Hotan) B4
Kiamusze (Jiamusi) 275,000 . M2
Kian (Ji'an) 100,000 .... J6
Kingtehchen (Jingdezhen)
300,000 .... J6
Kirin (Jilin) 1,200,000 .... L3
Kisi (Jixi) 350,000 .... M2
Kiukiang (Jiujiang) 120,000 .. J5
Kokiu (Gejiu) 250,000 .... F7
Kongmoon (Jiangmen) 150,000 . H7
Kuldja (Yining) 160,000 .... B3
Kunming 1,700,000 .... F6
Kwangchow (Canton)
2,300,000 .... H7
Kweilin (Guilin) 225,000 ...... G6
Kweisui (Hohhot) 700,000 ... H3
Kweiyang (Guiyang) 1,500,000 . G6
Lanzhou (Lanchow) 1,500,000 . F4
Leshan (Loshan) 250,000 .... F6
Lhasa 175,000 .... D6
Lhazê (Lhatse) C6
Lianyungang (Lienyünkang)
300,000 .... J4
Liaoyang 250,000 .... K3
Liaoyuan 300,000 .... K3
Linqing (Lintsing) J4
Liuzhou (Liuchow) 250,000 .. G7
Lopnur (Yuli) C3
Lüda (Dalian) 1,480,240 ...... K4
(continued on following page)

CHINA (TAIWAN)

AREA 13,971 sq. mi. (36,185 sq. km.)
POPULATION 16,609,961
CAPITAL Taipei
LARGEST CITY Taipei
HIGHEST POINT Yü Shan 13,113 ft. (3,997 m.)
MONETARY UNIT new Taiwan yüan (dollar)
MAJOR LANGUAGES Chinese, Formosan
MAJOR RELIGIONS Confucianism, Buddhism, Taoism, Christianity, tribal religions

MONGOLIA

AREA 606,163 sq. mi. (1,569,962 sq. km.)
POPULATION 1,594,800
CAPITAL Ulaanbaatar
LARGEST CITY Ulaanbaatar
HIGHEST POINT Tabun Bogdo 14,288 ft. (4,355 m.)
MONETARY UNIT tughrik
MAJOR LANGUAGES Khalkha Mongolian, Kazakh (Turkic)
MAJOR RELIGION Buddhism

HONG KONG

AREA 403 sq. mi. (1,044 sq. km.)
POPULATION 5,022,000
CAPITAL Victoria
MONETARY UNIT Hong Kong dollar
MAJOR LANGUAGES Chinese, English
MAJOR RELIGIONS Confucianism, Buddhism, Christianity

MACAU

AREA 6 sq. mi. (16 sq. km.)
POPULATION 271,000
CAPITAL Macau
MONETARY UNIT pataca
MAJOR LANGUAGES Chinese, Portuguese
MAJOR RELIGIONS Confucianism, Buddhism, Taoism, Christianity

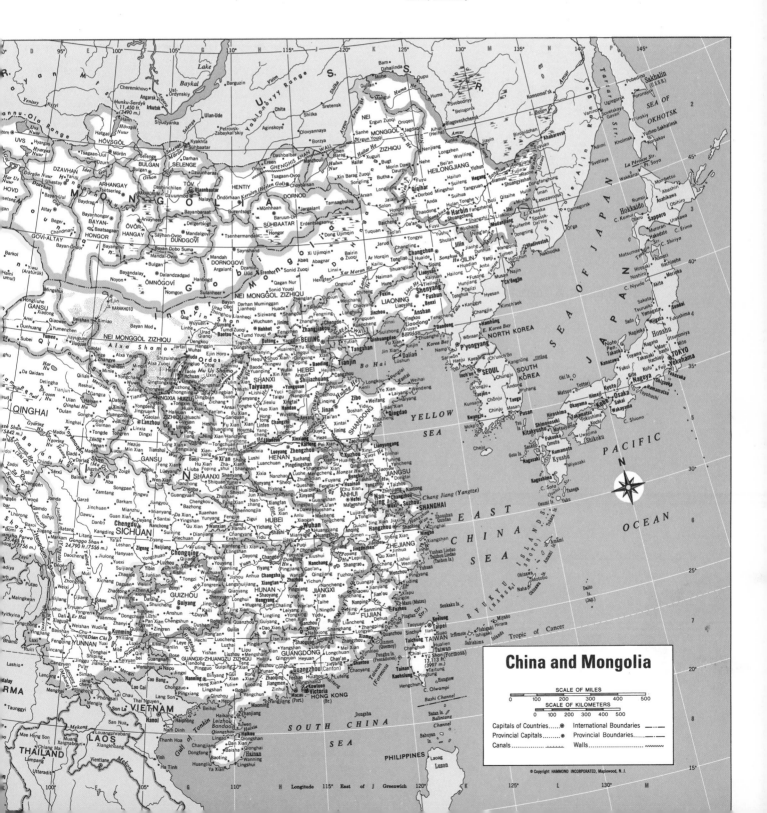

China and Mongolia

SCALE OF MILES
0 100 200 300 400 500

SCALE OF KILOMETERS
0 100 200 300 400 500

Capitals of Countries......⊛   International Boundaries _____
Provincial Capitals........⊛   Provincial Boundaries......_____
Canals ....   Walls .... ∿∿∿∿∿

© Copyright HAMMOND INCORPORATED, Maplewood, N.J.

(continued)

Luoyang (Loyang) 750,000 ..... H5
Lüshun K4
Luzhou (Luchol) 225,000 ..... G6
Ma'anshan J5
Manzhouli (Manchouli) J2
Maoming (Mowming) H7
Mengzi F7
Mianyang G5
Minfeng (Niya) B4
Moyu (Karakax) A4
Mudanjiang (Mutankiang) 400,000 ..... M3
Mukden (Shenyang) 3,750,000 K3
Nanchang 900,000 ..... J6
Nanchong (Nanchung) 275,000 G5
Nanjing (Nanking) 2,000,000 ..... J5
Nanning 375,000 ..... G7
Nanping J6
Nantong 300,000 ..... K5
Nanyang H5
Neijiang (Neikiang) 240,000 ..... G6
Nenjiang L2
Ningbo (Ningpo) 350,000 ..... K6
Ningsia (Yinchuan, Yinchwan) 175,000 ..... G4
Paicheng (Baicheng) K2
Pakhoi (Beihai) 175,000 ..... G7
Paoki (Baoji) 275,000 ..... G5
Paoting (Baoding) 350,000 ..... J4
Paotow (Baotou) 800,000 ..... G3
Pehan (Bei'an) 130,000 ..... L2
Peking (Beijing) (cap.)○ 8,500,000 ..... J3
Pengpu (Bengbu) 400,000 ..... J5
Penki (Benxi) 750,000 ..... K3
Pingdingshan H5
Pingliang G4
Pingtung 165,360 ..... K7
Pingxiang, Guangxi Zhuangzu G7
Pingxiang, Jiangxi H6
Piqan (Shanshan) D3
Qamdo E5
Qarkilik (Ruoqiang) C4
Qiemo (Qarqan) C4
Qingdao (Tsingtao) 1,900,000 . K4
Qingjiang 110,000 ..... J5
Qinhuangdao (Chinwangtao) 400,000 ..... K4
Qiqihar (Tsitsihar) 1,500,000 ..... K2
Qitai C3
Qoqek (Tacheng) B2
Quanzhou (Chüanchow) 130,000 ..... J7
Ruijin (Juichin) J6
Ruoqiang (Qarkilik) C4
Shache (Yarkand) A4
Shanghai○ 10,980,000 ..... K5
Shangqui (Shangkiu) 250,000 .. J5
Shangrao (Shangjao) 100,000 . J6
Shangshui 100,000 ..... J5
Shanshan (Piqan) D3
Shantou (Swatow) 400,000 ..... J7
Shaoguan (Shiukwan) 125,000 H7
Shaoxing (Shaohing) 225,000 .. K5
Shaoyang 275,000 ..... H6
Shashi 125,000 ..... H5
Shenyang (Mukden) 3,750,000 K3
Shigatse (Xigazê) C6
Shihezi (Shihhotzu) C3
Shijiazhuang (Shihkiachwang) 1,500,000 . J4
Shiyan H5
Shizuishan (Shihsuishan) G4
Shuangcheng L2
Shuangyashan 150,000 ..... M2
Siakwan (Xiaguan) E6
Sian (Xi'an) 1,900,000 ..... G5
Siangfan (Xiangfan) 150,000 ... H5
Siangtan (Xiangtan) 300,000 ... H6
Sienyang (Xianyang) 125,000 .. G5
Simao (Fusingchen) F7
Sinchu 208,038 ..... K7
Singtai (Xingtai) H4
Sining (Xining) 250,000 ..... F4
Sinsiang (Xinxiang) 300,000 .... H4
Sinyang (Xinyang) 125,000 ..... H5
Siping (Szeping) 180,000 ..... K3
Soche (Shache) A4
Suao K7
Süchow (Xuzhou) 1,500,000 ... J5
Suifenhe M3
Suihua L2
Suining G5
Suzhou (Soochow) 1,300,000 . K5
Swatow (Shantou) 400,000 ..... J7
Tacheng (Qoqek) B2
Tai'an J4
Taichung 565,255 ..... K7
Tainan 541,390 ..... J7
Taipei 2,108,193 ..... K7
Taitung K7
Taiyuan 2,725,000 ..... H4
Taizhou (Taichow) 275,000 ..... K5
Tali (Dali) E6
Tangshan 1,200,000 ..... J4
Tantung (Dandong) 450,000 ... K3
Tao'an K2
Taoyuan 105,841 ..... K6
Tatung (Datong) 300,000 ..... H3
Tehchow (Dezhou) J4
Tianjin (Tientsin)○ 7,210,000 ... J4
Tianshui 100,000 ..... F5
Tieling K3
Tientsin (Tianjin)○ 7,210,000 ... J4
Tongchuan (Tungchwan) G5
Tonghua (Tunghwa) 275,000 ... L3
Tongjiang (Tungkiang) M2
Tongliao K3
Tongling J5
Tsiaotso (Jiaozuo) 300,000 ..... H4
Tsinan (Jinan) 1,500,000 ..... J4
Tsingkiang (Qingjiang) 110,000 ..... J5
Tsingshih (Jinshi) 100,000 ..... H6
Tsingtao (Qingdao) 1,900,000 . K4
Tsining (Jining) 160,000 ..... H3
Tsitsihar (Qiqihar) 1,500,000 ..... K2
Tsunyi (Zunyi) 275,000 ..... G6
Tumen M3
Tunxi (Tunki) J6
Turpan (Turfan) C3
Tzekung (Zigong) 350,000 ..... F6
Tzepo (Zibo) 1,750,000 ..... J4
Uch Turfan (Wushi) A3
Ulanhot (Horquin Youyi Qianqi) 100,000 ..... K2
Ulughchat (Wuqia) A4
Ürümqi (Urumchi) 500,000 ..... C3
Usu B3
Wanxian (Wanhsien) 175,000 .. G5
Weifang 260,000 ..... J4
Weihai (Weihaiwei) K4
Wenzhou 250,000 ..... J6
Wuda G4
Wuhan 4,250,000 ..... H5
Wuhu 300,000 ..... J5
Wuqi G4
Wuqia A4
Wushi A3
Wuxi (Wusih) 900,000 ..... K5
Wuxing (Wuhing) 160,000 ..... K5
Wuzhong (Wuchung) G4
Wuzhou (Wuchow) 150,000 .... H7
Xiaguan (Siakwan) E6
Xiamen (Amoy) 400,000 ..... J7
Xi'an (Sian) 1,900,000 ..... G5
Xiangfan (Siangfan) 150,000 ... H5
Xiangtan (Siangtan) 300,000 ... H6
Xianyang (Sienyang) 125,000 .. G5
Xiapu (Siapu) K6
Xichang (Sichang) F6
Xigazê (Shigatse) C6
Xingtai (Singtai) H4
Xining (Sining) 250,000 ..... F4
Xinxiang (Sinsiang) 300,000 .... H4
Xinyang (Sinyang) 125,000 ..... H5
Xuzhou (Süchow) 1,500,000 ... J5
Ya'an 100,000 ..... F6
Yadong C6
Yan'an (Yenan) G4
Yanji (Yenki) 130,000 ..... L3
Yangquan (Yangchüan) 350,000 ..... H4
Yangzhou (Yangchow) 210,000 ..... J5
Yantai (Chefoo) 180,000 ..... K4
Yarkand (Shache) A4
Ya Xian G8
Yecheng A4
Yenan (Yan'an) G4
Yibin (Ipin) 275,000 ..... F6
Yichang (Ichang) 150,000 ..... H5
Yichun 200,000 ..... L2
Yinchuan (Ningsia) 175,000 .... G4
Yingkou 215,000 ..... K3
Yining 160,000 ..... B3
Yiyang H6
Yuci (Yütze) H4
Yuli (Lopnur) C3
Yumen 325,000 ..... E4
Yungkia (Wenzhou) 250,000 ... J6
Yutian B4
Zhangjiakou (Kalgan) 1,000,000 ..... J3
Zhangzhou (Changchow) J7
Zhanjiang (Chankiang) 220,000 ..... H7
Zhaoqing H7
Zhengzhou (Chengchow) 1,500,000 ..... H5
Zhenjiang (Chinkiang) 250,000 ..... J5
Zhongshan (Chungshan) 135,000 ..... H7
Zhuzhou (Chuchow) 350,000 ... H6
Zibo (Tzepo) 1,750,000 ..... J4
Zigong (Tzekung) 350,000 ..... F6
Zunyi (Tsunyi) 275,000 ..... G6

OTHER FEATURES

Altun Shan (range) C4
Alxa Shamo (des.) F4
Amur (Heilong Jiang) (riv.) L2
A'nyêmaqên Shan (mts.) E5
Argun' (Ergun He) (riv.) K1
Bashi (chan.) K7
Bayan Har Shan (range) E5
Bo Hai (gulf) J4
Bosten (Bagrax) Hu (lake) C3
Chang Jiang (Yangtze) (riv.) K5
Da Hingan Ling (range) J3
Dian Chi (lake) F7
Dongsha (isl.) J7
Dongting Hu (riv.) H6
East China (sea) L6
Ergun He (Argun') (riv.) K1
Er Hai (lake) F6
Everest (mt.) C6
Formosa (Taiwan) (str.) J7
Gangdisê Shan (range) B5
Ghenghis Khan Wall (ruin) H2
Gobi (des.) G3
Grand (canal) J4
Great Wall (ruins) G4,J
Gurla Mandhada (mt.) B5
Hainan (isl.) H8
Hangzhou Wan (bay) K5
Heilong Jiang (Amur) (riv.) L2
Himalaya (mts.) C6
Hotan He (riv.) B4
Huang He (Yellow) (riv.) J4
Hulun Nur (lake) J2
Inner Mongolia (reg.) H3
Jinmen (Quemoy) (isl.) J7
Jinsha Jiang (Yangtze) (riv.) E5
Junggar Pendi (desert basin) C2
Karakhoto (ruins) F3
Karamiran Shankou (pass) C4
Keriya Shankou (pass) B4
Khanka (lake) M3
Kongur Shan (mt.) A4
Künes He (riv.) B3
Kunlun Shan (range) B4
Kuruktag Shan (range) C3
Lancang Jiang (riv.) F7
Leizhau Bandao (pen.) G7
Liaodong Bandao (pen.) K3
Liao He (riv.) K3
Lop Nor (Lop Nur) (lake) D3
Manas He (riv.) C3
Mazu (Matsu) (isl.) K6
Mekong (Lancang Jiang) (riv.) F7
Muztag (mt.) B4
Muztagata (mt.) A4
Nam Co (lake) D5
Namzha Parwa (mt.) E6
Nan Ling (mts.) H6
Nu Jiang (riv.) E6
Nyainqêntanglha Shan (range) D5
Olwampi (cape) K7
Ordos (reg.) G4
Penghu (Pescadores) (isls.) J7
Pobeda (peak) A3
Poyang Hu (lake) J6
Pratas (Dongsha) (isl.) J7
Qaidam Pendi (basin) (swamp) D4
Qarqan He (riv.) C4
Qilian Shan (range) E4
Qinghai Hu (lake) E4
Qiongzhou Haixia (str.) G7
Quemoy (Jinmen) (isl.) J7
Salween (Nu Jiang) (riv.) E6
Siling Co (lake) C5
Songhua Jiang (Sungari) (riv.) M2
South China (sea) J7
Tai Hu (lake) J5
Taiwan (Formosa) (str.) J7
Taizhou (Tachen) (isls.) K6
Takla Makan (Taklimakan Shamo) (des.) B4
Tanggula Shan (range) D5
Tangra Yumco (lake) C5
Tarim Pendi (basin) B4
Tian Shan (range) C3
Tibet (reg.) B5
Tongtian He (Zhi Qu) (riv.) E5
Tonkin (gulf) G7
Tumen (riv.) L3
Ulu Muztag (mt.) C4
Ussuri (Wusuli Jiang) (riv.) M2
Wei He (riv.) G5
Wusuli Jiang (Ussuri) (riv.) M2
Xiang Jiang (riv.) H6
Xi Jiang (riv.) H7
Yalong Jiang (riv.) F6
Yalu (riv.) L3
Yangtze (Chang Jiang) (riv.) K5
Yarkant He (riv.) A4
Yellow (Huang He) (riv.) J4
Yellow (sea) K4
Yü Shan (mt.) K7

HONG KONG

CITIES and TOWNS

Kowloon* 2,378,480 ..... H7
Victoria (cap.)* 1,026,870 ..... H7

MACAU (MACAO)

CITIES and TOWNS

Macau (Macao (cap.) 226,880 . H7

MONGOLIA

CITIES and TOWNS

Tamsagbulag J2
Ulaanbaatar (Ulan Bator) (cap.) 345,000 ..... G2

OTHER FEATURES

Altai (mts.) C2
Dzavhan Gol (riv.) D2
Hangayn Nuruu (mts.) E2
Har Us Nuur (lake) D2
Herlen Gol (Kerulen) (riv.) H2
Hovd Gol (riv.) D2
Hövsgöl Nuur (lake) F1
Hyargas Nuur (lake) D2
Karakorum (ruins) F2
Kerulen (riv.) H2
Munku-Sardyk (mt.) F1
Orhon Gol (riv.) F2
Selenge Mörön (riv.) G2
Tannu-Ola (range) D1
Tavan Bogd Uul (mt.) C2
Uvs Nuur (lake) D1

○Population of municipality. *City and suburbs †Populations of mainland cities excluding Peking (Beijing), Shanghai and Tianjin (Tientsin), courtesy of Kingsley Davis, Office of Int'l Population and Urban Research, Institute of Int'l Studies, Univ. of California.

Agriculture, Industry and Resources

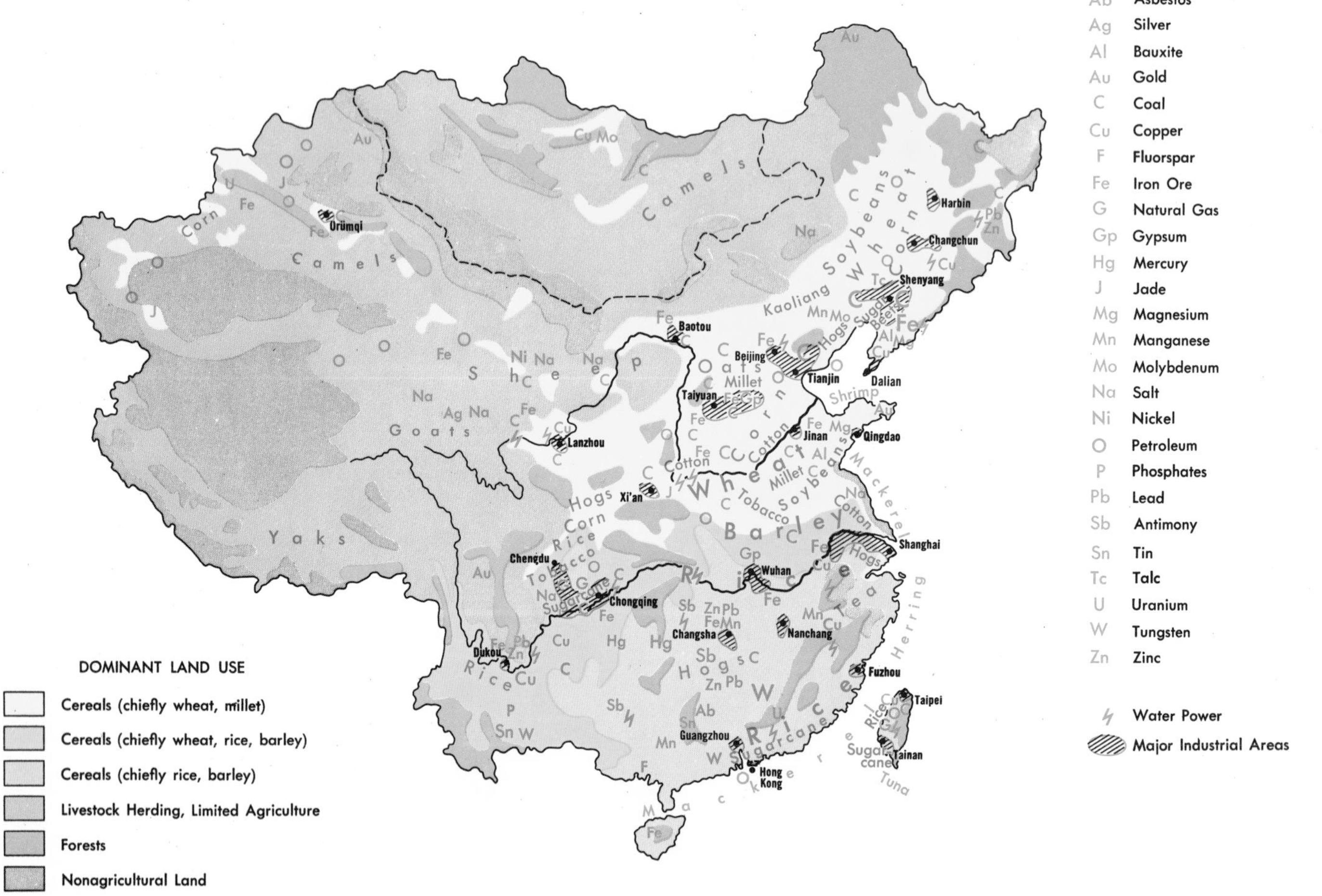

Ürümqi
Baotou
Harbin
Changchun
Shenyang
Beijing
Tianjin
Dalian
Taiyuan
Jinan
Qingdao
Lanzhou
Xi'an
Shanghai
Chengdu
Wuhan
Chongqing
Changsha
Nanchang
Dukou
Fuzhou
Taipei
Tainan
Guangzhou
Hong Kong
Camels
Yaks
Goats
Sheep
Hogs
Soybeans
Wheat
Barley
Rice
Corn
Millet
Oats
Cotton
Tobacco
Sugarcane
Kaoliang
Shrimp
Mackerel
Herring
Tuna
DOMINANT LAND USE
Cereals (chiefly wheat, millet)
Cereals (chiefly wheat, rice, barley)
Cereals (chiefly rice, barley)
Livestock Herding, Limited Agriculture
Forests
Nonagricultural Land
MAJOR MINERAL OCCURRENCES
Ab Asbestos
Ag Silver
Al Bauxite
Au Gold
C Coal
Cu Copper
F Fluorspar
Fe Iron Ore
G Natural Gas
Gp Gypsum
Hg Mercury
J Jade
Mg Magnesium
Mn Manganese
Mo Molybdenum
Na Salt
Ni Nickel
O Petroleum
P Phosphates
Pb Lead
Sb Antimony
Sn Tin
Tc Talc
U Uranium
W Tungsten
Zn Zinc
Water Power
Major Industrial Areas

BURMA

THAILAND

LAOS

CAMBODIA

VIETNAM

MALAYSIA

SINGAPORE

BURMA

AREA 261,789 sq. mi. (678,034 sq. km.)
POPULATION 32,913,000
CAPITAL Rangoon
LARGEST CITY Rangoon
HIGHEST POINT Hkakabo Razi 19,296 ft.
(5,881 m.)
MONETARY UNIT kyat
MAJOR LANGUAGES Burmese, Karen, Shan,
Kachin, Chin, Kayah, English
MAJOR RELIGIONS Buddhism, tribal religions

THAILAND

AREA 198,455 sq. mi. (513,998 sq. km.)
POPULATION 46,455,000
CAPITAL Bangkok
LARGEST CITY Bangkok
HIGHEST POINT Doi Inthanon 8,452 ft.
(2,576 m.)
MONETARY UNIT baht
MAJOR LANGUAGES Thai, Lao, Chinese,
Khmer, Malay
MAJOR RELIGIONS Buddhism, tribal religions

LAOS

AREA 91,428 sq. mi. (236,800 sq. km.)
POPULATION 3,721,000
CAPITAL Vientiane
LARGEST CITY Vientiane
HIGHEST POINT Phou Bia 9,252 ft. (2,820 m.)
MONETARY UNIT kip
MAJOR LANGUAGE Lao
MAJOR RELIGIONS Buddhism, tribal religions

CAMBODIA

AREA 69,898 sq. mi. (181,036 sq. km.)
POPULATION 5,200,000
CAPITAL Phnom Penh
LARGEST CITY Phnom Penh
HIGHEST POINT 5,948 ft. (1,813 m.)
MONETARY UNIT riel
MAJOR LANGUAGE Khmer (Cambodian)
MAJOR RELIGION Buddhism

VIETNAM

AREA 128,405 sq. mi. (332,569 sq. km.)
POPULATION 52,741,766
CAPITAL Hanoi
LARGEST CITY Ho Chi Minh City (Saigon)
HIGHEST POINT Fan Si Pan 10,308 ft.
(3,142 m.)
MONETARY UNIT dong
MAJOR LANGUAGES Vietnamese, Thai,
Muong, Meo, Yao, Khmer, French,
Chinese, Cham
MAJOR RELIGIONS Buddhism, Taoism,
Confucianism, Roman Catholicism,
Cao-Dai

MALAYSIA

AREA 128,308 sq. mi. (332,318 sq. km.)
POPULATION 13,435,588
CAPITAL Kuala Lumpur
LARGEST CITY Kuala Lumpur
HIGHEST POINT Mt. Kinabalu 13,455 ft.
(4,101 m.)
MONETARY UNIT ringgit
MAJOR LANGUAGES Malay, Chinese, English,
Tamil, Dayak, Kadazan
MAJOR RELIGIONS Islam, Confucianism,
Buddhism, tribal religions, Hinduism,
Taoism, Christianity, Sikhism

SINGAPORE

AREA 226 sq. mi. (585 sq. km.)
POPULATION 2,413,945
CAPITAL Singapore
LARGEST CITY Singapore
HIGHEST POINT Bukit Timah 581 ft. (177 m.)
MONETARY UNIT Singapore dollar
MAJOR LANGUAGES Chinese, Malay, Tamil,
English, Hindi
MAJOR RELIGIONS Confucianism, Buddhism,
Taoism, Hinduism, Islam, Christianity

Topography

0   200   400 MI.

0   200   400 KM.

5,000 m. | 2,000 m. | 1,000 m. | 500 m. | 200 m. | 100 m. | Sea | Below
16,404 ft. | 6,562 ft. | 3,281 ft. | 1,640 ft. | 656 ft. | 328 ft. | Level

BURMA

INTERNAL DIVISIONS

Arakan (state) 1,710,913	B3
Chin (state) 323,094	B2
Irrawaddy (div.) 4,152,521	B3
Kachin (state) 735,144	C1
Karen (state) 865,218	C3
Kayah (state) 126,492	C3
Magwe (div.) 2,632,144	B2
Mandalay (div.) 3,662,312	B2
Mon (state) 1,313,111	C3
Pegu (div.) 3,174,109	C3
Rangoon (div.) 3,186,886	C3
Sagaing (div.) 3,115,502	B1
Shan (state) 3,178,214	C2
Tenasserim (div.) 717,607	C4

CITIES and TOWNS

Akyab (Sittwe) 42,329	B2
Allanmyo 15,580	B3
Amarapura 11,268	B2
Amherst 6,000	C3
An	B3
Anin	C4
Bassein 126,045	B3
Bhamo 9,821	C1
Chauk 24,466	B2
Danubyu	B2
Falam	B2
Fort Hertz (Putao)	C1
Gawai	C1
Gokteik	C2
Gwa	B3
Gyobingauk 9,922	C3
Haka	B2
Henzada 61,972	B3
Hmawbi 23,032	C3
Homalin	B1
Hsenwi	C2
Hsipaw	C2
Htawgaw	C1
Insein 143,625	C3
Kamaing	C1
Karathuri	C5
Katha 7,648	C1
Kawludo	C3
Kawthaung 1,520	C5
Keng Hkam	C2
Keng Tung	C2
Koma	C4
Kunlong	C2
Kyaikto 13,154	C3
Kya-in Seikkyi	C3
Kyangin 6,073	B3
Kyaukme	C2
Kyaukpadaung 5,480	B2
Kyaukpyu 7,335	B3
Kyaukse 8,659	C2
Labutta 12,982	B3
Lai-hka	C2
Lamu	B3
Lashio	C2
Lenya	C5
Letpadan 15,896	C3
Lewe	B3
Loi-kaw	C3
Lonton	B1
Magwe 13,270	B2
Maingkwan	C1
Maliwun	C5
Mandalay 418,008	C2
Man Hpang	C2
Martaban 5,661	C3
Ma-ubin 23,362	B3
Maungdaw 3,772	B2
Mawkmai	C2
Mawlaik 2,993	B2
Mawlu	C1
Maymyo 22,287	C2
Meiktila 19,474	B2
Mergui 33,697	C4
Minbu 9,096	B2

Minhla 6,470	B3
Mogaung 2,920	C1
Mogok 8,334	C2
Mohnyin	C1
Möng Hsat	C2
Möng Maü	C3
Möng Mit	C2
Möng Pan	C2
Möng Si	C2
Möng Tön	C2
Möng Tung	C2
Monywa 26,279	B2
Moulmein 171,977	C3
Mudon 20,136	C3
Myanaung 11,155	B3
Myanmyra 24,532	B3
Myingyan 36,439	B2
Myitkyina 12,382	C1
Myohaung 6,534	B2
Naba	B2
Namhkam	C2
Namian	C2
Namtu	C2
Natmauk	B2
Okkan 14,443	B3
Okpo 12,155	C3
Pakokku 30,943	B2
Palaw 5,596	C4
Paletwa	B2
Pantha	B2
Papun	C3
Pasawng	C3
Paungde 17,286	B3
Pegu 47,378	C3
Prome (Pye) 36,997	B3
Putao	C1
Pyapon 19,174	B3
Pye 36,997	B3
Pyinmana 22,025	C3
Pyu 10,443	C3
Rangoon (cap.) 1,586,422	C3
Rangoon* 2,055,365	C3
Rathedaung 2,969	B2
Sadon	C1
Sagaing 15,382	B2
Samka	C2
Sandoway 5,172	B3
Shingbwiyang	B1
Shwebo 17,827	B2
Shwenyaung	C2
Singkaling Hkamti	B1
Singu 4,027	C2
Sinlumkaba	C1
Sittwe 42,329	B2
Sumprabum	C1
Syriam 15,296	C3
Taungdwingyi 16,233	C2
Taunggyi	C2
Tavoy 40,312	C4
Tharrawaddy 8,977	C3
Thaton 38,047	C3
Thaungdut	B1
Thayetmyo 11,649	B3
Thazi 7,531	C2
Thongwa 10,829	C3
Toungoo 31,589	C3
Wakema 20,716	B3
Yamethin 11,167	C2
Yandoon 15,245	B3
Ye 12,852	C4
Yenangyaung 24,416	B2
Yesagyo 7,880	B2
Ye-u 5,307	B2
Ywathit	C3
Zadi	C4
Zalun 899	B3

OTHER FEATURES

Amya (pass)	C4
Andaman (sea)	B4
Arakan Yoma (mts.)	B3
Ataran (riv.)	C4
Bengal, Bay of (sea)	B3
Bentinck (isl.)	C5

(continued on following page)

(continued)

Bilauktaung (range) C4
Chaukan (pass) C1
Cheduba (isl.) B3
Chin (hills) B2
Chindwin (riv.) B2
Coco (chan.) B4
Combermere (bay) B3
Daung Kyun (isl.) C4
Dawna (range) C3
Great Coco (isl.) B4
Great Tenasserim (riv.) C4
Heinze Chaung (bay) C4
Heywood (chan.) B3
Hka, Nam (riv.) C2
Hkakabo Razi (mt.) C1
Indawgyi (lake) C1
Inle (lake) C2
Irrawaddy (riv.) B3
Irrawaddy, Mouths of the (delta) B4
Kadan Kyun (isl.) C4
Kaladan (riv.) B2
Kalegauk (isl.) C4
Khao Luang (mt.) C5
Lanbi Kyun (isl.) C5
Launglon Bok (isls.) C4
Loi Leng (mt.) C2
Manipur (riv.) B2
Martaban (gulf) C4
Mekong (riv.) D2
Mergui (arch.) C5
Mon (riv.) B2
Mu (riv.) B2
Negrais (cape) B3
Pakchan (riv.) C5
Pangsau (pass) C1
Pawn, Nam (riv.) C2
Pegu Yoma (mts.) B3
Preparis (isl.) B4
Ramree (isl.) B3
Salween (riv.) C3
Shan (plat.) C2
Sittang (riv.) C3
Taungthonton (mt.) B1
Tavoy (pt.) C4
Tenasserim (isl.) C4
Teng, Nam (riv.) C2
Three Pagodas (pass) C4
Victoria (mt.) B2

CAMBODIA (KAMPUCHEA)

CITIES and TOWNS

Batdambang (Battambang) D4
Choam Khsant E4
Kampong Cham E4
Kampong Chhnang D4
Kampong Khleang E4
Kampong Saom D5
Kampong Spoe E5
Kampong Thum E4
Kampong Trabek E5
Kampot E5
Kaoh Nhek E4
Kracheh E4
Krong Kaoh Kong D4
Krong Keb E5
Kulen E4
Lumphat E4
Moung Roessei D4
Pailin D4
Paoy Pet D4
Phnom Penh (cap.) c. 300,000 E5
Phnum Tbeng Meanchey E4
Phsar Ream D5
Phumi Banam E5
Phumi Phsar E4
Phumi Prek Kak E4
Phumi Samraong D4
Pouthisat D4
Prek Pouthi E5
Prey Veng E5
Pursat (Pouthisat) D4
Rovieng Tbong E4
Sambor E4
Senmonoron E4
Siempang E4
Siemreab D4
Sisophon D4
Sre Ambel D5
Sre Khtum E4
Stoeng Treng E4
Suong E5
Svay Rieng E5
Takev E5
Virochey E4

OTHER FEATURES

Angkor Wat (ruins) E4
Dangrek (mts.) D4
Drang, Ia (riv.) E4
Joncs (plain) E5
Khong, Se (riv.) E4
Kong, Kaoh (isl.) D5
Mekong (riv.) E4
Rung, Kaoh (isl.) D5
San, Se (riv.) E4
Sen, Stoeng (riv.) E4
Srepok (riv.) E4
Tang, Kaoh (isl.) D5
Thailand (gulf) D5
Tonle Sap (lake) D4
Wai, Poulo (isls.) D5

LAOS

CITIES and TOWNS

Attapu 2,750 E4
Ban Khon E4
Ban Lahanam E3
Borikan D3
Champasak 3,500 E4
Dônghén E3
Khamkeut⊙ 31,206 E3
Louang Namtha 1,459 D2
Louangphrabang 7,596 D3
Muang Hinboun 1,750 E3
Muang Kènthao D3
Muang Khammoun 5,500 E3
Muang Không 1,750 E4
Muang Khôngxédôn 2,000 E4
Muang Khoua D2
Muang May E4
Muang Ou Tai D2
Muang Paktha D2
Muang Phin E3
Muang Tahoi E3
Muang Vapi E4
Muang Xaignabouri (Sayaboury) 2,500 D3
Mounlapamôk E4
Napè E3
Nong Het E3
Pakxé 8,000 E4
Phiafai⊙ 17,216 E4
Phôngsali 2,500 D2
San Nua (Sam Neua) 3,000 E2
Saravan 2,350 E4
Savannakhét 8,500 E3
Sayaboury (Muang Xaignabouri) 2,500 D3
Thakhek (Muang Khammouan) 5,500 E3
Tourakom D3
Viangchan (Vientiane) 132,253 D3
Vientiane (cap.) 132,253 D3
Xiangkhoang 3,500 D3

OTHER FEATURES

Bolovens (plat.) E4
Hou, Nam (riv.) D2
Jars (plain) D3
Mekong (riv.) D3
Ou, Nam (riv.) D2
Phou Bia (mt.) D3
Phou Cô Pi (mt.) E3
Phou Loi (mt.) D2
Rao Co (mt.) E3
Se Khong (riv.) E4
Tha, Nam (riv.) D2
Xianghoang (plat.) D3

MALAYA, MALAYSIA*

STATES

Federal Territory 937,875 D7
Johor (Johore) 1,601,504 D7
Kedah 1,102,200 D6
Kelantan 877,575 D6
Melaka 453,153 D7
Negeri Sembilan 563,955 D7
Pahang 770,644 D7
Perak 1,762,288 D6
Perlis 147,726 D6
Pinang (Penang) 911,586 D6
Selangor 1,467,441 D7
Terengganu 542,280 D6

CITIES and TOWNS

Alor Gajah 2,222 D7
Alor Setar 66,260 D6
Bandar Maharani (Muar) 61,218 D7
Bandar Penggaram (Batu Pahat) 53,291 D7
Batu Gajah 10,692 D6
Batu Pahat 53,291 D7
Bentong 22,683 D7
Butterworth 61,187 D6
Chukai 12,514 D6
Gemas 5,214 D7
George Town (Pinang) 269,603 C6
Ipoh 247,953 D6
Johor Baharu (Johore Bharu) 136,234 F5
Kampar 26,591 D6
Kangar 8,758 D6
Kelang 113,611 D7
Keluang 43,272 D7
Kota Baharu 55,124 D6
Kota Tinggi 8,725 F5
Kuala Dungun 17,560 D6
Kuala Lipis 9,270 D6
Kuala Lumpur (cap.) 451,977 D7
Kuala Lumpur* 937,875 D7
Kuala Pilah 12,508 D7
Kuala Rompin 1,384 D7
Kuala Selangor 3,132 D7
Kuala Terengganu 53,320 D6
Kuantan 43,358 D7
Kulai 11,841 F5
Lumut 3,255 D6
Malacca (Melaka) 87,160 D7
Mawai F5
Melaka 87,160 D7
Mersing 18,246 E7
Muar 61,218 D7
Pekan 4,682 D7
Pekan Nanas 9,003 E5
Pinang (George Town) 269,603 C6
Pontian Kechil 8,349 E5
Port Dickson 10,300 D7
Port Kelang D7
Port Weld 3,233 D6
Raub 18,433 D7
Segamat 17,796 D7
Seremban 80,921 D7
Sungai Petani 35,959 C6
Taiping 54,645 D6
Tanah Merah 7,012 D6
Telok Anson 44,524 D6
Tumpat 10,673 D6

OTHER FEATURES

Aur, Pulau (isl.) E7
Belumut, Gunong (mt.) D7
Gelang, Tanjong (pt.) D6
Johor, Sungai (riv.) F5
Johore (str.) E6
Kelantan, Sungai (riv.) D6
Langkawi, Pulau (isl.) C6
Ledang, Gunong (mt.) D7
Lima, Pulau (isl.) F6
Malacca (str.) D7
Malay (pen.) D6
Pahang, Sungai (riv.) D7
Pangkor, Pulau (isl.) D6
Perak, Gunong (mt.) D6
Perhentian, Kepulauan (isls.) D6
Pulai, Sungai (riv.) E5
Ramunia, Tanjong (pt.) F6
Redang, Pulau (isl.) D6
Sedili Kechil, Tanjong (pt.) F5
Tahan, Gunong (mt.) D6
Temiang, Bukit (mt.) D6
Tenggol, Pulau (isl.) D6
Tinggi, Pulau (isl.) E7

SINGAPORE

CITIES and TOWNS

Jurong 50,974 E6
Nee Soon 37,641 F6
Serangoon 89,558 F6
Singapore (cap.) 2,413,945 F6

OTHER FEATURES

Keppel (harb.) F6
Main (str.) F6
Singapore (str.) F6
Tekong Besar, Pulau (isl.) F6

THAILAND (SIAM)

CITIES and TOWNS

Ang Thong 7,267 C4
Ayutthaya (Phra Nakhon Si Ayutthaya) 37,213 D4
Ban Aranyaprathet 12,276 D4
Bangkok (cap.) 1,867,297 D4
Bangkok* 2,495,312 D4
Bang Lamung D4
Bang Saphan C5
Ban Kantang 9,247 C6
Ban Kapong C5
Ban Khlong Yai D5
Ban Kui Nua D4
Ban Ngon D3
Ban Pak Phanang 13,590 D5
Banphot Phisai C3
Ban Pua D3
Ban Sattahip D4
Ban Tha Uthen D3
Bua Chum D4
Buriram 16,431 D4
Chachoengsao 22,106 D4
Chai Badan D4
Chai Buri D3
Chainat 9,944 D4
Chaiya C5
Chaiyaphum 12,540 D4
Chang Khoeng C3
Chanthaburi 15,479 D4
Chiang Dao C3
Chiang Khan D3
Chiang Mai 83,729 C3
Chiang Rai 13,927 C3
Chiang Saen C2
Chon Buri 39,367 D4
Chumphon 11,643 C5
Den Chai C3
Hat Yai 47,953 C6
Hot C3
Hua Hin 21,426 D4
Kalasin 14,960 D3
Kamphaeng Phet 12,378 C3
Kanchanaburi 16,397 C4
Khanu C3
Khemmarat E4
Khon Kaen 29,431 D3
Khorat (Nakhon Ratchasima) 66,071 D4
Krabi 8,764 C5
Krung Thep (Bangkok) (cap.) 1,867,297 D4
Kumphawapi D3
Lae D3
Lampang 40,100 C3
Lamphun 11,309 C3
Lang Suan 4,020 C5
Loei 10,137 D3
Lom Sak 10,597 D3
Lop Buri 23,112 D4
Mae Hong Son 3,981 C3
Maha Sarakham 19,707 D3
Mukdahan E3
Nakhon Nayok 8,185 D4
Nakhon Pathom 34,300 C4
Nakhon Phanom 20,385 D3
Nakhon Ratchasima 66,071 D4
Nakhon Sawan 46,853 D4
Nakhon Si Thammarat 40,671 D5
Nan 17,738 D3
Nang Rong D4
Narathiwat 21,256 D6
Ngao D3
Nong Khai 21,150 D3
Pattani 21,938 D6
Phanat Nikhom 10,514 D4
Phangnga 5,738 C5
Phatthalung 13,336 D6
Phayao 20,346 C3
Phet Buri 27,755 C4
Phetchabun 6,240 D3
Phichai D3
Phichit 10,814 D3
Phitsanulok 33,883 D3
Phon Phisai D3
Phrae 17,555 D3
Phra Nakhon Si Ayutthaya 37,213 D4
Phuket 34,362 C6
Phutthaisong D4
Prachin Buri 14,167 D4
Prachuap Khiri Khan 9,075 D5
Pran Buri D4
Rahaeng (Tak) 16,317 C3
Ranong 10,301 C5
Rat Buri 32,271 C4
Rayong 14,846 D4
Roi Et 20,242 D4
Rong Kwang D3
Sakon Nakhon 18,943 E3
Samut Prakan 46,632 D4
Samut Sakhon 33,619 D4
Samut Songkhram 23,574 C4
Sara Buri 25,025 D4
Satun 7,315 C6
Sawankhalok 8,387 C3
Selaphum E3
Sing Buri 9,050 D4
Singora (Songkhla) 41,193 D6
Sisaket 13,662 E4
Songkhla 41,193 D6
Sukhothai 15,488 D3
Suphan Buri 18,768 C4
Surat Thani 24,923 C5
Surin 16,342 D4
Suwannaphum D4
Tak 16,317 C3
Takua Pa 7,825 C5
Thoen C3
Thon Buri 628,015 D4
To Mo D6
Trang 32,985 C6
Trat 7,917 D4
Ubon 40,650 E4
Udon Thani 56,218 D3
Uthai Thani 10,525 C4
Uttaradit 12,022 D3
Warin Chamrap 21,520 E4
Yala 30,051 D6
Yasothon 12,079 D4

OTHER FEATURES

Amya (pass) C4
Bilauktaung (range) C4
Chang, Ko (isl.) D4
Chao Phraya, Mae Nam (riv.) D4
Chi, Mae Nam (riv.) D3
Dangrek (Dong Rak) (mts.) D4
Doi Inthanon (mt.) C3
Doi Pha Hom Pok (mt.) C2
Doi Pia Fai (mt.) D4
Kao Prawa (mt.) C3
Khao Luang (mt.) C5
Khwae Noi, Mae Nam (riv.) C4
Kra (isth.) C5
Kut, Ko (isl.) D5
Laem Pho (cape) D6
Laem Talumphuk (cape) D5
Lanta, Ko (isl.) C6
Luang (mt.) C5
Mae Klong, Mae Nam (riv.) C4
Mekong (riv.) E3
Mun, Mae Nam (riv.) D4
Nan, Mae Nam (riv.) D3
Nong Lahan (lake) D3
Pakchan (riv.) C5
Pa Sak, Mae Nam (riv.) D4
Phangan, Ko (isl.) D5
Phuket, Ko (isl.) C5
Ping, Mae Nam (riv.) C3
Samui (str.) D5
Samui, Ko (isl.) D5
Siam (Thailand) (gulf) D5
Tao, Ko (isl.) C5
Tapi, Mae Nam (riv.) C5
Terutao, Ko (isl.) C6
Tha Chin, Mae Nam (riv.) C4
Thale Luang (lag.) D6
Thalu, Ko (isls.) C5
Three Pagodas (pass) C4
Wang, Mae Nam (riv.) C3

Agriculture, Industry and Resources

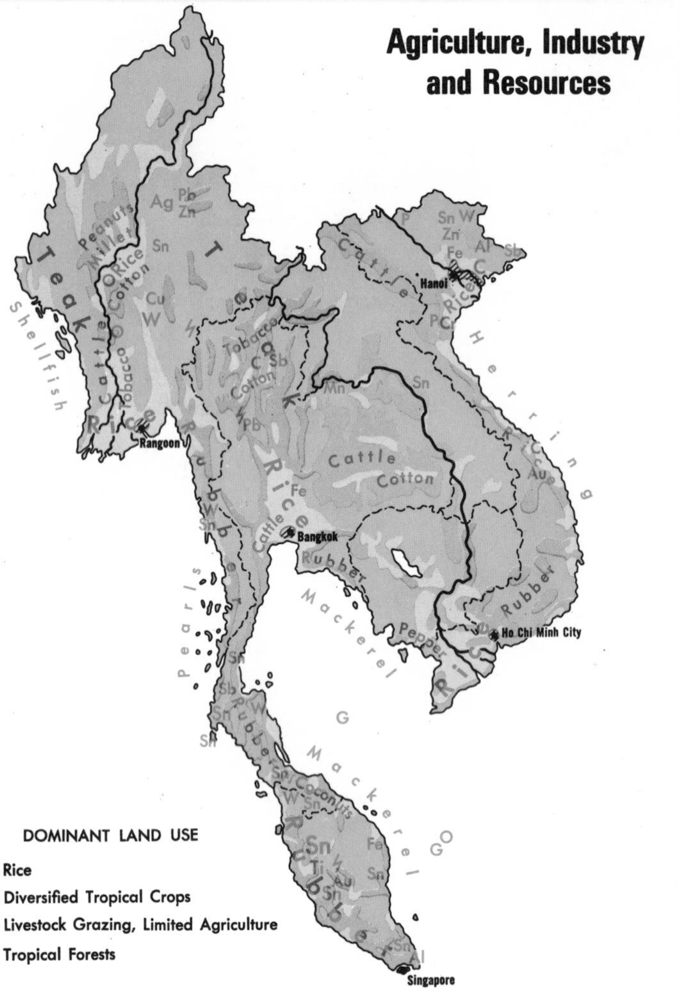

Teak
Shellfish
Peanuts
Millet
Rice
Cotton
Tobacco
Cattle
Ag
Pb
Zn
Sn
Cu
W
Sb
Mn
Fe
Au
Ti
Al
C
PC
Cr
G
O
Rangoon
Hanoi
Bangkok
Ho Chi Minh City
Singapore
Rubber
Pearls
Mackerel
Herring
Pepper
Coconuts

DOMINANT LAND USE

- Rice
- Diversified Tropical Crops
- Livestock Grazing, Limited Agriculture
- Tropical Forests

MAJOR MINERAL OCCURRENCES

Ag	Silver	Cu	Copper	O	Petroleum	Sn	Tin
Al	Bauxite	Fe	Iron Ore	P	Phosphates	Ti	Titanium
Au	Gold	G	Natural Gas	Pb	Lead	W	Tungsten
C	Coal	Mn	Manganese	Sb	Antimony	Zn	Zinc
Cr	Chromium						

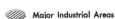

Water Power

Major Industrial Areas

VIETNAM

CITIES and TOWNS

An Loc (Binh Long) 15,276 E5
An Nhon F4
An Tuc (An Khe) F4
Ap Long Ha F5
Ap Vinh Hao F5
Bac Can E2
Bac Giang E2
Bac Lieu 53,841 E5
Bac Ninh 22,560 E2
Ba Don E3
Bai Thuong E3
Ban Me Thuot 68,771 F4
Bao Ha D2
Bao Lac E2
Bien Hoa 87,135 E5
Binh Long (An Loc) 15,276 E5
Binh Son F4
Bo Duc E4
Bong Son (Hoai Nhon) F4
Cam Ranh 118,111 F5
Can Tho 182,424 E5
Cao Bang E2
Cao Lanh 16,482 E5
Chau Phu 37,175 E5
Chu Lai F4
Con Cuong E3
Cua Rao E3
Da Lat 105,072 F5
Dam Doi E5
Da Nang 492,194 E3
Dien Bien Phu D2
Dong Hoi E3
Duong Dong D5
Gia Dinh E5
Go Cong 33,191 E5
Ha Giang E2
Haiphong* 1,279,067 E2
Hanoi (cap.)* 2,570,905 E2
Ha Tien E5
Ha Tinh E3
Hau Bon E4
Hoa Binh E2
Hoa Da F5
Hoai Nhon F4
Ho Chi Minh City (Saigon)* 3,419,678 E5
Hoi An 45,059 F4
Hoi Xuan E2
Hon Chong E5
Hon Gai 100,000 E2
Hue 209,043 E3
Huong Khe E3
Ke Bao E2
Khanh Hoa F4
Khanh Hung 59,015 E5
Khe Sanh E3
Kien Hung E5
Kontum 33,554 E4
Lac Giao (Ban Me Thuot) 68,771 E4
Lai Chau D2
Lang Son 15,071 E2
Lao Cai E2
Loc Ninh E5
Long Xuyen 72,658 E5
Mo Duc F4
Mong Cai E2
Muong Khuong E2
My Tho 119,892 E5
Nam Dinh E2
Nghia Lo D2
Nha Trang 216,227 F4
Ninh Binh E3
Phan Rang 33,377 F5
Phan Thiet 80,122 F5
Phu Cuong 28,267 E5
Phu Lang Thuong (Bac Giang) E2
Phuc Loi E3
Phu Dien E3
Phu Ly E2
Phu My F4
Phu Qui E3
Phu Rieng E5
Phu Tho 10,888 E2
Phu Vinh 48,485 E5
Pleiku 23,720 E4
Quang Nam E4
Quang Ngai 14,119 F4
Quang Tri 15,874 E3
Quang Yen E2
Quan Long 59,331 E5
Qui Nhon 213,757 F4
Rach Gia 104,161 E5
Ron E3
Sa Dec 51,867 E5
Saigon (Ho Chi Minh City)* 3,419,678 E5
Song Cau F4
Son Ha F4
Son La D2
Son Tay 19,213 E2
Tam Ky 38,532 F4
Tam Quan F4
Tan An 38,082 E5
Tay Ninh 22,957 E5
Thai Binh 14,739 E2
Thai Nguyen E2
Thanh Hoa 31,211 E3
Thanh Tri E5
That Khe E2
Tien Yen E2
Tra Vinh (Phu Vinh) 48,485 E5
Truc Giang 68,629 E5
Trung Khanh Phu E2
Tuyen Quang E2
Tuy Hoa 63,552 F4
Van Hoa E2
Van Ninh F4
Van Yen E2
Vinh 43,954 E3
Vinh Long 30,667 E5
Vinh Yen E2
Vu Liet E3
Vung Tau 108,436 E5
Xuan Loc
Yen Bai

OTHER FEATURES

Bach Long Vi, Dao (isl.)
Ba Den, Nui (mt.)
Bai Bung, Mui (Ca Mau) (pt.)
Black (riv.)
Ca Mau (Mui Bai Bung) (pt.)
Cam Ranh, Vinh (bay)
Cat Ba, Dao (isl.)
Chon May, Vung (bay)
Cu Lao, Hon (isls.)
Deux Frères, Les (isls.)
Dinh, Mui (cape)
Fan Si Pan (mt.)
Ia Drang (riv.)
Joncs (plain)
Kontum (plat.)
Khoai, Hon (isl.)
Lang Bian, Nui (mts.)
Lay, Mui (cape)
Mekong, Mouths of the (delta)
Nam Tram, Mui (cape)
Nightingale (Bach Long Vi) (isl.)
Panjang, Hon (Hon Tho Chau) (isl.)
Phu Quoc, Dao (isl.)
Rao Co (mt.)
Red (riv.)
Se San (riv.)
Sip Song Chau Thai (mts.)
Song Ba (riv.)
Song Ca (riv.)
Song Cai (riv.)
South China (sea)
Tonkin (gulf)
Varella, Mui (cape)
Wai, Poulo (isls.)
Yang Sin, Chu (mt.)

*See Southeast Asia, p. 84 for other part of Malaysia.

*City and suburbs.

⊙Population of district.

Burma, Thailand, Indochina and Malaya

CONIC PROJECTION

SCALE OF MILES

SCALE OF KILOMETERS

International Boundaries	....
Division and State Boundaries	....
Capitals of Countries	.... ☆
Division and State Capitals	.... ⊙

© Copyright HAMMOND INCORPORATED, Maplewood, N.J.

Longitude East 96° of Greenwich

PHILIPPINES

AREA 115,707 sq. mi. (299,681 sq. km.)
POPULATION 48,098,460
CAPITAL Manila
LARGEST CITY Manila
HIGHEST POINT Apo 9,692 ft. (2,954 m.)
MONETARY UNIT piso
MAJOR LANGUAGES Pilipino (Tagalog), English, Spanish, Bisayan, Ilocano, Bikol
MAJOR RELIGIONS Roman Catholicism, Islam, Protestantism, tribal religions

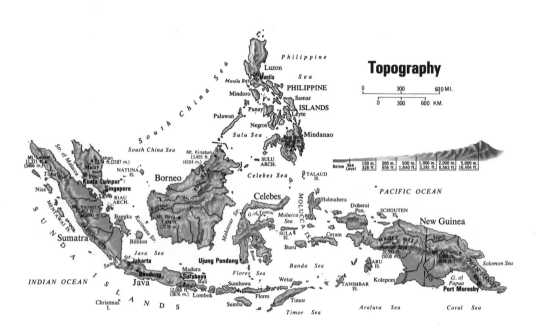

Topography

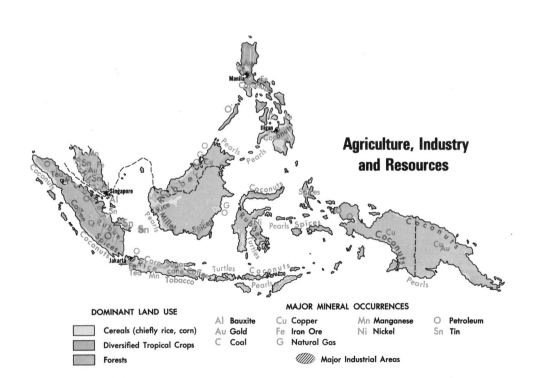

Agriculture, Industry and Resources

DOMINANT LAND USE

Cereals (chiefly rice, corn)

Diversified Tropical Crops

Forests

MAJOR MINERAL OCCURRENCES

Al Bauxite	Cu Copper	Mn Manganese	O Petroleum
Au Gold	Fe Iron Ore	Ni Nickel	Sn Tin
C Coal	G Natural Gas		

Major Industrial Areas

© Copyright HAMMOND INCORPORATED, Maplewood, N.J.

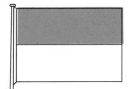

INDONESIA

BRUNEI

PAPUA NEW GUINEA

AREA 788,430 sq. mi. (2,042,034 sq. km.)
POPULATION 147,490,298
CAPITAL Jakarta
LARGEST CITY Jakarta
HIGHEST POINT Puncak Jaya 16,503 ft. (5,030 m.)
MONETARY UNIT rupiah
MAJOR LANGUAGES Bahasa Indonesia, Indonesian and Papuan languages, English
MAJOR RELIGIONS Islam, tribal religions, Christianity, Hinduism

AREA 2,226 sq. mi. (5,765 sq. km.)
POPULATION 192,832
CAPITAL Bandar Seri Begawan
LARGEST CITY Bandar Seri Begawan
HIGHEST POINT Pagon 6,070 ft. (1,850 m.)
MONETARY UNIT Brunei Dollar
MAJOR LANGUAGES Malay, English, Chinese
MAJOR RELIGIONS Islam, Buddhism, Christianity, tribal religions

AREA 183,540 sq. mi. (475,369 sq. km.)
POPULATION 3,010,727
CAPITAL Port Moresby
LARGEST CITY Port Moresby
HIGHEST POINT Mt. Wilhelm 15,400 ft. (4,694 m.)
MONETARY UNIT kina
MAJOR LANGUAGES pidgin English, Hiri Motu, English
MAJOR RELIGIONS Tribal religions, Christianity

BRUNEI

CITIES and TOWNS

Bandar Seri Begawan 63,868 E 4
Seria 23,511 E 5

CHINA

OTHER FEATURES

Amphitrite (isls.) E 2
Crescent (isls.) E 2
Duncan (isls.) E 2
Lincoln (isl.) E 2
Money (isl.) E 2
Paracel (isls.) E 2
Robert (isl.) E 2
Triton (isl.) E 2
Xisha (isls.) E 2
Woody (isl.) E 2

INDONESIA

CITIES AND TOWNS

Agats K 7
Amahai H 6
Ambon (Amboina) 208,898 H 6
Ampana G 6
Amurang G 5
Atambua G 7
Auba H 7
Baa G 8
Babo K 7
Bagansiapiapi C 5
Balige B 5
Balikpapan 280,675 F 6
Banda Aceh 72,090 A 4
Bandanaira H 6
Bandung 1,462,637 H 2
Banggai G 6
Bangil •49,438 K 2
Bangkalan •41,639 K 2
Banjarmasin 381,286 E 6
Bantul •40,585 J 2
Banyumas J 2
Banyuwangi •76,596 L 2
Barabai •33,688 F 6
Barus •46,120 B 5
Batang •69,577 J 2
Batavia (Jakarta) (cap.) 6,503,449 H 1
Baturaja •48,350 C 6
Batusangkar C 6
Baubau G 7
Baukau H 7
Bekasi •123,264 H 2
Belawan B 5
Bengkalis •14,072 C 5
Bengkayang •15,404 E 5
Bengkulu 64,783 C 6
Benteng F 7
Beo H 5
Biak K 6
Binjai 76,464 B 5
Bintuhan C 6
Bireuen B 4
Bitung •59,507 H 5
Blitar 78,503 K 2
Blora •67,853 K 2
Bogor 247,409 H 2
Bojonegoro •74,241 J 2
Bondowoso •50,317 L 2
Bonthain •30,377 F 7
Brebes •87,918 H 2
Bukittinggi 70,771 B 6
Bula J 6
Buli H 5
Bulukumba •63,932 G 7
Bumiayu •65,403 H 2
Buntok F 6
Buol G 5
Calang B 5
Ciamis •105,434 H 2
Cianjur •132,058 H 2
Cijulang •44,487 H 2
Cilacap •118,815 H 2
Cimahi •157,222 H 2
Cirebon 223,776 H 2
Curup •71,965 C 6
Demak •57,676 J 2
Demta L 6
Denpasar •98,005 E 7
Dili H 7
Djambi (Jambi) 230,373 C 6
Djokjakarta (Yogyakarta) 398,727 J 2
Dobo J 7
Dompu •14,103 F 7
Donggala F 6
Ende G 7
Fakfak J 6
Galela •11,554 H 5
Garut •93,340 H 2
Genting D 5
Gorontalo 97,628 G 5
Gresik •48,561 K 2
Hollandia (Jayapura) •45,786 K 6
Indramayu •69,441 H 2
Isimu G 5
Jailolo •17,243 H 5
Jakarta (cap.) 6,503,449 H 1
Jambi 230,373 C 6
Jayapura •45,786 L 6
Jember •115,201 K 2
Jeneponto •6,883 F 7
Jepara •75,124 J 2
Jogjakarta (Yogyakarta) 398,727 J 2
Jombang •80,643 K 2
Kaimana J 6
Kayuagung •37,319 D 6
Kalianda •42,609 D 7
Kampung Baru (Tolitoli) •10,071 G 5
Karangasem •15,177 F 7
Karosa F 6
Kau H 5
Kebumen •81,571 J 2
Kediri 221,830 K 2
Kendal •32,544 J 2
Kendari •28,628 G 6
Kepi K 7
Ketapang E 6
Klaten •58,870 J 2
Kokonau K 6
Kolaka •10,384 G 6
Kolonodale G 6
Kotaagung •20,154 C 7
Kotabaharu E 6
Kotabaru •23,443 F 6
Kotabumi C 7
Kotawaringin E 6
Kragan •33,389 K 2
Krawang •99,552 H 2
Kualakapuas E 6
Kudus •79,186 J 2
Kumai E 6
Kumai •13,564 E 6
Kuningan •105,255 H 2
Kupang •49,354 G 8
Kutaraja (Banda Aceh) 72,090 A 4
Kutoarjo •52,989 J 2
Labuha H 6
Labuhan •34,274 G 2
Laham F 5
Lahat •48,136 C 6
Laiwui H 6
Lamongan •38,897 K 2
Langsa •58,060 B 5
Larantuka G 7
Lawang •59,071 K 2
Lekitobi G 6
Letong D 5
Longiram F 5
Longnawan F 5
Lubuklinggau •43,011 C 6
Lubuksikaping •24,244 B 5
Lumajang •79,641 K 2
Madiun 150,562 K 2
Majalengka •80,999 H 2
Magelang 123,484 J 2
Magetan •59,507 K 2
Makassar (Ujung Pandang) 709,038 F 7
Malang 511,780 K 2
Malili G 6
Malinau •14,130 F 5
Mamuju •17,345 F 6
Manado 217,159 G 5
Manokwari J 6
Maros F 6
Martapura •55,011 F 6
Masamba •16,571 G 6
Mataram •46,846 F 7
Maumere G 7
Medan 1,378,955 B 5
Menggala •20,878 D 6
Merauke •21,366 K 7
Mindiptana L 7
Mojokerto 68,849 K 2
Muarabungo •26,304 C 6
Muarasiberut B 6
Muaratewe F 6
Muntok •31,719 D 6
Nabire K 6
Nangapinoh •19,983 E 6
Nangatayap E 6
Negara •65,762 E 7
Ngabang •33,190 D 5
Ngawi K 2
Okaba K 7
Pacitan •51,993 J 2
Padang 480,922 B 6
Padangpanjang 34,517 B 6
Padangsidempuan •134,611 B 5
Painan C 6
Pakanbaru 186,262 C 5
Palangkaraya 60,447 E 6
Palaumerak •58,655 G 1
Paleleh •7,603 G 5
Palembang 787,187 D 6
Palopo F 6
Pamangkat •62,402 D 5
Pamekasan •55,409 L 2
Pameungpeuk •41,449 H 2
Panarukan •37,482 K 2
Pandeglang •35,550 G 1
Pangkalanberandan •60,299 B 5
Pangkalanbuun E 6
Pangkalpinang 90,096 D 6
Pare •107,806 K 2
Parepare 86,450 F 6
Pariaman •44,428 B 6
Pasangkayu F 6
Pasuruan 95,864 K 2
Pati •75,397 J 2
Payakumbuh 78,836 C 6
Pekalongan 132,558 J 2
Pemalang •110,206 J 2
Pematangsiantar 150,376 B 5
Perabumulih •88,031 C 6
Pinrang F 6
Piru H 6
Plaju D 6
Ponorogo •58,321 J 2
Pontianak 304,778 D 6
Poso G 6
Prapat •7,723 B 5
Praya •89,266 F 7
Probolinggo 100,296 K 2
Purbolinggo •41,031 J 2
Purwakarta •93,016 H 2
Purwodadi •75,713 J 2
Purwokerto •125,464 H 2
Purworejo •28,663 J 2
Putussibau •12,408 E 5
Raha G 6
Rangkasbitung •78,685 G 2
Ransiki J 6
Rantauprapat C 5
Rembang •33,610 K 2
Rengat •33,559 C 6
Ruteng •12,294 G 7
Sabang, Celebes F 5
Sabang, Weh 23,821 B 4
Salatiga 85,849 J 2
Samarinda 264,718 F 6
Sambas •48,253 D 5
Samboja F 6
Sampang •60,136 K 2
Sampit E 6
Sanggau •7040 E 5
Sangkulirang •8,769 F 5
Saparua H 6
Sarmi K 6
Saumlaki J 7
Sawahlunto 13,561 C 6
Seba G 8
Semarang 1,026,671 J 2
Semitau •7,165 E 5
Serang •79,675 G 1
Serui K 6
Siaksriinderapura C 5
Sibolga 59,897 B 5
Sidoharjo •59,942 K 2
Sigli •10,623 B 4
Sinabang B 5
Sindangbarang •70,603 D 7
Singaraja F 7
Singkawang •93,650 D 5
Sinjai G 7
Sintang •24,842 E 5
Situbondo •36,094 L 2
Soe G 7
Solo (Surakarta) 469,888 J 2
Solok 31,724 C 6
Sorong •23,763 J 6
Sragen •50,515 J 2
Subang •35,077 H 2
Sukabumi 109,994 H 2
Sukadana •9,741 E 6
Sumbawa Besar F 7
Sumedang H 2
Sumenep •46,659 L 2
Surabaya 2,027,913 K 2
Surakarta 469,888 J 2
Takalar F 7
Takingeun B 5
Talangbetutu C 6
Tanahgrogot F 6
Tanahmerah K 7
Tangerang G 1
Tanjungbalai 41,894 C 5
Tanjungkarang 284,275 D 7
Tanjungpandan •61,225 D 6
Tanjungpinang C 5
Tanjungpriok •147,824 H 1
Tanjungpura •30,992 B 5
Tanjungredeb F 5
Tanjungselor F 5
Tapaktuan B 5
Tarakan •31,118 F 5
Tarutung B 5
Tasikmalaya •135,919 H 2
Tebingtinggi 92,087 B 5
Tegal 131,728 J 2
Telukbayur C 6
Temanggung •85,492 J 2
Tenggarong •15,081 F 6
Tepa H 7
Terempa D 5
Ternate •34,539 H 5
Tjilatjap (Cilacap) •118,815 H 2
Tjirebon (Cirebon) 223,776 H 2
Tobelo H 5
Tolitoli •10,071 G 5
Tondano •35,978 H 5
Trenggalek •49,065 K 2
Tual J 7
Tuban •54,212 K 2
Tulungagung •53,880 K 2
Turen •76,018 K 2
Ujung Pandang 709,038 F 7
Vikeke H 7
Wahai H 6
Waikabubak F 7
Waingapu G 7
Wajabula H 5
Waren K 6
Wasior K 6
Watampone G 6
Weda H 5
Wonogiri •56,435 J 2
Wonosobo •47,650 J 2
Wonreli H 7
Yogyakarta 398,727 J 2

OTHER FEATURES

Adi (isl.) J 6
Adonara (isl.) 71,462 G 7
Alas (str.) F 7
Alor (isl.) 86,136 G 7
Ambelau (isl.) H 6
Anambas (isls.) 29,572 D 5
Arafura (sea) J 8
Aru (isls.) 34,195 K 7
Asahan (riv.) B 5
Asia (isls.) J 5
Ayu (isls.) J 5
Babar (isl.) H 7
Babar (isls.) 28,636 H 7
Bacan (isls.) 29,137 H 6
Balabalagan (isls.) F 6
Bali (isl.) 2,074,438 F 7
Bali (sea) F 7
Bali (str.) E 7
Banda (isls.) 13,638 H 6
Banda (sea) H 7
Banggai (arch.) 169,025 G 6
Bangka (isl.) 298,017 D 6
Bangka (str.) C 6
Banyak (isls.) 1,980 B 5
Barbar (isls.) J 7
Barisan (mts.) C 6
Barito (riv.) E 6
Batu (isls.) 16,390 B 6
Bawean (isl.) 64,551 K 1
Belitung (Billiton) (isl.) 128,694 D 6
Benggala (str.) A 4
Berau (bay) J 6
Berhala (str.) C 6
Biak (isl.) K 6
Billiton (isl.) 128,694 D 6
Binongko (isl.) 11,549 G 7
Bintan (isl.) 102,644 C 5
Blackwood (Ngundju) (cape) F 8
Boano (isl.) H 6
Bone (gulf) G 7
Borneo (isl.) E 5
Bosch, van den (cape) J 6
Bungalaut (chan.) B 6
Bunguran (Great Natuna) (isl.) D 5
Bunguran (Natuna) (isls.) D 5
Bunyu (isl.) F 5
Buru (isl.) 23,034 H 6
Buru (sea) H 6
Butung (isl.) 188,173 G 6
Celebes (Sulawesi) (isl.) 7,732,383 G 5
Celebes (sea) G 5
Cenderawasih (bay) K 6
Ceram (isl.) 158,591 H 6
Ciremay (mt.) H 2
Damar (isl.) H 7
Damar (isls.) H 7
Dampier (str.) J 6
Dempo (mt.) C 6
Digul (riv.) K 7
Doberai (pen.) J 6
Enggano (isl.) 1,082 C 7
Ewab (Kai) (isls.) 108,328 J 7
Fatagar Tuting (cape) J 6
Flores (isl.) 860,328 G 7
Flores (sea) F 7
Frederik Hendrik (Kolepom) (isl.) K 7
Gebe (isl.) 8,607 H 6
Gede (mt.) H 2
Geelvink (Cenderawasih) (bay) K 6
Gorong (isl.) J 6
Gorong (isls.) J 6
Great Kai (isl.) 38,748 J 7
Great Natuna (isl.) D 5
Gunungapi (isl.) H 7
Halmahera (isl.) 122,521 H 5
Halmahera (sea) H 5
Hari (riv.) C 6
Indian Ocean E 8
Indramayu (pt.) H 1
Irian Jaya (reg.) 923,440 J 6
Jambuair (cape) B 4
Jamursba (cape) J 5
Java (head) C 7
Java (isl.) 73,712,411 J 2
Java (sea) D 6
Jaya, Puncak (mt.) K 6
Jayawijaya (range) K 6
Jemaja (isl.) 5,628 D 5
Kabaena (isl.) G 7
Kahayan (riv.) E 6
Kai (isls.) 108,328 J 7
Kalao (issl.) G 7
Kalaotoa (isl.) G 5
Kalimantan (reg.) 4,956,865 E 5
Kampar (riv.) C 5
Kangean (isl.) F 7
Kangean (isls.) 89,060 F 7
Kapuas (riv.) D 6
Karakelong (isl.) H 5
Karimata (arch.) 9,398 D 6
Karimata (isl.) D 6
Karimata (str.) D 6
Karimunjawa (isls.) 5,025 J 1
Kawi (mt.) K 2
Kawio (isls.) G 5
Kayan (riv.) F 5
Kelasa (str.) D 6
Kengah (isls.) F 7
Kerinci (mt.) C 6
Kisar (isl.) H 7
Kobroor (isl.) K 7
Kolepom (isl.) K 7
Komodo (isl.) 30,407 F 7
Komoran (isl.) K 7
Krakatau (Rakata) (isl.) C 7
Kur (isl.) J 7
Lakor (isl.) H 7
Larat (isl.) J 7
Laurot (Laut Kecil) (isls.) E 7
Laut (isl.) 55,711 F 6
Laut (North Natuna) (isl.) D 5
Laut Kecil (isls.) E 7
Lawu (mt.) J 2
Leti (isls.) H 7
Leuser (mt.) B 5
Lima (isls.) F 7
Lingga (arch.) 46,658 D 5
Lingga (isl.) 18,027 D 6
Little Kai (isl.) J 7
Liukang Tenggaja (isls.) F 7
Lomblen (isl.) 62,572 G 7
Lombok (isl.) 1,581,193 F 7
Lombok (str.) E 7
Macan (isls.) G 7
Madura (isl.) 1,509,774 K 2
Madura (str.) K 2
Maffin (bay) K 6
Mahakam (riv.) F 6
Makassar (str.) F 6
Malacca (str.) C 5
Malangka (cape) G 5
Mamberamo (riv.) K 6
Mandar (cape) F 6
Mangkalihat (cape) F 5
Mangole (isl.) H 6
Manipa (str.) H 6
Manui (isl.) G 6
Maoke (mts.) K 6
Mapia (isls.) J 5
Maras (mt.) D 6
Maratua (isl.) F 5
Masela (isl.) H 7
Mega (isl.) C 6
Mentawai (isls.) 30,107 B 6
Misool (isl.) J 6
Moa (isl.) H 7
Molucca (sea) H 6
Moluccas (isls.) 944,240 H 6
Morotai (isl.) 27,333 H 5
Muli (str.) K 7
Müller (mts.) E 5
Muna (isl.) 156,186 G 7
Muryo (mt.) J 2
Musi (riv.) C 6
Natuna (isls.) 23,893 D 5
Ngunju (cape) F 8
Nias (isl.) 356,093 B 5
Nila (isl.) H 7
North Natuna (isl.) D 4
North Pagai ((isl.) C 6
Numfoor (isl.) J 6
Nusa Barung (isl.) K 3
Obi (isl.) H 6
Obi (isls.) 12,437 H 6
Ombai (str.) H 7
Panaitan (isl.) C 7
Pantar (isl.) 28,259 G 7
Patuha (mt.) H 2
Pegun (isl.) J 5
Pelabuhan Ratu (bay) G 2
Peleng (isl.) G 6
Pembuang (riv.) E 6
Penyu (isls.) H 7
Perkam (cape) K 6
Pujut (pt.) G 1
Puting, Borneo (cape) E 6
Puting, Sumatra (cape) C 7
Raja Ampat Group (isls.) H 6
Rakata (isl.) C 7
Rangasa (cape) F 6
Rantekombola (mt.) F 6
Raung (mt.) L 2
Raya (mt.) E 6
Rewataya (reef) F 7
Riau (arch.) 483,230 C 5
Rokan (riv.) C 5
Romang (isl.) H 7
Roti (isl.) 76,270 G 8
Rupat (isl.) 17,672 C 5
Sabra (cape) J 6
Salabangka (isls.) G 6
Salawati (isl.) J 6
Sandalwood (Sumba) (isl.) 291,190 F 7
Sanding (isl.) C 6
Sangeang (isl.) F 7
Sanggabuwana (mt.) G 2
Sangihe (isl.) H 5
Sangihe (isls.) 183,000 G 5
Saweba (cape) J 6
Sawu (isl.) G 8
Sawu (isls.) 51,002 G 8
Sawu (sea) G 7
Schouten (isls.) 110,148 K 6
Schwaner (mts.) E 6
Sebatik (isll.) F 5
Sebuku (bay) F 5
Selaru (isl.) J 7
Selatan (cape) E 6
Selayar (isl.) 92,342 G 7
Semeru (mt.) K 2
Sera (isl.) J 7
Serasan (isl.) 5,024 D 5
Sermata (isl.) H 7
Serua (isl.) H 7
Siak (riv.) C 5
Siau (isl.) 46,801 H 5
Siberut (isl.) 14,732 B 6
Siberut (str.) B 6
Simeulue (isl.) 29,147 A 5
Singkep (isl.) 28,631 D 6
Sipura (isl.) 6,051 B 6
Sisi (cape) F 6
Slamet (mt.) J 2
Solor (isl.) 24,586 G 7
Sopi (cape) H 5
Sorikmerapi (mt.) B 5
South China (sea) D 4
South Natuna (isls.) D 5
South Pagai (isl.) C 6
Subi Besar (isl.) D 5
Sudirman (range) K 6
Sula (isls.) 36,922 H 6
Sulawesi (isl.) 7,732,383 G 6
Sumatra (isl.) 19,360,400 B 5
Sumba (isl.) 291,190 F 7
Sumba (str.) F 7
Sumbawa (isl.) 621,140 F 7
Sumbing (mt.) J 2
Sunda (str.) C 7
Supiori (isl.) K 6
Tahulandang (isl.) 21,493 H 5
Talaud (isls.) 46,395 H 5
Taliabu (isl.) 18,303 G 6
Tambelan (isls.) 4,032 D 5
Tanimbar (isls.) 55,405 J 7
Tariku (riv.) K 6
Taritatu (riv.) K 6
Tidore (isl.) 28,655 H 5
Tiger (Macan) (isls.) G 7
Timor (reg.) 1,435,527 H 7
Timor (sea) H 7
Toba (lake) B 5
Togian (isls.) 13,913 G 6
Tolo (gulf) G 6
Tomini (gulf) G 6
Torawitan (cape) G 5
Towuti (lake) G 6
Trangan (isl.) J 7
Tukangbesi (isls.) 73,106 G 7
Turtle (Penju) (isls.) H 7
Vals (cape) K 7
Vogelkop (Doberai) (pen.) J 6
Waigeo (isl.) J 5
Wakde (isl.) K 6
Wangiwangi (isl.) 28,469 G 7
Watubela (isls.) J 6
We (isl.) B 4
Wetar (isl.) H 7
Wokam (isl.) K 7
Workai (isl.) K 7
Wowoni (isl.) G 6
Yamdena (isl.) J 7
Yapen (isl.) 50,888 K 6
Yapen (str.) K 6

MALAYSIA

STATES

Labuan 26,453 F 4
(North Borneo) Sabah 1,002,608 F 3
Sarawak 1,294,753 E 5

CITIES and TOWNS

Beaufort 2,709 F 4
Bintulu 4,424 E 5
Kabong E 5
Kampong Sibuti E 5
Kapit 1,929 E 5
Keningau 2,037 F 4
Kota Kinabalu 40,939 F 4
Kuching 63,535 E 5
Kudat 5,089 F 4
Labuan 7,216 E 4
Lahad Datu 5,169 F 5
Lamag F 4
Marudi 4,700 E 5
Miri 35,702 E 5
Mukah 1,717 E 5
Papar 1,855 F 4
Ranau 2,024 F 4
Sandakan 42,413 F 4
Sematan D 5
Semporna 3,371 F 5
Serian 2,209 E 5
Sibu 50,635 E 5
Simanggang 8,445 E 5
Suai E 5
Tawau 24,247 F 5
Weston F 4

OTHER FEATURES

Balambangan (isl.) F 4
Banggi (isl.) F 4
Barut, Tanjong (cape) E 5
Borneo (isl.) E 5
Iran (mts.) E 5
Kinabalu (mt.) F 4
Labuan (isl.) 17,189 E 4
Labuk (bay) F 4
Malay (pen.) B 4
Rajang (riv.) E 5
Sebatik (isl.) F 5
Sirik (cape) E 5
South China (sea) D 4

PAPUA NEW GUINEA

CITIES and TOWNS

Abau C 7
Aitape 3,368 B 6
Ambunti 1,035 B 6
Angoram 1,846 B 6
Baniara C 7
Bogia 755 B 6
Bulolo 6,730 B 7
Buna C 7
Daru 7,127 B 7
Finschhafen 756 C 7
Gaima B 7
Gehua C 8
Gona C 7
Goroka 18,511 B 7
Ihu 541 B 7
Ioma C 7
Kaiapit 515 B 7
Kairuku B 7
Kerema 3,389 B 7
Kikori 763 B 7
Kiunga 1,407 B 7
Kokoda C 7
Kundiawa 4,299 B 7
Lae 61,617 B 7
Madang 21,335 B 7
Marienberg B 6
Mendi 4,130 B 7
Morobe C 7
Mount Hagen 13,441 B 7
Popondetta 6,429 C 7
Port Moresby (cap.) 123,624 B 7
Rigo C 7
Rouka B 7
Saidor 500 B 7
Samarai 864 C 8
Telefomin B 7
Tufi C 7
Vanimo 3,071 B 6
Wau 2,349 B 7
Wedau C 7
Wewak 19,890 B 6

OTHER FEATURES

Coral (sea) B 7
Dampier (str.) C 7
D'Entrecasteaux (isls.) C 7
Fly (riv.) A 7
Huon (gulf) C 7
Karkar (isl.) B 6
Kiriwina (isl.) C 7
Long (isl.) B 7
Louisiade (arch.) D 8
Milne (bay) C 8
Misima (isl.) C 8
Murray (lake) B 7
New Britain (isl.) 148,773 C 7
Ramu (riv.) B 7
Rossel (isl.) D 8
Schouten (isls.) B 6
Sepik (riv.) B 6
Solomon (sea) C 7
Tagula (isl.) C 8
Torres (str.) A 7
Trobriand (isls.) C 7
Vitiaz (str.) B 7
Wilhelm (mt.) B 7
Woodlark (isl.) C 7

PHILIPPINES

CITIES and TOWNS

Aparri 45,070 G 2
Bacolod 262,415 G 3
Baguio 119,009 G 2
Bangued 28,666 G 2
Bangui 11,122 G 2
Batangas 143,570 G 3
Baybay 74,640 H 3
Bayombong 32,066 G 2
Bislig 81,615 H 4
Bontoc 17,091 G 2
Butuan 172,489 H 4
Cabanatuan 138,298 G 2
Cagayan de Oro 227,312 G 4
Calapan 67,370 G 3
Catbalogan 58,737 H 3
Cateel 20,084 H 4
Cavite 87,666 G 3
Cebu 490,281 G 3
Cotabato 83,871 G 4
Daet 54,785 G 3
Davao 610,375 H 4
Dumaguete 63,411 G 4
Glan 48,882 G 4
Iba 22,791 F 2
Iloilo 244,827 G 3
Laoag 69,648 F 2
Legazpi 99,766 G 3
Lingayen 65,187 F 2
Lucena 107,880 G 3
Manila (cap.) 1,630,485 G 3
Marawi 53,812 G 4
Mati 78,178 H 4
Mondragon 20,423 H 3
Naga 90,712 G 3
Oroquieta 47,328 G 4
Palanan 10,295 G 2
Puerto Princesa 60,234 F 4
Roxas 81,183 G 3
San Jose 66,262 G 3
Siocon (Siokun) 29,515 G 4
Sorsogon 60,574 G 3
Surigao 79,745 H 4
Tacloban 102,523 H 3
Tarlac 175,691 G 2
Taytay 22,980 G 3
Tuguegarao 73,507 G 2
Vigan 33,483 F 2
Zamboanga 343,722 G 4

OTHER FEATURES

Babuyan (isls.) G 2
Balabac (isl.) F 4
Balabac (str.) F 4
Basilan (isl.) G 4
Batan (isls.) G 1
Bohol (isl.) G 4
Bugsuk (isl.) F 4
Bulilyan (cape) F 4
Busuanga (isl.) F 3
Cagayan (isls.) F 4
Cagayan Sulu (isl.) F 4
Calamian Group (isls.) F 3
Catanduanes (isl.) H 3
Cebu (isl.) G 3
Cuyo (isls.) G 3
Davao (gulf) H 4
Dinagat (isl.) H 3
Dumaran (isl.) G 3
Espiritu Santo (cape) H 3
Jolo (isl.) G 4
Leyte (isl.) H 3
Lubang (isls.) F 3
Luzon (isl.) G 2
Masbate (isl.) G 3
Matutum (mt.) G 4
Mindanao (isl.) H 4
Mindanao (sea) G 4
Mindoro (isl.) G 3
Mindoro (str.) F 3
Moro (gulf) G 4
Negros (isl.) G 4
Olutanga (isl.) G 4
Palawan (isl.) F 4
Palawan (passg.) F 4
Panay (isl.) G 3
Pangutaran Group (isls.) G 4
Philippine (sea) G 2
Polillo (isl.) G 3
Samar (isl.) H 3
San Agustin (cape) H 4
San Miguel (isls.) F 4
Sarangani (isls.) G 4
Siargao (isl.) H 4
Sibutu (passg.) F 4
Sibuyan (isl.) G 3
Sibuyan (sea) G 3
South China (sea) D 4
Sulu (arch.) G 4
Sulu (sea) G 4
Tagolo (pt.) G 4
Tapul Group (isls.) G 4
Tawitawi Group (isls.) G 4
Tinaca (pt.) H 4
Tubbataha (reefs) G 4
Visayan (sea) G 3

•Population of district, sub-district or division.

AUSTRALIA

AREA 2,966,136 sq. mi. (7,682,300 sq. km.)
POPULATION 14,576,330
CAPITAL Canberra
LARGEST CITY Sydney
HIGHEST POINT Mt. Kosciusko 7,310 ft.
(2,228 m.)
LOWEST POINT Lake Eyre -39 ft. (-12 m.)
MONETARY UNIT Australian dollar
MAJOR LANGUAGE English
MAJOR RELIGIONS Protestantism,
Roman Catholicism

NEW ZEALAND

AREA 103,736 sq. mi. (268,676 sq. km.)
POPULATION 3,175,737
CAPITAL Wellington
LARGEST CITY Auckland
HIGHEST POINT Mt. Cook 12,349 ft.
(3,764 m.)
MONETARY UNIT New Zealand dollar
MAJOR LANGUAGES English, Maori
MAJOR RELIGIONS Protestantism,
Roman Catholicism

AUSTRALIA

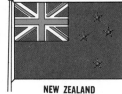

NEW ZEALAND

AUSTRALIA

STATES and TERRITORIES

Ashmore and Cartier Is., Terr.
of .... C 2
Australian Capital Territory
221,609 .... H 7
Coral Sea Islands Territory ... H 2
New South Wales 5,126,217... H 6
Norfolk Island 2,175 .... L 5
Northern Territory 123,324 ... E 3
Queensland 2,295,123 .... G 4
South Australia 1,285,033 .... F 6
Tasmania 418,957 .... H 8
Victoria 3,832,443 .... G 7
Western Australia 1,273,624.. B 5

CITIES and TOWNS

Adelaide (cap.), S. Aust.
882,520 .... D 8
Albany, W. Aust. 15,222 ...... B 6
Albury, N.S.W. 35,072 .... H 7
Alice Springs, N. Terr. 18,395. E 4
Altona, Vic. 30,909 .... J 3
Ararat, Vic. 8,336 .... G 7
Armidale, N.S.W. 18,922 ..... J 6
Ashfield, N.S.W. 41,253 ...... K 4
Auburn, N.S.W. 46,622 .... K 4
Ayr, Queens. 8,787 .... H 3
Bairnsdale, Vic. 9,459 .... H 7
Ballarat, Vic. 35,681 .... G 7
Bankstown, N.S.W. 152,636 .. K 4
Bathurst, N.S.W. 19,640 ..... H 6
Bega, N.S.W. 4,388 .... J 7
Bendigo, Vic. 31,841 .... G 7
Blackall, Queens. 1,609 ...... H 4
Blacktown, N.S.W. 181,139... K 4

Blue Mountains, N.S.W.
55,877 .... J 6
Bordertown, S. Aust. 2,138 ... F 7
Botany, N.S.W. 34,703 .... L 4
Boulder-Kalgoorlie, W. Aust.
19,848 .... C 6
Bourke, N.S.W. 3,326 .... H 6
Bowen, S. Aust. 7,663 .... H 3
Box Hill, Vic. 47,579 .... K 2
Brighton, S. Aust. 19,441 .... D 8
Brighton, Vic. 33,697 .... K 3
Brisbane (cap.), Queens.
942,836 .... K 3
Brisbane Water, N.S.W.
71,984 .... J 6
Broadmeadows, Vic. 103,540. J 2
Broken Hill, N.S.W. 26,913 ... G 6
Broome, W. Aust. 3,666 ...... C 3
Brunswick, Vic. 44,464 .... K 2
Bunbury, W. Aust. 21,749 .... B 6
Bundaberg, Queens. 32,560.. J 4
Burnie-Somerset, Tas.
19,994 .... H 8
Burnside, S. Aust. 37,593 .... E 8
Burwood, N.S.W. 28,896 ..... K 4
Busselton, W. Aust. 6,463 .... A 6
Cairns, Queens. 48,557 ...... H 3
Camberwell, Vic. 85,883 ..... K 2
Campbelltown, S. Aust.
43,084 .... E 8
Canberra (cap.), A.C.T.
*220,822 .... H 7
Canterbury, N.S.W. 126,741.. K 4
Carnarvon, W. Aust. 5,053 ... A 4
Casino, N.S.W. 9,743 .... J 5
Caulfield, Vic. 69,922 .... K 2
Ceduna, S. Aust. 2,794 ...... E 6
Cessnock-Bellbird, N.S.W.
16,916 .... J 6
Charleville, Queens. 3,523 ... H 5

Charters Towers, Queens.
6,823 .... H 4
Chelsea, Vic. 26,034 .... K 3
Clermont, Queens. 1,659 ..... H 4
Cloncurry, Queens. 1,961 .... G 4
Cobar, N.S.W. 3,583 .... H 6
Coburg, Vic. 55,035 .... K 2
Coffs Harbour, N.S.W. 16,020. J 6
Collie, W. Aust. 2,667 .... B 6
Collinsville, Queens. 2,756 ... H 4
Concord, N.S.W. 23,926 ...... K 4
Condobolin, N.S.W. 3,355 .... H 6
Coober Pedy, S. Aust. 2,078.. E 5
Cooma, N.S.W. 7,978 .... H 7
Coonamble, N.S.W. 3,090 .... H 6
Cootamundra, N.S.W. 6,540.. H 6
Cowra, N.S.W. 7,900 .... H 6
Croydon, Vic. 36,210 .... L 2
Cunnamulla, Queens. 1,627.. H 5
Dalby, Queens. 8,784 .... J 5
Dandenong, Vic. 54,962 ..... L 3
Darwin (cap.), N. Terr. 56,482. E 2
Deniliquin, N.S.W. 7,354 ..... G 7
Derby, W. Aust. 2,933 .... C 3
Devonport, Tas. 21,424 ...... H 8
Doncaster and Templestowe,
Vic. 90,660 .... K 2
Drummoyne, N.S.W. 30,961 .. K 4
Dubbo, N.S.W. 23,986 .... H 6
Echuca, Vic. 7,943 .... G 7
Elizabeth, S. Aust. 32,608.... E 7
Eltham, Vic. 34,648 .... K 2
Enfield, S. Aust. 66,797 ...... D 7
Esperance, W. Aust. 6,375 ... C 6
Essendon, Vic. 56,380 .... J 2
Fairfield, N.S.W. 129,557 .... K 4
Footscray, Vic. 49,756 .... J 2
Forbes, N.S.W. 8,029 .... H 6
Fremantle, W. Aust. 22,484.. B 6
Gawler, S. Aust. 9,433 .... F 6

Geelong, Vic. 14,471 .... G 7
Geraldton, W. Aust. 20,895... A 5
Gladstone, Queens. 22,083 .. J 4
Glen Innes, N.S.W. 6,052 .... J 5
Glenorchy, Tas. 41,019 ...... H 8
Gold Coast, Queens.
135,437 .... J 5
Goondiwindi, Queens. 3,576 . H 5
Goulburn, N.S.W. 21,755 ..... J 6
Grafton, N.S.W. 17,005 ...... J 5
Griffith, N.S.W. 13,187 .... H 6
Gunnedah, N.S.W. 8,909 ..... H 6
Gympie, Queens. 10,768 ..... J 5
Hamilton, Vic. 9,751 .... G 7
Hawthorne, Vic. 30,689 ...... K 2
Hay, N.S.W. 2,958 .... H 6
Heidelberg, Vic. 64,757 ...... K 2
Hindmarsh, S. Aust. 7,593 ... D 8
Hobart (cap.), Tas. 128,603.. H 8
Holyroyd, N.S.W. 80,116 ..... K 4
Home Hill, Queens. 3,138 .... H 3
Hornsby, N.S.W. 111,081..... K 3
Horsham, Vic. 12,034 .... G 7
Hughenden, Queens. 1,657 .. G 4
Hurstville, N.S.W. 64,910 .... K 4
Ingham, Queens. 5,598 ...... H 3
Innisfail, Queens. 7,933 ...... H 3
Inverell, N.S.W. 9,734 .... J 5
Kadina, S. Aust. 2,943 .... F 6
Kalgoorlie, W. Aust. 9,145 ... C 6
Katanning, W. Aust. 4,413 ... B 6
Katherine, N. Terr. 3,737 .... E 2
Keilor, Vic. 81,762 .... J 2
Kempsey, N.S.W. 9,037 ...... J 6
Kensington and Norwood, S.
Aust. 8,950 .... E 8
Kew, Vic. 28,870 .... K 2
Kingaroy, Queens. 5,134 ..... J 5
Knox, Vic. 88,902 .... L 2
Kogarah, N.S.W. 46,322 ..... K 4

Kwinana-Newtown, W. Aust.
12,355 .... B 2
Lane Cove, N.S.W. 29,113 ... L 4
Launceston, Tas. 31,273 ..... H 8
Leichhardt, N.S.W. 57,332 ... L 4
Leigh Creek, S. Aust.
1,635 .... F 6
Leonora, W. Aust. 524 .... C 5
Lismore, N.S.W. 24,033 ...... J 5
Lithgow, N.S.W. 12,793 ...... J 6
Liverpool, N.S.W. 92,715..... K 4
Longreach, Queens. 2,971 ... G 4
Mackay, Queens. 35,361..... H 4
Maitland, N.S.W. 38,865 ..... J 6
Malvern, Vic. 43,211 .... K 2
Mandurah, W. Aust. 10,978.. B 3
Maralinga, S. Aust. .... E 6
Mareeba, Queens. 6,309 ..... G 3
Marion, S. Aust. 66,580 ...... D 8
Maroochydore-Mooloolaba,
Queens. 17,460 .... J 5
Marrickville, N.S.W. 83,448... L 4
Maryborough, Queens.
20,111 .... J 5
Maryborough, Vic. 7,858 ..... G 7
Meekatharra, W. Aust. 989 .. B 5
Melbourne (cap.), Vic.
2,578,759 .... K 2
Merredin, W. Aust. 3,520 .... B 6
Mildura, Vic. 15,763 .... G 6
Mingenew, W. Aust. 368 ..... B 5
Mitcham, S. Aust. 60,309 .... D 8
Moora, W. Aust. 1,677 .... B 6
Moorabbin, Vic. 97,810 ...... K 3
Mordialloc, Vic. 27,869 ...... K 3
Moree, N.S.W. 10,459 .... H 5
Mossman, Queens. 1,614 ... G 3
Mount Gambier, S. Aust.
18,193 .... G 7
Mount Isa, Queens. 23,679... F 4

Mount Morgan, Queens.
2,974 .... J 4
Mudgee, N.S.W. 6,015 .... J 6
Murray Bridge, S. Aust. 8,664. F 7
Murwillumbah, N.S.W. 7,807.. J 5
Muswellbrook, N.S.W. 8,548.. J 6
Naracoorte, S. Aust. 4,758 .. F 7
Narrabri, N.S.W. 7,296 .... J 6
Narrandera, N.S.W. 5,813.... H 6
Narrogin, W. Aust. 4,969 ..... B 6
Narromine, N.S.W. 2,994..... H 6
Nedlands, W. Aust. 20,257 .. B 2
Newcastle, N.S.W. 135,207... J 6
New Norfolk, Tas. 6,243 ..... H 8
Northam, W. Aust. 6,791 .... B 6
Northampton, W. Aust. 750 .. A 5
Northcote, Vic. 51,235 .... K 2
North Sydney, N.S.W. 48,500. L 4
Nowra-Bomaderry, N.S.W.
17,887 .... K 2
Nunawading, Vic. 97,052 .... K 2
Nyngan, N.S.W. 2,485 .... H 6
Oakleigh, Vic. 55,612 .... K 2
Orange, N.S.W. 27,626 ...... H 6
Orbost, Vic. 2,586 .... H 7
Parkes, N.S.W. 9,047 .... H 6
Parramatta, N.S.W. 130,943 . K 4
Penrith, N.S.W. 108,720 ..... J 6
Perth (cap.), W. Aust. 809,035. B 2
Peterborough, S. Aust. 2,575. F 6
Port Adelaide, S. Aust.
35,407 .... D 7
Port Augusta, S. Aust. 15,566. F 6
Port Hedland, W. Aust.
12,948 .... B 3
Portland, Vic. 9,353 .... G 7
Port Lincoln, S. Aust. 9,846.. E 6
Port Melbourne, Vic. 8,585 .. K 2
Port Macquarie, N.S.W.
19,581 .... J 6

Port Pirie, S. Aust. 14,695.... F 6
Prahan, Vic. 45,018 .... K 2
Preston, Vic. 84,519 .... K 2
Proserpine, Queens. 3,058 .. H 4
Queenstown, Tas. 3,714 ..... H 8
Randwick, N.S.W. 116,202 .. L 4
Red Cliffe, Queens. 42,223 .. J 5
Renmark, S. Aust. 3,475 ..... G 6
Richmond, Vic. 24,506 .... K 2
Ringwood, Vic. 38,665 .... K 2
Rockdale, N.S.W. 83,719..... K 4
Rockhampton, Queens.
50,146 .... H 4
Rockingham, W. Aust. 24,932. B 2
Roebourne, W. Aust. 1,688 .. B 4
Roma, Queens. 5,706 .... H 5
Ryde, N.S.W. 88,948 .... L 4
Saint George, Queens. 2,204. H 5
Saint Kilda, Vic. 49,366 ...... K 2
Sale, Vic. 12,968 .... H 7
Salisbury, S. Aust. 86,451 ... E 7
Sandringham, Vic. 31,175 ... K 3
Sarina, Queens. 2,815 .... H 4
Seymour, Vic. 6,494 .... H 7
Shepparton-Maoopna, Vic.
†27,373 .... G 7
South Sydney, N.S.W. 30,776. L 4
Springvale, Vic. 80,186 ...... K 3
Stanthorpe, Queens. 3,966 .. J 5
Stirling, W. Aust. 161,858 ... B 2
Strathfield, N.S.W. 25,882 ... K 4
Sunshine, Vic. 94,419 .... J 2
Sutherland, N.S.W. 165,336 . K 5
Swan Hill, Vic. 8,398 .... G 7
Sydney (cap.), N.S.W.
2,876,508 .... L 4
Tamworth, N.S.W. 29,657 ... J 6
Taree, N.S.W. 14,697 .... J 6
Tea Tree Gully, S. Aust.
67,237 .... E 7

(continued on following page)

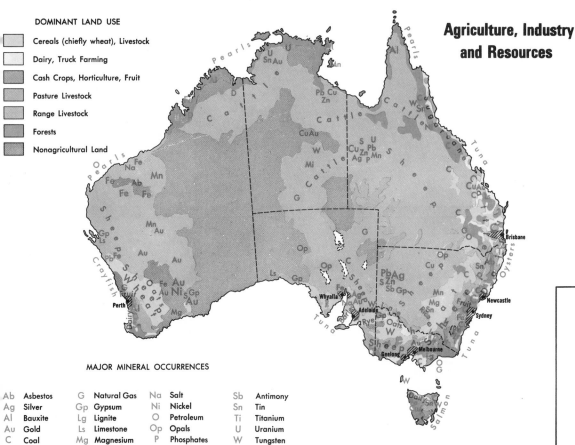

DOMINANT LAND USE

- Cereals (chiefly wheat), Livestock
- Dairy, Truck Farming
- Cash Crops, Horticulture, Fruit
- Pasture Livestock
- Range Livestock
- Forests
- Nonagricultural Land

Agriculture, Industry and Resources

MAJOR MINERAL OCCURRENCES

Ab	Asbestos	G	Natural Gas	Na	Salt
Ag	Silver	Gp	Gypsum	Ni	Nickel
Al	Bauxite	Lg	Lignite	O	Petroleum
Au	Gold	Ls	Limestone	Op	Opals
C	Coal	Mg	Magnesium	P	Phosphates
Cu	Copper	Mi	Mica	Pb	Lead
D	Diamonds	Mn	Manganese	S	Sulfur, Pyrites
Fe	Iron Ore				

Sb	Antimony
Sn	Tin
Ti	Titanium
U	Uranium
W	Tungsten
Zn	Zinc
Zr	Zirconium

⚡ Water Power
▨ Major Industrial Areas

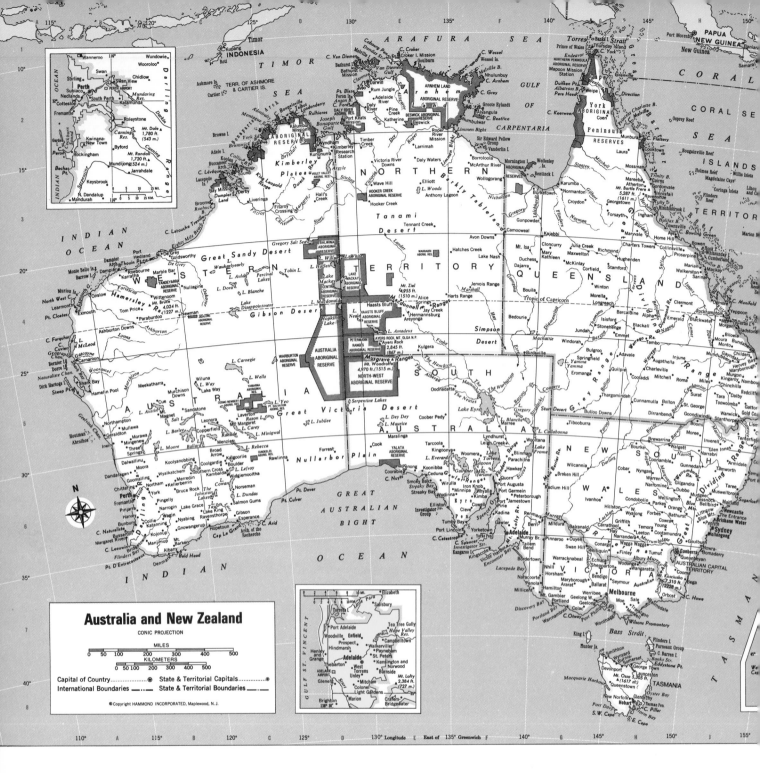

Australia and New Zealand

CONIC PROJECTION

MILES

KILOMETERS

Capital of Country ....⊛   State & Territorial Capitals ....⊛
International Boundaries ——   State & Territorial Boundaries —

⊛Copyright HAMMOND INCORPORATED, Maplewood, N.J.

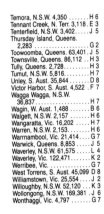

Population Distribution

- Cities with over 1,000,000 inhabitants (including suburbs)
- Cities with over 100,000 inhabitants (including suburbs)

DENSITY PER

SQ. KILOMETER	SQ. MILE
Over 50	Over 130
10-50	25-130
1-10	3-25
Under 1	Under 3

Topography

5,000 m. 2,000 m. 1,000 m. 500 m. 200 m. 100 m. Sea Level Below
16,404 ft. 6,562 ft. 3,281 ft. 1,640 ft. 656 ft. 328 ft.

0 150 300 MI.
0 150 300 KM.

New Zealand — Same Scale as main map

FIJI

AREA 7,055 sq. mi. (18,272 sq. km.)
POPULATION 588,068
CAPITAL Suva
LARGEST CITY Suva
HIGHEST POINT Tomaniivi 4,341 ft.
(1,323 m.)
MONETARY UNIT Fijian dollar
MAJOR LANGUAGES Fijian, Hindi, English
MAJOR RELIGIONS Protestantism, Hinduism

KIRIBATI

AREA 291 sq. mi. (754 sq. km.)
POPULATION 56,213
CAPITAL Bairiki (Tarawa)
HIGHEST POINT (on Banaba I.) 285 ft. (87 m.)
MONETARY UNIT Australian dollar
MAJOR LANGUAGES I-Kiribati, English
MAJOR RELIGIONS Protestantism, Roman
Catholicism

NAURU

AREA 7.7 sq. mi. (20 sq. km.)
POPULATION 7,254
CAPITAL Yaren (district)
MONETARY UNIT Australian dollar
MAJOR LANGUAGES Nauruan, English
MAJOR RELIGION Protestantism

SOLOMON ISLANDS

AREA 11,500 sq. mi. (29,785 sq. km.)
POPULATION 221,000
CAPITAL Honiara
HIGHEST POINT Mount Popomanatseu
7,647 ft. (2,331 m.)
MONETARY UNIT Solomon Islands dollar
MAJOR LANGUAGES English, pidgin English,
Melanesian dialects
MAJOR RELIGIONS Tribal religions,
Protestantism, Roman Catholicism

TONGA

AREA 270 sq. mi. (699 sq. km.)
POPULATION 90,128
CAPITAL Nuku'alofa
LARGEST CITY Nuku'alofa
HIGHEST POINT 3,389 ft. (1,033 m.)
MONETARY UNIT pa'anga
MAJOR LANGUAGES Tongan, English
MAJOR RELIGION Protestantism

TUVALU

AREA 9.78 sq. mi. (25.33 sq. km.)
POPULATION 7,349
CAPITAL Fongafale (Funafuti)
HIGHEST POINT 15 ft. (4.6 m.)
MONETARY UNIT Australian dollar
MAJOR LANGUAGES English, Tuvaluan
MAJOR RELIGION Protestantism

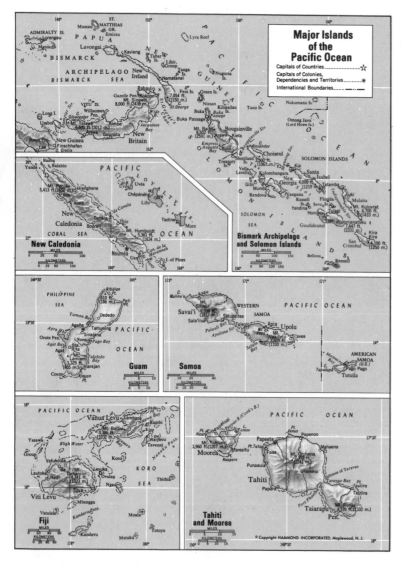

Major Islands
of the
Pacific Ocean

Capitals of Countries . . . . ☆
Capitals of Colonies,
Dependencies and Territories . . . . . ⊛
International Boundaries . . . .

© Copyright HAMMOND INCORPORATED, Maplewood, N. J.

VANUATU

AREA 5,700 sq. mi. (14,763 sq. km.)
POPULATION 112,596
CAPITAL Vila
HIGHEST POINT Mt. Tabwemasana
6,165 ft. (1,879 m.)
MONETARY UNIT vatu
MAJOR LANGUAGES Bislama, English,
French
MAJOR RELIGIONS Christian, animist

WESTERN SAMOA

AREA 1,133 sq. mi. (2,934 sq. km.)
POPULATION 158,130
CAPITAL Apia
LARGEST CITY Apia
HIGHEST POINT Mt. Silisili 6,094 ft.
(1,857 m.)
MONETARY UNIT tala
MAJOR LANGUAGES Samoan, English
MAJOR RELIGIONS Protestantism,
Roman Catholicism

*City and suburbs.
•Population of urban area.

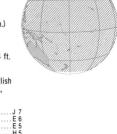

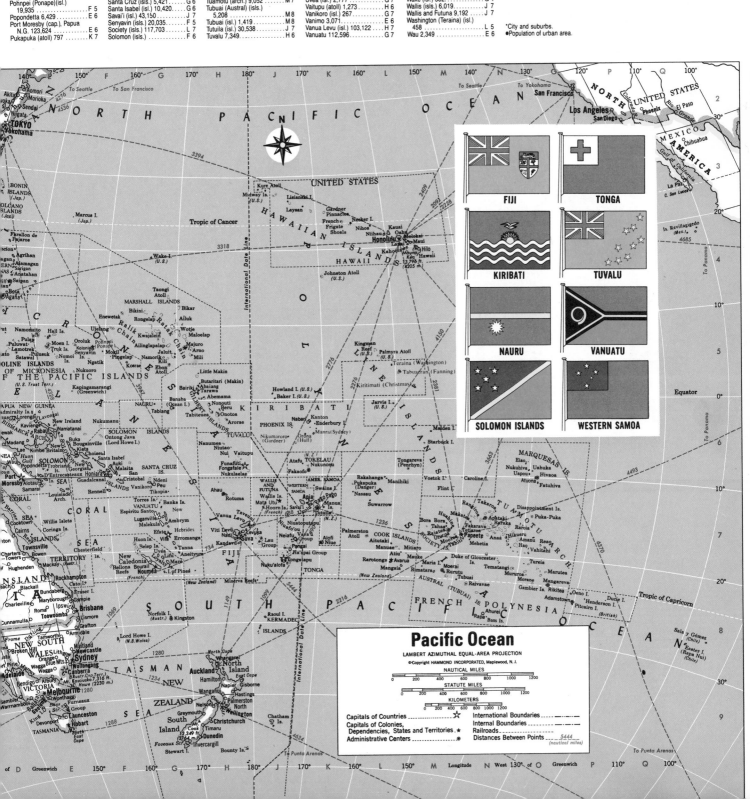

Pacific Ocean

LAMBERT AZIMUTHAL EQUAL-AREA PROJECTION
©Copyright HAMMOND INCORPORATED, Maplewood, N.J.

NAUTICAL MILES
0   200   400   600   800   1000   1200

STATUTE MILES
0   200   400   600   800   1000   1200

KILOMETERS
0   200   400   600   800   1000   1200

Capitals of Countries . . . . ☆
Capitals of Colonies,
  Dependencies, States and Territories . ★
Administrative Centers . . . .
International Boundaries . . . .
Internal Boundaries . . . .
Railroads . . . .
Distances Between Points 5444
(nautical miles)

South America
Northern Part

LAMBERT AZIMUTHAL EQUAL-AREA PROJECTION

SCALE OF MILES

SCALE OF KILOMETRES

Capitals of Countries......... ☆
Other Capitals .... △
International Boundaries........ ——————
Other Boundaries.............. ------

© Copyright HAMMOND INCORPORATED, Maplewood, N.J.

ARGENTINA

PROVINCES

Buenos Aires 10,796,036... H 11	
Catamarca 206,204....... G 9	
Chaco 692,410........... H 8	
Chubut 262,196.......... G 12	
Córdoba 2,407,135....... H 10	
Corrientes 657,716....... J 9	
Distrito Federal 2,908,001... J 10	
Entre Ríos 902,241....... J 10	
Formosa 292,479......... H 8	
Jujuy 408,514........... G 8	
La Pampa 207,132....... G 11	
La Rioja 163,342......... G 9	
Mendoza 1,187,305....... G 10	
Misiones 579,579........ K 9	
Neuquén 241,904........ G 11	
Río Negro 383,896....... G 12	
Salta 662,369........... G 10	
San Juan 469,973........ G 10	
San Luis 212,837........ G 10	
Santa Cruz 114,479...... G 13	
Santa Fe 2,457,188...... J 10	
Santiago del Estero 652,318.. H 9	
Tierra del Fuego, Antártida, e Islas del Atlántico Sur 29,451........... G 14	
Tucumán 968,066........ G 9	

CITIES and TOWNS

Azul 43,582............ J 11
Bahía Blanca *220,765.... J 11
Balcarce 28,985......... J 11
Bell Ville 26,559......... H 10
Bolívar 16,382.......... H 11
Buenos Aires (cap.) *9,927,404........ H 10
Campana 51,498........ H 10
Catamarca *88,432...... H 9
Chivilcoy 43,779........ H 11
Comodoro Rivadavia 96,865 G 13
Concepción del Uruguay 46,065............ J 10
Concordia 93,618....... J 10
Córdoba *982,018....... G 10
Corrientes 179,590...... J 9
Cruz del Eje 23,473...... H 10
Curuzú Cuatiá 24,955.... J 9
Embarcación 9,016...... G 8
Esperanza 22,838...... H 10
Formosa 95,067........ J 9
Gaimán 2,651.......... G 12
Gastre................ G 12
General Alvear 21,250... H 11
General Pico 30,180..... H 11
General Roca 38,296.... G 11
Godoy Cruz 141,553.... G 10
Goya 47,357........... J 9
Jáchal 8,832........... G 10
Jujuy 124,487.......... J 11
La Plata *560,341...... J 11
La Rioja 66,826........ G 9
Liberador General San Martín 30,814.......... H 8
Lincoln 19,009......... H 10
Maquinchao 1,295...... G 12
Mar del Plata 407,024... J 11
Mendoza 596,796....... G 10
Mercedes 50,856....... G 10

Miramar 15,473......... J 11
Necochea 50,939....... J 11
Neuquén 90,037....... G 11
Olavarría 63,686....... H 11
Paraná 159,581........ J 10
Pehuajó 25,613........ H 11
Pergamino 68,989...... H 10
Plaza Huincul 7,988.... G 11
Posadas 139,941....... J 9
Presidencia Roque Sáenz Peña 49,261........ J 9
Puerto Madryn 20,709... G 12
Punta Alta 54,375...... H 11
Rafaela 53,152........ H 10
Rawson 12,981........ G 12
Reconquista 32,442.... H 9
Resistencia *218,438.... J 9
Rinconada............ G 8
Río Cuarto 110,148..... H 10
Río Gallegos 43,479.... G 14
Río Grande 13,271..... G 14
Rivadavia............. H 8
Rosario *954,606...... H 10
Rosario de la Frontera 13,531 H 9
Salta 260,323......... G 8
San Antonio de los Cobres 2,357............ G 8
San Carlos de Bariloche 48,222........... F 12
San Francisco *58,616... H 10
San Juan *290,479..... G 10
San Julián 4,278....... G 13
San Luis 70,632....... G 10
San Miguel de Tucumán 496,914.......... H 9
San Nicolás 96,313..... J 10

San Rafael 7,047....... G 10
Santa Cruz 2,353...... G 14
Sante Fe 287,240...... J 10
Santa Rosa 51,689..... H 11
Santiago del Estero 148,357.. H 9
Tandil 78,821......... J 9
Tartagal 31,367....... H 8
Trelew 52,073........ G 12
Trenque Lauquen 22,504.. H 11
Tres Arroyos 42,118.... J 11
Ushuaia 10,988....... G 14
Valcheta 2,994....... G 12
Venado Tuerto 46,775... H 10
Viedma 24,338....... H 12
Villa Dolores 21,508.... G 10
Villa María *67,490.... H 10

OTHER FEATURES

Aconcagua (mt.)....... F 10
Andes de Patagonia (mts.).. F 12
Argentino (lake)....... G 14
Bermejo (riv.)......... H 9
Colorado (riv.)........ G 11
Estados, Los (isl.)..... H 14
Gran Chaco (reg.)..... H 8
Iguassú (falls)........ K 9
Magellan (str.)........ G 14
Maipo (mt.).......... G 11
Nahuel Huapí (lake).... F 12
Negro (riv.).......... G 12
Ojos del Salado (mt.)... G 9
Pampas (plain)........ H 11
Patagonia (reg.)....... G 12
Plata, Río de la (est.)... J 11
Salado (riv.)......... J 10

Salado (riv.)......... H 9
San Antonio (cape).... J 11
San Martín (lake)..... F 13
San Matías (gulf)..... H 12
Santiago del Estero (isl.).. H 14
Tierra del Fuego (isl.)... G 14
Uruguay (riv.)........ J 9
Valdés (pen.)........ H 12

BOLIVIA

CITIES and TOWNS

Cochabamba 204,684.... G 7
Guaqui 2,266......... G 7
Guayaramerin 1,470.... G 6
Huanchaca........... G 7
La Paz (cap.) 635,283... G 7
Oruro 124,213........ G 7
Potosí 77,397........ G 7
Puerto Suárez 1,159.... J 7
Santa Cruz 254,682.... H 7
Sucre (cap.) 63,625.... G 7
Tarija 38,916........ H 8

OTHER FEATURES

Abuná (riv.)......... F 5
Beni (riv.).......... G 6
Desaguadero (riv.).... G 7
Grande (riv.)........ H 7
Guaporé (riv.)....... H 6
Illampu (mt.)........ G 7
Mamoré (riv.)....... H 6
Poopó (lake)........ G 7

Real, Cordillera (mts.)... G 7
Titicaca (lake)....... F 7

BRAZIL

STATES

Acre 301,605......... F 5
Alagoas 1,987,581.... N 5
Amapá (terr.) 175,634... K 3
Amazonas 1,432,066... G 5
Bahia 9,474,263...... M 6
Ceará 5,294,876...... N 5
Distrito Federal 1,177,393.. L 7
Espírito Santo 2,023,821.. M 8
Goiás 3,865,482..... L 6
Maranhão 4,002,599... L 5
Mato Grosso 1,141,661.. J 6
Mato Grosso do Sul 1,370,333......... J 8
Minas Gerais 13,390,805.. M 7
Pará 3,411,868...... K 4
Paraíba 2,772,600.... N 5
Paraná 7,630,466.... L 8
Pernambuco 6,147,102.. N 5
Piauí 2,140,066..... M 5
Rio de Janeiro 11,297,327.. M 8
Rio Grande do Norte 1,899,720......... N 5
Rio Grande do Sul 7,777,212......... K 9
Rondônia 492,810.... H 6
Roraima (terr.) 79,153... H 3
Santa Catarina 3,628,751.. L 9
São Paulo 25,040,698.. N 6
Sergipe 1,141,834.... N 6

CITIES and TOWNS

Alagoinhas 76,377..... N 6
Alcobaça 3,430....... N 7
Alegrete 54,786...... J 9
Amapá 2,676........ J 3
Amarante 6,848....... M 5
Anápolis 160,520..... L 7
Andradina 42,036..... K 8
Aracaju 288,106..... N 6
Araçatuba 1,113,486... K 8
Araguari 73,302...... L 7
Araquara 77,202..... L 8
Araxá 51,339........ L 7
Bacabal 43,229...... J 5
Bagé 66,743......... K 10
Bahia (Salvador) 1,496,276... N 6
Barcelos 1,846...... H 4
Barra do Garças...... K 7
Barretos 65,294..... L 8
Baurú 178,861...... L 8
Bebedouro 39,070.... L 8
Belém 758,117...... L 4
Belo Horizonte †2,541,788.. M 7
Benjamin Constant 6,563... G 4
Blumenau 144,819.... L 9
Boa Vista 43,131..... H 3
Borba 5,366......... H 4
Botucatu 56,316..... L 8
Bragança 1,208...... L 4
Brasiléia 4,835...... F 6
Brasília (cap.) 411,305... L 7
Brejo 5,859......... M 5
Brumado 24,663..... M 6

(continued on following page)

AREA 6,875,000 sq. mi. (17,806,250 sq. km.)
POPULATION 245,000,000
LARGEST CITY São Paulo
HIGHEST POINT Cerro Aconcagua 22,831 ft. (6,959 m.)
LOWEST POINT Salina Grande -131 ft. (-40 m.)

Topography

0   300   600 MI.
0   300   600 KM.

Flags:
ARGENTINA BOLIVIA
BRAZIL CHILE
COLOMBIA ECUADOR
FRENCH GUIANA GUYANA PARAGUAY
PERU SURINAME URUGUAY VENEZUELA

ARGENTINA
AREA 1,072,070 sq. mi. (2,776,661 sq. km.)
POPULATION 28,438,000
CAPITAL Buenos Aires
LARGEST CITY Buenos Aires
HIGHEST POINT Cerro Aconcagua 22,831 ft. (6,959 m.)
MONETARY UNIT austral
MAJOR LANGUAGE Spanish
MAJOR RELIGION Roman Catholicism

BOLIVIA
AREA 424,163 sq. mi. (1,098,582 sq. km.)
POPULATION 5,600,000
CAPITALS La Paz, Sucre
LARGEST CITY La Paz
HIGHEST POINT Nevada Ancohuma 21,489 ft. (6,550 m.)
MONETARY UNIT Bolivian peso
MAJOR LANGUAGES Spanish, Quechua, Aymara
MAJOR RELIGION Roman Catholicism

BRAZIL
AREA 3,284,426 sq. mi. (8,506,663 sq. km.)
POPULATION 119,098,992
CAPITAL Brasília
LARGEST CITY São Paulo (greater)
HIGHEST POINT Pico da Neblina 9,889 ft. (3,014 m.)
MONETARY UNIT cruzeiro
MAJOR LANGUAGE Portuguese
MAJOR RELIGION Roman Catholicism

CHILE
AREA 292,257 sq. mi. (756,946 sq. km.)
POPULATION 11,275,440
CAPITAL Santiago
LARGEST CITY Santiago
HIGHEST POINT Ojos del Salado 22,572 ft. (6,880 m.)
MONETARY UNIT Chilean escudo
MAJOR LANGUAGE Spanish
MAJOR RELIGION Roman Catholicism

COLOMBIA
AREA 439,513 sq. mi. (1,138,339 sq. km.)
POPULATION 27,520,000
CAPITAL Bogotá
LARGEST CITY Bogotá
HIGHEST POINT Pico Cristóbal Colón 19,029 ft. (5,800 m.)
MONETARY UNIT Colombian peso
MAJOR LANGUAGE Spanish
MAJOR RELIGION Roman Catholicism

ECUADOR
AREA 109,483 sq. mi. (283,561 sq. km.)
POPULATION 8,354,000
CAPITAL Quito
LARGEST CITY Guayaquil
HIGHEST POINT Chimborazo 20,561 ft. (6,267 m.)
MONETARY UNIT sucre
MAJOR LANGUAGES Spanish, Quechua
MAJOR RELIGION Roman Catholicism

FRENCH GUIANA
AREA 35,135 sq. mi. (91,000 sq. km.)
POPULATION 73,022
CAPITAL Cayenne
LARGEST CITY Cayenne
HIGHEST POINT 2,723 ft. (830 m.)
MONETARY UNIT French franc
MAJOR LANGUAGE French
MAJOR RELIGIONS Roman Catholicism, Protestantism

GUYANA
AREA 83,000 sq. mi. (214,970 sq. km.)
POPULATION 820,000
CAPITAL Georgetown
LARGEST CITY Georgetown
HIGHEST POINT Mt. Roraima 9,094 ft. (2,772 m.)
MONETARY UNIT Guyana dollar
MAJOR LANGUAGES English, Hindi
MAJOR RELIGIONS Christianity, Hinduism, Islam

PARAGUAY
AREA 157,047 sq. mi. (406,752 sq. km.)
POPULATION 2,973,000
CAPITAL Asunción
LARGEST CITY Asunción
HIGHEST POINT Amambay Range 2,264 ft. (690 m.)
MONETARY UNIT guaraní
MAJOR LANGUAGES Spanish, Guaraní
MAJOR RELIGION Roman Catholicism

PERU
AREA 496,222 sq. mi. (1,285,215 sq. km.)
POPULATION 17,031,221
CAPITAL Lima
LARGEST CITY Lima
HIGHEST POINT Huascarán 22,205 ft. (6,768 m.)
MONETARY UNIT sol
MAJOR LANGUAGES Spanish, Quechua, Aymara
MAJOR RELIGION Roman Catholicism

SURINAME
AREA 55,144 sq. mi. (142,823 sq. km.)
POPULATION 354,860
CAPITAL Paramaribo
LARGEST CITY Paramaribo
HIGHEST POINT Julianatop 4,200 ft. (1,280 m.)
MONETARY UNIT Suriname guilder
MAJOR LANGUAGES Dutch, Hindi, Indonesian
MAJOR RELIGIONS Christianity, Islam, Hinduism

URUGUAY
AREA 72,172 sq. mi. (186,925 sq. km.)
POPULATION 2,899,000
CAPITAL Montevideo
LARGEST CITY Montevideo
HIGHEST POINT Mirador Nacional 1,644 ft. (501 m.)
MONETARY UNIT Uruguayan peso
MAJOR LANGUAGE Spanish
MAJOR RELIGION Roman Catholicism

VENEZUELA
AREA 352,143 sq. mi. (912,050 sq. km.)
POPULATION 14,313,000
CAPITAL Caracas
LARGEST CITY Caracas
HIGHEST POINT Pico Bolívar 16,427 ft. (5,007 m.)
MONETARY UNIT Bolívar
MAJOR LANGUAGE Spanish
MAJOR RELIGION Roman Catholicism

OTHER FEATURES

CHILE

CITIES and TOWNS

OTHER FEATURES

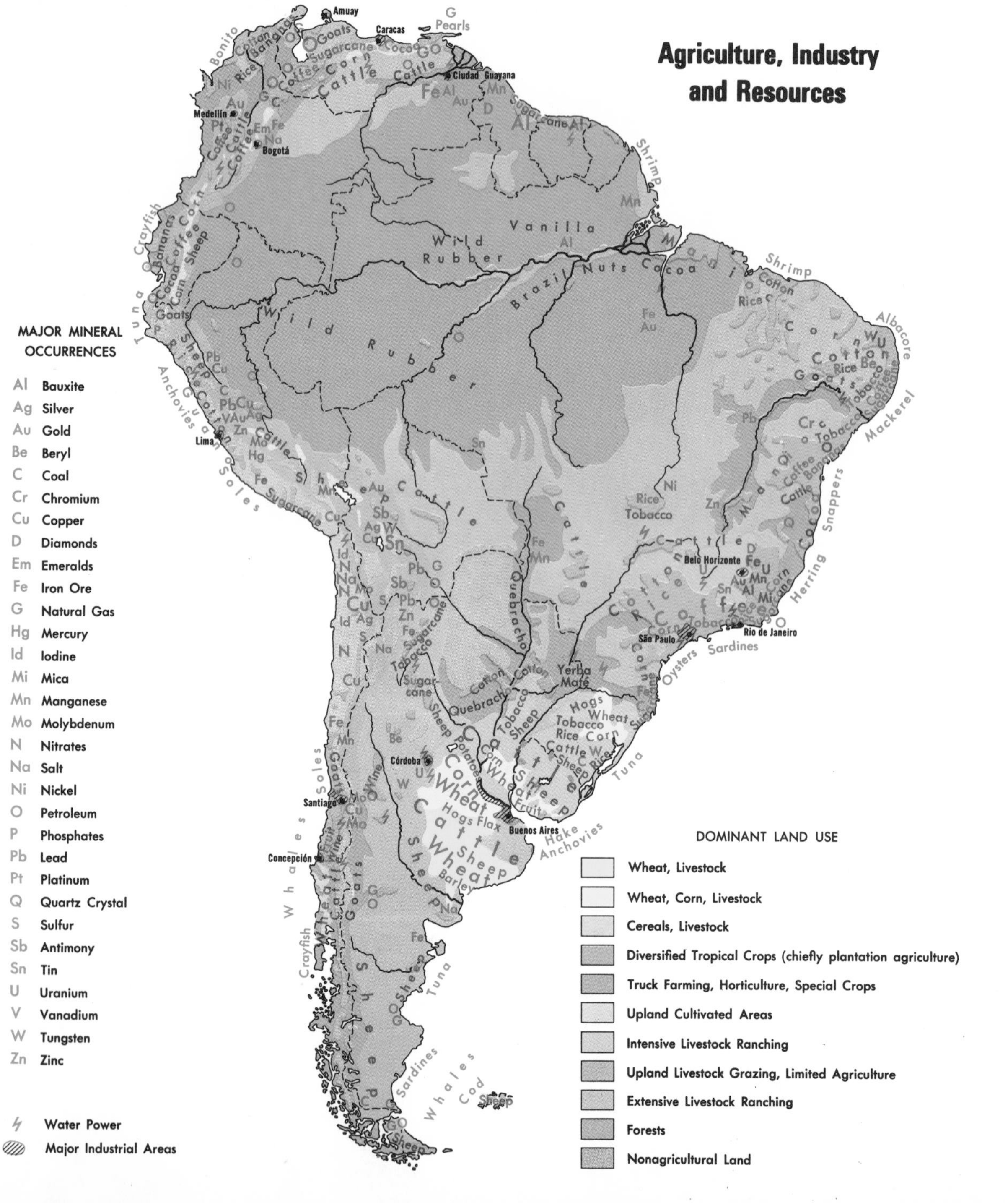

Agriculture, Industry and Resources
MAJOR MINERAL OCCURRENCES
Al Bauxite
Ag Silver
Au Gold
Be Beryl
C Coal
Cr Chromium
Cu Copper
D Diamonds
Em Emeralds
Fe Iron Ore
G Natural Gas
Hg Mercury
Id Iodine
Mi Mica
Mn Manganese
Mo Molybdenum
N Nitrates
Na Salt
Ni Nickel
O Petroleum
P Phosphates
Pb Lead
Pt Platinum
Q Quartz Crystal
S Sulfur
Sb Antimony
Sn Tin
U Uranium
V Vanadium
W Tungsten
Zn Zinc
Water Power
Major Industrial Areas
DOMINANT LAND USE
Wheat, Livestock
Wheat, Corn, Livestock
Cereals, Livestock
Diversified Tropical Crops (chiefly plantation agriculture)
Truck Farming, Horticulture, Special Crops
Upland Cultivated Areas
Intensive Livestock Ranching
Upland Livestock Grazing, Limited Agriculture
Extensive Livestock Ranching
Forests
Nonagricultural Land
Amuay
Caracas
Pearls
Ciudad Guayana
Medellín
Bogotá
Lima
Belo Horizonte
São Paulo
Rio de Janeiro
Córdoba
Santiago
Buenos Aires
Concepción
Wild Rubber
Vanilla
Brazil Nuts
Cocoa
Shrimp
Albacore
Mackerel
Snappers
Herring
Sardines
Oysters
Yerba Maté
Quebracho
Hake
Anchovies
Tuna
Whales
Crayfish
Soles
Cod

Loa (riv.) ....F 8
Magellan (str.) ....E 14
Maipo (mt.) ....O 10
Navarino (isl.) ....G 14
O'Higgins (lake) ....F 13
Ojos del Salado (mt.).....G 9
Penas (gulf) ....E 13
Taitao (pen.) ....E 13
Tierra del Fuego (isl.)...G 14

COLOMBIA
CITIES and TOWNS
Arauca 7,613 ....F 2
Barrancabermeja 87,191 ..F 2
Barranquilla 661,009 .....F 1
Bogotá (cap.) 2,696,270 ..F 3
Bolivar ....E 3
Bucaramanga 291,661 ....F 2
Buenaventura 115,770 ....E 3
Buga 71,016 ....E 3
Cali 898,253 ....E 1
Cartagena 292,512 ....F 1
Chiquinquirá 21,727 .....F 2
Ciénaga 42,546 ....F 1
Cúcuta 219,772 ....F 2
Facatativá 27,892 ....F 3
Florencia 31,817 ....E 3
Ibagué 176,223 ....E 3
Ipiales 30,871 ....E 3
Leticia 6,285 ....F 4
Magangué 34,396 ....E 2
Manizales 199,904 ....E 2
Medellín 1,070,924 ......F 2
Mitú 1,637 ....F 3
Mocoa 6,221 ....E 3
Montería 89,583 ....F 3
Neiva 105,476 ....F 3
Ocaña 38,352 ....F 2
Palmira 140,481 ....E 3
Pamplona 31,817 ....F 2
Pasto 119,339 ....E 3
Pereira 174,128 ....E 3
Popayán 77,669 ....E 3
Puerto Carreño 2,172 ....G 2
Puerto Wilches 5,282 ....F 2
Quibdó 28,040 ....E 2
San Marcos 26,542 ......E 2
Santa Marta 102,484 ....F 1
Sincelejo 68,797 ....E 2
Sogamoso 48,891 ....F 2
Tulua 86,736 ....E 3
Tumaco 38,742 ....E 3
Tunja 51,620 ....F 3
Villavicencio 82,869 ....F 3
Yarumal 21,333 ....E 2

OTHER FEATURES
Alto Ritacuva (mt.) ......F 2
Apaporis (riv.) ....F 3
Arauca (riv.) ....F 2
Caquetá (riv.) ....F 4
Casanare (riv.) ....F 2
Cauca (riv.) ....E 2
Central, Cordillera (mts.).E 2
Guainía (riv.) ....G 3
Guajira (pen.) ....F 1
Guaviare (riv.) ....F 3
Huila (mt.) ....E 3
Inírida (riv.) ....G 3
Magdalena (riv.) ....F 2
Meta (riv.) ....G 2
Occidental, Cordillera (mts.)..E 3
Oriental, Cordillera (mts.)..F 3
Orinoco (riv.) ....G 2
Putumayo (riv.) ....F 3
Tolima (mt.) ....E 3
Vaupés (riv.) ....F 3
Vichada (riv.) ....F 3

ECUADOR
CITIES and TOWNS
Ambato 77,955 ....E 4
Babahoyo 28,914 ....D 4
Baquerizo Moreno 1,311 ..D 7
Cuenca 104,470 ....E 4
Esmeraldas 60,364 .....D 3
Guayaquil 823,219 .....D 4
Ibarra 41,335 ....E 3
Jipijapa 19,996 ....D 4
Latacunga 21,921 ......E 4
Loja 47,697 ....E 4
Macas 1,934 ....E 4
Machala 69,170 ....D 4
Manta 64,519 ....D 4
Pasaje 20,790 ....E 4
Portoviejo 59,550 ......D 4
Puerto Villamil ....D 7
Quito (cap.) 599,828 ...E 4
Riobamba 58,087 ......E 4
Santa Elena 7,687 .....D 4
Santa Rosa 19,696 .....E 4
Tena ....E 4
Tulcán 24,398 ....E 4

OTHER FEATURES
Chimborazo (mt.) ......E 4
Cotopaxi (mt.) ....E 4
Guayaquil (gulf) ....D 4
Morona (riv.) ....E 4
Napo (riv.) ....E 4
Occidental, Cordillera (mts.)..E 4
Pastaza (riv.) ....E 4
Real, Cordillera (mts.) ..E 4
Santiago (riv.) ....E 4

FALKLAND ISLANDS
CITIES and TOWNS
Stanley (cap.) ....J 14

OTHER FEATURES
East Falkland (isl.) .....J 14
Falkland (sound) ....H 14
West Falkland (isl.) ....H 14

FRENCH GUIANA
CITIES and TOWNS
Cayenne (cap.) 37,097 ..K 2
Guisanbourg ....K 3
Iracoubo 483 ....K 2
Mana 623 ....K 2
Saint-Georges 921 .....K 3
St-Laurent du Maroni 5,042. K 2

OTHER FEATURES
Devils (isl.) ....K 2
Maroni (riv.) ....K 3
Oyapock (riv.) ....K 3

GUYANA
CITIES and TOWNS
Corriverton ●10,502 ....J 2
Georgetown (cap.) 63,184 .J 2
Morawhanna ●292 ......J 2
New Amsterdam 17,782 ..J 2

OTHER FEATURES
Courantyne (riv.) ......J 3
Cuyuni (riv.) ....H 2
Essequibo (riv.) ....J 2
Kaieteur (falls) ....J 3
Mazaruni (riv.) ....J 3
Roraima (mt.) ....H 2
Rupununi (riv.) ....J 3

PARAGUAY
CITIES and TOWNS
Asunción (cap.) 387,676 ..J 9
Concepción 19,392 .....J 8
Encarnación 23,343 ....J 9
Fuerte Olimpo 3,063 ....J 8
Mariscal Estigarribia 3,150 ..H 8
Puerto Casado 4,078 ....J 8
Puerto Guaraní 302 ....J 8
Puerto Sastre 160 ......J 8
Villarrica 17,687 ......J 9

OTHER FEATURES
Gran Chaco (reg.) .....H 8
Itaipu (res.) ....K 8
Paraguay (riv.) ....J 8
Paraná (riv.) ....K 9
Pilcomayo (riv.) ....H 8

PERU
CITIES and TOWNS
Arequipa 447,431 ......F 7
Ayacucho 68,535 ......F 6
Cajamarca 60,280 .....E 5
Callao 441,374 ....E 6
Cañete 15,277 ....E 6
Catacaos 30,927 ......D 5
Cerro de Pasco 71,558 ..E 6
Chiclayo 280,244 ......E 5
Chimbote 216,406 .....E 5
Chincha Alta 37,475 ....E 6
Coracora 4,598 ....F 7
Cusco 181,604 ....F 6
Huacho 43,402 ....E 6
Huancavelica 20,889 ...E 6
Huancayo 165,132 .....F 6

Huánuco 52,628 ....E 6
Huaraz 45,116 ....E 6
Ica 111,087 ....E 6
Ilo 31,549 ....F 7
Iquitos 173,629 ....F 4
Jauja 14,630 ....E 6
Juliaca 77,976 ....F 6
Lima (cap.) 375,957 ...E 6
Machupicchu 544 .....F 6
Matarani ....F 7
Mollendo 21,206 ......F 7
Moquegua 21,488 .....F 7
Nazca 22,756 ....F 6
Pacasmayo 17,588 ....D 5
Paita 18,749 ....D 5
Pisco 53,414 ....E 6
Piura 186,354 ....D 5
Pucallpa 91,953 ......E 5
Puerto Maldonado 12,609..G 6
Puno 66,477 ....F 7
Sechura (bay) ....D 5
Sullana 80,947 ....D 4
Supe 10,061 ....E 6
Tacna 92,862 ....F 7
Talara 55,122 ....D 4
Tarma 34,369 ....E 6
Trujillo 354,557 ....E 5
Tumbes 48,187 ....D 4

OTHER FEATURES
Aguja (pt.) ....D 5
Altiplano (plat.) ....F 7
Apurímac (riv.) ....F 6
Central, Cordillera (mts.)..E 5
Huascarán (mt.) ......E 5
Madre de Dios (riv.) ...G 6
Marañón (riv.) ....E 4
Misti, El (mt.) ....F 7
Montaña, La (reg.) .....F 5
Napo (riv.) ....F 4

Occidental, Cordillera (mts.)..F 6
Oriental, Cordillera (mts.)..E 6
Paracas (pen.) ....E 6
Putumayo (riv.) ....F 4
Real, Cordillera (mts.) ..F 6
Titicaca (lake) ....F 7
Ucayali (riv.) ....E 5
Urubamba (riv.) ....F 6
Vilcanota (mt.) ....F 6

SURINAME
CITIES and TOWNS
Albina 1,000 ....K 3
Groningen 600 ....J 2
Nieuw-Nickerie 7,400 ...J 2
Paramaribo (cap.) ●67,905..K 2
Totness 1,300 ....J 2

OTHER FEATURES
Coeroeni (riv.) ....J 3
Tapanahoni (riv.) ......J 3

URUGUAY
CITIES and TOWNS
Artigas 29,256 ....J 10
Canelones 15,938 .....J 10
Colonia 16,895 ....J 10
Durazno 25,811 ....J 10
Florida 25,030 ....J 10
Fray Bentos 19,569 ....J 10
Maldonado 32,159 .....K 11
Melo 38,260 ....K 10
Mercedes 34,667 .....J 10
Minas 35,433 ....K 10

Montevideo (cap.) 1,173,254. J 11
Paysandú 62,412 ......J 10
Rivera 49,013 ....J 10
Rocha 21,612 ....K 10
Salto 72,948 ....J 10
San José 28,427 ......J 10
Tacuarembó 34,152 ....J 10
Treinta y Tres 25,757 ..K 10
Trinidad 17,598 ....J 10

OTHER FEATURES
Mirim (lag.) ....K 10
Negro (riv.) ....J 10
Plata, Río de la (est.) ...J 11
Uruguay (riv.) ....J 9

VENEZUELA
CITIES and TOWNS
Barcelona 78,201 .....H 2
Barinas 56,329 ....G 2
Barquisimeto 330,815 ..F 2
Bruzual 941 ....G 2
Calabozo 37,282 ......G 2
Caracas (cap.) 1,035,499..G 1
Carora 36,115 ....F 1
Carúpano 50,935 .....H 1
Ciudad Bolívar 103,728 ..H 2
Ciudad Piar 3,965 .....H 2
Coro 68,701 ....G 1
Cumaná 119,751 ......H 1
El Tigre 49,801 ....H 2
El Tocuyo 19,351 .....G 2
Guanare 34,148 ......G 2
La Guaira 20,344 .....G 1
Los Teques 63,106 ....G 1
Maracaibo 651,574 ....F 1
Maracay 255,134 .....G 1
Maturín 98,188 ....H 2

Mérida 74,214 ....F 2
Puerto Ayacucho 10,417 ..G 2
Puerto Cabello 72,103 ...G 1
Puerto La Cruz 63,276 ..H 1
San Carlos 21,029 .....G 2
San Cristóbal 151,717 ..F 2
San Felipe 43,801 .....G 1
San Fernando 38,960 ...G 2
Trujillo 25,921 ....F 2
Tucacas 4,780 ....G 1
Tucupita 21,417 ......H 2
Valencia 367,171 ......G 2
Valera 76,740 ....F 2
Valle de la Pascua 36,809 ..G 2
Villa de Cura 27,832 ...G 2

OTHER FEATURES
Angel (fall) ....H 2
Arauca (riv.) ....F 2
Apure (riv.) ....F 2
Bolívar (mt.) ....F 2
Caroní (riv.) ....H 3
Casiquiare, Brazo (riv.) ..G 3
Maracaibo (lake) ......F 2
Margarita (isl.) ....H 1
Mérida (mts.) ....F 2
Orinoco (riv.) ....G 2
Paraguana (pen.) ......F 1
Paria (gulf) ....H 1
Serpents Mouth (str.) ..H 2
Tortuga, La (isl.) ......G 1
Venezuela (gulf) ......F 1

*City and suburb.
†Population of metropolitan area.
△Population of commune.
●Population of district, sub-district or division.

South America
Southern Part
LAMBERT AZIMUTHAL EQUAL-AREA PROJECTION
SCALE OF MILES
0   100   200   300   400   500
SCALE OF KILOMETERS
0   100 200 300 400 500

Capitals of Countries ....☆
Other Capitals ....△
International Boundaries ....
Other Boundaries ....

© Copyright HAMMOND INCORPORATED, Maplewood, N.J.

North America

LAMBERT AZIMUTHAL EQUAL-AREA PROJECTION

MILES
0 100 200 400 600 800

KILOMETERS
0 100 200 400 600 800

Capitals of Countries .... ●
Other Capitals .... ◉
International Boundaries .... —·—·—
Other Boundaries .... — — —

● Copyright HAMMOND INCORPORATED, Maplewood, N.J.

Population Distribution

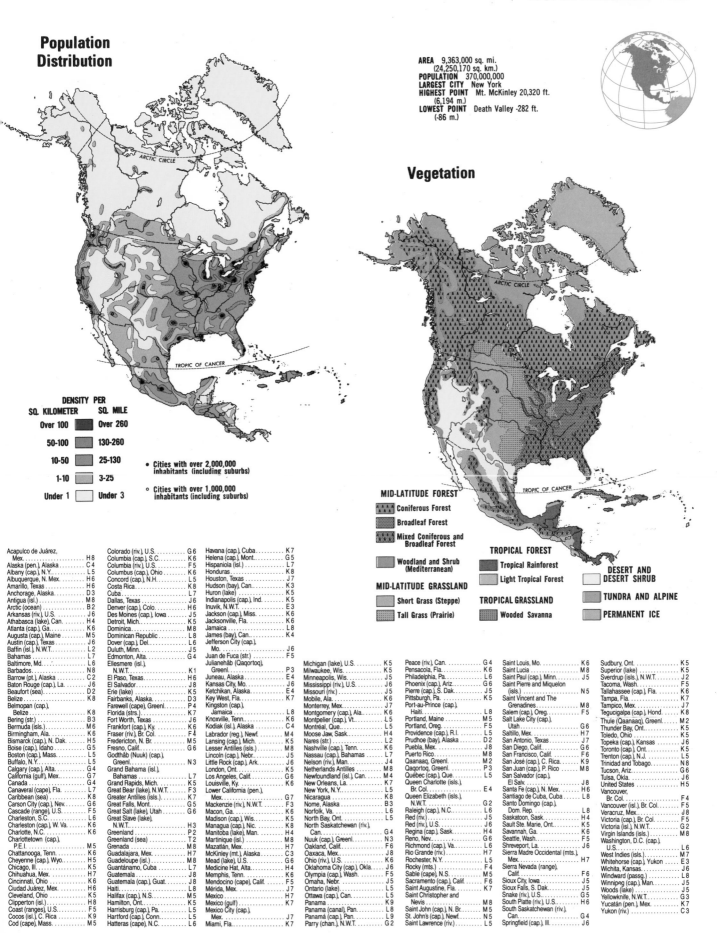

AREA 9,363,000 sq. mi.
(24,250,170 sq. km.)
POPULATION 370,000,000
LARGEST CITY New York
HIGHEST POINT Mt. McKinley 20,320 ft.
(6,194 m.)
LOWEST POINT Death Valley -282 ft.
(-86 m.)

Vegetation

DENSITY PER

SQ. KILOMETER	SQ. MILE
Over 100	Over 260
50-100	130-260
10-50	25-130
1-10	3-25
Under 1	Under 3

• Cities with over 2,000,000 inhabitants (including suburbs)
○ Cities with over 1,000,000 inhabitants (including suburbs)

MID-LATITUDE FOREST
- Coniferous Forest
- Broadleaf Forest
- Mixed Coniferous and Broadleaf Forest
- Woodland and Shrub (Mediterranean)

MID-LATITUDE GRASSLAND
- Short Grass (Steppe)
- Tall Grass (Prairie)

TROPICAL FOREST
- Tropical Rainforest
- Light Tropical Forest

TROPICAL GRASSLAND
- Wooded Savanna

DESERT AND DESERT SHRUB

TUNDRA AND ALPINE

PERMANENT ICE

Canada

CONIC PROJECTION

SCALE OF MILES

0 50 100 200 300

SCALE OF KILOMETERS

0 50 100 200 300 400 500

Capitals of Countries	☆
Provincial & Territorial Capitals	△
Administrative Centers	⊙
International Boundaries	
Provincial Boundaries	
Regional Boundaries	

Scale 1:19,600,000

© Copyright HAMMOND INCORPORATED, Maplewood, N. J.

AREA 3,851,787 sq. mi. (9,976,139 sq. km.)
POPULATION 24,343,181
CAPITAL Ottawa
LARGEST CITY Montréal
HIGHEST POINT Mt. Logan 19,524 ft. (5,951 m.)
MONETARY UNIT Canadian dollar
MAJOR LANGUAGES English, French
MAJOR RELIGIONS Protestantism, Roman Catholicism

Population Distribution

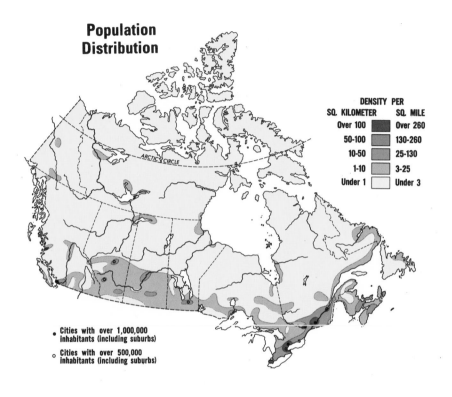

DENSITY PER

SQ. KILOMETER	SQ. MILE
Over 100	Over 260
50-100	130-260
10-50	25-130
1-10	3-25
Under 1	Under 3

● Cities with over 1,000,000 inhabitants (including suburbs)

○ Cities with over 500,000 inhabitants (including suburbs)

Vegetation

MID-LATITUDE FOREST
Coniferous Forest
Broadleaf Forest
Mixed Coniferous and Broadleaf Forest

MID-LATITUDE GRASSLAND
Short Grass (Steppe)
Tall Grass (Prairie)

DESERT AND DESERT SHRUB
TUNDRA AND ALPINE
PERMANENT ICE

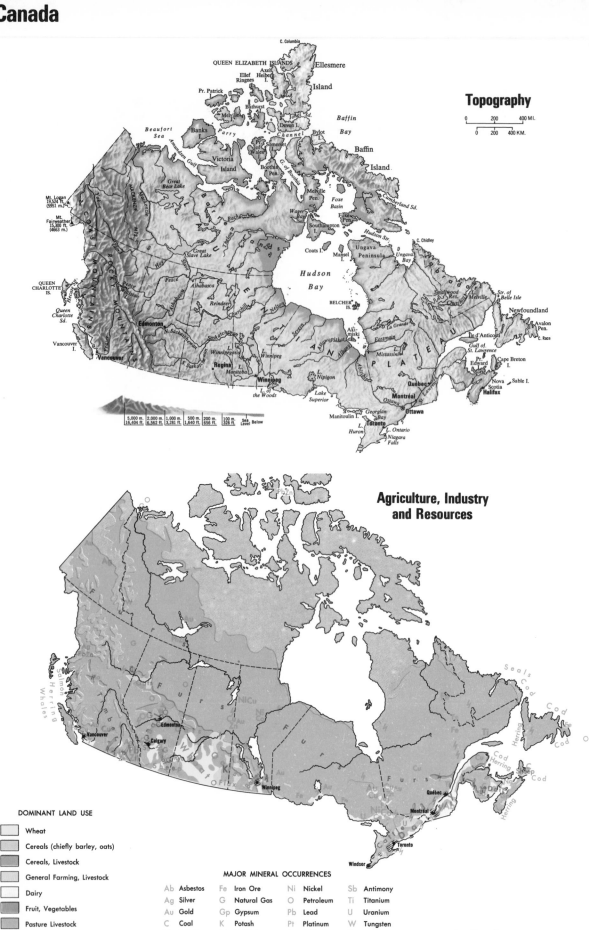

Topography

0 200 400 MI.
0 200 400 KM.

C. Columbia

QUEEN ELIZABETH ISLANDS

Ellesmere
Island

Ellef
Ringnes
Axel
Heiberg
Pr. Patrick
Bathurst
Melville
Devon I.
Jones
Baffin
Bay

Beaufort
Sea
Banks
Parry
Channel
Somerset
Pr. of
Wales
Bylot

Baffin
Island

Amundsen Gulf

Victoria
Island

Boothia
Pen.

G. of Boothia

Cumberland Sd.

Mt. Logan
19,524 ft.
(5951 m.)

Great
Bear Lake

MACKENZIE MTS.

Back

Melville
Pen.

Foxe
Basin

C. Chidley

Mt. Fairweather
15,300 ft.
(4663 m.)

Great
Slave Lake

Wager
Bay
Southampton
I.
Foxe
Pen.

Hudson Str.

Ungava
Peninsula

Ungava
Bay

Peace
Liard
Peace

Athabasca

Reindeer
Lake
Coats I.
Mansel
I.

QUEEN
CHARLOTTE
IS.

Edmonton

N. Saskatchewan
Churchill
Nelson

Hudson
Bay

BELCHER
IS.

Smallwood
Res.
Churchill
Melville

Str. of
Belle Isle

Queen
Charlotte
Sd.

Hecate Str.

COAST MOUNTAINS

ROCKY MOUNTAINS

Fraser

Saskatchewan

Winnipegosis

L.
Winnipeg

Severn
Albany
Akimiski
I.

La Grande
Eastmain
Mistassini

Newfoundland

Avalon
Pen.
C. Race

Île d'Anticosti

Vancouver
I.

Vancouver

S. Saskat.
Regina

Manitoba

L.
Manitoba

LAURENTIAN

Attawapiskat

Abitibi

PLATEAU

Gulf of
St. Lawrence

Pr.
Edward
I.
Cape Breton
I.

Nova
Scotia
Sable I.
Halifax

Winnipeg

L.
of the Woods
L.
Nipigon
Lake
Superior

Québec

Montréal
St. Lawrence
Ottawa

Georgian
Bay

Manitoulin I.
Toronto
L. Huron
L. Ontario
Niagara
Falls

5,000 ft. 2,000 m. 1,000 m. 500 m. 200 m. 100 m. Sea
16,404 ft. 6,562 ft. 3,281 ft. 1,640 ft. 656 ft. 328 ft. Level Below

Agriculture, Industry and Resources

Pb Zn

Seals
Cod

Salmon
Herring
Whales

Cod

Edmonton

Calgary

Ni Cu

Furs

Au

Herring
Cod
Cod

Cod
Herring
Sheep
Cod

Winnipeg

Furs

Cu

Québec

Montréal

Herring

Toronto

Windsor

DOMINANT LAND USE

Wheat

Cereals (chiefly barley, oats)

Cereals, Livestock

General Farming, Livestock

Dairy

Fruit, Vegetables

Pasture Livestock

Range Livestock

Forests

Nonagricultural Land

MAJOR MINERAL OCCURRENCES

Ab	Asbestos	Fe	Iron Ore	Ni	Nickel	Sb	Antimony
Ag	Silver	G	Natural Gas	O	Petroleum	Ti	Titanium
Au	Gold	Gp	Gypsum	Pb	Lead	U	Uranium
C	Coal	K	Potash	Pt	Platinum	W	Tungsten
Co	Cobalt	Mo	Molybdenum	S	Sulfur	Zn	Zinc
Cu	Copper	Na	Salt				

Water Power

Major Industrial Areas

AREA 156,184 sq. mi. (404,517 sq. km.)
POPULATION 567,681
CAPITAL St. John's
LARGEST CITY St. John's
HIGHEST POINT in Torngat Mountains
5,420 ft. (1,652 m.)
SETTLED IN 1610
ADMITTED TO CONFEDERATION 1949
PROVINCIAL FLOWER Pitcher Plant

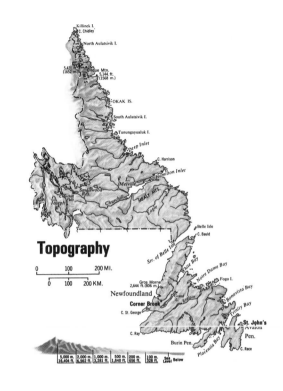

Topography

0 100 200 MI.
0 100 200 KM.

Newfoundland

© Copyright by HAMMOND INCORPORATED, Maplewood, N.J.

Newfoundland

SCALE
0 10 20 40 60 80 100 MI.
0 1020 40 60 80 100KM.
Provincial Capital.....................⊛
Provincial Boundaries........._____

Agriculture, Industry and Resources

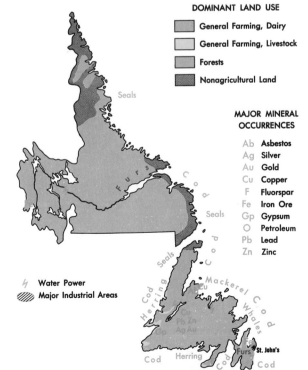

DOMINANT LAND USE

- General Farming, Dairy
- General Farming, Livestock
- Forests
- Nonagricultural Land

MAJOR MINERAL OCCURRENCES

Ab	Asbestos
Ag	Silver
Au	Gold
Cu	Copper
F	Fluorspar
Fe	Iron Ore
Gp	Gypsum
O	Petroleum
Pb	Lead
Zn	Zinc

⚡ Water Power
▨ Major Industrial Areas

NOVA SCOTIA

COUNTIES

Annapolis 22,522 .... C 4
Antigonish 18,110 .... F 3
Cape Breton 127,035 .... H 3
Colchester 43,224 .... D 3
Cumberland 35,231 .... D 3
Digby 21,689 .... C 4
Guysborough 12,752 .... F 3
Halifax 288,126 .... D 4
Hants 33,121 .... D 4
Inverness 22,337 .... G 2
Kings 49,739 .... C 4
Lunenburg 45,746 .... D 4
Pictou 50,350 .... F 3
Queens 13,126 .... C 4
Richmond 12,284 .... H 3
Shelburne 17,328 .... C 5
Victoria 8,432 .... H 2
Yarmouth 26,290 .... C 5

CITIES and TOWNS

Alder Point 651 .... H 2
Aldershot .... D 3
Amherst 9,684 .... D 3
Annapolis Royal® 631 .... C 4
Antigonish® 5,205 .... F 3
Arichat 824 .... H 3
Aylesford 744 .... D 3
Baddeck® 972 .... H 2
Barrington Passage 722 .... C 5
Bear River-Sissiboo 854 .... C 4
Beaverbank 1,322 .... E 4
Berwick 1,699 .... D 3
Bridgetown 1,047 .... C 4
Bridgewater 6,669 .... D 4
Brookfield 619 .... E 3
Brooklyn 1,269 .... C 4
Cambridge Station 799 .... D 3
Canning 763 .... D 3
Canso 1,255 .... H 3
Centreville 765 .... C 4
Chéticamp 1,022 .... G 2
Chester 1,131 .... D 4
Chester Basin 639 .... D 4
Church Point 318 .... B 4
Clark's Harbour 1,059 .... C 5
Coldbrook Station 617 .... D 3
Cow Bay 670 .... E 4
Dartmouth 62,277 .... E 4
Debert 618 .... E 3
Digby® 2,558 .... C 4
Dominion 2,856 .... J 2
Donkin 873 .... J 2
Ellershouse-Hartville 662 .... D 4
Elmsdale 1,172 .... E 4
Enfield 1,510 .... E 4
Fall River 1,897 .... E 4
Falmouth 1,110 .... D 3
Glace Bay 21,466 .... J 2
Guysborough® 496 .... G 3
Halifax (cap.)® 114,594 .... E 4
Halifax ®277,727 .... E 4
Hantsport 1,395 .... D 3
Herring Cove 1,323 .... E 4
Hilden 1,262 .... E 3

Ingonish 471 .... H 2
Inverness 2,013 .... G 2
Judique 925 .... G 3
Kentville® 4,974 .... D 3
Kingston 1,612 .... D 4
Lakeside 936 .... E 4
Lantz 1,172 .... E 4
Liverpool® 3,304 .... C 4
Lockeport 929 .... C 5
Louisbourg 1,410 .... J 3
Louisdale 979 .... G 3
Lower West Pubnico 790 .... C 5
Lunenburg® 3,014 .... D 4
Mahone Bay 1,228 .... D 4
Meteghan 890 .... B 4
Middleton 1,834 .... C 4
Milford Station 748 .... E 3
Milton 1,678 .... C 4
Mount Uniacke 1,145 .... E 4
Mulgrave 1,099 .... G 3
Musquodoboit Harbour 936 .... E 4
New Glasgow 10,464 .... F 3
New Victoria 1,374 .... H 2

New Waterford 8,808 .... J 2
North Sydney 7,820 .... H 2
Oxford 1,470 .... E 3
Parrsboro 1,799 .... D 3
Pictou® 4,628 .... F 3
Port Hastings 312 .... G 3
Port Hawkesbury 3,850 .... G 3
Port Hood® 701 .... G 2
Port Morien 717 .... J 2
Port Williams 1,227 .... D 3
Prospect 693 .... E 4
Pugwash 648 .... E 3
Reserve Mines 2,472 .... H 2
River Hébert 835 .... D 3
Saint Peters 669 .... H 3
Sandy Point 691 .... C 5
Scotchtown 2,037 .... H 2
Sheet Harbour 819 .... F 4
Shelburne® 2,303 .... C 5
Shubenacadie 984 .... E 3
Springhill 4,896 .... E 3
Stellarton 5,435 .... F 3

Stewiacke 1,174 .... E 3
Sydney® 29,444 .... H 2
Sydney Mines 8,501 .... H 2
Terence Bay 960 .... E 4
Thorburn 1,014 .... F 3
Three Mile Plains 1,355 .... D 4
Timberlea 1,159 .... E 4
Trenton 3,154 .... F 3
Truro® 12,552 .... E 3
Waterville 687 .... D 3
Waverley 1,699 .... E 4
Wedgeport 827 .... C 5
Western Shore 1,712 .... D 4
Westmount 3,097 .... J 2
Westville 4,522 .... F 3
Wileville 746 .... D 4
Windsor® 3,646 .... D 3
Wolfville 3,235 .... D 3
Yarmouth® 7,475 .... B 5

OTHER FEATURES

Advocate (bay) .... D 3
Ainslie (lake) .... G 2
Amet (sound) .... E 3
Andrew (isl.) .... H 3
Annapolis (basin) .... C 4
Annapolis (riv.) .... D 3
Antigonish (harb.) .... G 3
Argos (cape) .... H 2
Aspy (bay) .... H 2
Avon (riv.) .... D 4
Baccaro (pt.) .... C 5
Baddeck (riv.) .... G 2
Barachois (pt.) .... G 4
Barren (isl.) .... G 4
Barrington (bay) .... C 5
Berry (head) .... E 4
Bedford (basin) .... E 4
Boularderie (isl.) .... H 2
Bras d'Or (lake) .... H 2
Breton (cape) .... H 3
Brier (isl.) .... B 4
Canso (cape) .... G 3
Canso (str.) .... G 3
Cap d'Or (cape) .... D 3

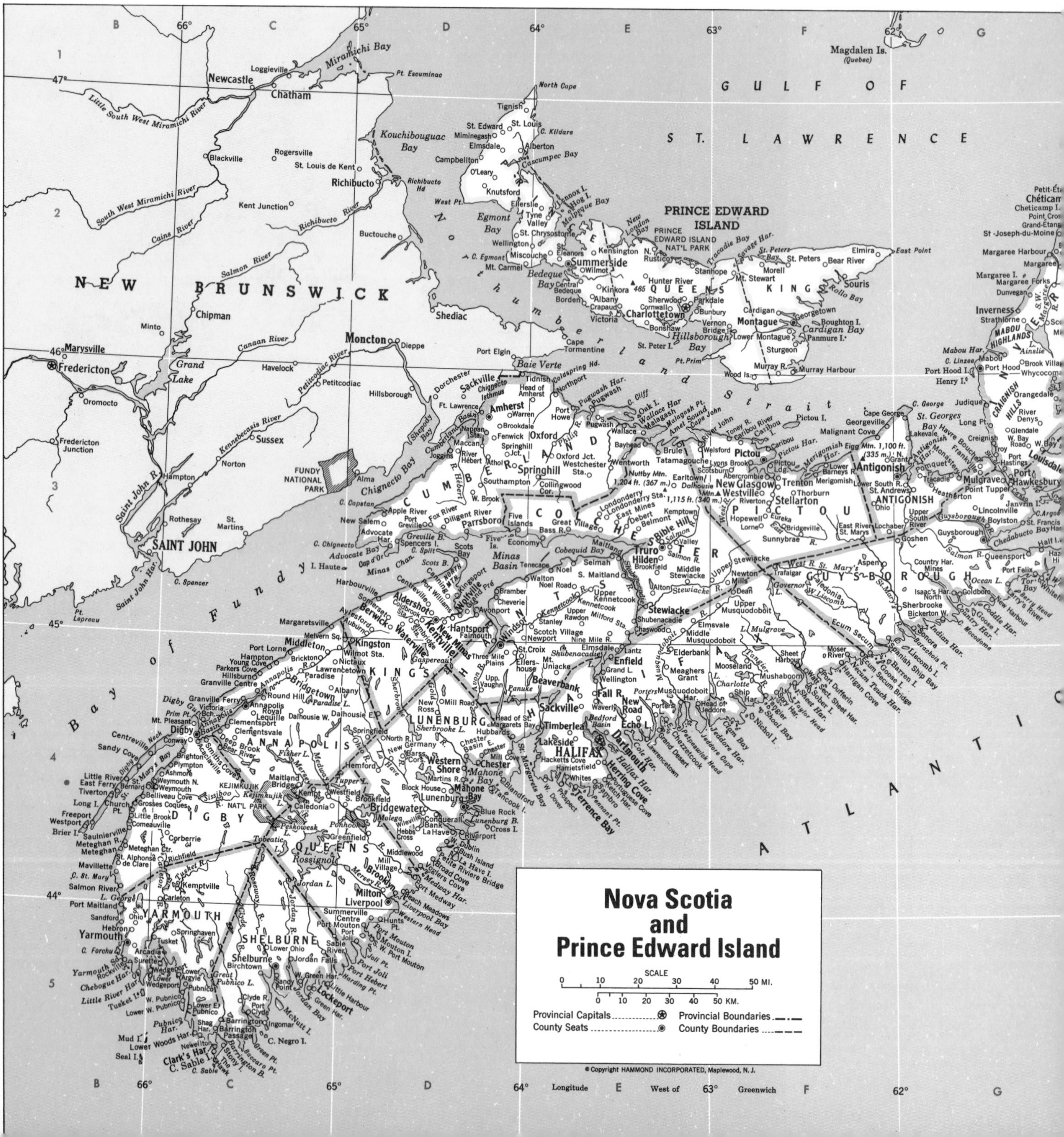

Cape Breton (isl.) . . . . J 2
Cape Breton Highlands Nat'l Park . . . . H 2
Cape Negro (isl.) . . . . C 5
Cape Sable (isl.) . . . . C 5
Capstan (cape) . . . . D 3
Caribou (isl.) . . . . F 3
Carleton (riv.) . . . . C 4
Charlotte (lake) . . . . F 4
Chebogue (harb.) . . . . B 5
Chedabucto (bay) . . . . G 3
Chéticamp (isl.) . . . . G 2
Chignecto (bay) . . . . D 3
Chignecto (cape) . . . . C 3
Chignecto (isth.) . . . . D 3
Clam (bay) . . . . F 4
Cliff (cape) . . . . E 3
Clyde (riv.) . . . . C 5
Cobequid (bay) . . . . E 3
Coddle (harb.) . . . . G 3
Coldspring (head) . . . . E 3
Cole (harb.) . . . . E 4
Country (harb.) . . . . G 3
Craignish (hills) . . . . G 3
Cross (isl.) . . . . D 4
Cumberland (basin) . . . . D 3
Dalhousie (mt.) . . . . E 3
Dauphin (cape) . . . . H 2
Digby Gut (chan.) . . . . C 4
Digby Neck (pen.) . . . . B 4
East (bay) . . . . H 3
East (riv.) . . . . F 3
East Bay (hills) . . . . H 3
Egmont (cape) . . . . H 2
Eigg (mt.) . . . . F 3
Fisher (lake) . . . . C 4
Five (isls.) . . . . D 3
Forchu (bay) . . . . H 3
Forchu (cape) . . . . B 5
Framboise Cove (bay) . . . . H 3
Fundy (bay) . . . . C 3
Gabarus (bay) . . . . H 3
Gabarus (cape) . . . . J 3
Gaspereau (lake) . . . . D 4
George (cape) . . . . G 3
George (lake) . . . . B 5

PRINCE EDWARD ISLAND

AREA 2,184 sq. mi. (5,657 sq. km.)
POPULATION 122,506
CAPITAL Charlottetown
LARGEST CITY Charlottetown
HIGHEST POINT 465 ft. (142 m.)
SETTLED IN 1720
ADMITTED TO CONFEDERATION 1873
PROVINCIAL FLOWER Lady's Slipper

NOVA SCOTIA

AREA 21,425 sq. mi. (55,491 sq. km.)
POPULATION 847,442
CAPITAL Halifax
LARGEST CITY Halifax
HIGHEST POINT Cape Breton Highlands 1,747 ft. (532 m.)
SETTLED IN 1605
ADMITTED TO CONFEDERATION 1867
PROVINCIAL FLOWER Trailing Arbutus or Mayflower

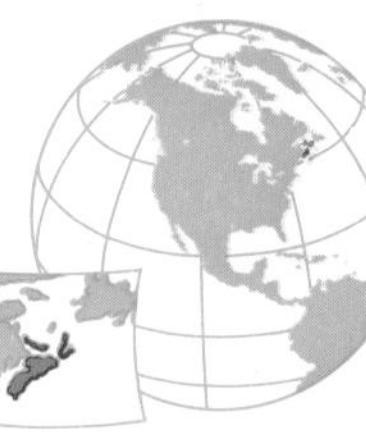

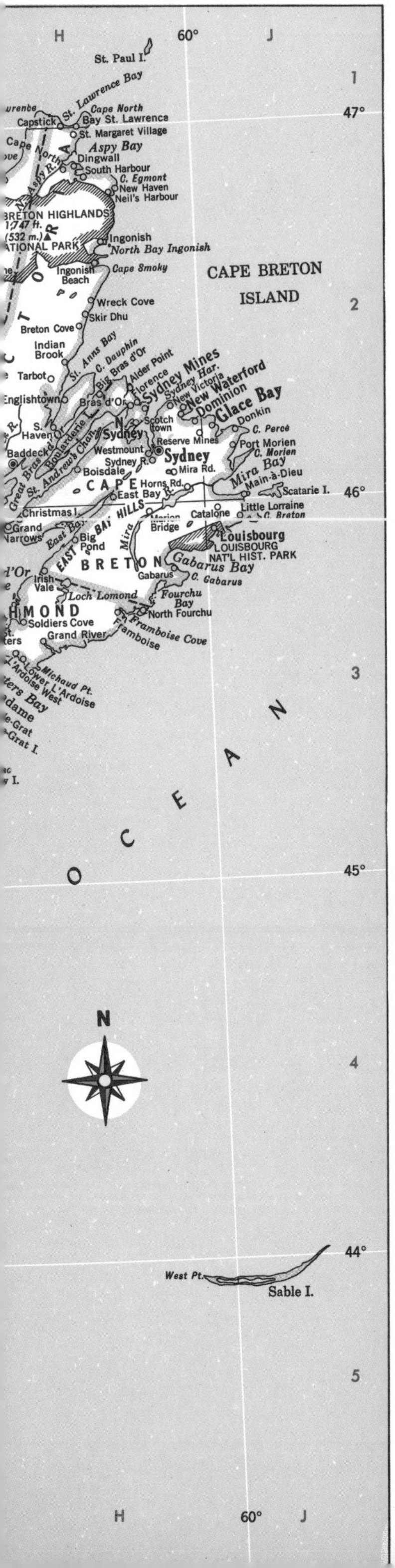

H
60°
J
St. Paul I.
St. Lawrence Bay
Cape North
Bay St. Lawrence
St. Margaret Village
Aspy Bay
Dingwall
South Harbour
C. Egmont
New Haven
Neil's Harbour
BRETON HIGHLANDS
Ingonish
North Bay Ingonish
Cape Smoky
Ingonish Beach
CAPE BRETON
ISLAND
Wreck Cove
Skir Dhu
Breton Cove
Indian Brook
Tarbot
St. Anns Bay
C. Dauphin
Alder Point
Sydney Mines
Florence
New Victoria
New Waterford
Dominion
Glace Bay
Donkin
C. Percé
Port Morien
C. Morien
Reserve Mines
Sydney
Westmount
Mira Rd.
Mira Bay
Main-à-Dieu
Scatarie I.
Little Lorraine
C. Breton
East Bay
Louisbourg
LOUISBOURG NAT'L HIST. PARK
Gabarus Bay
Gabarus
C. Gabarus
Fourchu Bay
North Fourchu
Loch Lomond
Soldiers Cove
Grand River
Framboise Cove
Framboise
Irish Vale
Big Pond
Christmas I.
Grand Narrows
West Pt.
Sable I.
47°
46°
45°
44°
O C E A N
N
1
2
3
4
5

Topography

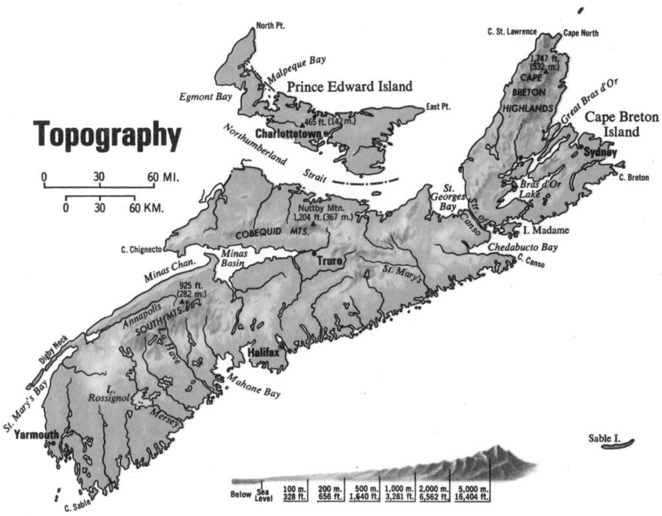

North Pt.
Malpeque Bay
Prince Edward Island
Egmont Bay
465 ft. (142 m.)
Charlottetown
East Pt.
Northumberland Strait
C. St. Lawrence
Cape North
1,747 ft. (532 m.)
CAPE BRETON HIGHLANDS
Great Bras d'Or
Cape Breton Island
Sydney
C. Breton
Bras d'Or Lake
St. Georges Bay
I. Madame
Chedabucto Bay
C. Canso
Nuttby Mtn. 1,204 ft. (367 m.)
COBEQUID MTS.
C. Chignecto
Minas Basin
Minas Chan.
Truro
St. Mary's
925 ft. (282 m.)
Annapolis
SOUTH MTS.
Digby Neck
St. Mary's Bay
L. Rossignol
Halifax
Mahone Bay
Yarmouth
C. Sable
Sable I.
0 30 60 MI.
0 30 60 KM.
Below Sea Level
100 m. 328 ft.
200 m. 656 ft.
500 m. 1,640 ft.
1,000 m. 3,281 ft.
2,000 m. 6,562 ft.
5,000 m. 16,404 ft.

Gold (riv.) . . . . D 4
Goose (isl.) . . . . F 4
Goose (isl.) . . . . G 3
Governor (lake) . . . . F 3
Great Bras d'Or (chan.) . . . . . . H 2
Great Pubnico (lake) . . . . C 5
Green (pt.) . . . . C 5
Greville (bay) . . . . D 3
Guysborough (riv.) . . . . G 3
Halifax (harb.) . . . . E 4
Harding (pt.) . . . . D 5
Haute (isl.) . . . . C 3
Hebert (riv.) . . . . D 3
Henry (isl.) . . . . G 3
Indian (harb.) . . . . G 3
Ingonish North (bay) . . . . H 2
Janvrin (isl.) . . . . G 3
Jeddore (harb.) . . . . F 4
John (cape) . . . . E 3
Joli (pt.) . . . . D 5
Jordan (bay) . . . . C 5
Jordan (lake) . . . . C 4
Jordan (riv.) . . . . C 5
Kejimkujik (lake) . . . . C 4
Kejimkujik Nat'l Park . . . . C 4
Kennetcook (riv.) . . . . E 3
La Have (isl.) . . . . D 4
La Have (riv.) . . . . D 4
Linzee (cape) . . . . G 2
Liscomb (isl.) . . . . G 4
Little River (harb.) . . . . B 5
Liverpool (bay) . . . . D 5
Lomond, Loch (lake) . . . . H 3
Long (isl.) . . . . B 4
Louisbourg Nat'l Hist. Park . . . J 3
Lunenburg (bay) . . . . D 4
Mabou (harb.) . . . . G 2
Mabou Highlands (hills) . . . . . . G 2
Madame (isl.) . . . . H 3
Mahone (bay) . . . . D 4
Malagash (pt.) . . . . E 3
Margaree (isl.) . . . . F 4
McNutt (isl.) . . . . C 5
Medway (harb.) . . . . D 4
Medway (riv.) . . . . C 4
Merigomish (harb.) . . . . F 3
Mersey (riv.) . . . . C 4
Michaud (pt.) . . . . H 3
Minas (basin) . . . . D 3
Minas (chan.) . . . . D 3
Mira (bay) . . . . J 2
Mira (riv.) . . . . H 3
Mocodome (cape) . . . . G 3
Molega (lake) . . . . D 4
Morien (cape) . . . . J 2
Mouton (isl.) . . . . D 5
Mud (isl.) . . . . B 5
Mulgrave (lake) . . . . F 3
Musquodoboit (riv.) . . . . E 4
Necum Teuch (harb.) . . . . F 4
Nichol (isl.) . . . . F 4
North (cape) . . . . H 1
North (mt.) . . . . D 3
North Aspy (riv.) . . . . H 2
North Bay Ingonish (bay) . . . . . H 2
North East Margaree (riv.) . . . . H 2
Northumberland (str.) . . . . E 2
Nuttby (mt.) . . . . E 3
Oak (isl.) . . . . E 3
Ocean (lake) . . . . G 3
Ohio (riv.) . . . . D 4
Panuke (lake) . . . . D 4
Paradise (lake) . . . . C 4
Pennant (pt.) . . . . E 4
Percé (cape) . . . . J 2
Peskowesk (lake) . . . . C 4
Petit-de-Grat (isl.) . . . . H 3
Petpeswick (head) . . . . E 4
Philip (riv.) . . . . E 3
Pictou (harb.) . . . . F 3
Pictou (isl.) . . . . F 3
Pleasant (bay) . . . . H 2
Ponhook (lake) . . . . D 4
Porters (lake) . . . . E 4
Port Hebert (harb.) . . . . D 5
Port Hood (isl.) . . . . G 2
Port Joli (harb.) . . . . D 5
Port Mouton (harb.) . . . . D 5
Poulet Cove (bay) . . . . H 2
Prim (pt.) . . . . C 4
Pubnico (harb.) . . . . C 5
Pugwash (harb.) . . . . E 3
Roseway (riv.) . . . . C 4
Rossignol (lake) . . . . C 4
Sable (cape) . . . . C 5
Sable (isl.) . . . . J 5
Saint Andrews (chan.) . . . . H 2
Saint Anns (bay) . . . . H 2
Saint Georges (bay) . . . . G 3
Saint Lawrence (bay) . . . . H 1
Saint Lawrence (cape) . . . . H 1
Saint Margarets (bay) . . . . E 4
Saint Mary (cape) . . . . B 4
Saint Marys (bay) . . . . B 4
Saint Mary's (riv.) . . . . F 3
Saint Patrick (chan.) . . . . G 3
Saint Paul (isl.) . . . . H 1
Saint Peters (bay) . . . . H 3
Salmon (riv.) . . . . E 3
Salmon (riv.) . . . . G 3
Scatarie (isl.) . . . . J 2
Scots (bay) . . . . D 3
Seall (isl.) . . . . B 5
Sheet (harb.) . . . . F 4
Sherbrooke (lake) . . . . D 4
Sherbrooke (riv.) . . . . D 4
Shoal (bay) . . . . F 4
Shubenacadie (lake) . . . . E 4
Shubenacadie (riv.) . . . . E 3
Sissiboo (riv.) . . . . C 4
Smoky (cape) . . . . H 2
Sober (isl.) . . . . F 4
South West Margaree (riv.) . . . G 2
Split (cape) . . . . D 3
Spry (harb.) . . . . F 4
Stewiacke (riv.) . . . . E 3
Sydney (harb.) . . . . H 2
Tangier (riv.) . . . . F 4
Taylor (head) . . . . F 4
Tobeatic (lake) . . . . C 4
Tor (bay) . . . . G 3
Tupper (lake) . . . . D 4
Tusket (isl.) . . . . B 5
Tusket (riv.) . . . . C 4
Verte (bay) . . . . D 2
Wallace (harb.) . . . . E 3
West (bay) . . . . G 3
West (pt.) . . . . H 5
West (riv.) . . . . F 3
Western (head) . . . . D 5
West Liscomb (riv.) . . . . F 3
West Saint Mary's (riv.) . . . . F 3
Whitehaven (harb.) . . . . G 3
Yarmouth (sound) . . . . B 5

PRINCE EDWARD ISLAND

COUNTIES

Kings 19,215 . . . . F 2
Prince 42,821 . . . . D 2
Queens 60,470 . . . . E 2

CITIES and TOWNS

Alberton 1,020 . . . . E 2
Bunbury 1,024 . . . . F 2
Charlottetown (cap.)⊙ 15,282 . E 2
Cornwall 1,838 . . . . E 2
Georgetown⊙ 737 . . . . F 2
Kensington 1,143 . . . . E 2
Miscouche 752 . . . . D 2
Montague 1,957 . . . . F 2
Murray Harbour 443 . . . . F 2
North Rustico 688 . . . . E 2
O'Leary 736 . . . . D 2
Parkdale 2,018 . . . . E 2
Saint Edward 650 . . . . D 2
Saint Eleanors 2,716 . . . . E 2
Sherwood 5,681 . . . . E 2
Souris 1,413 . . . . F 2
Summerside⊙ 7,828 . . . . E 2
Tignish 982 . . . . D 2
Wilmot 1,563 . . . . E 2

OTHER FEATURES

Bedeque (bay) . . . . E 2
Boughton (isl.) . . . . F 2
Cardigan (bay) . . . . F 2
Cascumpeque (bay) . . . . E 2
East (pt.) . . . . G 2
Egmont (bay) . . . . D 2
Egmont (cape) . . . . D 2
Hillsborough (bay) . . . . E 2
Hog (isl.) . . . . E 2
Kildare (cape) . . . . E 2
Lennox (isl.) . . . . E 2
Malpeque (bay) . . . . E 2
New London (bay) . . . . E 2
North (pt.) . . . . E 1
Northumberland (str.) . . . . D 2
Panmure (isl.) . . . . F 2
Prim (pt.) . . . . E 2
Prince Edward Island Nat'l Park . . . . E 2
Rollo (bay) . . . . F 2
Saint Lawrence (gulf) . . . . F 2
Saint Peters (bay) . . . . F 2
Saint Peters (isl.) . . . . E 2
Savage (harb.) . . . . F 2
Tracadie (bay) . . . . F 2
West (pt.) . . . . D 2
Wood (isls.) . . . . F 3

⊙County seat.
*Population of metropolitan area.

Agriculture, Industry and Resources

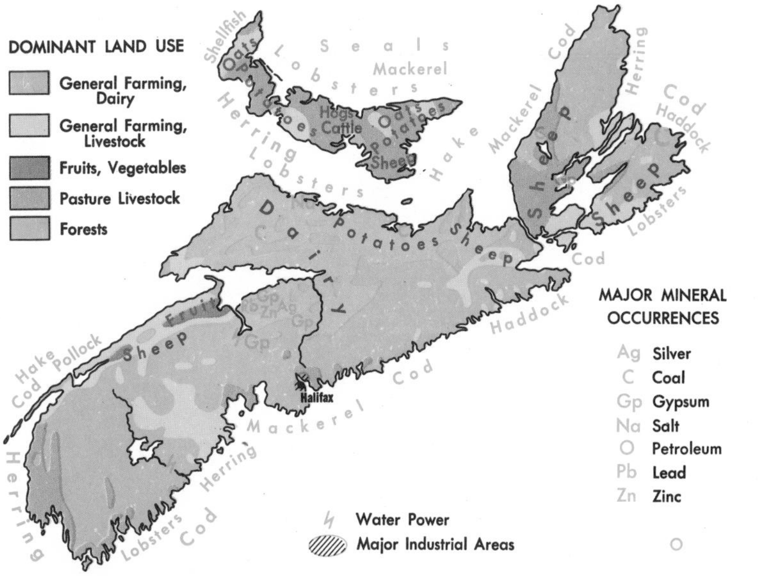

DOMINANT LAND USE
General Farming, Dairy
General Farming, Livestock
Fruits, Vegetables
Pasture Livestock
Forests
Shellfish
Seals
Mackerel
Lobsters
Oats
Potatoes
Hogs
Cattle
Sheep
Herring
Hake
Cod
Haddock
Dairy
Fruit
Pollock
Halifax
MAJOR MINERAL OCCURRENCES
Ag Silver
C Coal
Gp Gypsum
Na Salt
O Petroleum
Pb Lead
Zn Zinc
Water Power
Major Industrial Areas

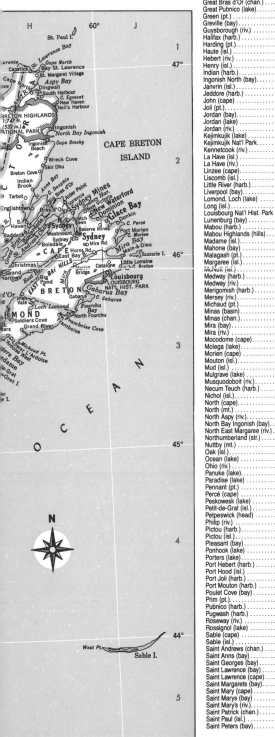

COUNTIES

Albert 23,632............F 3
Carleton 24,659..........C 2
Charlotte 26,571.........C 3
Gloucester 86,156........E 1
Kent 30,799.............E 2
King's 51,114............E 3
Madawaska 34,892.........B 1
Northumberland 54,134....D 2
Queen's 12,485...........D 3
Restigouche 40,593.......C 1
Saint John 86,148........E 3
Sunbury 21,012...........D 3
Victoria 20,815..........C 1
Westmorland 107,640......F 2
York 74,213.............C 3

CITIES and TOWNS

Acadie Siding 64.........E 2
Acadieville 176..........E 2
Adamsville 94............E 2
Albert Mines 120.........F 3
Alcida 174..............E 1
Aldouane 64.............E 2
Allardville 478.........E 1
Alma 329................F 3
Anagance 114............E 3
Anse-Bleue 562..........E 1

Apohaqui 341............E 3
Argyle 63...............C 2
Armstrong Brook 191.....E 1
Aroostook 403...........C 2
Arthurette 178..........C 2
Astle 201...............D 2
Atholville 1,694........D 1
Aulac 113...............F 3
Back River 455..........D 3
Baie-Sainte-Anne 709....F 1
Baie-Verte 175..........F 2
Bairdsville 81..........C 2
Baker Brook 527.........B 1
Balmoral 1,823..........D 1
Barachois 686...........F 2
Barnaby River 38........E 2
Barnettville 117........E 2
Bartibog Bridge 122.....E 1
Bas-Caraquet 1,859......F 1
Bass River 112..........E 2
Bath 794................C 2
Bathurst⊛ 15,705........E 1
Bayfield 81.............G 2
Bayside................C 3
Beaubois 211............E 1
Beaver Brook Station 95..E 1
Beaver Harbour 316......D 3
Beechwood 111...........C 2
Beersville 52...........E 2
Belledune 690...........E 1

Bellefleur 83...........C 1
Bellefond 243...........E 1
Belleisle Creek 145.....E 3
Benjamin River 171......D 1
Ben Lomond.............E 3
Benton 101..............C 2
Beresford 3,652.........E 1
Berry Mills 238.........E 2
Bertrand 1,268..........E 1
Berwick 129.............E 3
Black Point 131.........D 1
Black River 150.........E 3
Blacks Harbour 1,356....D 3
Blackville 892..........D 2
Blissfield 119..........D 2
Bloomfield Ridge 153....D 2
Bloomfield Station 62...E 3
Bocabec 34..............C 3
Boiestown 299...........D 2
Bonny River 153.........D 3
Bossé 193...............B 1
Bourgeois 215...........F 2
Brantville 1,066........E 1
Breau-Village 293.......F 2
Brest 94................E 2
Brewers Mills 199.......C 2
Briggs Corner 89........E 2
Bristol 824.............C 2
Brockway (Lower Brockway-
  Brockway) 97..........C 3

Browns Flat 295.........D 3
Buctouche 2,476.........F 2
Burnsville 156..........E 1
Burton⊛ 291.............D 2
Burtts Corner 484.......D 2
Cambridge-Narrows 433...E 3
Campbellton 9,818.......D 1
Canaan 115..............E 2
Canaan Forks 78.........E 2
Canaan Road 86..........E 2
Canterbury 474..........C 3
Cap-Bateau 417..........F 1
Cape Tormentine 229.....G 2
Cap Lumière 262.........F 2
Cap-Pelé 2,199..........F 2
Caraquet 4,315..........E 1
Carlingford 229.........C 2
Carlisle 75.............C 2
Caron Brook 171.........B 1
Carrolls Crossing 119...D 2
Castalia 145............D 4
Central Blissville 155..D 3
Centre-Saint-Simon (St.
  Simon) 991............E 1
Centreville 577.........C 2
Chance Harbour 63.......D 3
Charlo 1,603............D 1
Chatham 6,779...........E 2
Chatham Head............E 2
Chipman 1,829...........E 2

Clair 915...............B 1
Clarendon 80............D 3
Cliffordvale (Limestone-
  Cliffordvale) 69......C 2
Clifton 194.............E 1
Coal Branch 90..........E 2
Coal Creek 61...........E 2
Cocagne Cape 278........F 2
Cocagne-Cocagne Sud 600.F 2
Codys 125...............E 3
Coldstream 217..........C 2
Coles Island 160........E 3
College Bridge 536......F 2
Collette 198............E 2
Connell 58..............C 2
Connors 96..............B 1
Cork 54.................D 3
Cornhill 181............E 3
Coughlan 181............D 2
Cross Creek 192.........D 2
Cumberland Bay 231......E 2
Dalhousie⊛ 4,958........D 1
Dalhousie Junction 105..D 1
Darlington 749..........D 1
Daulnay 398.............E 1
Dawsonville 278.........E 1
Debec 200...............C 2
Dieppe 8,511............F 2
Dipper Harbour 166......D 3
Doaktown 1,009..........D 2

Dorchester⊛ 1,101.......F 3
Dorchester Crossing 605.F 2
Douglasville 1,091......D 1
Drummond 849............C 1
Duguayville 337.........E 1
Dumfries 150............C 3
Dupuis Corner 303.......F 2
Durham Bridge 255.......D 2
East Riverside-Kingshurst
  989...................E 3
Edmundston⊛ 12,044......B 1
Eel River Bridge 377....C 1
Eel River Crossing 1,431.D 1
Elgin 301...............E 3
Enniskillen 63..........D 3
Escuminac 194...........F 1
Evandale 58.............E 3
Evangeline 356..........F 1
Everett 48..............C 1
Fairfield 250...........E 2
Fairhaven 142...........C 4
Fairisle 415............E 1
Fairvale 3,960..........E 3
Ferry Road 325..........E 1
Fielding 197............C 2
Five Fingers 189........C 1
Flatlands 249...........D 1
Florenceville 709.......C 2
Forest City 25..........C 3
Fosterville 58..........C 3

Four Falls 69...........C 2
Fredericton (cap.)⊛ 43,723.D 3
Fredericton Junction 711.D 3
Gagetown⊛ 618...........D 3
Gardner Creek 56........E 3
Geary 654...............D 3
Germantown 62...........F 3
Gillespie 96............C 1
Glassville 147..........C 2
Glencoe 147.............D 1
Glenlivet 284...........D 1
Gloucester Junction 36..E 1
Gondola Point 3,076.....E 3
Grafton 385.............C 2
Grand Bay 3,173.........D 3
Grande-Anse 817.........E 1
Grand Falls 6,203.......C 1
Grand Falls Hill 152....C 1
Grand Harbour 614.......D 4
Gray Rapids 266.........E 2
Hampstead 87............D 3
Hampton⊛ 3,141..........E 3
Harcourt 127............E 2
Hardwick 114............F 1
Hardwood Ridge 191......D 2
Hartland 846............C 2
Harvey, Albert 58.......F 3
Harvey, York 356........D 3
Hatfield Point 176......E 3

New Brunswick

AREA 28,354 sq. mi. (73,437 sq. km.)
POPULATION 696,403
CAPITAL Fredericton
LARGEST CITY Saint John
HIGHEST POINT Mt. Carleton 2,690 ft.
   (820 m.)
SETTLED IN 1611
ADMITTED TO CONFEDERATION 1867
PROVINCIAL FLOWER Purple Violet

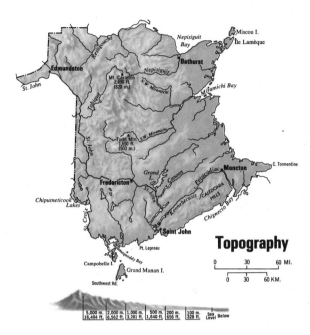

Topography

0   30   60 MI.
0   30   60 KM.

5,000 m. / 16,404 ft. | 2,000 m. / 6,562 ft. | 1,000 m. / 3,281 ft. | 500 m. / 1,640 ft. | 200 m. / 656 ft. | 100 m. / 328 ft. | Sea Level | Below

Agriculture, Industry and Resources

DOMINANT LAND USE

Cereals, Livestock

Dairy

Potatoes

General Farming, Livestock

Pasture Livestock

Forests

MAJOR MINERAL OCCURRENCES

Ag Silver   Pb Lead
C Coal   Sb Antimony
Cu Copper   Zn Zinc

⚡ Water Power
▨ Major Industrial Areas

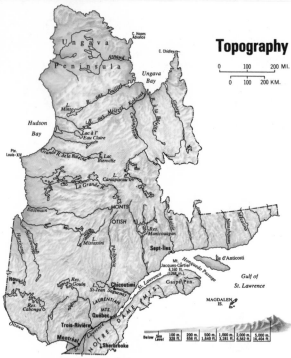

Topography

0   100   200 MI.

0   100   200 KM.

Below Sea Level | 100 m. 328 ft. | 200 m. 656 ft. | 500 m. 1,640 ft. | 1,000 m. 3,281 ft. | 2,000 m. 6,562 ft. | 5,000 m. 16,404 ft.

COUNTIES

Argenteuil 32,454..........C 4
Arthabaska 59,277..........E 4
Bagot 26,840..........E 4
Beauce 73,427..........G 3
Beauharnois 54,034..........C 4
Bellechasse 23,559..........G 3
Berthier 31,096..........C 3
Bonaventure 40,487..........C 2
Brome 17,436..........E 4
Chambly 307,090..........J 4
Champlain 119,595..........E 2
Charlevoix-Est 17,448..........G 2
Charlevoix-Ouest 14,172..........G 2
Châteauguay 59,968..........D 4
Chicoutimi 174,441..........G 1
Compton 20,536..........F 4
Deux-Montagnes 71,252..........C 4
Dorchester 33,949..........C 3
Drummond 69,770..........E 4
Frontenac 26,814..........G 4

Gaspé-Est 41,173..........D 1
Gaspé-Ouest 18,943..........C 1
Gatineau 54,229..........B 3
Hull 131,213..........B 4
Huntingdon 16,953..........C 4
Iberville 23,180..........D 4
Île-de-Montréal 1,760,122..........H 4
Île-Jésus 268,335..........H 4
Joliette 60,384..........C 3
Kamouraska 28,642..........H 2
Labelle 34,395..........B 3
Lac-Saint-Jean-Est 47,891..........F 1
Lac-Saint-Jean-Ouest 62,952..........E 1
Laprairie 105,962..........H 4
L'Assomption 109,705..........D 4
Lévis 94,104..........J 3
L'Islet 22,062..........G 2
Lotbinière 29,653..........F 3
Maskinongé 20,763..........D 3
Matane 29,955..........B 1
Matapédia 23,715..........B 2
Mégantic 57,892..........F 3

Missisquoi 36,161..........D 4
Montcalm 27,557..........C 3
Montmagny 25,622..........G 3
Montmorency No. 1 23,048..........F 2
Montmorency No. 2 6,436..........G 3
Napierville 13,562..........D 4
Nicolet 33,513..........E 3
Papineau 37,975..........B 4
Pontiac 20,283..........A 3
Portneuf 58,843..........E 3
Québec 458,980..........J 4
Richelieu 53,058..........D 4
Richmond 40,871..........E 4
Rimouski 69,099..........J 1
Rivière-du-Loup 41,250..........H 2
Rouville 42,391..........D 4
Saguenay 115,881..........H 1
Saint-Hyacinthe 55,888..........D 4
Saint-Jean 55,576..........D 4
Saint-Maurice 107,703..........D 3
Shefford 70,733..........E 4
Sherbrooke 115,983..........E 4

CITIES and TOWNS

Soulanges 15,429..........C 4
Stanstead 38,186..........F 4
Témiscouata 52,570..........J 2
Terrebonne 193,865..........H 4
Vaudreuil 50,043..........C 4
Verchères 63,353..........J 4
Wolfe 15,635..........F 4
Yamaska 14,797..........E 3

Acton Vale 4,371..........E 4
Albanel 992..........E 1
Alma® 26,322..........F 1
Amqui® 4,048..........B 2
Ancienne-Lorette 12,935..........H 3
Angers..........B 4
Anjou 37,346..........H 4
Annaville 712..........E 3
Armagh 878..........G 3
Arthabaska® 6,827..........F 3
Arvida..........F 1
Asbestos 7,967..........F 4
Ascot Corner 847..........F 4
Audet 760..........G 4
Ayer's Cliff 810..........E 4
Aylmer 26,695..........B 4
Baie-Comeau 12,866..........A 1
Baie-d'Urfé 3,674..........H 4
Baie-Saint-Paul® 3,961..........G 2
Baie-Trinité 749..........B 1
Beaconsfield 19,613..........H 4
Beauceville 4,302..........G 3
Beauharnois® 7,025..........D 4
Beaumont 791..........F 3
Beauport 60,447..........J 3
Beaupré 2,740..........G 2
Bécancour® 10,247..........E 3
Bedford® 2,832..........E 4
Beebe Plain 1,072..........E 4
Bélair (Val-Bélair) 12,695..........H 3
Beloeil 17,540..........D 4
Bernierville 2,120..........F 3
Berthier-en-Bas 562..........G 3
Berthierville® 4,049..........D 3
Bic 2,994..........J 1
Biencourt 824..........J 2
Black Lake 5,148..........F 3
Blainville 14,682..........H 4
Boischatel 3,345..........J 3
Bois-des-Filion 4,943..........H 4
Bolduc 1,565..........G 4
Bonaventure 1,371..........C 2
Boucherville 29,704..........J 4
Bromont 2,731..........E 4
Bromptonville 3,035..........F 4
Brossard 52,232..........H 4
Brownsburg 2,875..........C 4
Buckingham 7,992..........B 4
Cabano 3,291..........J 2
Cacouna 1,160..........H 2
Calumet 729..........C 4
Candiac 8,502..........J 4
Cap-à-l'Aigle 819..........G 2
Cap-Chat 3,464..........B 1
Cap-de-la-Madeleine 32,626..........E 3
Caplan-Rivière Caplan 1,139..........C 2
Cap-Saint-Ignace 1,485..........G 2
Cap-Santé® 671..........F 3
Carignan 4,544..........J 4
Carleton 2,710..........C 2
Causapscal 2,501..........B 2
Chambly 12,190..........J 4
Chambord 961..........E 1

Chandler 3,946..........D 2
Charlemagne 4,827..........H 4
Charlesbourg 68,326..........J 3
Charny 8,240..........J 3
Châteauguay 36,928..........H 4
Château-Richer® 3,628..........F 3
Chénéville 633..........B 4
Chicoutimi® 60,064..........G 1
Chicoutimi-Jonquière
  *135,172..........G 1
Chute-aux-Outardes 2,280..........A 1
Clermont 3,621..........G 2
Coaticook 6,271..........F 4
Coleraine 1,660..........F 4
Compton 728..........F 4
Contrecoeur 5,449..........D 4
Cookshire® 1,480..........F 4
Coteau-du-Lac 1,247..........C 4
Coteau-Landing® 1,386..........C 4
Côte-Saint-Luc 27,531..........H 4
Courcelles 608..........G 4
Courville..........J 3
Cowansville 12,240..........E 4
Crabtree 1,950..........D 4
Danville 2,200..........E 4
Daveluyville 1,257..........E 3
Deauville 942..........E 4
Dégelis 3,477..........J 2
Delisle 4,011..........F 1
Delson 4,935..........H 4
Desbiens 1,541..........E 1
Deschaillons-sur-Saint-
  Laurent 950..........E 3
Deschambault 977..........E 3
Deschênes..........B 4
Deux-Montagnes 9,944..........H 4
Didyme 667..........E 1
Disraëli 3,181..........F 4
Dolbeau 8,766..........E 1
Dollard-des-Ormeaux 39,940..........H 4
Donnacona 5,731..........F 3
Dorion 5,749..........C 4
Dorval 17,727..........H 4
Dosquet 703..........F 3
Douville..........D 4
Drummondville 27,347..........E 4
Drummondville-Sud 9,220..........E 4
Dunham 2,887..........E 4
Durham-Sud 1,045..........E 4
East Angus 4,016..........F 4
East Broughton 1,397..........F 4
East Broughton Station 1,302..........F 3
Eastman 612..........E 4
Entrelacs 1,735..........C 3
Farnham 6,498..........E 4
Ferme-Neuve 2,266..........B 3
Forestville 4,271..........H 1
Frampton 684..........G 3
Francoeur 1,427..........F 3
Gaspé 17,261..........D 1
Gatineau 74,988..........B 4
Giffard..........J 3
Girardville 1,128..........E 1
Gracefield 869..........A 3
Granby 38,069..........E 4
Grand Mère 15,442..........E 3
Grande-Rivière 4,420..........D 2
Grandes-Bergeronnes 748..........H 1
Grande-Vallée 700..........D 1
Greenfield Park 18,527..........J 4
Grenville 1,417..........C 4
Gros-Morne 672..........C 1
Hampstead 7,598..........H 4
Ham-Sud® 62..........F 4
Hauterive 13,995..........A 1
Hébertville 2,515..........F 1
Hébertville-Station 1,442..........F 1
Hemmingford 737..........D 4
Henryville 595..........D 4
Howick 639..........C 4
Hudson 4,414..........C 4
Hull® 56,225..........B 4
Huntingdon® 3,018..........C 4
Île-Perrot 5,945..........G 4
Iberville® 8,587..........D 4
Inverness® 329..........F 3
Joliette® 16,987..........D 3
Jonquière 60,354..........F 1
Jonquière-Chicoutimi
  *135,172..........F 1
Kingsey Falls 818..........E 4
Kirkland 10,476..........H 4
Knowlton (Lac-Brome)®
  4,316..........E 4
La Baie 20,935..........G 1
Labelle 1,534..........C 3
Lac-à-la-Croix 1,017..........F 1
Lac-Alouette-Lac-Brière 1,356..........D 4
Lac-au-Saumon 1,332..........B 2
Lac-aux-Sables 838..........E 3
Lac-Beaufort..........F 3
Lac-Bouchette 1,703..........E 1
Lac-Carré 717..........C 3
Lac-des-Écorces 766..........B 3
Lac-Drolet 1,120..........G 4
Lac-Etchemin 2,729..........G 3
Lachenaie 8,631..........D 4
Lachine 37,521..........H 4
Lachute® 11,729..........C 4
Lac-Mégantic® 6,119..........G 4
Lacolle 1,319..........D 4
Lac-Saint-Charles 5,837..........H 3
Lafontaine 4,799..........C 4
La Guadeloupe 1,692..........F 4
La Malbaie® 4,030..........G 2
Lambton 1,559..........F 4
L'Annonciation 2,384..........C 3
Lanoraie (Lanoraie-d'Autray)
  1,613..........D 4
La Pêche 4,977..........B 4
La Pérade 1,039..........E 3
La Pocatière 4,560..........H 2

La Prairie® 10,627..........J 4
La Providence..........E 4
Larouche 662..........F 1
La Salle 76,299..........H 4
L'Ascension 1,287..........F 1
L'Assomption® 4,844..........D 4
La Station-du-Coteau 892..........C 4
Laterrière 788..........F 1
La Tuque 11,556..........D 2
Laurentides 1,947..........D 4
Laurier-Station 1,123..........F 3
Laurierville 939..........F 3
Lauzon 13,362..........J 3
Laval 268,335..........H 4
Lavaltrie 2,053..........D 4
L'Avenir 1,116..........E 4
Lawrenceville 562..........E 4
Le Moyne 6,137..........J 4
L'Épiphanie 2,971..........D 4
Léry 2,239..........H 4
Lévis 17,895..........J 3
Lennoxville 3,922..........F 4
Les Méchins 803..........B 1
Linière 1,168..........G 3
L'Islet 1,070..........G 2
L'Islet-sur-Mer 774..........G 2
L'Isle-Verte 1,142..........G 1
Longueuil 124,320..........J 4
Loretteville® 15,060..........H 3
Lorraine 6,881..........H 4
Louiseville® 3,735..........E 3
Luceville 1,524..........J 1
Lyster 830..........F 3
Magog 13,604..........E 4

Maniwaki 5,424..........B 3
Manseau 626..........E 3
Maple Grove 2,009..........H 4
Maria 1,178..........C 2
Marieville 4,877..........D 4
Mascouche 20,345..........H 4
Maskinongé 1,005..........E 3
Masson 4,264..........B 4
Massueville 671..........E 4
Matane® 13,612..........B 1
Matapédia 586..........C 2
Melocheville 1,892..........C 4
Mercier 6,352..........H 4
Metabetchouan 3,406..........F 1
Mirabel® 14,080..........H 4
Mistassini 6,682..........E 1
Montauban 557..........E 3
Mont-Carmel 807..........H 2
Montcerf 570..........A 3
Montebello 1,229..........B 4
Mont-Joli 6,359..........J 1
Mont-Laurier® 8,405..........B 3
Mont-Louis 756..........C 1
Montmagny® 12,405..........G 3
Montréal® 980,354..........H 4
Montréal *2,828,349..........H 4
Montréal-Est 3,778..........J 4
Montréal-Nord 94,914..........H 4
Mont-Rolland 1,517..........C 4
Mont-Royal 19,247..........H 4
Mont-Saint-Hilaire 10,066..........D 4
Morin Heights 592..........C 4
Murdochville 3,396..........C 1
Nantes 1,167..........G 4

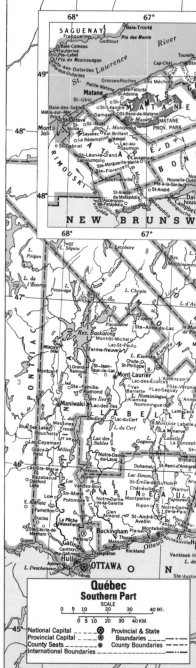

Québec Southern Part

SCALE

0 5 10   20   30   40 MI.

0 5 10   20   30   40 KM.

National Capital ......⊛
Provincial Capital ......⊛
County Seats ......⊛
Provincial & State Boundaries ------
County Boundaries ------
International Boundaries ------

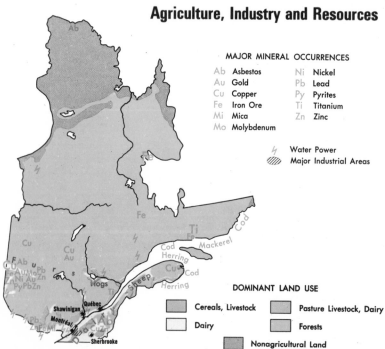

Agriculture, Industry and Resources

MAJOR MINERAL OCCURRENCES

Ab   Asbestos   Ni   Nickel
Au   Gold   Pb   Lead
Cu   Copper   Py   Pyrites
Fe   Iron Ore   Ti   Titanium
Mi   Mica   Zn   Zinc
Mo   Molybdenum

⚡ Water Power
▨ Major Industrial Areas

DOMINANT LAND USE

▨ Cereals, Livestock   ▨ Pasture Livestock, Dairy
☐ Dairy   ▨ Forests
▨ Nonagricultural Land

Napierville⊙ 2,343 ....D 4	Pincourt 8,750 ....D 4	Rivière-à-Pierre 615 ....E 3	Saint-Anselme 1,808 ....F 3
Neuville 996 ....F 3	Pintendre 1,849 ....J 3	Rivière-au-Renard 2,211 ....D 1	Saint-Antoine 7,012 ....H 4
New Carlisle⊙ 1,292 ....D 2	Plaisance 748 ....B 4	Rivière-Bleue 1,690 ....J 2	Saint-Antonin 941 ....H 2
New Richmond 4,257 ....C 2	Plessisville 7,249 ....F 3	Rivière-Bois-Clair 604 ....F 3	Saint-Aubert 884 ....G 2
Nicolet 4,880 ....E 3	Pohénégamooke 3,702 ....H 2	Rivière-du-Loup⊙ 13,459 ....H 2	Saint-Augustin-de-Québec
Nominingue 881 ....B 3	Pointe-à-la-Croix 1,481 ....C 2	Rivière-du-Moulin ....G 1	2,475 ....E 3
Normandin 4,041 ....E 1	Pointe-au-Père 796 ....J 1	Rivière-Éternité 659 ....J 1	Saint-Basile-Sud 1,719 ....J 3
North Hatley 689 ....F 4	Pointe-au-Pic 1,054 ....G 2	Rivière-Portneuf-Portneuf-sur-	Saint-Basile-le-Grand 7,658 ....J 4
Notre-Dame-de-la-Doré 1,064 E 1	Pointe-aux-Outardes 1,056 ....A 1	Mer 1,255 ....H 1	Saint-Benjamin 1,027 ....G 3
Notre-Dame-des-Laurentides H 3	Pointe-aux-Trembles 36,270 ....H 4	Robertsonville 1,987 ....F 3	Saint-Bernard 585 ....F 3
Notre-Dame-des-Prairies	Pointe-Calumet 2,935 ....G 4	Roberval⊙ 11,429 ....E 1	Saint-Bernard-sur-Mer 711 ....G 2
6,150 ....D 3	Pointe-Claire 24,571 ....H 4	Rock Island 1,179 ....E 4	Saint-Boniface-de-Shawinigan
Notre-Dame-du-Bon-Conseil	Pointe-du-Lac 5,359 ....E 3	Rosemère 7,778 ....H 4	3,164 ....D 3
1,089 ....E 4	Pointe-Gatineau ....B 4	Rougemont 972 ....D 4	Saint-Bruno 2,580 ....F 1
Notre-Dame-du-Lac⊙ 2,258 ....J 2	Pointe-Lebel 1,573 ....A 1	Roxboro 6,292 ....H 4	Saint-Bruno-de-Montarville
Nouvelle 669 ....C 2	Pont-Rouge 3,580 ....F 3	Roxton Falls 1,245 ....E 4	22,880 ....J 4
Oka 1,538 ....C 4	Port-Alfred 8,621 ....G 1	Sacré-Coeur-de-Saguenay	
Omerville 1,398 ....E 4	Portneuf 1,333 ....F 3	1,678 ....H 1	Saint-Dominique 2,068 ....E 4
Ormstown 1,659 ....D 4	Portneuf-sur-Mer (Rivière-	Saint-Adelme 618 ....B 1	Saint-Donat-de-Montcalm
Orsainville ....H 3	Portneuf-sur-Mer) 1,255 ....H 1	Saint-Adelphe 1,159 ....E 3	1,521 ....C 3
Otis 673 ....G 1	Price 2,273 ....A 1	Saint-Adolphe-d'Howard	Sainte-Adèle 4,675 ....C 4
Otterburn Park 4,268 ....D 4	Princeville 4,023 ....F 3	1,686 ....C 4	Sainte-Agathe 709 ....G 3
Outremont 24,338 ....H 4	Proulxville 588 ....E 3	Saint-Adrien 597 ....F 4	Sainte-Agathe-des-Monts
Pabos 1,295 ....D 2	Québec (cap.) 166,474 ....H 3	Saint-Agapitville 2,954 ....F 3	5,641 ....C 3
Pabos-Mills 1,565 ....D 2	Québec⊙ *576,075 ....H 3	Saint-Aimé-des-Lacs 861 ....G 2	Sainte-Anne-de-Beaupré
Papineauville 1,481 ....C 4	Quyon 744 ....A 4	Saint-Alban 673 ....E 3	3,292 ....F 2
Paspébiac 1,914 ....D 2	Rawdon 2,958 ....D 3	Saint-Alexandre-de-	Sainte-Anne-de-Bellevue
Percé 4,839 ....D 1	Repentigny 34,419 ....J 4	Kamouraska 1,048 ....H 2	3,981 ....H 4
Petit-Cap 1,023 ....D 1	Richelieu 1,832 ....D 4	Saint-Alexis-des-Monts 1,984 D 3	Sainte-Anne-des-Monts⊙
Petite-Matane 1,065 ....B 1	Richmond⊙ 3,568 ....E 4	Saint-Amable 2,424 ....J 4	6,062 ....C 1
Petit-Saguenay (Saint-	Rigaud 2,268 ....C 4	Saint-Ambroise 3,606 ....F 1	Sainte-Anne-des-Plaines
François-d'Assise) 804 ....G 1	Rimouski⊙ 29,120 ....J 1	Saint-Anaclet 1,377 ....J 1	4,258 ....H 4
Pierrefonds 38,390 ....H 4	Rimouski-Est 2,506 ....J 1	Saint-André-Avellin 1,312 ....B 4	Sainte-Anne-du-Lac 686 ....B 3
Pierreville 1,212 ....E 3	Ripon 620 ....B 4	Saint-André-Est 1,293 ....C 4	Sainte-Aurélie 1,045 ....G 3

Saint-Camille-de-Bellechasse	Sainte-Catherine 1,474 ....F 3	Sainte-Martine 2,196 ....D 4
1,744 ....G 3	Sainte-Claire 1,566 ....G 3	Saint-Émile 5,216 ....H 3
Saint-Casimir 1,133 ....E 3	Sainte-Croix 1,814 ....F 3	Sainte-Monique 705 ....F 1
Saint-Césaire 2,935 ....D 4	Sainte-Félicité 711 ....B 1	Sainte-Pétronille 982 ....J 3
Saint-Charles 1,019 ....G 3	Sainte-Foy 68,883 ....H 3	Saint-Ephrem-de-Tring 973 ....G 3
Saint-Charles-de-Mandeville	Sainte-Geneviève 2,573 ....H 4	Saint-Épiphane 647 ....H 2
1,392 ....D 3	Sainte-Geneviève-de-	Saint-Ephrem-de-Tring 973 ....G 3
Saint-Chrysostome 1,018 ....D 4	Batiscan⊙ 356 ....E 3	Saint-Épiphane 647 ....H 2
Saint-Côme 660 ....D 3	Sainte-Hélène-de-Bagot	Saint-Pudentienne 866 ....E 4
Saint-Constant 9,938 ....H 4	1,328 ....E 4	Saint-Rosalie 2,862 ....E 4
Saint-Cyprien 860 ....H 2	Sainte-Hénédine 3,981 ....F 3	Saint-Esprit 1,068 ....D 4
Saint-Cyrille 1,041 ....E 4	Sainte-Julie-de-Verchères	Saint-Thérèse 18,750 ....H 4
Saint-Damien-de-Buckland	14,243 ....J 4	Saint-Thérèse-Ouest
1,522 ....G 3	Sainte-Julienne⊙ 750 ....D 4	(Boisbriand) 13,471 ....H 4
Saint-David 5,380 ....G 3	Sainte-Justine 1,080 ....G 3	Sainte-Thècle 1,703 ....E 3
Saint-David-de-Falardeau	Saint-Élie 639 ....E 3	Saint-Étienne-de-Grès 845 ....E 3
1,876 ....F 1	Saint-Élzéar 743 ....F 3	Saint-Étienne-de-Lauzon
Saint-Denis 861 ....D 4	Sainte-Marie 8,937 ....G 3	1,218 ....J 3

AREA 594,857 sq. mi. (1,540,680 sq. km.)
POPULATION 6,438,403
CAPITAL Québec
LARGEST CITY Montréal
HIGHEST POINT Mont D'Iberville 5,420 ft.
(1,652 m.)
SETTLED IN 1608
ADMITTED TO CONFEDERATION 1867
PROVINCIAL FLOWER White Garden Lily

Internal divisions represent Municipal Counties

COUNTIES
indicated by numbers:

1 Iberville ....D 4
2 Napierville ....D 4
3 Rouville ....D 4
4 St-Hyacinthe ....D 4
5 Île-de-Montréal ....H 4
6 Deux-Montagnes ....C 4
7 Soulanges ....C 4
8 Beauharnois ....D 4
9 Hull ....A 4
10 Jésus ....H 4
11 Richelieu ....D 4
12 Vaudreuil ....C 4

Gaspé Peninsula

Gulf of St. Lawrence

NEW BRUNSWICK

MAINE

NEW YORK   VERMONT   N.H.

Saint-Eustache 29,716......H 4
Saint-Fabien 1,361......J 1
Saint-Félicien 9,058......E 1
Saint-Félix-de-Valois 1,462......D 3
Saint-Ferréol-les-Neiges
1,758......G 2
Saint-Flavien 734......F 3
Saint-François-de-Sales 831......E 1
Saint-François-du-Lac 942......E 3
Saint-Fulgence 950......G 1
Saint-Gabriel 3,161......D 3
Saint-Gabriel-de-Rimouski
779......J 1
Saint-Gédéon, Frontenac
1,569......F 4
Saint-Gédéon, Lac-St-Jean-E.
1,000......F 1
Saint-Georges, Beauce
10,342......G 3
Saint-Georges, Champlain
3,444......F 3
Saint-Georges-Ouest 6,378......G 3
Saint-Germain-de-Grantham
1,373......E 4
Saint-Gervais 973......G 3
Saint-Gilles 912......F 3
Saint-Grégoire (Mont-St-
Grégoire) 740......D 4
Saint-Henri 1,970......J 3
Saint-Honoré, Beauce 1,116......G 4
Saint-Honoré, Chicoutimi
1,790......F 1
Saint-Hubert 60,573......J 4
Saint-Hubert-de-Témiscouata
871......J 2
Saint-Hyacinthe® 38,246......D 4
Saint-Isidore 811......H 4
Saint-Isidore-de-Laprairie 769......D 4
Saint-Jacques 2,152......D 3
Saint-Jacques-le-Mineur
1,203......H 4
Saint-Jean-Chrysostome
6,930......J 3
Saint-Jean-de-Dieu 1,377......J 1
Saint-Jean-de-Matha 931......D 3
Saint-Jean-Port-Joli 1,813......G 2
Saint-Jean-sur-Richelieu®
35,640......D 4
Saint-Jérôme 25,123......H 4
Saint-Joachim 1,139......G 2
Saint-Joseph-de-Beauce
3,216......G 3
Saint-Joseph-de-Sorel 2,545......D 3
Saint-Jovite 3,841......C 3
Saint-Lambert 20,557......J 4
Saint-Laurent 65,900......H 4

Saint-Lazare 731......G 3
Saint-Léonard 79,429......H 4
Saint-Léonard-d'Aston 992......E 3
Saint-Léon-de-Chicoutimi 749......F 1
Saint-Léon-le-Grand 722......B 2
Saint-Liboire® 746......E 4
Saint-Louis-de-Gonzague
615......D 4
Saint-Louis-de-Terrebonne
14,172......H 2
Saint-Louis-du-Ha! Ha! 809......H 2
Saint-Luc 8,815......D 4
Saint-Luc-de-Matane 598......B 1
Saint-Marc-des-Carrières
2,822......E 3
Saint-Méthode-de-Frontenac
925......F 3
Saint-Michel-de-Bellechasse
963......G 3
Saint-Michel-des-Saints
1,584......D 3
Saint-Nazaire-de-Chicoutimi
962......F 1
Saint-Nérée 970......G 3
Saint-Nicolas 5,074......H 3
Saint-Noël 666......B 1
Saint-Odilon 580......G 3
Saint-Omer 718......C 2
Saint-Ours 625......D 4
Saint-Pacôme 1,996......G 2
Saint-Pamphile 3,428......H 3
Saint-Pascal 2,763......H 2
Saint-Paul-de-Montminy 602......G 3
Saint-Paulin 663......D 3
Saint-Paul-l'Ermite (Le
Gardeur) 8,312......J 4
Saint-Philippe-de-Néri 715......H 2
Saint-Pie 1,328......E 4
Saint-Pierre 5,305......H 4
Saint-Pierre-d'Orléans 880......G 3
Saint-Polycarpe 602......C 4
Saint-Prime 2,522......E 1
Saint-Prosper-de-Dorchester
2,150......G 3
Saint-Raphaël 1,346......G 3
Saint-Raymond 3,605......F 3
Saint-Rédempteur 4,463......J 3
Saint-Régis 1,370......C 4
Saint-Rémi 5,146......D 4
Saint-Roch-de-l'Achigan
1,160......D 4
Saint-Roch-de-Richelieu
1,650......D 4
Saint-Romuald-d'Etchemin®
9,849......J 3

Saint-Sauveur-des-Monts
2,348......C 4
Saint-Siméon 1,152......C 2
Saint-Simon 602......H 1
Saint-Stanislas 1,443......E 3
Saint-Sylvère 1,006......E 3
Saint-Timothée 2,113......D 4
Saint-Tite 3,031......E 3
Saint-Tite-des-Caps 626......G 2
Saint-Ubald 1,605......E 3
Saint-Ulric 792......B 1
Saint-Urbain-de-Charlevoix
1,079......G 2
Saint-Victor 1,104......G 3
Saint-Zacharie 1,284......G 3
Saint-Zotique 1,774......C 4
Sault-au-Mouton 828......H 1
Sawyerville 939......F 4
Sayabec 1,721......B 1
Scotstown 762......F 4
Senneville 1,221......G 4
Shannon 3,488......F 3
Shawbridge 942......C 4
Shawinigan 23,011......E 3
Shawinigan-Sud 11,325......E 3
Shawville 1,608......A 4
Sherbrooke® 74,075......E 4
Sherrington 614......D 4
Sillery 12,825......J 3
Sorel® 20,347......D 4
Squatec 1,000......J 2
Stanstead Plain 1,093......E 4
Sutton 1,599......E 4
Tadoussac® 900......H 1
Templeton 3,081......B 4
Terrebonne 11,769......H 4
Thetford Mines 19,965......F 3
Thurso 2,780......B 4
Tourelle (Tourelle-Grand-
Tourelle) 942......C 1
Tourville 659......H 2
Tracy 12,843......D 4
Tring-Jonction 1,315......F 3
Trois-Pistoles 4,445......H 1
Trois-Rivières 50,466......E 3
Trois-Rivières® 111,453......E 3
Trois-Rivières-Ouest 13,107......E 3
Upton 926......E 4
Val-Barrette 609......C 3
Val-Brillant 687......B 1
Valcourt 2,601......E 4
Val-David 2,336......C 3
Vallée-Jonction 1,200......G 3
Valleyfield (Salaberry-de-
Valleyfield) 29,574......C 4
Vanier 10,725......J 3

Varennes 8,764......J 4
Vaudreuil® 7,608......C 4
Verchères® 4,473......J 4
Verdun 61,287......H 4
Victoriaville 21,838......E 3
Villeneuve......J 3
Warwick 2,847......F 4
Waterloo® 4,664......E 4
Waterville 1,397......F 4
Weedon-Centre 1,263......F 4
Westmount 20,480......H 4
Wickham 2,043......E 4
Windsor 5,233......F 4
Wottonville 673......F 4
Yamachiche® 1,258......E 3

OTHER FEATURES

Alma (isl.)......F 1
Aylmer (lake)......B 4
Baskatong (res.)......B 3
Batiscan (riv.)......E 3
Bécancour (riv.)......E 3
Bonaventure (isl.)......D 1
Bonaventure (riv.)......C 1
Brome (lake)......E 4
Brompton (lake)......E 4
Cascapédia (riv.)......C 1
Chaleur (bay)......C 1
Champlain (lake)......D 4
Chaudière (riv.)......G 4
Chic-Chocs (mts.)......C 1
Chicoutimi (riv.)......F 2
Coudres (isl.)......G 2
Deschênes (lake)......A 4
Deux Montagnes (lake)......H 4
Ditton (riv.)......F 4
Forillon Nat'l Park......D 1
Fort Chambly Nat'l Hist. Park......J 4
Gaspé (bay)......D 1
Gaspé (cape)......D 1
Gaspé (pen.)......C 1
Gaspésie Prov. Park......C 1
Gatineau (riv.)......B 3
Îles (lake)......B 3
Jacques-Cartier (mt.)......C 1
Jacques-Cartier (riv.)......F 3
Kénogami (lake)......F 1
Kiamika (lake)......C 3
La Maurice Nat'l Park......D 3
Laurentides Prov. Park......F 2
Lièvre (riv.)......B 3
Lièvres (isl.)......H 2
Maskinongé (riv.)......D 3
Matane (riv.)......B 1
Matane Prov. Park......B 1

Matapédia (riv.)......B 2
Mégantic (lake)......G 4
Memphremagog (lake)......E 4
Mercier (dam)......F 1
Métabetchouane (riv.)......F 1
Mille Îles (riv.)......H 4
Montmorency (riv.)......F 2
Mont-Tremblant Prov. Park......C 3
Nicolet (riv.)......E 3
Nominingue (lake)......C 3
Nord (riv.)......C 4
Orléans (isl.)......G 3
Ottawa (riv.)......B 4
Ouareau (riv.)......D 3
Ouelle (riv.)......H 2
Patapédia (riv.)......B 2
Péribonca (riv.)......F 1
Petite Nation (riv.)......B 3
Prairies (riv.)......H 4
Rimouski (riv.)......J 1
Ristigouche (riv.)......B 1
Saguenay (riv.)......G 1
Sainte-Anne (riv.)......F 3
Sainte-Anne (riv.)......C 1
Saint-François (lake)......F 4
Saint-François (riv.)......F 4
Saint-Jean (lake)......E 1
Saint Lawrence (gulf)......D 1
Saint Lawrence (riv.)......H 1
Saint-Louis (lake)......H 4
Saint-Maurice (riv.)......E 3
Saint-Pierre (lake)......E 3
Shawinigan (riv.)......E 3
Shipshaw (riv.)......F 1
Soeurs (riv.)......H 4
Témiscouata (lake)......H 2
Tremblant (lake)......C 3
Trente et un Milles (lake)......B 3
Verte (isl.)......H 1
Yamaska (riv.)......D 4
York (riv.)......D 1

® County seat.
*Population of metropolitan area.

QUÉBEC, NORTHERN

INTERNAL DIVISIONS

Abitibi (county) 93,529......B 2
Abitibi (terr.)......B 2
Berthier (county) 31,096......B 3
Bonaventure (county) 40,487......D 3
Champlain (county) 119,595......C 3
Charlevoix-Est (co.) 17,348......C 3

Charlevoix-Ouest (county)
14,172......C 3
Chicoutimi (county) 174,441......C 2
Gaspé-Est (county) 41,173......E 2
Gaspé-Ouest (county) 18,943......D 1
Gatineau (county) 54,229......B 3
Joliette (county) 60,384......C 3
Lac-Saint-Jean-Est (county)
47,891......C 3
Lac-Saint-Jean-Ouest
(county) 62,952......C 3
Maskinongé (county) 20,763......C 3
Matane (county) 29,955......D 3
Matapédia (county) 23,715......D 3
Mistassini (terr.)......B 2
Montcalm (county) 27,557......C 3
Montmorency No. I (county)
23,048......C 3
Nouveau-Québec (terr.)......E 1
Pontiac (county) 20,283......C 3
Portneuf (county) 58,843......C 3
Québec (county) 458,980......C 3
Rimouski (county) 69,099......D 3
Saguenay (county) 115,881......D 2
Saint-Maurice (co.) 107,703......C 3
Témiscamingue (co.) 52,570......B 3

CITIES and TOWNS

Alma® 26,322......C 3
Amos® 9,421......B 3
Baie-Comeau 12,866......D 2
Baie-du-Poste 1,690......C 2
Chicoutimi® 60,064......C 3
Gaspé 17,261......E 3
Hauterive 13,995......D 2
Jonquière 60,354......C 3
Lévis 17,895......C 3
La Tuque 11,556......C 3
Manicouagan......D 2
Maniwaki® 5,424......B 3
Matane® 13,612......D 3
Mistassini (Baie-du-Poste)
1,690......C 2
Mont-Laurier® 8,405......B 3
Montmagny® 12,405......C 3
New Carlisle® 781......E 3
Nouveau-Comptoir......E 1
Percé® 4,839......E 3
Port-Cartier-Ouest......D 2
Port-Menier® 275......D 2
Povungnituk 745......E 1
Québec (cap.)® 166,474......C 3
Rimouski 29,120......D 3
Rivière-au-Tonnerre 480......D 2
Rivière-du-Loup 13,459......D 3

Rouyn 17,224......B 3
Sept-Îles 29,262......D 2
Seven Islands (Sept-Îles)
29,262......D 2
Shawinigan 23,011......C 3
Tadoussac 900......C 3
Val d'Or 21,371......B 3
Ville-Marie 2,651......B 3

OTHER FEATURES

Allard (lake)......E 2
Anticosti (isl.)......E 2
Baleine, Grand Rivière de la
(riv.)......B 1
Bell (riv.)......B 3
Betsiamites (riv.)......C 2
Bienville (lake)......C 2
Broadback (riv.)......B 2
Cabonga (res.)......B 3
Caniapiscau (riv.)......D 1
Eastmain (riv.)......B 2
Eau Claire (lake)......C 1
Feuilles (riv.)......D 1
Gaspésie Prov. Park......D 3
George (riv.)......D 1
Gouin (res.)......C 3
Grande Rivière, La (riv.)......B 2
Honguedo (passage)......E 3
Hudson (bay)......A 1
Hudson (str.)......F 1
Jacques-Cartier (passage)......D 2
James (bay)......A 2
Koksoak (riv.)......D 1
Laurentides Prov. Park......C 3
Louis-XIV (pt.)......A 2
Manicouagan (res.)......D 2
Minto (lake)......D 1
Mistassibi (riv.)......C 2
Mistassini (lake)......C 2
Moisie (riv.)......D 2
Natashquan (riv.)......E 2
Nottaway (riv.)......B 2
Nouveau-Québec (crater)......F 1
Otish (mts.)......C 2
Ottawa (riv.)......B 3
Péribonca (riv.)......C 2
Plétipi (lake)......C 2
Saguenay (riv.)......C 3
Saint-Jean (lake)......C 3
Saint Lawrence (gulf)......E 3
Ungava (pen.)......E 1

® County seat.
*Population of metropolitan area.

Northern Québec

SCALE
0   50   100   150   200 MI.
0   50 100 150 200 KM.

Provincial Capital............⊛   Provincial Boundaries ———
County Seats............⊛   County Boundaries ———
International Boundaries ———   Territorial Boundaries ·—·—

ONTARIO, NORTHERN

INTERNAL DIVISIONS

Algoma (terr. dist.) 133,553...D 3
Cochrane (terr. dist.) 96,875...D 2
Kenora (terr. dist.) 59,421...C 2
Manitoulin (terr. dist.) 11,001...D 3
Nipissing (terr. dist.) 80,268...E 3
Parry Sound (terr. dist.)
33,528...E 3
Rainy River (terr. dist.) 22,798 B 3
Renfrew (county) 87,484...E 3
Sudbury (reg. munic.)
159,779...D 3
Sudbury (terr. dist.) 27,068...D 3
Thunder Bay (terr. dist.)
153,997...C 3
Timiskaming (terr. dist.)
41,288...D 3

CITIES and TOWNS

Chalk River 1,010...E 3
Elliot Lake 16,723...D 3
Fort Albany 482...D 2
Fort Frances⊛ 8,906...B 3
Kapuskasing 12,014...D 3
Kenora⊛ 9,817...B 3
Kirkland Lake 12,219...D 3
Moose Factory 1,452...D 2
Moosonee 1,433...D 2
Nickel Centre 12,318...D 3
North Bay⊛ 51,268...E 3
Pembroke 14,026...E 3
Sault Sainte Marie⊛ 82,697..D 3
Sudbury 91,829...D 3
Thunder Bay⊛ 112,486...C 3
Timmins 46,114...D 3
Valley East 20,433...D 3

OTHER FEATURES

Abitibi (lake)...E 3
Abitibi (riv.)...D 2
Albany (riv.)...C 2
Algonquin Prov. Park...E 3
Asheweig (riv.)...C 2
Attawapiskat (lake)...C 2
Attawapiskat (riv.)...C 2
Basswood (lake)...B 3
Berens (riv.)...A 2
Big Trout (lake)...B 2
Black Duck (riv.)...C 1
Bloodvein (riv.)...A 2
Caribou (isl.)...C 3

Cobham (riv.)...A 2
Eabamet (lake)...C 2
Ekwan (riv.)...C 2
English (riv.)...B 2
Fawn (riv.)...C 2
Finger (lake)...B 2
Georgian (bay)...D 3
Hannah (bay)...D 2
Henrietta Maria (cape)...D 1
Hudson (bay)...D 1
Huron (lake)...D 3
James (bay)...D 2
Kapiskau (riv.)...D 2
Kapuskasing (riv.)...D 3
Kenogami (riv.)...C 2
Kesagami (riv.)...E 2
Lake of the Woods (lake)...B 3
Lake Superior Prov. Park...C 2
Little Current (riv.)...C 2
Long (lake)...C 3
Manitoulin (isl.)...D 3
Mattagami (riv.)...D 3
Michipicoten (isl.)...C 3
Mille Lacs (lake)...B 3
Missinaibi (lake)...D 3
Missinaibi (riv.)...D 2
Missisa (lake)...D 2
Nipigon (lake)...C 3
Nipissing (lake)...E 3
North (chan.)...D 3
North Caribou (lake)...B 2
Nungesser (lake)...B 2
Ogidaki (mt.)...D 3
Ogoki (riv.)...C 2
Opazatika (riv.)...D 2
Opinnagau (riv.)...D 2
Otoskwin (riv.)...B 2
Ottawa (riv.)...E 3
Pipestone (riv.)...B 2
Polar Bear Prov. Park...D 2
Pukaskwa Prov. Park...C 3
Quetico Prov. Park...B 3
Rainy (lake)...B 3
Red (lake)...B 2
Sachigo (riv.)...B 2
Saganaga (lake)...B 3
Saint Ignace (isl.)...C 3
Saint Joseph (lake)...B 2
Sandy (lake)...B 2
Savant (lake)...B 2
Seine (riv.)...B 3
Seul (lake)...B 2
Severn (lake)...B 2
Severn (riv.)...B 2
Shamattawa (riv.)...C 2
Shibogama (lake)...C 2

Sibley Prov. Park...C 3
Slate (isls.)...C 3
Stout (lake)...B 2
Superior (lake)...C 3
Sutton (lake)...D 2
Sutton (riv.)...D 2
Timagami (lake)...D 3
Timiskaming (lake)...E 3
Trout (lake)...B 2
Wabuk (pt.)...D 1
Winisk (lake)...C 2
Winisk (riv.)...C 2
Winnipeg (riv.)...A 2
Woods (lake)...B 3

ONTARIO

INTERNAL DIVISIONS

Algoma (terr. dist.) 133,553...J 5
Brant (county) 104,427...D 4
Bruce (county) 60,020...C 3
Cochrane (terr. dist.) 96,875...J 4
Dufferin (county) 31,145...D 3
Dundas (county) 18,946...J 2
Durham (reg. munic.) 283,639 F 3
Elgin (county) 69,707...C 5
Essex (county) 312,467...B 5
Frontenac (county) 108,133..H 3
Glengarry (county) 20,254..K 2
Grenville (county) 27,176...J 3
Grey (county) 73,824...D 3
Haldimand-Norfolk (reg.
munic.) 89,456...E 5
Haliburton (county) 11,361...F 2
Halton (reg. munic.) 253,883..E 4
Hamilton-Wentworth (reg.
munic.) 411,445...D 4
Hastings (county) 106,883..G 3
Huron (county) 56,127...C 4
Kenora (terr. dist.) 59,421...J 5
Kent (county) 107,022...B 5
Lambton (county) 123,445..B 5
Lanark (county) 45,676...H 3
Leeds (county) 53,765...H 3
Lennox and Addington
(county) 33,040...G 3
Manitoulin (terr. dist.) 11,001 B 2
Middlesex (county) 318,184...C 4
Muskoka (dist. munic.)
38,370...E 3
Niagara (reg. munic.) 368,288 E 4
Nipissing (terr. dist.) 80,268..F 2
Northumberland (county)
64,966...G 3

Ottawa-Carleton (reg. munic.)
546,849...J 2
Oxford (county) 85,920...D 4
Parry Sound (terr. dist.)
33,528...D 2
Peel (reg. munic.) 490,731..E 4
Perth (county) 66,096...C 4
Peterborough (county)
102,452...F 3
Prescott (county) 30,365...K 2
Prince Edward (county)
22,336...G 3
Rainy River (terr. dist.) 22,798 G 5
Renfrew (county) 87,484...G 2
Russell (county) 22,412...J 2
Simcoe (county) 225,071...E 3
Stormont (county) 61,927...K 2
Sudbury (reg. munic.)
159,779...K 6
Sudbury (terr. dist.) 27,068...J 5
Thunder Bay (terr. dist.)
153,997...H 5
Timiskaming (terr. dist.)
41,288...K 4
Toronto (metro. munic.)
2,137,395...K 4
Victoria (county) 47,854...F 3
Waterloo (reg. munic.)
305,496...D 4
Wellington (county) 129,432..D 4
York (reg. munic.) 252,053...E 4

CITIES and TOWNS

Ailsa Craig 765...C 4
Ajax 25,475...E 4
Alban 342...D 1
Alexandria 3,271...K 2
Alfred 1,057...K 2
Alliston 4,712...E 3
Almonte 3,855...H 2
Alvinston 736...C 4
Amherstburg 5,685...A 5
Amherst View 6,110...H 3
Ancaster 14,428...D 4
Angus 3,085...E 3
Apsley 264...F 3
Arkona 473...C 4
Armstrong 378...H 4
Arnprior 5,828...H 2
Aroland 291...H 4
Arthur 1,700...D 4
Astorville 340...E 1
Athens 948...J 3
Atherley 366...E 3
Atikokan 4,452...G 5

Atwood 723...D 4
Aurora 16,267...J 3
Avonmore 273...K 2
Aylmer 5,254...C 5
Ayr 1,295...D 4
Ayton 424...D 3
Baden 945...D 4
Bala 525...D 2
Bancroft 2,329...G 2
Barrie⊛ 38,423...E 3
Barry's Bay 1,216...G 2
Batawa 430...G 3
Bath 1,071...H 3
Bayfield 649...C 4
Beachburg 682...H 2
Beachville 917...D 4
Beardmore 583...H 5
Beaverton 1,952...E 3
Beeton 1,989...E 3
Belle River 3,568...B 5
Belleville 34,881...G 3
Belmont 831...C 5
Bethany 365...F 3
Bewdley 508...F 3
Binbrook 306...E 4
Blackstock 720...F 3
Blenheim 4,044...C 5
Blind River 3,444...J 5
Bloomfield 718...G 4
Blyth 926...C 4
Bobcaygeon 1,625...F 3
Bonfield 540...E 1
Bothwell 915...C 5
Bourget 1,057...J 2
Bracebridge⊛ 9,063...E 2
Bradford 7,370...E 3
Braeside 492...H 2
City View...J 2
Clarence Creek 796...J 2
Bridgenorth 1,633...F 3

Brigden 635...B 5
Brighton 3,147...G 3
Britt 419...D 2
Brockville⊛ 19,896...J 3
Bruce Mines 635...J 5
Brussels 962...C 4
Burford 1,461...D 4
Burgessville 302...D 4
Burk's Falls 922...E 2
Burlington 114,853...E 4
Cache Bay 665...D 1
Caesarea 551...F 3
Calabogie 256...H 2
Caledon 26,645...E 4
Callander 1,158...E 1
Cambridge 77,183...D 4
Campbellford 3,409...G 3
Cannington 1,623...E 3
Capreol 3,845...K 5
Caramat 265...H 5
Cardinal 1,753...J 3
Carleton Place 5,626...H 2
Carlisle 781...D 4
Carlsbad Springs 616...J 2
Carp 707...H 2
Cartier 302...J 5
Casselman 1,675...J 2
Castleton 346...F 3
Chalk River 1,010...G 1
Chapleau 3,243...J 5
Charing Cross 443...B 5
Chatham 40,952...B 5
Chatsworth 383...D 3
Cherry Valley 289...G 4
Chesley 1,840...C 3
Chesterville 1,430...J 2
Chute-à-Blondeau 365...K 2

Clifford 645...D 4
Clinton 3,081...C 4
Cobalt 1,759...K 5
Cobden 997...H 2
Coboconk 426...F 3
Cobourg⊛ 11,385...F 4
Cochrane⊛ 4,848...K 4
Colborne 1,796...G 4
Colchester 711...B 6
Coldwater 964...E 3
Collingwood 12,064...D 3
Comber 667...B 5
Consecon 295...G 3
Cookstown 918...E 3
Cornwall⊛ 46,144...K 2
Cottam 404...B 5
Courtland 647...D 5
Courtright 1,024...B 5
Crediton 370...C 4
Creemore 1,182...D 3
Crysler 540...J 2
Cumberland 248...J 2
Cumberland Beach-Bramshot-
Buena Vista 679...E 3
Dashwood 426...C 4
Deep River 5,095...G 1
Delaware 481...C 4
Delhi 4,043...D 5
Delta 360...H 3
Deseronto 1,740...G 3
Douglas 303...H 2
Drayton 809...D 4
Dresden 2,550...B 5
Drumbo 476...D 4
Dryden 6,640...G 5
Dublin 295...C 4
Dubreuilville △988...J 5
Dundalk 1,250...D 3
Dundas 19,586...D 4
Dungannon 284...C 4
Dunnville 11,353...E 5
Durham 2,458...D 3
Dutton 1,115...C 5
Earlton 1,028...K 5
East York 101,974...J 4
Echo Bay 786...J 5
Eden Mills 318...D 4
Eganville 1,245...G 2
Egmondville 465...C 4
Elgin 327...H 3
Elk Lake 526...K 5
Elliot Lake 16,723...B 1
Elmira 7,063...D 4
Elmvale 1,183...E 3
Elmwood 364...C 3
Elora 2,666...D 4
Embro 727...C 4
Embrun 1,883...J 2
Emeryville-Puce 1,611...B 5
Emo 762...F 5
Englehart 1,689...K 5
Enterprise 357...H 3
Erieau 430...C 5
Erin 2,313...D 4
Espanola 5,836...J 5
Essex 6,295...B 5
Etobicoke 298,713...J 4
Everett 570...E 3
Exeter 3,732...C 4
Fauquier 561...J 5
Fenelon Falls 1,701...F 3
Fergus 6,064...D 4
Field 462...E 1
Finch 353...J 2
Fingal 380...C 5
Fitzroy Harbour 446...H 2
Flesherton 565...D 3
Foleyet 484...J 5
Fordwich 365...C 4
Forest 2,671...C 4
Formosa 393...C 3
Fort Erie 24,096...E 4
Foxboro 597...G 3
Frankford 1,919...G 3
Fraserdale 303...J 4
Freelton 307...D 4
Gananoque 4,863...H 3
Garden Village 270...E 1
Geraldton 2,956...H 5
Glencoe 1,694...C 5
Glen Miller 639...G 3
Glen Robertson 378...K 2
Glen Walter 710...K 2
Goderich⊛ 7,322...C 4
Gogama 652...J 5
Goodwood 335...E 3
Gore Bay⊛ 777...C 2
Gorrie 468...C 4
Grafton 409...G 4
Grand Bend 680...C 4
Grand Valley 1,226...D 4
Granton 315...C 4
Gravenhurst 8,532...E 3
Greely 567...J 2
Green Valley 459...K 2
Grimsby 15,797...E 4
Guelph⊛ 71,207...D 4

(continued on following page)

AREA 412,580 sq. mi. (1,068,582 sq. km.)
POPULATION 8,625,107
CAPITAL Toronto
LARGEST CITY Toronto
HIGHEST POINT in Timiskaming Dist.
2,275 ft. (693 m.)
SETTLED IN 1749
ADMITTED TO CONFEDERATION 1867
PROVINCIAL FLOWER White Trillium

Northern Ontario

SCALE
0 25 50   100   150   200 MI.
0 25 50   100   150 200 KM.

Provincial Capital...⊛ Provincial and
County Seats...⊙ State Boundaries
International Boundaries...County Boundaries

Longitude West B of Greenwich

Ontario
Central Part

SCALE
0 25 50 75 100 125 MI.
0 25 50 75 100 125 KM.

® Copyright HAMMOND INCORPORATED, Maplewood, N. J.

Longitude 80° West of E Greenwich 79°

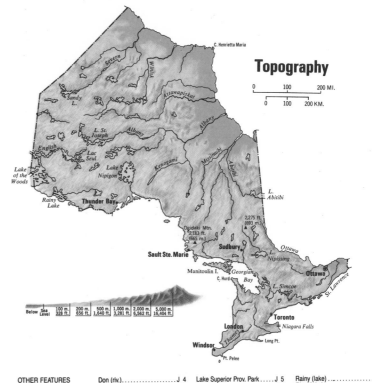

Topography

Ontario
Southern Part

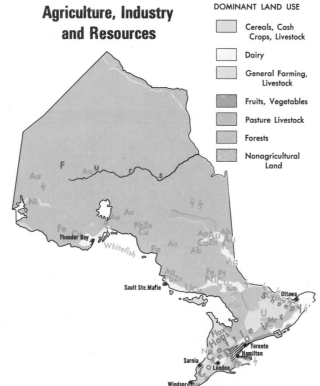

Agriculture, Industry and Resources

DOMINANT LAND USE

- Cereals, Cash Crops, Livestock
- Dairy
- General Farming, Livestock
- Fruits, Vegetables
- Pasture Livestock
- Forests
- Nonagricultural Land

MAJOR MINERAL OCCURRENCES

Ab	Asbestos	Mg	Magnesium
Ag	Silver	Mr	Marble
Au	Gold	Na	Salt
Co	Cobalt	Ni	Nickel
Cu	Copper	Pb	Lead
Fe	Iron Ore	Pt	Platinum
G	Natural Gas	U	Uranium
Gr	Graphite	Zn	Zinc

⚡ Water Power
▨ Major Industrial Areas

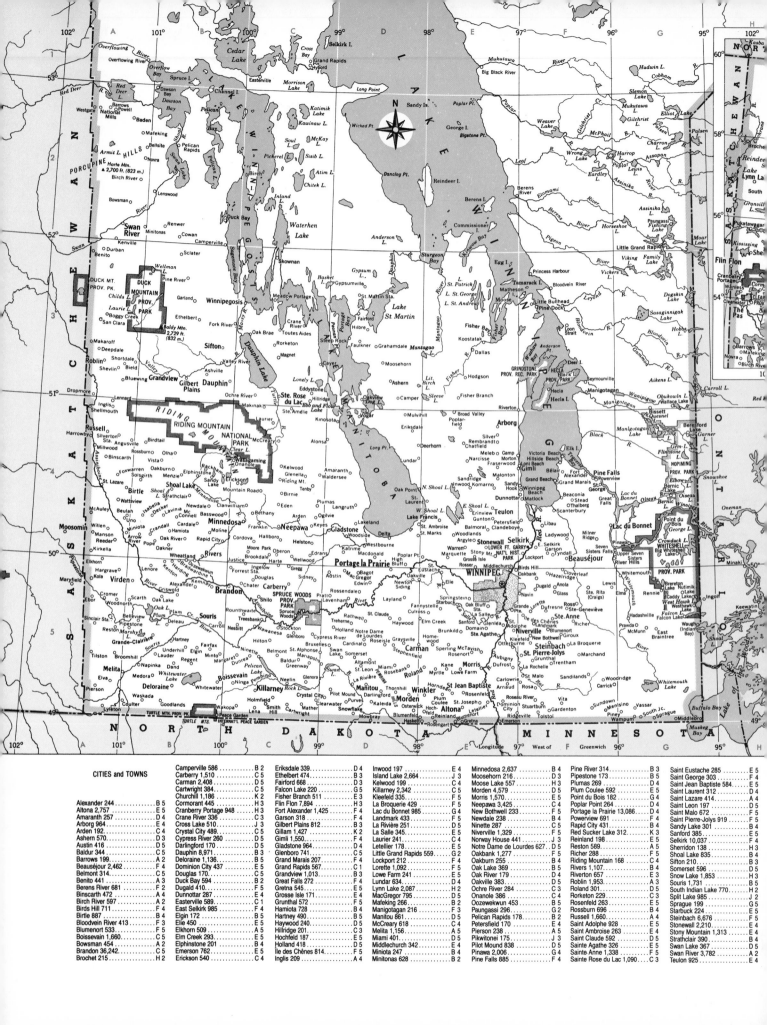

CITIES and TOWNS

Manitoba Northern Part

0 40 80 120 MI.
0 40 80 120 KM.

HUDSON BAY

ONTARIO

Manitoba
Southern Part
SCALE

0 5 10 20 40 60 MI.
0 5 10 20 40 60 KM.

Provincial Capital .... ⊛
International Boundaries .—.—.—
Provincial Boundaries .——.——

© Copyright HAMMOND INCORPORATED, Maplewood, N.J.

The Pas 6,390 .... H 3
Thicket Portage 195 .... J 3
Thompson 14,288 .... J 2
Treherne 743 .... D 5
Tyndall 421 .... F 4
Virden 2,940 .... A 5
Vita 364 .... F 5
Wabowden 655 .... J 3
Wallace Lake ●2,044 .... G 3
Wanless 193 .... H 3
Warren 459 .... E 4
Waskada 239 .... B 5
Wawanesa 492 .... C 5
Whitemouth 320 .... E 5
Whitewater ●856 .... B 5
Winkler 5,046 .... E 5
Winnipeg (cap.) 564,473 ...... E 5
Winnipeg *584,842 .... E 5
Winnipeg Beach 565 .... F 4
Winnipegosis 855 .... B 3
Woodlands 185 .... E 4
Wooddridge 170 .... F 5
York Landing 229 .... J 2

OTHER FEATURES

Aikens (lake) .... G 3
Anderson (lake) .... D 2
Anderson (pt.) .... F 3
Armit (lake) .... A 2
Assapan (riv.) .... G 2
Assiniboine (riv.) .... C 5
Assinika (lake) .... G 2
Assinika (riv.) .... G 2
Atim (lake) .... C 2
Baldy (mt.) .... B 3
Basket (lake) .... C 3
Beaverhill (lake) .... J 3
Berens (isl.) .... E 2
Berens (riv.) .... E 2
Bernic (lake) .... G 4
Big Sand (lake) .... H 2
Bigstone (lake) .... J 3
Bigstone (pt.) .... E 2
Bigstone (riv.) .... J 3
Birch (isl.) .... C 2
Black (isl.) .... F 3
Black (riv.) .... F 4
Bloodvein (riv.) .... F 3
Bonnet (lake) .... G 4
Buffalo (bay) .... G 5
Burntwood (riv.) .... J 2
Caribou (riv.) .... J 1
Carroll (lake) .... G 3
Cedar (lake) .... B 1
Channel (isl.) .... B 2
Charron (lake) .... G 2
Childs (lake) .... A 3
Chitek (lake) .... C 2
Churchill (cape) .... K 2
Churchill (riv.) .... J 2
Clear (lake) .... C 4
Clearwater Lake Prov. Park .. H 3
Cobham (riv.) .... G 1
Cochrane (riv.) .... H 2
Commissioner (isl.) .... E 2
Cormorant (lake) .... H 3
Cross (bay) .... C 1
Cross (lake) .... J 3
Crowduck (lake) .... G 4
Dancing (pt.) .... D 2
Dauphin (lake) .... C 3
Dauphin (riv.) .... D 3
Dawson (bay) .... B 2
Dog (lake) .... D 3
Dogskin (lake) .... F 3
Duck Mountain Prov. Park .. B 3
Eardley (lake) .... F 2

East Shoal (lake) .... E 4
Ebb and Flow (lake) .... C 3
Egg (isl.) .... E 3
Elbow (lake) .... G 4
Elk (isl.) .... F 4
Elliot (lake) .... G 2
Etawney (lake) .... J 2
Etomami (riv.) .... F 2
Falcon (lake) .... G 5
Family (lake) .... G 3
Fisher (bay) .... E 3
Fisher (riv.) .... E 3
Fishing (lake) .... G 2
Flintstone (lake) .... G 4
Fox (riv.) .... K 2
Gammon (riv.) .... G 3
Garner (lake) .... G 4
Gem (lake) .... G 4
George (isl.) .... E 2
George (lake) .... G 4
Gilchrist (creek) .... F 2
Gilchrist (lake) .... G 2
Gods (lake) .... K 3
Gods (riv.) .... K 3
Granville (lake) .... H 2
Grass (riv.) .... J 3
Grass River Prov. Park .... H 3
Grindstone Prov. Rec. Park .. F 3
Gunisao (lake) .... J 3
Gypsum (lake) .... D 3
Harrop (lake) .... G 2
Harte (mt.) .... A 2
Hayes (riv.) .... K 3
Hecla (isl.) .... E 3
Hecla Prov. Park .... F 3
Hobbs (lake) .... G 3
Horseshoe (lake) .... G 2
Hubbart (pt.) .... K 2
Hudson (bay) .... K 2
Hudwin (lake) .... G 1
Inland (lake) .... C 2
International Peace Garden .. B 5
Island (lake) .... K 3
Katimik (lake) .... C 2
Kawinaw (lake) .... C 2
Kinwow (bay) .... E 2
Kississing (lake) .... H 2
Knee (lake) .... E 2
Lake of the Woods (lake) ... H 5
La Salle (riv.) .... E 5
Laurie (lake) .... A 3
Leaf (riv.) .... F 2
Lewis (lake) .... G 2
Leyond (riv.) .... F 3
Little Birch (lake) .... E 3
Lonely (lake) .... C 3
Long (lake) .... G 4
Long (pt.) .... D 1
Long (pt.) .... D 4
Manigotagan (lake) .... G 4

Manigotagan (riv.) .... G 3
Manitoba (lake) .... D 4
Mantagao (riv.) .... E 3
Marshy (lake) .... B 5
McKay (lake) .... C 2
McPhail (riv.) .... F 2
Minnedosa (riv.) .... B 4
Moar (riv.) .... G 2
Molson (lake) .... J 3
Moose (isl.) .... E 3
Morrison (lake) .... C 1
Mossy (riv.) .... C 3
Mukutawa (lake) .... E 1
Mukutawa (riv.) .... E 1
Muskeg (bay) .... G 6
Nejanilini (lake) .... J 1
Nelson (riv.) .... J 2
Nopiming Prov. Park .... G 4
Northern Indian (lake) ...... J 2
North Knife (lake) .... J 2
North Knife (riv.) .... H 2
North Seal (riv.) .... H 2
North Shoal (lake) .... E 4
Nueltin (lake) .... H 1
Oak (lake) .... B 5
Obukowin (lake) .... G 3
Oiseau (lake) .... G 4
Oiseau (riv.) .... G 4
Overflow (bay) .... A 1
Overflowing (riv.) .... A 1
Owl (riv.) .... K 2
Oxford (lake) .... J 3
Paint (lake) .... J 2
Palsen (riv.) .... G 2
Pelican (bay) .... B 2
Pelican (lake) .... B 2
Pelican (lake) .... C 5
Pembina (hills) .... D 5
Pembina (riv.) .... C 5
Peonan (pt.) .... D 3
Pickerel (lake) .... C 2
Pigeon (riv.) .... F 2
Pipestone (creek) .... A 5
Plum (creek) .... B 5
Plum (lake) .... B 5
Poplar (riv.) .... E 2
Porcupine (hills) .... A 2
Portage (bay) .... D 3
Punk (isl.) .... F 3
Quesnel (lake) .... G 4
Rat (riv.) .... *E 5
Red (riv.) .... F 4
Red Deer (lake) .... A 2
Red Deer (riv.) .... A 2
Reindeer (isl.) .... E 3
Reindeer (lake) .... H 2
Reindeer (lake) .... E 3
Riding (mt.) .... B 4
Riding Mountain Nat'l Park .. B 4
Rock (lake) .... C 5
Ross (isl.) .... J 3
Sagemace (bay) .... B 3

Saint Andrew (lake) .... E 3
Saint George (lake) .... D 4
Saint Martin (lake) .... D 3
Saint Patrick (lake) .... D 3
Sale (riv.) .... E 5
Sandy (isls.) .... D 2
Sasaginnigak (lake) .... G 3
Seal (riv.) .... J 2
Selkirk (isl.) .... C 1
Setting (lake) .... H 3
Shoal (lake) .... G 5
Shoal (riv.) .... B 2
Sipiwesk (lake) .... J 3
Sisib (lake) .... C 2
Sleeve (lake) .... E 3
Slemon (lake) .... G 1
Snowshoe (lake) .... G 4
Soul (lake) .... C 2
Souris (riv.) .... B 5
Southern Indian (lake) ...... H 2
South Knife (riv.) .... J 2
South Seal (riv.) .... J 2
Split (lake) .... J 2
Spruce (isl.) .... B 1
Spruce Woods Prov. Park .... C 5
Stevenson (lake) .... J 3
Sturgeon (bay) .... E 3
Swan (lake) .... B 2
Swan (lake) .... D 5
Swan (riv.) .... A 3
Tadoule (lake) .... J 2
Tamarack (lake) .... F 3
Tatnam (cape) .... K 2
Traverse (bay) .... F 4
Turtle (mts.) .... B 5
Turtle (riv.) .... C 3
Turtle Mountain Prov. Park .. B 5
Valley (riv.) .... B 3
Vickers (lake) .... F 3
Viking (lake) .... G 3
Wanipigow (riv.) .... G 3
Washow (bay) .... F 3
Waterhen (lake) .... C 2
Weaver (lake) .... F 2
Wellman (lake) .... A 3
West Hawk (lake) .... G 5
West Shoal (lake) .... E 4
Whitemouth (lake) .... G 5
Whitemouth (riv.) .... G 5
Whiteshell Prov. Park ...... G 4
Whitewater (lake) .... B 5
Wicked (pt.) .... D 2
Winnipeg (lake) .... E 2
Winnipeg (riv.) .... G 4
Winnipegosis (lake) .... C 2
Woods (lake) .... H 5
Wrong (lake) .... F 2

*Population of metropolitan area.
●Population of rural municipality.

AREA 250,999 sq. mi. (650,087 sq. km.)
POPULATION 1,026,241
CAPITAL Winnipeg
LARGEST CITY Winnipeg
HIGHEST POINT Baldy Mtn. 2,729 ft. (832 m.)
SETTLED IN 1812
ADMITTED TO CONFEDERATION 1870
PROVINCIAL FLOWER Prairie Crocus

Topography

0 75 150 MI.
0 75 150 KM.

Below Sea Level | 100 m. 328 ft. | 200 m. 656 ft. | 500 m. 1,640 ft. | 1,000 m. 3,281 ft. | 2,000 m. 6,562 ft. | 5,000 m. 16,404 ft.

Agriculture, Industry and Resources

DOMINANT LAND USE

Cereals (chiefly barley, oats)
Cereals, Livestock
Dairy
Livestock
Forests
Nonagricultural Land

MAJOR MINERAL OCCURRENCES

Au Gold
Co Cobalt
Cu Copper
Na Salt
Ni Nickel
O Petroleum
Pb Lead
Pt Platinum
Zn Zinc

⚡ Water Power
▨ Major Industrial Areas

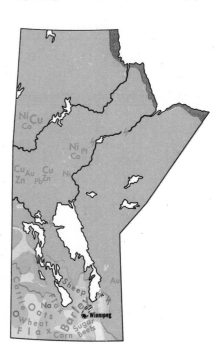

Topography

0   60   120 MI.

0   60   120 KM.

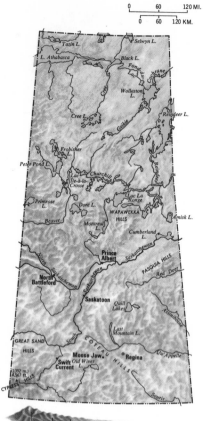

5,000 m. / 2,000 m. / 1,000 m. / 500 m. / 200 m. / 100 m. / Sea Level / Below
16,404 ft. / 6,562 ft. / 3,281 ft. / 1,640 ft. / 656 ft. / 328 ft.

CITIES and TOWNS

Abbey 218 .... C 5
Aberdeen 496 .... E 3
Abernethy 300 .... H 5
Air Ronge 557 .... M 3
Alameda 318 .... J 6
Alida 169 .... K 6
Allan 871 .... E 4
Alsask 652 .... B 4
Annaheim 209 .... G 3
Antelope ●231 .... C 5
Arborfield 439 .... H 2
Archerwill 286 .... H 3
Arcola 493 .... J 6
Arlington Beach ●432 . F 4
Asquith 507 .... D 3
Assiniboia 2,924 .... E 6
Avonlea 442 .... G 5
Baildon ●799 .... F 5
Balcarres 739 .... H 5
Balgonie 777 .... G 5
Batoche .... E 3
Battleford 3,565 ...... C 3
Beauval 606 .... L 3
Beechy 279 .... D 5
Bengough 536 .... F 6
Bethune 369 .... F 5
Bienfait 835 .... J 6
Biggar 2,561 .... C 3
Big River 819 .... D 2
Birch Hills 957 ...... F 3
Bjorkdale 269 .... H 3
Blaine Lake 653 .... D 3
Borden 197 .... D 3
Brabant Lake 245 .. M 3
Bradwell 168 .... E 4
Bredenbury 467 .... K 5
Briercrest 151 ..... F 5
Broadview 840 ..... J 5
Brock 184 .... C 4
Browning ●687 ..... J 6
Bruno 772 .... F 3
Buchanan 392 ...... J 4
Buffalo Gap ●598 ... F 6
Buffalo Narrows 1,088 L 3
Burstall 550 .... B 5
Cabri 632 .... C 5
Cadillac 173 ...... D 6
Calder 164 .... K 4
Cana ●1,238 ...... J 5
Candle Lake 219 .. F 2
Cando 163 .... C 3
Canoe Lake 182 .. L 2
Canora 2,667 ..... J 4
Canwood 340 ..... E 2
Carievale 246 .... K 6
Carlyle 1,074 .... J 6
Carnduff 1,043 ... K 6
Carrot River 1,169 . H 2

Central Butte 548 ...... E 5
Ceylon 184 .... G 6
Chaplin 389 .... E 5
Chitek Lake 170 .... D 2
Choiceland 543 .... G 2
Christopher Lake 227 . F 2
Churchbridge 972 ..... J 5
Clavet 234 .... E 4
Climax 207 .... C 6
Cochin 221 .... C 2
Codette 236 .... H 2
Coleville 383 .... B 4
Colonsay 594 .... F 4
Connaught Heights ●982 . G 3
Conquest 256 .... D 4
Consul 153 .... B 6
Coronach 1,032 ..... F 6
Craik 565 .... F 4
Craven 206 .... G 5
Creelman 184 ...... H 6
Creighton 1,636 .... N 4
Cudworth 947 ...... F 3
Cumberland House 831 . J 2
Cupar 669 .... G 5
Cut Knife 624 ...... B 3
Dalmeny 1,064 ..... E 3
Davidson 1,166 .... E 4
Debden 403 .... E 2
Delisle 980 .... D 4
Denare Beach 592 . M 4
Denzil 199 .... B 3
Deschambault Lake 386 . M 3
Dinsmore 398 .... D 4
Dodsland 272 .... C 4
Domremy 209 .... F 3
Drake 211 .... F 4
Duck Lake 699 .. E 3
Dundurn 531 .... E 4
Dysart 275 ...... H 5
Earl Grey 303 ... G 5
Eastend 723 ..... C 6
Eatonia 528 ..... B 4
Ebenezer 164 ... J 4
Edam 384 .... C 2
Edenwold 143 ... G 5
Elbow 313 ...... E 4
Eldorado 229 ... L 2
Elfros 199 ...... H 4
Elrose 624 ...... D 4
Elstow 143 ...... E 4
Endeavour 199 .. J 3
Englefeld 271 ... G 3
Erwood 149 ..... J 3
Eston 1,413 .... C 4
Estevan 9,174 .. J 6
Esterhazy 3,065 . K 5
Eyebrow 168 .... E 5
Fillmore 396 .... H 6
Fleming 141 .... K 5
Flin Flon 367 ... N 4

Foam Lake 1,452 .... H 4
Fond du Lac 494 .... L 2
Fort Qu'Appelle 1,827 . H 5
Fox Valley 380 .... B 5
Francis 182 .... H 5
Frobisher 166 .... J 6
Frontier 619 .... C 6
Gainsborough 308 .... K 6
Gerald 197 .... K 5
Glaslyn 430 .... C 2
Glenavon 284 .... J 5
Glen Ewen 168 ..... K 6
Goodsoil 263 ...... L 4
Govan 394 .... G 4
Grand Coulee 208 . G 5
Gravelbourg 1,338 . E 6
Grayson 264 ...... J 5
Green Acres 139 .. F 2
Green Lake 634 ... L 4
Grenfell 1,307 ... J 5
Guernsey 198 .... F 4
Gull Lake 1,095 .. C 5
Hafford 557 ...... D 3
Hague 625 .... E 3
Hanley 484 ...... E 4
Harris 259 .... D 4
Hawarden 137 ... E 4
Hearts Hill ●552 . B 3
Hepburn 411 .... E 3
Herbert 1,019 ... D 5
Hodgeville 329 .. E 5
Holdfast 297 .... F 5
Hudson Bay 2,361 . J 3
Humboldt 4,705 .. F 3
Hyas 165 .... J 4
Île-à-la-Crosse 1,035 . L 3
Imperial 501 .... F 4
Indian Head 1,889 . H 5
Invermay 353 ... J 4
Ituna 870 ...... H 4
Jansen 223 .... G 4
Jasmin ●14 .... H 4
Kamsack 2,688 . K 4
Kelliher 397 ... H 4
Kelvington 1,054 . H 3
Kenaston 345 .. E 4
Kennedy 275 ... J 5
Kerrobert 1,141 . C 4
Kincaid 256 .... D 6
Kindersley 3,969 . B 4
Kinistino 783 ... F 3
Kipling 1,016 ... J 5
Kisbey 228 .... J 6
Kronau 154 .... G 5
Kyle 516 .... C 5
Lac Pelletier ●586 . C 6
Lafleche 583 ... E 6
Laird 233 ...... E 3
Lake Lenore 361 . G 3
La Loche 1,632 . L 3
Lampman 651 .. J 6
Lancer 156 .... C 5
Landis 277 .... C 3
Lang 219 ...... G 6
Langenburg 1,324 . K 5
Langham 1,151 .. E 3
Lanigan 1,732 .. F 4
La Ronge 2,579 . L 3
Lashburn 813 .. B 2
Leader 1,108 .. B 5
Leask 478 ..... E 2
Lebret 274 .... H 5
Lemberg 414 .. H 5
Leoville 393 .. D 2
Leroy 504 .... G 4
Lestock 402 .. G 4
Limerick 164 . E 6
Lintlaw 234 .. H 3

Lipton 364 .... H 5
Lloydminster 6,034 .... A 2
Loon Lake 369 .... B 1
Loreburn 201 .... E 4
Lucky Lake 333 ...... D 5
Lumsden 1,303 ...... G 5
Luseland 704 .... B 3
Macdowall 171 ..... F 3
Macklin 976 ...... A 3
Macoun 190 ...... H 6
Maidstone 1,001 ... B 2
Mankota 375 .... D 6
Manor 368 ...... K 6
Maple Creek 2,470 . B 6
Marcelin 238 .... E 3
Margo 153 ...... H 4
Marriott ●627 ... D 4
Marsden 229 ... B 3
Marshall 453 .. B 2
Martensville 1,966 . E 3
Maryfield 431 .. K 6
Maymont 212 .. D 3
McLean 189 ... G 5
Meacham 178 . F 3
Meadow Lake 3,857 . C 1
Meath Park 262 .. F 2
Medstead 163 ... C 2
Melfort 6,010 ... G 3
Melville 5,092 .. J 5
Meota 381 ..... C 2
Mervin 155 .... C 2
Midale 564 .... H 6
Middle Lake 275 . F 3
Milden 251 .... D 4
Milestone 602 .. G 5
Montmartre 544 . H 5
Montreal Lake 448 . F 1
Moose Jaw 33,941 . F 5
Moose Range ●679 . H 2
Moosomin 2,579 .. K 5
Morse 416 ..... D 5
Mortlach 293 .. E 5
Mossbank 464 .. E 6
Muenster 385 .. F 3
Naicam 886 ... G 3
Neilburg 354 .. B 3
Neuanlage 144 . E 3
Neudorf 425 .. J 5
Neuhorst 146 . E 3
Nipawin 4,376 . H 2
Nokomis 524 . F 4
Norquay 552 .. J 4
North Battleford 14,030 . C 3
North Portal 164 .. J 6
Odessa 232 .... H 5
Ogema 441 .... G 6
Osler 527 ..... E 3
Outlook 1,976 .. E 4
Oxbow 1,191 .. J 6
Paddockwood 211 . F 2
Pangman 227 ... G 6
Paradise Hill 421 . B 2
Patuanak 173 .. L 3
Paynton 210 ... B 2
Pelican Narrows 331 . N 3
Pelly 391 ..... K 4
Pennant 202 .. C 5
Pense 472 .... G 5
Perdue 407 ... D 3
Pierceland 425 . K 4
Pilger 150 .... F 3
Pilot Butte 1,255 . G 5
Pine House 612 . M 3
Plenty 175 .... C 4
Plunkett 150 .. F 4
Ponteix 769 ... D 6
Porcupine Plain 937 . H 3
Preeceville 1,243 .. J 4

Prelate 317 .... B 5
Prince Albert 31,380 ... F 2
Prud'homme 222 .... F 3
Punnichy 394 .... G 4
Qu'Appelle 653 .... H 5
Quill Lake 514 .... G 3
Quinton 169 .... G 4
Rabbit Lake 159 ..... D 2
Radisson 439 .... D 3
Radville 1,012 ...... G 6
Rama 133 .... H 4
Raymore 635 ...... G 4
Redvers 859 ...... K 6
Regina (cap.) 162,613 . G 5
Regina ●164,313 .. G 5
Regina Beach 603 . G 5
Rhein 271 .... J 4
Richmound 188 .. B 5
Riverhurst 193 .. E 5
Rocanville 934 .. K 5
Roche Percé 142 . J 6
Rockglen 511 ... F 6
Rosetown 2,664 . D 4
Rose Valley 538 . H 3
Rosthern 1,609 .. E 3
Rouleau 443 .... F 5
Saint Benedict 157 . F 3
Saint Brieux 401 .. G 3
Saint Louis 448 .. F 3
Saint Philips ●538 . K 4
Saint Walburg 802 . B 2
Saltcoats 549 ... J 4
Sandy Bay 756 .. N 3
Saskatoon 154,210 . E 3
Saskatoon ●154,210 . E 3
Sceptre 169 .... C 5
Scott 203 ...... C 3
Sedley 373 .... H 5
Semans 344 ... G 4
Shaunavon 2,112 . C 6
Sheho 285 ..... H 4
Shell Lake 220 . D 2
Shellbrook 1,228 . E 2
Simpson 231 ... F 4
Sintaluta 215 .. H 5
Smeaton 246 .. G 2
Southey 697 .. G 5
Spalding 337 .. G 3
Spiritwood 926 . D 2
Springside 533 . J 4
Spy Hill 354 ... K 5
Star City 527 .. G 3
Stenen 143 .... J 4
Stockholm 391 . J 5
Stonehenge ●701 . F 6
Storthoaks 142 . K 6
Stoughton 716 .. J 6
Strasbourg 842 . G 4
Sturgis 789 .... J 4
Swift Current 14,747 . D 5
Tantallon 196 ... K 5
Theodore 473 .. J 4
Timber Bay 152 . F 1
Tisdale 3,107 .. H 3
Togo 181 ...... K 4
Tompkins 215 .. C 5
Torch River ●2,440 . G 2
Torquay 311 ... H 6
Tramping Lake 178 . B 3
Tugaske 175 ... E 5
Turnor Lake 166 . L 3
Turtleford 505 . B 2
Unity 2,408 .... B 3
Uranium City 2,507 . L 1
Val Marie 236 .. D 6
Vanguard 292 .. D 6
Vanscoy 298 .. D 4
Vibank 369 .... H 5

Viscount 386 .... F 4
Vonda 313 .... F 3
Wadena 1,495 .... H 4
Wakaw 1,030 .... F 3
Waldeck 292 .... D 5
Waldheim 758 ...... E 3
Walpole ●711 ...... K 6
Wapella 487 ...... K 5
Warman 2,076 .... E 3
Waseca 169 ..... B 2
Waskesiu Lake 176 . E 2
Watrous 1,830 .. F 4
Watson 901 .... G 3
Wawota 622 ... J 6
Weldon 279 ... F 3
Welwyn 170 .. K 5
Weyburn 9,523 . H 6
White City 602 . G 5
White Fox 394 . H 2
Whitewood 1,003 . J 5
Wilcox 202 ... G 5
Wilkie 1,501 .. C 3
Willow Bunch 494 . F 6
Willow Creek ●1,218 . E 5
Windthorst 254 . J 5
Wiseton 195 .. D 4
Wishart 212 .. H 4
Wollaston Lake 248 . N 2
Wolseley 904 . J 5
Wymark 162 .. D 5
Wynyard 2,147 . G 4
Yarbo 158 .... K 5

Yellow Grass 477 ...... H 6
Yorkton 15,339 .... J 4
Young 456 .... F 4
Zenon Park 273 ..... H 2

OTHER FEATURES

Allan (hills) .... E 4
Amisk (lake) .... M 4
Antelope (lake) ...... C 5
Antler (riv.) .... K 5
Arm (riv.) .... F 5
Assiniboine (riv.) ... J 4
Athabasca (lake) .. L 2
Bad (lake) .... C 5
Bad (hills) .... F 3
Basin (lake) ...... G 3
Batoche Nat'l Hist. Site . E 3
Battle (creek) .... B 6
Battle (riv.) ...... B 3
Bear (hills) ...... H 4
Beaver (hills) .. C 1
Beaver (riv.) .. L 2
Beaverlodge (lake) . L 2
Big Muddy (lake) . G 6
Bigstick (lake) .. B 5
Birch (lake) .... B 3
Bitter (lake) ... B 5
Black (lake) .. M 2
Boundary (plat.) . B 6
Brightsand (lake) . B 2
Bronson (lake) .. B 2

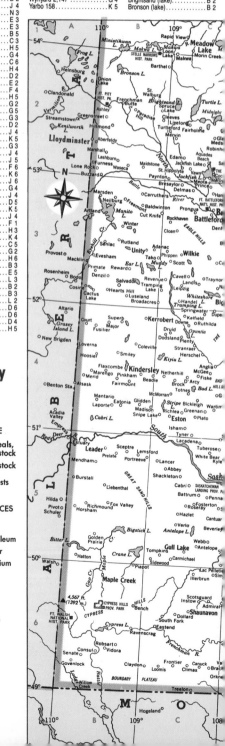

Agriculture, Industry and Resources

DOMINANT LAND USE

- Wheat
- Cereals (chiefly barley, oats)
- Forests
- Cereals, Livestock
- Livestock

MAJOR MINERAL OCCURRENCES

Au Gold
Cu Copper
G   Natural Gas
He Helium
K   Potash
Lg Lignite

Na Salt
O   Petroleum
S   Sulfur
U   Uranium
Zn Zinc

⚡ Water Power

▨ Major Industrial Areas

AREA 251,699 sq. mi. (651,900 sq. km.)
POPULATION 968,313
CAPITAL Regina
LARGEST CITY Regina
HIGHEST POINT Cypress Hills 4,567 ft.
  (1,392 m.)
SETTLED IN 1774
ADMITTED TO CONFEDERATION 1905
PROVINCIAL FLOWER Prairie Lily

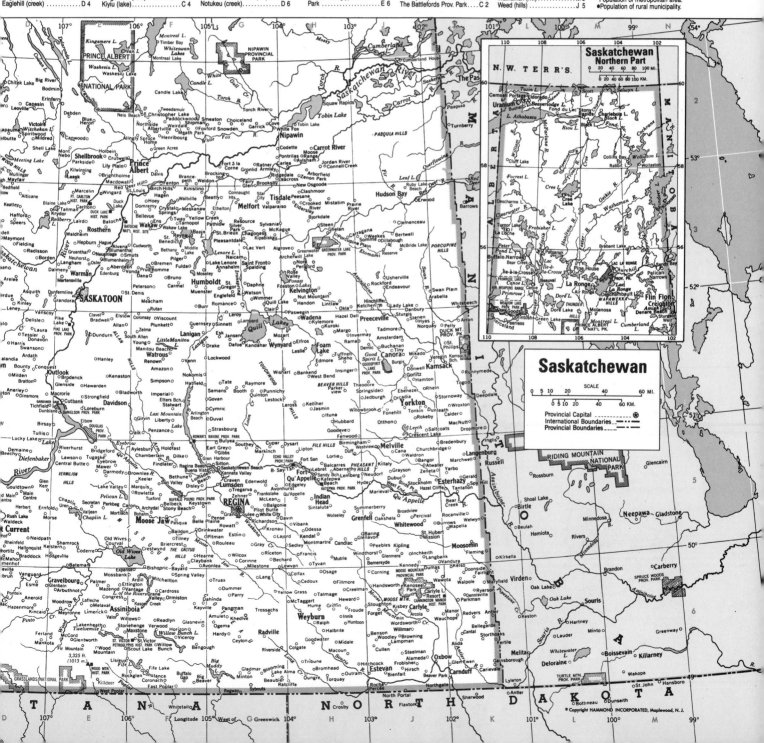

AREA 255,285 sq. mi. (661,185 sq. km.)
POPULATION 2,237,724
CAPITAL Edmonton
LARGEST CITY Edmonton
HIGHEST POINT Mt. Columbia 12,294 ft. (3,747 m.)
SETTLED IN 1861
ADMITTED TO CONFEDERATION 1905
PROVINCIAL FLOWER Wild Rose

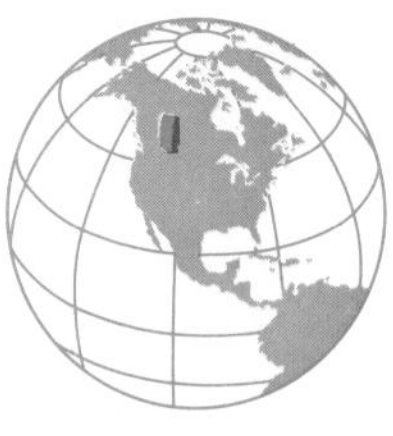

Topography

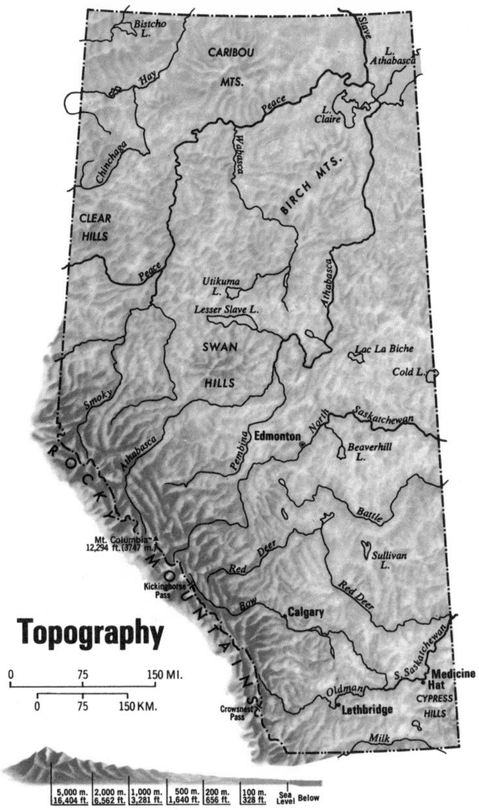

Bistcho L.
CARIBOU MTS.
Hay
Slave
L. Athabasca
Peace
L. Claire
Chinchaga
Wabasca
BIRCH MTS.
CLEAR HILLS
Peace
Athabasca
Utikuma L.
Lesser Slave L.
SWAN HILLS
Lac La Biche
Cold L.
Smoky
Athabasca
North Saskatchewan
Pembina
Edmonton
Beaverhill L.
ROCKY MOUNTAINS
Battle
Mt. Columbia 12,294 ft. (3747 m.)
Red Deer
Sullivan L.
Kickinghorse Pass
Red Deer
Bow
Calgary
S. Saskatchewan
Oldman
Medicine Hat
CYPRESS HILLS
Crowsnest Pass
Lethbridge
Milk
0 75 150 MI.
0 75 150 KM.
5,000 m. 16,404 ft.
2,000 m. 6,562 ft.
1,000 m. 3,281 ft.
500 m. 1,640 ft.
200 m. 656 ft.
100 m. 328 ft.
Sea Level
Below

CITIES and TOWNS

Acme 457 . . . . . D 4
Airdrie 8,414 . . . . . C 4
Alberta Beach 485 . . . . . C 3
Alix 837 . . . . . D 3
Andrew 548 . . . . . D 3
Antler Lake 334 . . . . . D 3
Ardmore 224 . . . . . E 2
Arrowwood 156 . . . . . D 4
Athabasca 1,731 . . . . . D 2
Banff 4,208 . . . . . C 4
Barnwell 359 . . . . . D 5
Barons 315 . . . . . D 4
Barrhead 3,736 . . . . . C 2
Bashaw 875 . . . . . D 3
Bassano 1,200 . . . . . D 4
Bawlf 350 . . . . . D 3
Beaumont 2,638 . . . . . D 3
Beaverlodge 1,937 . . . . . A 2
Beiseker 580 . . . . . D 4
Bentley 823 . . . . . C 3
Berwyn 557 . . . . . B 1
Big Valley 360 . . . . . D 3
Black Diamond 1,444 . . . . . C 4
Blackfalds 1,488 . . . . . D 3
Blackfoot 220 . . . . . E 3
Blackie 298 . . . . . D 4
Bon Accord 1,376 . . . . . D 3
Bonnyville 4,454 . . . . . E 2
Bowden 989 . . . . . C 4
Bow Island 1,491 . . . . . E 5
Boyle 638 . . . . . D 2
Bragg Creek 505 . . . . . C 4
Breton 552 . . . . . C 3
Brooks 9,421 . . . . . E 4
Bruce 88 . . . . . E 3
Bruderheim 1,136 . . . . . D 3
Burdett 220 . . . . . E 5
Calgary 592,743 . . . . . C 4
Calgary *592,743 . . . . . C 4
Calmar 1,003 . . . . . D 3
Camrose 12,570 . . . . . D 3
Canmore 3,484 . . . . . C 4
Carbon 434 . . . . . D 4
Cardston 3,267 . . . . . D 5
Carmangay 266 . . . . . D 4
Caroline 436 . . . . . C 3
Carseland 484 . . . . . D 4
Carstairs 1,587 . . . . . D 4
Castor 1,123 . . . . . D 3
Cereal 249 . . . . . E 4
Champion 339 . . . . . D 4
Chauvin 298 . . . . . E 3
Chipman 266 . . . . . D 3
Clairmont 469 . . . . . A 2
Claresholm 3,493 . . . . . D 4
Clive 364 . . . . . D 3
Clyde 364 . . . . . D 2
Coaldale 4,579 . . . . . D 5
Coalhurst 882 . . . . . D 5
Cochrane 3,544 . . . . . C 4
Cold Lake 2,110 . . . . . E 2
College Heights 267 . . . . . D 3
Consort 632 . . . . . E 3
Cooking Lake 218 . . . . . D 3
Coronation 1,309 . . . . . E 3
Coutts 400 . . . . . D 5
Cowley 304 . . . . . D 5
Cremona 382 . . . . . C 4
Crossfield 1,217 . . . . . C 4
Daysland 679 . . . . . D 3
Delburne 574 . . . . . D 3
Desmarais 260 . . . . . D 2
Devon 3,885 . . . . . D 3
Didsbury 3,095 . . . . . C 4
Donalda 280 . . . . . D 3
Donnelly 336 . . . . . B 2
Drayton Valley 5,042 . . . . . C 3
Drumheller 6,508 . . . . . D 4
Duchess 429 . . . . . E 4
East Coulee 218 . . . . . D 4
Eckville 870 . . . . . C 3
Edgerton 387 . . . . . E 3
Edmonton (cap.) 532,246 . . . . . D 3
Edmonton *657,057 . . . . . D 3
Edmonton Beach 280 . . . . . C 3
Edson 5,835 . . . . . B 3
Elk Point 1,022 . . . . . E 3
Elnora 249 . . . . . D 3
Entwistle 462 . . . . . C 3
Erskine 259 . . . . . D 3
Evansburg 779 . . . . . C 3
Exshaw 353 . . . . . C 4
Fairview 2,869 . . . . . A 1
Falher 1,102 . . . . . B 2
Faust 399 . . . . . C 2
Foremost 568 . . . . . E 5
Forestburg 924 . . . . . E 3
Fort Assiniboine 207 . . . . . C 2
Fort Chipewyan 944 . . . . . C 5
Fort Macleod 3,139 . . . . . D 5
Fort McKay 267 . . . . . E 1
Fort McMurray 31,000 . . . . . E 1
Fort Saskatchewan 12,169 . . . . . D 3
Fort Vermilion 752 . . . . . B 5
Fox Creek 1,978 . . . . . B 2
Fox Lake 634 . . . . . B 5
Gibbons 2,276 . . . . . D 3
Gift Lake 428 . . . . . C 2
Girouxville 325 . . . . . B 2
Gleichen 381 . . . . . D 4
Glendon 430 . . . . . E 2
Glenwood 259 . . . . . D 5
Grand Centre 3,146 . . . . . E 2
Grande Cache 4,523 . . . . . A 3
Grande Prairie 24,263 . . . . . A 2
Granum 399 . . . . . D 5
Grimshaw 2,316 . . . . . B 1
Grouard Mission 221 . . . . . C 2
Hanna 2,806 . . . . . E 4
Hardisty 641 . . . . . E 3
Hay Lakes 302 . . . . . D 3
Heisler 212 . . . . . D 3
High Level 2,194 . . . . . A 5
High Prairie 2,506 . . . . . B 2
High River 4,792 . . . . . D 4
Hines Creek 575 . . . . . A 1
Hinton 8,342 . . . . . B 3
Holden 430 . . . . . D 3
Hughenden 267 . . . . . E 3
Hythe 639 . . . . . A 2
Innisfail 5,247 . . . . . D 3
Innisfree 255 . . . . . E 3
Irma 474 . . . . . E 3
Irricana 558 . . . . . D 4
Irvine 360 . . . . . E 5
Jasper 3,269 . . . . . B 3
John d'Or Prairie 437 . . . . . B 5
Joussard 330 . . . . . B 2
Killam 1,005 . . . . . E 3
Kinuso 285 . . . . . C 2
Kitscoty 497 . . . . . E 3
Lac La Biche 2,007 . . . . . E 2
Lacombe 5,591 . . . . . D 3
La Crete 479 . . . . . B 5
Lake Louise 355 . . . . . B 4
Lamont 1,563 . . . . . D 3
Leduc 12,471 . . . . . D 3
Legal 1,022 . . . . . D 3
Lethbridge 54,072 . . . . . D 5
Linden 407 . . . . . D 4
Little Buffalo Lake 253 . . . . . B 1
Lloydminster 8,997 . . . . . E 3
Longview 301 . . . . . C 4
Lougheed 226 . . . . . E 3
Lundbreck 244 . . . . . C 5
Magrath 1,576 . . . . . D 5
Manning 1,173 . . . . . B 1
Mannville 788 . . . . . E 3
Marlboro 211 . . . . . B 3
Marwayne 500 . . . . . E 3
Mayerthorpe 1,475 . . . . . C 3
McLennan 1,125 . . . . . B 2
Medicine Hat 40,380 . . . . . E 4
Milk River 894 . . . . . D 5
Millet 1,120 . . . . . D 3
Mirror 507 . . . . . D 3
Monarch 212 . . . . . D 5
Morinville 4,657 . . . . . D 3
Morrin 244 . . . . . D 4
Mundare 604 . . . . . D 3
Myrnam 397 . . . . . E 3
Nacmine 369 . . . . . D 4
Nampa 334 . . . . . B 1
Nanton 1,641 . . . . . D 4
New Norway 291 . . . . . D 3
New Sarepta 417 . . . . . D 3
Nobleford 534 . . . . . D 5
North Calling Lake 234 . . . . . D 2
Okotoks 3,847 . . . . . C 4
Olds 4,813 . . . . . D 4
Onoway 621 . . . . . C 3
Oyen 975 . . . . . E 4
Peace River 5,907 . . . . . B 1
Penhold 1,531 . . . . . D 3
Picture Butte 1,404 . . . . . D 5
Pincher Creek 3,757 . . . . . D 5
Plamondon 259 . . . . . D 2
Pollockville 19 . . . . . E 4
Ponoka 5,221 . . . . . D 3
Provost 1,645 . . . . . E 3
Rainbow Lake 504 . . . . . A 5
Ralston 357 . . . . . E 4
Raymond 2,837 . . . . . D 5
Redcliff 3,876 . . . . . E 4
Red Deer 46,393 . . . . . D 3
Redwater 1,932 . . . . . D 3
Rimbey 1,685 . . . . . C 3
Robb 230 . . . . . B 3
Rockyford 329 . . . . . D 4
Rocky Mountain House 4,698 . C 3
Rosemary 328 . . . . . E 4
Rycroft 649 . . . . . A 2
Ryley 483 . . . . . D 3
Saint Albert 31,996 . . . . . D 3
Saint Paul 4,884 . . . . . E 3
Sangudo 398 . . . . . C 3
Sedgewick 879 . . . . . E 3
Sexsmith 1,180 . . . . . A 2
Shaughnessy 270 . . . . . D 5
Sherwood Park 29,285 . . . . . D 3
Slave Lake 4,506 . . . . . C 2
Smith 216 . . . . . D 2
Smoky Lake 1,074 . . . . . D 2
Spirit River 1,104 . . . . . A 2
Spruce Grove 10,326 . . . . . D 3
Standard 379 . . . . . D 4
Stavely 504 . . . . . D 4
Stettler 5,136 . . . . . D 3
Stirling 688 . . . . . D 5
Stony Plain 4,839 . . . . . C 3
Strathmore 2,986 . . . . . D 4
Strome 281 . . . . . E 3
Sundre 1,742 . . . . . C 4
Swan Hills 2,497 . . . . . C 2
Sylvan Lake 3,779 . . . . . C 3
Taber 5,988 . . . . . E 5
Thorhild 576 . . . . . D 2
Thorsby 737 . . . . . C 3
Three Hills 1,787 . . . . . D 4
Tilley 345 . . . . . E 4
Tofield 1,504 . . . . . D 3
Trochu 880 . . . . . D 4
Turner Valley 1,311 . . . . . C 4
Two Hills 1,193 . . . . . E 3
Valleyview 2,061 . . . . . B 2
Vauxhall 1,049 . . . . . D 4
Vegreville 5,251 . . . . . E 3
Vermilion 3,766 . . . . . E 3
Veteran 314 . . . . . E 3
Viking 1,232 . . . . . E 3
Vilna 345 . . . . . E 2
Vulcan 1,489 . . . . . D 4
Wabamun 662 . . . . . C 3
Wabasca 701 . . . . . D 2
Wainwright 4,266 . . . . . E 3
Warburg 501 . . . . . C 3
Warner 477 . . . . . D 5
Waskatenau 290 . . . . . D 2
Wembley 1,169 . . . . . A 2
Westlock 4,424 . . . . . C 2
Wetaskiwin 9,597 . . . . . D 3
Whitecourt 5,585 . . . . . C 2
Wildwood 441 . . . . . C 3
Willingdon 366 . . . . . E 3
Youngstown 297 . . . . . E 4

OTHER FEATURES

Abraham (lake) . . . . . B 3
Alberta (mt.) . . . . . B 3
Assiniboine (mt.) . . . . . C 4
Athabasca (lake) . . . . . C 5
Athabasca (riv.) . . . . . D 1
Banff Nat'l Park . . . . . B 4
Battle (riv.) . . . . . D 3
Bear (lake) . . . . . A 2
Beaver (riv.) . . . . . E 2
Beaverhill (lake) . . . . . D 3
Behan (lake) . . . . . E 2
Belly (riv.) . . . . . D 5
Berland (riv.) . . . . . A 3
Berry (creek) . . . . . E 4
Biche (lake) . . . . . E 2
Big (isl.) . . . . . B 5
Big Horn (dam) . . . . . B 3
Bighorn (range) . . . . . B 3
Birch (hills) . . . . . A 2
Birch (lake) . . . . . E 3
Birch (mts.) . . . . . B 5
Birch (riv.) . . . . . B 5
Bison (lake) . . . . . B 1
Bittern (lake) . . . . . D 3
Botha (riv.) . . . . . B 1
Bow (riv.) . . . . . D 4
Boyer (riv.) . . . . . A 5
Brazeau (mt.) . . . . . B 3
Brazeau (riv.) . . . . . B 3
Buffalo (lake) . . . . . D 3
Buffalo Head (hills) . . . . . B 5
Burnt (lakes) . . . . . C 1
Cadotte (lake) . . . . . B 1
Cadotte (riv.) . . . . . B 1
Calling (lake) . . . . . D 2
Canal (creek) . . . . . E 5
Cardinal (lake) . . . . . B 1
Caribou (mts.) . . . . . B 5
Chinchaga (riv.) . . . . . A 5
Chip (lake) . . . . . C 3
Chipewyan (lake) . . . . . D 1
Chipewyan (riv.) . . . . . D 1
Christina (lake) . . . . . E 2
Christina (riv.) . . . . . E 1
Claire (lake) . . . . . B 5
Clear (hills) . . . . . A 1
Clearwater (riv.) . . . . . C 4
Clearwater (riv.) . . . . . E 1
Clyde (lake) . . . . . E 2
Cold (lake) . . . . . E 2
Columbia (mt.) . . . . . B 3
Crowsnest (pass) . . . . . C 5
Cypress (hills) . . . . . E 5
Cypress Hills Prov. Park . . . . . E 5
Dillon (riv.) . . . . . E 2
Dowling (lake) . . . . . D 4
Dunkirk (riv.) . . . . . D 1
Eisenhower (mt.) . . . . . C 4
Elbow (riv.) . . . . . C 4
Elk Island Nat'l Park . . . . . D 3
Ells (riv.) . . . . . D 1
Etzikom Coulee (riv.) . . . . . E 5
Eva (lake) . . . . . B 5
Farrell (lake) . . . . . D 4
Firebag (riv.) . . . . . E 1
Forbes (mt.) . . . . . B 4
Freeman (riv.) . . . . . C 2
Frog (lake) . . . . . E 3
Garson (lake) . . . . . E 1
Gipsy (lake) . . . . . E 1
Gordon (lake) . . . . . E 1
Gough (lake) . . . . . D 3
Graham (lake) . . . . . C 1
Gull (lake) . . . . . C 3
Haig (lake) . . . . . B 1
Hawk (hills) . . . . . B 1
Hay (lake) . . . . . A 5
Hay (riv.) . . . . . A 5
Heart (lake) . . . . . E 2
Highwood (riv.) . . . . . C 4
House (mt.) . . . . . C 2
House (riv.) . . . . . D 2
Iosegun (lake) . . . . . B 2
Iosegun (riv.) . . . . . B 2
Jackfish (riv.) . . . . . B 5
Jasper Nat'l Park . . . . . A 3
Kakwa (riv.) . . . . . A 2
Kickinghorse (pass) . . . . . B 4
Kimiwan (lake) . . . . . B 2
Kirkpatrick (lake) . . . . . E 4
Kitchener (mt.) . . . . . B 3
Legend (lake) . . . . . D 1
Lesser Slave (lake) . . . . . C 2
Liége (riv.) . . . . . D 1
Little Bow (riv.) . . . . . D 4
Little Cadotte (riv.) . . . . . B 1
Little Smoky (riv.) . . . . . B 2
Livingstone (range) . . . . . C 4
Logan (lake) . . . . . E 2
Loon (lake) . . . . . C 1
Loon (riv.) . . . . . C 1
Lubicon (lake) . . . . . C 1
Lyell (mt.) . . . . . B 4
MacKay (riv.) . . . . . D 1
Maligne (lake) . . . . . B 3
Margaret (lake) . . . . . B 5
Marie (lake) . . . . . E 2
Marion (lake) . . . . . D 3
Marten (mt.) . . . . . C 2
McClelland (lake) . . . . . E 1
McGregor (lake) . . . . . D 4
McLeod (riv.) . . . . . B 3
Meikle (riv.) . . . . . A 1
Mikkwa (riv.) . . . . . B 5
Milk (riv.) . . . . . D 5
Mistehae (lake) . . . . . C 2
Muriel (lake) . . . . . E 2
Muskwa (lake) . . . . . C 1
Muskwa (riv.) . . . . . C 1
Namur (lake) . . . . . D 1
Newell (lake) . . . . . E 4
Nordegg (riv.) . . . . . C 3
North Saskatchewan (riv.) . . . . . E 3
North Wabasca (lake) . . . . . D 1
Notikewin (riv.) . . . . . A 1
Oldman (riv.) . . . . . D 5
Otter (lakes) . . . . . B 1
Pakowki (lake) . . . . . E 5
Panny (riv.) . . . . . C 1
Peace (riv.) . . . . . B 1
Peerless (lake) . . . . . C 1
Pelican (lake) . . . . . D 2
Pelican (mts.) . . . . . D 2
Pembina (riv.) . . . . . C 3
Pigeon (lake) . . . . . D 3
Pinehurst (lake) . . . . . E 2
Porcupine (hills) . . . . . C 4
Primrose (lake) . . . . . E 2
Rainbow (lake) . . . . . A 5
Red Deer (lake) . . . . . D 3
Red Deer (riv.) . . . . . D 4
Richardson (riv.) . . . . . C 5
Rocky (mts.) . . . . . B-C 4
Rosebud (riv.) . . . . . D 4
Russell (lake) . . . . . C 1
Saddle (hills) . . . . . A 2
Sainte Anne (lake) . . . . . C 3
Saint Mary (res.) . . . . . D 5
Saint Mary (riv.) . . . . . D 5
Saulteaux (riv.) . . . . . C 2
Seibert (lake) . . . . . E 2
Simonette (riv.) . . . . . A 2
Slave (riv.) . . . . . C 5
Smoky (riv.) . . . . . A 2
Snake Indian (riv.) . . . . . A 3
Snipe (lake) . . . . . B 2
Sounding (creek) . . . . . E 4
South Saskatchewan (riv.) . . . . . E 4
South Wabasca (lake) . . . . . D 2
Spencer (lake) . . . . . E 2
Spray (mts.) . . . . . C 4
Sturgeon (lake) . . . . . B 2
Sullivan (lake) . . . . . D 3
Swan (hills) . . . . . C 2
Swan (riv.) . . . . . C 2
Temple (mt.) . . . . . B 4
The Twins (mt.) . . . . . B 3
Thickwood (hills) . . . . . D 1
Touchwood (lake) . . . . . E 2
Travers (res.) . . . . . D 4
Trout (mt.) . . . . . C 1
Trout (riv.) . . . . . C 1
Utikuma (lake) . . . . . C 2
Utikuma (riv.) . . . . . C 1
Utikumasis (lake) . . . . . C 2
Vermilion (riv.) . . . . . E 3
Wabasca (riv.) . . . . . C 1
Wallace (mt.) . . . . . C 2
Wapiti (riv.) . . . . . A 2
Wappau (lake) . . . . . E 2
Watchusk (lake) . . . . . E 1
Waterton-Glacier Int'l Peace Park . . . . . C 5
Waterton Lakes Nat'l Park . . . . . C 5
Whitemud (riv.) . . . . . A 1
Wildhay (riv.) . . . . . B 3
Willmore Wilderness Prov. Park . . . . . A 3
Winagami (lake) . . . . . B 2
Winefred (lake) . . . . . E 2
Winefred (riv.) . . . . . E 2
Wolf (lake) . . . . . E 2
Wolverine (riv.) . . . . . B 1
Wood Buffalo Nat'l Park . . . . . B 5
Yellowhead (pass) . . . . . A 3
Zama (lake) . . . . . A 5

*Population of metropolitan area.

Agriculture, Industry and Resources

DOMINANT LAND USE

- Wheat
- Cereals (chiefly barley, oats)
- Cereals, Livestock
- Dairy
- Pasture Livestock
- Range Livestock
- Forests
- Nonagricultural Land

MAJOR MINERAL OCCURRENCES

- C Coal
- G Natural Gas
- Na Salt
- O Petroleum
- S Sulfur

- Water Power
- Major Industrial Areas

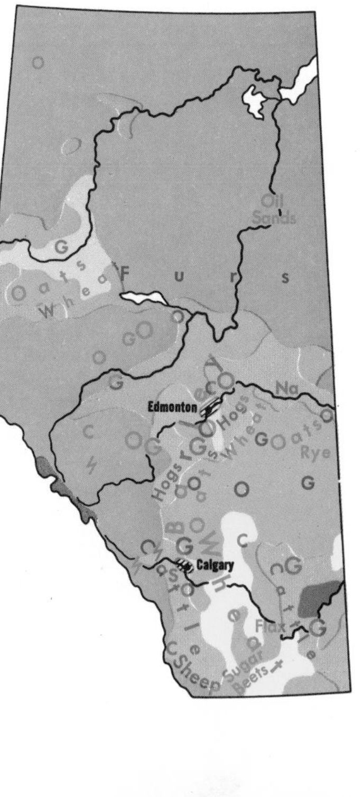

Oil Sands
Furs
Oats
Wheat
Edmonton
Hogs
Na
Oats
Rye
Calgary
Cattle
Sheep
Sugar Beets
Flax

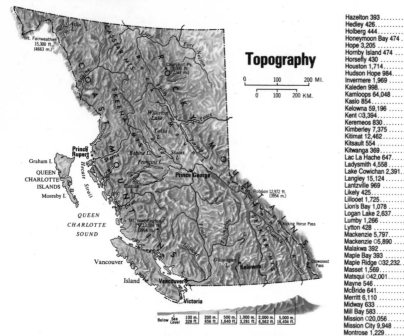

Topography

```
0    100    200 MI.
0    100    200 KM.
```

Below Sea Level | 100 m. 328 ft. | 200 m. 656 ft. | 500 m. 1,640 ft. | 1,000 m. 3,281 ft. | 2,000 m. 6,562 ft. | 5,000 m. 16,404 ft.

CITIES and TOWNS

Abbotsford 12,745 ....L 3
Alert Bay 626 ....D 5
Armstrong 2,683 ....H 5
Ashcroft 2,156 ....G 5
Ashton Creek 452 ....G 4
Balfour 472 ....J 5
Barlow 441 ....J 5
Barrière 1,370 ....H 4
Blueberry Creek 635 .....J 5
Blue River 384 ....H 4
Boston Bar 498 ....G 5
Bowen Island 1,125 ......K 3
Brackendale 1,719 ....J 3
Burnaby ○136,494 ....K 3
Burns Lake 1,777 ....D 3
Cache Creek 1,308 ....G 5
Campbell River 15,370 ...E 5
Canal Flats 919 ....J 5
Canyon 698 ....J 5
Cassiar 1,045 ....K 2
Castlegar 6,902 ....J 5

Cawston 785 ....H 5
Central Saanich ○9,890 ..K 3
Chase 1,777 ....H 5
Chemainus 2,069 ....J 3
Cherry Creek 450 ....G 5
Chetwynd 2,553 ....G 2
Chilliwack ○40,642 ......M 3
Clearwater 1,461 ....G 4
Clinton 804 ....G 4
Coldstream ○6,450 ....H 5
Comox 6,607 ....H 2
Coquitlam ○61,077 ....K 3
Courtenay 8,992 ....E 5
Cranbrook 15,915 ....K 5
Creston 4,190 ....J 5
Crofton 1,303 ....J 3
Cultus Lake 481 ....M 3
Cumberland 1,947 ....E 5
Dawson Creek 11,373 .....G 2
Delta ○74,692 ....K 3
Duncan 4,228 ....J 3
Elkford 3,126 ....K 5
Enderby 1,816 ....H 5
Erickson 972 ....J 5

Errington 609 ....J 3
Esquimalt ○15,870 ....K 4
Falkland 478 ....H 5
Fernie 5,444 ....K 5
Forest Grove 444 ....G 4
Fort Fraser 574 ....E 3
Fort Langley 2,326 ......L 3
Fort Nelson 3,724 ....M 2
Fort Saint James 2,284 ..E 3
Fort Saint John 13,891 ..G 2
Fraser Lake 1,543 ....E 3
Fruitvale 1,904 ....J 5
Gabriola 1,627 ....J 3
Galiano 669 ....K 3
Ganges 1,118 ....J 3
Gibsons 2,594 ....K 3
Gold River 2,225 ....D 5
Golden 3,476 ....J 4
Grand Forks 3,486 ....H 6
Granisle 1,430 ....D 3
Greenwood 856 ....H 5
Hagensborg 350 ....D 4
Harrison Hot Springs 569 .M 3
Hatzic 1,055 ....L 3

Hazelton 393 ....D 2
Hedley 426 ....G 5
Holberg 444 ....C 5
Honeymoon Bay 474 ....J 3
Hope 3,205 ....M 3
Hornby Island 474 ....H 2
Horsefly 430 ....G 4
Houston 1,714 ....D 3
Hudson Hope 984 ....F 2
Invermere 1,969 ....J 5
Kaleden 998 ....H 5
Kamloops 64,048 ....G 5
Kaslo 854 ....J 5
Kelowna 59,196 ....H 5
Kent ○3,394 ....M 3
Keremeos 830 ....G 5
Kimberley 7,375 ....K 5
Kitimat 12,462 ....C 3
Kitsault 554 ....C 2
Kitwanga 369 ....D 2
Lac La Hache 647 ....G 4
Ladysmith 4,558 ....J 3
Lake Cowichan 2,391 .....J 3
Lantzville 969 ....J 3
Likely 425 ....G 4
Lillooet 1,725 ....G 5
Lion's Bay 1,078 ....K 3
Logan Lake 2,637 ....G 5
Lumby 1,266 ....H 5
Lytton 428 ....G 5
Mackenzie 5,797 ....F 2
Mackenzie ○5,890 ....F 2
Malakwa 392 ....H 5
Maple Bay 393 ....K 3
Maple Ridge ○32,232 .....L 3
Masset 1,569 ....B 3
Matsqui ○42,001 ....L 3
Mayne 546 ....K 3
McBride 641 ....G 3
Merritt 6,110 ....G 5
Midway 633 ....H 6
Mill Bay 583 ....K 3
Mission ○20,056 ....L 3
Mission City 9,948 ......L 3
Montrose 1,229 ....J 5
Nakusp 1,495 ....J 5
Nanaimo 47,069 ....J 3
Naramata 876 ....H 5
Nelson 9,143 ....J 5
New Denver 642 ....J 5
New Hazelton 792 ....D 2
New Westminster 38,550 ..K 3
Nicomen Island 360 ......L 3
Nootka ....D 5
North Cowichan ○18,210 ..K 3
North Pender Island 906 ..K 3
North Saanich ○6,117 ....K 3
North Vancouver 33,952 ..K 3
North Vancouver ○65,367 ..K 3
Oak Bay ○16,990 ....K 4
Okanagan Falls 1,030 ....H 5
Okanagan Landing 834 ....H 5
Okanagan Mission ....H 5
Old Barkerville 11 ......G 3
Oliver 1,893 ....H 5
One Hundred Mile House
  1,925 ....G 4
Osoyoos 2,738 ....H 5
Oyama 430 ....H 5
Parksville 5,216 ....J 3
Peachland ○2,865 ....G 5

Penticton 23,181 ....H 5
Pitt Meadows ○6,209 .....L 3
Port Alberni 19,892 .....H 3
Port Alice 1,668 ....D 5
Port Clements 380 ....B 3
Port Coquitlam 27,535 ...L 3
Port Edward 989 ....B 3
Port Hardy ○3,778 ....D 5
Port McNeill 2,474 ......D 5
Port Moody 14,917 ....L 3
Pouce-Coupé 821 ....G 2
Powell River ○13,423 ....E 5
Prince George 67,559 ....F 3
Prince Rupert 16,197 ....B 3
Princeton 3,051 ....G 5
Qualicum Beach 2,844 ....J 3
Queen Charlotte 1,070 ...A 3
Quesnel 8,240 ....F 3
Radium Hot Springs 419 ..J 5
Revelstoke 5,544 ....J 5
Richmond ○96,154 ....K 3
Roberts Creek 926 ....K 3
Robson 1,008 ....J 5
Rossland 3,967 ....H 6
Royston 754 ....H 2
Saanich ○78,710 ....K 3
Salmo 1,169 ....J 5
Salmon Arm 1,946 ....H 5
Salmon Arm ○10,780 .....H 5
Saltair 1,356 ....J 3
Sandspit 794 ....B 3
Sayward 482 ....D 5
Sechelt 1,096 ....J 2
Shawnigan Lake 419 ......J 3
Shoreacres 555 ....J 5
Sicamous 1,057 ....H 5
Sidney 7,946 ....K 3
Slocan 351 ....J 5
Slocan Park 414 ....J 5
Smithers 4,570 ....D 2
Sointula 567 ....D 5
Sooke 852 ....J 4
Sorrento 659 ....H 5
South Hazelton 500 ......D 2
South Wellington 620 ....J 3
Spallumcheen 4,213 ......H 5
Sparwood 3,267 ....K 5
Sproat Lake 440 ....H 3
Squamish 1,590 ....F 5
Stewart ○1,456 ....C 2
Summerland ○7,473 ......G 5
Surrey ○147,138 ....K 3
Tahsis 1,739 ....D 5
Taylor 966 ....G 2
Telkwa 840 ....D 3
Terrace 8,893 ....C 3
Terrace ○10,914 ....C 3
Thornhill 4,281 ....C 3
Thrums 360 ....J 5
Tofino 705 ....H 2
Trail 9,599 ....J 6
Ucluelet 1,593 ....E 6
Union Bay 601 ....H 2
Valemount 1,130 ....H 4
Vancouver 414,281 ......K 3
Vancouver (Greater)
  *1,169,831 ....K 3
Vanderhoof 2,323 ....E 3
Vavenby 479 ....H 4
Vernon 19,987 ....H 5
Victoria (cap.) 64,379 ...K 4
Victoria *233,481 ....K 4
Warfield 1,969 ....J 5
Wasa 345 ....K 5
Wells 417 ....G 3
Westbank 1,271 ....H 5
West Vancouver ○35,728 ..K 3
Westwold 409 ....G 5
Whistler ○1,365 ....F 5
White Rock 13,550 ....K 3
Williams Lake 8,362 .....F 4
Wilson Creek 611 ....J 2
Windermere 611 ....K 5
Winlaw 435 ....J 5
Woss Lake 395 ....D 5
Wynndel 566 ....J 5
Yarrow 1,201 ....M 3
Youbou 965 ....J 3

OTHER FEATURES

Adams (lake) ....H 4
Adams (riv.) ....H 4
Alberni (inlet) ....H 3
Alsek (riv.) ....H 1
Aristazabal (isl.) ......C 4
Assiniboine (mt.) ....K 5
Atlin (lake) ....J 1
Azure (lake) ....G 4
Babine (lake) ....E 3
Babine (riv.) ....D 2
Banks (isl.) ....B 3
Barkley (sound) ....E 6
Beale (cape) ....E 6
Beatton (riv.) ....G 1
Bella Coola (riv.) ......D 4
Bennett, W.A.C. (dam) ...F 2
Birkenhead Lake Prov. Park .F 5
Bowron Lake Prov. Park ..G 3
Bowser (lake) ....C 2
Brooks (pen.) ....D 5
Browning Entrance (str.) .B 3
Bryce (mt.) ....J 4
Bugaboo Glacier Prov. Park .J 4
Bulkley (riv.) ....D 2
Burke (chan.) ....D 4
Burnaby (isl.) ....B 4
Bute (inlet) ....E 5
Caamaño (sound) ....C 4
Calvert (isl.) ....C 4
Canim (lake) ....G 4
Canoe (riv.) ....H 4
Cariboo (mts.) ....G 3
Carpenter (lake) ....F 5
Carp Lake Prov. Park ....F 3
Cassiar (mts.) ....K 2
Castle (mt.) ....A 2

Charlotte (lake) ....E 4
Chatham (sound) ....B 3
Chehalis (lake) ....L 3
Chilcotin (riv.) ....E 4
Chilko (lake) ....F 4
Chilko (riv.) ....E 4
Chilkoot (pass) ....J 1
Chuchi (lake) ....E 2
Churchill (peak) ....L 2
Clayoquot (sound) ....D 5
Clearwater (lake) ....G 4
Clearwater (riv.) ....G 4
Coast (mts.) ....D 3
Columbia (lake) ....K 5
Columbia (mt.) ....J 4
Columbia (riv.) ....H 4
Cook (cape) ....C 5
Cowichan (lake) ....J 3
Crowsnest (pass) ....K 5
Cypress Prov. Park ......K 3
Dean (chan.) ....D 4
Dean (riv.) ....D 4
Dease (lake) ....K 2
Dease (riv.) ....K 2
Devils Thumb (mt.) ......A 1
Dixon Entrance (chan.) ..A 3
Douglas (chan.) ....C 3
Duncan (riv.) ....J 5
Dundas (isl.) ....B 3
Elk (riv.) ....K 5
Elk Lakes Prov. Park ....K 5
Eutsuk (lake) ....D 3
Fairweather (mt.) ....H 1

Cathedral Prov. Park ....H 5
Finlay (riv.) ....E 1
Fitzhugh (sound) ....D 4
Flathead (riv.) ....K 6
Flores (isl.) ....D 5
Fontas (riv.) ....M 2
Forbes (mt.) ....M 2
Fort Nelson (riv.) ......M 2
François (lake) ....D 3
Fraser (chan.) ....E 3
Fraser (riv.) ....F 4
Fraser Reach (chan.) ....C 3
Galiano (isl.) ....K 3
Gardner (canal) ....C 3
Garibaldi Prov. Park ....F 5
Georgia (str.) ....J 3
Germansen (lake) ....E 2
Gil (isl.) ....C 3
Glacier Nat'l Park ......J 4
Golden Ears Prov. Park ..L 2
Gordon (riv.) ....H 3
Graham (isl.) ....A 3
Graham Reach (chan.) ....C 3
Grenville (chan.) ....C 3
Halfway (riv.) ....F 2
Hamber Prov. Park ....H 4
Harrison (lake) ....M 2
Hawkesbury (isl.) ....C 3
Hazelton (mts.) ....C 2
Hecate (str.) ....B 3
Hobson (lake) ....H 4
Homathko (riv.) ....E 5
Horsefly (lake) ....G 4

Agriculture, Industry and Resources

DOMINANT LAND USE

Cereals, Livestock
Dairy
Fruits, Vegetables
Pasture Livestock
Forests
Nonagricultural Land

MAJOR MINERAL OCCURRENCES

Ab Asbestos
Ag Silver
Au Gold
C Coal
Cu Copper
Fe Iron Ore
G Natural Gas

Gp Gypsum
Mo Molybdenum
Ni Nickel
O Petroleum
Pb Lead
S Sulfur
Sn Tin
Zn Zinc

Water Power
Major Industrial Areas

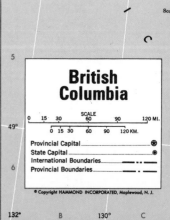

British Columbia

```
SCALE
0   15   30        60        90        120 MI.
0  15 30   60        90      120 KM.
```

Provincial Capital ....⊛
State Capital ....⊛
International Boundaries .....
Provincial Boundaries ....

AREA 366,253 sq. mi. (948,596 sq. km.)
POPULATION 2,744,467
CAPITAL Victoria
LARGEST CITY Vancouver
HIGHEST POINT Mt. Fairweather 15,300 ft.
(4,663 m.)
SETTLED IN 1806
ADMITTED TO CONFEDERATION 1871
PROVINCIAL FLOWER Dogwood

*Population of metropolitan area.
○Population of municipality.

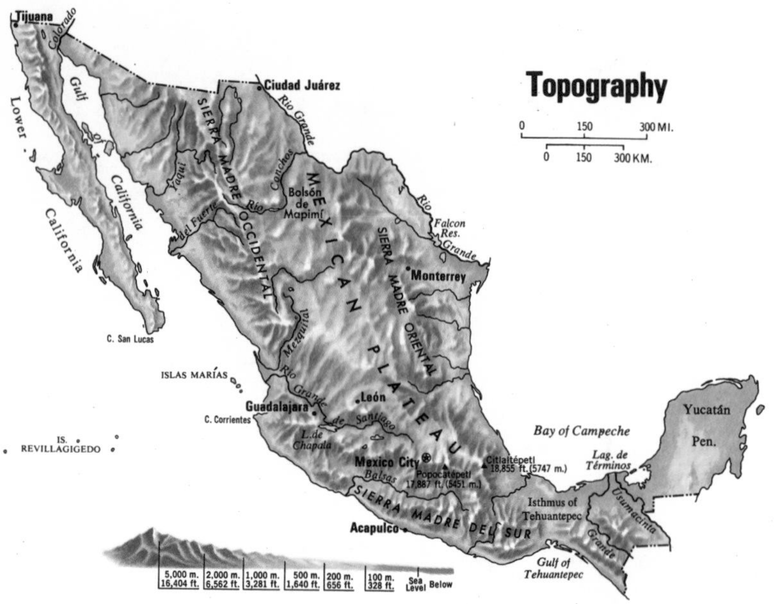

STATES

Aguascalientes 504,300 H6
Baja California 1,227,400 B1
Baja California Sur 221,000 C3
Campeche 371,800 O7
Chiapas 2,097,500 N8
Chihuahua 1,935,100 F2
Coahuila 1,561,000 H3
Colima 339,400 G7
Distrito Federal 9,377,300 L1
Durango 1,160,300 G4
Guanajuato 3,045,600 J6
Guerrero 2,174,200 J8
Hidalgo 1,518,200 K6
Jalisco 4,296,500 H6
México 7,542,300 K7
Michoacán 3,049,400 H7
Morelos 931,400 K7
Nayarit 729,500 G6
Nuevo León 2,463,500 K4
Oaxaca 2,517,500 L8
Puebla 3,285,300 L7
Querétaro 730,900 J6
Quintana Roo 209,900 P7
San Luis Potosí 1,669,900 J5
Sinaloa 1,882,200 F4
Sonora 1,498,100 D2
Tabasco 1,150,000 N7
Tamaulipas 1,924,900 K4
Tlaxcala 548,500 N1
Veracruz 5,263,800 L7
Yucatán 1,034,300 P6
Zacatecas 1,144,700 H5

CITIES and TOWNS

Acala 11,483 N8
Acámbaro 32,257 J7
Acaponeta 11,844 G5
Acapulco de Juárez 309,254 K8
Acatlán de Osorio 7,624 K7
Acatzingo de Hidalgo 6,905 N2
Acayucan 21,173 M8
Aconchi 1,596 D2
Actopan, Hidalgo 11,037 K6
Actopan, Veracruz 2,265 Q1
Agua Dulce 21,060 M7
Agualeguas 2,502 J3
Agua Prieta 20,754 E1
Aguascalientes 181,277 H6
Aguililla 5,715 H7
Ahome 4,182 E4
Ahuacatitlán 6,436 L1
Ahuacatlán 5,350 G6
Ahumada 6,466 F1
Ajalpan 8,238 L7
Alamo 9,954 L6
Álamos 4,269 E3
Aldama, Chihuahua 6,047 G2
Aldama, Tamaulipas 3,033 L5
Aljojuca 3,204 O1
Allende, Coahuila 11,076 J2
Allende, Nuevo León 9,914 J4
Almoloya del Río 3,714 K1
Altamira 6,053 L5
Altar 2,519 D1
Altepexi 6,661 L7
Alto Lucero 3,698 P1
Altotonga 6,754 P1
Alvarado 15,592 M7
Amatlán de los Reyes 3,664 P2
Amealco 2,960 K6
Ameca 21,018 H6
Amecameca de Juárez 16,276 L1
Amozoc de Mota 9,203 N2
Anáhuac, Chihuahua 10,886 F2
Anáhuac, Nuevo León 8,168 J3
Angostura 2,663 E4
Antiguo Morelos 1,569 K5
Apan 13,705 M1
Apatzingán de la Constitución 44,849 H7
Apizaco 21,189 N1
Aquiles Serdán 2,565 G2
Aramberri 1,786 J5
Arandas 18,934 H6
Arcelia 10,024 J7
Ario de Rosales 8,774 J7
Arizpe 1,736 D1
Armería 10,616 G7
Arriaga 13,193 N8
Arteaga 5,324 H7
Ascensión 4,104 E1
Asunción Nochixtlán 3,235 L8
Atlixco 41,967 M2
Atotonilco el Alto 16,271 H6
Atoyac de Álvarez 8,874 J8
Autlán de Navarro 20,398 G7
Axochiapan 8,283 M2
Ayutla de los Libres 3,618 K8
Azcapotzalco 534,554 L1
Azoyú 3,446 K8
Bacadéhuachi 1,514 E2
Bacalar 2,121 P7
Bachíniva 1,809 F2
Bácum 2,668 D3
Bahía Tortugas 1,457 B3
Balancán de Domínguez 3,669 O8
Bamoa 5,866 E4
Banderilla 3,488 P1
Baviácora 2,049 E2
Benjamín Hill 5,366 D1
Bernardino de Sahagún 12,327 M1
Boca del Río 2,354 Q2
Bolonchén de Rejón 2,342 O7
Buenaventura 3,924 F2
Burgos 673 K4
Cabo San Lucas 1,534 E5
Cacahoatán 5,079 N9
Cadereyta Jiménez 13,586 K4
Calkiní 6,870 O6
Calnali 3,318 K6
Calpulálpan 8,659 M1
Calvillo 6,453 H6
Campeche 69,506 O7
Cananea 17,518 D1
Canatlán 5,983 G4
Cancún 326 Q6
Candela 1,689 J3
Candelaria 1,982 O7
Cañitas de Felipe Pescador 4,885 H5
Capulhuac de Mirafuentes 8,289 K1
Carbo 2,804 D2
Cárdenas, San Luis Potosí 12,020 K6
Cárdenas, Tabasco 15,643 N8
Carichic 1,520 F2
Castaños 8,996 J3
Catemaco 11,786 M7
Ceballos 2,937 H3
Cedral 4,057 J5
Celaya 79,977 J6
Celestún 1,490 O6
Cerritos 10,421 J5
Cerro Azul 20,259 L6
Chahuites 5,218 M8
Chalchihuites 1,894 G5
Chalco de Díaz Covarrubias 12,172 M1
Champotón 6,606 O7
Charcas 10,491 J5
Chetumal 23,685 Q7
Chiapa de Corzo 8,571 N8
Chiautempan 12,327 N1
Chietla 4,602 M2
Chignahuapan 3,805 N1
Chihuahua 327,313 F2
Chilapa de Álvarez 9,204 K8
Chilpancingo de los Bravos 36,193 K8
China, Nuevo León 4,958 K4
Chocomán 5,114 P2
Choix 2,503 E3
Cholula de Rivadavia 15,399 M1
Cihuatlán 9,451 G7
Cintalapa de Figueroa 12,036 N8
Ciudad Acuña (Villa Acuña) 30,276 J2
Ciudad Altamirano 8,694 J7
Ciudad Camargo, Chihuahua 24,030 G3
Ciudad Camargo, Tamaulipas 5,953 K3
Ciudad del Carmen 34,656 N7
Ciudad Delicias 52,446 G2
Ciudad del Maíz 5,241 K5
Ciudad de Río Grande 11,651 H5
Ciudad Guerrero 3,110 F2
Ciudad Guzmán 48,166 H7
Ciudad Hidalgo, Chiapas 4,105 N9
Ciudad Hidalgo, Michoacán 24,692 J7
Ciudad Juárez 424,135 F1
Ciudad Lerdo 19,803 H4
Ciudad Madero 115,302 L5
Ciudad Mante 51,247 K5
Ciudad Mendoza 18,696 O2
Ciudad Miguel Alemán 11,259 K3
Ciudad Obregón 144,795 E3
Ciudad Río Bravo 39,018 K4
Ciudad Satélite 35,083 L1
Ciudad Serdán 9,581 O2
Ciudad Valles 47,587 K5
Ciudad Victoria 83,897 K5
Coalcomán de Matamoros 4,875 H7
Coatepec 21,542 P1
Coatetelco 5,268 L2
Coatzacoalcos 69,753 M7
Coatzingo 3,038 N2
Cocorit 4,478 E3
Colima 58,450 H7
Colón 3,346 K6
Colotlán 6,135 H5
Comala 5,592 H7
Comalcalco 14,963 N7
Comitán de Domínguez 21,249 O8
Compostela 9,801 G6
Concepción del Oro 8,144 J4
Concordia 3,947 G5
Contla 7,517 N1
Copala 3,783 K8
Coquimatlán 6,212 G7
Córdoba 78,495 P2
Cosalá 2,279 F4
Cosamaloapan de Carpio 19,766 M7
Cosautlán de Carvajal 2,039 P1
Coscomatepec de Bravo 6,023 P2
Coslo 2,680 H5
Costa Rica 11,795 F4
Cotija de la Paz 9,178 H7
Coyoacán 339,446 L1
Coyotepec 8,888 L1
Coyuca de Benítez 6,328 J8
Coyuca de Catalán 2,926 J7
Coyutla 3,726 L6
Cozumel 5,858 Q6
Creel 2,449 E3
Cuatrociénagas de Carranza 5,523 H3
Cuauhtémoc 26,598 F2
Cuautepec de Hinojosa 5,501 K6
Cuautitlán de Romero Rubio 11,439 L1
Cuautla Morelos 13,946 L2
Cuencamé de Ceniceros 3,774 H4
Cuernavaca 239,813 L2
Cuicatlán 2,733 L8
Cuitlahuac 4,813 P2
Culiacán 228,001 F4
Cumpas 2,395 E1
Cunduacán 4,397 N7
Dimas 2,194 F5
Doctor Arroyo 4,290 K5
Dolores Hidalgo de la Independencia Naci 16,849 J6
Durango 182,633 G1
Dzibalchén 1,917 P7
Dzidzantún 7,064 P6
Dzitbalché 4,393 P6
Ebano 17,489 K5
Ecatepec de Morelos 11,899 L1
Ejutla de Crespo 5,263 L8
Eldorado 8,115 E4
El Fuerte 7,179 E3
El Porvenir 3,030 G1
El Potosí 2,032 J4
El Salto 7,818 G5
El Zacatón 2,686 J5
Empalme 24,927 D2
Encarnación de Díaz 10,474 H6
Ensenada 77,687 A1
Escalón 2,998 G3
Escarcega 7,248 O7
Escuinapa de Hidalgo 16,442 G5
Escuintla 4,111 N9
Esperanza, Puebla 4,258 O2
Esperanza, Sonora 11,762 E3
Espita 5,394 Q6
Esqueda 1,458 E1
Etchojoa 4,398 E3
Ezequiel Montes 3,139 K6
Fortín de las Flores 9,358 P2
Francisco I. Madero 12,613 H4
Fresnillo de González Echererría 44,475 H5
Frontera 10,066 N7
Galeana, Nuevo León 3,429 J4
General Bravo 2,894 K4
General Cepeda 3,486 J4
General Terán 5,354 K4
Gómez Farías 3,030 F2
Gómez Palacio 79,650 G4
González 6,440 K5
Guadalajara 1,478,383 H6
Guadalajara* 2,343,034 H6
Guadalupe, Nuevo León 51,899 K4
Guadalupe, Zacatecas 13,246 H5
Guadalupe Bravo 3,333 F1
Guadalupe Victoria, Durango 7,931 H4
Guadalupe Victoria, Puebla 3,946 O1
Guamúchil 17,151 E4
Guanajuato 36,809 J6
Guasave 26,080 E4
Guaymas 57,492 D3
Gustavo Díaz Ordaz 10,154 K3
Gutiérrez Zamora 9,099 L6
Halachó 4,804 O6
Hecelchakán 4,279 O6
Hermosillo 232,691 D2
Heroica Caborca 20,771 C1
Heroica Nogales 52,108 D1
Hidalgo, Tamaulipas 2,450 K4
Hidalgo del Parral (Parral) 57,619 G3
Hopelchén 3,699 P7
Huajuapan de León 13,822 L8
Huamantla 15,565 N1
Huaquechula 2,294 M2
Huatabampo 18,506 D3
Huatusco de Chicuellar 9,501 P2
Huauchinango 16,826 L6
Huautla de Jiménez 6,132 L7
Huehuetlán el Chico 2,667 M2
Huejotzingo 8,552 M1
Huejutla 6,854 K6
Huetamo 9,333 J7
Hueyotlipan de Hidalgo 2,353 M1
Huimanguillo 7,075 N8
Huitzilán 3,573 O1
Huitzuco de los Figueroa 9,406 K7
Huixcolotla 4,039 N2
Huixtepec 5,927 L8
Huixtla 15,737 N9
Hunucmá 8,020 O6
Ignacio de la Llave 3,962 Q2
Iguala de la Independencia 45,355 K7
Imuris 1,958 D1
Irapuato 135,596 J6
Isla Mujeres 2,663 Q6
Isla, Veracruz 8,075 M7
Ixmiquilpan 6,048 K6
Ixtapa J8
Ixtapalapa 522,095 L1
Ixtenco 5,035 N1
Ixtepec 14,025 M8
Ixtlán del Río 10,986 G6
Izamal 9,749 P6
Izúcar de Matamoros 21,164 M2
Jala 4,535 G6
Jalacingo 3,427 P1
Jalapa Enríquez 161,352 P1
Jalpa 9,904 H6
Jalpa de Méndez 4,785 N7
Jalpan 1,878 K6
Jáltipan de Morelos 15,170 M8
Jantetelco 2,015 L2
Jaumave 3,072 K5
Jerez de García Salinas 20,325 H5
Jico 7,269 P1
Jilotepec de Abasolo 4,252 K7
Jiménez, Chihuahua 18,095 G3
Joachín 3,918 Q2
Jojutla de Juárez 14,438 L2
Jonacatepec 3,868 M2
Jonuta 2,746 N7
José Cardel 5,396 Q1
Juan Aldama 9,667 H4
Juchipila 6,328 H6
Juchitán de Zaragoza 30,218 M8
Kantunilkin 1,970 Q6
La Barca 18,055 H6
La Barra de Navidad 1,829 G7
La Concordia 3,559 N9
La Cruz, Sinaloa 4,218 F5
Lagos de Moreno 33,782 J6
La Huerta 4,328 G7
La Paz, Baja California Sur 46,011 D5
La Paz, San Luis Potosí 3,735 J5
La Piedad Cavadas 34,963 H6
Las Choapas 20,166 M7
Las Hadas G7
Las Nieves 2,262 G3
Las Rosas 7,658 N8
León 468,887 J6
Lerdo de Tejada 11,628 M8
Lerma 4,158 O7
Libres 4,830 O1
Linares 24,456 K4
Llera de Canales 3,564 K5
Loma Bonita 15,804 M7
Loreto, Baja California 2,570 D4
Loreto, Zacatecas 7,132 J5
Los Mochis 67,953 E4
Los Reyes de Salgado 19,452 H7
Macuspana 12,293 N8
Madera 9,759 F2
Magdalena de Kino 10,281 D1
Maltrata 5,457 O2
Manzanillo 20,777 G7
Mapastepec 5,907 N9
Mapimí 2,737 G4
Martínez de la Torre 17,203 L6
Mascota 5,674 G6
Matamoros, Coahuila 15,125 H4
Matamoros, Tamaulipas 165,124 L4
Matehuala 28,799 J5
Matías Romero 13,200 M8
Maxcanú 6,505 O6
Mazatlán 147,010 F5
Melchor Múzquiz 18,868 H3
Melchor Ocampo del Balsas 4,766 H8
Meoquí 12,308 G2
Mérida 233,912 P6
Metepec 4,625 M2
Metlatonoc 1,870 K8
Mexicali 317,228 B1
Mexico City (cap.) 9,377,300 L1
Mexico City* 13,993,866 L1
Miacatlán 3,980 K2
Mier 5,636 K3
Miguel Auza 9,303 H4
Minatitlán 68,397 M8
Mineral del Monte 8,887 K6
Miquihuana 1,971 J5
Misantla 8,799 P1
Miahuatlán de Porfirio Díaz 5,714 L8
Mocorito 3,993 F4
Moctezuma, San Luis Potosí 1,734 J5
Moctezuma, Sonora 2,700 E2
Monclova 78,134 J3
Montemorelos 18,642 K4
Monterrey 1,006,221 J4
Monterrey* 1,923,402 J4
Morelia 199,099 J7
Morelos 4,241 J2
Morelos Cañada 2,288 O2
Moroleón 25,620 J6
Motozintla de Mendoza 4,682 N9
Motul de Felipe Carillo Puerto 12,949 P6
Muna 5,491 P6
Naco 3,580 D1
Nacozari 2,976 E1
Nadadores 2,461 H3
Naica 7,190 G2
Namiquipa 4,875 F2
Nanacamilpa 6,356 M1
Naolinco de Victoria 4,365 P1
Naranjos 14,732 L6
Naucalpan de Juárez 9,425 L1
Nautla 1,935 L6
Nava 4,097 J2
Navojoa 43,817 E3
Navolato 12,799 E4
Nazas 2,881 G4
Netzahualcóyotl 580,436 L1
Nieves 3,966 H5
Nochistlán 8,780 H6
Nogales 14,254 P2
Nombre de Dios 3,188 G5
Nopalucan de la Granja 3,002 O1
Nueva Casas Grandes 20,023 F1
Nueva Ciudad Guerrero 3,300 K3
Nueva Italia de Ruiz 14,718 J7
Nueva Rosita 34,706 J2
Nuevo Ideal 5,252 G4
Nuevo Laredo 184,622 J3
Oaxaca de Juárez 114,948 L8
Ocampo, Coahuila 1,613 H3
Ocampo, Tamaulipas 4,801 K5
Ocosingo 2,946 O8
Ocotlán 35,361 H6
Ocotlán de Morelos 5,882 L8
Ojinaga 12,757 G2
Ojocaliente 7,582 H5
Ometepec 7,342 K8
Oriental 6,009 O1
Orizaba 105,150 P2
Otumba de Gómez Farías 3,198 M1
Oxkutzcab 8,182 P6
Ozuluama 2,851 L6
Ozumba de Alzate 6,876 M1
Pachuca de Soto 83,892 K6
Padilla 4,581 K5
Palenque 2,595 O8
Palizada 2,332 O7
Palomas 2,129 F1

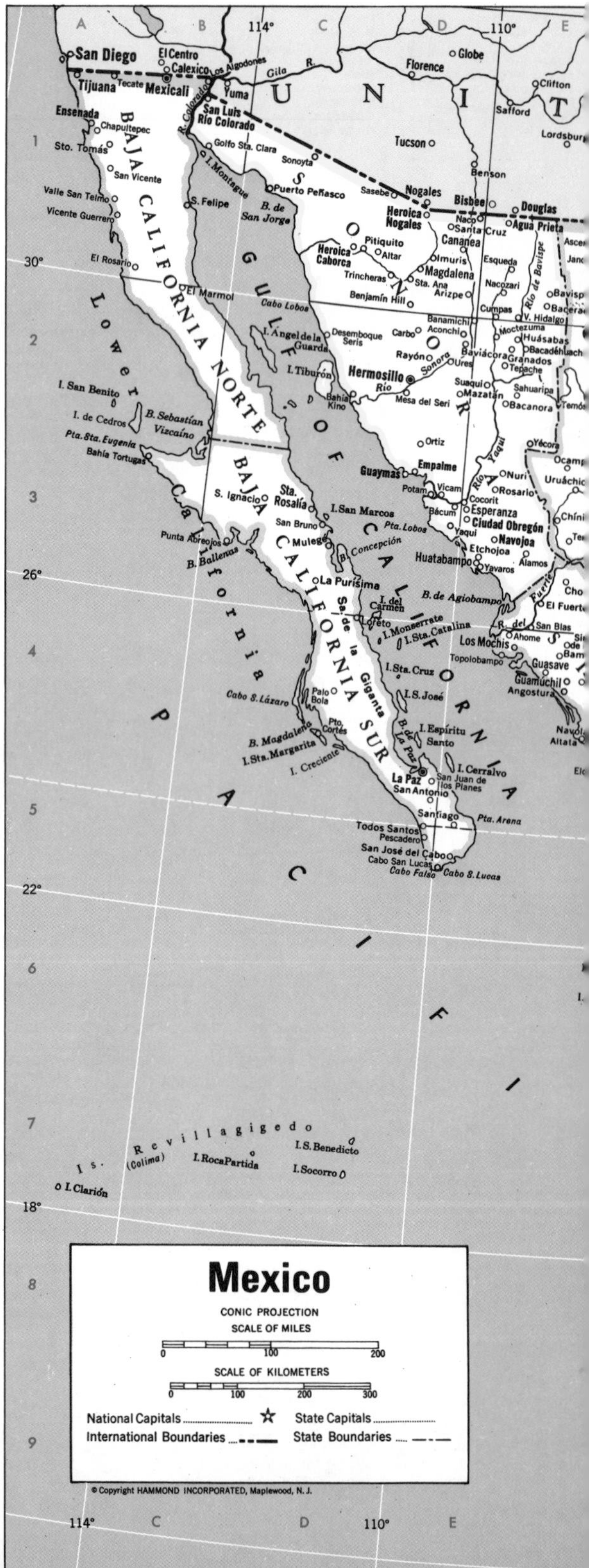

(continued on following page)

AREA 761,601 sq. mi. (1,972,546 sq. km.)
POPULATION 67,395,826
CAPITAL Mexico City
LARGEST CITY Mexico City
HIGHEST POINT Citlaltépetl 18,855 ft. (5,747 m.)
MONETARY UNIT Mexican peso
MAJOR LANGUAGE Spanish
MAJOR RELIGION Roman Catholicism

States Indicated by Numbers

1	Tlaxcala	6	Querétaro
2	Morelos	7	Guanajuato
3	Distrito Federal	8	Aguascalientes
4	México	9	Nayarit
5	Hidalgo	10	Colima

Rosario, Sinaloa 10,276 ... G5
Rosario, Sonora 1,887 ... E3
Ruiz 8,954 ... G6
Sabancuy 1,819 ... O7
Sabinas 20,538 ... J3
Sabinas Hidalgo 17,439 ... J3
Sahuaripa 4,710 ... E2
Sahuayo de Díaz 28,727 ... H7
Sain Alto 3,628 ... H5
Salamanca 61,039 ... J6
Salina Cruz 22,004 ... M9
Salinas 7,471 ... J5
Saltillo 200,712 ... J4
Salvatierra 18,975 ... J6
San Andrés Tuxtla 24,267 ... M7
San Blas, Nayarit 3,443 ... G6
San Blas, Sinaloa 6,222 ... E3
San Buenaventura 9,188 ... J3
San Carlos, Coahuila 1,960 ... J2
San Cristóbal de las Casas 25,700 ... N8
San Felipe, Baja California 160 ... B1
San Felipe, Guanajuato 10,129 ... J6
San Fernando, Tamaulipas 27,656 ... L4
San Francisco del Oro 12,116 ... F3
San Francisco del Rincón 27,079 ... H6
San Gabriel Chilac 6,707 ... K7
San Ignacio, Sinaloa 1,804 ... F5
San Jerónimo de Juárez 5,204 ... J8
San José del Cabo 2,571 ... D5
San Juan 15,422 ... K6
San Juan de los Lagos 19,570 ... H6
San Juan Xiutetelco 3,306 ... O1
San Luis de la Paz 12,654 ... J6
San Luis del Cordero 2,203 ... H4
San Luis Potosí 271,123 ... J5
San Luis Río Colorado 49,990 ... B1
San Marcos 5,861 ... K8
San Martín de las Pirámides 4,575 ... M1
San Martín Texmelucan 23,355 ... M1
San Miguel de Allende 24,286 ... J6
San Nicolás de los Garza 28,803 ... J3
San Pedro de las Colonias 26,882 ... H4
San Pedro Pochutla 4,395 ... L9
San Rafael 8,974 ... M1
San Salvador el Seco 7,729 ... O1
Santa Ana 7,020 ... D1
Santa Ana Chiautempan (Chiautèmpan) 12,327 ... N1
Santa Bárbara 16,978 ... F3
Santa Clara 3,449 ... H4
Santa María del Oro 4,231 ... G3
Santa María del Río 4,972 ... J6
Santa María del Tule 1,674 ... L8
Santander Jiménez 3,586 ... K4
Santa Rosalía 7,356 ... C3
Santiago Ixcuintla 17,321 ... G6
Santiago Jamiltepec 5,280 ... K8
Santiago Juxtlahuaca 2,923 ... K8
Santiago Miahuatlán 4,917 ... O2
Santiago Papasquiaro 6,636 ... F4
Santiago Pinotepa Nacional 9,382 ... K8
Santiago Tuxtla 9,426 ... M7
Saucillo 8,467 ... G2
Sayula 14,339 ... H7
Sayula de Alemán 4,896 ... M8
Seybaplaya 4,439 ... O7
Silao 31,825 ... J6
Simojovel de Allende 3,779 ... N8
Sinaloa de Leyva 1,998 ... E4
Soledad de Doblado 6,612 ... Q2
Soledad Díez
Gutiérrez 9,622 ... J5
Sombrerete 11,077 ... H5
Sonoyta 2,463 ... C1
Sotuta 3,772 ... P6
Tabasco 3,197 ... H6
Tacámbaro de Codallos 9,695 ... J7
Tacotalpa 2,019 ... N8
Tala 15,744 ... H6
Talpa de Allende 4,264 ... G6
Tamazulapan del Progreso 2,870 ... L8
Tamazunchale 12,302 ... K6
Tamiahua 6,264 ... L6
Tampico 212,188 ... L5
Tamuín 7,251 ... K6
Tantoyuca 11,902 ... L6
Tapachula 60,620 ... N9
Taxco de Alarcón 27,089 ... K7
Tayoltita 2,697 ... G4
Teapa 6,534 ... N8
Tecamachalco 3,319 ... O2
Tecate 14,738 ... A1
Tecomán 31,625 ... H7
Tecpan de Galeana 8,095 ... J8
Tecuala 12,461 ... G5
Tehuacán 47,497 ... L7
Tehuantepec 16,179 ... M8
Tekax de Álaro Obregón 10,326 ... P6
Teloloapan 10,335 ... J7
Temax 4,915 ... P6
Temósachic 1,738 ... E2
Tenabo 3,278 ... P6
Tenancingo de Degollado 12,807 ... K7
Tenango de Río Blanco 12,302 ... O2
Tenosique de Pino Suárez 11,393 ... O8
Teocaltiche 13,745 ... H6
Teocelo 4,572 ... P1
Teotihuacán de Arista 2,238 ... L1
Teotitlán del Camino 3,106 ... L8
Tepache 1,591 ... E2
Tepalcingo 5,968 ... M2
Tepatitlán de Morelos 29,292 ... H6
Tepeaca 7,466 ... N2
Tepeapulco 7,027 ... M1
Tepehuanes 2,531 ... G4
Tepeji del Río 10,365 ... L1
Tepexi de Rodríguez 2,618 ... N2
Tepic 108,924 ... G6
Tepoztlán 6,851 ... L1
Tequixquitla 4,825 ... O1
Terán 5,215 ... N8
Terrenate 1,515 ... N1
Texcoco de Mora 18,044 ... M1
Teziutlán 23,948 ... O1
Tezonapa 3,506 ... P2
Tezontepec 2,762 ... M1
Ticul 14,341 ... P6
Tierra Blanca 22,727 ... L7
Tila 2,633 ... N8
Tijuana 363,154 ... A1
Tixtla de Guerrero 10,334 ... K8
Tizayuca 6,262 ... L1
Tizimín 18,343 ... Q6
Tlachichuca 3,721 ... O1
Tlacolula de Matamoros 8,300 ... L8
Tlacotepec de Mejiá 1,595 ... P1
Tlahualilo de Zaragoza 8,951 ... H3
Tlalancaneca 5,090 ... M1
Tlalixcoyan 3,211 ... Q2
Tlalmanalco de Velásquez 5,744 ... L1
Tlalnepantla de Comonfort 45,575 ... L1
Tlalpan 130,719 ... L1
Tlaltenango de Sánchez Román 7,698 ... H6
Tlaltizapan 6,384 ... L2
Tlapacoyan 13,172 ... P1
Tlapa de Comonfort 6,676 ... K8

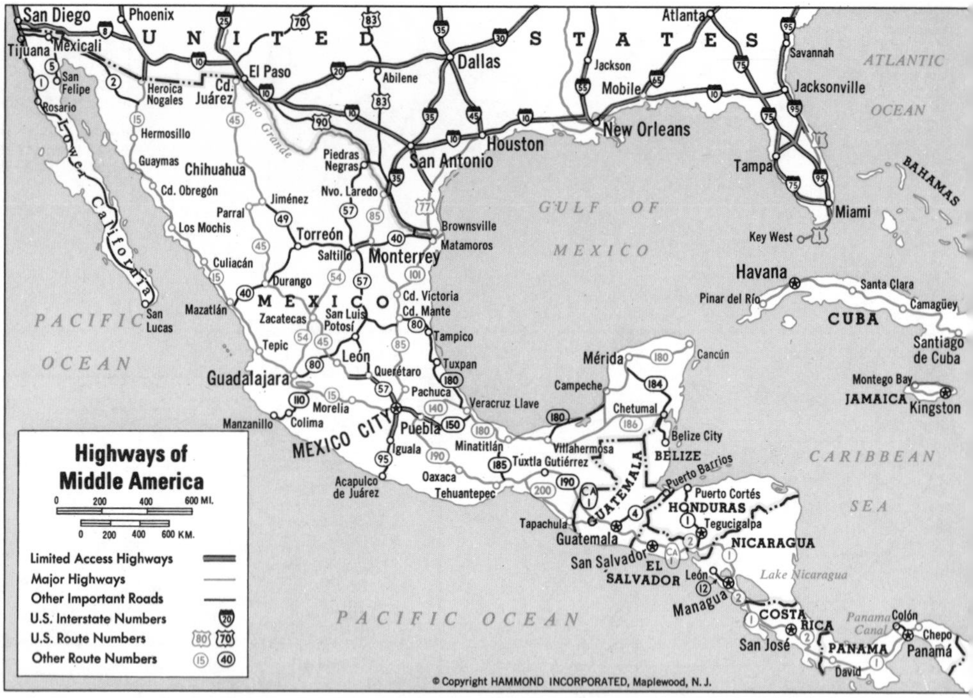
Highways of Middle America
0 200 400 600 MI.
0 200 400 600 KM.
Limited Access Highways
Major Highways
Other Important Roads
U.S. Interstate Numbers
U.S. Route Numbers
Other Route Numbers
UNITED STATES
MEXICO
San Diego
Phoenix
Tijuana
Mexicali
San Felipe
Rosario
Heroica Nogales
Cd. Juárez
El Paso
Abilene
Dallas
Atlanta
Jackson
Mobile
Savannah
Jacksonville
Houston
New Orleans
San Antonio
Tampa
Miami
Key West
Hermosillo
Guaymas
Chihuahua
Cd. Obregón
Los Mochis
Parral
Jiménez
Piedras Negras
Nvo. Laredo
Brownsville
Matamoros
Torreón
Saltillo
Monterrey
Culiacán
Durango
Mazatlán
Zacatecas
San Luis Potosí
Cd. Victoria
Cd. Mante
Tampico
Tuxpan
San Lucas
Tepic
León
Querétaro
Guadalajara
Pachuca
Veracruz Llave
Manzanillo
Colima
Morelia
MEXICO CITY
Puebla
Iguala
Minatitlán
Tuxtla Gutiérrez
Villahermosa
Acapulco de Juárez
Oaxaca
Tehuantepec
Tapachula
Mérida
Campeche
Cancún
Chetumal
Belize City
BELIZE
GUATEMALA
Guatemala
Puerto Barrios
Puerto Cortés
HONDURAS
Tegucigalpa
San Salvador
EL SALVADOR
NICARAGUA
León
Managua
Lake Nicaragua
COSTA RICA
San José
PANAMA
Panama Canal
Colón
Chepo
Panamá
David
Havana
Pinar del Río
Santa Clara
Camagüey
CUBA
Santiago de Cuba
Montego Bay
JAMAICA
Kingston
BAHAMAS
Lower California
Rio Grande
ATLANTIC OCEAN
GULF OF MEXICO
CARIBBEAN SEA
PACIFIC OCEAN
© Copyright HAMMOND INCORPORATED, Maplewood, N. J.

Tlaquepaque 59,760 ... G6
Tlatlauquitepec 4,272 ... O1
Tlaquiltenango 8,625 ... L2
Tlaxcala de Xicotencatl 9,972 ... M1
Tlaxco 4,969 ... N1
Tlaxiaco 4,477 ... L8
Tlayacapan 3,538 ... L1
Tochimilco 3,190 ... M2
Todos Santos 2,400 ... D5
Toluca de Lerdo 136,092 ... K7
Tomatlán 2,695 ... G6
Tonalá 15,611 ... N8
Topolobampo 4,685 ... E4
Torreón 244,309 ... H4
Tula, Tamaulipas 5,407 ... K5
Tula de Allende 10,720 ... K6
Tulancingo 35,799 ... K7
Tulcingo del Valle 2,983 ... M2
Tultepec 8,321 ... L1
Tuxpan, Jalisco 14,693 ... H7
Tuxpan, Nayarit 20,322 ... G6
Tuxpan de Rodríguez Cano 33,901 ... L6
Tuxtepec 17,701 ... L7
Tuxtla Gutiérrez 66,851 ... N8
Tzucabab 4,876 ... P7
Umán 8,371 ... P6
Unión de Tula 6,399 ... G7
Unión Hidalgo 8,658 ... M8
Ures 3,681 ... D2
Ursulo Galván 2,637 ... Q1
Uruapan del Progreso 108,124 ... H7
Valladolid 14,663 ... P6
Valle de Allende 4,973 ... G3
Valle de Bravo 7,628 ... J7
Valle Hermoso 19,278 ... L4
Vanegas 2,042 ... J5
Venado 2,790 ... J5
Venustiano Carranza 23,624 ... N8
Veracruz 255,646 ... Q1
Vicam 4,104 ... D3
Vicente Guerrero, Durango 8,451 ... G5
Victor Rosales 7,629 ... H5
Viesca 2,923 ... H4
Villa Acuña 30,276 ... J2
Villa Cuauhtémoc 6,611 ... L5
Villa de Cos 1,850 ... H5
Villa de Guadelupe Hidalgo 88,537 ... L1
Villa Frontera 25,761 ... J3
Villa García 2,765 ... J5
Villahermosa 133,181 ... N8
Villa Hidalgo 2,126 ... E1
Villaldama 2,350 ... J3
Villa Matamoros 1,998 ... G3
Villanueva 5,895 ... H5
Villa Unión, Coahuila 4,058 ... J2
Villa Unión, Durango 4,042 ... H5
Villa Unión, Sinaloa 6,789 ... F5
Villa Vicente Guerrero 18,280 ... N1
Xaltocan 2,524 ... N1
Xicoténcatl 6,374 ... K5
Xicotepec de Juárez 12,656 ... L6
Xochihuehuetlán 3,268 ... K8
Xochimilco 116,493 ... L1
Xochitlán 3,312 ... N2
Yajalón 4,506 ... N8
Yanga 3,843 ... P2
Yaqui 8,061 ... D3
Yautepec 13,952 ... L2
Yavaros 1,959 ... E3
Yécora ... E2
Yecuatla 2,816 ... P1
Yehualtepec 2,558 ... O2
Zaachila 7,270 ... L8
Zacapoaxtla 4,527 ... O1
Zacapu 31,989 ... J7
Zacatepec 16,839 ... L2
Zacatecas 50,251 ... H5
Zacatelco 14,117 ... N1
Zacatlán 7,909 ... N1
Zacoalco de Torres 11,343 ... H6
Zamora de Hidalgo 5,775 ... H7
Zaragoza, Coahuila 6,797 ... J2
Zaragoza, Chihuahua 3,984 ... F1
Zaragoza, Puebla 4,754 ... O1
Zempoala 5,064 ... Q1
Zihuatenejo 4,879 ... J8
Zimatlán de Álvarez 5,746 ... L8
Zitácuaro 36,911 ... J7
Zongolica 2,378 ... P2
Zumpango de Ocampo 12,923 ... L1
Zumpango del Río 8,162 ... J8

OTHER FEATURES

Agiobampo (bay) ... E3
Aguanaval (riv.) ... H4
Amistad (res.) ... J2
Ángel de la Guarda (isl.) ... C2
Antigua (riv.) ... Q1
Arena (pt.) ... E5
Arenas (cay) ... O5
Atoyac (riv.) ... N2
Atoyac (riv.) ... Q2
Babia (riv.) ... J2
Bacalar (lake) ... P7
Ballenas (bay) ... C3
Balsas (riv.) ... J7
Banderas (bay) ... G6
Bavispe, Río de (riv.) ... E1
Blanco (riv.) ... Q2
Bravo (Grande) (riv.) ... G2
Burro (mts.) ... J2
California (gulf) ... D3
Campeche (bank) ... O6
Campeche (bay) ... N7
Candelaria (riv.) ... O8
Carmen (isl.) ... D3
Casas Grandes (riv.) ... F1
Catoche (cape) ... Q6
Cedros (isl.) ... B2
Cerralvo (isl.) ... E4
Chamela (bay) ... G7
Chapala (lake) ... H6
Chetumal (bay) ... P8
Chichén-Itzá (ruin) ... P6
Citlaltépetl (mt.) ... O2
Clarión (isl.) ... B7
Colorado (riv.) ... B1
Conchos (riv.) ... G2
Corrientes (cape) ... F6
Coyuca (riv.) ... O1
Creciente (isl.) ... D5
Cuitzeo (lake) ... J7
Delgada (pt.) ... L7
Dzibichaltún (ruin) ... P6
El Azúcar (res.) ... K3
Espíritu Santo (isl.) ... D4
Falcón (res.) ... K
Falso (cape) ... D
Fuerte (riv.) ... E
Giganta, Sierra de la (mts.) ... D
Grande (riv.) ... G
Grande (riv.) ... N
Grande de Santiago (riv.) ... G
Grijalva (riv.) ... N
Guzmán (lake) ... F
Herrero (pt.) ... O
Hondo (riv.) ... P
Jesús María (reef) ... L
La Boquilla (res.) ... G
La Paz (bay) ... D
Lobos (cape) ... C
Lobos (pt.) ... D
Lower California (pen.) ... C
Madre (lag.) ... L
Madre del Sur, Sierra (mts.) ... K
Madre Occidental, Sierra (mts.) ... F
Madre Oriental, Sierra (mts.) ... J
Magdalena (bay) ... C
Maldonado (pt.) ... K
Mapimí (depr.) ... G
María Cleófas (isl.) ... F
María Madre (isl.) ... F
María Magdalena (isl.) ... F
Mexico (gulf) ... N
Mezquital (riv.) ... G
Mita (pt.) ... G
Mitla (ruin) ... M
Moctezuma (riv.) ... K
Monserrate (isl.) ... D
Montague (isl.) ... B
Muerto, Mar (lag.) ... N
Nauhcampatépetl (mt.) ... O
Nayarit, Sierra (mts.) ... G
Nazas (riv.) ... G
Nuevo, Bajo (reef) ... O
Orizaba (Citlaltépetl) (mt.) ... O
Palenque (ruin) ... O
Palmito de la Virgen (isl.) ... F
Palmito del Verde (isl.) ... F
Pánuco (riv.) ... K
Paricutín (vol.) ... H
Pátzcuaro (lake) ... J
Pérez (isl.) ... P
Petacalco (bay) ... H
Popocatépetl (mt.) ... M
Ramos (riv.) ... G4
Revillagigedo (isls.) ... C7
Roca Partida (isl.) ... C7
Sabinas (riv.) ... J
San Antonio (reef) ... L4
San Benedicto (isl.) ... D7
San Benito (isl.) ... B2
San Jorge (bay) ... C1
San José (isl.) ... D4
San Lázaro (cape) ... C4
San Lucas (cape) ... E5
San Marcos (isl.) ... D3
San Rafael (reef) ... L4
Santa Ana (reef) ... N7
Santa Catalina (isl.) ... D4
Santa Cruz (isl.) ... D4
Santa Eugenia (pt.) ... B3
Santa Margarita (isl.) ... C4
Santa María (lake) ... F1
Santa María (riv.) ... F1
Santiaguillo (lake) ... G4
Sebastián Vizcaíno (bay) ... B2
Socorro (isl.) ... D7
Sonora (riv.) ... D2
Superior (lag.) ... M9
Teacapán (inlet) ... F5
Tehuantepec (gulf) ... M9
Tehuantepec (isth.) ... M8
Teotihuacán (ruin) ... M1
Términos (lag.) ... O7
Tiburón (isl.) ... C2
Triángulo Este (isl.) ... N6
Triángulo Oeste (isl.) ... N6
Tula (riv.) ... L1
Urique (riv.) ... F3
Usumacinta (riv.) ... O8
Uxmal (ruins) ... P6
Valsequillo (res.) ... N2
Verde (riv.) ... F3
Verde (riv.) ... L8
Yaqui (riv.) ... E2

*City and suburbs.

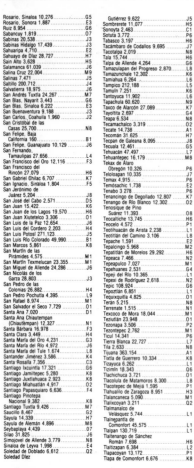

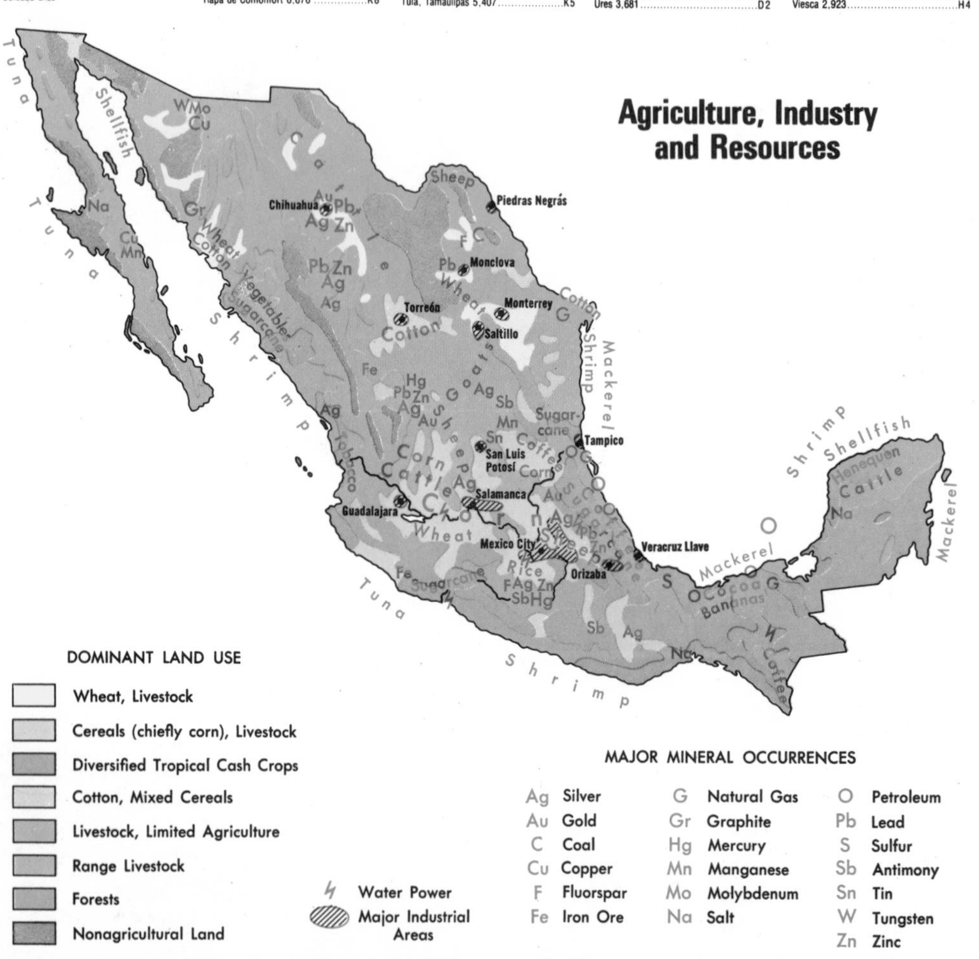
Agriculture, Industry and Resources
DOMINANT LAND USE
Wheat, Livestock
Cereals (chiefly corn), Livestock
Diversified Tropical Cash Crops
Cotton, Mixed Cereals
Livestock, Limited Agriculture
Range Livestock
Forests
Nonagricultural Land
Water Power
Major Industrial Areas
MAJOR MINERAL OCCURRENCES
Ag Silver
Au Gold
C Coal
Cu Copper
F Fluorspar
Fe Iron Ore
G Natural Gas
Gr Graphite
Hg Mercury
Mn Manganese
Mo Molybdenum
Na Salt
O Petroleum
Pb Lead
S Sulfur
Sb Antimony
Sn Tin
W Tungsten
Zn Zinc
Chihuahua
Piedras Negrás
Monclova
Torreón
Monterrey
Saltillo
Tampico
San Luis Potosí
Salamanca
Guadalajara
Mexico City
Veracruz Llave
Orizaba
Tuna
Shellfish
Shrimp
Mackerel
Wheat
Cotton
Vegetables
Sugarcane
Sheep
Cattle
Goats
Corn
Coffee
Rice
Tobacco
Henequen
Cacao
Bananas

GUATEMALA

AREA 42,042 sq. mi. (108,889 sq. km.)
POPULATION 7,262,419
CAPITAL Guatemala
LARGEST CITY Guatemala
HIGHEST POINT Tajumulco 13,845 ft. (4,220 m.)
MONETARY UNIT quetzal
MAJOR LANGUAGES Spanish, Quiché
MAJOR RELIGION Roman Catholicism

BELIZE

AREA 8,867 sq. mi. (22,966 sq. km.)
POPULATION 144,857
CAPITAL Belmopan
LARGEST CITY Belize City
HIGHEST POINT Victoria Peak 3,681 ft. (1,122 m.)
MONETARY UNIT Belize dollar
MAJOR LANGUAGES English, Spanish, Mayan
MAJOR RELIGIONS Roman Catholicism, Protestantism

EL SALVADOR

AREA 8,260 sq. mi. (21,393 sq. km.)
POPULATION 4,813,000
CAPITAL San Salvador
LARGEST CITY San Salvador
HIGHEST POINT Santa Ana 7,825 ft. (2,385 m.)
MONETARY UNIT colón
MAJOR LANGUAGE Spanish
MAJOR RELIGION Roman Catholicism

HONDURAS

AREA 43,277 sq. mi. (112,087 sq. km.)
POPULATION 3,691,000
CAPITAL Tegucigalpa
LARGEST CITY Tegucigalpa
HIGHEST POINT Las Minas 9,347 ft. (2,849 m.)
MONETARY UNIT lempira
MAJOR LANGUAGE Spanish
MAJOR RELIGION Roman Catholicism

NICARAGUA

AREA 45,698 sq. mi. (118,358 sq. km.)
POPULATION 2,703,000
CAPITAL Managua
LARGEST CITY Managua
HIGHEST POINT Cerro Mocotón 6,913 ft. (2,107 m.)
MONETARY UNIT córdoba
MAJOR LANGUAGE Spanish
MAJOR RELIGION Roman Catholicism

COSTA RICA

AREA 19,575 sq. mi. (50,700 sq. km.)
POPULATION 2,245,000
CAPITAL San José
LARGEST CITY San José
HIGHEST POINT Chirripó Grande 12,530 ft. (3,819 m.)
MONETARY UNIT colón
MAJOR LANGUAGE Spanish
MAJOR RELIGION Roman Catholicism

PANAMA

AREA 29,761 sq. mi. (77,082 sq. km.)
POPULATION 1,830,175
CAPITAL Panamá
LARGEST CITY Panamá
HIGHEST POINT Vol. Baru 11,401 ft. (3,475 m.)
MONETARY UNIT balboa
MAJOR LANGUAGE Spanish
MAJOR RELIGION Roman Catholicism

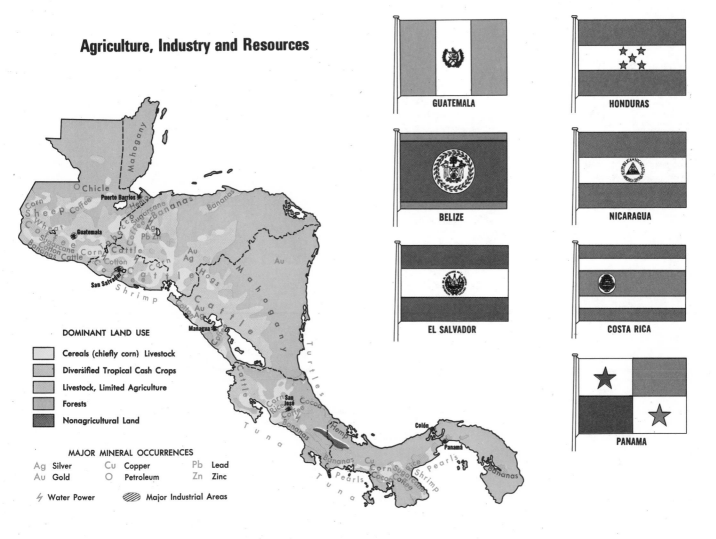

Agriculture, Industry and Resources

DOMINANT LAND USE

- Cereals (chiefly corn) Livestock
- Diversified Tropical Cash Crops
- Livestock, Limited Agriculture
- Forests
- Nonagricultural Land

MAJOR MINERAL OCCURRENCES

Ag Silver
Au Gold
Cu Copper
O Petroleum
Pb Lead
Zn Zinc

⚡ Water Power
▨ Major Industrial Areas

Flags: GUATEMALA, HONDURAS, BELIZE, NICARAGUA, EL SALVADOR, COSTA RICA, PANAMA

(continued on following page)

OTHER FEATURES		San Miguel 59,304	D4	Antigua 17,994	B3	Jacaltenango 4,517	B3	San Luis Jilotepeque 6,055	C3	Pasión (riv.)	B2
		San Salvador (cap.) 337,171	C4	Asunción Mita 7,477	C3	Jalapa 13,788	B3	San Marcos 5,700	B3	Petén-Itzá (lake)	B2
Blanca (pt.)	F5	Santa Ana 96,306	C4	Cahabón 1,344	B3	Jutiapa 8,210	B3	San Martín Jilotepeque 3,770	B3	San Pedro (riv.)	B2
Blanco (cape)	F6	Santa Rosa de Lima 5,707	C4	Chajul 4,329	B3	La Gomera 2,394	B3	San Mateo Ixtatán 1,834	B3	Sarstún (riv.)	B2
Blanco (peak)	F6	San Vicente 18,872	C4	Champerico 5,722	B3	La Libertad 908	C2	San Pedro Carchá 4,465	B3	Tacaná (vol.)	B3
Burica (pt.)	F6	Sensuntepeque 7,226	C4	Chichicastenango 2,635	B3	Livingston 2,898	C2	Santa Cruz del Quiché 7,651	B3	Tajumulco (vol.)	B3
Caño (isl.)	F6	Sonsonate 33,562	C4	Chimaltenango 12,860	B3	Los Amates 1,383	C3	Santa Rosa de Lima 1,161	B3	Tres Puntas (cape)	C2
Carreta (pt.)	F6	Texistepeque 1,722	C3	Chiquimula 16,126	C3	Masagua 1,178	B3	Sololá 3,960	B3	Usumacinta (riv.)	B2
Chirripó Grande (mt.)	F6	Usulután 19,616	C4	Coatepeque 15,979	A3	Mazatenango 23,285	B3	Tacaná 1,280	B3		
Coronada (bay)	F6	Zacatecoluca 15,718	C4	Cobán 11,418	B3	Momostenango 5,210	B3	Tejutla 1,205	B3	HONDURAS	
Cuilapa Miravalles (vol.)	E5			Comalapa 10,980	B3	Morales 2,113	C3	Tikal	B2		
Dulce (gulf)	F6	OTHER FEATURES		Cubulco 2,021	B3	Ocós 741	A3	Totonicapán 8,568	B3	CITIES and TOWNS	
Góngora (pt.)	E6			Cuilapa 4,287	B3	Panzós 1,643	C3	Zacapa 12,688	C3		
Guiones (pt.)	E6	Fonseca (gulf)	D4	Cuilco 862	B3	Puerto Barrios 22,598	C3			Amapala 2,274	D4
Irazú (mt.)	F6	Güija (lake)	C3	Dolores 973	C3	Quezaltenango 53,021	B3	ATITLÁN (lake)	B3	Brus Laguna 933	E3
Judas (pt.)	F6	Lempa (riv.)	C3	El Estor 2,324	B3	Quezaltepeque 2,222	B3	Atitlán (vol.)	B3	Catacamas 9,134	E3
Llerena (pt.)	F6	Remedios (pt.)	C4	El Progreso 4,009	B3	Rabinal 4,625	B3	Azul (riv.)	C2	Cedros 917	D3
Matapalo (cape)	F6	Santa Ana (mt.)	C4	Escuintla 33,205	B3	Retalhuleu 19,060	B3	Chixoy (riv.)	B2	Choloma 961	D3
Nicoya (gulf)	E6			Flores 1,477	C2	Río Hondo 1,416	C3	Güija (lake)	C3	Choluteca 26,152	D4
Nicoya (pen.)	E6	GUATEMALA		Guatán 5,169	C3	Sacapulas 1,439	B3	Honduras (gulf)	D2	Comayagua 15,941	D3
Papagayo (gulf)	E6			Guatemala (cap.)		Salamá 5,529	B3	Izabal (lake)	C3	Corquín 2,629	C3
Salinas (bay)	D5	CITIES and TOWNS		700,538	B3	San Andrés 1,066	B3	Minas (mts.)	C3	Danlí 10,825	D3
San Juan (riv.)	E5			Huehuetenango 12,570	B3	San Felipe 3,210	B3	Motagua (riv.)	C3	El Dulce Nombre 1,297	D3
Santa Elena (cape)	D5	Amatitlán 15,251	B3	Ipala 3,386	C3	San José 9,402	B4				
				Iztapa 1,237	B4	San Luis 1,136	C2				

EL SALVADOR	
CITIES and TOWNS	
Acajutla 8,598	B4
Ahuachapán 17,242	C4
Atiquizaya 7,035	C3
Chalatenango 7,633	C3
Chinameca 6,303	C4
Cojutepeque 20,615	C4
Estanzuelas 2,548	C4
Ilobasco 6,572	C4
Jucuarán 1,443	C4
La Libertad	C4
La Palma 1,998	C3
La Unión 17,207	D4
Metapán 7,704	C3
Nueva San Salvador 35,106	C4
Puerto de la Concordia	C4
San Francisco Gotera 4,725	C4

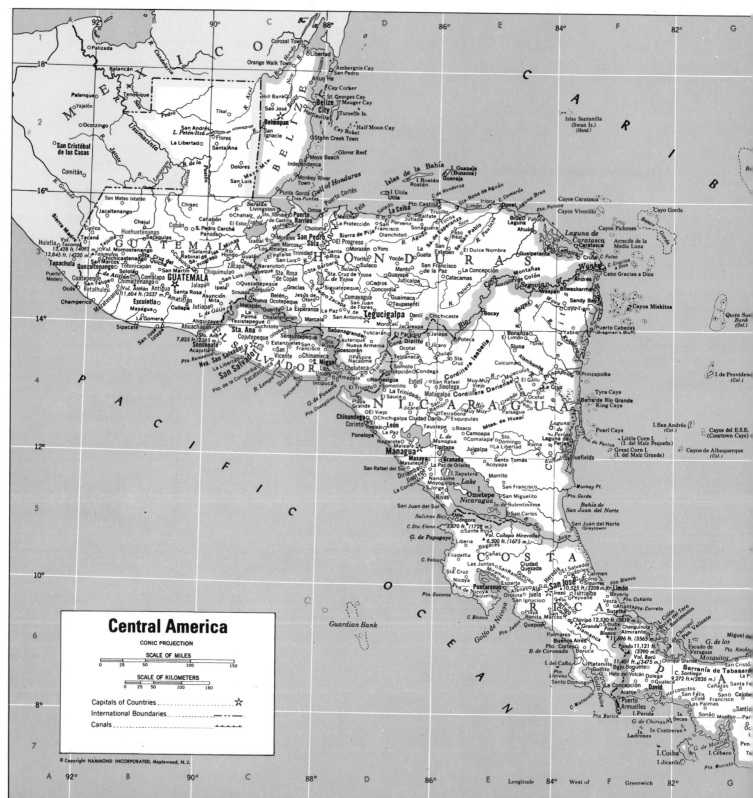

Topography

0   75   150 MI.

0   75   150 KM.

5,000 m.	2,000 m.	1,000 m.	500 m.	200 m.	100 m.	Sea	Below
16,404 ft.	6,562 ft.	3,281 ft.	1,640 ft.	656 ft.	328 ft.	Level	

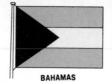

BAHAMAS | CUBA | HAITI | DOMINICAN REPUBLIC | JAMAICA

BAHAMAS
AREA 5,382 sq. mi. (13,939 sq. km.)
POPULATION 209,505
CAPITAL Nassau
LARGEST CITY Nassau
HIGHEST POINT Mt. Alvernia 206 ft. (63 m.)
MONETARY UNIT Bahamian dollar
MAJOR LANGUAGE English
MAJOR RELIGIONS Roman Catholicism, Protestantism

CUBA
AREA 44,206 sq. mi. (114,494 sq. km.)
POPULATION 9,706,369
CAPITAL Havana
LARGEST CITY Havana
HIGHEST POINT Pico Turquino 6,561 ft. (2,000 m.)
MONETARY UNIT Cuban peso
MAJOR LANGUAGE Spanish
MAJOR RELIGION Roman Catholicism

JAMAICA
AREA 4,411 sq. mi. (11,424 sq. km.)
POPULATION 2,161,000
CAPITAL Kingston
LARGEST CITY Kingston
HIGHEST POINT Blue Mountain Peak 7,402 ft. (2,256 m.)
MONETARY UNIT Jamaican dollar
MAJOR LANGUAGE English
MAJOR RELIGIONS Protestantism, Roman Catholicism

GRENADA
AREA 133 sq. mi. (344 sq. km.)
POPULATION 103,103
CAPITAL St. George's
LARGEST CITY St. George's
HIGHEST POINT Mt. St. Catherine 2,757 ft. (840 m.)
MONETARY UNIT East Caribbean dollar
MAJOR LANGUAGES English, French patois
MAJOR RELIGIONS Roman Catholicism, Protestantism

DOMINICA
AREA 290 sq. mi. (751 sq. km.)
POPULATION 74,089
CAPITAL Roseau
HIGHEST POINT Morne Diablotin 4,747 ft. (1,447 m.)
MONETARY UNIT Dominican dollar
MAJOR LANGUAGES English, French patois
MAJOR RELIGION Roman Catholicism

SAINT VINCENT AND THE GRENADINES
AREA 150 sq. mi. (388 sq. km.)
POPULATION 124,000
CAPITAL Kingstown
HIGHEST POINT Soufrière 4,000 ft. (1,219
MONETARY UNIT East Caribbean dollar
MAJOR LANGUAGE English
MAJOR RELIGIONS Protestantism, Roman Catholicism

HAITI
AREA 10,694 sq. mi. (27,697 sq. km.)
POPULATION 5,009,000
CAPITAL Port-au-Prince
LARGEST CITY Port-au-Prince
HIGHEST POINT Pic La Selle 8,793 ft. (2,680 m.)
MONETARY UNIT gourde
MAJOR LANGUAGES Creole French, French
MAJOR RELIGION Roman Catholicism

TRINIDAD AND TOBAGO
AREA 1,980 sq. mi. (5,128 sq. km.)
POPULATION 1,067,108
CAPITAL Port of Spain
LARGEST CITY Port of Spain
HIGHEST POINT Mt. Aripo 3,084 ft. (940 m.)
MONETARY UNIT Trinidad and Tobago dollar
MAJOR LANGUAGES English, Hindi
MAJOR RELIGIONS Roman Catholicism, Protestantism, Hinduism, Islam

DOMINICAN REPUBLIC
AREA 18,704 sq. mi. (48,443 sq. km.)
POPULATION 5,647,977
CAPITAL Santo Domingo
LARGEST CITY Santo Domingo
HIGHEST POINT Pico Duarte 10,417 ft. (3,175 m.)
MONETARY UNIT Dominican peso
MAJOR LANGUAGE Spanish
MAJOR RELIGION Roman Catholicism

BARBADOS
AREA 166 sq. mi. (430 sq. km.)
POPULATION 248,983
CAPITAL Bridgetown
LARGEST CITY Bridgetown
HIGHEST POINT Mt. Hillaby 1,104 ft. (336 m.)
MONETARY UNIT Barbadian dollar
MAJOR LANGUAGE English
MAJOR RELIGION Protestantism

SAINT LUCIA
AREA 238 sq. mi. (616 sq. km.)
POPULATION 115,783
CAPITAL Castries
HIGHEST POINT Mt. Gimie 3,117 ft. (950
MONETARY UNIT East Caribbean dollar
MAJOR LANGUAGES English, French patois
MAJOR RELIGIONS Roman Catholicism, Protestantism

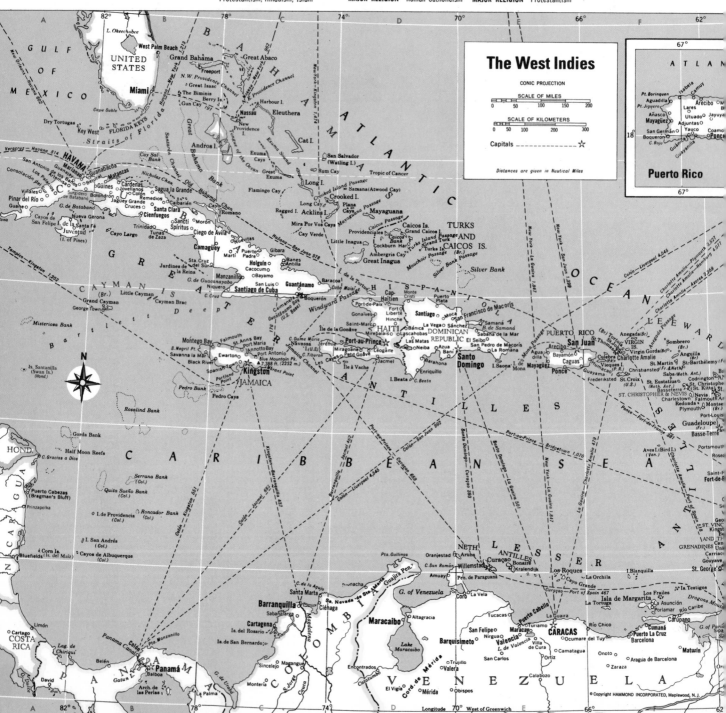

The West Indies
CONIC PROJECTION

SCALE OF MILES
0 50 100 150 200

SCALE OF KILOMETERS
0 50 100 200 300

Capitals ☆ - - - - - -

Distances are given in Nautical Miles

Puerto Rico

© Copyright HAMMOND INCORPORATED, Maplewood, N.J.

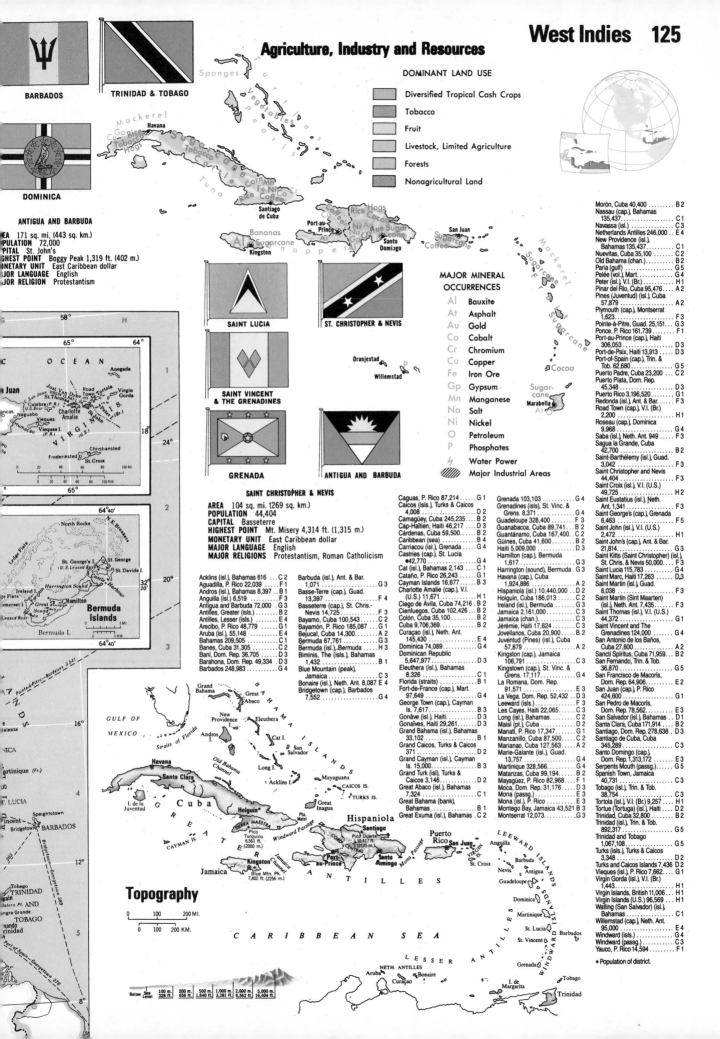

Agriculture, Industry and Resources

DOMINANT LAND USE

- Diversified Tropical Cash Crops
- Tobacco
- Fruit
- Livestock, Limited Agriculture
- Forests
- Nonagricultural Land

BARBADOS

TRINIDAD & TOBAGO

DOMINICA

ANTIGUA AND BARBUDA
AREA 171 sq. mi. (443 sq. km.)
POPULATION 72,000
CAPITAL St. John's
HIGHEST POINT Boggy Peak 1,319 ft. (402 m.)
MONETARY UNIT East Caribbean dollar
MAJOR LANGUAGE English
MAJOR RELIGION Protestantism

SAINT LUCIA

ST. CHRISTOPHER & NEVIS

SAINT VINCENT & THE GRENADINES

GRENADA

ANTIGUA AND BARBUDA

MAJOR MINERAL OCCURRENCES

Al	Bauxite
At	Asphalt
Au	Gold
Co	Cobalt
Cr	Chromium
Cu	Copper
Fe	Iron Ore
Gp	Gypsum
Mn	Manganese
Na	Salt
Ni	Nickel
O	Petroleum
P	Phosphates
⚡	Water Power
▨	Major Industrial Areas

SAINT CHRISTOPHER & NEVIS
AREA 104 sq. mi. (269 sq. km.)
POPULATION 44,404
CAPITAL Basseterre
HIGHEST POINT Mt. Misery 4,314 ft. (1,315 m.)
MONETARY UNIT East Caribbean dollar
MAJOR LANGUAGE English
MAJOR RELIGIONS Protestantism, Roman Catholicism

Bermuda Islands

Topography

Below Sea Level 100 m. 328 ft. / 200 m. 656 ft. / 500 m. 1,640 ft. / 1,000 m. 3,281 ft. / 2,000 m. 5,562 ft. / 5,000 m. 16,404 ft.

CARIBBEAN SEA

United States

POLYCONIC PROJECTION

SCALE OF MILES

SCALE OF KILOMETERS

Capitals of Countries .... ☆
State Capitals .... △
International Boundaries ....

© Copyright HAMMOND INCORPORATED, Maplewood, N.J.

Akron, Ohio‡ 660,328 ....K2	
Alabama (state) 3,890,061 ......J4	
Alaska (state) 400,481 ....C5	
Alaska (gulf), Alaska D6	
Alaska (range), Alaska C6	
Albany (cap.), N.Y.‡ 795,019 ...M2	
Albuquerque, N. Mex.‡ 454,499 ..E3	
Aleutian (isls.), Alaska D6	
Allentown, Pa.‡ 636,714 ....L2	
Anchorage, Alaska‡ 173,017 .....D6	
Annapolis (cap.), Md. 31,740 ...L3	
Ann Arbor, Mich.‡ 264,748 ......K2	
Appalachian (mts.) K3	
Appleton, Wis.‡ 291,325 ....J2	
Arizona (state) 2,717,866 ......D4	
Arkansas (state) 2,285,513 .....H3	
Arkansas (riv.) H3	
Atlanta (cap.), Ga.‡ 2,029,618 .K4	
Atlantic City, N.J.‡ 194,119 ...M3	
Attu (isl.), Alaska D6	
Augusta, Ga.‡ 327,372 ....K4	
Augusta (cap.), Maine 21,819 ...N2	
Austin (cap.), Texas‡ 536,450 ..G4	
Bakersfield, Calif.‡ 403,089 ...C3	
Baltimore, Md.‡ 2,174,023 ......L3	
Baton Rouge (cap.), La.‡ 493,973 ...H4	
Beaumont, Texas‡ 375,497 ....H4	
Bering (sea), Alaska C6	
Bering (str.), Alaska C5	
Bighorn (riv.) E2	
Binghamton, N.Y.‡ 301,336 ......L2	
Birmingham, Ala.‡ 847,360 ......J4	
Bismarck (cap.), N. Dak.‡ 79,988 ...G1	
Bitterroot (range) D1	
Black Hills (mts.) F2	
Boise (cap.), Idaho‡ 173,076 ...C2	
Borah (peak), Idaho D2	

Boston (cap.), Mass.‡ 2,763,357 ...M2	
Bridgeport, Conn.‡ 395,455 .....M2	
Brazos (riv.), Texas G4	
Brooks (range), Alaska C5	
Buffalo, N.Y.‡ 1,242,573 ....L2	
California (state) 23,668,562 ..B3	
Canadian (riv.) F3	
Canaveral (Kennedy) (cape)	
Canton, Ohio‡ 404,421 ....K2	
Cape Fear (riv.), N.C. L4	
Carson City (cap.), Nev. 32,022 ...C3	
Cascade (range) B1	
Cedar Rapids, Iowa‡ 169,775 ....H2	
Champlain (lake) M2	
Charleston, S.C.‡ 430,301 ......L4	
Charleston (cap.), W. Va.‡ 269,595 ...K3	
Charlotte, N.C.‡ 637,218 ....L3	
Chattahoochee (riv.) J4	
Chattanooga, Tenn.‡ 426,540 ....J3	
Chesapeake (bay) L3	
Cheyenne (cap.), Wyo. 47,283 ...F2	
Cheyenne (riv.) F2	
Chicago, Ill.‡ 7,102,328 ....J2	
Cimarron (riv.) G3	
Cincinnati, Ohio‡ 1,401,403 ....K3	
Cleveland, Ohio‡ 1,898,720 .....K2	
Coast (ranges) B2	
Cod (cape), Mass. N2	
Colorado (state) 2,888,834 .....E3	
Colorado (riv.) D4	
Colorado (riv.), Texas G4	
Colorado Springs, Colo.‡ 317,458 ...F3	
Columbia, S.C.‡ 408,176 ....K4	
Columbia (riv.) B1	
Columbus, Ga.‡ 239,196 ....K4	

Columbus (cap.), Ohio‡ 1,093,293 ...K3	
Concord (cap.), N.H. 30,400 ....M2	
Connecticut (state) 3,107,576 ..M2	
Connecticut (riv.) M2	
Corpus Christi, Texas‡ 326,228 .G5	
Cumberland (riv.) J3	
Dallas, Texas‡ 2,974,878 ....G4	
Davenport, Iowa‡ 383,958 ....H2	
Dayton, Ohio‡ 830,070 ....K3	
Death Valley (depr.) Calif. C3	
Delaware (state) 595,225 ....L3	
Delaware (bay) M3	
Denver (cap.), Colo.‡ 1,619,921 ...F3	
Des Moines (cap.), Iowa 338,048 ...H2	
Detroit, Mich.‡ 4,352,762 ......K2	
District of Columbia 637,651 ...L3	
Dover (cap.), Del. 23,512 ......L3	
Duluth, Minn.‡ 266,650 ....H1	
Durham, N.C.‡ 530,673 ....L3	
Elbert (mt.), Colo. E3	
El Paso, Texas‡ 479,899 ....E4	
Erie, Pa.‡ 279,780 ....K2	
Erie (lake) K2	
Eugene, Oreg.‡ 275,226 ....B2	
Evansville, Ind.‡ 309,408 ......J3	
Everglades, The (swamp) K5	
Fayetteville, N.C.‡ 247,160 ....L3	
Flint, Mich.‡ 521,589 ....K2	
Florida (state) 9,739,992 ......K5	
Florida (keys), Fla. K6	
Fort Smith, Ark.‡ 203,269 ......H3	
Fort Wayne, Ind.‡ 382,961 ......J2	
Fort Worth, Texas‡ 385,141 .....G4	
Frankfort (cap.), Ky. 25,973 ...K3	
Fresno, Calif.‡ 515,013 ....C3	
Galveston, Texas‡ 195,940 ......H5	
Gary, Ind.‡ 642,781 ....J2	

Georgia (state) 5,464,265 ......K4	
Gila (riv.) D4	
Glacier Nat'l Park, Mont. D1	
Golden Gate (chan.), Calif. B3	
Grand Canyon Nat'l Park, Ariz. ...D3	
Grand Rapids, Mich.‡ 601,680 ...K2	
Great Salt (lake), Utah D2	
Greensboro, N.C.‡ 827,385 ......L3	
Greenville, S.C.‡ 568,758 ......K4	
Harrisburg (cap.), Pa.‡ 446,072 ...L2	
Hartford (cap.), Conn.‡ 726,114 ...M2	
Hatteras (cape), N.C. M3	
Havasu (lake) D4	
Hawaii (state) 965,000 ....F5	
Hawaii (isl.), Hawaii F6	
Helena (cap.), Mont. 23,938 ....D1	
Honolulu (cap.), Hawaii 762,874 ...F5	
Houston, Texas‡ 2,905,350 ......G5	
Huntington, W. Va.‡ 311,350 ....K3	
Huntsville, Ala.‡ 308,593 ......J4	
Huron (lake), Mich. K2	
Idaho (state) 943,935 ....D2	
Illinois (state) 11,418,461 ....J3	
Indiana (state) 5,490,179 ......J3	
Indianapolis (cap.), Ind. J3	
Iowa (state) 2,913,387 ....H2	
Jackson (cap.), Miss.‡ 320,425 .J4	
Jacksonville, Fla.‡ 737,519 ....K4	
Jefferson City (cap.), Mo. 33,619 ...H3	
Jersey City, N.J.‡ 556,972 .....M2	
Johnstown, Pa.‡ 664,506 ....L2	
Juneau (cap.), Alaska 19,528 ...E6	
Kalamazoo, Mich.‡ 279,192 ......J2	
Kansas (state) 2,363,208 ....G3	
Kansas City.	

Kans.-Mo.‡ 1,327,020 ....G3	
Kauai (isl.), Hawaii E5	
Kentucky (state) 3,661,433 .....J3	
Kentucky (lake) J3	
Knoxville, Tenn.‡ 476,517 ......K3	
Lancaster, Pa.‡ 362,346 ....L2	
Lansing (cap.), Mich.‡ 476,511 .K2	
Las Vegas, Nev.‡ 461,816 ....C3	
Lawrence, Mass.‡ 281,981 ....M2	
Lexington, Ky.‡ 318,136 ....K3	
Lima, Ohio‡ 218,244 ....K2	
Lincoln (cap.), Nebr.‡ 192,884 .G2	
Little Rock (cap.), Ark.‡ 393,494 ...H4	
Long (isl.), N.Y. N2	
Long Beach, Calif.‡ 361,334 ....C4	
Los Angeles, Calif.‡ 7,477,657 .C4	
Louisiana (state) 4,203,972 ....H4	
Louisville, Ky.‡ 906,240 ....J3	
Lowell, Mass.‡ 233,410 ....M2	
Lubbock, Texas‡ 211,651 ....F4	
Macon, Ga.‡ 254,623 ....K4	
Madison (cap.), Wis.‡ 323,545 ..J2	
Maine (state) 1,124,660 ....N1	
Maryland (state) 4,216,446 .....L3	
Massachusetts (state) 5,737,037 ...M2	
Maui (isl.), Hawaii F5	
Mauna Kea (mt.), Hawaii G6	
Mauna Loa (mt.), Hawaii F6	
May (cape), N.J. M3	
McKinley (mt.), Alaska D5	
Memphis, Tenn.‡ 912,887 ....J3	
Mendocino (cape), Calif. B2	
Mexico (gulf)	
Miami, Fla.‡ 1,625,979 ....K5	
Michigan (state) 9,258,344 .....J1	
Michigan (lake) J2	
Milwaukee, Wis.‡ 1,397,143 .....J2	
Minneapolis, Minn.‡ 2,114,256 ..H1	

Minnesota (state) 4,077,148 ....H1	
Mississippi (state) 2,520,638 ..J4	
Mississippi (riv.) H4	
Missouri (state) 4,917,444 .....H3	
Missouri (riv.) H3	
Mitchell (mt.), N.C. K3	
Mobile, Ala.‡ 442,819 ....J4	
Montana (state) 786,690 ....E1	
Montgomery (cap.), Ala.‡ 272,687 ...J4	
Nantucket (isl.), Mass. N2	
Nashville (cap.), Tenn.‡ 850,505 ...J3	
Nebraska (state) 1,570,006 .....F2	
Nevada (state) 799,184 ....C3	
Newark, N.J.‡ 1,965,304 ....M2	
New Haven, Conn.‡ 417,592 ......M2	
New Jersey (state) 7,364,158 ...M3	
New Mexico (state) 1,299,968 ...E4	
New Orleans, La.‡ 1,186,725 ....H5	
Newport News, Va.‡ 364,449 .....L3	
New York (state) 17,557,288 ....M2	
New York, N.Y.‡ 9,119,737 ......M2	
Norfolk, Va.‡ 806,691 ....L3	
North Carolina (state) 5,874,429 ...L3	
North Dakota (state) 652,695 ...F1	
Oahu (isl.), Hawaii E5	
Oakland, Calif.‡ 3,252,721 .....B3	
Ohio (state) 10,797,419 ....J2	
Ohio (riv.) J3	
Oklahoma (state) 3,025,266 .....G3	
Oklahoma City (cap.), Okla.‡ 834,088 ...G3	
Olympia (cap.), Wash.‡ 124,264 .B1	
Olympic Nat'l Park, Wash. A1	
Omaha, Nebr.‡ 570,399 ....G2	
Ontario (lake), N.Y. L2	

Oregon (state) 2,632,663 ....B2	
Orlando, Fla.‡ 700,699 ....K5	
Ozark (mts.) H3	
Paterson, N.J.‡ 447,585 ....M2	
Pennsylvania (state) L2	
Pensacola, Fla.‡ 289,782 ....J4	
Peoria, Ill.‡ 365,864 ....J2	
Philadelphia, Pa.‡ 4,716,818 ...M2	
Phoenix (cap.), Ariz.‡ 1,508,030 ...D4	
Pierre (cap.), S. Dak. 11,793 ..F2	
Pikes (peak), Colo. F3	
Pittsburgh, Pa.‡ 2,263,894 .....L2	
Platte (riv.), Nebr. G2	
Portland, Maine‡ 183,625 ....L5	
Portland, Oreg.‡ 1,242,187 .....B1	
Potomac (riv.) L3	
Providence (cap.), R.I.‡ 919,216 ...M2	
Racine, Wis.‡ 173,132 ....J2	
Raleigh (cap.), N.C.‡ 530,673 ..L3	
Rainier (mt.), Wash. B1	
Reading, Pa.‡ 312,509 ....L2	
Red (riv.) H4	
Red River of the North (riv.) ...G1	
Rhode Island (state) 947,154 ...M2	
Richmond (cap.), Va.‡ 632,015 ..L3	
Rio Grande (riv.)	
Roanoke, Va.‡ 218,244 ....K3	
Rochester, N.Y.‡ 971,079 ....L2	
Rockford, Ill.‡ 279,514 ....J2	
Rocky (mts.) E3	
Sacramento (cap.), Calif.‡ 1,014,002 ...B3	
Saint Clair (lake), Mich. K2	
Saint Lawrence (riv.), N.Y. N1	
Saint Louis, Mo.‡ 2,355,276 ....H3	

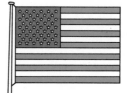

AREA 3,623,420 sq. mi.
(9,384,658 sq. km.)
POPULATION 226,504,825
CAPITAL Washington
LARGEST CITY New York
HIGHEST POINT Mt. McKinley 20,320 ft.
(6,194 m.)
MONETARY UNIT U.S. dollar
MAJOR LANGUAGE English
MAJOR RELIGIONS Protestantism,
Roman Catholicism, Judaism

Population Distribution

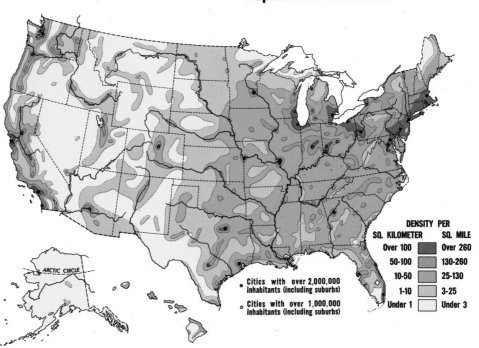

DENSITY PER

SQ. KILOMETER	SQ. MILE
Over 100	Over 260
50-100	130-260
10-50	25-130
1-10	3-25
Under 1	Under 3

● Cities with over 2,000,000
inhabitants (including suburbs)

○ Cities with over 1,000,000
inhabitants (including suburbs)

Vegetation

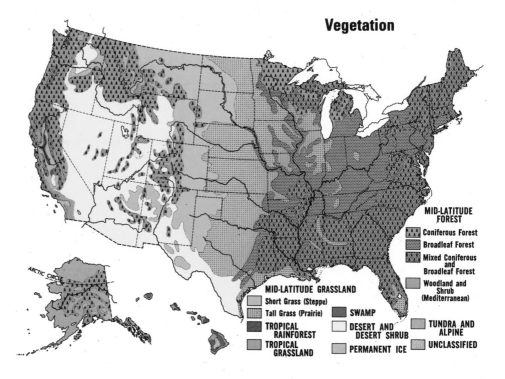

MID-LATITUDE FOREST

Coniferous Forest

Broadleaf Forest

Mixed Coniferous
and
Broadleaf Forest

Woodland and
Shrub
(Mediterranean)

MID-LATITUDE GRASSLAND

Short Grass (Steppe)

Tall Grass (Prairie)

SWAMP

TROPICAL
RAINFOREST

DESERT AND
DESERT SHRUB

PERMANENT ICE

TROPICAL
GRASSLAND

TUNDRA AND
ALPINE

UNCLASSIFIED

Topography

Agriculture, Industry and Resources

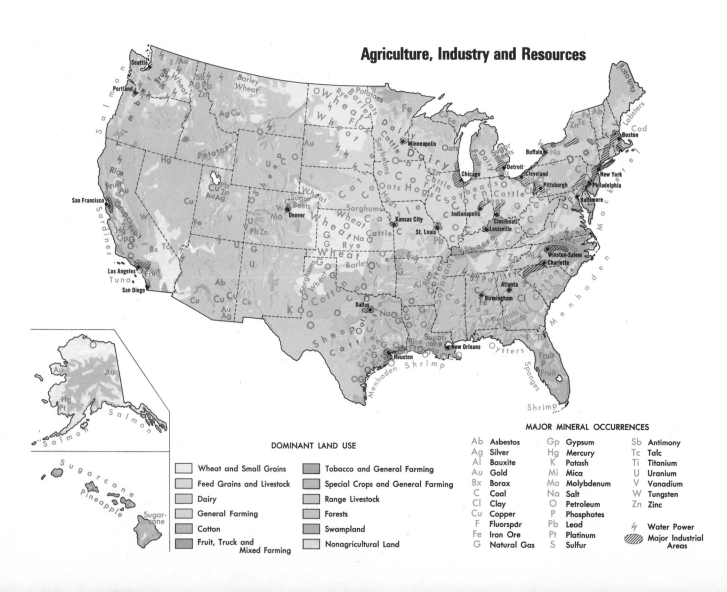

DOMINANT LAND USE

- Wheat and Small Grains
- Feed Grains and Livestock
- Dairy
- General Farming
- Cotton
- Fruit, Truck and Mixed Farming
- Tobacco and General Farming
- Special Crops and General Farming
- Range Livestock
- Forests
- Swampland
- Nonagricultural Land

MAJOR MINERAL OCCURRENCES

Ab	Asbestos	Gp	Gypsum	Sb	Antimony
Ag	Silver	Hg	Mercury	Tc	Talc
Al	Bauxite	K	Potash	Ti	Titanium
Au	Gold	Mi	Mica	U	Uranium
Bx	Borax	Mo	Molybdenum	V	Vanadium
C	Coal	Na	Salt	W	Tungsten
Cl	Clay	O	Petroleum	Zn	Zinc
Cu	Copper	P	Phosphates		
F	Fluorspar	Pb	Lead	⚡	Water Power
Fe	Iron Ore	Pt	Platinum	▨	Major Industrial Areas
G	Natural Gas	S	Sulfur		

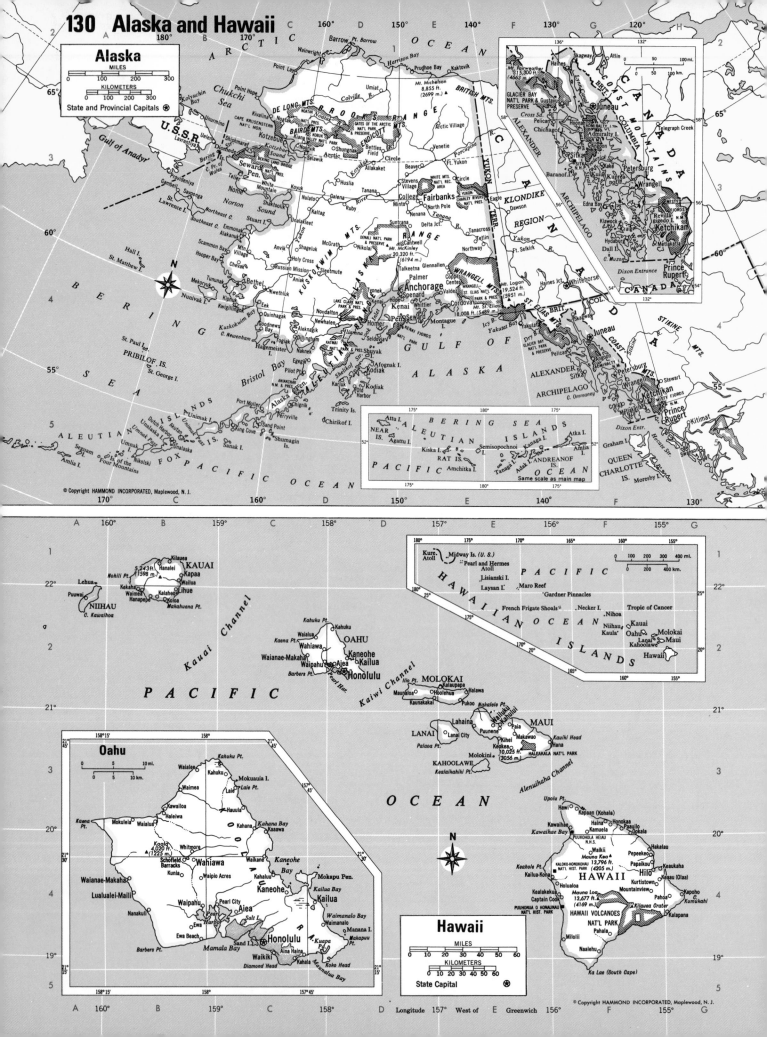

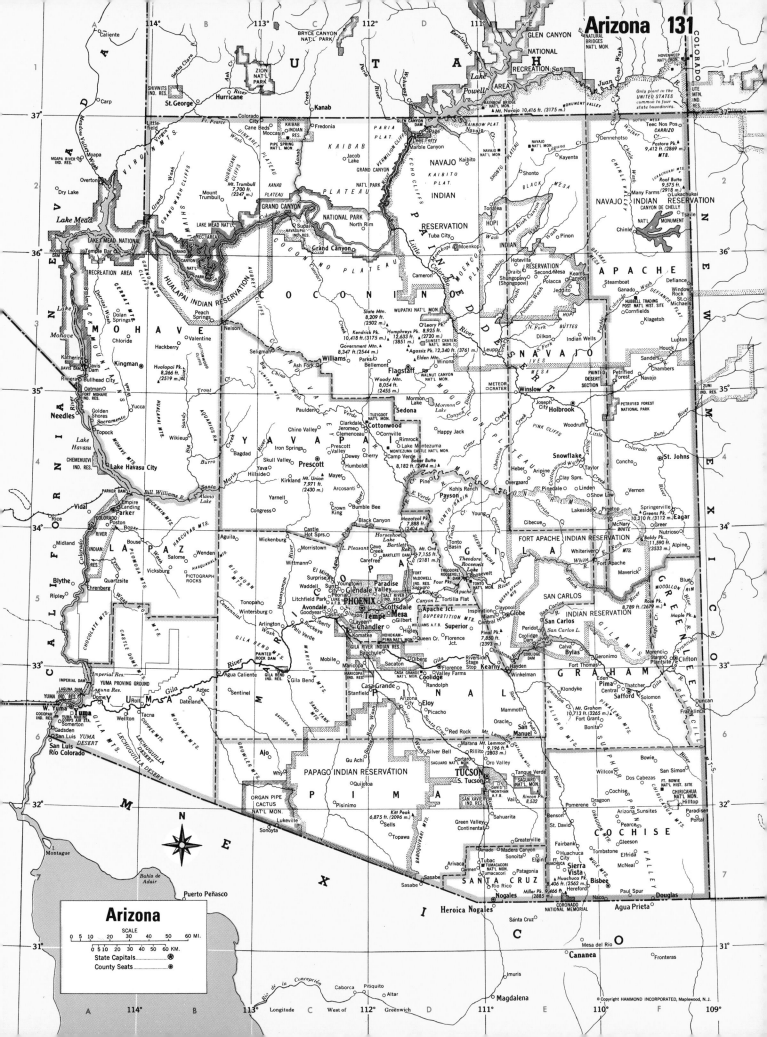

Arizona

SCALE

0 5 10   20   30   40   50   60 MI.

0 5 10 20 30 40 50 60 KM.

State Capitals .... ⊛

County Seats .... ◉

© Copyright HAMMOND INCORPORATED, Maplewood, N.J.

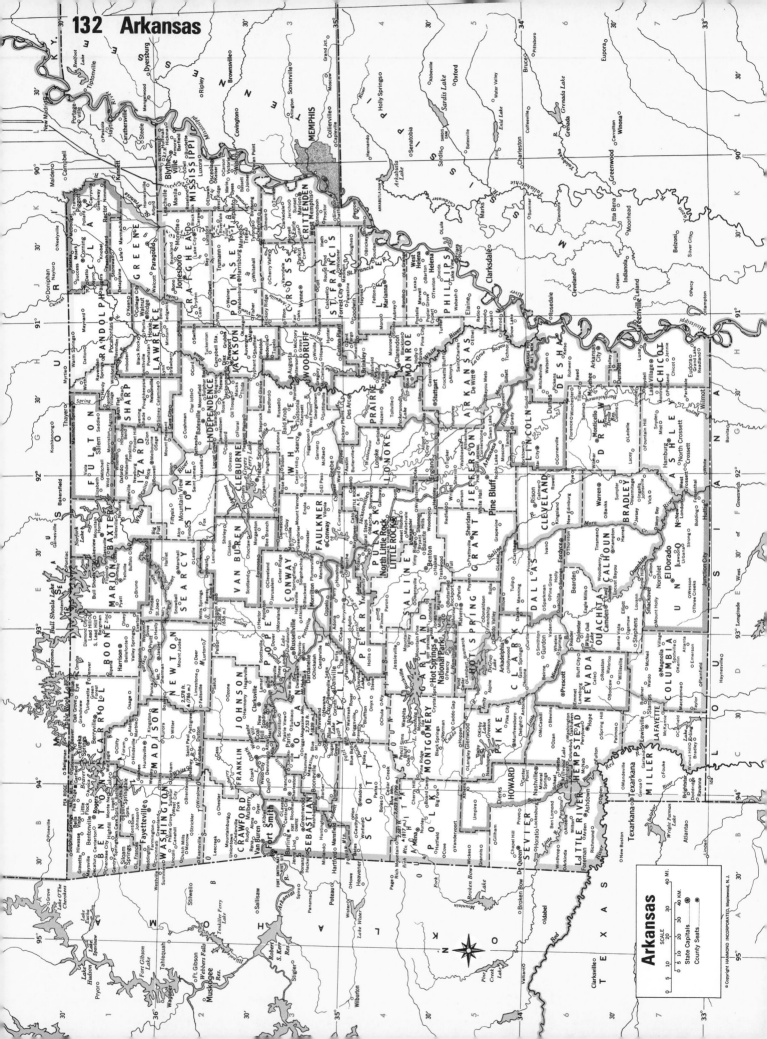

Arkansas

SCALE

State Capitals ⊛
County Seats ⊙

© Copyright HAMMOND INCORPORATED, Maplewood, N.J.

California 133

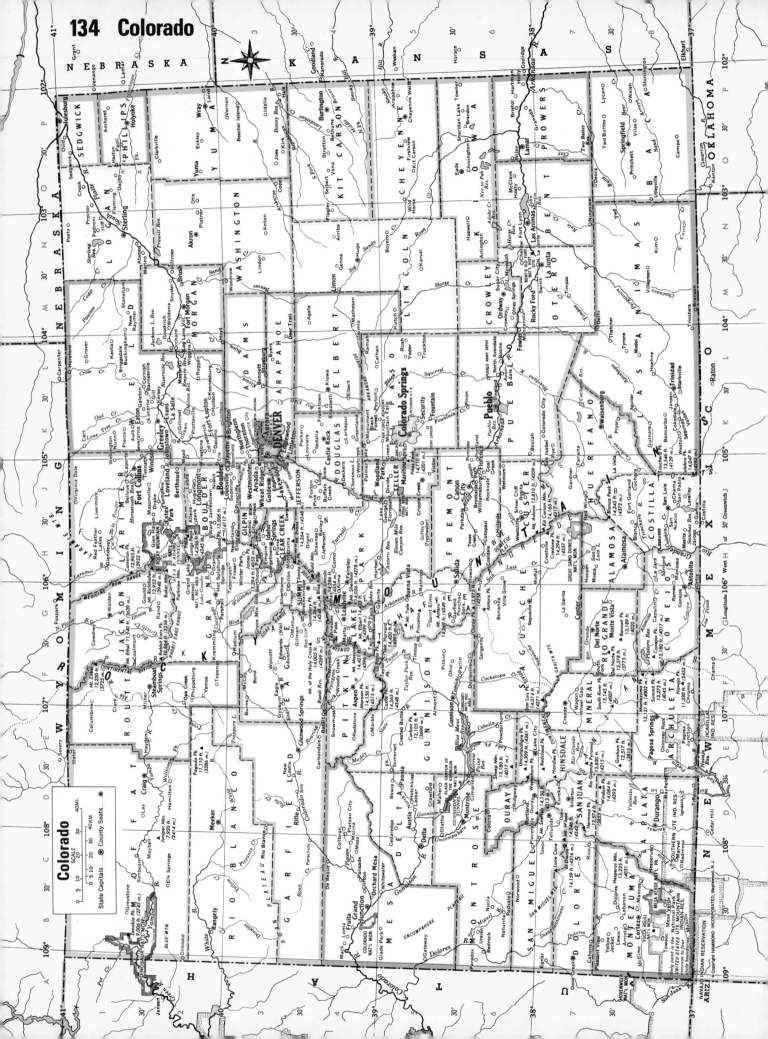

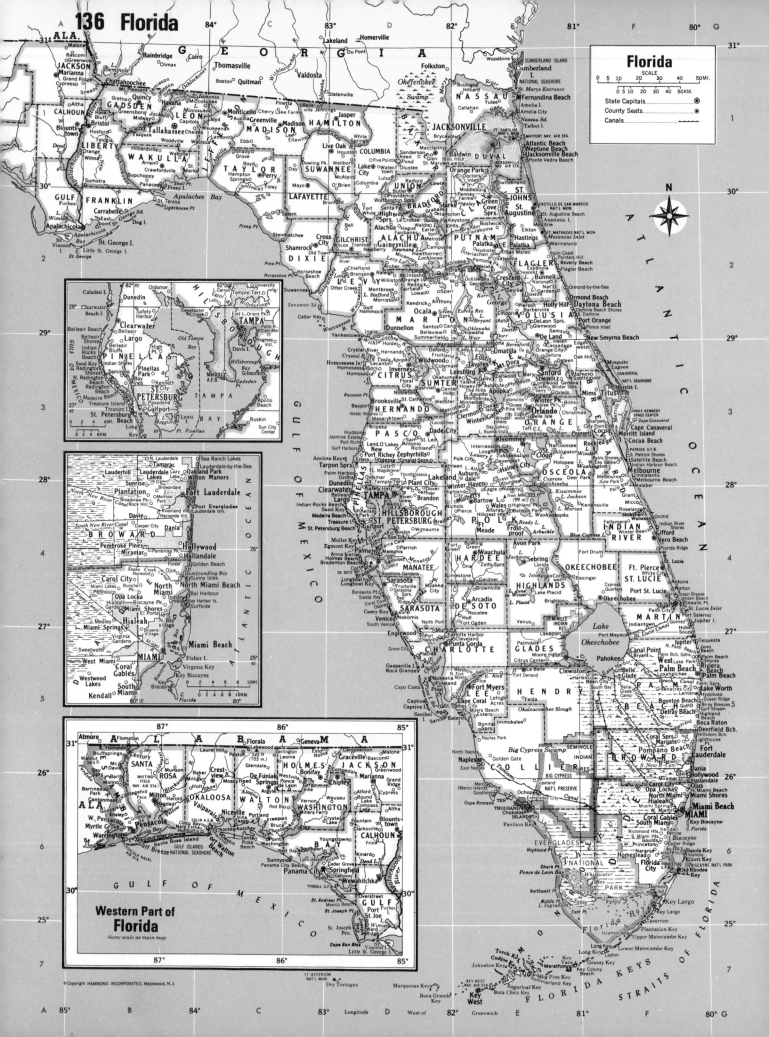

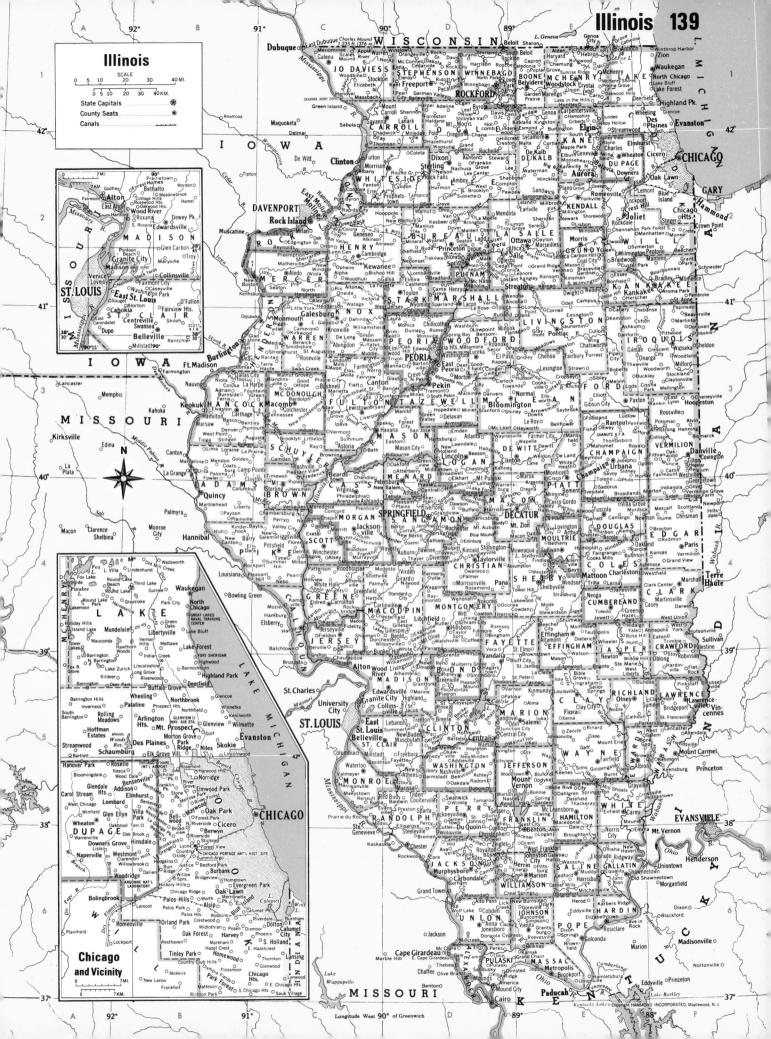

Illinois

SCALE

State Capitals ⊛
County Seats ⊙
Canals

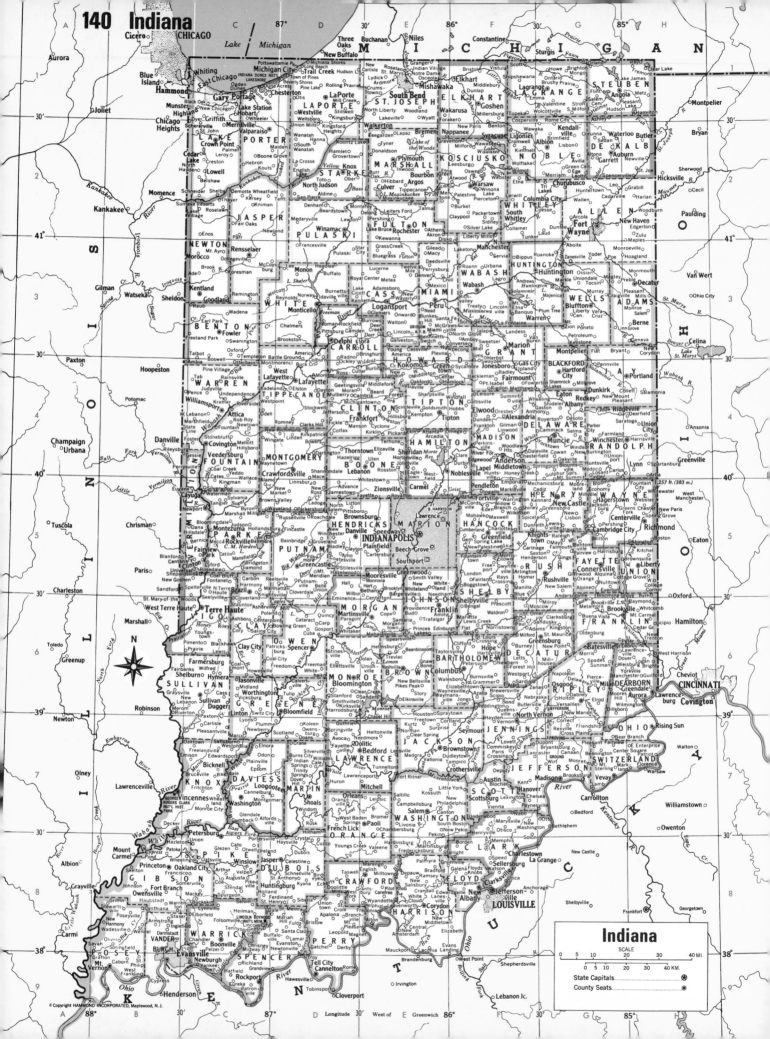

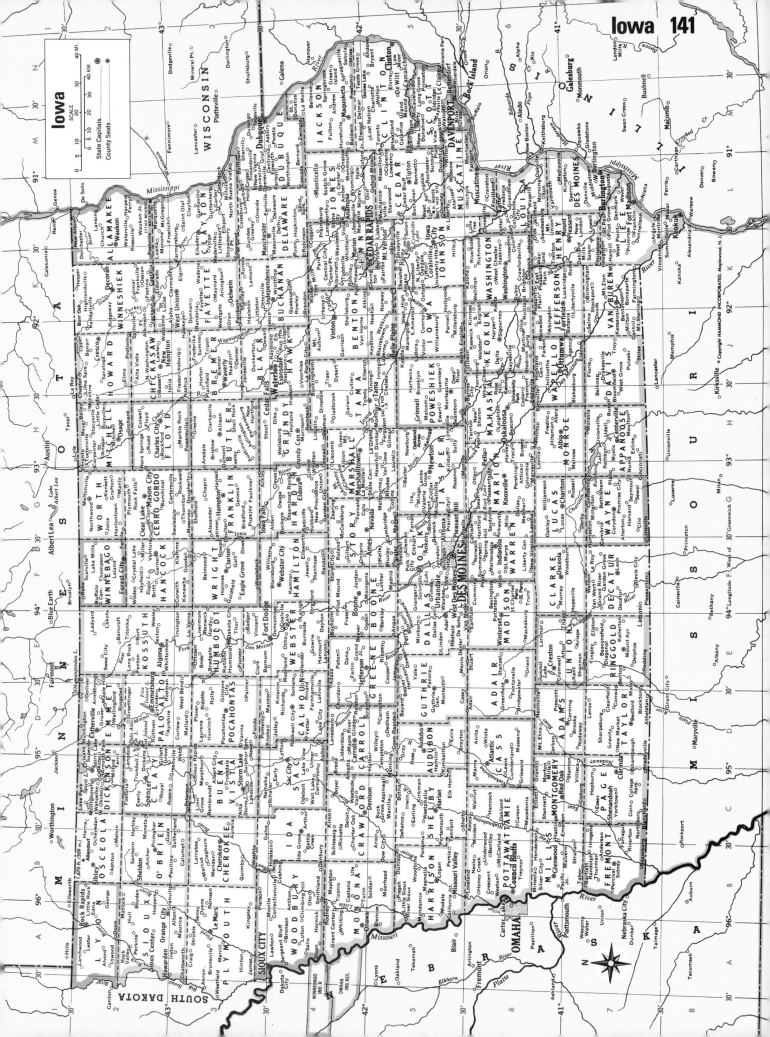

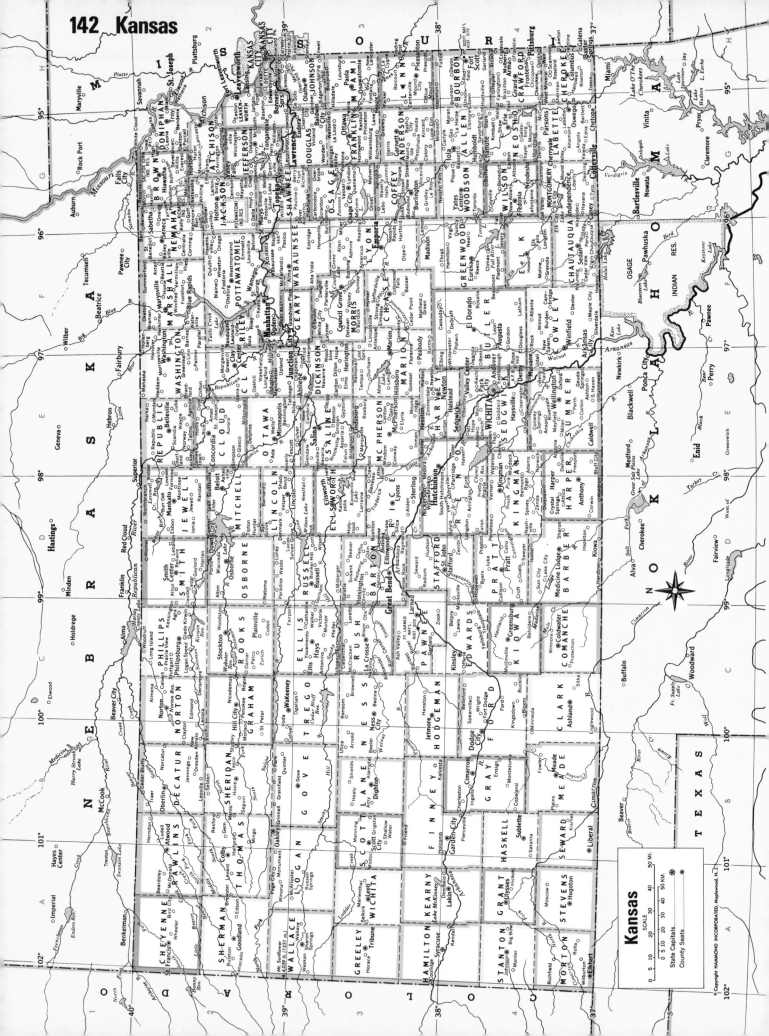

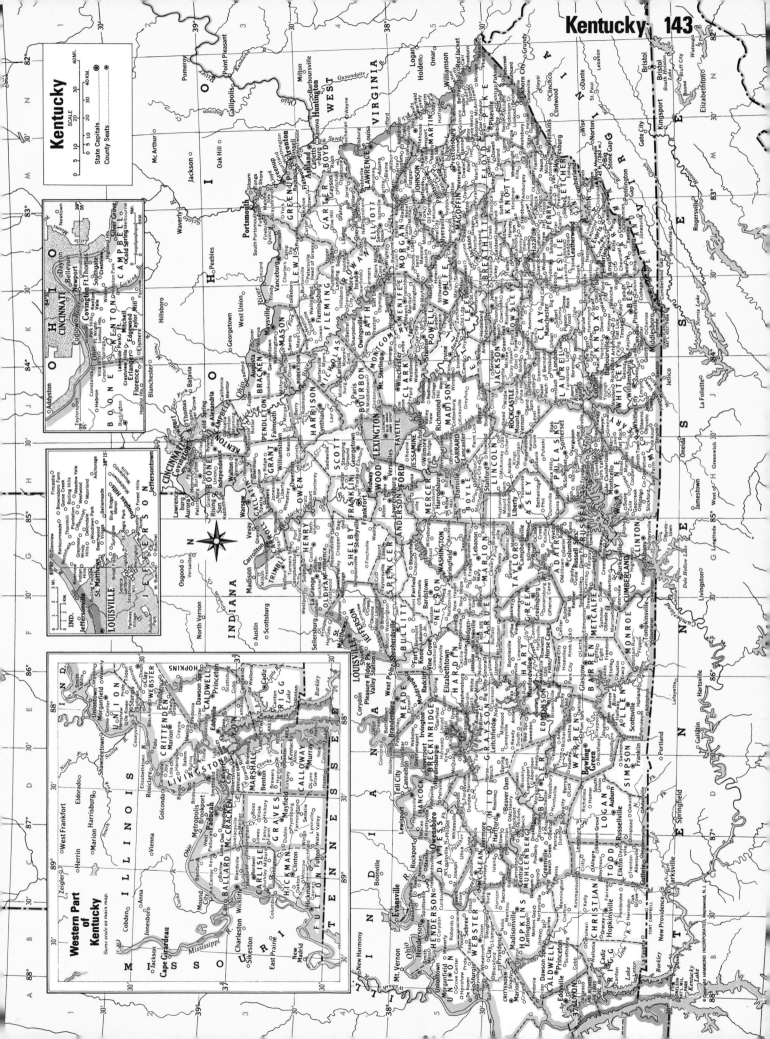

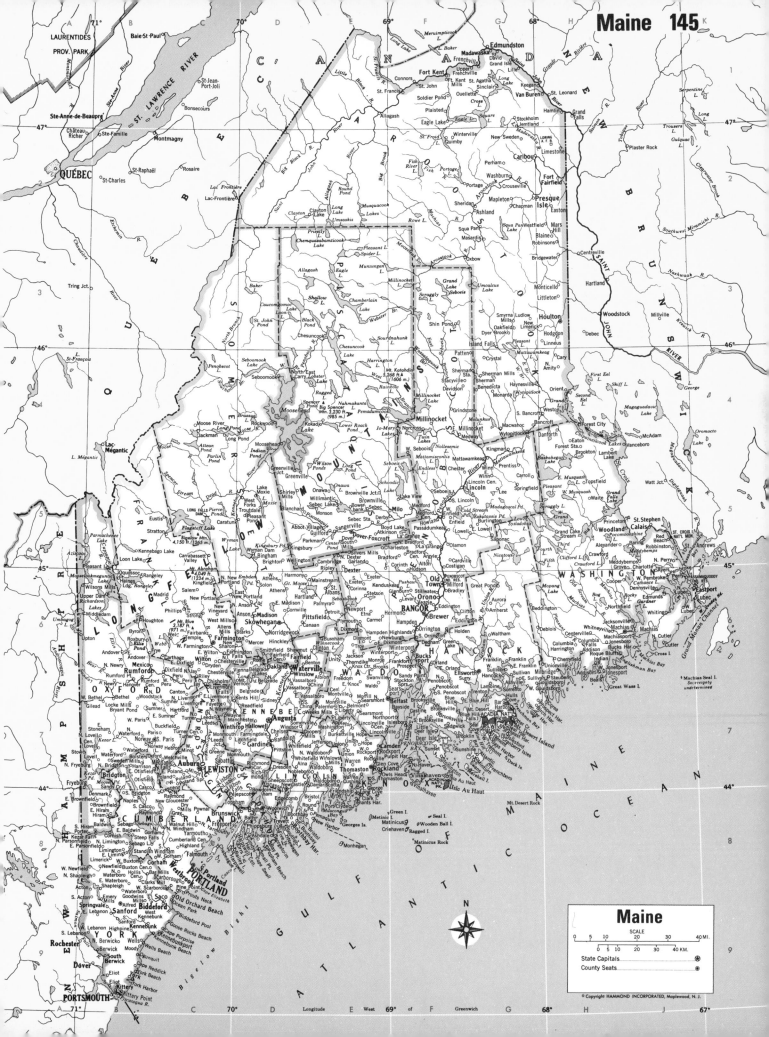

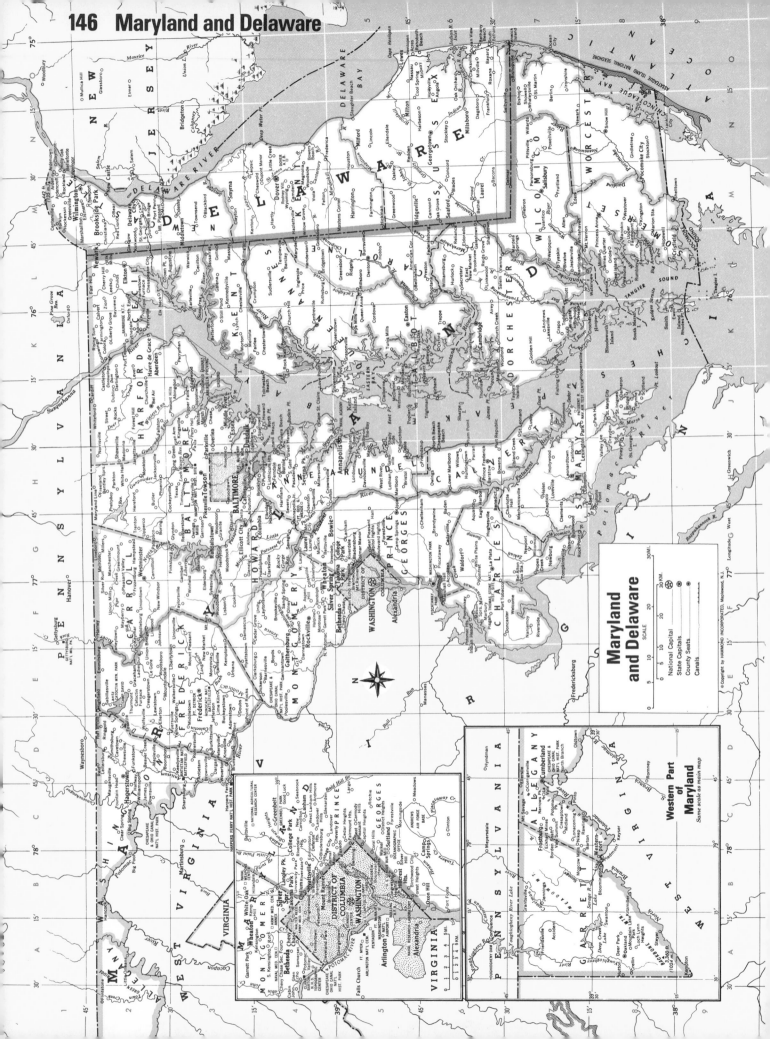

Maryland and Delaware

SCALE

National Capital
State Capitals
County Seats
Canals

© Copyright by HAMMOND INCORPORATED, Maplewood, N.J.

Western Part of Maryland

Same scale as main map

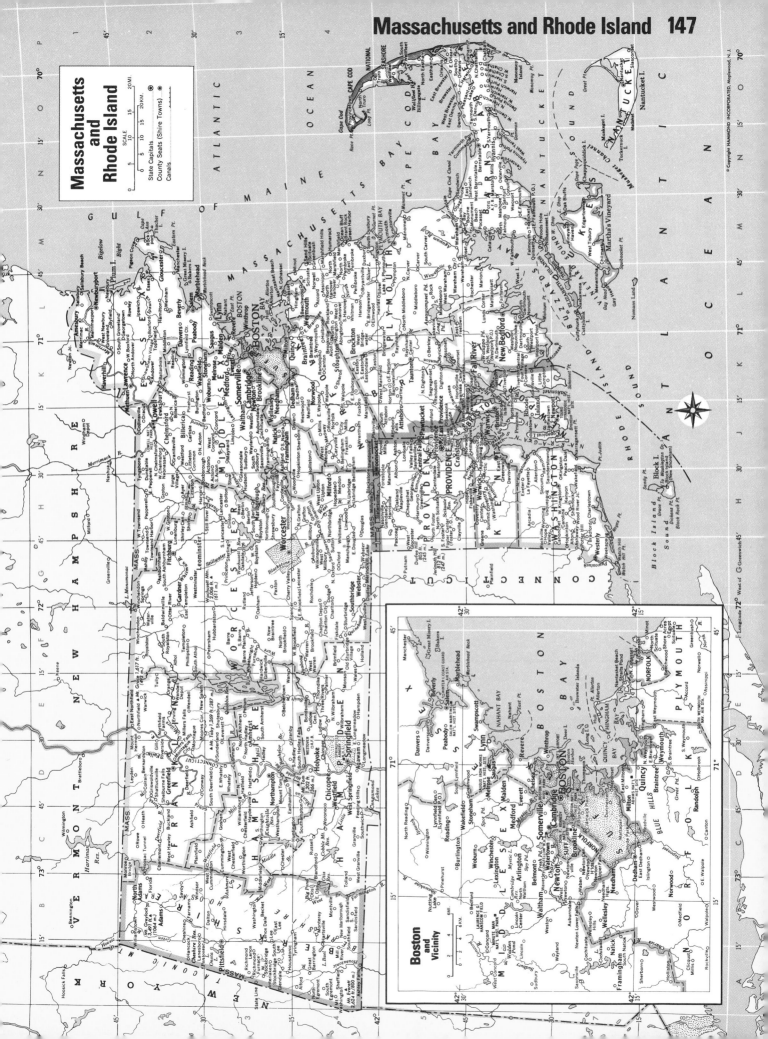

Massachusetts
and
Rhode Island

SCALE

State Capitals ⊛
County Seats (Shire Towns) ◉
Canals

Boston
and
Vicinity

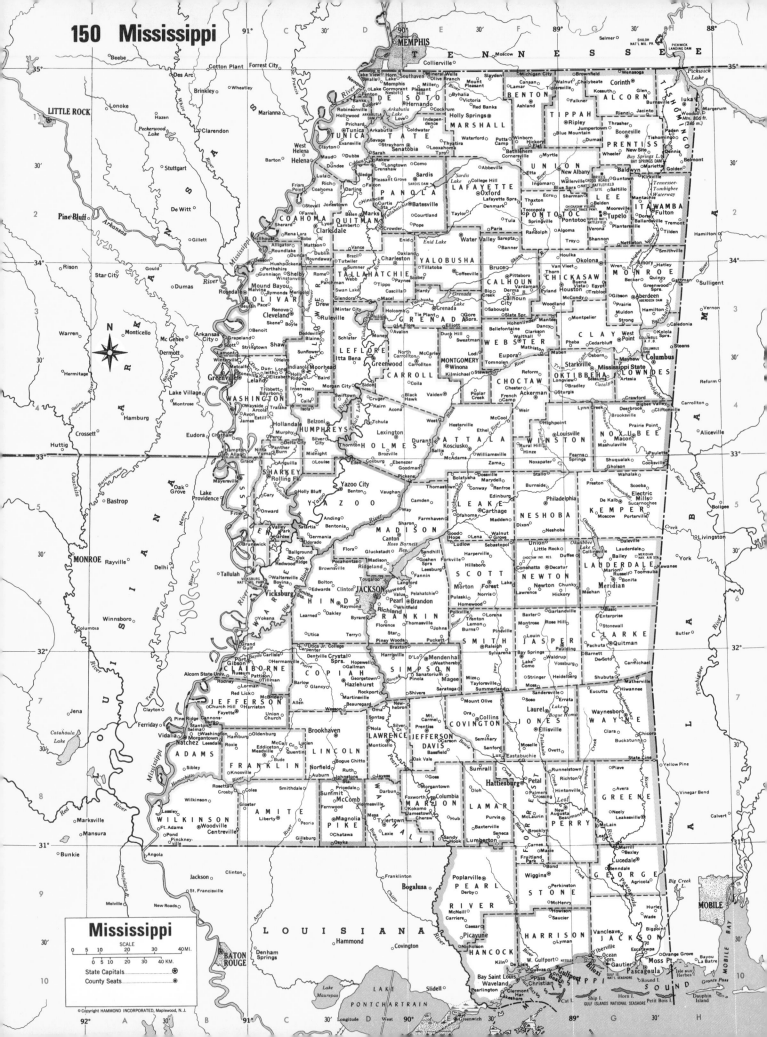

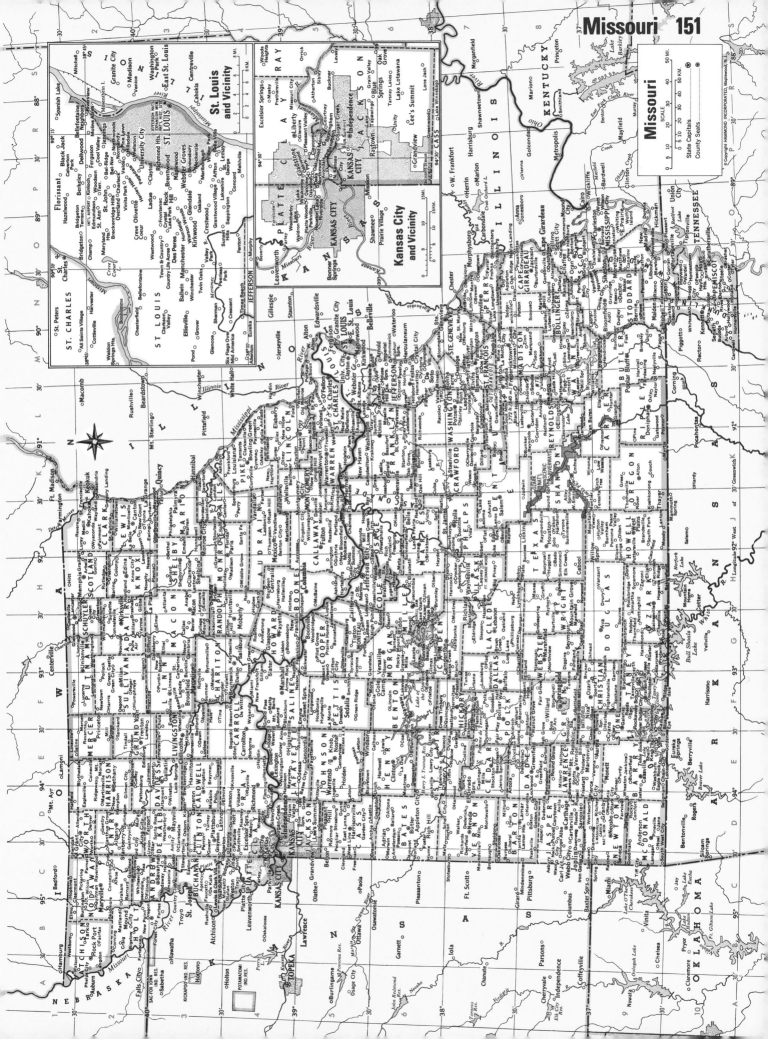

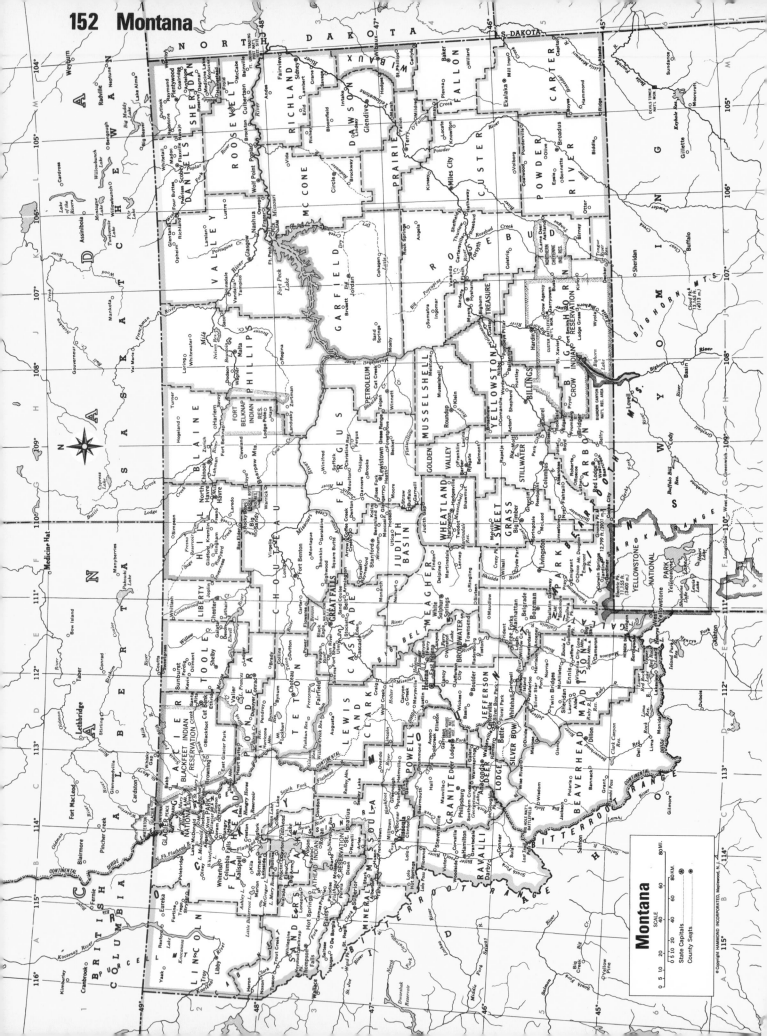

Montana

SCALE
0 5 10 20   40   60   80 MI.
0 5 10 20   40   60   80 KM.

⊗ State Capitals
⊙ County Seats

© Copyright HAMMOND INCORPORATED, Maplewood, N.J.

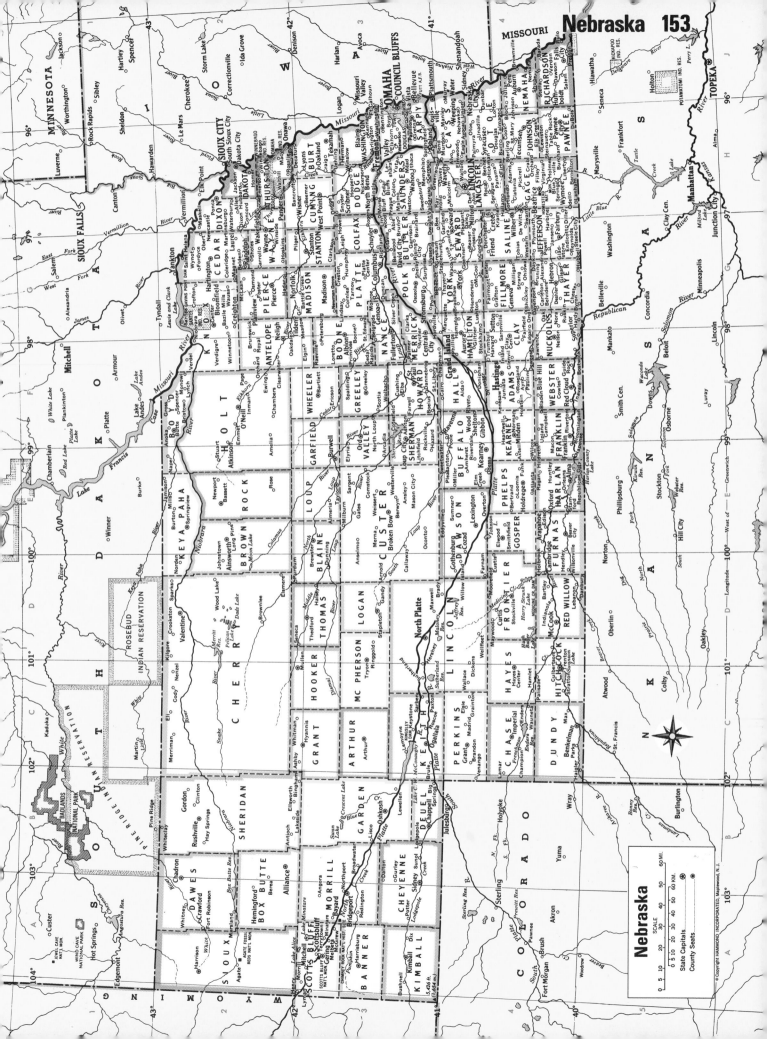

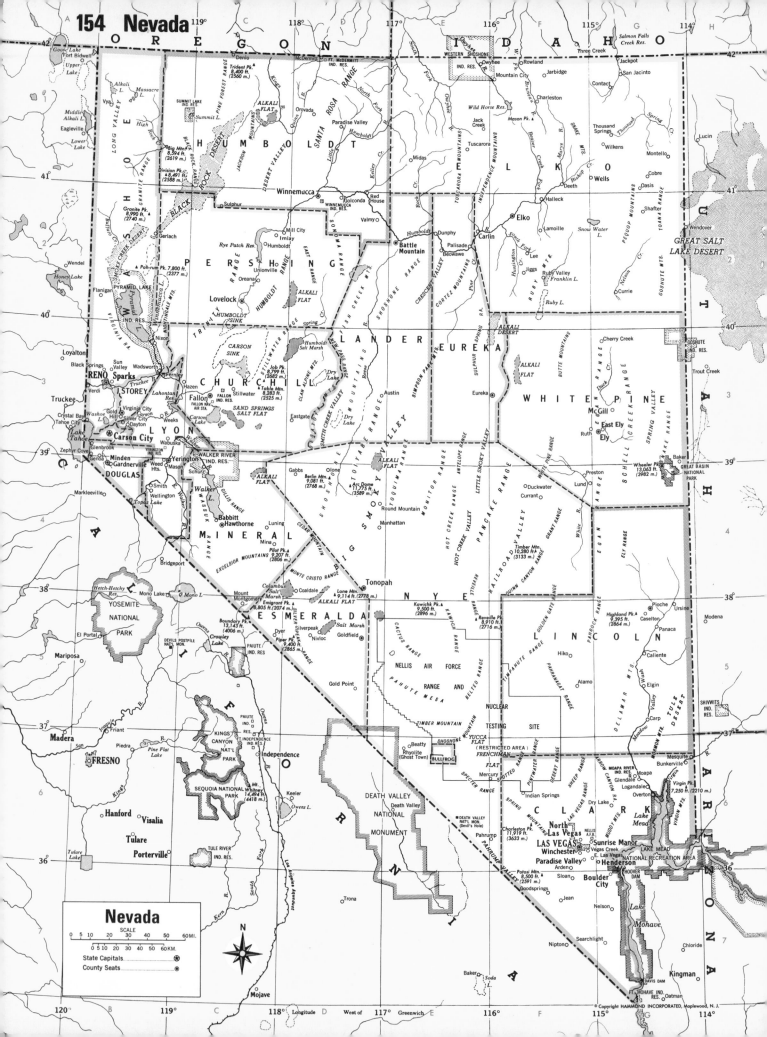

New Hampshire
and Vermont

SCALE
0   5   10   15   20   25MI.
0 5 10 15 20 25KM.

State Capitals .... ⊛
County Seats .... ◉

® Copyright HAMMOND INCORPORATED, Maplewood, N.J.

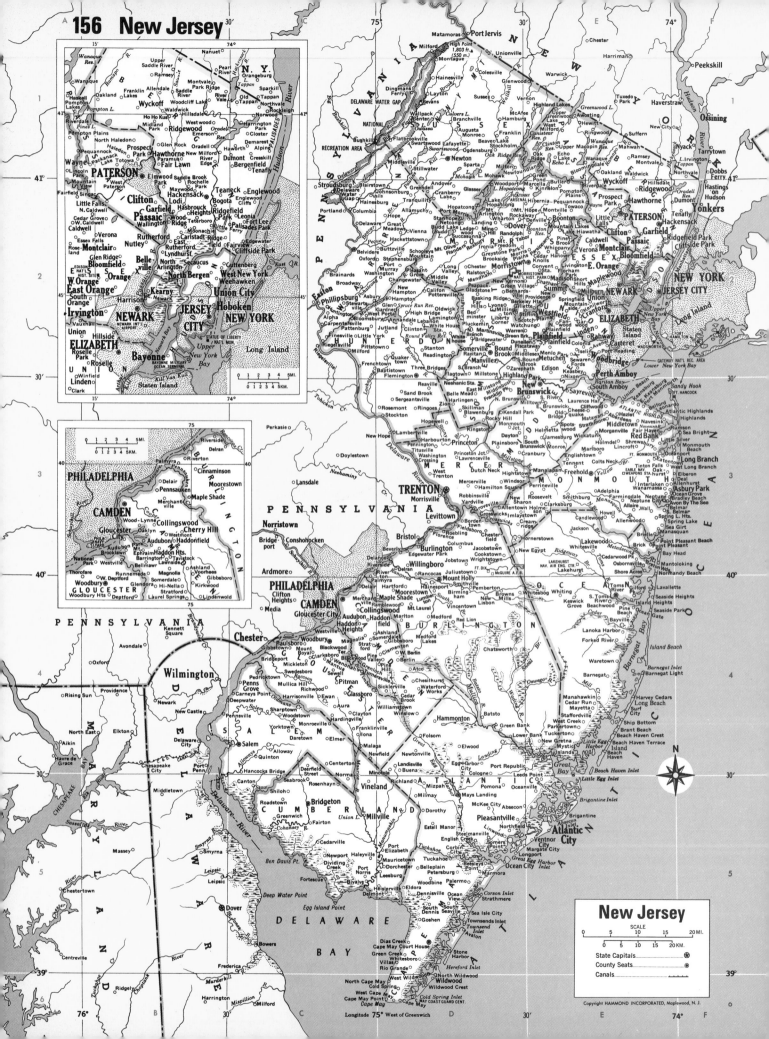

New Jersey

SCALE

0   5   10   15   20 MI.

0   5   10   15   20 KM.

State Capitals .... ⊛

County Seats .... ◉

Canals ....

Copyright HAMMOND INCORPORATED, Maplewood, N. J.

Longitude 75° West of Greenwich

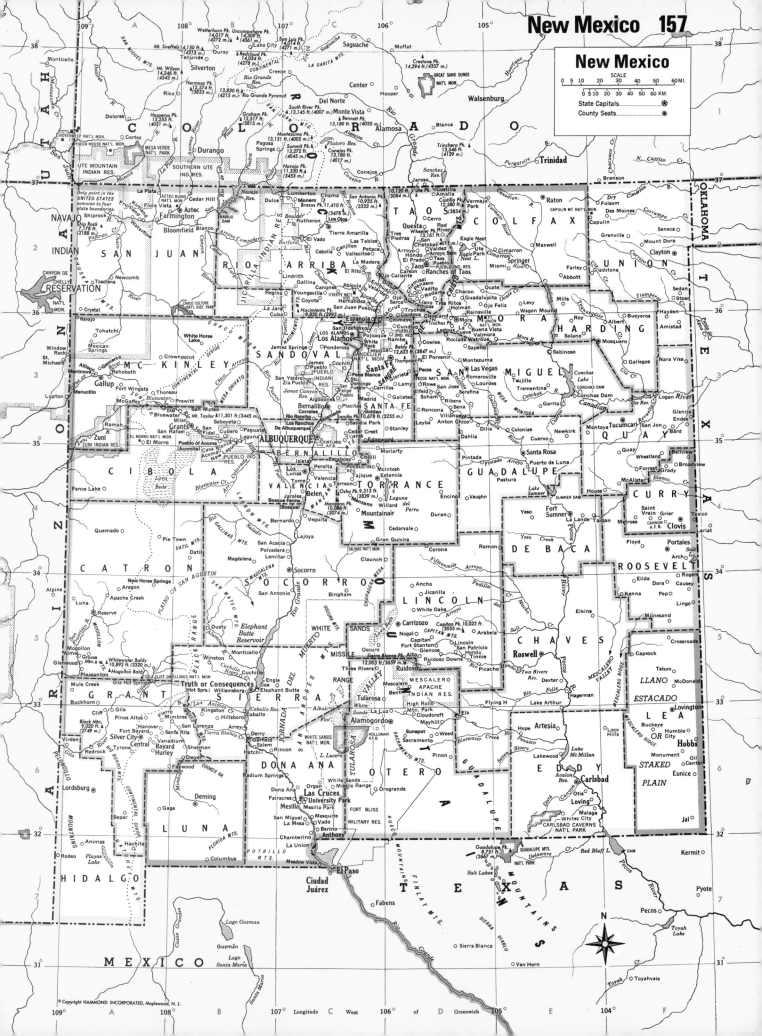

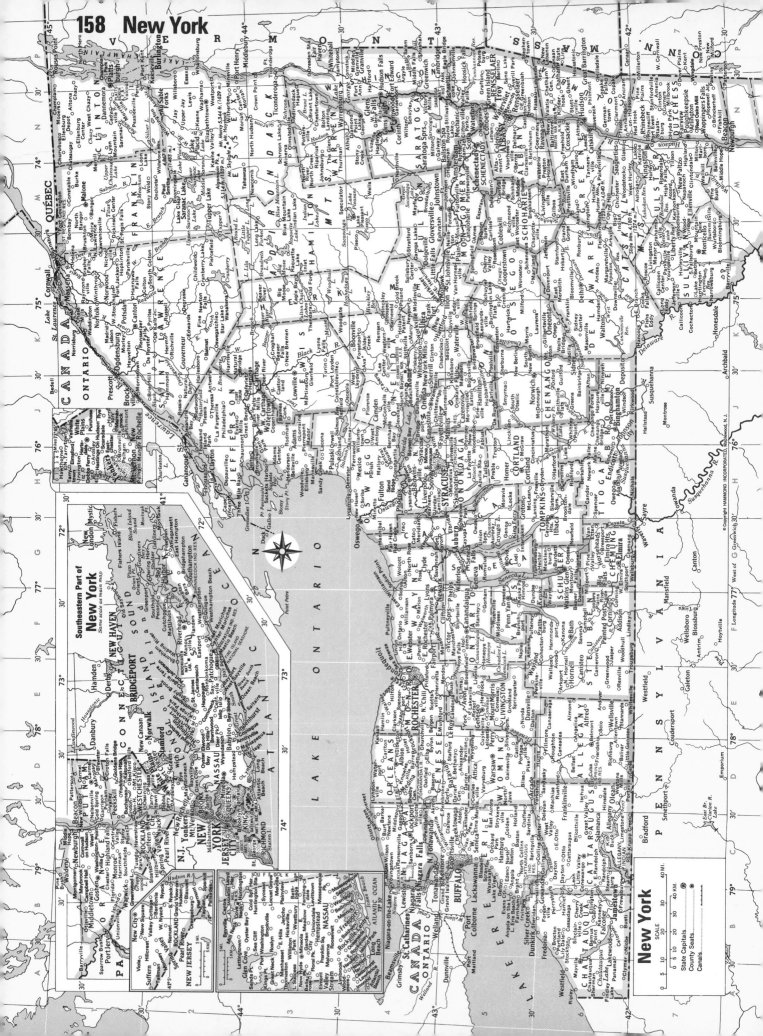

Southeastern Part of New York
Same scale as main map

New York

SCALE
0 5 10 20 30 40 MI.
0 5 10 20 30 40 KM.

State Capitals ⊛
County Seats ⊙
Canals

© COPYRIGHT HAMMOND INCORPORATED, Maplewood, N.J.

North Carolina

SCALE

MI.

KM.

State Capitals
County Seats
Canals

© Copyright HAMMOND INCORPORATED, Maplewood, N.J.

Western Part of
North Carolina

Same scale as main map.

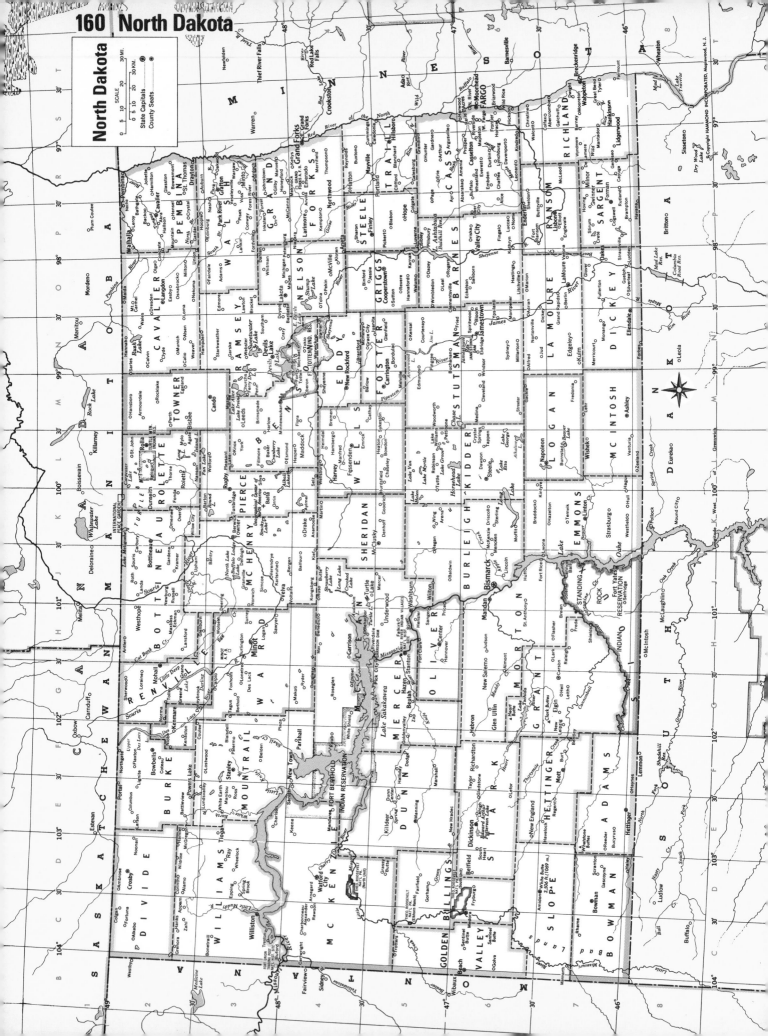

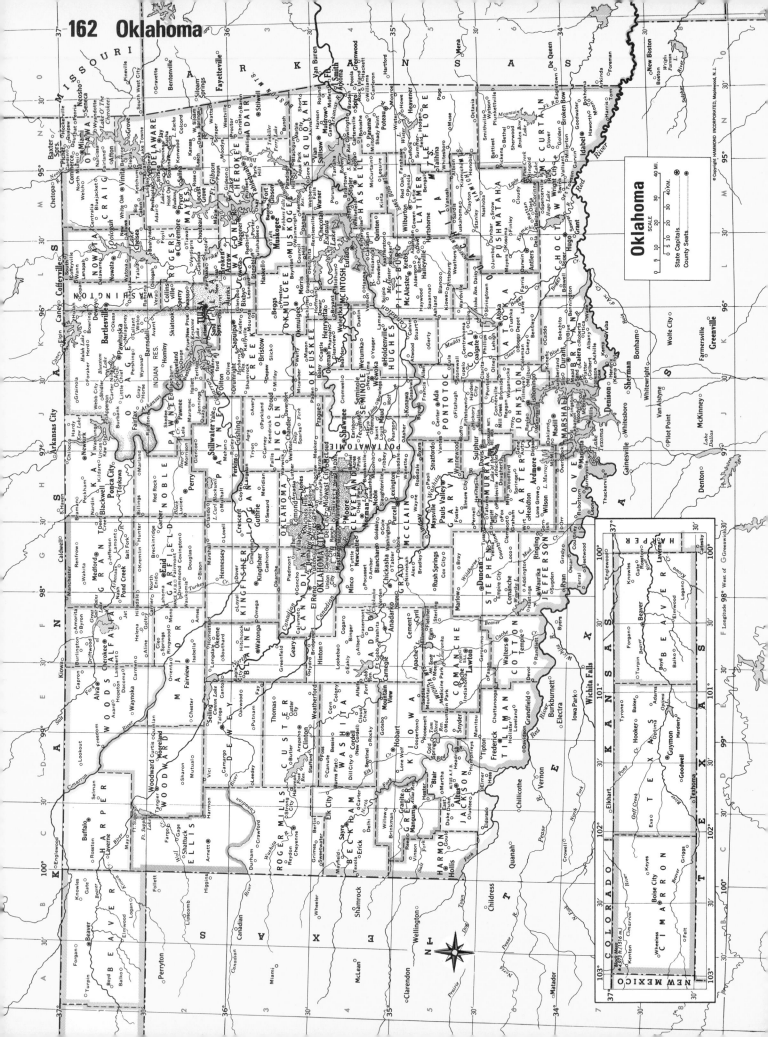

Oklahoma

SCALE

State Capitals........⊛
County Seats..........◉

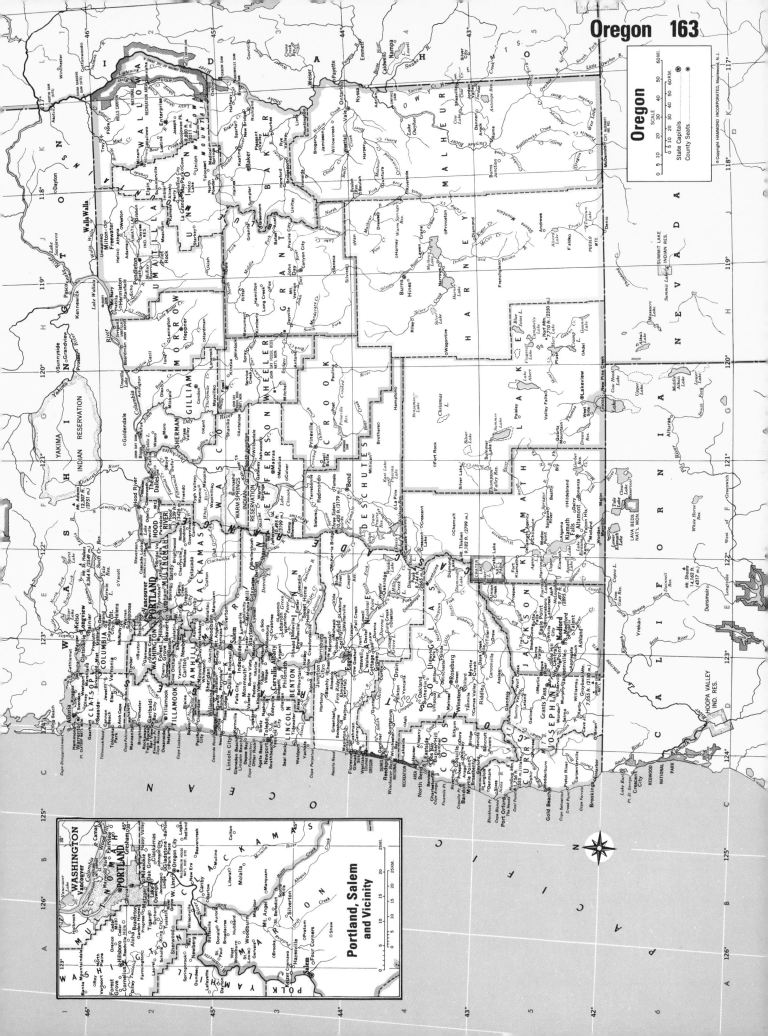

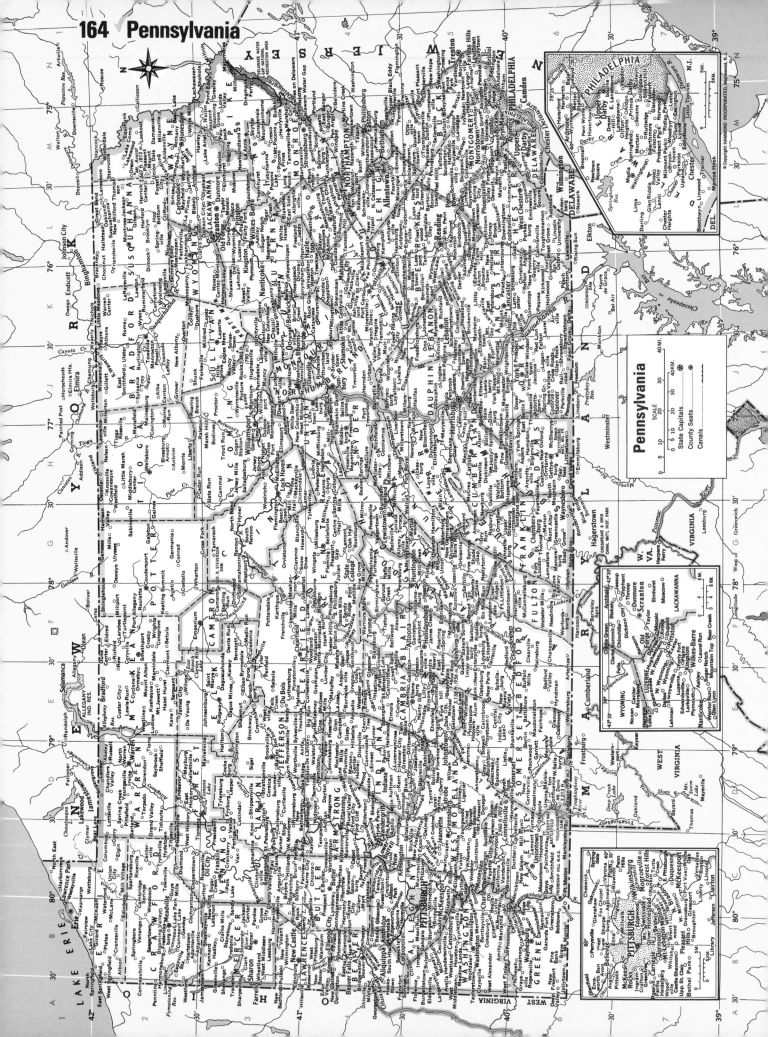

Pennsylvania

SCALE
5 10   20   30   40 MI.
0 5 10   20   30   40KM.
⊛ State Capitals
● County Seats
Canals

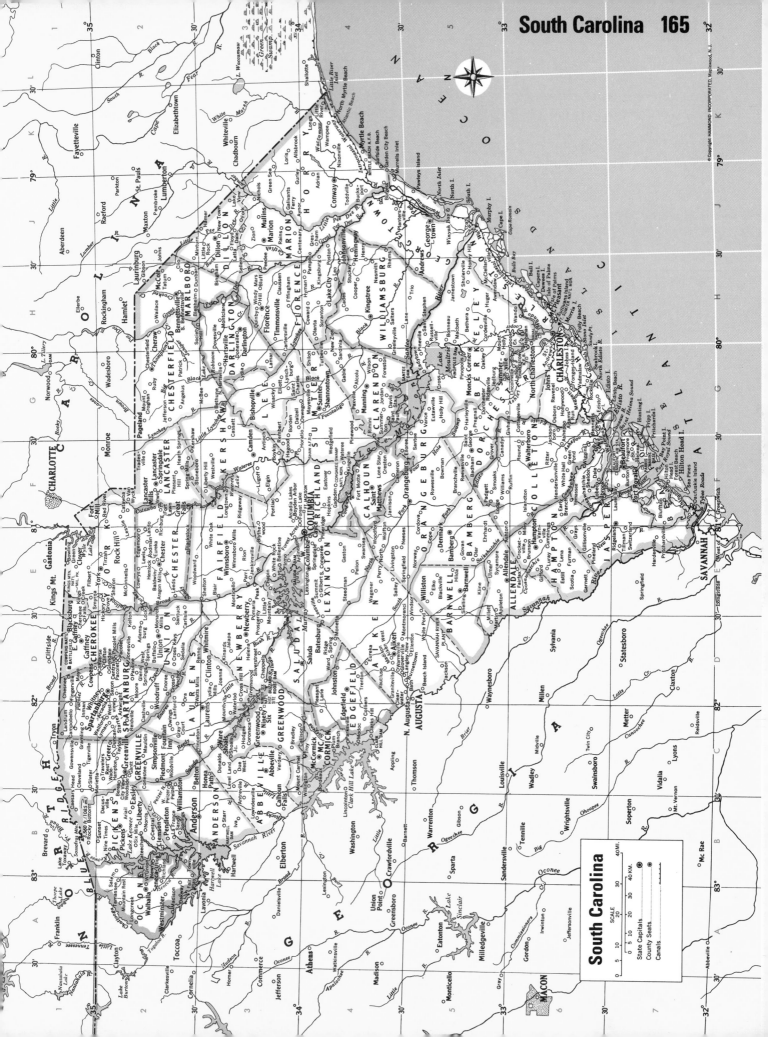

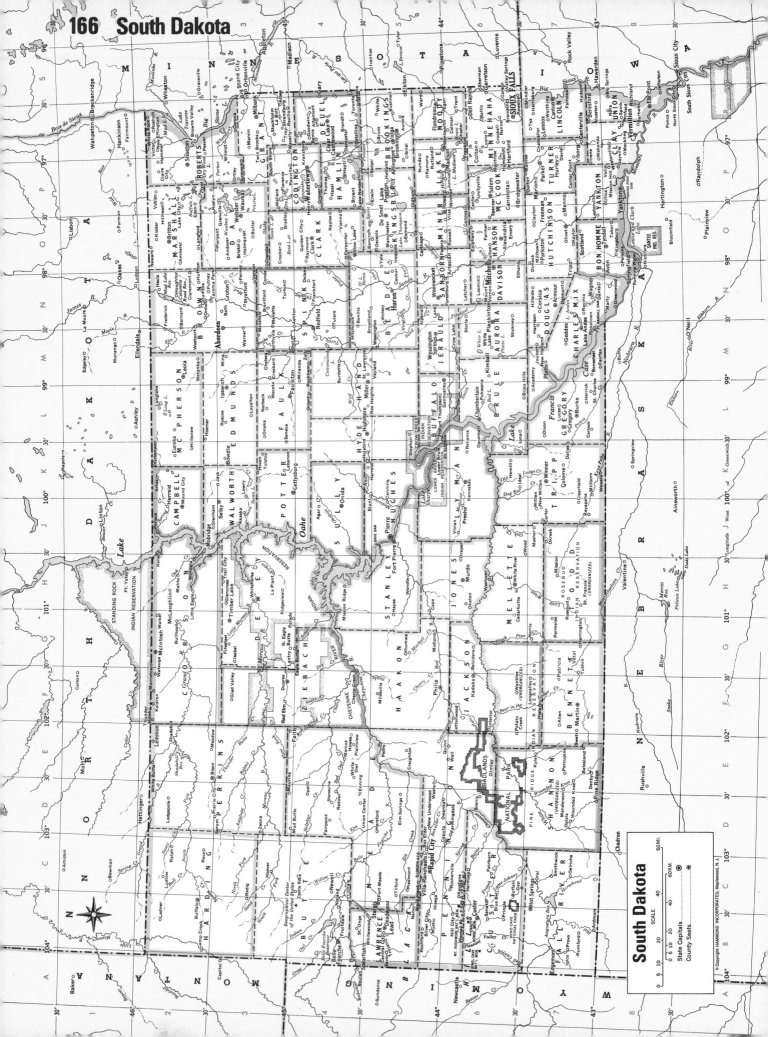

South Dakota

SCALE
0 5 10 20 40 60 MI.
0 5 10 20 40 60 KM.

State Capitals............⊛
County Seats.............◉

© Copyright HAMMOND INCORPORATED, Maplewood, N.J.

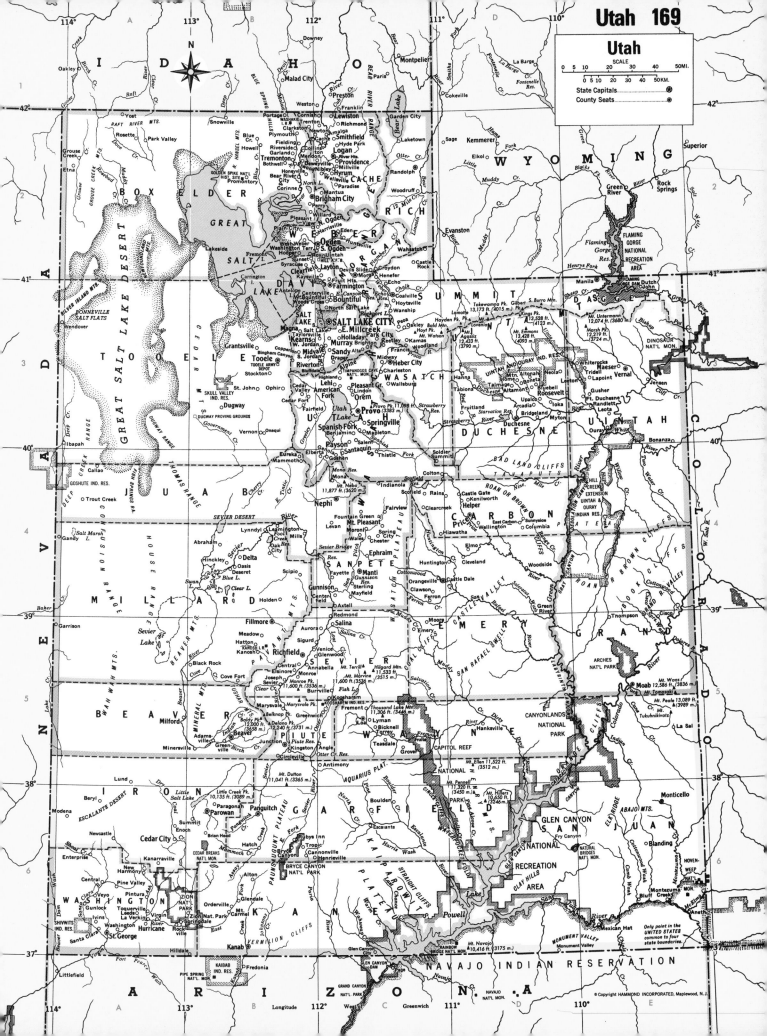

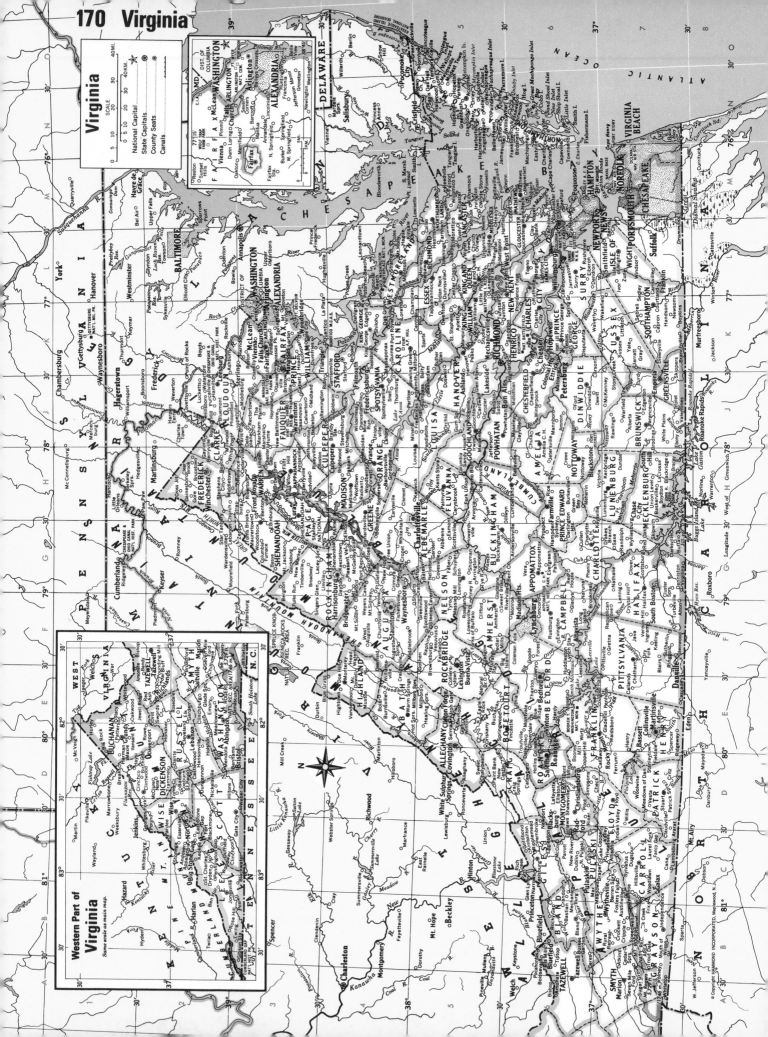

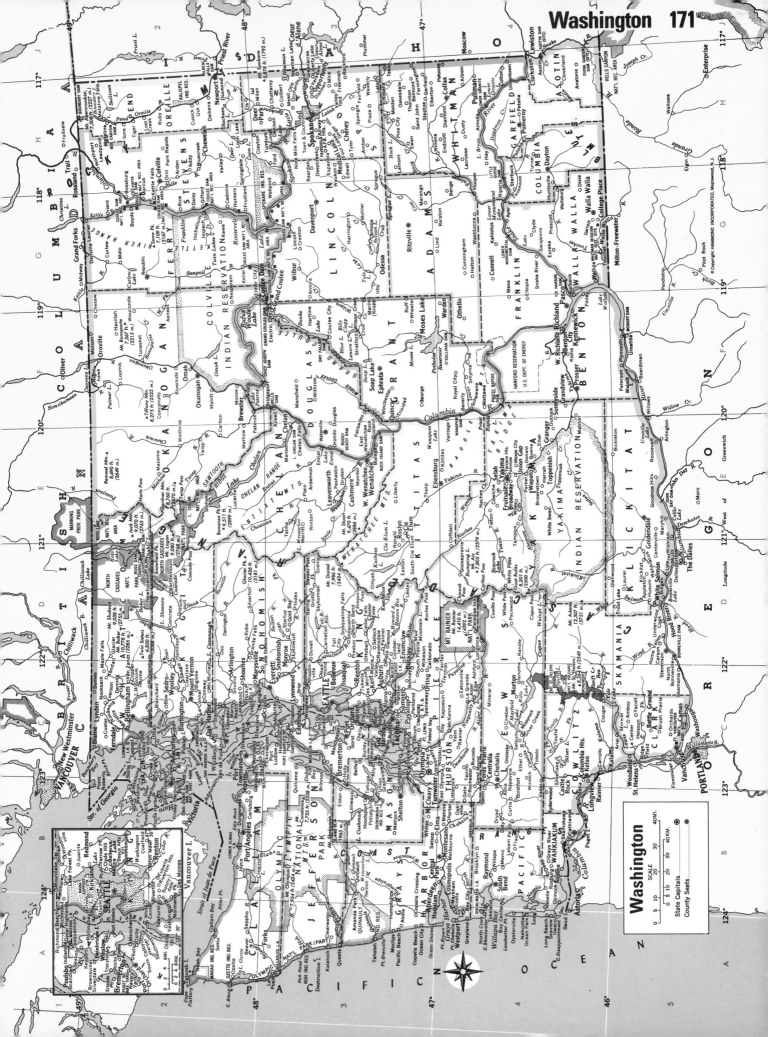

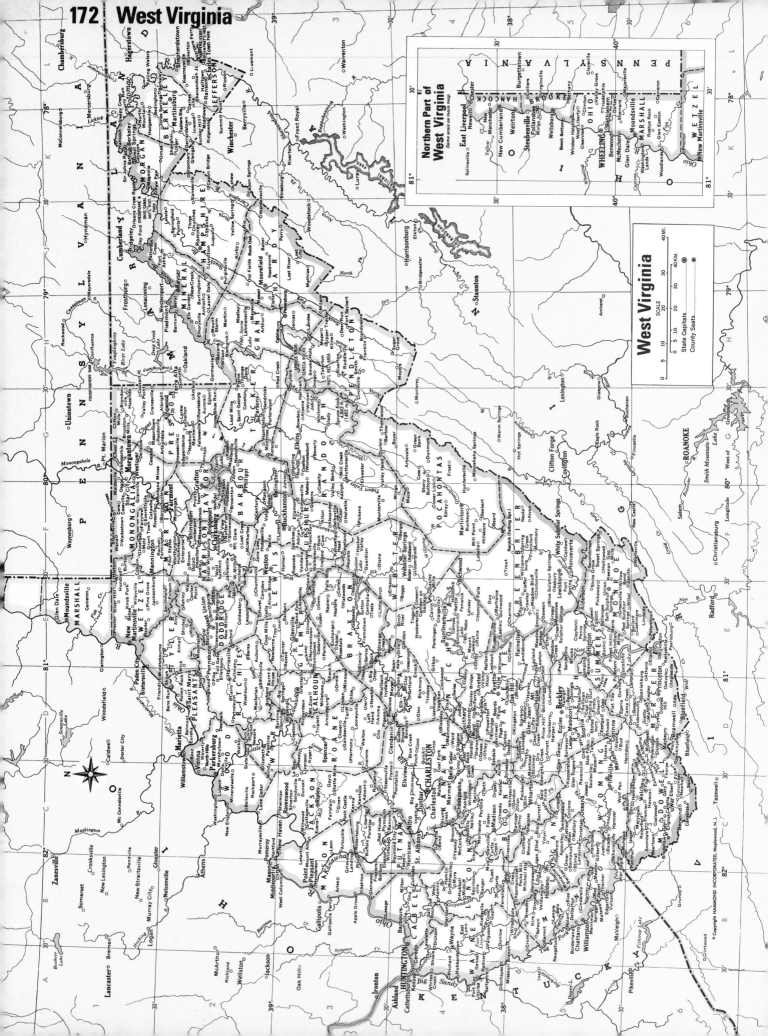

Northern Part of West Virginia
Same scale as main map

West Virginia
SCALE
State Capitals ⊛
County Seats ○

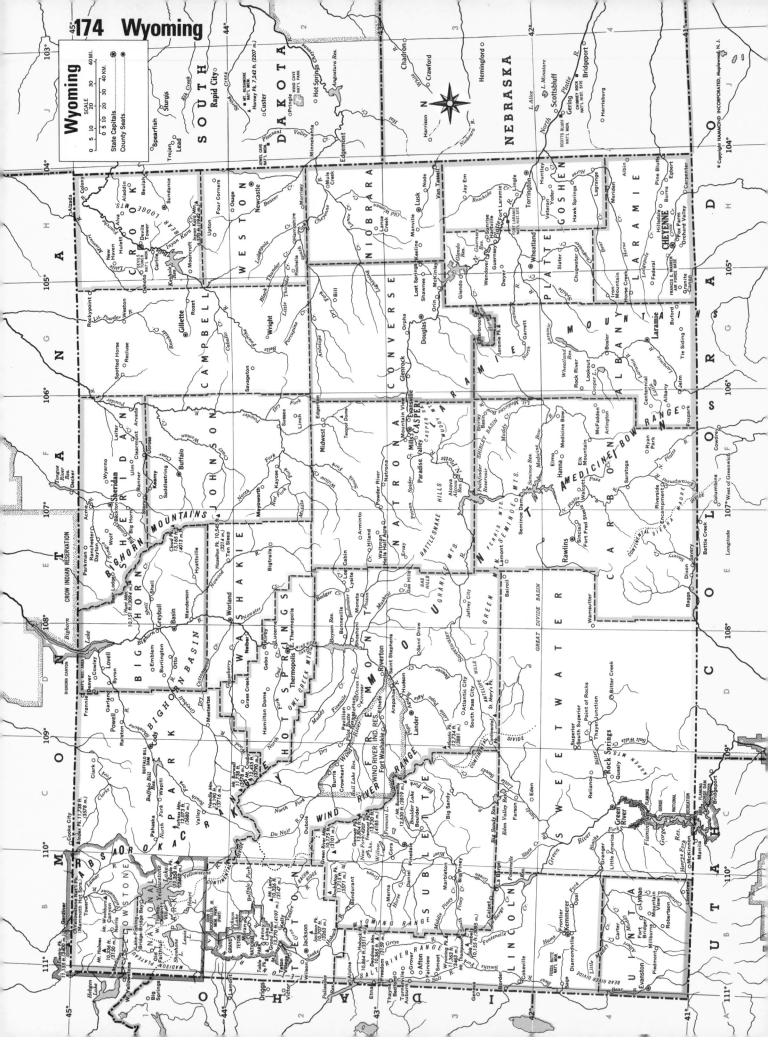

	LAND AREA IN SQUARE MILES	POPULATION 1980	CAPITAL	LARGEST CITY	STATE FLOWER	STATE BIRD
Alabama	51,705	3,893,888	Montgomery	Birmingham	Camellia	Yellowhammer
Alaska	591,004	401,851	Juneau	Anchorage	Forget-me-not	Willow Ptarmigan
Arizona	114,000	2,718,425	Phoenix	Phoenix	Saguaro Cactus Blossom	Cactus Wren
Arkansas	53,187	2,286,435	Little Rock	Little Rock	Apple Blossom	Mockingbird
California	158,706	23,667,565	Sacramento	Los Angeles	Golden Poppy	California Valley Quail
Colorado	104,091	2,889,735	Denver	Denver	Rocky Mountain Columbine	Lark Bunting
Connecticut	5,018	3,107,576	Hartford	Bridgeport	Mountain Laurel	Robin
Delaware	2,044	594,317	Dover	Wilmington	Peach Blossom	Blue Hen Chicken
Florida	58,664	9,746,342	Tallahassee	Jacksonville	Orange Blossom	Mockingbird
Georgia	58,910	5,463,105	Atlanta	Atlanta	Cherokee Rose	Brown Thrasher
Hawaii	6,471	964,691	Honolulu	Honolulu	Hibiscus	Nene (Hawaiian Goose)
Idaho	83,564	944,038	Boise	Boise	Syringa	Mountain Bluebird
Illinois	56,345	11,426,596	Springfield	Chicago	Native Violet	Cardinal
Indiana	36,185	5,490,260	Indianapolis	Indianapolis	Peony	Cardinal
Iowa	56,275	2,913,808	Des Moines	Des Moines	Wild Rose	Eastern Goldfinch
Kansas	82,277	2,364,236	Topeka	Wichita	Sunflower	Western Meadowlark
Kentucky	40,409	3,660,257	Frankfort	Louisville	Goldenrod	Cardinal
Louisiana	47,752	4,206,312	Baton Rouge	New Orleans	Magnolia	Eastern Brown Pelican
Maine	33,265	1,125,027	Augusta	Portland	White Pine Cone and Tassel	Chickadee
Maryland	10,460	4,216,975	Annapolis	Baltimore	Black-eyed Susan	Baltimore Oriole
Massachusetts	8,284	5,737,037	Boston	Boston	Mayflower	Chickadee
Michigan	58,527	9,262,078	Lansing	Detroit	Apple Blossom	Robin
Minnesota	84,402	4,075,970	St. Paul	Minneapolis	Pink and White Lady's-Slipper	Common Loon
Mississippi	47,689	2,520,638	Jackson	Jackson	Magnolia	Mockingbird
Missouri	69,697	4,916,759	Jefferson City	St. Louis	Hawthorn	Bluebird
Montana	147,046	786,690	Helena	Billings	Bitterroot	Western Meadowlark
Nebraska	77,355	1,569,825	Lincoln	Omaha	Goldenrod	Western Meadowlark
Nevada	110,561	800,493	Carson City	Las Vegas	Sagebrush	Mountain Bluebird
New Hampshire	9,279	920,610	Concord	Manchester	Purple Lilac	Purple Finch
New Jersey	7,787	7,364,823	Trenton	Newark	Purple Violet	Eastern Goldfinch
New Mexico	121,593	1,302,981	Santa Fe	Albuquerque	Yucca	Road Runner
New York	49,108	17,558,072	Albany	New York	Rose	Bluebird
North Carolina	52,669	5,881,813	Raleigh	Charlotte	Flowering Dogwood	Cardinal
North Dakota	70,702	652,717	Bismarck	Fargo	Wild Prairie Rose	Western Meadowlark
Ohio	41,330	10,797,624	Columbus	Cleveland	Scarlet Carnation	Cardinal
Oklahoma	69,956	3,025,290	Oklahoma City	Oklahoma City	Mistletoe	Scissor-tailed Flycatcher
Oregon	97,073	2,633,149	Salem	Portland	Oregon Grape	Western Meadowlark
Pennsylvania	45,308	11,863,895	Harrisburg	Philadelphia	Mountain Laurel	Ruffed Grouse
Rhode Island	1,212	947,154	Providence	Providence	Violet	Rhode Island Red
South Carolina	31,113	3,121,833	Columbia	Columbia	Carolina (Yellow) Jessamine	Carolina Wren
South Dakota	77,116	690,768	Pierre	Sioux Falls	Pasqueflower	Ring-necked Pheasant
Tennessee	42,144	4,591,120	Nashville	Memphis	Iris	Mockingbird
Texas	266,807	14,229,288	Austin	Houston	Bluebonnet	Mockingbird
Utah	84,899	1,461,037	Salt Lake City	Salt Lake City	Sego Lily	Sea Gull
Vermont	9,614	511,456	Montpelier	Burlington	Red Clover	Hermit Thrush
Virginia	40,767	5,346,818	Richmond	Norfolk	Dogwood	Cardinal
Washington	68,139	4,132,180	Olympia	Seattle	Western Rhododendron	Willow Goldfinch
West Virginia	24,231	1,950,279	Charleston	Charleston	Big Rhododendron	Cardinal
Wisconsin	56,153	4,705,521	Madison	Milwaukee	Wood Violet	Robin
Wyoming	97,809	469,557	Cheyenne	Casper	Indian Paintbrush	Meadowlark

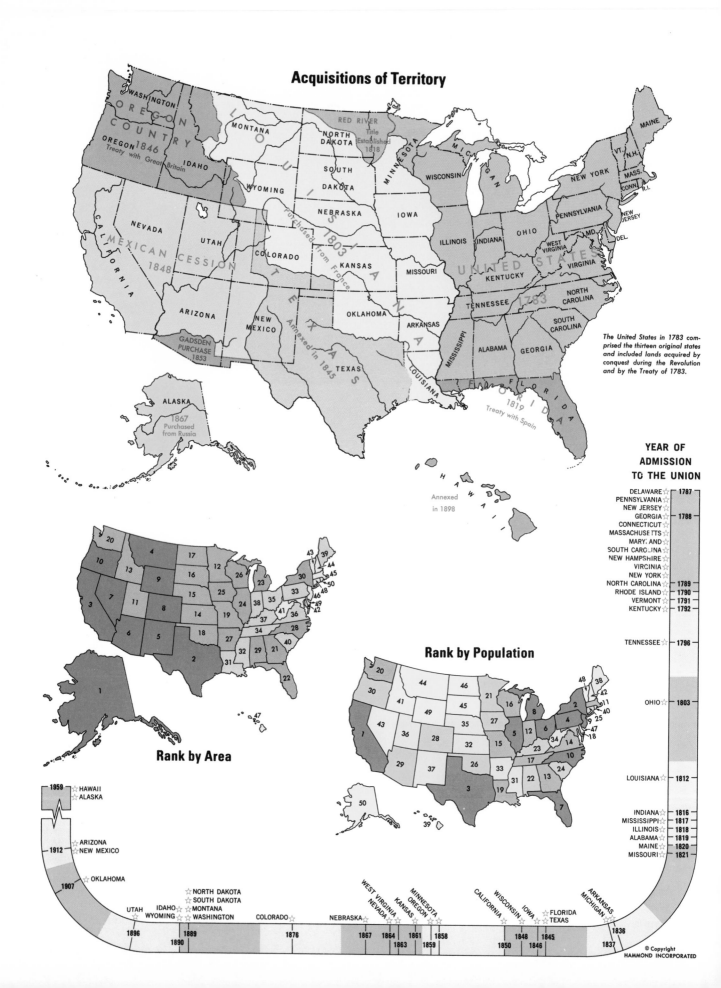

Acquisitions of Territory

The United States in 1783 comprised the thirteen original states and included lands acquired by conquest during the Revolution and by the Treaty of 1783.

Rank by Area

Rank by Population

YEAR OF ADMISSION TO THE UNION

DELAWARE ☆	1787
PENNSYLVANIA ☆	
NEW JERSEY ☆	
GEORGIA ☆	1788
CONNECTICUT ☆	
MASSACHUSETTS ☆	
MARY. AND ☆	
SOUTH CAROLINA ☆	
NEW HAMPSHIRE ☆	
VIRGINIA ☆	
NEW YORK ☆	1789
NORTH CAROLINA ☆	
RHODE ISLAND ☆	1790
VERMONT ☆	1791
KENTUCKY ☆	1792
TENNESSEE ☆	1796
OHIO ☆	1803
LOUISIANA ☆	1812
INDIANA ☆	1816
MISSISSIPPI ☆	1817
ILLINOIS ☆	1818
ALABAMA ☆	1819
MAINE ☆	1820
MISSOURI ☆	1821

1959 ☆ HAWAII ☆ ALASKA
1912 ☆ ARIZONA ☆ NEW MEXICO
1907 ☆ OKLAHOMA
☆ NORTH DAKOTA ☆ SOUTH DAKOTA
UTAH ☆ IDAHO ☆ MONTANA ☆ WASHINGTON
WYOMING ☆ COLORADO ☆ NEBRASKA ☆
WEST VIRGINIA ☆ NEVADA ☆ KANSAS ☆ MINNESOTA ☆ OREGON ☆
CALIFORNIA ☆ WISCONSIN ☆ IOWA ☆ FLORIDA ☆ TEXAS ☆
ARKANSAS ☆ MICHIGAN ☆

1896   1889   1876   1867   1864   1861   1858   1850   1848   1845   1836
   1890   1863   1859   1846   1837

© Copyright
HAMMOND INCORPORATED

This index, arranged in strict alphabetical order, includes grand divisions, countries, states, colonial possessions, major geographical areas, cities, towns and other features (both physical and man-made). Page number and index keys are given for the map on which they are shown at the largest scale. Note that inset maps continue the sequence of the keys from the main map. Population figures, where available, are also included for countries, some internal political divisions, islands and island groups, and for cities and towns. An asterisk preceding the population denotes that it represents an area larger than the city proper (i.e., metropolitan area, municipality, etc.).

LIST OF ABBREVIATIONS

A.F.B.	Air Force Base
Afghan.	Afghanistan
Ala.	Alabama
Alg.	Algeria
Alta.	Alberta
Ant. & Barb.	Antigua & Barbuda
Antarc.	Antarctica
arch.	archipelago
Arg.	Argentina
Ariz.	Arizona
Ark.	Arkansas
A.S.S.R.	Autonomous Soviet Socialist Republic
Austr.	Australia
aut.	autonomous
Bah.	Bahamas
Bang.	Bangladesh
Belg.	Belgium
Bol.	Bolivia
Bots.	Botswana
Braz.	Brazil
Br., Brit.	British
Br. Col.	British Columbia
Bulg.	Bulgaria
Burk. Faso	Burkina Faso
Calif.	California
Camb.	Cambodia
Can.	Canada
cap.	capital
Cent. Afr. Rep.	Central African Republic
chan.	channel
Chan. Is.	Channel Islands
Col.	Colombia
Colo.	Colorado
Conn.	Connecticut
C. Rica	Costa Rica
Czech.	Czechoslovakia
D.C.	District of Columbia
Del.	Delaware
Dem.	Democratic
Den.	Denmark
depr.	depression
des.	desert
dist.	district
Dom. Rep.	Dominican Republic
E.	East, Eastern
Ecua.	Ecuador
E. Ger.	East Germany
El Sal.	El Salvador
Eng.	England
Equat. Guin.	Equatorial Guinea
est.	estuary
Eth.	Ethiopia
Fed.	Federal, Federated
Fin.	Finland
Fla.	Florida
for.	forest
Fr.	France, French
Fr. Poly.	French Polynesia
Ft.	Fort
Ga.	Georgia
Ger.	Germany
Greenl.	Greenland
Gt.	Great
Guad.	Guadeloupe
Guat.	Guatemala
Guy.	Guyana
har., harb.	harbor
Hond.	Honduras
Hung.	Hungary
isl., isls.	isle, island, islands
Ill.	Illinois
Ind.	Indiana
Indon.	Indonesia
Int'l	International
Ire.	Ireland
Isr.	Israel
isth.	isthmus
Iv. Coast	Ivory Coast
Jam.	Jamaica
Kans.	Kansas
Ky.	Kentucky
La.	Louisiana
Leb.	Lebanon
Lux.	Luxembourg
Madag.	Madagascar
Man.	Manitoba
Mass.	Massachusetts
Maur.	Mauritania
Md.	Maryland
Mex.	Mexico
Mich.	Michigan
Minn.	Minnesota
Miss.	Mississippi
Mo.	Missouri
Mong.	Mongolia
Mont.	Montana
Mor.	Morocco
Moz.	Mozambique
mt., mtn., mts.	mount, mountain, mountains
N., No.	North, Northern
N. Amer.	North America
Nat'l Pk.	National Park
N. Br.	New Brunswick
N.C.	North Carolina
N. Dak.	North Dakota
Nebr.	Nebraska
Neth.	Netherlands
Neth. Ant.	Netherlands Antilles
Nev.	Nevada
Newf.	Newfoundland
N.H.	New Hampshire
Nic.	Nicaragua
N. Ire.	Northern Ireland
N.J.	New Jersey
N. Korea	North Korea
N. Mex.	New Mexico
Nor.	Norway
N.S.	Nova Scotia
N.W.T.	Northwest Territories (Canada)
N.Y.	New York
N.Z.	New Zealand
Okla.	Oklahoma
Ont.	Ontario
Oreg.	Oregon
Pa.	Pennsylvania
Pak.	Pakistan
Pan.	Panama
Papua N.G.	Papua New Guinea
Par.	Paraguay
P.D.R. Yemen	People's Democratic Republic of Yemen
P.E.I.	Prince Edward Island
pen.	peninsula
Phil.	Philippines
Pk.	Park
plat.	plateau
Pol.	Poland
Port.	Portugal, Portuguese
P. Rico	Puerto Rico
prom.	promontory
prov.	province, provincial
pt., pte.	point, pointe
Que.	Québec
reg.	region
Rep.	Republic
res.	reservoir
R.I.	Rhode Island
riv.	river
Rom.	Romania
S.	South, Southern
sa.	serra, sierra
S. Africa	South Africa
S. Amer.	South America
São T. & Pr.	São Tomé & Príncipe
Sask.	Saskatchewan
S.C.	South Carolina
Scot.	Scotland
S. Dak.	South Dakota
Sen.	Senegal
Sing.	Singapore
S. Korea	South Korea
S. Leone	Sierra Leone
Sol. Is.	Solomon Islands
Sp.	Spain, Spanish
S.S.R.	Soviet Socialist Republic
St., Ste.	Saint, Sainte
St. Chris. & Nevis	St. Christopher & Nevis
str.	strait
St. Vinc. & Grens.	Saint Vincent & The Grenadines
Switz.	Switzerland
Tanz.	Tanzania
Tenn.	Tennessee
terr.	territory
Thai.	Thailand
Trin. & Tob.	Trinidad & Tobago
Tun.	Tunisia
U.A.E.	United Arab Emirates
U.K.	United Kingdom
Urug.	Uruguay
U.S.	United States
U.S.S.R.	Union of Soviet Socialist Republics
Va.	Virginia
Ven., Venez.	Venezuela
V.I. (Br.)	Virgin Islands (British)
V.I. (U.S.)	Virgin Islands (U.S.)
Viet.	Vietnam
vol.	volcano
Vt.	Vermont
W.	West, Western
Wash.	Washington
W. Ger.	West Germany
W. Indies	West Indies
Wis.	Wisconsin
W. Samoa	Western Samoa
W. Va.	West Virginia
Wyo.	Wyoming
Yugo.	Yugoslavia
Zim.	Zimbabwe

A

	Pop.	Key	Pg.
Aachen, W. Ger.	242,453	B 3	20
Aare (riv.), Switz.		E 3	37
Aba, Nigeria	177,000	H10	54
Abadan, Iran	296,081	F 5	68
Abakan, U.S.S.R.	128,000	K 4	46
Abeokuta, Nigeria	253,000	G10	54
Aberdeen, Md.	11,533	K 2	146
Aberdeen, Scot.	210,362	F 3	13
Aberdeen, S. Dak.	25,851	M 3	166
Aberdeen, Wash.	18,739	B 3	171
Abidjan, Iv. Coast	685,828	E10	54
Abilene, Kans.	6,572	E 3	142
Abilene, Texas	98,315	E 5	168
Abington, Pa.	59,084	M 5	164
Abitibi (riv.), Ont.		J 5	108
Abraham Lincoln Birthplace Nat'l Hist. Site, Ky.		F 5	143
Abruzzi (reg.), Italy		D 3	32
Abu Dhabi (cap.), U.A.E.	347,000	F 5	60
Acadia Nat'l Pk., Maine		G 7	145
Acapulco, Mex.	309,254	K 8	119
Accra (cap.), Ghana	564,194	G11	54
Achinsk, U.S.S.R.	117,000	K 4	46
Aconcagua (mt.), Arg.		G10	93
Acre (riv.), Braz.		G 6	90
Acre, Isr.	34,400	C 2	67
Ada, Okla.	15,902	J 5	162
Adamawa (reg.), Africa		J10	54
Adams Nat'l Hist Site, Mass.		D 7	147
Adamstown (cap.), Pitcairn	54	N 8	89
Adana, Turkey	475,384	F 4	64
Addis Ababa (cap.), Eth.	1,196,300	O10	54
Addison, Ill.	29,759	B 5	139
Adelaide, Austr.	882,520	D 8	86
Aden (cap.), P.D.R. Yemen	240,370	E 7	60
Adige (riv.), Italy		C 2	32
Adirondack (mts.), N.Y.		M 3	158
Admiralty (isls.), Papua N.G.		E 6	89
Adrar (reg.), Maur.		D 7	54
Adrian, Mich.	21,186	F 7	148
Adriatic (sea), Europe		F 4	6
Aegean (sea)		G 6	43
Afars & Issas, see Djibouti			
Afghanistan	15,540,000	A 2	70
Africa	469,000,000		52-57
Agadir, Morocco	61,192	D 5	54
Agaña (cap.), Guam	896	E 4	89
Agate Fossil Beds Natl Mon., Nebr.		A 2	153
Agawam, Mass.	26,271	D 4	147
Ageo, Japan	146,358	O 2	75
Agra, India	591,917	D 3	70
Aguascalientes, Mex.	181,277	H 6	119
Ahaggar (mts.), Alg.		H 7	54
Ahmadabad, India	1,591,832	C 4	70
Ahwaz (Ahvaz), Iran	329,006	F 5	68
Aiea, Hawaii	32,879	C 4	130
Aiken, S.C.	14,978	D 4	165
Air (mts.), Niger		H 8	54
Air Force Acad., Colo.	8,655	K 5	134
Aix-en-Provence, France	91,655	F 6	26
Ajaccio, France	47,056	B 7	26
Ajmer, India	262,851	C 3	70
Akashi, Japan	234,905	H 8	75
Akita, Japan	261,246	J 4	75
Akola, India	168,436	D 4	70
Akron, Ohio	237,177	G 3	161
Aktyubinsk, U.S.S.R.	191,000	F 4	46
Alabama (riv.), Ala.		C 8	129
Alabama (state), U.S.	3,893,888		129
Alameda, Calif.	63,852	J 2	133
Alamogordo, N. Mex.	24,024	C 6	157
Alamosa, Colo.	6,830	H 8	156
Aland (isls.), Fin.		L 6	16
Alaska (gulf) Alaska		K 3	130
Alaska (state), U.S.	401,851		130
Albacete, Spain	82,607	F 3	31
Albania	2,590,600	E 5	43
Albany, Ga.	74,550	D 7	137
Albany (cap.), N.Y.	101,727	N 5	158
Albany, Oreg.	26,678	D 3	163
Albert (Mobutu Sese Seko) (lake), Africa		M11	57
Alberta (prov.), Can.	2,237,724		114
Albert Lea, Minn.	19,200	E 7	149
Alborg, Den.	154,582	D 4	19
Albuquerque, N. Mex.	331,767	C 3	157
Alderney (isl.), Chan. Is.	1,686	E 8	11
Aleppo, Syria	639,428	C 4	64
Aleutian (isls.), Alaska		D 4	130
Alexandria, Egypt	2,318,655	M 5	54
Alexandria, La.	51,565	E 4	144
Alexandria, Va.	103,217	N 3	170
Algeria	17,422,000	F 6	54
Algiers (cap.), Alg.	1,365,400	G 4	54
Alhambra, Calif.	64,615	C10	133
Alicante, Spain	177,918	F 3	30
Aligarh, India	252,314	D 3	70
Al Kuwait (cap.), Kuwait	181,774	E 4	60
Allahabad, India	440,622	E 3	70
Allen Park, Mich.	34,196	B 7	148
Allentown, Pa.	103,758	L 4	164
Allepey-Cochin, India	160,166	D 7	70
Alliance, Ohio	24,315	H 4	161
Alma-Ata, U.S.S.R.	910,000	H 5	46
Almería, Spain	104,008	E 4	30
Alps (mts.), Europe		E 4	6
Altadena, Calif.	40,983	C10	133
Altai (mts.), Asia		J 5	46
Alton, Ill.	34,171	A 2	139
Altoona, Pa.	57,078	F 4	164
Altun Shan (Altyn Tagh) (mts.), China		C 4	77
Altus, Okla.	23,101	D 5	162
Amagasaki, Japan	545,783	H 8	75
Amana, Iowa	300	K 5	141
Amarillo, Texas	149,230	C 2	168
Amazon (riv.), S. Amer.		J 4	90
American Fork, Utah	12,693	C 3	169
American Samoa	32,297	J 7	89
Americus, Ga.	16,120	D 6	137
Ames, Iowa	45,775	F 4	141
Amherst, N.S.	9,684	D 3	100
Amherst, Mass.	33,229	E 3	147
Amiens, France	129,453	D 3	26
Amistad Nat'l Rec. Area, Texas		D 8	168
Amman (cap.), Jordan	1,711,850	D 4	67
Amoy, see Xiamen, China			
Amravati, India	193,800	D 4	70
Amritsar, India	407,628	C 2	70
Amsterdam (cap.), Neth.	751,156	B 4	25
Amsterdam, N.Y.	21,872	M 5	158
Amudar'ya (riv.), Asia		G 5	46
Amur (riv.), Asia		D 4	46
Anaconda-Deer Lodge Co., Mont.	12,518	C 4	152
Anadyr', U.S.S.R.	7,703	S 3	46
Anaheim, Calif.	219,494	D11	133
Anchorage, Alaska	174,431	J 2	130
Ancona, Italy	88,427	D 3	32
Andalusia (reg.), Spain		C 4	31
Andaman (isls.), India		G 6	70
Anderson, Ind.	64,695	F 4	140
Anderson, S.C.	27,965	B 2	165
Andes (mts.), S. Amer.		F10	93
Andizhan, U.S.S.R.	230,000	H 5	46
Andorra	31,000	G 1	31
Andorra la Vella (cap.), Andorra	12,000	G 1	31
Andover, Mass.	26,370	K 2	147
Andrew Johnson, Nat'l Hist. Site, Tenn.		Q 2	167
Andrews A.F.B., Md.	10,064	C 5	146
Andropov, U.S.S.R.	239,000	E 3	50
Andros (isl.), Bah.	8,397	B 1	124
Angara (riv.), U.S.S.R.		K 4	46
Angarsk, U.S.S.R.	239,000	L 4	46
Angel (falls), Ven.		H 2	90
Angers, France	136,603	C 4	26
Angkor Wat (ruins), Camb.		D 4	81
Angola	7,078,000	K 4	57
Anguilla (isl.)	6,519	F 3	124
Ankara (cap.), Turkey	1,701,064	E 3	64
Ankeny, Iowa	15,429	F 5	141
Ann (cape), Mass.		M 2	147
Annaba, Alg.	255,900	H 4	54
An Najaf, Iraq	128,096	D 5	68
Annandale, Va.	49,524	N 3	170
Annapolis (cap.), Md.	31,740	H 5	146
Annapolis Royal, N.S.	631	C 4	100
Annapurna (mt.), Nepal		E 3	70
Ann Arbor, Mich.	107,966	F 6	148
Anniston, Ala.	29,523	G 3	129
Anqing, China	160,000	J 5	77
Anshan, China	1,500,000	K 3	77
Ansonia, Conn.	19,039	C 3	135
Antakya, Turkey	77,518	G 4	64
Antananarivo (cap.), Madag.	451,808	R15	57
Antarctica			5
Antibes, France	44,236	G 6	26
Anticosti (isl.), Que.		E 3	106
Antietam Nat'l Battlfld., Md.		H 3	146
Antigua and Barbuda	72,000	G 3	124
Antilles (isls.), W. Indies		B-F 2-4	124
Antioch, Calif.	42,683	L 1	133
Antofagasta, Chile	125,100	F 8	90
Antsiranana (Diégo-Suarez), Madag.	40,443	R14	57
Antwerp, Belg.	224,543	E 6	25
Anyang, China	225,000	H 4	77
Aomori, Japan	264,202	K 3	75
Apalachee (bay), Fla.		B 2	136
Apennines (mts.), Italy		B-F 2-5	32
Apia (cap.), W. Samoa	33,100	J 7	89
Apostle Is. Nat'l Lakeshore, Wis.		C 1	173
Appalachian (mts.), U.S.		K 3	126
Appleton, Wis.	58,913	J 7	173
Appomattox Court House Nat'l Hist. Pk., Va.		F 6	170
Aqaba (gulf), Asia		C 4	60

	Pop.	Key	Pg.
Arabian (sea), Asia		H 8	58
Arabian (des.), Egypt		N 6	54
Aracaju, Braz.	288,106	N 6	90
Arad, Rom.	161,568	E 2	43
Arafura (sea)		D 6	89
Aragón (reg.), Spain		F 2	31
Aral (sea), U.S.S.R.		F 5	46
Aran (isls.), Ire.	1,499	B 5	15
Ararat (mt.), Turkey		L 3	64
Arcadia, Calif.	45,994	C 10	133
Archangel, U.S.S.R.	385,000	F 2	50
Arches Nat'l Pk., Utah		E 5	169
Arctic Ocean			4
Ardabil, Iran	147,404	F 1	68
Ardennes (for.), Belg.		F 9	25
Ardmore, Okla.	23,689	H 6	162
Arecibo, P. Rico	48,779	G 1	124
Arequipa, Peru	447,431	F 7	90
Argenteuil, France	101,542	A 1	26
Argentina	28,438,000		93
Argonne Nat'l Lab., Ill.		B 6	139
Árgos, Greece	18,890	F 7	43
Arhus, Den.	245,941	D 5	19
Arica, Chile	87,700	F 7	90
Arizona (state), U.S.	2,718,425		131
Arkadelphia, Ark.	10,005	D 5	132
Arkansas (riv.), U.S.		H 3	126
Arkansas (state), U.S.	2,286,435		132
Arkansas Post Nat'l Mem., Ark.		H 5	132
Arles, France	37,337	F 6	26
Arlington, Mass.	48,219	C 6	147
Arlington, Texas	160,123	F 2	168
Arlington, Va.	152,599	O 3	170
Arlington Heights, Ill.	66,116	B 5	139
Armagh, N. Ire.	13,606	H 3	15
Armavir, U.S.S.R.	162,000	F 5	50
Armenian S.S.R., U.S.S.R.	3,031,000	F 6	50
Arnhem, Neth.	281,126	H 4	25
Arno (riv.), Italy		C 3	32
Arran (isl.), Scot.		C 5	13
Arthabaska, Que.	6,827	F 3	105
Aruba (isl.)	55,148	E 4	124
Arvada, Colo.	84,576	J 3	134
Asahikawa, Japan	320,526	L 2	75
Asansol, India	155,968	F 4	70
Asbury Park, N.J.	17,015	F 3	156
Ascension (isl.), St. Helena	719		1
Ashanti (reg.), Ghana		F 10	54
Ashdod, Isr.	40,500	B 4	67
Ashikaga, Japan	162,359	J 5	75
Asheville, N.C.	53,583	E 8	159
Ashkhabad, U.S.S.R.	312,000	F 2	46
Ashland, Ky.	27,064	M 4	143
Ashland, Oreg.	14,943	E 5	163
Ashtabula, Ohio	23,449	J 2	161
Asia	2,633,000,000		58
Asmara, Eth.	393,800	O 9	54
Aspen, Colo.	3,678	F 4	134
Aspen Hill, Md.	47,455	F 4	146
Assam (state), India		G 3	70
Assateague Isl. Nat'l Seashore, U.S.		O 4	170
Astoria, Oreg.	9,998	O 1	163
Astrakhan', U.S.S.R.	461,000	G 5	50
Asturias (reg.), Spain		C 1	31
Asunción (cap.), Par.	387,676	J 9	90
Aswân, Egypt	144,377	N 7	54
Asyût, Egypt	213,983	N 6	54
Atacama (des.), Chile		G 8	93
Atchison, Kans.	11,407	G 2	142
Athabasca (lake), Can.		F 4	96
Athens, Ga.	42,549	F 3	137
Athens (cap.), Greece	867,023	F 7	43
Athens, Ohio	19,743	F 7	161
Áthos (mt.), Greece		G 5	43
Atka (isl.), Alaska		M 4	130
Atlanta (cap.), Ga.	425,022	K 1	137
Atlantic City, N.J.	40,199	E 5	156
Atlantic Ocean			5
Atlas (mts.), Africa		E 5	54
Atsugi, Japan	108,955	O 2	75
Attleboro, Mass.	34,196	J 5	147
Attu (isl.), Alaska		J 2	130
Auburn, Ala.	28,471	H 5	129
Auburn, Maine	23,128	C 7	145
Auburn, N.Y.	32,548	G 5	158
Auburn, Wash.	26,417	C 3	171
Auckland, N.Z.	144,963	L 6	87
Augsburg, W. Ger.	243,943	D 4	20
Augusta, Ga.	47,532	J 4	137
Augusta (cap.), Maine	21,819	D 7	145
Aurangabad, India	150,483	D 5	70
Aurora, Colo.	158,588	K 3	134
Aurora, Ill.	81,293	E 2	139
Aurora, Ohio	8,177	H 3	161
Aurora, Minn.	23,020	E 7	149

	Pop.	Key	Pg.
Auschwitz, see Oświęcim, Poland			
Austin (cap.), Texas	354,496	G 7	168
Australia	14,576,330		86
Australian Alps (mts.), Austr.		H 7	86
Australian Cap. Terr., Austr.	221,609	H 7	86
Austria	7,507,000		39
Auvergne (mts.), France		E 5	26
Avalon (pen.), Newf.		D 4	99
Avignon, France	73,482	F 6	26
Avon (riv.), Eng.		F 7	11
Ayers Rock (mt.), Austr.		E 5	86
Azerbaidzhan S.S.R., U.S.S.R.	6,028,000	G 6	50
Azores (isls.), Port.			30
Azov (sea), U.S.S.R.		C 5	50
Aztec Ruins Nat'l Mon., N. Mex.		A 2	157
Azusa, Calif.	29,380	D 10	133

B

	Pop.	Key	Pg.
Bab el Mandeb (str.)		D 7	60
Bacău, Rom.	131,413	H 2	43
Bacolod, Phil.	262,415	G 3	83
Badalona, Spain	162,888	H 2	31
Baden-Baden, W. Ger.	49,718	C 4	20
Badlands Nat'l Pk., S. Dak.		E 6	166
Baffin (isl.), N.W.T.		J 1	96
Baghdad (cap.), Iraq	502,503	D 4	68
Bahamas	209,505	C 1	124
Bahawalpur, Pak.	133,956	C 3	70
Bahia (Salvador), Braz.	1,496,276	N 6	90
Bahía Blanca, Arg.	*220,765	H 11	90
Bahrain	358,857	F 4	60
Bairiki (cap.), Kiribati	1,777	H 5	89
Bakersfield, Calif.	105,735	G 8	133
Bakhtaran, Iran	290,861	E 3	68
Baku, U.S.S.R.	1,022,000	H 6	50
Balakovo, U.S.S.R.	152,000	G 4	50
Baldwin, N.Y.	31,630	B 4	158
Baldwin Park, Calif.	50,554	D 10	133
Balearic (isls.), Spain		H 3	31
Bali (isl.), Indon.	2,074,438	F 7	83
Balikpapan, Indon.	280,675	F 6	83
Balkan (mts.), Bulg.		G 4	43
Balkhash (lake), U.S.S.R.		H 5	46
Baltic (sea), Europe		F 3	6
Baltimore, Md.	786,755	H 3	146
Baluchistan (reg.), Pak.		B 3	70
Bamako (cap.), Mali	404,022	E 9	54
Banaba (isl.), Kiribati	2,314	G 7	89
Banda (sea), Indon.		H 7	83
Bandar Seri Begawan, (cap.), Brunei	63,868	E 4	83
Bandelier Nat'l Mon., N. Mex.		C 3	157
Bandung, Indon.	1,462,637	H 2	83
Banff Nat'l Pk., Alta.		B 4	114
Bangalore, India	1,540,741	D 6	70
Bangkok (cap.), Thai.	2,495,312	D 4	81
Bangladesh	87,052,024	G 4	70
Bangor, Maine	31,643	F 6	145
Bangui (cap.), Cent. Afr. Rep.	279,792	K 10	54
Banja Luka, Yugo.	85,786	C 3	43
Banjarmasin, Indon.	381,286	E 6	83
Banjul (cap.), Gambia	39,476	C 9	54
Banks (isl.), N.W.T.		D 1	96
Baoding, China	350,000	J 4	77
Baoji, China	275,000	G 5	77
Baotou, China	800,000	G 3	77
Baranovichi, U.S.S.R.	131,000	C 4	50
Barbados	248,983	G 4	124
Barberton, Ohio	29,751	G 4	161
Barbuda (isl.), see Antigua & Barbuda			
Barcelona, Spain	1,741,144	H 2	31
Barcelona, Ven.	78,201	G 2	90
Bareilly, India	296,248	D 3	70
Barents (sea), Europe		J 1	6
Bar Harbor, Maine	4,124	G 7	145
Bari, Italy	339,110	F 4	32
Barnaul, U.S.S.R.	533,000	J 4	46
Barnet, Eng.	305,200	H 7	11
Barnstable, Mass.	30,898	N 6	147
Barquisimeto, Ven.	330,815	F 2	90
Barranquilla, Col.	661,009	F 1	90
Barre, Vt.	9,824	C 3	155
Barrie, Ont.	38,423	E 3	108
Barrow (pt.), Alaska		G 1	130
Barstow, Calif.	17,690	H 9	133
Bartlesville, Okla.	34,568	K 1	162
Basel, Switz.	199,600	E 1	37
Basildon, Eng.	135,720	J 8	11
Basra, Iraq	313,327	E 5	68
Bassein, Burma	126,045	B 3	81
Basse-Terre (cap.), Guad.	13,397	F 4	124
Basseterre (cap.), St. Chris. & Nevis	14,725	F 3	124

	Pop.	Key	Pg.
Bastrop, La.	15,527	G 1	144
Bath, Eng.	83,100	E 6	11
Bathurst (Banjul) (cap.), Gambia	39,476	C 9	54
Bathurst, N. Br.	15,705	E 1	102
Bathurst (isl.), N.W.T.		M 3	96
Batna, Alg.	112,100	F 1	54
Baton Rouge (cap.), La.	219,419	K 2	144
Battle Creek, Mich.	35,724	D 6	148
Batumi, U.S.S.R.	123,000	F 6	50
Bat Yam, Isr.	124,100	B 3	67
Bavaria (state), W. Ger.		D 4	20
Bayamón, P. Rico	185,087	D 4	124
Bay City, Mich.	41,593	F 5	148
Bayeux, France	13,381	C 3	26
Baykal (lake), U.S.S.R.		L 4	46
Baykonur, U.S.S.R.		G 5	46
Bayonne, N.J.	65,047	B 2	156
Bayreuth, W. Ger.	67,035	D 4	20
Baytown, Texas	56,923	L 2	168
Bear (lake), U.S.		G 7	138
Bearpaw (mts.), Mont.		G 2	152
Beatrice, Nebr.	12,891	H 4	153
Beaufort (sea), N. Amer.		D 2	94
Beaufort, S.C.	8,634	F 7	165
Beaumont, Texas	118,102	K 7	168
Beaverhead (mts.), Idaho		E 4	138
Beaverton, Oreg.	30,582	A 2	163
Beckley, W. Va.	20,492	D 5	172
Beersheba, Isr.	101,000	B 5	67
Beihai, China	175,000	G 7	77
Beijing (Peking) (cap.), People's Rep. of China	*8,500,000	J 3	77
Beirut (cap.), Leb.	474,800	F 6	64
Belau (Palau)	12,116	D 5	89
Belém, Braz.	758,117	L 4	90
Belfast, Maine	6,243	F 7	145
Belfast (cap.), N. Ire.	353,700	J 2	15
Belgaum, India	192,427	C 5	70
Belgium	9,855,110		25
Belgorod, U.S.S.R.	240,000	E 4	50
Belgrade (cap.), Yugo.	727,945	E 3	43
Belize	144,857	C 2	122
Belize City, Belize	39,887	C 2	122
Bellary, India	125,183	D 5	70
Belleville, Ill.	41,580	B 3	139
Belleville, N.J.	35,367	B 2	156
Belleville, Ont.	34,881	G 3	108
Bellevue, Nebr.	21,813	J 3	153
Bellevue, Wash.	73,903	B 2	171
Bellflower, Calif.	53,441	C 11	133
Bellingham, Wash.	45,791	C 2	171
Bellingshausen (sea), Antarc.		C 14	5
Belmont, Mass.	26,100	C 6	147
Belmopan (cap.), Belize	144,857	C 2	122
Belo Horizonte, Braz.	*2,541,788	M 7	90
Beloit, Wis.	35,207	H 10	173
Beltsville, Md.	12,760	C 3	146
Bemidji, Minn.	10,949	D 3	149
Benares, see Varanasi, India			
Bend, Oreg.	17,263	F 3	163
Bengal (bay), Asia		K 8	58
Bengbu, China	400,000	J 5	77
Benghazi, Libya	286,943	K 5	54
Benguela, Angola	40,996	J 14	54
Benin	3,338,240	G 10	54
Bennington, Vt.	15,815	A 6	155
Benoni, S. Africa	*151,294	M 17	57
Benton, Ark.	17,717	E 4	132
Benton Harbor, Mich.	14,707	C 6	148
Bent's Old Fort Nat'l Hist. Site, Colo.		M 6	134
Benxi, China	750,000	K 3	77
Beppu, Japan	133,894	E 7	75
Berchtesgaden, W. Ger.	8,558	E 5	20
Berea, Ky.	8,226	J 5	143
Berezniki, U.S.S.R.	185,000	J 3	50
Bergamo, Italy	127,553	B 2	32
Bergen, Nor.	213,434	D 6	16
Bering (sea)		S 4	46
Bering (str.)		U 3	46
Berkeley, Calif.	103,328	J 2	133
Berkshire (hills), Mass.		B 4	147
Berlin, N.H.	13,084	E 3	155
Berlin, East (cap.), E. Ger.	1,094,147	F 4	20
Berlin, West, W. Ger.	1,983,837	E 4	20
Bermuda	67,761	H 3	124
Bern (cap.), Switz.	154,700	D 3	37
Berwyn, Ill.	46,849	B 6	139
Besançon, France	119,803	G 4	26
Bessemer, Ala.	31,729	D 4	129
Bethany, Okla.	22,130	G 3	162
Bethel, Conn.	16,004	B 3	135
Bethel Park, Pa.	34,755	B 7	164
Bethesda, Md.	62,736	A 4	146
Bethlehem, West Bank	14,439	C 4	67
Bethlehem, Pa.	70,419	M 4	164

	Pop.	Key	Pg.
Bettendorf, Iowa	27,381	N 5	141
Beverly, Mass.	37,655	E 5	147
Beverly Hills, Calif.	32,367	B 10	133
Bhagalpur, India	172,202	F 4	70
Bhavnagar, India	225,358	C 4	70
Bhilainagar, India	157,173	E 4	70
Bhopal, India	298,022	D 4	70
Bhutan	1,298,000	G 3	70
Bialystok, Pol.	166,619	F 2	45
Biarritz, France	27,453	C 6	26
Biddeford, Maine	19,638	B 9	145
Bielefeld, W. Ger.	316,058	C 2	20
Bielsko-Biala, Poland	105,601	D 4	45
Big Bend Nat'l Pk., Texas		A 8	168
Bighorn (riv.), U.S.		E 2	126
Big Spring, Texas	24,804	C 5	168
Bikaner, India	188,518	C 3	70
Bikini (atoll), Marshall Is.		G 4	89
Bilbao, Spain	393,170	E 1	31
Billerica, Mass.	36,727	J 2	147
Billings, Mont.	66,842	H 5	152
Biloxi, Miss.	49,311	G 10	150
Biminis, The (isls.), Bah.	1,432	B 1	124
Binghamton, N.Y.	55,860	J 6	158
Bioko (isl.), Equat. Guin.		H 11	54
Birkenhead, Eng.	135,750	G 2	11
Birmingham, Ala.	284,413	D 3	129
Birmingham, Eng.	1,058,800	F 5	11
Birmingham, Mich.	21,689	B 6	148
Bisbee, Ariz.	7,154	F 7	131
Biscay (bay), Europe		D 4	6
Biscayne Nat'l Pk., Fla.		F 6	136
Bisho, S. Africa		M 18	57
Bismarck (cap.), N. Dak.	44,485	J 6	160
Bismarck (arch.), Papua N.G.	218,339	E 6	89
Bissau (cap.), Guinea-Bissau	109,486	D 9	54
Bitterroot (range), U.S.		D 1	126
Biysk, U.S.S.R.	212,000	J 4	46
Bizerte, Tun.	62,856	J 4	54
Black (sea)		H 4	6
Black (for.), W. Ger.		C 4	20
Black Canyon of the Gunnison Nat'l Mon., Colo.		D 5	134
Blackfoot, Idaho	10,065	F 6	138
Black Hills (mts.), U.S.		F 2	126
Blackpool, Eng.	149,000	G 1	11
Blacksburg, Va.	30,638	D 6	170
Bladensburg, Md.	7,691	C 4	146
Blagoveshchensk, U.S.S.R.	172,000	N 4	46
Blanc (mt.), Europe		E 4	6
Blanca (peak), Colo.		H 7	134
Blantyre, Malawi	222,153	N 15	57
Blida, Alg.	160,900	G 4	54
Block (isl.), R.I.		H 8	147
Bloemfontein, S. Africa	149,836	L 17	57
Bloomfield, N.J.	47,792	B 2	156
Bloomington, Ill.	44,189	D 3	139
Bloomington, Ind.	52,044	D 6	140
Bloomington, Minn.	81,831	G 6	149
Blue (mts.), Oreg.		J 3	163
Bluefield, W. Va.	16,060	D 6	172
Blue Nile (riv.), Africa		N 9	54
Blue Springs, Mo.	25,927	R 6	151
Blytheville, Ark.	23,844	L 2	132
Bobo-Dioulasso, Burk. Faso	115,063	F 9	54
Bobruysk, U.S.S.R.	192,000	C 4	50
Boca Raton, Fla.	49,505	F 5	136
Bochum, W. Ger.	414,852	B 3	20
Bogalusa, La.	16,976	L 5	144
Bogor, Indon.	247,409	H 2	83
Bogotá (cap.), Col.	2,696,270	F 3	90
Bo Hai (gulf), China		J 4	77
Bohemia (for.), Czech.		B 2	39
Boise (cap.), Idaho	102,160	B 6	138
Bolívar (mt.), Ven.		F 2	90
Bolivia	5,600,000	G 7	90
Bologna, Italy	493,282	C 2	32
Bolton, Eng.	154,480	H 2	11
Bolzano, Italy	102,806	C 1	32
Bombay, India	*5,970,575	B 7	70
Bon (cape), Tun.		J 4	54
Bonaire (isl.), Neth. Ant.	8,087	E 4	124
Bonin (isls.), Japan	1,879	M 3	75
Bonn (cap.), W. Ger.	283,711	B 3	20
Bonneville (dam), U.S.		E 2	163
Booker T. Washington Nat'l Mon., Va.		E 6	170
Boone, Iowa	12,602	F 4	141
Bophuthatswana (aut rep.), S. Africa		L 17	57
Bora Bora (isl.), Fr. Poly.	2,579	L 7	89
Borah (peak), Idaho		E 5	138
Bordeaux, France	220,830	C 5	26
Borger, Texas	15,837	C 2	168

	Pop.	Key	Pg.
East Detroit, Mich.	38,280	B 6	148
Easter (isl.), Chile	1,598	Q 8	89
Eastern Ghats (mts.), India		D-F 4-6	70
East Frisian (isls.), W. Ger.		B 2	20
East Greenwich, R.I.	10,211	H 6	147
East Hampton, Conn.	8,572	E 2	135
East Hartford, Conn.	52,563	E 1	135
East Haven, Conn.	25,028	D 3	135
Eastlake, Ohio	22,104	J 8	161
East Lansing, Mich.	51,392	E 6	148
East Liverpool, Ohio	16,687	J 4	161
East London, S. Africa,	*126,671	M18	57
East Meadow, N.Y.	39,317	B 3	158
East Moline, Ill.	20,907	C 2	139
Easton, Pa.	26,027	M 4	164
East Orange, N.J.	77,690	B 2	156
East Peoria, Ill.	22,385	D 3	139
East Point, Ga.	37,486	K 2	137
East Providence, R.I.	50,980	J 5	147
East St. Louis, Ill.	55,200	A 2	139
East Siberian (sea), U.S.S.R.		R 2	46
Eau Claire, Wis.	51,569	D 6	173
Ebro (riv.), Spain		G 2	31
Ecorse, Mich.	14,447	B 7	148
Ecuador	8,354,000	E 4	90
Eden, N.C.	15,572	F 1	159
Eden Prairie, Minn.	16,623	G 6	149
Edenton, N.C.	5,367	M 2	159
Edgewood, Md.	19,455	J 3	146
Edina, Minn.	46,073	G 5	149
Edinburg, Texas	24,075	F 11	168
Edinburgh (cap.), Scot.	470,085	D 1	13
Edison, N.J.	70,193	E 2	156
Edison Nat'l Hist. Site., N.J.		A 2	156
Edmond, Okla.	34,637	H 3	142
Edmonds, Wash.	27,679	C 3	171
Edmonton (cap.), Alta.	*657,057	D 3	114
Edmundston, N. Br.	12,044	B 1	102
Edwards (plat.), Texas		C 7	168
Edwards A.F.B., Calif.	8,554	H 9	133
Edwardsville, Ill.	12,480	B 2	139
Eel (riv.), Calif.		B 4	133
Effigy Mounds, Nat'l Mon., Iowa		L 2	141
Effingham, Ill.	11,270	E 4	139
Eglin A.F.B., Fla.	7,574	C 6	136
Egmont (mt.), N.Z.		L 6	87
Egypt	41,572,000	M 6	54
		A 4	60
Eielson A.F.B., Alaska	5,232	K 1	130
Eindhoven, Neth.	192,565	G 6	25
El 'Alamein, Egypt		M 5	54
El Asnam, Alg.	106,100	G 4	54
Elat (Elath), Isr.	12,800	D 5	67
Elazig, Turkey	131,415	H 3	64
Elba (isl.), Italy		C 3	32
Elbe (riv.), Ger.		D 2	20
Elbert (mt.), Colo.		G 4	134
El'brus (mt.), U.S.S.R.		F 6	50
Elburz (mts.), Iran		G 2	68
El Cajon, Calif.	73,892	J 11	133
El Centro, Calif.	23,996	K 11	133
El Dorado, Ark.	25,270	E 7	132
Elektrostal', U.S.S.R.	139,000	E 3	50
Elephanta (isl.), India		B 7	70
Elephant Butte (res.), N. Mex.		B 5	157
Eleuthera (isl.), Bah.	8,326	C 1	124
El Faiyûm, Egypt	167,081	M 6	54
Elgin, Ill.	63,981	E 1	139
Elizabeth, N.J.	106,201	B 2	157
Elizabeth City, N.C.	14,004	N 2	159
El Karnak, Egypt		B 4	60
Elk Grove Village, Ill.	28,907	B 5	139
Elkhart, Ind.	41,305	F 1	140
Ellensburg, Wash.	11,752	E 3	171
Ellesmere (isl.), N.W.T.		N 3	96
El Mansûra, Egypt	257,866	B 3	60
Elmendorf A.F.B., Alaska		J 2	130
Elmhurst, Ill.	44,276	B 5	139
El Minya, Egypt	146,143	B 4	60
Elmira, N.Y.	35,327	G 6	158
El Monte, Calif.	79,494	D10	133
El Morro Nat'l Mon., N. Mex.		A 3	157
Elmwood Park, Ill.	24,016	B 5	139
El Paso, Texas	425,259	A 10	168
El Reno, Okla.	15,486	F 3	162
El Salvador	4,813,000	C 4	122
Elyria, Ohio	57,538	F 3	161
Emmaus, Pa.	11,001	M 4	164
Emporia, Kans.	25,287	F 3	142
Endicott, N.Y.	14,457	H 6	158
Enewetak (atoll)	542	G 4	89
Enfield, Conn.	42,695	E 1	135
Enfield, Eng.	260,900	H 7	11
England	46,220,955		11
Englewood, Colo.	30,021	K 3	134
Englewood, N.J.	23,701	C 2	156
English (chan.), Europe		D 8	11
Enid, Okla.	50,363	G 2	162
Enschede, Neth.	141,597	K 4	25
Entebbe, Uganda	21,096	N12	57
Enugu, Nigeria	187,000	H10	54
Enzeli (Bandar-e Anzali), Iran	55,978	F 2	68
Ephrata, Pa.	11,095	K 5	164
Equatorial Guinea	244,000	H11	57
Erbil, Iraq	90,320	D 2	68
Erfurt, E. Ger.	202,979	D 3	20
Erie (lake), N. Amer.		K 5	94
Erie, Pa.	119,123	B 1	164
Eritrea (reg.), Eth.		O 8	54
Erivan, U.S.S.R.	1,019,000	F 6	50
Erzgebirge (mts.), Europe		E 3	20
Erzurum, Turkey	162,973	J 3	64
Escalante (des.), Utah		A 6	169
Escanaba, Mich.	14,355	C 3	148
Escondido, Calif.	64,355	J 10	133
Eskişehir, Turkey	259,952	D 3	64
Espiritu Santo (isl.), Vanuatu	16,220	G 7	89
Essen, W. Ger.	677,568	B 3	20
Essex, Md.	39,614	J 3	146
Essex, Vt.	14,392	A 2	155
Estonian S.S.R., U.S.S.R.	1,466,000	C 1	51
Ethiopia	31,065,000	O 9	54
Etna (vol.), Italy		E 6	32
Eton, Eng.	4,950	G 8	11
Etosha (salt pan), Namibia		J 15	57
Euboea (Évvoia) (isl.), Greece		G 6	43
Euclid, Ohio	59,999	J 9	161
Eugene, Oreg.	105,624	D 3	163
Eunice, La.	12,749	F 6	144
Euphrates (riv.), Asia		D 4	68
Eureka, Calif.	24,153	A 3	133
Europe	676,000,000		6
Evans (mt.), Colo.		H 3	134
Evanston, Ill.	73,706	B 5	139
Evansville, Ind.	130,496	C 9	140
Everest (mt.), Asia		F 3	70
Everett, Mass.	37,195	D 6	147
Everett, Wash.	54,413	C 3	171
Everglades Nat'l Pk., Fla.		F 6	136
Évvoia (isl.), Greece		G 6	43
Ewa Beach, Hawaii	14,369	B 4	130
Exeter, Eng.	93,300	D 7	11
Exeter, N.H.	11,024	F 6	155
Eyre (lake), Austr.		F 5	86
Ez Zarqa', Jordan	263,400	E 3	67

F

	Pop.	Key	Pg.
Faeroe (isls.), Den.	41,969	B 2	19
Fairbanks, Alaska	22,645	K 1	130
Fairborn, Ohio	29,702	B 6	161
Fairfax, Va.	19,390	M 3	170
Fairfield, Calif.	58,099	K 1	133
Fairfield, Conn.	54,849	B 4	135
Fairfield, Ohio	30,777	A 7	161
Fair Lawn, N.J.	32,229	B 1	156
Fairmont, W. Va.	23,863	F 2	172
Fairweather (mt.), N. Amer.		L 3	130
Faisalabad, Pak.	822,263	C 2	70
Falcon (res.), N. Amer.		E 11	168
Falkland Islands	1,813	H14	93
Fall River, Mass.	92,574	K 6	147
Falmouth, Mass.	23,640	M 6	147
Famagusta, Cyprus	38,960	F 5	64
Fanning (Tabuaeran) (isl.), Kiribati	340	L 5	89
Farewell (cape), Greenl.		O 4	94
Farallon (isls.), Calif.		B 6	133
Fargo, N. Dak.	61,383	S 6	160
Faribault, Minn.	16,241	E 6	149
Farmington, N. Mex.	31,222	A 2	157
Farmington Hills, Mich.	58,056	F 6	148
Faro, Port.	20,470	B 4	30
Farrukhabad (Fatehgarh), India	102,768	D 3	70
Fayetteville, Ark.	36,608	B 1	132
Fayetteville, N.C.	59,507	H 4	159
Fear (cape), N.C.		K 7	159
Fergana, U.S.S.R.	176,000	H 5	46
Fergus Falls, Minn.	12,519	B 4	149
Ferrara, Italy	97,507	C 2	32
Fès, Mor.	325,327	F 5	54
Fezzan (reg.), Libya		J 6	54
Fianarantsoa, Madag.	68,054	R16	57
Fiji	588,068	H 8	89
Findlay, Ohio	35,594	C 3	161
Finisterre (cape), Spain		B 1	31
Finland	4,788,000		16
Finland (gulf), Europe		G 3	6
Finlay (riv.), Br. Col.		E 1	117
Fire Isl. Nat'l Seashore, N.Y.		F 2	158
Firenze (Florence), Italy	441,654	C 3	32
Fitchburg, Mass.	39,580	G 2	147
Fiume, see Rijeka, Yugo.			
Fiumicino, Italy	13,180	F 7	32
Flagstaff, Ariz.	34,743	D 3	131
Flaming Gorge (res.), U.S.		C 4	174
Flanders (provs.), Belg.		C-D 7	25
Flathead (lake), Mont.		C 3	152
Flattery (cape), Wash.		A 2	171
Flensburg, W. Ger.	92,313	C 1	20
Flint, Mich.	159,611	F 5	148
Floral Park, N.Y.	16,805	A 3	158
Florence, Ala.	37,029	C 1	129
Florence, Italy	441,654	C 3	32
Florence, Ky.	15,586	J 2	129
Florence, S.C.	29,176	H 3	165
Flores (isl.), Indon.	860,328	G 7	83
Florianópolis, Braz.	153,547	L 9	93
Florida (bay), Fla.		F 6	136
Florida (state), U.S.	4,788,000		136
Florissant, Mo.	55,372	P 2	151
Florissant Fossil Beds Nat'l Mon., Colo.		J 5	134
Flushing, Neth.	43,806	C 6	25
Foggia, Italy	136,436	E 4	32
Folkestone, Eng.	45,610	J 6	11
Fond du Lac, Wis.	35,863	K 8	173
Fongafale (cap.), Tuvalu		H 6	89
Fonseca (gulf), Cent. Amer.		O 4	122
Fontainebleau, France	16,436	E 3	26
Fontana, Calif.	37,107	E 10	133
Foochow, see Fuzhou, China			
Forlì, Italy	83,303	D 2	32
Formosa (Taiwan) (isl.), China	16,609,961	K 7	77
Fortaleza, Braz.	648,815	N 4	90
Ft. Belvoir, Va.	7,726	K 3	170
Ft. Benning, Ga.		B 6	137
Ft. Bliss, Texas	12,687	A 2	168
Ft. Bowie Nat'l Hist. Site, Ariz.		F 6	131
Ft. Bragg, N.C.	37,834	H 4	159
Ft. Campbell, U.S.		C 7	143
Ft. Caroline Nat'l Mem., Fla.		E 1	136
Ft. Clatsop Nat'l Mem., Oreg.		C 1	163
Ft. Collins, Colo.	65,092	J 1	134
Ft. Davis Nat'l Hist. Site, Texas		D11	168
Ft.-de-France (cap.), Martinique	97,649	G 4	124
Ft. Dodge, Iowa	29,423	E 3	141
Ft. Donelson Nat'l Mil. Pk., Tenn.		F 2	167
Ft. Frederica Nat'l Mon., Ga.		K 8	137
Ft. George G. Meade, Md.	14,083	G 4	146
Forth (firth), Scot.		F 4	13
Ft. Jefferson Nat'l Mon., Fla.		C 7	136
Ft. Knox, Ky.	31,055	F 5	143
Ft. Laramie Nat'l Hist. Site, Wyo.		H 3	174
Ft. Larned Nat'l Hist. Site, Kans.		C 3	142
Ft. Lauderdale, Fla.	153,279	C 4	136
Ft. Lee, N.J.	32,449	C 2	156
Ft. Lee, Va.	9,784	K 6	170
Ft. Leonard Wood, Mo.	21,262	H 7	151
Ft. Macleod, Alta.	3,139	D 5	114
Ft. Madison, Iowa	13,520	L 7	141
Ft. Matanzas Nat'l Mon., Fla.		E 2	136
Ft. McHenry Nat'l Mon., Md.		H 3	146
Ft. McMurray, Alta.	31,000	E 1	114
Ft. Myers, Fla.	36,638	E 5	136
Ft. Peck Lake (res.), Mont.		K 3	152
Ft. Pierce, Fla.	33,802	F 4	136
Ft. Point Nat'l Hist. Site, Calif.		J 2	133
Ft. Pulaski Nat'l Mon., Ga.		L 6	137
Ft. Raleigh Nat'l Hist. Site, N.C.		O 3	159
Ft. Riley, Kans.	18,233	F 2	142
Ft. Sill, Okla.	15,924	F 5	162
Ft. Smith, Ark.	71,626	B 3	132
Ft. Smith, N.W.T.	2,298	E 3	96
Ft. Sumter Nat'l Mon., S.C.		H 6	165
Ft. Thomas, Ky.	16,012	L 1	143
Ft. Union Nat'l Mon., N. Mex.		E 3	157
Ft. Union Trading Post Nat'l Hist. Site, N. Dak.		B 3	160
Ft. Vancouver Nat'l Hist. Site, Wash.		C 5	171
Ft. Walton Beach, Fla.	20,829	C 6	136
Ft. Wayne, Ind.	172,028	G 2	140
Ft. Worth, Texas	385,164	F 2	168
Fostoria, Ohio	15,743	D 3	161
Fountain Valley, Calif.	55,080	D11	133
Foxe (basin), N.W.T.		J 2	96
Framingham, Mass.	65,113	A 7	147
France	53,788,000		26
Francis Case (lake), S. Dak.		L 7	166
Francistown, Botswana	22,000	M16	57
Frankfort, Ind.	15,168	E 4	140
Frankfort (cap.), Ky.	25,973	H 4	143
Frankfurt-am-Main, W. Ger.	636,157	C 3	20
Frankfurt-an-der-Oder, E. Ger.	70,817	F 2	20
Franklin D. Roosevelt (lake), Wash.		G 2	171
Franz Josef Land (isls.), U.S.S.R.		E-G 1	46
Fraser (riv.), Br. Col.		F 4	117
Fraser, Mich.	14,560	B 6	148
Fredericia, Den.	36,157	C 6	19
Frederick, Md.	28,086	E 3	146
Fredericksburg, Va.	15,322	J 4	170
Fredericton (cap.), N. Br.	43,723	D 3	102
Frederiksberg, Den.	101,874	F 6	19
Frederikshavn, Den.	24,846	D 3	19
Freeport, Ill.	26,266	D 1	139
Freeport, N.Y.	38,272	B 4	158
Freetown (cap.), S. Leone	274,000	D10	54
Freiburg im Breisgau, W. Ger.	175,371	B 5	20
Fremantle, Austr.	22,484	B 2	86
Fremont, Calif.	131,945	K 3	133
Fremont, Nebr.	23,979	H 3	153
French Guiana	73,022	K 3	90
French Polynesia	137,382	M 8	89
Fresno, Calif.	217,289	F 7	133
Fribourg, Switz.	41,600	D 3	37
Fridley, Minn.	30,228	G 5	149
Friedrichshafen, W. Ger.	51,544	C 5	20
Friesland (prov.), Neth.		G 1	25
Frobisher Bay, N.W.T.	2,333	K 2	96
Front Royal, Va.	11,126	H 3	170
Frunze, U.S.S.R.	533,000	H 5	46
Fujairah, U.A.E.		G 4	61
Fuji (mt.), Japan		J 6	75
Fujian (Fukien) (prov.), China		J 6	77
Fujisawa, Japan	265,975	O 3	75
Fukui, Japan	231,634	G 5	75
Fukuoka, Japan	1,002,201	D 7	75
Fukushima, Japan	246,531	K 5	75
Fukuyama, Japan	329,714	F 6	75
Fullerton, Calif.	102,034	D11	133
Fulton, Mo.	11,046	J 5	151
Funabashi, Japan	423,101	P 2	75
Funchal, Port.	38,340	A 2	32
Fundy (bay), N. Amer.		E 3	102
Fundy Nat'l Pk., N. Br.		E 3	102
Fürth, W. Ger.	101,639	D 4	20
Fushun, China	1,700,000	K 3	77
Füssen, W. Ger.	10,506	D 5	20
Fuxin, China	350,000	K 3	77
Fuzhou, China	900,000	J 6	77

G

	Pop.	Key	Pg.
Gabès (gulf), Tun.		J 5	54
Gabon	551,000	J 12	57
Gaborone (cap.), Bots.	21,000	L 16	57
Gadsden, Ala.	47,565	G 2	129
Gaffney, S.C.	13,453	D 1	165
Gafsa, Tun.	42,225	H 5	54
Gainesville, Fla.	81,371	D 2	136
Gainesville, Ga.	15,280	E 2	137
Gaithersburg, Md.	26,424	F 4	146
Galápagos (isls.), Ecua.		J 9	94
Galaţi, Rom.	252,884	H 3	43
Galesburg, Ill.	35,305	C 3	139
Galicia (reg.), Spain		B 1	31
Galilee (reg.), Isr.		C 2	67
Gallatin, Tenn.	17,191	H 2	167
Galle, Sri Lanka	72,720	D 7	70
Gallipoli, Turkey	13,466	A 1	64
Gallup, N. Mex.	18,167	A 3	157
Galveston, Texas	61,902	L 3	168
Galway, Ire.	27,726	C 5	15
Gambia	601,000	C 9	54
Gander, Newf.	10,404	C 3	99
Ganges (riv.), Asia		F 3	70
Gangtok, India	12,000	F 3	70
Garda (lake), Italy		C 2	32
Garden City, Kans.	18,256	B 4	142
Garden City, N.Y.	22,927	B 3	158
Garden Grove, Calif.	123,307	D11	133
Garfield, N.J.	26,803	B 2	156
Garfield Heights, Ohio	34,938	J 9	161
Garland, Texas	138,857	H 2	168
Garmisch-Partenkirchen, W. Ger.	26,831	D 5	20
Garonne (riv.), France		C 5	26
Gary, Ind.	151,953	C 1	140
Gaspé (pen.), Que.		D 2	105
Gastonia, N.C.	47,333	C 4	159
Gates of the Arctic Nat'l Pk., Alaska		D 2	130
Gateway Nat'l Rec. Area, U.S.		D 3	158
Gauhati, India	123,783	G 3	70
Gaya, India	179,884	F 4	70

	Pop.	Key	Pg.
Gaza Strip, Egypt		A 5	67
Gaziantep, Turkey	300,882	G 4	64
Gdańsk, Pol.	364,385	D 1	45
Gdańsk (gulf), Pol.		D 1	45
Gdynia, Pol.	190,125	D 1	45
Gejiu, China	250,000	F 7	77
Gelsenkirchen, W. Ger.	322,584	B 3	20
General Grant Grove Section, Kings Canyon Nat'l Pk., Calif.		G 7	133
Geneva (lake), Europe		C 4	37
Geneva, N.Y.	15,133	G 5	158
Geneva, Switz.	163,100	B 4	37
Genoa (Genova), Italy	787,011	B 2	32
George Rogers Clark Nat'l Hist. Pk., Ind.		B 7	140
Georgetown (cap.), Cayman Is.	7,617	A 3	124
Georgetown (cap.), Guyana	63,184	J 2	90
George Town (Pinang), Malaysia	269,603	C 6	81
George Washington Birthplace Nat'l Mon., Va.		L 4	170
George Washington Carver Nat'l Mon., Mo.		D 9	151
Georgia (str.), Br. Col.		E 5	117
Georgia (state), U.S.	5,463,105		137
Georgian (bay), Ont.		C-D 2	108
Georgian S.S.R., U.S.S.R.	5,015,000	D 5	50
Geraldton, Austr.	20,895	A 5	86
Germany, East	16,737,000		20
Germany, West	61,658,000		20
Gettysburg, Pa.	7,194	H 6	164
Ghana	11,450,000	F 10	54
Ghazni, Afghan.	30,425	B 2	70
Ghent, Belg.	148,860	D 6	25
Gibraltar	29,760	D 4	31
Gibraltar (str.)		D 5	31
Gibson (des.), Austr.		D 4	86
Gifu, Japan	408,707	H 6	75
Gijón, Spain	159,806	D 1	31
Gila (riv.), U.S.		B 6	131
Gila Cliff Dwellings Nat'l Mon., N. Mex.		A 5	157
Gilbert Is. (Kiribati)	47,711	H 6	89
Gillette, Wyo.	12,134	G 1	174
Gironde (riv.), France		C 5	26
Giza, Egypt	1,246,713	B 4	60
Glace Bay, N.S.	21,466	J 2	100
Glacier Bay Nat'l Pk., Alaska		M 3	130
Glacier Nat'l Pk., Br. Col.		J 4	117
Glacier Nat'l Pk., Mont.		C 2	152
Glasgow, Scot.	880,617	B 2	13
Glassboro, N.J.	14,574	C 4	156
Glastonbury, Conn.	24,327	E 2	135
Glen Burnie, Md.	37,263	H 4	146
Glen Canyon Nat'l Rec. Area, U.S.		D 6	169
Glen Cove, N.Y.	24,618	A 3	158
Glendale, Ariz.	97,172	C 5	131
Glendale, Calif.	139,060	C 10	133
Glens Falls, N.Y.	15,897	N 4	158
Glenview, Ill.	32,060	B 5	139
Gliwice, Pol.	170,912	A 4	45
Gloucester, Eng.	91,600	E 6	11
Gloucester, Mass.	27,768	M 2	147
Gloversville, N.Y.	17,836	M 4	158
Goa (dist.), India		C 5	70
Gobi (des.), Asia		G 3	77
Godavari (riv.), India		D 5	70
Godhavn (Qeqertarsuaq), Greenl.	1,012	C 12	4
Godthab (Nuuk) (cap.), Greenl.	9,561	C 12	4
Godwin Austen (K2) (mt.), India		D 1	70
Goiânia, Braz.	703,263	L 7	90
Golan Heights, Syria		D 1	67
Golconda (ruins), India		D 5	70
Gold Coast, Austr.	135,437	J 5	86
Golden, Colo.	12,237	J 3	134
Golden Gate Nat'l Rec. Area, Calif.		H 2	133
Golden Spike Nat'l Hist. Site, Utah		B 2	169
Golden Valley, Minn.	22,775	G 5	149
Goldsboro, N.C.	31,871	K 4	159
Gomel', U.S.S.R.	383,000	D 4	50
Gonâve (isl.), Haiti		D 3	124
Gondar, Eth.	38,600	O 9	54
Good Hope (cape), S. Africa		C 20	57
Goose (lake), U.S.		G 5	163
Goose Bay-Happy Valley, Newf.	7,103	D 2	99
Gorakhpur, India	230,911	E 3	70
Gorham, Maine	10,101	C 8	145
Gor'kiy, U.S.S.R.	1,344,000	F 3	50
Gorlovka, U.S.S.R.	336,000	E 5	50
Goshen, Ind.	19,665	F 1	140
Göta (canal), Sweden		J 7	16
Göteborg, Sweden	444,540	G 8	16
Gotland (isl.), Sweden		D 3	16
Göttingen, W. Ger.	123,797	D 3	20
Gouda, Neth.	56,403	F 4	25
Granada, Spain	185,799	E 4	31
Gran Canaria (isl.), Spain		B 5	30
Gran Chaco (reg.), S. Amer.		H 9	93
Grand (canal), China		J 4	77
Grand Bahama (isl.), Bah.	33,102	B 1	124
Grand Canyon Nat'l Pk., Ariz.		C 2	131
Grand Cayman (isl.), Cayman Is.	15,000	B 3	124
Grande (riv.), Bol.		H 7	90
Grande, Rio (riv.), N. Amer.		H 7	94
Grande Prairie, Alta.	24,263	A 2	114
Grand Forks, N. Dak.	43,765	R 4	160
Grand Island, Nebr.	33,180	F 4	153
Grand Junction, Colo.	27,956	B 4	134
Grand Manan (isl.), N. Br.		D 4	102
Grand Portage Nat'l Mon., Minn.		G 2	149
Grand Prairie, Texas	71,462	G 2	168
Grand Rapids, Mich.	181,843	D 5	148
Grand Teton Nat'l Pk., Wyo.		B 2	174
Granite City, Ill.	36,815	A 2	139
Grants, N. Mex.	11,439	B 3	157
Grants Pass, Oreg.	15,032	D 5	163
Grasse, France	24,260	G 6	26
Gravesend, Eng.	53,500	J 8	11
Graz, Austria	251,900	C 3	39
Great Abaco (isl.), Bah.	7,324	C 1	124
Gt. Australian (bight), Austr.		D-E 6	86
Gt. Barrier (reef), Austr.		H-J 2-3	86
Gt. Bear (lake), N.W.T.		D 2	99
Great Bend, Kans.	16,608	D 3	142
Great Britain & Northern Ireland (United Kingdom)	55,672,000		8
Gt. Dividing (range), Austr.		H-J 4-5	86
Gt. Eastern Erg (des.), Africa		H 5	54
Gt. Exuma (isl.), Bah.		C 2	124
Great Falls, Mont.	56,725	E 3	152
Gt. Inagua (isl.), Bah.	939	D 2	124
Gt. Salt (lake), Utah		B 2-3	169
Gt. Sand Dunes Nat'l Mon., Colo.		H 7	134
Gt. Sandy (des.), Austr.		C 4	86
Gt. Slave (lake), N.W.T.		E 3	96
Gt. Smoky (mts.), U.S.		C 8	159
Gt. Smoky Mts. Nat'l Pk., Tenn.		C 8	159
Gt. Victoria (des.), Austr.		D-E 5	86
Gt. Wall (ruins), China		G 4	77
Gt. Western Erg (des.), Alg.		G 5	54
Greece	9,599,000		43
Greece, N.Y.	16,177	E 4	158
Greeley, Colo.	53,006	K 2	134
Green (riv.), U.S.		D 3	126
Green (mts.), Vt.		B1-4	155
Green Bay, Wis.	87,899	K 6	173
Greeneville, Tenn.	14,097	Q 2	167
Greenfield, Mass.	18,436	D 2	147
Greenfield, Wis.	31,467	L 2	173
Greenland	49,773	B 12	4
Greenland (sea)		B 10	4
Greensboro, N.C.	155,642	F 2	159
Greensburg, Pa.	17,558	D 5	164
Greenville, Miss.	40,613	B 4	150
Greenville, N.C.	35,740	L 3	159
Greenville, S.C.	581,242	C 2	165
Greenwich, Conn.	59,578	A 4	135
Greenwich, Eng.	207,200	H 8	11
Greenwood, Miss.	20,115	D 4	150
Greenwood, S.C.	21,613	C 3	165
Grenada	103,103	G 4	124
Grenadines (isls.), W. Indies		G 4	124
Grenoble, France	165,431	F 5	26
Gresham, Oreg.	33,005	B 2	163
Gretna, La.	20,615	O 4	144
Griffin, Ga.	20,728	D 4	137
Grodno, U.S.S.R.	195,000	B 4	50
Groningen, Neth.	163,357	K 2	25
Grosse Pointe Woods, Mich.	18,886	B 6	148
Grossglockner (mt.), Austria		B 3	39
Groton, Conn.	10,086	G 3	135
Groznyy, U.S.S.R.	375,000	G 6	50
Guadalajara, Mex.	1,478,383	H 6	119
Guadalajara, Spain	30,924	E 2	31
Guadalcanal (isl.), Sol. Is.	46,619	F 7	89
Guadalquivir (riv.), Spain		C 4	31
Guadalupe (mts.), U.S.		D 6	157
Guadalupe Mts. Nat'l Pk., Texas		C 10	168
Guadeloupe	328,400	F 3	124
Guainía (riv.), S. Amer.		G 3	90
Guajira (pen.), S. Amer.		F 1	90
Guam	105,979	E 4	89
Guanabacoa, Cuba	89,741	A 2	124
Guangdong (Kwangtung) (prov.), China		H 7	77
Guangzhou, China	2,300,000	H 7	77
Guantánamo, Cuba	178,129	C 2	124
Guantánamo (bay), Cuba		C 3	124
Guardafui (cape), Somalia		S 9	54
Guatemala	7,262,419	B 3	122
Guatemala (cap.), Guat.	700,538	B 3	122
Guayaquil, Ecua.	823,219	D 4	90
Guelph, Ont.	71,207	D 4	108
Guernsey (isl.), Chan. Is.	51,351	E 8	11
Guilford, Conn.	2,555	E 3	135
Guilin, China	225,000	G 6	77
Guinea	5,143,284	D 9	54
Guinea (gulf), Africa		F 11	57
Guinea-Bissau	777,214	C 9	54
Guiyang, China	1,500,000	G 6	77
Gujranwala, Pak.	360,419	C 2	70
Gulbarga, India	145,588	D 5	70
Gulf Isls. Nat'l Seashore, Fla.		B 6	136
Gulf Isls. Nat'l Seashore, Miss.		G 10	150
Gulfport, Miss.	39,696	F 10	150
Guntur, India	269,991	D 5	70
Gur'yev, U.S.S.R.	131,000	F 5	46
Guthrie, Okla.	10,312	H 3	162
Guyana	820,000	J 2	90
Gwalior, India	384,772	D 3	70
Gyor, Hung.	123,618	D 3	39

H

	Pop.	Key	Pg.
Haarlem, Neth.	164,172	F 4	25
Habik, Japan	94,160	J 8	75
Hachinohe, Japan	224,366	K 3	75
Hachioji, Japan	322,580	O 2	75
Hackensack, N.J.	36,039	D 2	156
Haddonfield, N.J.	12,337	B 3	156
Hadhramaut (reg.), P.D.R. Yemen		E-F 6	60
Haeju, N. Korea	140,000	B 4	74
Hagen, W. Ger.	229,224	B 3	20
Hagerstown, Md.	34,132	C 2	146
Hague, The (cap.), Neth.	479,369	E 4	25
Haifa, Isr.	227,800	B 2	67
Haikou, China	500,000	H 7	77
Hainan (isl.), China		H 8	77
Haiphong, Viet.	*1,279,067	E 2	81
Haiti	5,009,000	D 3	124
Hakodate, Japan	307,453	K 3	75
Haleakala Nat'l Pk., Hawaii		F 3	130
Haleb (Aleppo), Syria	639,428	G 4	64
Halifax (cap.), N.S.	*277,727	E 4	100
Hallandale, Fla.	36,517	B 4	136
Halle, E. Ger.	241,425	D 3	20
Halmahera (isl.), Indon.	122,521	H 5	83
Hama, Syria	137,421	G 5	64
Hamadan, Iran	155,846	F 3	68
Hamamatsu, Japan	468,884	H 6	75
Hamburg, W. Ger.	1,717,383	D 2	20
Hamden, Conn.	51,071	D 3	135
Hamersley (range), Austr.		B 4	86
Hamhŭng, N. Korea	484,000	C 4	74
Hamilton (cap.), Bermuda	1,617	G 3	124
Hamilton, N.Z.	91,109	L 6	87
Hamilton, Ohio	63,189	A 7	164
Hamilton, Ont.	*542,095	E 4	108
Hamm, W. Ger.	172,210	B 3	20
Hammerfest, Nor.	7,610	N 1	16
Hammond, Ind.	93,714	B 1	140
Hammond, La.	15,043	N 1	144
Hampton, Va.	122,617	M 6	170
Hamtramck, Mich.	21,300	B 6	148
Han (riv.), S. Korea		C 5	75
Handan, China	500,000	H 4	77
Hanford, Calif.	20,958	F 7	133
Hanford Atomic Energy Reservation, Wash.		F 4	171
Hangzhou (Hangchow), China	1,500,000	J 5	77
Hannibal, Mo.	18,811	K 3	151
Hannover, W. Ger.	552,955	C 2	20
Hanoi (cap.), Viet.	*2,570,905	E 2	81
Hanover, N.H.	6,861	C 4	155
Harare (cap.), Zim.	601,000	N 15	57
Harbin, China	2,750,000	L 2	77
Hardanger (fjord), Nor.		D 7	16
Hargeysa, Somalia	40,254	Q 10	54
Harlingen, Texas	43,543	G 11	168
Harpers Ferry Nat'l Hist. Site, W. Va.		L 2	172
Harper Woods, Mich.	16,361	B 6	148
Harrisburg (cap.), Pa.	53,264	H 5	164
Harrison, N.Y.	23,046	J 1	158
Harrisonburg, Va.	19,671	F 4	170
Harrodsburg, Ky.	7,265	H 5	143
Harrow, Eng.	200,200	G 8	11
Hartford (cap.), Conn.	136,392	E 1	135
Harvey, Ill.	35,810	B 6	139
Harz (mts.), Ger.		D 3	20
Hastings, Nebr.	23,045	F 4	153
Hatteras (cape), N.C.		P 4	159
Hattiesburg, Miss.	40,829	F 8	150
Havana (cap.), Cuba	1,924,886	A 2	124
Havasu (lake), U.S.		A 4	131
Haverhill, Mass.	46,865	K 1	147
Havre, Mont.	10,891	G 2	152
Hawaii (isl.), Hawaii		F 4	130
Hawaii (state), U.S.	964,691		130
Hawaiian (isls.), U.S.		J-L 3-4	89
Hawaii Volcanoes Nat'l Pk., Hawaii		F 4	130
Hawthorne, Calif.	56,447	C 11	133
Hawthorne, N.J.	18,200	B 2	156
Hay River, N.W.T.	2,863	E 3	96
Hays, Kans.	16,301	C 3	142
Hayward, Calif.	94,342	K 2	133
Hazel Park, Mich.	20,914	B 6	148
Hazleton, Pa.	27,318	L 4	164
Hebei (Hopei) (prov.), China		J 4	77
Hebrides (isls.), Scot.		C1-2	8
Hebron, West Bank	38,309	C 4	67
Hefei, China	400,000	J 5	77
Hegang, China	350,000	L 2	77
Heidelberg, W. Ger.	129,368	C 4	20
Hejaz (reg.), Saudi Arabia		C-D 4-5	60
Hekla (mt.), Iceland		B 1	19
Helena (cap.), Mont.	23,938	E 4	152
Helgoland (isl.), W. Ger.		C 1	20
Helmand (riv.), Afghan.		B 2	70
Helsingborg, Sweden	80,986	H 8	16
Helsinki (cap.), Fin.	502,961	O 6	16
Hempstead, N.Y.	40,404	B 3	158
Henan (Honan) (prov.), China		H 5	77
Henderson, Ky.	24,834	B 5	143
Henderson, Nev.	24,363	G 6	154
Henderson, N.C.	13,522	J 2	159
Hengyang, China	310,000	H 6	77
Herat, Afghan.	103,960	A 2	70
Herbert Hoover Nat'l Hist. Site, Iowa		L 5	141
Hermon (mt.), Asia		D 1	67
Hermosillo, Mex.	232,691	D 2	119
Herne, W. Ger.	190,561	B 3	20
Hershey, Pa.	13,249	J 5	164
Hesse (state), W. Ger.		C 3	20
Hialeah, Fla.	145,254	B 4	136
Hibbing, Minn.	21,193	F 3	149
Hickory, N.C.	20,757	C 3	159
Hicksville, N.Y.	43,245	B 3	158
Higashiosaka, Japan	524,750	J 8	75
Highland Park, Ill.	30,611	B 5	139
Highland Park, Mich.	27,909	B 6	148
High Point, N.C.	63,380	E 3	159
Hillsboro, Oreg.	27,664	A 2	163
Hillside, N.J.	21,440	B 2	156
Hilo, Hawaii	35,269	F 4	130
Himalaya (mts.), Asia		D-G 2-3	70
Himeji, Japan	436,086	G 6	75
Hindu Kush (mts.), Asia		B-C 1	70
Hingham, Mass.	20,339	E 8	147
Hinsdale, Ill.	16,726	B 6	139
Hirakata, Japan	297,618	J 7	75
Hiroshima, Japan	852,611	E 6	75
Hispaniola (isl.), W. Indies	10,440,000	D 2	124
Hitachi, Japan	202,383	K 5	75
Hobart, Austr.	128,603	H 8	86
Hobart, Ind.	22,987	C 1	140
Hobbs, N. Mex.	29,153	F 6	157
Hoboken, N.J.	42,460	C 2	156
Ho Chi Minh City, Viet.	3,419,678	E 5	81
Hodeida, Yemen Arab Rep.	80,314	D 7	60
Hoffman Estates, Ill.	37,272	A 5	139
Hofuf, Saudi Arabia	101,271	E 4	60
Hohhot, China	700,000	H 3	77
Holguín, Cuba	190,155	C 2	124
Holland, Mich.	26,281	C 6	148
Hollywood, Calif.		C 10	133
Hollywood, Fla.	121,323	B 4	136
Holon, Isr.	121,200	B 3	67
Holyoke, Mass.	44,678	D 4	147
Homestead, Fla.	20,668	F 6	136
Homestead Nat'l Mon., Nebr.		H 4	153
Homewood, Ala.	21,412	E 4	129
Homs, Libya	66,890	J 5	54
Homs, Syria	215,423	G 5	64
Honduras	3,691,000	D 3	122
Honduras (gulf), Cent. Amer.		D 2	122
Hong Kong	5,022,000	H 7	77
Honiara (cap.), Sol. Is.	14,942	F 6	89
Honolulu (cap.), Hawaii	365,048	C 4	130
Honshu (isl.), Japan		J 5	77
Hood (mt.), Oreg.		F 2	163
Hoover (dam), U.S.		G 7	154
Hope, Ark.	10,290	C 6	132
Hopewell, Va.	23,397	K 6	170
Hopkins, Minn.	15,336	G 5	149
Hopkinsville, Ky.	27,318	B 7	143
Horn (cape), Chile		G 15	93

	Pop.	Key	Pg.
Mwanza, Tanz.	110,611	N12	57
Mweru (lake), Africa		M13	57
Myrtle Beach, S.C.	18,446	K 4	165
Mysore, India	355,685	D 6	70

N

	Pop.	Key	Pg.
Nablus (Nabulus), West Bank	41,799	C 3	67
Nacogdoches, Texas	27,149	J 6	168
Nagaland (state), India		G 3	70
Nagano, Japan	306,637	J 5	75
Nagaoka, Japan	171,742	J 5	75
Nagasaki, Japan	450,194	D 7	75
Nagercoil, India	141,288	D 7	70
Nagoya, Japan	2,079,740	H 6	75
Nagpur, India	866,076	D 4	70
Naha, Japan	295,006	N 6	75
Nahuel Huapi (lake), Arg.		F 12	93
Nairobi (cap.), Kenya	509,286	O12	57
Nalchik, U.S.S.R.	207,000	E 6	50
Namangan, U.S.S.R.	227,000	H 5	46
Namib (des.), Namibia		J 15	57
Namibia	1,200,000	K16	57
Nampa, Idaho	25,112	B 6	138
Namp'o, N. Korea	140,000	D 3	74
Nanaimo, Br. Col.	47,069	J 3	117
Nanchang, China	900,000	J 6	77
Nanchong, China	275,000	G 5	77
Nancy, France	106,906	G 3	26
Nanda Devi (mt.), India		D 2	70
Nanga Parbat (mt.), Pak.		D 1	70
Nanjing (Nanking), China	2,000,000	J 5	77
Nanning, China	375,000	G 7	77
Nantes, France	252,537	C 4	26
Nantong, China	300,000	K 5	77
Nantucket (isl.), Mass.		O 7	147
Napa, Calif.	50,879	C 5	133
Naperville, Ill.	42,601	A 6	139
Naples, Fla.	17,581	E 5	136
Naples, Italy	1,214,775	E 4	32
Nara, Japan	257,538	J 8	75
Narmada (riv.), India		D 4	70
Narragansett (bay), R.I.		J 6	147
N.A.S.A. Space Center, Texas		K 2	168
Nashua, N.H.	67,865	D 6	155
Nashville (cap.), Tenn.	455,651	H 2	167
Nasik, India	176,091	C 5	70
Nassau (cap.), Bah.	135,437	C 1	124
Natal, Braz.	376,552	O 5	90
Natal (prov.), S. Africa		N17	57
Natchez, Miss.	22,015	B 7	150
Natchitoches, La.	16,664	D 3	144
Natick, Mass.	29,286	A 7	147
Natural Bridges Nat'l Mon., Utah		E 6	169
Naugatuck, Conn.	26,456	C 3	135
Nauru	7,254	G 6	89
Navarin (cape), U.S.S.R.		T 3	46
Navajo Nat'l Mon., Ariz.		E 2	131
Navarre (reg.), Spain		F 1	31
Náxos (isl.), Greece		G 7	43
Nazareth, Isr.	33,000	C 2	67
N'Djamena (cap.), Chad	179,000	K 9	54
Ndola, Zambia	282,439	M14	57
Neagh (lake), N. Ire.		J 2	15
Nebo (mt.), Jordan		D 4	67
Nebraska (state), U.S.	1,569,825		153
Neckar (riv.), W. Ger.		C 4	20
Needham, Mass.	27,901	B 7	147
Neenah, Wis.	22,432	J 7	173
Nefud (des.), Saudi Arabia		C-D 4	60
Negev (reg.), Isr.		D 5	67
Negro (riv.), S. Amer.		H 4	90
Negros (isl.), Phil.		G 4	83
Nei Monggol Zizhiqu (aut. reg.), China		H 3	77
Neisse (riv.), Europe		F 3	20
Neiva, Col.	105,476	F 3	90
Nejd (reg.), Saudi Arabia		C-E 4-5	60
Nelson, Br. Col.	9,143	J 5	117
Nelson (riv.), Man.		J 2	110
Nepal	14,179,301	E 3	70
Neptune, N.J.	28,366	E 3	156
Ness (lake), Scot.		D 3	13
Netherlands	14,227,000		25
Netherlands Antilles	246,000	E 4	124
		F 3	124
Netzahualcóyotl, Mex.	560,436	L 1	119
Nevada (state), U.S.	800,493		154
Nevada, Sierra (mts.), Spain		E 4	31
Nevada, Sierra (mts.), U.S.		B 3	126
Nevis (isl.), St. Chris. & Nevis		F 3	124
New Albany, Ind.	37,103	F 8	140
Newark, Calif.	32,126	K 3	133
Newark, Del.	25,247	L 2	146
Newark, N.J.	329,248	B 2	156
Newark, Ohio	41,200	F 5	161
New Bedford, Mass.	98,478	K 6	147
New Berlin, Wis.	30,529	K 2	173
New Bern, N.C.	14,557	L 4	159
New Braunfels, Texas	22,402	K10	168
New Brighton, Minn.	23,269	G 5	149
New Britain, Conn.	73,840	E 2	135
New Britain (isl.), Papua N.G.	148,773	F 6	89
New Brunswick (prov.), Can.	696,403		102
New Brunswick, N.J.	41,442	E 3	156
Newburgh, N.Y.	23,438	C 1	158
New Caledonia & Dependencies	133,233	G 8	89
New Canaan, Conn.	17,931	B 4	135
Newcastle, Austr.	135,207	J 6	86
Newcastle, Ind.	20,056	G 5	140
Newcastle, N. Br.	6,284	E 2	102
New Castle, Pa.	33,621	B 3	164
Newcastle upon Tyne, Eng.	295,800	H 3	11
New City, N.Y.	35,859	B 1	158
New Delhi (cap.), India	301,801	D 3	70
Newfoundland (prov.), Can.	567,681		99
Newfoundland (isl.), Newf.		B 2	99
New Georgia (isl.), Sol. Is.	16,472	F 6	89
New Glasgow, N.S.	10,464	F 3	100
New Guinea (isl.), Pacific		D-E 6	89
New Hampshire (state), U.S.	920,610		155
New Hanover (isl.), Papua N.G.		F 6	89
New Haven, Conn.	126,109	D 3	135
New Iberia, La.	32,766	G 6	144
Newington, Conn.	28,841	E 2	135
New Ireland (isl.), Papua N.G.	65,657	F 6	89
New Jersey (state), U.S.	7,364,823		156
New London, Conn.	28,842	G 3	135
Newmarket, Ont.	29,753	E 3	108
New Mexico (state), U.S.	1,302,981		157
New Milford, Conn.	19,420	B 2	135
New Orleans, La.	557,927	O 4	144
Newport, Ky.	21,587	L 1	143
Newport, R.I.	29,259	J 7	147
Newport Beach, Calif.	62,556	D11	133
Newport News, Va.	144,903	L 6	170
New Providence (isl.), Bah.	135,437	C 1	124
New Rochelle, N.Y.	70,794	J 1	158
New Siberian (isls.), U.S.S.R.		P 2	46
New South Wales (state), Austr.	5,126,217	H 6	86
Newton, Iowa	15,292	H 5	141
Newton, Kans.	16,332	E 3	142
Newton, Mass.	83,622	C 7	147
New Ulm, Minn.	13,755	D 6	149
New Waterford, N.S.	8,808	J 2	100
New Westminster, Br. Col.	38,550	K 3	117
New York, N.Y.	7,071,639	C 2	158
New York (state), U.S.	17,558,072		158
New Zealand	3,175,737	L 7	87
Neyagawa, Japan	254,311	J 7	75
Ngami (lake), Botswana		L 16	57
Nha Trang, Viet.	216,227	F 4	81
Niagara (riv.), N. Amer.		E 4	108
Niagara Falls, N.Y.	71,384	C 4	158
Niagara Falls, Ont.	70,960	E 4	108
Niamey (cap.), Niger	225,314	G 9	54
Nias (isl.), Indon.	356,093	B 5	83
Nicaragua	2,703,000	E 4	122
Nice, France	331,002	G 6	26
Nicobar (isls.), India		G 7	70
Nicosia (cap.), Cyprus	115,718	E 5	64
Niger	5,098,427	H 8	54
Niger (riv.), Africa		G 9	54
Nigeria	82,643,000	H10	54
Niigata, Japan	423,188	J 5	75
Niihau (isl.), Hawaii		A 2	130
Nijmegen, Neth.	148,493	H 5	25
Nikolayev, U.S.S.R.	440,000	D 5	50
Nile (riv.), Africa		N 7	54
Niles, Ill.	30,363	B 5	139
Niles, Ohio	23,088	J 3	161
Nîmes, France	123,914	F 6	26
Ningbo (Ningpo), China	350,000	K 6	77
Nipawin, Sask.	4,376	H 2	113
Nipigon (lake), Ont.		H 5	108
Nipissing (lake), Ont.		E 1	108
Niš, Yugo.	128,231	F 4	43
Nishinomiya, Japan	400,622	H 8	75
Niterói, Braz.	386,185	M 8	93
Niue	3,578	K 7	89
Nizhniy Tagil, U.S.S.R.	398,000	G 4	46
Njazidja (isl.), Comoros		P14	57
Nogales, Ariz.	15,683	E 7	131
Nome, Alaska	2,301	E 1	130
Nordkapp (cape), Nor.		E 1	16
Norfolk, Nebr.	19,449	G 2	153
Norfolk, Va.	266,979	M 7	170
Norfolk I. (terr.), Austr.	2,175	L 5	86
Noril'sk, U.S.S.R.	180,000	J 3	46
Normal, Ill.	35,672	E 3	139
Norman, Okla.	68,020	H 4	162
Norman Wells, N.W.T.	420	D 2	96
Norristown, Pa.	34,684	M 5	164
Norrköping, Sweden	85,244	K 7	16
North (sea), Europe		E 3	6
North (isl.), N.Z.	2,322,989	K 6	86
North Adams, Mass.	18,063	B 2	147
North America	370,000,000		94
Northampton, Eng.	128,290	F 5	11
Northampton, Mass.	29,286	D 3	147
North Attleboro, Mass.	21,095	J 5	147
North Battleford, Sask.	14,030	C 3	113
North Bay, Ont.	51,268	E 1	108
North Bergen, N.J.	47,019	B 2	156
Northbrook, Ill.	30,778	B 5	139
North Brunswick, N.J.	22,220	D 3	156
North Carolina (state), U.S.	5,881,813		159
North Cascades Nat'l Pk., Wash.		D 2	171
North Charleston, S.C.	62,534	G 6	165
North Chicago, Ill.	38,774	B 4	139
North Dakota (state), U.S.	652,717		160
Northern Ireland, U.K.	1,543,000	H 2	15
Northern Territory, Austr.	123,324	E 3	86
Northfield, Minn.	12,562	E 6	149
North Frisian (isls.), Europe		C 1	20
Northglenn, Colo.	29,847	K 3	134
North Korea	17,914,000		74
North Haven, Conn.	22,080	D 3	135
North Highlands, Calif.	37,825	B 8	133
North Las Vegas, Nev.	42,739	F 6	154
North Little Rock, Ark.	64,288	F 4	132
North Magnetic Pole, N.W.T.		M 3	96
North Miami, Fla.	42,566	B 4	136
North Miami Beach, Fla.	36,553	C 4	136
North Olmsted, Ohio	36,486	G 9	161
North Plainfield, N.J.	19,108	E 2	156
North Platte, Nebr.	24,509	D 3	153
North Platte (riv.), U.S.		F 2	126
Northport, Ala.	14,291	C 4	129
North Providence, R.I.	29,188	J 5	147
North Saskatchewan (riv.), Can.		E-F 5	96
North Tonawanda, N.Y.	35,760	C 4	158
Northumberland (str.), Can.		D 2	96
North Vancouver, Br. Col.	*65,367	K 3	117
North West (cape), Austr.		A 4	86
Northwest Territories, Can.	45,741	E 2	96
Norton Shores, Mich.	22,025	C 5	148
Norwalk, Calif.	85,286	C11	133
Norwalk, Conn.	77,767	B 4	135
Norway	4,092,000		16
Norwegian (sea), Europe		D-E 2	6
Norwich, Conn.	38,074	G 2	135
Norwich, Eng.	119,200	J 5	11
Norwood, Mass.	29,711	B 8	147
Norwood, Ohio	26,342	C 9	161
Nottingham, Eng.	280,300	F 5	11
Nouakchott (cap.), Mauritania	134,986	C 8	54
Nouméa (cap.), New Caledonia	56,078	G 8	89
Nouveau-Québec (crater), Que.		F 1	106
Nova Scotia (prov.), Can.	847,442		100
Novato, Calif.	43,916	H 1	133
Novaya Zemlya (isls.), U.S.S.R.		F 2	46
Novgorod, U.S.S.R.	186,000	D 3	50
Novi, Mich.	22,525	F 6	148
Novi Sad, Yugo.	143,591	D 3	43
Novocherkassk, U.S.S.R.	183,000	F 5	50
Novokuznetsk, U.S.S.R.	541,000	J 4	46
Novomoskovsk, U.S.S.R.	147,000	E 4	50
Novorossiysk, U.S.S.R.	159,000	E 6	50
Novosibirsk, U.S.S.R.	1,312,000	J 4	46
Nubia (lake), Sudan		N 7	54
Nubian (des.), Sudan		N 7	54
Nueces (riv.), Texas		F 9	168
Nuevo Laredo, Mex.	184,622	J 3	119
Nuku'alofa (cap.), Tonga	18,356	J 8	89
Numazu, Japan	199,325	J 6	75
Nunivak (isl.), Alaska		E 3	130
Nuremberg (Nürnberg), W. Ger.	499,060	D 4	20
Nutley, N.J.	28,998	B 2	156
Nuuk (cap.), Greenl.	9,561	C12	4
Nyasa (lake), Africa		N14	57
Nyasaland, see Malawi			
Nyíregyháza, Hung.	108,156	F 3	39

O

	Pop.	Key	Pg.
Oahe (lake), U.S.		G 1	126
Oahu (isl.), Hawaii		B 3	130
Oak Creek, Wis.	16,932	M 2	173
Oak Forest, Ill.	26,096	B 6	139
Oakland, Calif.	339,337	J 2	133
Oakland Park, Fla.	23,035	B 3	136
Oak Lawn, Ill.	60,590	B 6	139
Oak Park, Ill.	54,887	B 5	139
Oak Park, Mich.	31,537	B 6	148
Oak Ridge, Tenn.	27,662	N 2	167
Oakville, Ont.	75,773	E 4	108
Oaxaca de Juárez, Mex.	114,948	L 8	119
Ob' (riv.), U.S.S.R.		G 3	46
Oberammergau, W. Ger.	4,704	D 5	20
Oberhausen, W. Ger.	237,147	B 3	20
Oberlin, Ohio	8,660	F 3	161
Ocala, Fla.	37,170	D 2	136
Ocean (Banaba) (isl.), Kiribati	2,314	G 6	89
Ocean City, N.J.	13,949	D 5	156
Oceanside, Calif.	76,698	H10	133
Oceanside, N.Y.	33,639	B 4	158
Ocmulgee Nat'l Mon., Ga.		F 5	137
Odense, Den.	168,178	D 7	19
Oder (riv.), Europe		L 5	20
Odessa, Texas	90,027	B 6	168
Odessa, U.S.S.R.	1,046,000	D 5	50
Ogaden (reg.), Eth.		P-R10	54
Ogbomosho, Nigeria	432,000	H10	54
Ogden, Utah	64,407	C 2	169
O'Higgins (lake), Chile		F13	93
Ohio (riv.), U.S.		J 3	126
Ohio (state), U.S.	10,797,624		161
Ohrid (lake), Europe		E 5	43
Oise (riv.), France		E 3	26
Oita, Japan	320,237	E 7	75
Ojos del Salado (mt.), S. Amer.		G 9	93
Okayama, Japan	513,471	F 6	75
Okazaki, Japan	234,510	H 6	75
Okeechobee (lake), Fla.		F 5	136
Okefenokee (swamp), U.S.		H 9	137
Okhotsk (sea), U.S.S.R.		P 4	46
Okinawa (isl.), Japan		N 6	75
Oklahoma (state), U.S.	3,025,290		162
Oklahoma City (cap.), Okla.	403,136	G 4	162
Okmulgee, Okla.	16,263	K 3	162
Öland (isl.), Sweden		K 8	16
Olathe, Kans.	37,258	H 3	142
Oldenburg, W. Ger.	134,706	C 2	20
Old Bridge, N.J.	51,515	E 3	156
Olds, Alta.	4,813	D 4	114
Olean, N.Y.	18,207	D 6	158
Olinda, Braz.	266,392	N 5	90
Olsztyn, Pol.	94,119	E 2	45
Olympia (cap.), Wash.	27,447	C 3	171
Olympic Nat'l Pk., Wash.		B 3	171
Olympus (mt.), Greece		F 5	43
Omaha (beach), France		C 3	26
Omaha, Nebr.	313,911	J 3	153
Oman	891,000	G 5	60
Oman (gulf), Asia		G 5	60
Omdurman, Sudan	299,000	N 8	54
Omiya, Japan	327,698	O 2	75
Omsk, U.S.S.R.	1,014,000	H 4	46
Omuta, Japan	165,969	E 7	75
Onega (lake), U.S.S.R.		E 2	50
Onitsha, Nigeria	220,000	H10	54
Ontario, Calif.	88,820	D10	133
Ontario (prov.), Can.	8,625,107		107,108
Ontario (lake), N. Amer.		D-G 3	94
Opelika, Ala.	21,896	H 5	129
Opelousas, La.	18,903	G 5	144
Opole, Pol.	86,510	C 3	45
Oporto, see Porto, Port.			
Oradea, Rom.	175,400	E 2	43
Oran, Alg.	491,000	F 4	54
Orange (riv.), Africa		K17	57
Orange, Austr.	27,626	H 6	86
Orange, Calif.	91,450	D11	133
Orange, N.J.	31,136	B 2	156
Orange, Texas	23,628	L 7	168
Orange Free State (prov.), S. Africa		M17	57
Orangeville, Ont.	13,740	D 4	108
Ordos (reg.), China		G 4	77
Ordzhonikidze, U.S.S.R.	279,000	E 6	50
Örebro, Sweden	117,877	J 7	16
Oregon (state), U.S.	2,633,149		163
Oregon Caves Nat'l Mon., Oreg.		D 5	163
Oregon City, Oreg.	14,673	B 2	163
Oregon Dunes Nat'l Rec. Area, Oreg.		C 4	163
Orel, U.S.S.R.	305,000	E 4	50
Orem, Utah	52,399	C 3	169
Orenburg, U.S.S.R.	459,000	J 4	50
Orillia, Ont.	23,955	E 3	108
Orinoco (riv.), S. Amer.		G 2	90
Orissa (state), India		E-F 4-5	70
Orlando, Fla.	128,291	E 3	136
Orléans, France	88,503	D 3	26

	Pop.	Key	Pg.
Qattâra (depr.), Egypt		M 6	54
Qazvin, Iran	138,527	F 2	68
Qeqertarsuaq, Greenl.	1,012	C 12	4
Qilian Shan (range), China		E 4	77
Qingdao (Tsingtao), China	1,900,000	K 4	77
Qinghai Hu (lake), China		E 4	77
Qiqihar, China	1,500,000	K 2	77
Qiryat Shemona, Isr.	15,200	C 1	67
Qom (Qum), Iran	246,831	G 3	68
Qonduz, Afghan.	107,191	B 1	70
Qu'Appelle (riv.), Sask.		J 5	113
Québec (prov.), Can.	6,438,403		105, 106
Québec (cap.), Que.	*576,075	H 3	105
Queen Charlotte (isls.), Br. Col.		B 3	117
Queens (borough), N.Y.	1,891,325	D 2	158
Queensland (state), Austr.	2,295,123	G 4	86
Quesnel, Br. Col.	8,240	F 4	117
Quetico Prov. Pk., Ont.		G 5	108
Quetta, Pak.	156,000	B 2	70
Quincy, Ill.	42,554	B 4	139
Quincy, Mass.	84,743	D 7	147
Qui Nhon, Viet.	213,757	F 4	81
Quito (cap.), Ecua.	599,828	E 3	90

R

	Pop.	Key	Pg.
Rabat (cap.), Mor.	367,620	E 5	54
Rabaul, Papua N.G.	14,954	F 6	89
Race (cape), Newf.		D 4	99
Racine, Wis.	85,725	M 3	173
Radom, Pol.	158,640	E 3	45
Radville, Sask.	1,012	G 6	113
Rahway, N.J.	26,723	E 2	156
Rainbow Bridge Nat'l Mon., Utah		C 6	169
Rainier (mt.), Wash.		D 4	171
Rainy (lake), N. Amer.		E 2	149
Raipur, India	174,518	E 4	70
Rajahmundry, India	165,912	E 5	70
Rajkot, India	300,612	C 4	70
Raleigh (cap.), N.C.	150,225	H 3	159
Ramat Gan, Isr.	120,900	B 3	67
Rampur, India	161,417	D 3	70
Ranchi, India	175,934	F 4	70
Rancho Cucamonga, Calif.	55,250	E 10	133
Randallstown, Md.	25,927	G 3	146
Randolph, Mass.	28,218	D 8	147
Rangoon (cap.), Burma	1,586,422	C 3	81
Rantoul, Ill.	20,161	E 3	139
Rapa (isl.), Fr. Poly.	398	M 8	89
Rapa Nui (Easter) (isl.), Chile	1,598	Q 8	89
Rapid City, S. Dak.	46,492	C 5	166
Rappahannock (riv.), Va.		L 4	170
Raritan (riv.), N.J.		D 2	156
Rarotonga (isl.), Cook Is.	9,477	K 8	89
Ras Dashan (mt.), Eth.		O 9	54
Rasht, Iran	187,203	F 2	68
Ras Tanura, Saudi Arabia		F 4	60
Ravenna, Italy	75,153	D 2	32
Ravensburg, W. Ger.	42,725	C 5	20
Ravi (riv.), Asia		C 2	70
Rawalpindi, Pak.	615,392	C 2	70
Rawlins, Wyo.	11,547	E 4	174
Ray (cape), Newf.		A 4	99
Raytown, Mo.	31,759	P 6	151
Reading, Eng.	131,200	G 8	11
Reading, Pa.	78,686	L 5	164
Real (mts.), S. Amer.		G 7	90
Recife, Braz.	1,184,215	O 5	90
Red (sea)		C5-6	60
Red (riv.), Asia		E 2	81
Red (riv.), U.S.		H 4	126
Red Deer, Alta.	46,393	D 3	114
Red Deer (riv.), Alta.		D 4	114
Redding, Calif.	41,995	C 3	133
Redlands, Calif.	43,619	H 9	133
Redmond, Wash.	23,318	B 1	171
Redondo Beach, Calif.	57,102	B 11	133
Red River of the North (riv.), U.S.		A 2	96
Red Volta (riv.), Africa		F 9	54
Redwood City, Calif.	54,965	J 3	133
Redwood Nat'l Pk., Calif.		A 2	133
Ree (lake), Ire.		F 5	15
Regensburg, W. Ger.	131,886	E 4	20
Reggio di Calabria, Italy	110,291	E 5	32
Reggio nell'Emilia, Italy	102,337	C 2	32
Regina (cap.), Sask.	*164,313	G 5	113
Registan (des.), Afghan.		A-B 2	70
Reims, France	77,320	E 3	26
Reindeer (lake), Can.		N 3	96
Renfrew, Ont.	8,283	H 2	108
Rennes, France	194,094	C 3	26
Reno, Nev.	100,756	B 3	154
Renton, Wash.	30,612	B 2	171
Republican (riv.), U.S.		F 2	126
Resolution (isl.), N.W.T.		K 3	96
Réunion	491,000	R 20	57
Reutlingen, W. Ger.	95,289	C 4	20
Revelstoke, Br. Col.	5,544	J 5	117
Revere, Mass.	42,423	D 6	147
Revillagigedo (isls.), Mex.		C 7	119
Rexburg, Idaho	11,559	G 6	138
Reykjavík (cap.), Iceland	81,693	B 1	19
Reynosa, Mex.	206,500	K 3	119
Rhaetian Alps (mts.), Europe		J 3	37
Rhine (riv.), Europe		B 3	20
Rhode Island (state), U.S.	947,154		147
Rhodope (mts.), Europe		G 5	43
Rhône (riv.), Europe		F 5	26
Rialto, Calif.	37,474	E 10	133
Riau (arch.), Indon.	483,230	C 5	83
Ribeirão Preto, Braz.	300,704	L 8	90
Richardson, Texas	72,496	G 2	168
Richfield, Minn.	37,851	G 6	149
Richibucto, N. Br.	1,722	E 2	102
Richland, Wash.	33,578	F 4	171
Richmond, Calif.	74,676	J 1	133
Richmond, Ind.	41,349	H 5	140
Richmond, Ky.	21,705	J 5	143
Richmond (cap.), Va.	219,214	K 5	170
Rideau (riv.), Ont.		J 3	108
Riding Mtn. Nat'l Pk., Man.		B 4	110
Ridgefield, Conn.	20,120	B 3	135
Ridgewood, N.J.	25,208	B 1	156
Riga, U.S.S.R.	835,000	C 2	51
Rijeka, Yugo.	128,883	B 3	43
Rimini, Italy	101,579	D 2	32
Rimouski, Que.	29,120	J 1	105
Rio de Janeiro, Braz.	*9,018,637	M 8	93
Rio Grande (riv.), N. Amer.		H 7	94
Río Muni (reg.), Equat. Guin.		J 11	54
Riverside, Calif.	170,591	E 11	133
Riviera (reg.), Europe		G 6	26
Riviera Beach, Fla.	26,489	G 5	136
Rivière-du-Loup, Que.	13,459	H 2	105
Riyadh (cap.), Saudi Arabia	666,840	E 5	60
Road Town (cap.), V.I. (Br.)	2,200	H 1	124
Roanoke (isl.), N.C.		O 3	159
Roanoke, Va.	100,220	D 6	170
Roanoke Rapids, N.C.	14,702	K 2	159
Roberval, Que.	11,429	E 1	105
Rochester, Minn.	57,890	F 6	149
Rochester, N.H.	21,560	E 5	155
Rochester, N.Y.	241,741	E 4	158
Rockall (isl.), Scot.		C 3	6
Rockford, Ill.	139,712	D 1	139
Rock Hill, S.C.	35,344	E 2	165
Rock Island, Ill.	46,928	C 2	139
Rock Springs, Wyo.	19,458	C 4	174
Rockville, Md.	43,811	F 4	146
Rockville Centre, N.Y.	25,412	B 4	158
Rocky (mts.), N. Amer.		F-G 4	94
Rocky Mount, N.C.	41,283	K 3	159
Rocky Mountain House, Alta.	4,698	C 3	114
Rocky Mountain Nat'l Pk., Colo.		H 2	134
Rogers, Ark.	17,429	B 1	132
Romania	22,048,305		43
Rome, Ga..	29,654	B 2	137
Rome (cap.), Italy	2,535,018	F 6	32
Rome, N.Y.	43,826	J 4	158
Roosevelt (isl.), Antarc.		A 10	5
Roosevelt (riv.), Braz.		H 5	90
Rosa (mt.), Europe		A 1	32
Rosario, Arg.	*954,606	H 10	93
Roseau (cap.), Dominica	9,968	G 4	124
Roseburg, Oreg.	16,644	D 4	163
Rosemead, Calif.	42,604	C 10	133
Rosetown, Sask.	2,664	D 4	113
Rosetta, Egypt	42,962	B 3	60
Roseville, Mich.	54,311	B 6	148
Roseville, Minn.	35,820	G 5	149
Ross (sea), Antarc.		B 10	5
Ross Lake Nat'l Rec. Area, Wash.		E 2	171
Rostock, E. Ger.	210,167	E 1	20
Rostov-na-Donu, U.S.S.R.	934,000	F 5	50
Roswell, Ga.	23,337	D 2	137
Roswell, N. Mex.	39,676	E 5	157
Rotterdam, Neth.	614,767	E 5	25
Rotuma (isl.), Fiji	2,805	H 7	89
Rouen, France	113,536	D 3	26
Rouyn, Que.	17,224	B 3	106
Rovno, U.S.S.R.	179,000	C 4	50
Roy, Utah	19,694	C 2	169
Royal Gorge (canyon), Colo.		J 6	134
Royal Oak, Mich.	70,893	B 6	148
Rub' al Khali (des.), Asia		F 5	60
Ruda Śląska, Pol.	142,407	B 4	45
Rufus Woods (lake), Wash.		F 2	171
Rügen (isl.), E. Ger.		E 1	20
Ruhr (riv.), W. Ger.		B 3	20
Rukwa (lake), Tanz.		N 13	57
Rum (cay), Bah.		C 2	124
Rum (Rhum) (isl.), Scot.		B 3	13
Rupert (riv.), Que.		B 2	106
Ruse, Bulg.	160,351	H 4	43
Russell Cave Nat'l Mon., Ala.		G 1	129
Russian S.F.S.R., U.S.S.R.	137,551,000	D-S 4	46
Ruston, La.	20,585	E 1	144
Rutland, Vt.	18,436	B 4	155
Rwanda	4,819,317	N 12	57
Ryazan', U.S.S.R.	453,000	E 4	50
Rybinsk (Andropov), U.S.S.R.	239,000	E 3	50
Ryde, Austr.	88,948	K 4	86
Ryukyu (isls.), Japan		L 7	75

S

	Pop.	Key	Pg.
Saanich, Br. Col.	*78,710	K 3	117
Saar (riv.), Europe		B 4	20
Saarbrücken, W. Ger.	205,336	B 4	20
Saaremaa (isl.), U.S.S.R.		B 1	51
Saarland (state), W. Ger.		B 4	20
Sabadell, Spain	148,273	H 2	31
Sabah (state), Malaysia	1,002,608	F 4	83
Sabine (riv.), U.S.		H 4	126
Sable (cape), Fla.		E 6	136
Sable (cape), N.S.		C 5	100
Sable (isl.), N.S.		J 5	100
Sacajawea (lake), Wash.		G 4	171
Sackville, N. Br.	5,654	F 3	102
Sacramento (cap.), Calif.	275,741	B 8	133
Sacramento (riv.), Calif.		D 5	133
Sacramento (mts.), N. Mex.		D 6	157
Saga, Japan	152,258	E 7	75
Sagamihara, Japan	377,398	O 2	75
Sagamore Hill Nat'l Hist. Site, N.Y.		B 2	158
Saginaw, Mich.	77,508	K 2	148
Saguaro Nat'l Mon., Ariz.		E 6	131
Saguenay (riv.), Que.		G 1	105
Sahara (des.), Africa		E-M 7	54
Saharanpur, India	225,396	D 3	70
Saigon (Ho Chi Minh City), Viet.	*3,419,678	E 5	81
St. Albert, Alta.	31,996	D 3	114
St. Andrews, N. Br.	1,760	C 3	102
St. Augustine, Fla.	11,985	E 2	136
St. Catharines, Ont.	124,018	E 4	108
St. Charles, Mo.	37,379	N 1	151
St. Christopher (isl.), St. Chris. & Nevis		F 3	124
St. Christopher & Nevis	44,404	F 3	124
St. Clair (lake), N. Amer.		K 2	126
St. Clair Shores, Mich.	76,210	B 6	148
St. Cloud, Minn.	42,566	D 5	149
St. Croix (isl.), V.I. (U.S.)	49,725	H 2	124
St. Croix (riv.), U.S.		J 5	145
St. Croix Isl. Nat'l Mon., Maine		J 5	145
St-Denis, France	95,808	B 1	26
St-Denis (cap.), Réunion	80,075	P 19	57
Ste-Agathe-des-Monts, Que.	5,641	C 3	105
Ste-Anne-de-Beaupré, Que.	3,292	F 2	105
Ste-Foy, Que.	68,883	H 3	105
Ste-Geneviève, Que.	2,573	H 4	105
St. Elias (mt.), N. Amer.		L 2	130
Ste-Thérèse, Que.	18,750	H 4	105
St-Étienne, France	218,289	F 5	26
St-Eustache, Que.	29,716	H 4	105
St. George (cape), Newf.		A 3	99
St. George's (chan.), Europe		B 5	11
St. George's (cap.), Grenada	6,463	F 5	124
St. Gotthard (tunnel), Switz.		G 3	37
St. Helena & Dependencies	5,147		1
St. Helens (mt.), Wash.		C 4	171
St. Helier (cap.), Jersey, Chan. Is.	28,135	E 8	11
St-Hyacinthe, Que.	38,246	D 4	105
St-Jean (lake), Que.		E 1	105
St-Jerôme, Que.	25,123	H 4	105
St. John, N. Br.	80,521	E 3	102
St. John (riv.), N. Amer.		N 1	126
St. John (isl.), V.I. (U.S.)	2,472	H 1	124
St. Johns (cap.), Antigua & Barbuda	21,814	G 3	124
St. Johns (riv.), Fla.		E 2	136
St. John's (cap.), Newf.	*154,820	D 4	99
St. Joseph, Mo.	76,691	C 3	151
St-Joseph-de-Sorel, Que.	2,545	D 3	105
St. Kilda, Austr.	49,366	K 2	86
St. Kitts, see St. Christopher			
St-Lambert, Que.	20,557	J 4	105
St-Laurent, Que.	65,900	H 4	105
St. Lawrence (isl.), Alaska		D 2	130
St. Lawrence (gulf), Can.		K 6	96
St. Lawrence (riv.), N. Amer.		K 6	94
St-Léonard, Que.	79,429	H 4	105
St. Louis, Mo.	453,085	R 3	151
St. Louis Park, Minn.	42,931	G 5	149
St. Lucia	115,783	G 4	124
St-Maurice (riv.), Que.		E 2	105
St-Nazaire, France	65,228	B 4	26
St. Paul (cap.), Minn.	270,230	G 6	149
St. Peter Port (cap.), Guernsey, Chan. Is.	16,303	E 8	11
St. Petersburg, Fla.	238,647	B 3	136
St. Pierre & Miquelon	6,041	B 4	99
St. Simons (isl.), Ga.		K 8	137
St. Stephen, N. Br.	5,120	C 3	102
St. Thomas, Ont.	28,165	C 5	108
St. Thomas (isl.), V.I. (U.S.)	44,572	G 11	124
St. Vincent & the Grenadines	124,000	G 4	124
Saipan (isl.), N. Marianas	14,549	E 4	89
Sakai, Japan	750,688	J 8	75
Sakakawea (lake), N. Dak.		G 5	160
Sakhalin (isl.), U.S.S.R.		P 4	46
Salamanca, Spain	125,132	D 2	31
Sala y Gómez (isl.), Chile		Q 8	89
Salem, India	308,716	D 6	70
Salem, Mass.	38,220	E 5	147
Salem, N.H.	24,124	E 6	155
Salem (cap.), Oreg.	89,233	A 3	163
Salem, Va.	23,958	D 6	170
Salem Maritime Nat'l Hist. Site, Mass.		E 5	147
Salerno, Italy	146,534	E 4	32
Salina, Kans.	41,843	E 3	142
Salinas, Calif	80,479	D 7	133
Salinas Nat'l Mon., N. Mex.		C 4	157
Salisbury, Austr.	86,451	E 7	86
Salisbury, Md.	16,429	M 7	146
Salisbury (Harare) (cap.), Zim.	601,000	N 15	57
Salmon (riv.), Idaho		B 4	138
Salta, Arg.	260,323	G 8	93
Saltillo, Mex.	200,712	J 4	119
Salt Lake City (cap.), Utah	163,697	C 3	169
Salton Sea (lake), Calif.		K 10	133
Saluda (riv.), S.C.		D 3	165
Salvador, Braz.	1,496,276	N 6	90
Salween (riv.), Asia		L 8	58
Salzburg, Austria	213,430	B 3	39
Samar (isl.), Phil.		H 3	83
Samaria (reg.), Jordan		C 3	67
Samarinda, Indon.	264,718	F 6	83
Samarkand, U.S.S.R.	477,000	G 6	46
Sámos (isl.), Greece		H 7	43
Samothráki (isl.), Greece		G 5	43
Samsun, Turkey	168,478	F 2	64
San'a (cap.), Yemen Arab Rep.	134,588	D 6	60
San Andrés (isl.), Col.		D 1	90
San Angelo, Texas	73,240	D 6	168
San Antonio, Texas	786,023	J 11	168
San Bernardino, Calif.	118,794	E 10	133
San Bernardino (mts.), Calif.		J 10	133
San Blas (gulf), Pan.		H 6	122
San Bruno, Calif.	35,417	J 2	133
San Clemente, Calif.	27,325	H 10	133
San Clemente (isl.), Calif.		G 11	133
San Cristobal (isl.), Solomon Is.	11,212	G 7	89
San Cristóbal, Ven.	151,717	F 2	90
Sandia (peak), N. Mex.		C 3	157
San Diego, Calif.	875,538	H 11	133
Sand Springs, Okla.	13,246	K 2	162
Sandusky, Ohio	31,360	E 3	161
Sandy, Utah	52,210	C 3	169
Sandy Hook (spit), N.J.		F 3	156
San Fernando, Calif.	17,731	C 10	133
Sanford, Fla.	23,176	E 3	136
Sanford, Maine	18,020	B 9	145
Sanford, N.C.	14,773	G 4	159
San Francisco, Calif.	678,974	H 2	133
San Francisco (bay), Calif.		J 2	133
San Gabriel, Calif.	30,072	C 10	133
Sangre de Cristo (mts.), U.S.		H 6	134
San Joaquin (riv.), Calif.		E 6	133
San Jose, Calif.	629,546	L 3	133
San José (cap.), C. Rica	215,441	F 5	122
San Juan, Arg.	*290,479	G 10	93
San Juan (cap.), P. Rico	424,600	G 1	124
San Juan (riv.), U.S.		E 3	126
San Juan Island Nat'l Hist. Pk., Wash.		B 2	171
San Leandro, Calif.	63,952	J 2	133
San Lucas (cape), Mex.		E 5	119
San Luis Obispo, Calif.	34,252	E 8	133
San Luis Potosí, Mex.	271,123	J 5	119
San Marcos, Texas	23,420	F 8	168
San Marino	19,149	D 3	32
San Mateo, Calif.	77,640	J 3	133
San Miguel de Tucumán, Arg.	*496,914	H 9	93
San Nicolas (isl.), Calif.		F 10	133

MAP PROJECTIONS

by Erwin Raisz

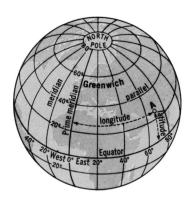

Our earth is rotating around its *axis* once a day. The two end points of its axis are the *poles;* the line circling the earth midway between the poles is the *equator.* The arc from either of the poles to the equator is divided into 90 *degrees.* The distance, expressed in degrees, from the equator to any point is its *latitude* and circles of equal latitude are the *parallels.* On maps it is customary to show parallels of evenly-spaced degrees such as every fifth or every tenth.

The equator is divided into 360 degrees. Lines circling from pole to pole through the degree points on the equator are called *meridians.* They are all equal in length but by international agreement the meridian passing through the Greenwich Observatory in London has been chosen as *prime meridian.* The distance, expressed in degrees, from the prime meridian to any point is its *longitude.* While meridians are all equal in length, parallels become shorter and shorter as they approach the poles. Whereas one degree of latitude represents everywhere approximately 69 miles, one degree of longitude varies from 69 miles at the equator to nothing at the poles.

Each degree is divided into 60 minutes and each minute into 60 seconds. One minute of latitude equals a nautical mile.

The map is flat but the earth is nearly spherical. Neither a rubber ball nor any part of a rubber ball may be flattened without stretching or tearing unless the part is very small. To present the curved surface of the earth on a flat map is not difficult as long as the areas under consideration are small, but the mapping of countries, continents, or the whole earth requires some kind of *projection.* Any regular set of parallels and meridians upon which a map can be drawn makes a map projection. Many systems are used.

In any projection only the parallels or the meridians or some other set of lines can be *true* (the same length as on the globe of corresponding scale); all other lines are too long or too short. Only on a globe is it possible to have both the parallels and the meridians true. The scale given on a flat map cannot be true everywhere. The construction of the various projections begins usually with laying out the parallels or meridians which have true lengths.

RECTANGULAR PROJECTION — This is a set of evenly-placed meridians and horizontal parallels. The central or *standard parallel* and all meridians are true. All other parallels are either too long or too short. The projection is used for simple maps of small areas, as city plans, etc.

MERCATOR PROJECTION — In this projection the meridians are evenly-spaced vertical lines. The parallels are horizontal, spaced so that their length has the same relation to the meridians as on a globe. As the meridians converge at higher latitudes on the globe, while on the map they do not, the parallels have to be drawn also farther and farther apart to maintain the correct relationship. When every very small area has the same shape as on a globe we call the projection *conformal.* The most interesting quality of this projection is that all *compass directions* appear as straight lines. For this reason it is generally used for marine charts. It is also frequently used for world maps in spite of the fact that the high latitudes are very much exaggerated in size. Only the equator is true to scale; all other parallels and meridians are too long. The Mercator projection did *not* derive from projecting a globe upon a cylinder.

SINUSOIDAL PROJECTION — The parallels are truly-spaced horizontal lines. They are divided truly and the connecting curves make the meridians. It does not make a good world map because the outer regions are distorted, but the

Rectangular Projection

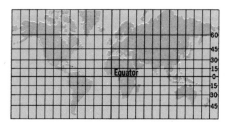

Mercator Projection

Sinusoidal Projection

Mollweide Projection

central portion is good and this part is often used for maps of Africa and South America. Every part of the map has the same area as the corresponding area on the globe. It is an *equal-area* projection.

MOLLWEIDE PROJECTION — The meridians are equally-spaced ellipses; the parallels are horizontal lines spaced so that every belt of latitude should have the same area as on a globe. This projection is popular for world maps, especially in European atlases.

GOODE'S INTERRUPTED PROJECTIONS—Only the good central part of the Mollweide or sinusoidal (or both) projection is used and the oceans are cut. This makes an equal-area map with little distortion of shape. It is commonly used for world maps.

Goode's Interrupted Projection

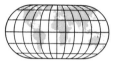

Eckert Projection

ECKERT PROJECTIONS — These are similar to the sinusoidal or the Mollweide projections, but the poles are shown as lines half the length of the equator. There are several variants; the meridians are either sine curves or ellipses; the parallels are horizontal and spaced either evenly or so as to make the projection equal area. Their use for world maps is increasing. The figure shows the elliptical equal-area variant.

CONIC PROJECTION — The original idea of the conic projection is that of capping the globe by a cone upon which both the parallels and meridians are projected from the center of the globe. The cone is then cut open and laid flat. A cone can be made tangent to any chosen *standard parallel*.

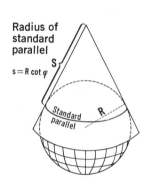

Radius of standard parallel

$s = R \cot \varphi$

Standard parallel

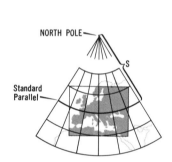

NORTH POLE

Standard Parallel

Conic Projection

The actually-used conic projection is a modification of this idea. The radius of the standard parallel is obtained as above. The meridians are straight radiating lines spaced truly on the standard parallel. The parallels are concentric circles spaced at true distances. All parallels except the standard are too long. The projection is used for maps of countries in middle latitudes, as it presents good shapes with small scale error.

There are several variants: The use of *two standard parallels*, one near the top, the other near the bottom of the map, reduces the scale error. In the *Albers projection* the parallels are spaced unevenly, to make the projection equal-area. This is a good projection for the United States. In the *Lambert conformal conic projection* the parallels are spaced so that any small quadrangle of the grid should have the same shape as on the globe. This is the best projection for air-navigation charts as it has relatively straight azimuths.

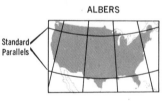

ALBERS

Standard Parallels

Albers Projection

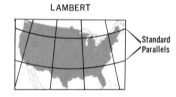

LAMBERT

Standard Parallels

Lambert Conformal Conic Projection

An *azimuth* is a great-circle direction reckoned clockwise from north. A *great-circle direction* points to a place along the shortest line on the earth's surface. This is not the same as compass direction. The center of a great circle is the center of the globe.

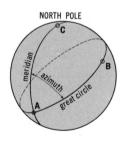

NORTH POLE

meridian azimuth great circle

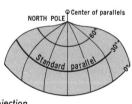

Center of parallels
NORTH POLE
Standard parallel

Bonne Projection

BONNE PROJECTION — The parallels are laid out exactly as in the conic projection. All parallels are divided truly and the connecting curves make the meridians. It is an equal-area projection. It is used for maps of the northern continents, as Asia, Europe, and North America.

POLYCONIC PROJECTION — The central meridian is divided truly. The parallels are non-concentric circles, the radii of which are obtained by drawing tangents to the globe as though the globe were covered by several cones rather than by only one. Each parallel is divided truly and the connecting curves make the meridians. All meridians except the central one are too long. This projection is used for large-scale topographic sheets — less often for countries or continents.

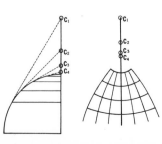

Polyconic Projection

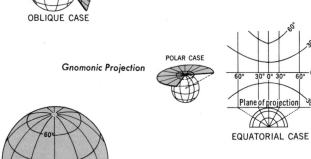

POLAR CASE

Plane of projection

EQUATORIAL CASE

eyepoint   axis   center of projection

rays

Plane of projection

OBLIQUE CASE

center

The Azimuthal Projections

THE AZIMUTHAL PROJECTIONS — In this group a part of the globe is projected from an eyepoint onto a plane. The eyepoint can be at different distances, making different projections. The plane of projection can be tangent at the equator, at a pole, or at any other point on which we want to focus attention. The most important quality of all azimuthal projections is that they show every point at its true direction (azimuth) from the center point, and all points equally distant from the center point will be equally distant on the map also.

GNOMONIC PROJECTION — This projection has the eyepoint at the center of the globe. Only the central part is good; the outer regions are badly distorted. Yet the projection has one important quality, all great circles being shown as straight lines. For this reason it is used for laying out the routes for long range flying or trans-oceanic navigation.

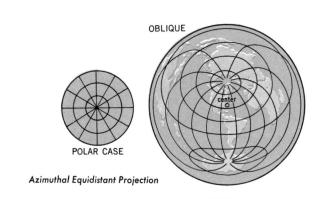

POLAR CASE

Gnomonic Projection

EQUATORIAL CASE

Plane of projection

60°   30° 0° 30°   60° 0°

30°

60°   30° 0° 30°   60°

30°

60°
30°
center
0°
30°

Orthographic Projection

ORTHOGRAPHIC PROJECTION — This projection has the eyepoint at infinite distance and the projecting rays are parallel. The polar or equatorial varieties are rare but the oblique case became very popular on account of its visual quality. It looks like a picture of a globe. Although the distortion on the peripheries is extreme, we see it correctly because the eye perceives it not as a map but as a picture of a three-dimensional globe. Obviously only a hemisphere (half globe) can be shown.

Some azimuthal projections do not derive from the actual process of projecting from an eyepoint, but are arrived at by other means:

OBLIQUE

center

POLAR CASE

Azimuthal Equidistant Projection

AZIMUTHAL EQUIDISTANT PROJECTION — This is the only projection in which every point is shown both at true great-circle direction and at true distance from the center point, but all other directions and distances are distorted. The principle of the projection can best be understood from the polar case. Most polar maps are in this projection. The oblique case is used for radio direction finding, for earthquake research, and in long-distance flying. A separate map has to be constructed for each central point selected.

LAMBERT AZIMUTHAL EQUAL-AREA PROJECTION—The construction of this projection can best be understood from the polar case. All three cases are widely used. It makes a good polar map and it is often extended to include the southern continents. It is the most common projection used for maps of the Eastern and Western Hemispheres, and it is a good projection for continents as it shows correct areas with relatively little distortion of shape. Most of the continent maps in this atlas are in this projection.

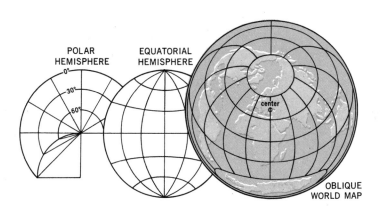

POLAR HEMISPHERE

EQUATORIAL HEMISPHERE

0°
30°
60°

center

OBLIQUE WORLD MAP

Lambert Azimuthal Equal-Area Projection

IN THIS ATLAS, on almost all maps, parallels and meridians have been marked because they are useful for the following:

(a) They show the north-south and east-west directions which appear on many maps at oblique angles especially near the margins.

(b) With the help of parallels and meridians every place can be exactly located; for instance, New York City is at 41° N and 74° W on any map.

(c) They help to measure distances even in the distorted parts of the map. The scale given on each map is true only along certain lines which are specified in the foregoing discussion for each projection. One degree of latitude equals nearly 69 statute miles or 60 nautical miles. The length of one degree of longitude varies (1° long. = 1° lat. × cos lat.).

AIR DISTANCES BETWEEN MAJOR WORLD CITIES
SOURCE: USAF Aeronautical Chart and Information Center (in statute miles)

	Bangkok	Berlin	Cairo	Cape Town	Caracas	Chicago	Hong Kong	Honolulu	Istanbul	Lima	London	Madrid	Melbourne
Accra	6,850	3,330	2,672	2,974	4,576	5,837	7,615	10,052	3,039	5,421	3,169	2,412	9,325
Amsterdam	5,707	360	2,015	5,997	4,883	4,118	5,772	7,254	1,372	6,538	222	921	10,286
Anchorage	6,022	4,545	6,116	10,478	5,353	2,858	5,073	2,778	5,388	6,385	4,491	5,181	7,729
Athens	4,930	1,121	671	4,957	5,815	5,447	5,316	8,353	352	7,312	1,488	1,474	9,297
Auckland	4,645	9,995	8,825	6,574	9,620	9,507	4,625	5,346	9,203	7,989	10,570	10,884	1,610
Baghdad	3,756	2,029	798	4,924	7,020	6,430	4,260	8,399	1,006	8,487	2,547	2,675	8,105
Bangkok	—	5,351	4,521	6,301	10,558	8,569	1,076	6,610	4,648	12,241	5,929	6,334	4,579
Beirut	4,272	1,689	341	4,794	6,520	6,097	4,756	8,536	614	7,972	2,151	2,190	8,579
Belgrade	5,073	623	1,147	5,419	5,587	5,000	5,327	7,882	500	7,169	1,053	1,263	9,578
Berlin	5,351	—	1,768	5,958	5,242	4,415	5,443	7,323	1,075	6,893	580	1,162	9,929
Bombay	1,870	3,915	2,717	5,103	9,034	8,066	2,679	8,036	3,000	10,389	4,478	4,689	6,101
Buenos Aires	10,490	7,395	7,360	4,285	3,155	5,582	11,478	7,554	7,608	1,945	6,907	6,236	7,219
Cairo	4,521	1,768	—	4,510	6,337	6,116	5,057	8,818	741	7,725	2,158	2,069	8,700
Cape Town	6,301	5,958	4,510	—	6,361	8,489	7,377	11,534	5,204	6,074	5,988	5,306	6,428
Caracas	10,558	5,242	6,337	6,361	—	2,500	10,171	6,024	6,050	1,699	4,662	4,351	9,703
Chicago	8,569	4,415	6,116	8,489	2,500	—	7,797	4,256	5,485	3,772	3,960	4,192	9,667
Copenhagen	5,361	222	1,964	6,179	5,215	4,263	5,392	7,101	1,252	6,886	595	1,289	9,936
Denver	8,409	5,092	6,846	9,331	3,078	920	7,476	3,346	6,164	3,986	4,701	5,028	8,755
Frankfurt	5,305	50	1,730	5,944	5,290	4,460	5,403	7,341	1,032	6,940	628	1,193	9,882
Helsinki	4,903	689	2,069	6,490	5,658	4,442	4,867	6,818	1,330	7,349	1,135	1,835	9,448
Hong Kong	1,076	5,443	5,057	7,377	10,171	7,797	—	5,557	4,989	11,415	5,986	6,556	4,605
Honolulu	6,610	7,323	8,818	11,534	6,024	4,256	5,557	—	8,118	5,944	7,241	7,874	5,501
Houston	9,261	5,337	7,005	8,608	2,262	942	8,349	3,902	6,400	3,123	4,860	5,014	8,979
Istanbul	4,648	1,075	741	5,204	6,050	5,485	4,989	8,118	—	7,593	1,551	1,701	9,100
Karachi	2,305	3,365	2,222	5,153	8,502	7,564	2,977	8,059	2,457	9,943	3,928	4,152	6,646
Keflavik	6,300	1,505	3,267	7,107	4,269	2,942	6,044	6,085	2,578	5,965	1,188	1,802	10,552
Kinshasa	5,974	3,916	2,618	2,047	5,752	7,085	6,904	11,178	3,241	6,322	3,951	3,305	8,112
Leningrad	4,718	826	2,034	6,500	5,843	4,589	4,687	6,816	1,306	7,534	1,307	1,985	9,263
Lima	12,241	6,893	7,725	6,074	1,699	3,772	11,415	5,944	7,593	—	6,316	5,907	8,052
Lisbon	6,651	1,442	2,352	5,301	4,040	4,001	6,862	7,835	2,015	5,591	989	317	11,049
London	5,929	580	2,158	5,988	4,662	3,960	5,986	7,241	1,551	6,316	—	786	10,508
Madrid	6,334	1,162	2,069	5,306	4,351	4,192	6,556	7,874	1,701	5,907	786	—	10,766
Melbourne	4,579	9,929	8,700	6,428	9,703	9,667	4,605	5,501	9,100	8,052	10,508	10,766	—
Mexico City	9,793	6,054	7,677	8,516	2,234	1,688	8,789	3,791	7,106	2,635	5,558	5,642	8,420
Montreal	8,337	3,740	5,403	7,920	2,443	746	7,736	4,919	4,798	3,967	3,256	3,449	10,390
Moscow	4,394	1,001	1,770	6,277	6,176	4,984	4,443	7,049	1,087	7,855	1,556	2,140	8,965
Nairobi	4,481	3,947	2,217	2,543	7,179	8,012	5,447	10,740	2,957	7,821	4,229	3,840	7,159
New Delhi	1,812	3,598	2,752	5,769	8,837	7,486	2,339	7,413	2,837	10,430	4,178	4,528	6,340
New York City	8,669	3,980	5,598	7,801	2,124	714	8,061	4,969	5,022	3,635	3,473	3,596	10,352
Oslo	5,395	523	2,243	6,477	5,167	4,050	5,342	6,801	1,518	6,857	-718	1,485	9,934
Panama City	10,871	5,856	7,118	7,021	867	2,321	10,089	5,254	6,756	1,454	5,285	5,081	9,027
Paris	5,877	549	1,973	5,782	4,735	4,145	5,992	7,452	1,400	6,367	215	652	10,442
Peking	2,027	4,600	4,687	8,034	8,978	6,625	1,195	5,084	4,407	10,365	5,089	5,759	5,632
Rabat	6,652	1,623	2,230	4,954	4,111	4,282	6,954	8,177	2,008	5,590	1,254	474	10,856
Rio de Janeiro	9,987	6,207	6,153	3,773	2,805	5,288	11,002	8,295	6,378	2,351	5,751	5,045	8,218
Rome	5,493	735	1,305	5,231	5,198	4,823	5,773	8,040	853	6,748	892	849	9,940
Saigon (Ho Chi Minh City)	467	5,771	4,987	6,534	10,905	8,695	938	6,302	5,102	12,180	6,345	6,779	4,168
San Francisco	7,930	5,673	7,436	10,248	3,908	1,860	6,904	2,397	6,711	4,516	5,369	5,806	7,850
Santiago	10,967	7,772	7,967	4,947	3,033	5,295	11,615	6,861	8,135	1,528	7,241	6,639	7,017
Seattle	7,455	5,060	6,809	10,205	4,096	1,737	6,481	2,681	6,077	4,961	4,799	5,303	8,176
Shanghai	1,797	5,231	5,188	8,062	9,508	7,071	760	4,947	4,975	10,665	5,728	6,386	4,991
Shannon	6,256	940	2,534	6,188	4,320	3,583	6,246	7,006	1,938	5,992	387	884	10,826
Singapore	887	6,167	5,143	6,007	11,408	9,376	1,608	6,728	5,379	11,689	6,747	7,079	3,767
St. Louis	8,763	4,676	6,370	8,549	2,414	265	7,949	4,134	5,744	3,589	4,215	4,426	9,476
Stockholm	5,141	505	2,084	6,422	5,422	4,288	5,115	6,873	1,347	7,109	892	1,613	9,693
Teheran	3,392	2,184	1,220	5,240	7,322	6,502	3,844	8,072	1,274	8,850	2,739	2,974	7,838
Tokyo	2,865	5,557	5,937	9,155	8,813	6,313	1,792	3,860	5,574	9,628	5,956	6,704	5,070
Vienna	5,252	323	1,455	5,656	5,374	4,696	5,432	7,632	791	6,990	767	1,124	9,802
Warsaw	5,032	322	1,588	5,934	5,563	4,679	5,147	7,368	858	7,212	901	1,425	9,609
Washington D.C.	8,807	4,182	5,800	7,892	2,051	2,598	8,157	4,839	5,225	3,504	3,676	3,794	10,174

Mexico City	Montreal	Moscow	Nairobi	New Delhi	New York	Paris	Peking	Rio de Janeiro	Rome	San Francisco	Singapore	Stockholm	Teheran	Tokyo	Vienna	Warsaw
6,677	5,146	4,038	2,603	5,279	5,126	2,988	7,359	3,501	2,624	7,688	7,183	3,835	3,874	8,594	3,100	3,440
5,735	3,426	1,337	4,136	3,958	3,654	271	4,890	5,938	807	5,465	6,526	701	2,533	5,788	581	681
3,776	3,133	4,364	8,287	5,709	3,373	4,697	3,997	8,145	5,263	2,005	6,678	4,102	5,654	3,463	4,856	4,601
7,021	4,737	1,387	2,827	3,120	4,938	1,305	4,757	6,030	654	6,792	5,629	1,498	1,539	5,924	801	996
8,274	10,231	9,018	7,315	6,420	10,194	10,519	5,626	8,259	10,048	7,692	3,848	9,732	7,935	5,017	9,886	9,676
8,082	5,768	1,583	2,431	1,966	6,007	2,405	3,925	6,938	1,836	7,466	4,427	2,164	431	5,199	1,781	1,752
9,793	8,337	4,394	4,481	1,812	8,669	5,877	2,027	9,987	5,493	7,930	887	5,141	3,392	2,865	5,252	5,032
7,707	5,405	1,514	2,420	2,479	5,622	1,987	4,352	6,478	1,368	7,302	4,935	1,931	913	5,598	1,401	1,459
6,610	4,305	1,066	3,328	3,270	4,526	902	4,634	6,145	449	6,296	5,833	1,010	1,741	5,720	309	516
6,054	3,740	1,001	3,947	3,598	3,980	549	4,600	6,207	735	5,673	6,167	505	2,184	5,557	323	322
9,739	7,524	3,132	2,811	722	7,811	4,367	2,953	8,334	3,846	8,406	2,427	3,880	1,743	4,196	3,725	3,601
4,580	5,597	8,369	6,479	9,823	5,279	6,857	11,994	1,231	6,925	6,455	9,870	7,799	8,565	11,411	7,334	7,656
7,677	5,403	1,770	2,217	2,752	5,598	1,973	4,687	6,153	1,305	7,436	5,143	2,084	1,220	5,937	1,455	1,588
8,516	7,920	6,277	2,543	5,769	7,801	5,782	8,034	3,773	5,231	10,248	6,007	6,422	5,240	9,155	5,656	5,934
2,234	2,443	6,176	7,179	8,837	2,124	4,735	8,978	2,805	5,198	3,908	11,408	5,422	7,322	8,813	5,374	5,563
1,688	746	4,984	8,012	7,486	714	4,145	6,625	5,288	4,823	1,860	9,376	4,288	6,502	6,313	4,696	4,679
5,918	3,605	971	4,156	3,640	3,857	642	4,503	6,321	953	5,473	6,195	325	2,287	5,415	540	417
1,438	1,639	5,501	8,867	7,730	1,631	4,900	6,385	5,866	5,887	953	9,079	4,879	7,033	5,815	5,395	5,322
6,127	3,787	961	3,915	3,550	4,028	589	4,567	6,237	729	5,709	6,119	502	2,135	5,533	296	274
6,101	3,845	554	4,282	3,247	4,126	1,192	3,956	6,872	1,370	5,435	5,759	248	2,062	4,872	895	569
8,789	7,736	4,443	5,447	2,339	8,061	5,992	1,195	11,002	5,773	6,904	1,608	5,115	3,844	1,792	5,432	5,147
3,791	4,919	7,049	10,740	7,413	4,969	7,452	5,084	8,295	8,040	2,397	6,728	6,873	8,072	3,860	7,632	7,368
749	1,605	5,925	8,746	8,388	1,419	5,035	7,244	5,015	5,702	1,648	9,954	5,227	7,442	6,685	5,609	5,609
7,106	4,798	1,087	2,957	2,837	5,022	1,400	4,407	6,378	853	6,711	5,379	1,347	1,274	5,574	791	858
9,249	6,997	2,600	2,708	678	7,277	3,817	3,020	8,082	3,306	8,078	2,942	3,340	1,194	4,313	3,175	3,052
4,614	2,317	2,083	5,404	4,749	2,597	1,402	4,951	6,090	2,068	4,196	7,181	1,352	3,568	5,497	1,813	1,745
7,915	6,378	4,328	4,234	4,692	6,378	3,742	7,002	4,105	3,186	8,920	6,132	4,388	3,612	8,307	3,619	3,910
6,276	4,005	396	1,505	3,069	4,291	1,350	3,789	7,028	1,460	5,523	5,575	431	1,926	4,733	986	642
2,635	3,967	7,855	7,821	10,430	3,635	6,367	10,365	2,351	6,748	4,516	11,689	7,109	8,850	9,628	6,990	7,212
5,396	3,255	2,433	4,013	4,844	3,377	904	6,040	4,777	1,163	5,679	7,393	1,862	3,288	6,943	1,432	1,720
5,558	3,256	1,556	4,229	4,178	3,473	215	5,089	5,751	892	5,369	6,747	892	2,739	5,956	767	901
5,642	3,449	2,140	3,840	4,528	3,596	652	5,759	5,045	849	5,806	7,079	1,613	2,974	6,704	1,124	1,425
8,420	10,390	8,965	7,159	6,340	10,352	10,442	5,632	8,218	9,940	7,850	3,767	9,693	7,838	5,070	9,802	9,609
—	2,315	6,671	9,218	9,119	2,086	5,723	7,772	4,769	6,374	1,889	10,331	5,965	8,182	7,036	6,316	6,335
2,315	—	4,397	7,267	7,012	333	3,432	6,541	5,082	4,102	2,544	9,207	3,667	5,879	6,470	4,007	4,021
6,671	4,397	—	3,928	2,703	4,680	1,550	3,627	7,162	1,477	5,884	5,236	764	1,534	4,663	1,039	716
9,218	7,267	3,928	—	3,371	7,365	4,020	5,720	5,556	3,340	9,598	4,636	4,299	2,709	6,996	3,625	3,800
9,119	7,012	2,703	3,317	—	7,319	4,103	2,350	8,747	3,684	7,691	2,574	3,466	1,584	3,638	3,467	3,277
2,086	333	4,680	7,365	7,319	—	3,638	6,867	4,805	4,293	2,574	9,539	3,939	6,141	6,757	4,233	4,271
5,722	3,418	1,024	4,446	3,726	3,686	838	4,395	6,462	1,248	5,196	6,249	260	2,462	5,238	839	661
1,496	2,542	6,720	8,043	9,422	2,213	5,388	8,939	3,296	5,916	3,326	11,692	5,956	8,011	8,441	6,031	6,175
5,723	3,432	1,550	4,020	4,103	3,638	—	5,138	5,681	688	5,579	6,676	964	2,624	6,054	643	853
7,772	6,541	3,627	5,720	2,350	6,867	5,138	—	10,778	5,076	5,934	2,754	4,197	3,496	1,305	4,664	4,340
5,612	3,537	2,579	3,733	4,841	3,636	1,125	6,206	4,589	1,184	5,995	7,348	2,084	3,263	7,174	1,546	1,866
4,769	5,082	7,162	5,556	8,747	4,805	5,681	10,778	—	5,704	6,621	9,776	6,638	7,368	11,535	6,124	6,453
6,374	4,102	1,477	3,340	3,684	4,293	688	5,076	5,704	—	6,259	6,231	1,229	2,126	6,140	476	819
9,718	8,558	4,798	4,874	2,268	8,889	6,303	2,072	10,290	5,943	7,829	682	5,534	3,851	2,689	5,687	5,454
1,889	2,544	5,884	9,598	7,691	2,574	5,579	5,934	6,621	6,259	—	8,449	5,372	7,362	5,148	5,992	5,854
4,094	5,436	8,770	7,180	10,518	5,106	7,224	11,859	1,820	7,391	5,926	10,190	8,120	9,185	10,711	7,760	8,059
2,340	2,289	5,217	9,006	7,046	2,409	5,012	5,432	6,890	5,680	679	8,074	4,731	6,686	4,793	5,381	5,222
8,033	7,067	4,248	5,951	2,646	7,384	5,772	645	11,339	5,679	6,150	2,363	4,837	3,974	1,097	5,281	4,963
5,172	2,873	1,863	4,563	4,529	3,086	563	5,288	5,597	1,247	5,040	7,089	1,135	3,117	6,064	1,153	1,258
10,331	9,207	5,236	4,636	2,574	9,539	6,676	2,754	9,776	6,231	8,449	—	5,993	4,106	3,304	6,039	5,846
1,425	978	5,248	8,231	7,736	878	4,398	6,792	5,218	5,073	1,744	9,544	4,552	6,766	6,407	4,955	4,942
5,965	3,667	764	4,299	3,466	3,939	964	4,197	6,638	1,229	5,372	5,993	—	2,217	5,091	771	504
8,182	5,879	1,534	2,709	1,584	6,141	2,624	3,496	7,386	2,126	7,362	4,106	2,217	—	4,775	1,983	1,878
7,036	6,479	4,663	6,996	3,638	6,757	6,054	1,305	11,535	6,140	5,148	3,304	5,091	4,775	—	5,689	5,346
6,316	4,007	1,039	3,625	3,467	4,233	643	4,664	6,124	476	5,992	6,039	771	1,983	5,689	—	347
6,335	4,021	716	3,800	3,277	4,271	853	4,340	6,453	819	5,854	5,846	504	1,878	5,346	347	—
1,883	490	4,873	7,550	7,500	203	3,841	6,965	4,783	4,496	2,444	9,667	4,135	6,340	6,792	4,436	4,471

Elements of the Solar System

	Mean Distance from Sun: in Miles	in Kilometers	Period of Revolution around Sun	Period of Rotation on Axis	Equatorial Diameter: in Miles	in Kilometers	Surface Gravity (Earth = 1)	Mass (Earth = 1)	Mean Density (Water = 1)	Number of Satellites
MERCURY	35,990,000	57,900,000	87.97 days	59 days	3,032	4,880	0.38	0.055	5.5	0
VENUS	67,240,000	108,200,000	224.70 days	243 days†	7,523	12,106	0.90	0.815	5.25	0
EARTH	93,000,000	149,700,000	365.26 days	23h 56m	7,926	12,755	1.00	1.00	5.5	1
MARS	141,730,000	228,100,000	687.00 days	24h 37m	4,220	6,790	0.38	0.107	4.0	2
JUPITER	483,880,000	778,700,000	11.86 years	9h 50m	88,750	142,800	2.87	317.9	1.3	16
SATURN	887,130,000	1,427,700,000	29.46 years	10h 39m	74,580	120,020	1.32	95.2	0.7	23
URANUS	1,783,700,000	2,870,500,000	84.01 years	17h 24m†	31,600	50,900	0.93	14.6	1.3	15
NEPTUNE	2,795,500,000	4,498,800,000	164.79 years	17h 50m	30,200	48,600	1.23	17.2	1.8	2
PLUTO	3,667,900,000	5,902,800,000	247.70 years	6.39 days (?)	1,500	2,400	0.03 (?)	0.01(?)	0.7(?)	1

†Retrograde motion

Facts About the Sun

Equatorial diameter	865,000 miles	1,392,000 kilometers
Period of rotation on axis	25-35 days*	
Orbit of galaxy	every 225 million years	
Surface gravity (Earth = 1)	27.8	
Mass (Earth = 1)	333,000	
Density (Water = 1)	1.4	
Mean distance from Earth	93,000,000 miles	149,700,000 kilometers

*Rotation of 25 days at Equator, decreasing to about 35 days at the poles.

Facts About the Moon

Equatorial diameter	2,160 miles	3,476 kilometers
Period of rotation on axis	27 days, 7 hours, 43 minutes	
Period of revolution around Earth (sidereal month)	27 days, 7 hours, 43 minutes	
Phase period between new moons (synodic month)	29 days, 12 hours, 44 minutes	
Surface gravity (Earth = 1)	0.16	
Mass (Earth = 1)	0.0123	
Density (Water = 1)	3.34	
Maximum distance from Earth	252,710 miles	406,690 kilometers
Minimum distance from Earth	221,460 miles	356,400 kilometers
Mean distance from Earth	238,860 miles	384,400 kilometers

Dimensions of the Earth

	Area in Sq. Miles	Sq. Kilometers
Superficial area	197,751,000	512,175,090
Land surface	57,970,000	150,142,300
Water surface	139,781,000	362,032,790

	Miles	Kilometers
Equatorial circumference	24,902	40,075
Polar circumference	24,860	40,007
Equatorial diameter	7,926.68	12,756.4
Polar diameter	7,899.99	12,713.4
Equatorial radius	3,963.34	6,378.2
Polar radius	3,949.99	6,356.7

Volume of the Earth	2.6×10^{11} cubic miles	10.84×10^{11} cubic kilometers
Mass or weight	6.6×10^{21} short tons	6.0×10^{21} metric tons
Maximum distance from Sun	94,600,000 miles	152,000,000 kilometers
Minimum distance from Sun	91,300,000 miles	147,000,000 kilometers

The Continents

	Area in: Sq. Miles	Sq. Km.	Percent of World's Land
Asia	17,128,500	44,362,815	29.5
Africa	11,707,000	30,321,130	20.2
North America	9,363,000	24,250,170	16.2
South America	6,875,000	17,806,250	11.8
Antarctica	5,500,000	14,245,000	9.5
Europe	4,057,000	10,507,630	7.0
Australia	2,966,136	7,682,300	5.1

Oceans and Major Seas

	Area in: Sq. Miles	Sq. Km.	Greatest Depth in: Feet	Meters
Pacific Ocean	64,186,000	166,241,700	36,198	11,033
Atlantic Ocean	31,862,000	82,522,600	28,374	8,648
Indian Ocean	28,350,000	73,426,500	25,344	7,725
Arctic Ocean	5,427,000	14,056,000	17,880	5,450
Caribbean Sea	970,000	2,512,300	24,720	7,535
Mediterranean Sea	969,000	2,509,700	16,896	5,150
Bering Sea	875,000	2,266,250	15,800	4,800
Gulf of Mexico	600,000	1,554,000	12,300	3,750
Sea of Okhotsk	590,000	1,528,100	11,070	3,370
East China Sea	482,000	1,248,400	9,500	2,900
Sea of Japan	389,000	1,007,500	12,280	3,740
Hudson Bay	317,500	822,300	846	258
North Sea	222,000	575,000	2,200	670
Black Sea	185,000	479,150	7,365	2,245
Red Sea	169,000	437,700	7,200	2,195
Baltic Sea	163,000	422,170	1,506	459

Major Ship Canals

	Length in: Miles	Kms.	Minimum Feet	Depth in: Meters
Volga-Baltic, U.S.S.R.	225	362	—	—
Baltic-White Sea, U.S.S.R.	140	225	16	5
Suez, Egypt	100.76	162	42	13
Albert, Belgium	80	129	16.5	5
Moscow-Volga, U.S.S.R.	80	129	18	6
Volga-Don, U.S.S.R.	62	100	—	—
Göta, Sweden	54	87	10	3
Kiel (Nord-Ostsee), W. Ger.	53.2	86	38	12
Panama Canal, Panama	50.72	82	41.6	13
Houston Ship, U.S.A.	50	81	36	11

Largest Islands

	Area in: Sq. Mi.	Sq. Km.		Area in: Sq. Mi.	Sq. Km.		Area in: Sq. Mi.	Sq. Km.
Greenland	840,000	2,175,600	South I., New Zealand	58,393	151,238	Hokkaido, Japan	28,983	75,066
New Guinea	305,000	789,950	Java, Indonesia	48,842	126,501	Banks, Canada	27,038	70,028
Borneo	290,000	751,100	North I., New Zealand	44,187	114,444	Ceylon, Sri Lanka	25,332	65,610
Madagascar	226,400	586,376	Newfoundland, Canada	42,031	108,860	Tasmania, Australia	24,600	63,710
Baffin, Canada	195,928	507,454	Cuba	40,533	104,981	Svalbard, Norway	23,957	62,049
Sumatra, Indonesia	164,000	424,760	Luzon, Philippines	40,420	104,688	Devon, Canada	21,331	55,247
Honshu, Japan	88,000	227,920	Iceland	39,768	103,000	Novaya Zemlya (north isl.), U.S.S.R.	18,600	48,200
Great Britain	84,400	218,896	Mindanao, Philippines	36,537	94,631	Marajó, Brazil	17,991	46,597
Victoria, Canada	83,896	217,290	Ireland	31,743	82,214	Tierra del Fuego, Chile & Argentina	17,900	46,360
Ellesmere, Canada	75,767	196,236	Sakhalin, U.S.S.R.	29,500	76,405	Alexander, Antarctica	16,700	43,250
Celebes, Indonesia	72,986	189,034	Hispaniola, Haiti & Dom. Rep.	29,399	76,143			

Principal Mountains of the World

Mountain	Feet	Meters
Everest, Nepal-China	29,028	8,848
Godwin Austen (K2), Pakistan-China	28,250	8,611
Kanchenjunga, Nepal-India	28,208	8,598
Lhotse, Nepal-China	27,923	8,511
Makalu, Nepal-China	27,824	8,481
Dhaulagiri, Nepal	26,810	8,172
Nanga Parbat, Pakistan	26,660	8,126
Annapurna, Nepal	26,504	8,078
Gasherbrum, Pakistan-China	26,740	8,068
Nanda Devi, India	25,645	7,817
Rakaposhi, Pakistan	25,550	7,788
Kamet, India	25,447	7,756
Gurla Mandhada, China	25,355	7,728
Kongur Shan, China	25,325	7,719
Tirich Mir, Pakistan	25,230	7,690
Gongga Shan, China	24,790	7,556
Muztagata, China	24,757	7,546
Communism Peak, U.S.S.R.	24,599	7,498
Pobeda Peak, U.S.S.R.	24,406	7,439
Chomo Lhari, Bhutan-China	23,997	7,314
Muztag, China	23,891	7,282
Cerro Aconcagua, Argentina	22,831	6,959
Ojos del Salado, Chile-Argentina	22,572	6,880
Bonete, Chile-Argentina	22,541	6,870
Tupungato, Chile-Argentina	22,310	6,800
Pissis, Argentina	22,241	6,779
Mercedario, Argentina	22,211	6,770
Huascarán, Peru	22,205	6,768
Llullaillaco, Chile-Argentina	22,057	6,723
Nevada Ancohuma, Bolivia	21,489	6,550
Illampu, Bolivia	21,276	6,485
Chimborazo, Ecuador	20,561	6,267
McKinley, Alaska	20,320	6,194
Logan, Canada (Yukon)	19,524	5,951
Cotopaxi, Ecuador	19,347	5,897
Kilimanjaro, Tanzania	19,340	5,895
El Misti, Peru	19,101	5,822
Pico Cristóbal Colón, Colombia	19,029	5,800
Huila, Colombia	18,865	5,750
Citlaltépetl (Orizaba), Mexico	18,855	5,747
El'brus, U.S.S.R.	18,510	5,642
Damavand, Iran	18,376	5,601
St. Elias, Alaska-Canada (Yukon)	18,008	5,489
Vilcanota, Peru	17,999	5,486
Popocatépetl, Mexico	17,887	5,452
Dykhtau, U.S.S.R.	17,070	5,203
Kenya, Kenya	17,058	5,199
Ararat, Turkey	16,946	5,165
Vinson Massif, Antarctica	16,864	5,140
Margherita (Ruwenzori), Africa	16,795	5,119
Kazbek, U.S.S.R.	16,512	5,033
Puncak Jaya, Indonesia	16,503	5,030
Tyree, Antarctica	16,289	4,965
Blanc, France	15,771	4,807
Klyuchevskaya Sopka, U.S.S.R.	15,584	4,750
Fairweather (Br. Col., Canada)	15,300	4,663
Dufourspitze (Mte. Rosa), Italy-Switzerland	15,203	4,634
Ras Dashan, Ethiopia	15,157	4,620
Matterhorn, Switzerland	14,691	4,478
Whitney, California, U.S.A.	14,494	4,418
Elbert, Colorado, U.S.A.	14,433	4,399
Rainier, Washington, U.S.A.	14,410	4,392
Shasta, California, U.S.A.	14,162	4,350
Pikes Peak, Colorado, U.S.A.	14,110	4,301
Finsteraarhorn, Switzerland	14,022	4,274
Mauna Kea, Hawaii, U.S.A.	13,796	4,205
Mauna Loa, Hawaii, U.S.A.	13,677	4,169
Jungfrau, Switzerland	13,642	4,158
Cameroon, Cameroon	13,350	4,069
Grossglockner, Austria	12,457	3,797
Fuji, Japan	12,389	3,776
Cook, New Zealand	12,349	3,764
Etna, Italy	11,053	3,369
Kosciusko, Australia	7,310	2,228
Mitchell, North Carolina, U.S.A.	6,684	2,037

Longest Rivers of the World

River	Length in: Miles	Kms.
Nile, Africa	4,145	6,671
Amazon, S. Amer.	3,915	6,300
Chang Jiang (Yangtze), China	3,900	6,276
Mississippi-Missouri-Red Rock, U.S.A.	3,741	6,019
Ob'Irtysh-Black Irtysh, U.S.S.R.	3,362	5,411
Yenisey-Angara, U.S.S.R.	3,100	4,989
Huang He (Yellow), China	2,877	4,630
Amur-Shilka-Onon, Asia	2,744	4,416
Lena, U.S.S.R.	2,734	4,400
Congo (Zaire), Africa	2,718	4,374
Mackenzie-Peace-Finlay, Canada	2,635	4,241
Mekong, Asia	2,610	4,200
Missouri-Red Rock, U.S.A.	2,564	4,125
Niger, Africa	2,548	4,101
Paraná-La Plata, S. Amer.	2,450	3,943
Mississippi, U.S.A.	2,348	3,778
Murray-Darling, Australia	2,310	3,718
Volga, U.S.S.R.	2,194	3,531
Madeira, S. Amer.	2,013	3,240
Purus, S. Amer.	1,995	3,211
Yukon, Alaska-Canada	1,979	3,185
St. Lawrence, Canada-U.S.A.	1,900	3,058
Rio Grande, Mexico-U.S.A.	1,885	3,034
Syrdar'ya-Naryn, U.S.S.R.	1,859	2,992
São Francisco, Brazil	1,811	2,914
Indus, Asia	1,800	2,897
Danube, Europe	1,775	2,857
Salween, Asia	1,770	2,849
Brahmaputra, Asia	1,700	2,736
Euphrates, Asia	1,700	2,736
Tocantins, Brazil	1,677	2,699
Xi (Si), China	1,650	2,655
Amudar'ya, Asia	1,616	2,601
Nelson-Saskatchewan, Canada	1,600	2,575
Orinoco, S. Amer.	1,600	2,575
Zambezi, Africa	1,600	2,575
Paraguay, S. Amer.	1,584	2,549
Kolyma, U.S.S.R.	1,562	2,514
Ganges, Asia	1,550	2,494
Ural, U.S.S.R.	1,509	2,428
Japurá, S. Amer.	1,500	2,414
Arkansas, U.S.A.	1,450	2,334
Colorado, U.S.A.-Mexico	1,450	2,334
Negro, S. Amer.	1,400	2,253
Dnieper, U.S.S.R.	1,368	2,202
Orange, Africa	1,350	2,173
Irrawaddy, Burma	1,325	2,132
Brazos, U.S.A.	1,309	2,107
Ohio-Allegheny, U.S.A.	1,306	2,102
Kama, U.S.S.R.	1,262	2,031
Red, U.S.S.R.	1,222	1,966
Don, U.S.S.R.	1,222	1,967
Columbia, U.S.A.-Canada	1,214	1,953
Saskatchewan, Canada	1,205	1,939
Peace-Finlay, Canada	1,195	1,923
Tigris, Asia	1,181	1,901
Darling, Australia	1,160	1,867
Angara, U.S.S.R.	1,135	1,827
Sungari, Asia	1,130	1,819
Pechora, U.S.S.R.	1,124	1,809
Snake, U.S.A.	1,000	1,609
Churchill, Canada	1,000	1,609
Pilcomayo, S. Amer.	1,000	1,609
Magdalena, Colombia	1,000	1,609
Uruguay, S. Amer.	994	1,600
Platte-N. Platte, U.S.A.	990	1,593
Ohio, U.S.A.	981	1,578
Pecos, U.S.A.	926	1,490
Oka, U.S.S.R.	918	1,477
Canadian, U.S.A.	906	1,458
Colorado, Texas, U.S.A.	894	1,439
Dniester, U.S.S.R.	876	1,410

Principal Natural Lakes

Lake	Area in: Sq. Miles	Sq. Km.	Max. Depth in: Feet	Meters
Caspian Sea, U.S.S.R.-Iran	143,243	370,999	3,264	995
Lake Superior, U.S.A.-Canada	31,820	82,414	1,329	405
Lake Victoria, Africa	26,724	69,215	270	82
Aral Sea, U.S.S.R.	25,676	66,501	256	78
Lake Huron, U.S.A.-Canada	23,010	59,596	748	228
Lake Michigan, U.S.A.	22,400	58,016	923	281
Lake Tanganyika, Africa	12,650	32,764	4,700	1,433
Lake Baykal, U.S.S.R.	12,162	31,500	5,316	1,620
Great Bear Lake, Canada	12,096	31,328	1,356	413
Lake Nyasa (Malawi), Africa	11,555	29,928	2,320	707
Great Slave Lake, Canada	11,031	28,570	2,015	614
Lake Erie, U.S.A.-Canada	9,940	25,745	210	64
Lake Winnipeg, Canada	9,417	24,390	60	18
Lake Ontario, U.S.A.-Canada	7,540	19,529	775	244
Lake Ladoga, U.S.S.R.	7,104	18,399	738	225
Lake Balkhash, U.S.S.R.	7,027	18,200	87	27
Lake Maracaibo, Venezuela	5,120	13,261	100	31
Lake Chad, Africa	4,000-10,000	10,360-25,900	25	8
Lake Onega, U.S.S.R.	3,710	9,609	377	115
Lake Eyre, Australia	3,500-0	9,000-0	—	—
Lake Titicaca, Peru-Bolivia	3,200	8,288	1,000	305
Lake Nicaragua, Nicaragua	3,100	8,029	230	70
Lake Athabasca, Canada	3,064	7,936	400	122
Reindeer Lake, Canada	2,568	6,651	—	—
Lake Turkana (Rudolf), Africa	2,463	6,379	240	73
Issyk-Kul', U.S.S.R.	2,425	6,281	2,303	702
Lake Torrens, Australia	2,230	5,776	—	—
Vänern, Sweden	2,156	5,584	328	100
Nettilling Lake, Canada	2,140	5,543	—	—
Lake Winnipegosis, Canada	2,075	5,374	38	12
Lake Mobutu Sese Seko (Albert), Africa	2,075	5,374	160	49
Kariba Lake, Zambia-Zimbabwe	2,050	5,310	295	90
Lake Nipigon, Canada	1,872	4,848	540	165
Lake Mweru, Zaire-Zambia	1,800	4,662	60	18
Lake Manitoba, Canada	1,799	4,659	12	4
Lake Taymyr, U.S.S.R.	1,737	4,499	85	26
Lake Khanka, China-U.S.S.R.	1,700	4,403	33	10
Lake Kioga, Uganda	1,700	4,403	25	8

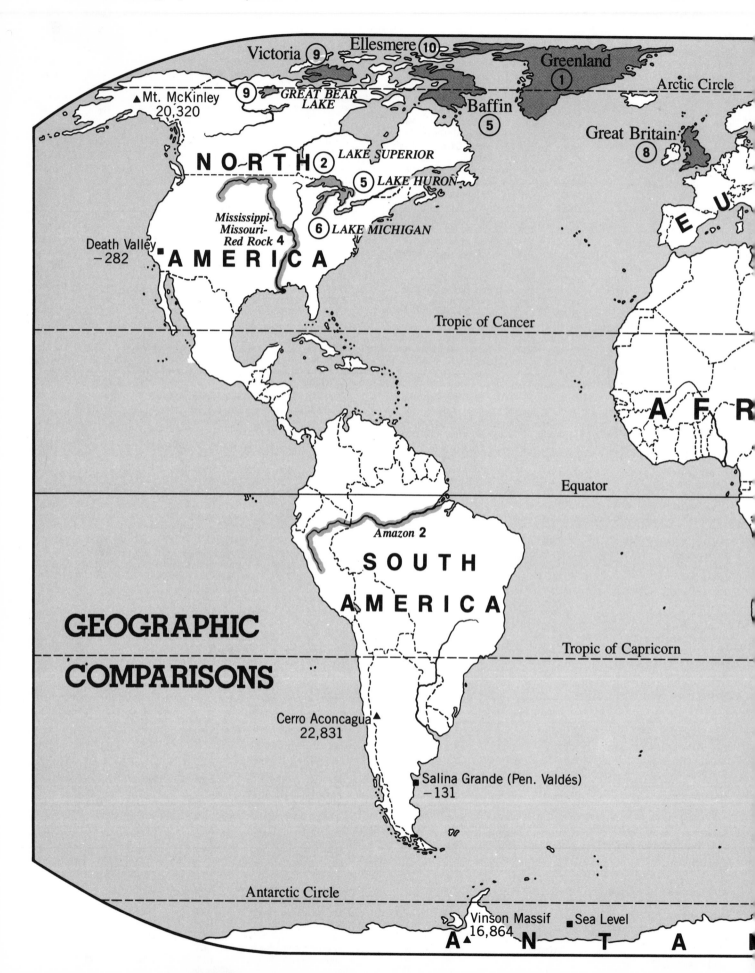

Victoria **9**
Ellesmere **10**
Greenland **1**
Arctic Circle

▲Mt. McKinley
20,320

9

GREAT BEAR LAKE

Baffin **5**

Great Britain **8**

N O R T H

2 *LAKE SUPERIOR*

5 *LAKE HURON*

E U

*Mississippi-
Missouri-
Red Rock* **4**

6 *LAKE MICHIGAN*

Death Valley
−282

A M E R I C A

A F R

Tropic of Cancer

Equator

Amazon **2**

S O U T H

A M E R I C A

GEOGRAPHIC

Tropic of Capricorn

COMPARISONS

Cerro Aconcagua ▲
22,831

Salina Grande (Pen. Valdés)
−131

Antarctic Circle

Vinson Massif ■Sea Level
▲16,864

A ▲ N T A I

Yenisey-Angara 6

Lena 9

Ob'-Irtysh 5

LAKE BAYKAL (8)

Amur-Shilka-Onon 8

P E

Caspian Sea (1) 92 ■

(4) ARAL SEA

El'brus ▲ 18,510

CASPIAN SEA

I A

Honshu (7)

Dead Sea -1,296 ■

S

Huang 7

Mt. Everest -29,028 ▲

Chang 3

C A

Nile 1

Lake Assal -512 ■

Borneo (3)

New Guinea (2)

Sumatra (6)

go

(3) LAKE VICTORIA

▲ Kilimanjaro 19,340

(7) LAKE TANGANYIKA

(10) LAKE NYASA

Madagascar (4)

AUSTRALIA

Lake Eyre -39 ■

Mt. Kosciuśko ▲ 7,310

▲ Highest Point of Continent (in feet)

■ Lowest Point of Continent (in feet)

⬭ Ten Largest Islands of the World

⬭ Ten Largest Lakes of the World

⬳ Ten Longest Rivers of the World

© Copyright MCMLXXXVIII by HAMMOND INCORPORATED, Maplewood, N.J.

C T I C A

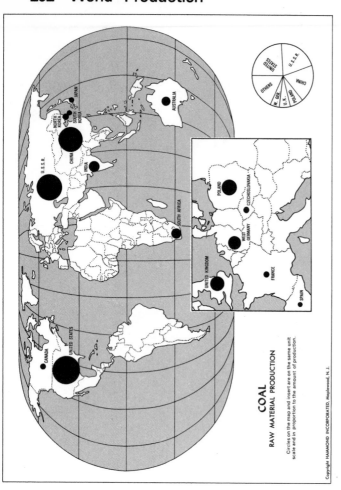

COAL
RAW MATERIAL PRODUCTION

Circles on the map and insert are on the same unit scale and in proportion to the amount of production.

Copyright HAMMOND INCORPORATED, Maplewood, N. J.

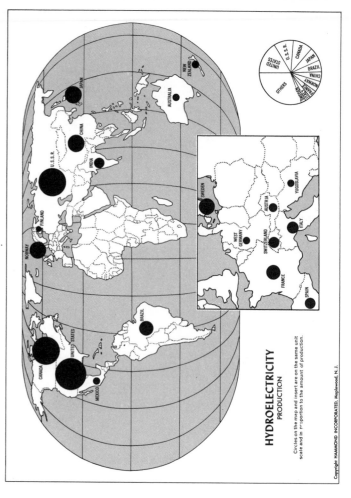

HYDROELECTRICITY
PRODUCTION

Circles on the map and insert are on the same unit scale and in proportion to the amount of production.

Copyright HAMMOND INCORPORATED, Maplewood, N. J.

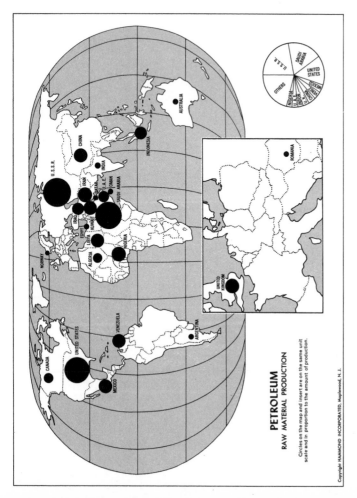

PETROLEUM
RAW MATERIAL PRODUCTION

Circles on the map and insert are on the same unit scale and in proportion to the amount of production.

Copyright HAMMOND INCORPORATED, Maplewood, N. J.

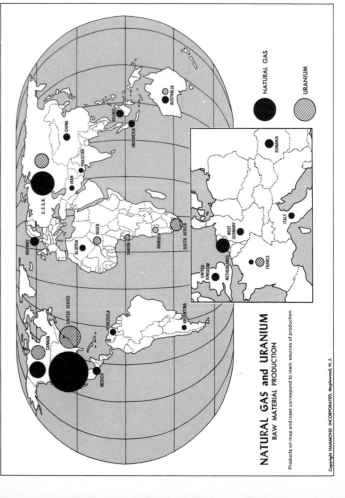

NATURAL GAS

URANIUM

NATURAL GAS and URANIUM
RAW MATERIAL PRODUCTION

Products on map and inset correspond to main sources of production.

Copyright HAMMOND INCORPORATED, Maplewood, N. J.

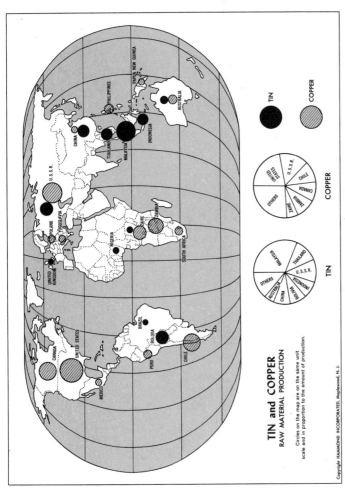

TIN and COPPER
RAW MATERIAL PRODUCTION

Circles on the map are on the same unit scale and in proportion to the amount of production.

Copyright HAMMOND INCORPORATED, Maplewood, N. J.

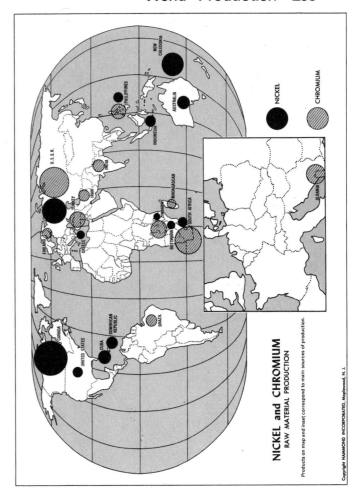

NICKEL and CHROMIUM
RAW MATERIAL PRODUCTION

Products on map and inset correspond to main sources of production.

Copyright HAMMOND INCORPORATED, Maplewood, N. J.

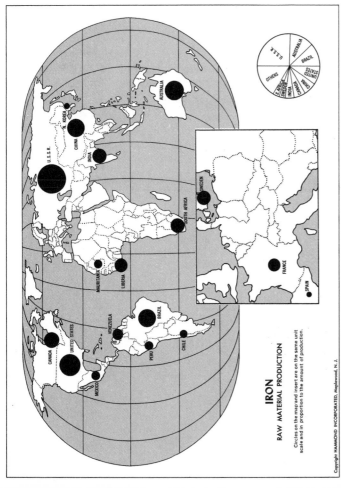

IRON
RAW MATERIAL PRODUCTION

Circles on the map and insert are on the same unit scale and in proportion to the amount of production.

Copyright HAMMOND INCORPORATED, Maplewood, N. J.

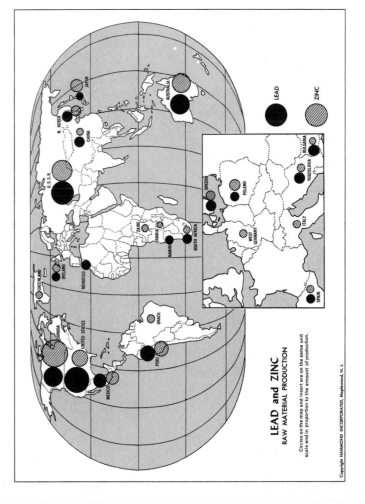

LEAD and ZINC
RAW MATERIAL PRODUCTION

Circles on the map and insert are on the same unit scale and in proportion to the amount of production.

Copyright HAMMOND INCORPORATED, Maplewood, N. J.

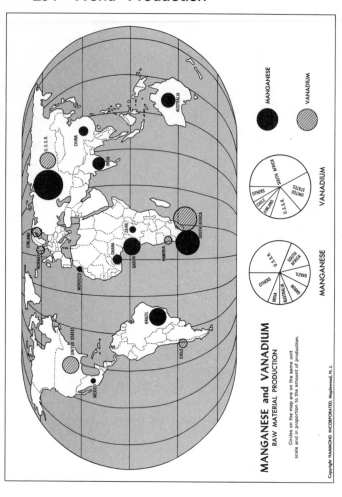

MANGANESE and VANADIUM
RAW MATERIAL PRODUCTION

Circles on the map are on the same unit scale and in proportion to the amount of production.

Copyright HAMMOND INCORPORATED, Maplewood, N.J.

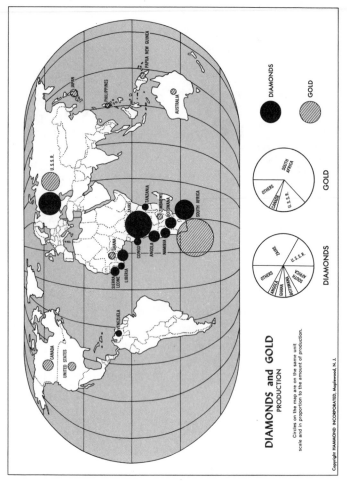

DIAMONDS and GOLD
PRODUCTION

Circles on the map are on the same unit scale and in proportion to the amount of production.

Copyright HAMMOND INCORPORATED, Maplewood, N.J.

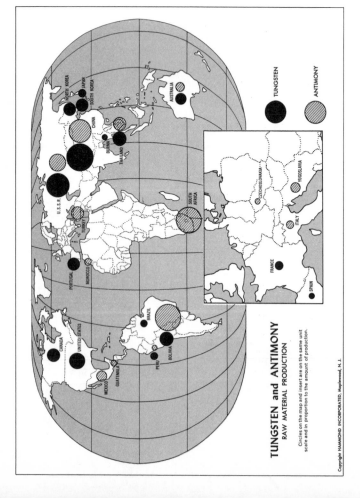

TUNGSTEN and ANTIMONY
RAW MATERIAL PRODUCTION

Circles on the map and insert are on the same unit scale and in proportion to the amount of production.

Copyright HAMMOND INCORPORATED, Maplewood, N.J.

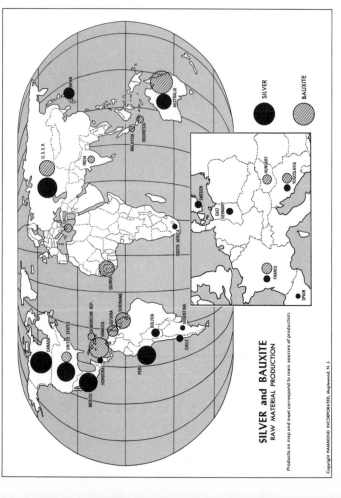

SILVER and BAUXITE
RAW MATERIAL PRODUCTION

Products on map and inset correspond to main sources of production.

Copyright HAMMOND INCORPORATED, Maplewood, N.J.

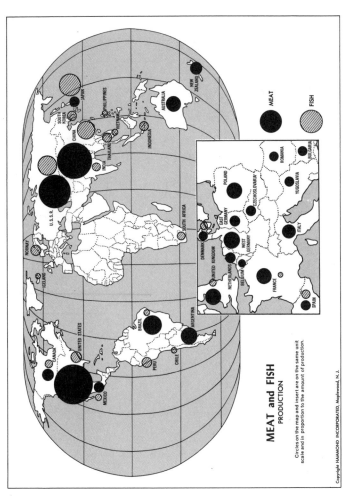

MEAT and FISH
PRODUCTION

Circles on the map and insert are on the same unit
scale and in proportion to the amount of production.

Copyright HAMMOND INCORPORATED, Maplewood, N. J.

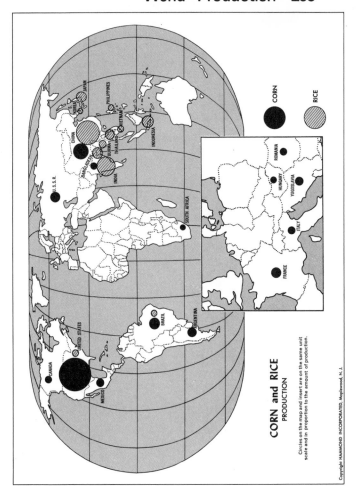

CORN and RICE
PRODUCTION

Circles on the map and insert are on the same unit
scale and in proportion to the amount of production.

Copyright HAMMOND INCORPORATED, Maplewood, N. J.

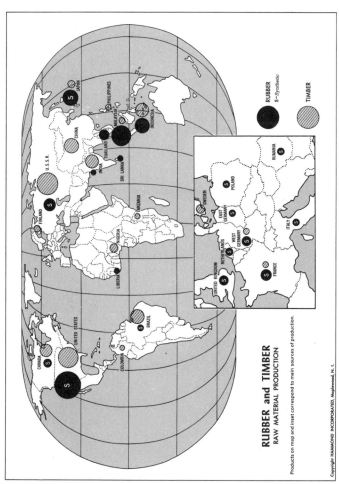

RUBBER and TIMBER
RAW MATERIAL PRODUCTION

Products on map and inset correspond to main sources of production.

Copyright HAMMOND INCORPORATED, Maplewood, N. J.

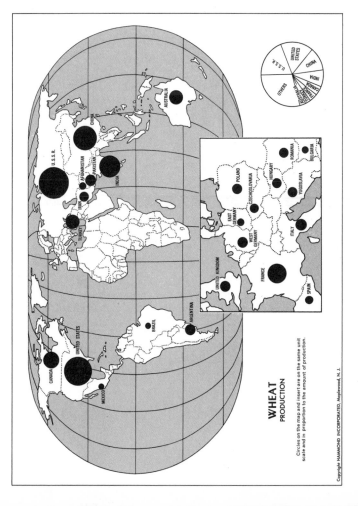

WHEAT
PRODUCTION

Circles on the map and insert are on the same unit
scale and in proportion to the amount of production.

Copyright HAMMOND INCORPORATED, Maplewood, N. J.

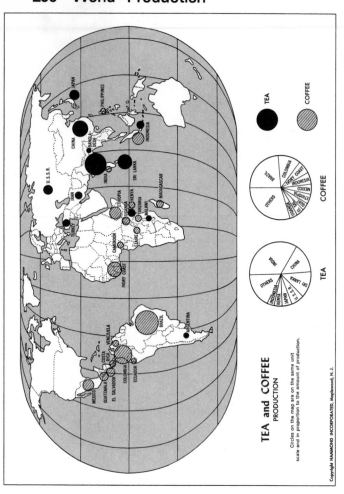

TEA and COFFEE
PRODUCTION

Circles on the map are on the same unit
scale and in proportion to the amount of production.

Copyright HAMMOND INCORPORATED, Maplewood, N.J.

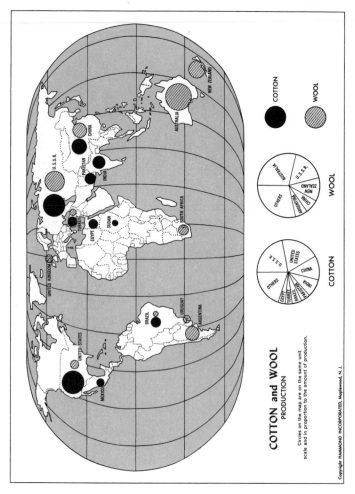

COTTON and WOOL
PRODUCTION

Circles on the map are on the same unit
scale and in proportion to the amount of production.

Copyright HAMMOND INCORPORATED, Maplewood, N.J.

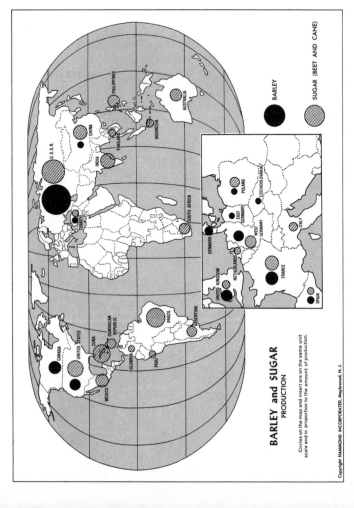

BARLEY and SUGAR
PRODUCTION

Circles on the map and insert are on the same unit
scale and in proportion to the amount of production.

Copyright HAMMOND INCORPORATED, Maplewood, N.J.

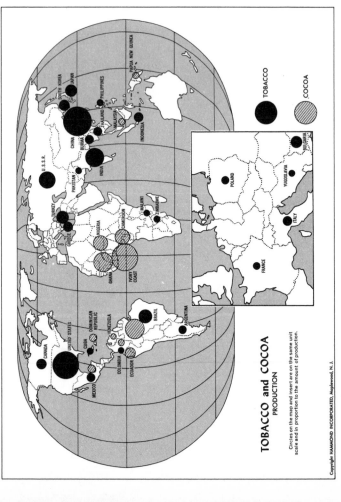

TOBACCO and COCOA
PRODUCTION

Circles on the map and insert are on the same unit
scale and in proportion to the amount of production.

Copyright HAMMOND INCORPORATED, Maplewood, N.J.

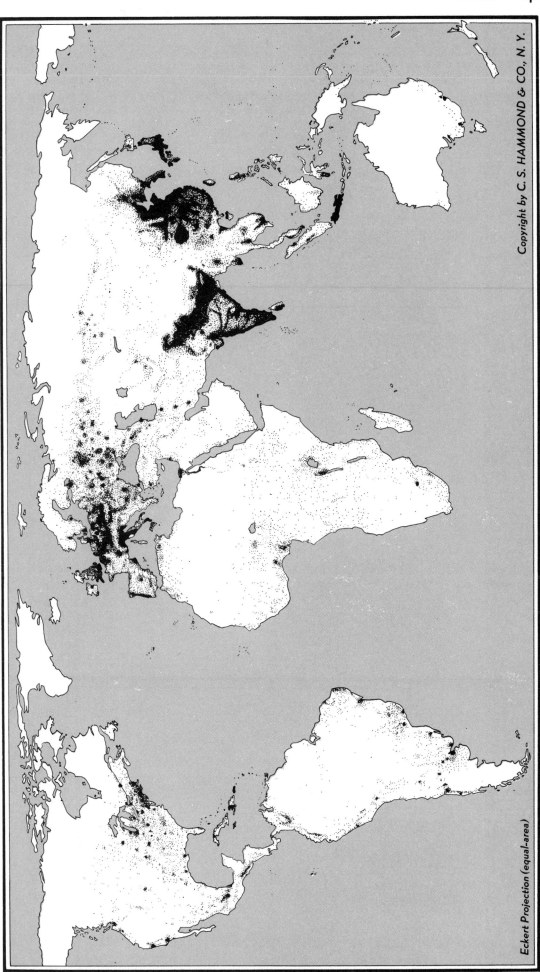

Eckert Projection (equal-area)

Copyright by C. S. HAMMOND & CO., N. Y.

DENSITY OF POPULATION. One of the most outstanding facts of human geography is the extremely uneven distribution of people over the Earth. One-half of the Earth's surface has less than 3 people per square mile, while in the lowlands of India, China, Java and Japan rural density reaches the incredible congestion of 2000-3000 per square mile. Three-fourths of the Earth's population live in four relatively small areas; Northeastern United States, North-Central Europe, India and the Far East.

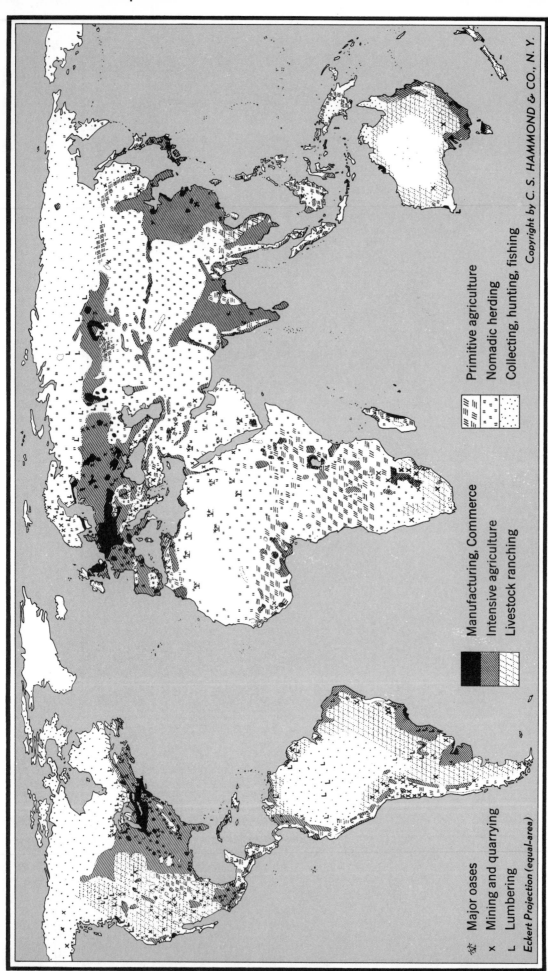

Major oases

× Mining and quarrying

L Lumbering

Eckert Projection (equal-area)

Manufacturing, Commerce

Intensive agriculture

Livestock ranching

Primitive agriculture

Nomadic herding

Collecting, hunting, fishing

Copyright by C. S. HAMMOND & CO., N. Y.

OCCUPATIONS. Correlation with the density of population shows that the most densely populated areas fall into the regions of manufacturing and intensive farming. All other economies require considerable space. The most sparsely inhabited areas are those of collecting, hunting and fishing. Areas with practically no habitation are left blank.

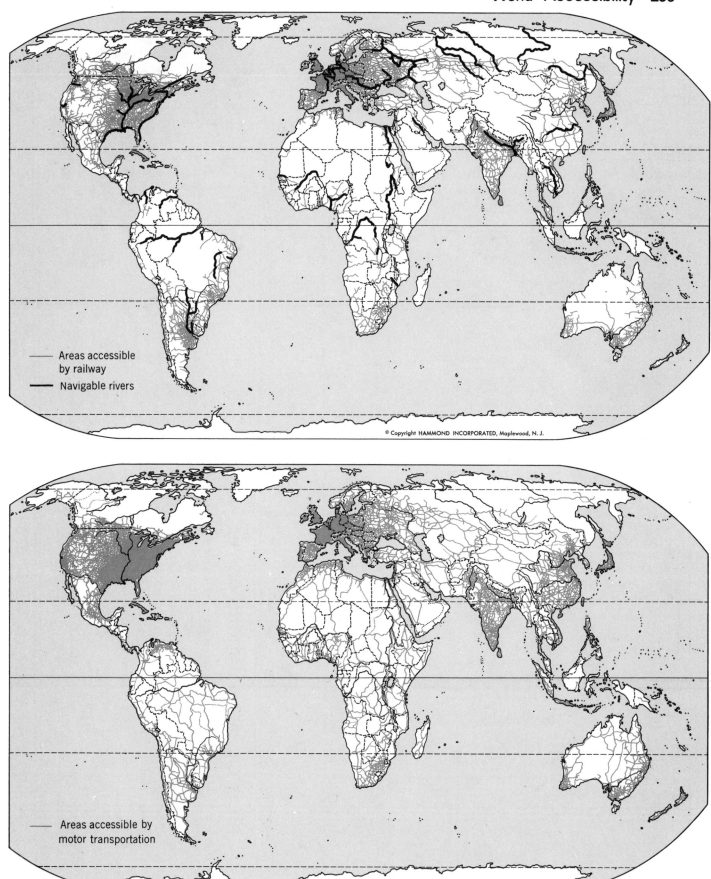

Areas accessible
by railway
Navigable rivers

© Copyright HAMMOND INCORPORATED, Maplewood, N. J.

Areas accessible by
motor transportation

© Copyright HAMMOND INCORPORATED, Maplewood, N. J.

ACCESSIBILITY. *Many regions in the world are far from railways, roads, navigable rivers or the seas. Their economic development is retarded because their products can be brought to the world's markets only at great expense. Such areas are in the tundra (alpine), the boreal forest and in the equatorial rain* *forest regions. Desert areas, if not too mountainous, can be crossed by tractors. The largest inaccessible area is in Tibet, on account of high mountains, the alpine climate and isolationist attitude of the people. Airplane transportation is helping to bring these inaccessible areas into the orbit of civilization.*

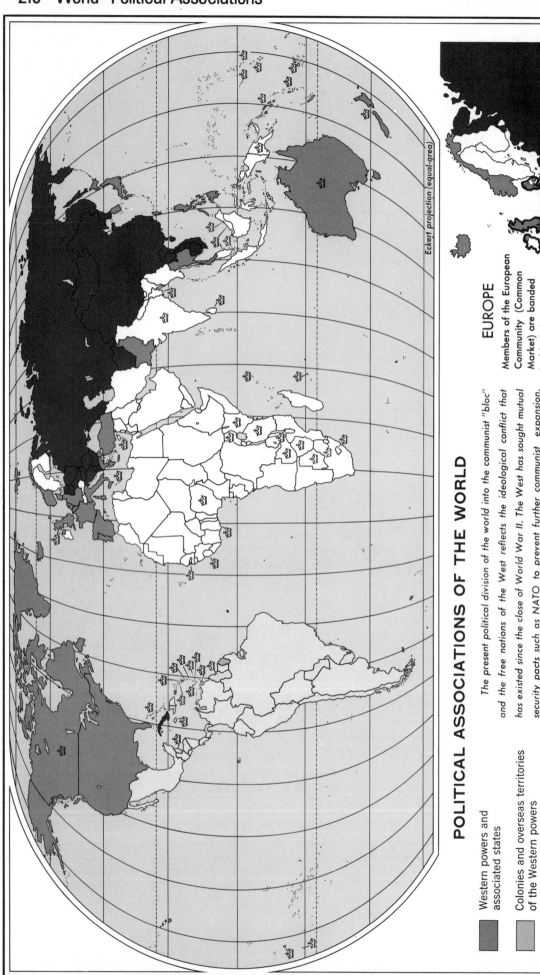

Eckert projection (equal-area)

POLITICAL ASSOCIATIONS OF THE WORLD

The present political division of the world into the communist "bloc" and the free nations of the West reflects the ideological conflict that has existed since the close of World War II. The West has sought mutual security pacts such as NATO to prevent further communist expansion.

A third group, that of the uncommitted or neutral nations has grown in numbers as colonial territories in Africa and Asia have become independent. A regional association, the European Community or Common Market, has made substantial progress in achieving trade and economic cooperation among its members. Further integration along political and social lines is planned.

EUROPE

Members of the European Community (Common Market) are banded by black line thus: ——

Western powers and associated states

Colonies and overseas territories of the Western powers

Members of Organization of American States (OAS) (U.S. also a member)

Communist states

Independent members of the British Commonwealth

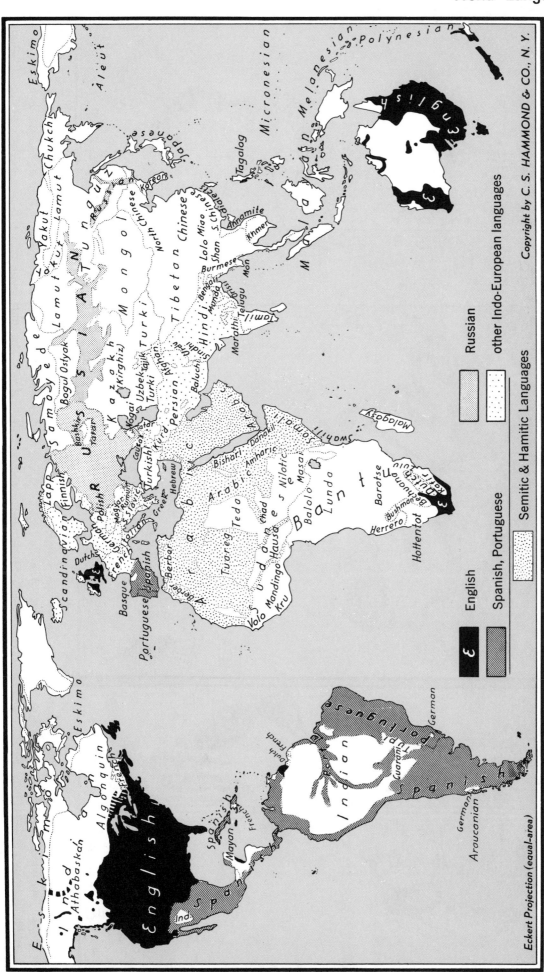

LANGUAGES. Several hundred different languages are spoken in the World, and in many places two or more languages are spoken, sometimes by the same people. The map above shows the dominant languages in each locality. English, French, Spanish, Russian, Arabic and Swahili are spoken by many people as a second language for commerce or travel.

Copyright by C. S. HAMMOND & CO., N.Y.

English

Spanish, Portuguese

Russian

other Indo-European languages

Semitic & Hamitic Languages

Eckert Projection (equal-area)

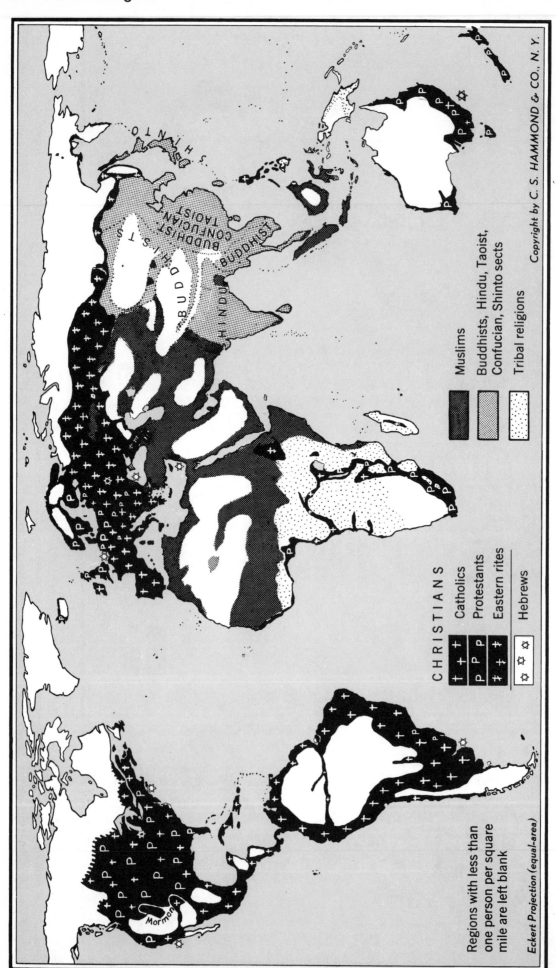

RELIGIONS. Most people of the Earth belong to four major religions: Christians, Muslims, Brahmans, Bhuddhists and derivatives. The Eastern rites of the Christians include the Greek Orthodox, Greek Catholic, Armenian, Syrian, Coptic and more minor churches. The lamaism of Tibet and Mongolia differs a great deal from Buddhism in Burma and Thailand. In the religion of China the teachings of Buddha, Confucius and Tao are mixed, while in Shinto rites of the Christians ancestor and emperor worship is added. About 11 million Hebrews live scattered over the globe, chiefly in cities and in the state of Israel.

CHRISTIANS

Catholics

Protestants

Eastern rites

Hebrews

Muslims

Buddhists, Hindu, Taoist, Confucian, Shinto sects

Tribal religions

Regions with less than one person per square mile are left blank

Eckert Projection (equal-area)

Copyright by C. S. HAMMOND & CO., N. Y.

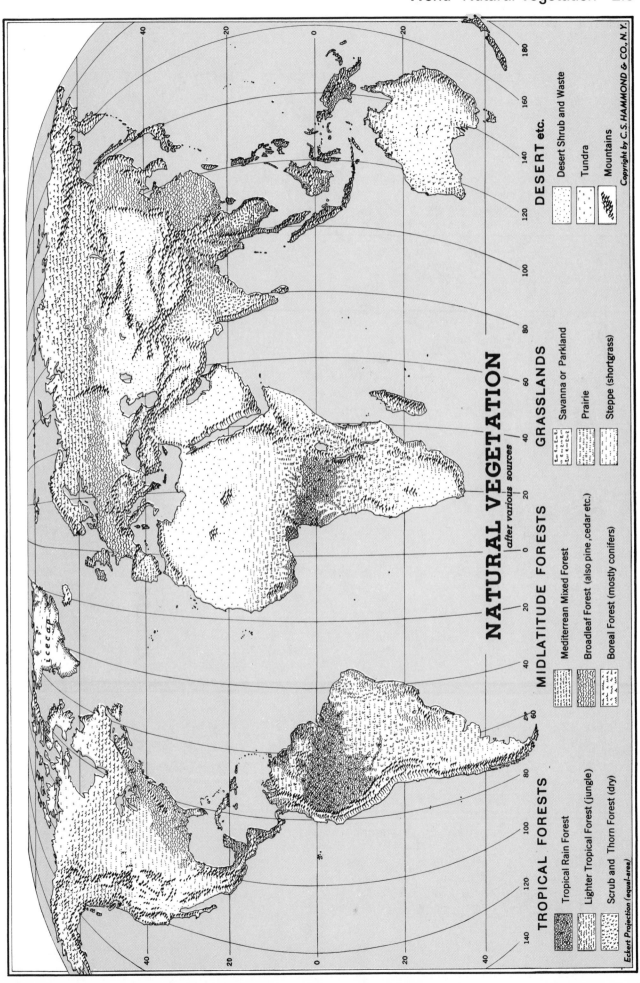

NATURAL VEGETATION
after various sources

TROPICAL FORESTS
Tropical Rain Forest
Lighter Tropical Forest (jungle)
Scrub and Thorn Forest (dry)

MIDLATITUDE FORESTS
Mediterranean Mixed Forest
Broadleaf Forest (also pine, cedar etc.)
Boreal Forest (mostly conifers)

GRASSLANDS
Savanna or Parkland
Prairie
Steppe (shortgrass)

DESERT etc.
Desert Shrub and Waste
Tundra
Mountains

Copyright by C. S. HAMMOND & CO., N.Y.

Eckert Projection (equal-area)

icecap

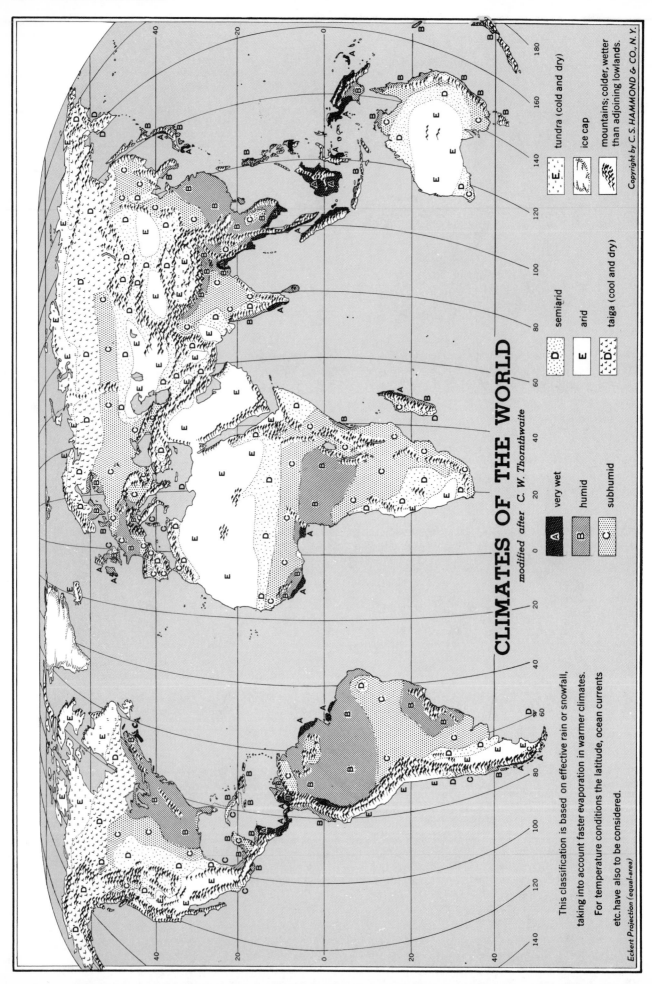

CLIMATES OF THE WORLD
modified after C. W. Thornthwaite

	very wet		semiarid
A		**D**	
B	humid	**E**	arid
C	subhumid	**D**	taiga (cool and dry)

E	tundra (cold and dry)
	ice cap
	mountains; colder, wetter than adjoining lowlands.

This classification is based on effective rain or snowfall, taking into account faster evaporation in warmer climates. For temperature conditions the latitude, ocean currents etc. have also to be considered.

Eckert Projection (equal-area)

Copyright by C.S. HAMMOND & CO., N.Y.

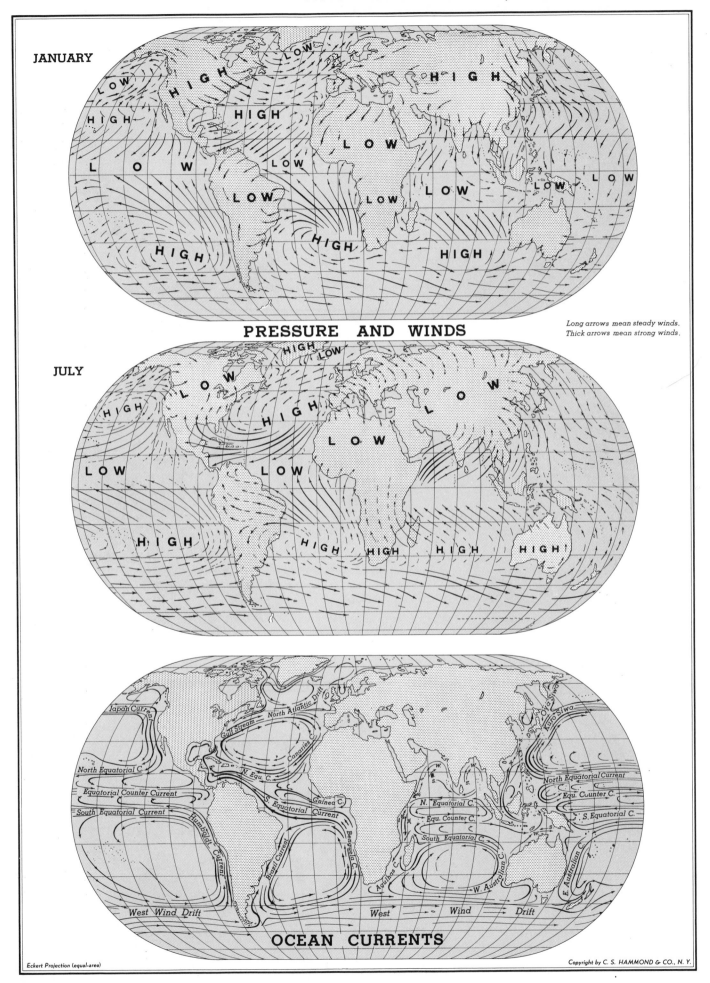

JANUARY

LOW HIGH LOW LOW HIGH HIGH
HIGH HIGH
LOW LOW
LOW LOW LOW
LOW LOW LOW LOW
HIGH
HIGH HIGH

PRESSURE AND WINDS

Long arrows mean steady winds.
Thick arrows mean strong winds.

JULY

HIGH LOW LOW
LOW HIGH HIGH LOW LOW
LOW LOW
HIGH HIGH HIGH HIGH HIGH

OCEAN CURRENTS

Japan Current · North Atlantic Drift · Gulf Stream · Kuro Siwo · O Siwo
North Equatorial C. · Canaries C. · North Equatorial Current
Equatorial Counter Current · N. Equ. C. · Equ. Counter C.
South Equatorial Current · Guinea C. · S. Equatorial C.
Humboldt Current · S. Equatorial Current · N. Equatorial C.
Brazil Current · Equ. Counter C.
Benguela C. · South Equatorial C.
Agulhas C. · W. Australian C. · E. Australian C.
West Wind Drift · West Wind Drift

Eckert Projection (equal-area)

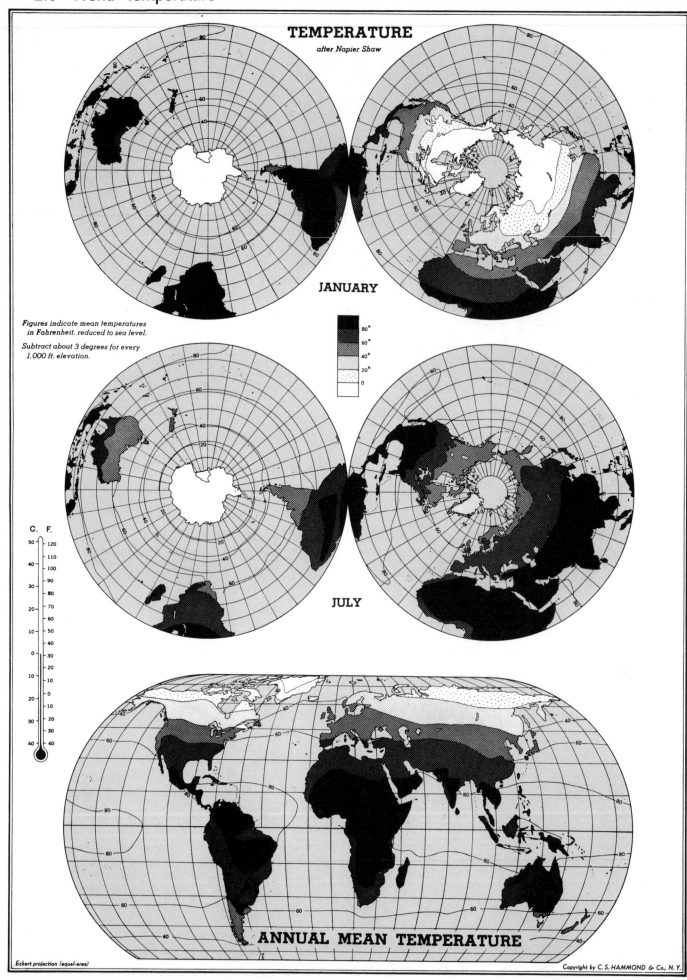

TEMPERATURE
after Napier Shaw

JANUARY

JULY

ANNUAL MEAN TEMPERATURE

Figures indicate mean temperatures in Fahrenheit, reduced to sea level.

Subtract about 3 degrees for every 1,000 ft. elevation.

80°
60°
40°
20°
0

C. F.

Eckert projection (equal-area)

Copyright by C. S. HAMMOND & Co., N. Y.

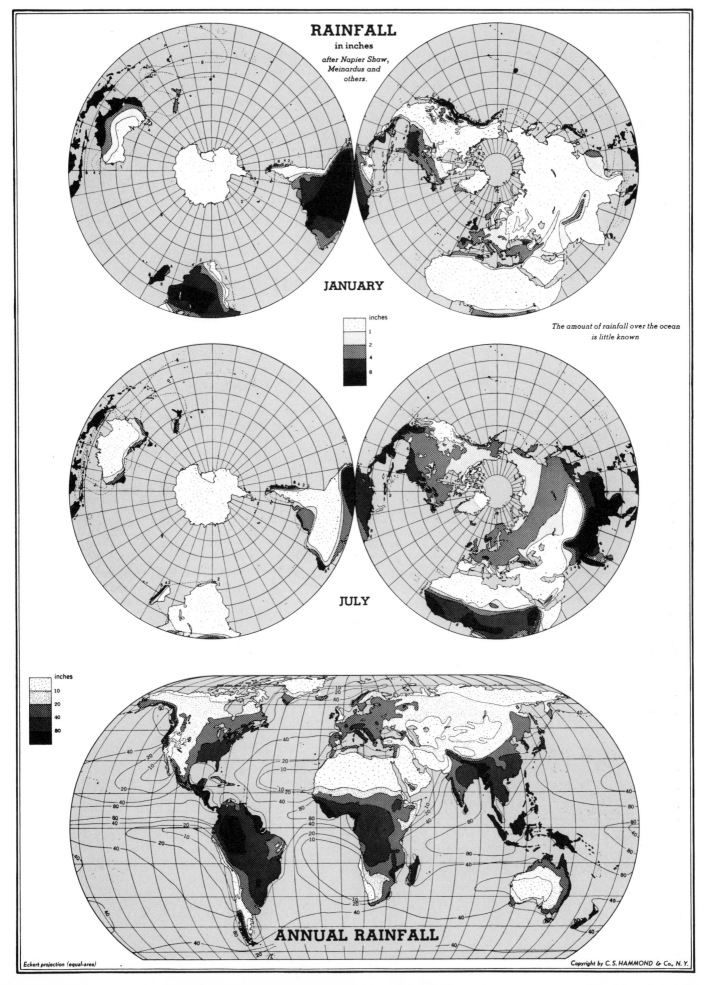

RAINFALL
in inches
after Napier Shaw,
Meinardus and
others.

JANUARY

inches
1
2
4
8

The amount of rainfall over the ocean
is little known

JULY

inches
10
20
40
80

ANNUAL RAINFALL

Eckert projection (equal-area)

Copyright by C. S. HAMMOND & Co., N. Y.

If we can envision the continents of the world as seated firmly on massive rafts of rock and moving across the surface of the earth at a rate of about 6 feet every 60 years we have a basic notion of what is meant by continental drift and the manner in which land and sea masses have been formed.

The original concept of continental drift was proposed in the 1920s, but only during the past three years or so have geologists and geophysicists accepted as fact the seemingly preposterous notion that the surface of the earth is constantly in motion.

The making of the continents began more than 200 million years ago during the Permian period with the splitting of a gigantic landmass known as Pangaea. Two continents, Laurasia to the north and Gondwana to the south, were formed by the initial division. Over a period of many millions of years these landmasses subdivided into smaller parts approximately the shapes of Africa, Eurasia, North and South America, Australia, and Antarctica as we know them today.

CONTINENTAL DRIFT

Source: R. S. Dietz and J. C. Holden

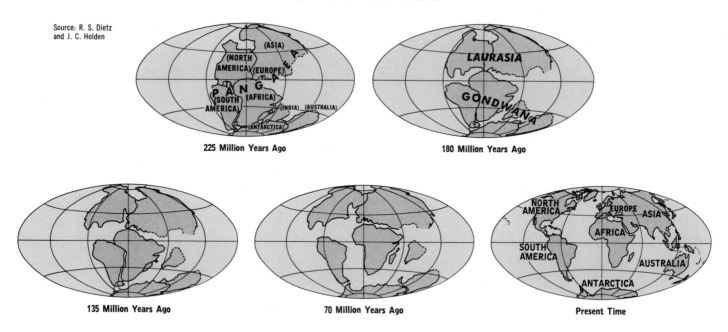

225 Million Years Ago

180 Million Years Ago

135 Million Years Ago

70 Million Years Ago

Present Time

CRUSTAL MOVEMENT

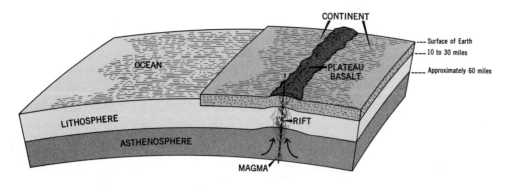

The concept of movement within the earth's crust assumes that the earth's outer layer has a firm lithosphere divided up into individual pieces called plates. These plates "float" above a weaker interior layer, the **asthenosphere**, and over vast periods of time noticeably change position, shape, size and direction depending upon forces exerted from within the earth.

Far from being an isolated instance, the movement of glaciers over the face of the earth has been a natural phenomenon for many thousands of years. Stimulated by changes in climate and resulting changes in sea level — perhaps induced by shifts in the earth's axis — glaciers have followed a rather unpredictable course of advance and retreat continuing into the 20th century.

At some point in unrecorded history during the greatest ice age, or the Pleistocene epoch, as much as 27 percent of the earth's surface was covered by glacial ice to a depth of up to 10,000 feet. The icy masses moved across the earth as far south as New York City and the Missouri River in North America, burying much of Europe and blanketing vast areas in northern Asia.

Many of the great ice sheets retreated as the climate became warmer, leaving deposits of soil and rock picked up as they traveled southward in the Northern Hemisphere. The landscape changed as the glaciers left behind their typical U-shaped valleys, amphitheater-like hollows and jagged mountain ridges, altering to a large extent the former ecological zones which changed again and again as the ice reformed and melted.

Although not enough is known about glaciers to predict accurately their future behavior, we do know that they react to climatic changes. Glaciers were advancing in Alpine regions during the 19th century until a global warm up in the beginning of this century caused their retreat. Recently the trend has been toward cooler and moister climate and, on a limited scale, glaciers are beginning to advance once more.

EXTENT OF GLACIATION
IN THE NORTHERN HEMISPHERE
DURING THE ICE AGES

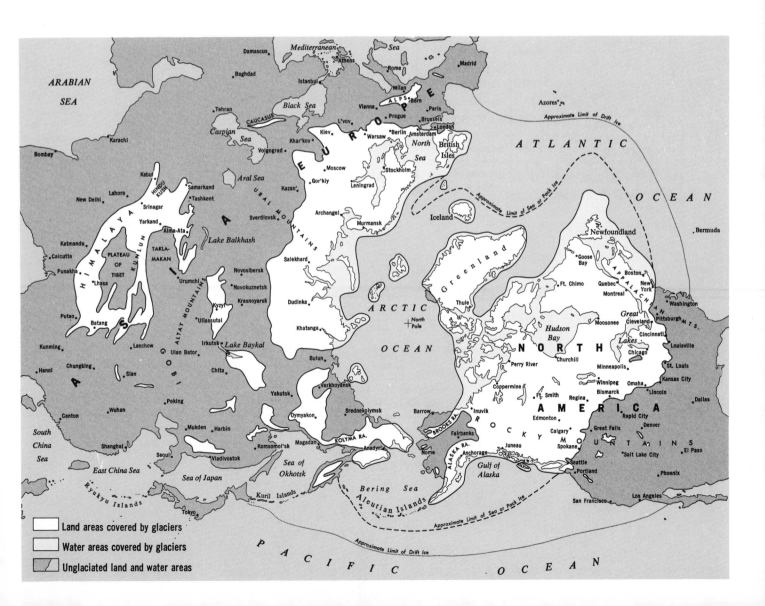

GEOLOGIC TIME

TIME DIVISION			YEARS AGO	MAJOR GEOLOGIC DEVELOPMENTS
CENOZOIC ERA	QUATERNARY PERIOD	RECENT	10,000	GREAT LAKES
CENOZOIC ERA	QUATERNARY PERIOD	PLEISTOCENE	1-2 million	NORWEGIAN FJORDS ICE AGES BLACK SEA
CENOZOIC ERA	TERTIARY PERIOD	PLIOCENE	11 million	CASPIAN SEA
CENOZOIC ERA	TERTIARY PERIOD	MIOCENE	25 million	HIMALAYAS
CENOZOIC ERA	TERTIARY PERIOD	OLIGOCENE	40 million	ALPS
CENOZOIC ERA	TERTIARY PERIOD	EOCENE	60 million	
CENOZOIC ERA	TERTIARY PERIOD	PALEOCENE	70 million	ANDES MOUNTAINS ROCKY MOUNTAINS CHALK DEPOSITS
MESOZOIC ERA		CRETACEOUS PERIOD	135 million	COAST RANGES SIERRA NEVADA JURA MOUNTAINS
MESOZOIC ERA		JURASSIC PERIOD	180 million	NEW JERSEY PALISADES
MESOZOIC ERA		TRIASSIC PERIOD	225 million	CAUCASUS URAL MOUNTAINS APPALACHIAN MOUNTAINS
PALEOZOIC ERA		PERMIAN PERIOD	270 million	POTASH DEPOSITS
PALEOZOIC ERA		PENNSYLVANIAN PERIOD	300 million	COAL DEPOSITS
PALEOZOIC ERA		MISSISSIPPIAN PERIOD	350 million	ACADIAN MOUNTAINS
PALEOZOIC ERA		DEVONIAN PERIOD	400 million	
PALEOZOIC ERA		SILURIAN PERIOD	440 million	NIAGARA FALLS CAPROCK TACONIC MOUNTAINS
PALEOZOIC ERA		ORDOVICIAN PERIOD	500 million	LIMESTONE DEPOSITS VERMONT MOUNTAINS
PALEOZOIC ERA		CAMBRIAN PERIOD	600 million	ARIZONA MOUNTAINS
		PRE-CAMBRIAN		METALLIC ORE DEPOSITS LAURENTIAN MOUNTAINS ADIRONDACK MOUNTAINS

Like a giant Rosetta stone the secrets of the earth's creation lie spread in strata beneath our feet, revealing their hieroglyphic message to a few of the initiated.

For billions of years layers of rock — the sedimentary deposits of ages — have piled up on the earth's surface, entrapping the characteristics of time. Time when a lifeless nature prepared for the first microscopic living organisms; time when these organisms were destroyed or became extinct, time when, through endless subtle mutations, they evolved into new forms of life.

The Paleozoic, ancient era; Mesozoic, middle era; and

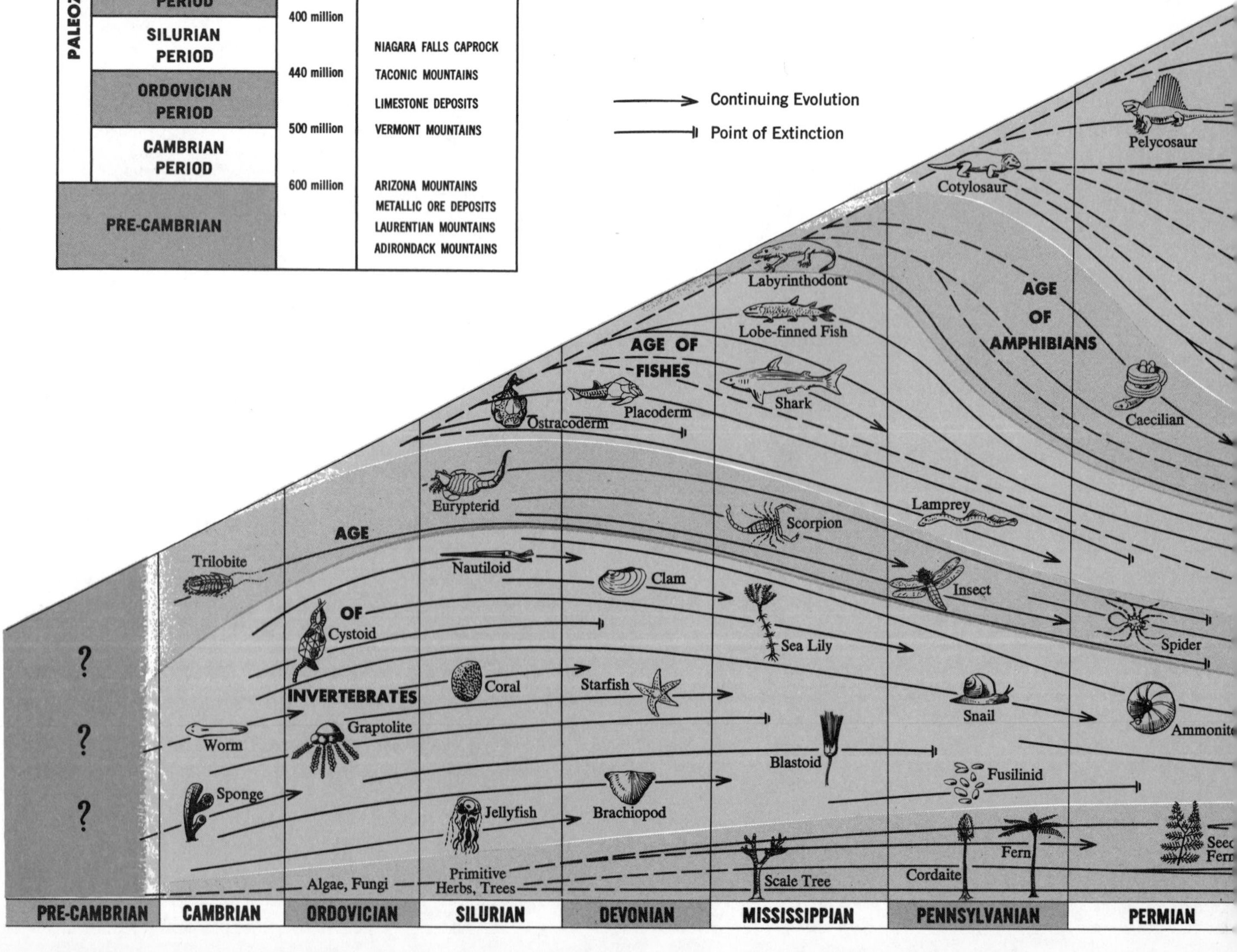

⟶ Continuing Evolution

⊣ Point of Extinction

| PRE-CAMBRIAN | CAMBRIAN | ORDOVICIAN | SILURIAN | DEVONIAN | MISSISSIPPIAN | PENNSYLVANIAN | PERMIAN |

Cenozoic, recent era, are the designations used for the broad periods of time during which life evolved. Locked within strata of rock, vestiges of life are found in the fossilized remains of creatures over a billion years old. In succeeding layers geologists and anthropologists find other clues to the mystery of time and life: the appearance of the lowest forms of animal life; the evolution of fish, amphibians, reptiles, birds and mammals. Late in the schedule of creation traces of a strange and wonderful animal appear, for it was only one million years ago that man left his first imprint on the geologic record.

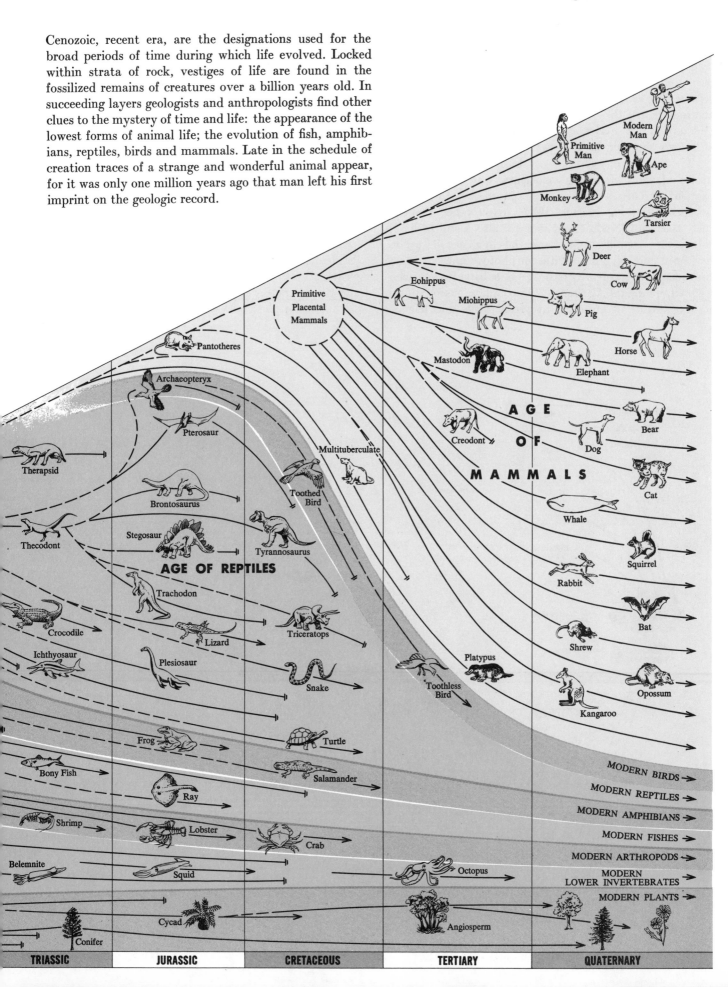

TRIASSIC   JURASSIC   CRETACEOUS   TERTIARY   QUATERNARY

With an intuition clearly beyond their scientific knowledge, the ancients of India developed a theory of reincarnation which, in some philosophic ways, parallels what science has learned of the workings of the biosphere. In the remarkable thrift of nature nothing is lost — in tremendous complex cycles atoms from the first life on earth still move through the biosphere.

The miracle of energy is constantly performed in the cycles of the "life-giving" elements. Carbon, hydrogen, oxygen, nitrogen, sulfur and phosphorus act together to produce all living matter. While many other elements such as calcium, iodine and iron are also found in living things, they are not absolute essentials in all cases. Carbon, hydrogen and oxygen are vital for photosynthesis and are the components of the basic food substances — carbohydrates and fats. Carbon, in its common gaseous form, carbon dioxide, is absorbed by green plants and triggers

the production of carbohydrate compounds by reacting with molecules of water.

Some "energy" is stored within the plant in the form of new tissue; other "energy," in the form of oxygen is released into the air to be used by other organisms. The seemingly inexhaustible supply of carbon dioxide available for use is replenished in the atmosphere through the respiration of all living things, and in the soil as bacteria and fungi break down plant and animal cells,

Nitrogen, sulfur and phosphorus are essential to animals and plants for the production and maintenance of protein. Nitrogen, with carbon, hydrogen and oxygen, is used for the growth and repair of tissue. Sulfur acts as a "stiffening" agent in all protein. To perform their functions proteins must be folded and shaped in a particular way, and their structure is maintained by bonds between sulfur atoms. While phosphorus is not a constituent of protein,

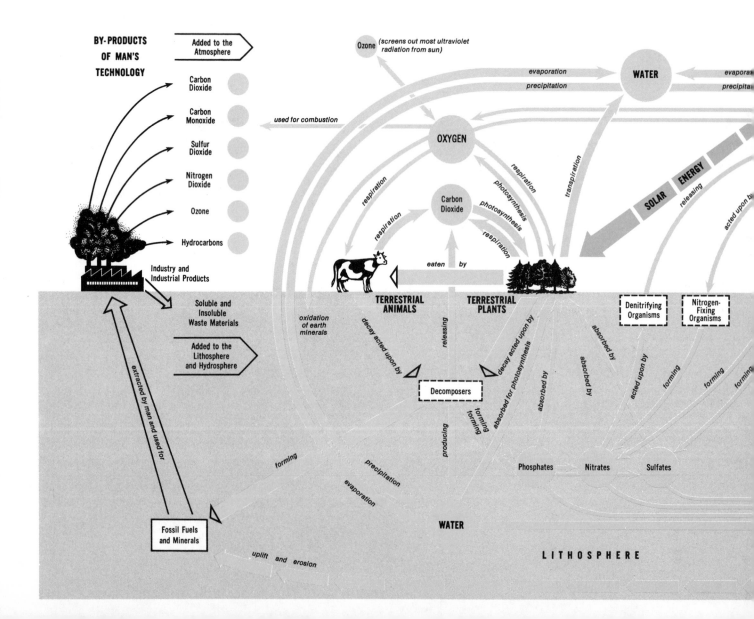

no protein can be made without it. Special phosphate compounds are the "fuel" for all biochemical work within the cell.

Although about four-fifths of the atmosphere is nitrogen, higher forms of life cannot make use of it in its "free" state and must absorb it at one or more points in its biospheric cycle. The decomposers — bacteria and fungi — act on waste matter, breaking down complex compounds into simpler usable forms including nitrogen. Some nitrogen-fixing bacteria are able to utilize atmospheric nitrogen in their own metabolism, while others convert it to those nitrogen-enriched substances necessary for all plant growth.

In nature, no part is greater than the whole and almost every element is dependent on another for some essential part of its cycle. Water, which is incorporated into every organism, is essential in the formation of free oxygen which in turn sustains the life of that organism. Water is also the principal "carrier" in the cycling of all elements. When it evaporates, water returns certain elements to the atmosphere; when it seeps through the soil on its return to the sea, water distributes nutrients to plant roots.

Carbon monoxide, sulfur and nitrogen oxides, hydrocarbons — by-products of man's industry — are being injected into the biosphere in ever-increasing amounts. There, as the "new compounds," they must in some way co-exist with the life-support cycles established throughout millions of years of evolution. Their compatability with these cycles and the organisms they nurture will determine the future of life on our planet.

Already man has learned one thing. Although the question of reincarnation or any form of life after death remains unanswered for many, science has proved that there is no natural end to the raw materials of nature or to the "new compounds" man has made from them.

INTERLOCKING CYCLES OF THE BIOSPHERE

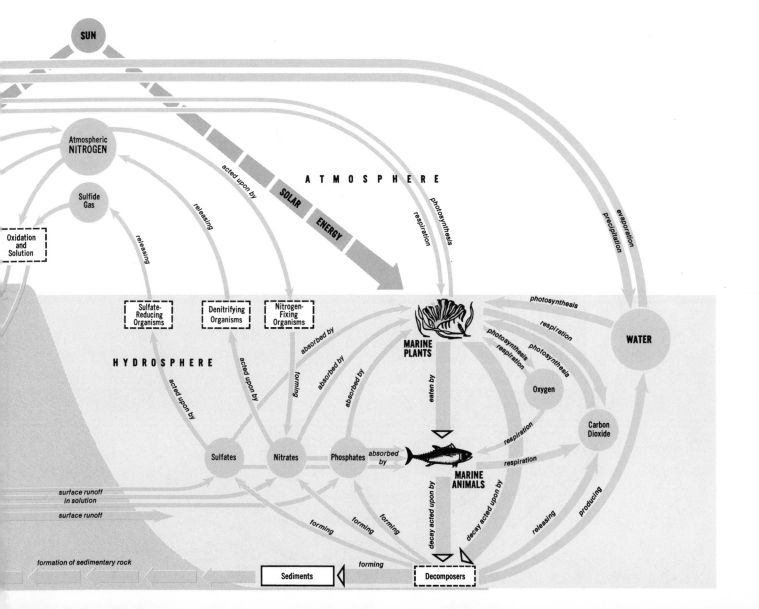

Since he could think man has been at war with death. He has fought his battles against destruction with science and technology as his weapons, virtually eliminating his own annihilation by predatory animals and from diseases such as leprosy, tuberculosis and diphtheria. He has walked into many valleys of death to fight malaria and yellow fever, and he has resolved that each year more of his own kind will live to finish out their threescore years and ten.

However, the victory over nature, which had balanced population with food supply and space, is bitter, for the population has "exploded" leaving man with the seemingly insolvable problem of providing more food and space for himself or reducing his numbers by starvation or by war.

Man outsmarted himself in many ways as he worked toward creating a more perfect world for himself without understanding that natural laws go beyond human manipulation. He has destroyed forests and meadows, polluted the water and air, eliminated organisms that tried to share his bread. However, he has yet to learn to recreate the wood and brush or the interdependent communities of bacteria, insects and animals that he learned — too late — enrich the air, the soil and the water and without which he cannot function.

Modern man knows how to manufacture "miraculous" materials to work for his pleasure or his seemingly insatiable needs, but the sophistications of technology have yet to control effectively the by-products. These new materials, still subject to the order of nature's cycles, penetrate the biosphere and eventually come to roost in his own vulnerable body.

New battles are being fought throughout the world and new standards bearing the slogans of ecology float in the "unsafe" air. It is somehow ironic to find that many people now believe that man has been fighting the wrong fight in his gigantic struggle with nature. That, after all, nature never was his enemy.

Man cannot turn back to his beginnings when he lived with, and not against, the natural world. But a compromise between technology and nature must take place for our "plundered planet" cries out for the day of reckoning.

POLLUTION CIRCLE

TYPES OF POLLUTION AND THEIR EFFECT ON THE TOTAL ENVIRONMENT

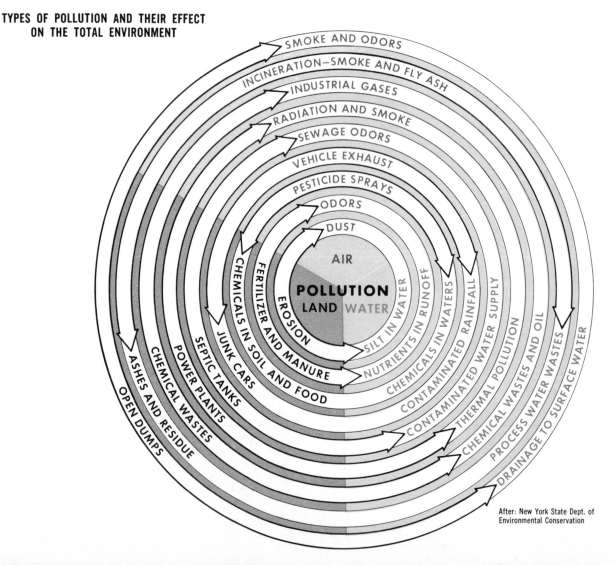

After: New York State Dept. of Environmental Conservation